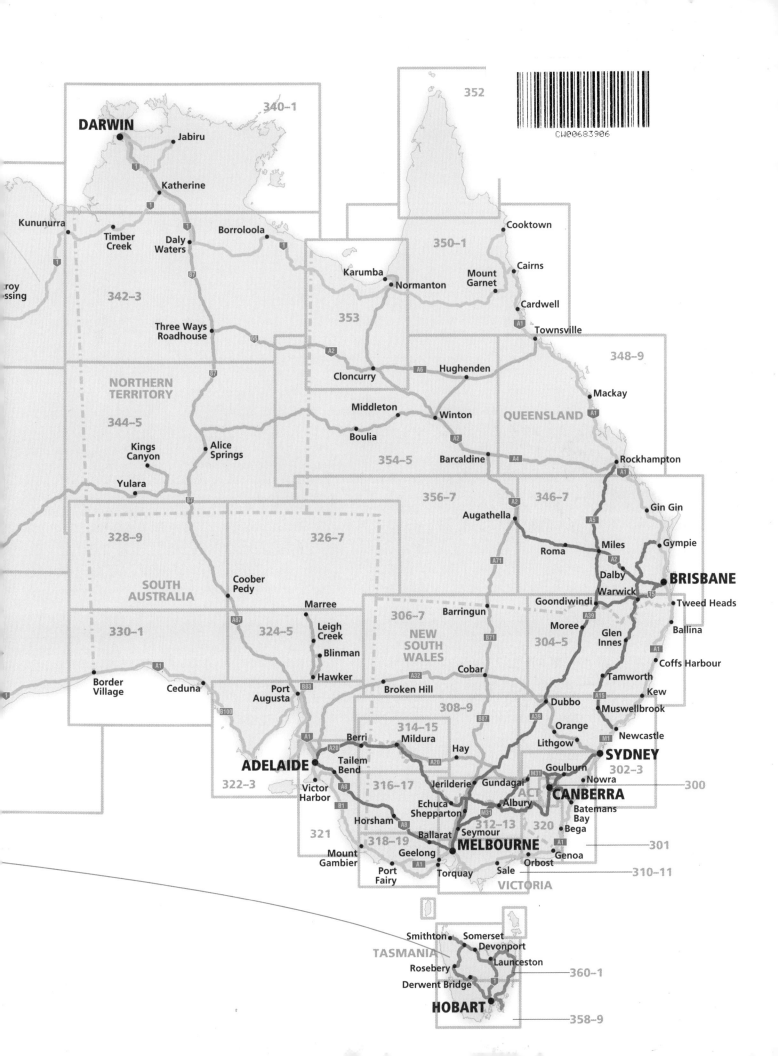

EXPLORE AUSTRALIA BY

CARA VAN & MOTOR HOME

6th

BRENDAN BATTY

EXPLORE
AUSTRALIA

CONTENTS

HOW TO USE THIS BOOK

Explore Australia by Caravan & Motorhome
is divided into sections.

Festivals
This section tells you what is on in major
centres in Australia during the year.
Events are listed by month within states
and territories.

Chapters 1, 2, 3 and 4
Chapter 1 takes you around Australia on
Highway One. It is divided into touring
routes, such as Melbourne to Sydney
(see below right), with each segment then
divided into smaller tour sections, such as
Melbourne to Phillip Island (see example on
facing page), and all provide the same details
pictured here. Chapters 2, 3 and 4 follow the
same format. Chapter 2 covers the outback
routes, Chapter 3 great rural trips, and
Chapter 4 Tasmania.

Making the most of your trip
Essential information on preparing for
and planning your trip.

CHAPTER OPENING

Brief description of what travellers can expect
on the touring routes covered in the chapter,
including major highlights.

Overview of the different touring
routes covered in this chapter.

TOURING ROUTES

Roads, highways and freeways
covered in the trip, and total
number of kilometres.

Brief overview of each section
of the trip; information on the
landscape and towns, cities
and attractions.

Weather details for the region,
to give you an idea of the best
time of year to visit.

Information on the smaller touring sections that make up the larger touring routes.

TOURING SECTION

Practical notes on the roads, highways and freeways you will travel on.

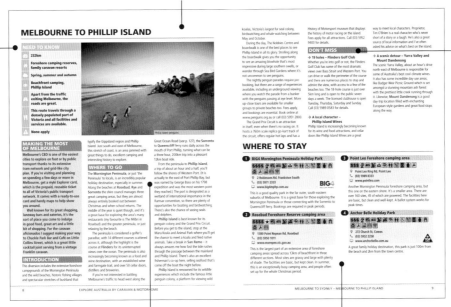

Descriptions of attractions in the area, with relevant contact details.

Overview of the major towns on or near the route, with details of the best places to visit.

Directory of recommended caravan parks on or near the touring route. Each listing includes contact details, facilities symbols and a brief description. Each caravan park is identified by a number. This number appears on the relevant maps in the atlas section.

ATLAS SECTION

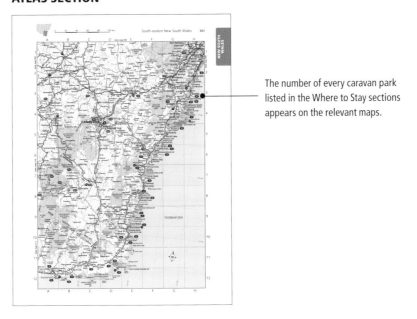

The number of every caravan park listed in the Where to Stay sections appears on the relevant maps.

FESTIVALS

JANUARY

ACT
Canberra: Summernats Car Festival

NSW
Bungendore: Show
Brunswick Heads: Festival of the Fish 'n' Chips and Woodchop Carnival
Bulli: Illawarra Folk Festival
Guyra: Lamb and Potato Festival
Moruya: Rodeo
Parkes: Elvis Festival
Sydney: Festival
Tamworth: Country Music Festival
Taree: Taste Fest on Manning
Wingham: Summer Rodeo

Qld
Charters Towers: Goldfield Ashes Cricket Carnival
Surfers Paradise: Conrad Jupiters Magic Millions Carnival
Yandina: Ginger Flower Food Festival

SA
Adelaide: Schutzenfest
Cape Jaffa: Seafood and Wine Fest
Port Lincoln: Tunarama Festival (family fun festival)
Port MacDonnell: Bayside Festival
Victor Harbor: Rotary Art Show

Tas.
Burnie: Athletic Carnival
Cygnet: Folk Festival
Devonport: Taste the Harvest Summer Style
Latrobe: Henley-on-the-Mersey
Strahan: Mount Lyell Picnic

Vic.
Ballarat: Organs of the Ballarat Goldfields
Geelong: Festival of Sails (sailing)
Lorne: Pier to Pub Swim; Mountain to Surf Footrace
Melbourne: Australian Open Tennis Championships; Midsumma
Tatura: International Dairy Week

WA
Busselton: Beach Festival of Busselton
Lancelin: Ocean Classic (windsurfing)
Perth: Cup (horseracing); Hopman Cup (tennis)

FEBRUARY

ACT
Canberra: National Multicultural Festival; Canberra Show; Summerfest; Big Canberra Bike Ride

NSW
Bega: Far South Coast National Show
Goulburn: Australia Blues Music Festival
Murrurundi: King of the Ranges Stockman's Challenge
Orange: Banjo Paterson Festival (Feb)
Sydney: Gay and Lesbian Mardi Gras (Feb–March); Laneway Festival; Tropfest

Qld
Chinchilla: Melon Festival (odd-numbered years)

SA
Adelaide: Fringe; Laneway Festival
Loxton: Loxton Gift Carnival
Peterborough: Rodeo
Port Lincoln: Teakle Classic Adelaide to Port Lincoln Yacht Race

Tas.
Evandale: Village Fair and National Penny Farthing Championships
Hobart: Australian Wooden Boat Festival (odd-numbered years); Cup Carnival; Royal Hobart Regatta
Launceston: Cup (horse racing); Festivale (food and wine festival)
Rosebery: Folk Festival

Vic.
Bunyip: Country Music Festival
Echuca-Moama: Riverboats Music Festival
Heywood: Wood, Wine and Roses Festival
Melbourne: Laneway Festival; Sustainable Living Festival
Mildura: Wentworth Arts Festival (Feb–Mar)
Nagambie: Rowing Regatta
Paynesville: Music Festival
Shepparton: Summer City Market
Warrnambool: Wonta Fiesta (family fun festival)

WA
Boyup Brook: Country Music Festival
Broome: Saltwater Music Festival
Margaret River: Leeuwin Estate Concert (Feb/Mar)
Perth: International Arts Festival; Writers Week

MARCH

ACT
Canberra: Balloon Spectacular; Enlighten Festival; Chinese Lantern Festival; Craft Beer and Cider Fest; Skyfire (fireworks)

NSW
Albury: Gold Cup Carnival
Armidale: Cup
Bega: Bega Cheese Pro-Am (golf)
Bermagui: Seaside Fair
Broken Hill: St Patricks Day Races
Bungendore: Harvest Festival
Cooma: Show
Glen Innes: Minerama (gem and mineral show)
Katoomba: Blue Mountains Festival of Folk, Roots and Blues
Kiama: Jazz Festival
Lithgow: Show
Narrandera: John O'Brien Bush Festival
Newcastle: Regional Show
Queanbeyan: Multicultural Festival
Wingham: Agricultural Show; Rodeo

NT
Alice Springs: Easter in the Alice Mountain Bike Race

Qld
Warwick: Show

SA
Adelaide: Fringe; Glendi Greek Festival; WOMAdelaide (world music and dance)
Mount Gambier: South East Country Music Festival

Tas.
Hobart: Ten Days on the Island (arts festival; Mar-Apr; odd-numbered years)
Wynyard: Agricultural Show

Vic.
Ararat: Jailhouse Rock Festival
Ballarat: Begonia Festival
Castlemaine: State Festival
Geelong: Highland Gathering
Kilmore: Country Music Festival
Melbourne: AFLW Grand Final; Australian Formula One Grand Prix; Food and Wine Festival: Moomba Festival: Fashion Festival: Queer Film Festival; International Comedy Festival (Mar/April); International Flower and Garden Show

Sydney Mardi Gras

Port Fairy: Folk Festival
Rosebud: Kite Festival
Seymour: Labour Day Bush Market
Shepparton: Arts Festival
Tallangatta: Show

WA
Albany: West Australian Great Southern
    Wine Festival
Augusta: Live Lighter Augusta River Festival
Broome: Staircase to the Moon (Mar–Oct)
Kalbarri: Sport Fishing Classic
Margaret River: World Surf League
    Championship Event
Norseman: Cup
Perth: Festival

EASTER

ACT
Canberra: National Folk Festival

NSW
Adaminaby: Easter Fair
Byron Bay: Bluesfest
Central Tilba: Easter Festival
Huskisson: White Sands Carnival
Maclean: Highland Gathering
Sydney: Autumn Racing Carnival; Royal
    Easter Show; Rosehill Caravan Supershow
Taree: Easter Powerboat Spectacular
Ulladulla: Blessing of the Fleet
Wollongong: Autumn Jazzfest

Qld
Augathella: Races

Bundaberg: Bundy Easter Round Up
Burketown: World Barramundi Fishing
    Championships
Emerald: Easter Sunflower Festival Rodeo
Gladstone: Harbour Festival (includes finish
    of Brisbane-Gladstone Yacht Race)
Normanton: Barra Classic
Roma: Easter in the Country
Warwick: Rock Swap Meet

SA
Barmera: Lake Bonney Yachting Regatta
Barossa Valley: Vintage Festival
    (odd-numbered years)

Vic.
Bells Beach: World Surf League Event;
    Music Festival
Bendigo: Easter Festival
Mildura: Mildura 100 Ski Race
Stawell: Gift (professional footrace)

WA
Donnybrook: Apple Festival
    (even-numbered years)
York: Easter Fair

APRIL

ACT
Canberra: National Folk Festival; Canberra
    District Wine Harvest Festival

NSW
Bathurst: Royal Bathurst Show
Boggabri: Drovers Campfire
Collector: Pumpkin Festival (Apr/May)
Maitland: Hunter Steam Fest
Morpeth: Chapel Jazz Festival
Toronto: Lakemac Heritage Festival
    (Mar–Apr)

WOMAdelaide

Julia Creek Dirt and Dust Festival

NT
Alice Springs: Heritage Festival

Qld
Julia Creek: Dirt and Dust Festival

SA
Adelaide: Tasting Australia (Apr–May)
Kapunda: Farm Fair (even-numbered years)
Yankalilla: Fleurieu Festival (odd-numbered years)

Vic.
Apollo Bay: Music Festival
Barmah State Forest: Barmah Muster
Corryong: Man from Snowy River Bush Festival
Koroit: Irish Festival
Melbourne: International Comedy Festival (Mar–Apr)
Stratford: Shakespeare on the River Festival (Apr–May)

WA
Bunbury: Agricultural Show
Margaret River: Drug Aware Margaret River Pro (surfing)
Pinjarra: Fairbridge Music Festival

MAY

NSW
Broken Hill: Outback Challenge (4WD competition)
Collector: Pumpkin Festival
Dubbo: Agricultural Show

Glen Innes: Australian Celtic Festival
Lovedale: Long Lunch
Moree: On A Plate Festival
Narooma: Oyster Festival
Narrabri: Show Rodeo
Port Macquarie: Ironman 70.3
Sydney: Writers' Festival; Archibald Prize Exhibition (national portrait prize; May–Sept)
Wagga Wagga: Australian International Animation Festival

NT
Alice Springs: Camel Cup
Daly Waters: Campdraft, Rodeo and Gymkhana
Mataranka: Never Never Festival

Qld
Ballandean: Opera in the Vineyard
Barcaldine: Show
Blackall: Barcoo Show
Brisbane: Queensland Winter Racing Carnival (May–June)
Cairns: Tropical Garden Show
Charleville: Show
Charters Towers: Country Music Festival
Goondiwindi: Show
Gregory Downs: Gregory River Canoe Race
Maryborough: Fraser Coast Agricultural Show
Miles: Show
Mount Garnet: Races and Rodeo
Mount Morgan: Golden Mount Festival

Richmond: Outback Fossil Festival
Seventeen Seventy: Captain Cook 1770 Festival
Winton: Outback Art Show

SA
Mount Gambier: Generations in Jazz
Penola: Coonawarra Arts Festival
Waikerie: Riverland Rock 'n' Roll Festival

Vic.
Bairnsdale: East Gippsland Field Day
Halls Gap: Grampians Grape Escape
Warrnambool: Grand Annual Day

WA
Exmouth: Ningaloo Whale Shark Festival
Gascoyne Junction: Gascoyne River Music Festival
Kununurra: Ord River Muster
Perth: International Jazz Festival

JUNE

ACT
Canberra: Canberra Region Truffle Fest

NSW
Merimbula: Jazz Festival
Sydney: Film Festival
Tweed Heads: Cooly Rocks On; Wintersun 2.0
Wagga Wagga: Veteran and Vintage Motor Club Rally

NT
Adelaide River: Country Show
Alice Springs: Finke Desert Race (car and motorbike racing); Top Half Folk Festival
Pine Creek: Gold Rush Festival

Qld
Caboolture: Agricultural Show
Caloundra: Arts and Craft Fair
Cloncurry: Show
Croydon: Poddy Dodgers Festival
McKinlay: Annual Race Meeting
Mount Isa: Show
Mount Larcom: Show
Normanton: Rodeo and Campdraft
Proserpine: Agricultural Show
Winton: Outback Writers' Festival

SA
Adelaide: Cabaret Festival
Barmera: South Australian Country Music Festival
Coober Pedy: Opal Festival
McLaren Vale: Sea and Vines Festival

Tas.
Hobart: Atlantic Midwinter Festival

Vic.
Echuca: Steam, Horse and Vineyard Rally
Kilmore: Celtic Festival
Melbourne: Cabaret Festival; International Jazz Festival; Emerging Writers' Festival
Portarlington: National Celtic Festival
Rutherglen: Winery Walkabout

WA
Carnarvon: Tropicool Festival
Derby: Mowanjum Festival; Mad Hatters Race Day

JULY

NSW
Byron Bay: Splendour in the Grass
Evans Head: Fishing Classic
Tamworth: Hats off to Country

NT
Alice Springs: Camel Cup; Beanie Festival; Show
Darwin: Lions Beer Can Regatta; Royal Darwin Show
Katherine: Agricultural Show
Tennant Creek: Show

Qld
Birdsville: Big Red Bash
Boulia: Camel Races
Brisbane: International Film Festival (July–Aug)
Cairns: The Cairns Show
Childers: Festival
Cloncurry: Stockman's Challenge and Campdraft
Ingham: Herbert River Show
Mackay: Festival of Arts; Mackay Cup
Malanda: Show
Mareeba: Rodeo
Pomona: King of the Mountain Festival
Rockhampton: River Festival
Sarina: Country Music Festival
Townsville: Winter Racing Carnival
Tully: Agricultural Show
Yowah: Opal Festival

SA
Fleurieu Peninsula: Fleurieu Art Prize (odd-numbered years)
Maree: Australian Camel Cup
Willunga: Almond Blossom Festival

Tas.
Devonport: Jazz Weekend

Vic.
Melbourne: International Film Festival (July–Aug)
Swan Hill: Italian Fiesta

WA
Derby: Boab Festival (June–July)
Fitzroy Crossing: Rodeo and Campdraft
Kununurra: Agricultural Show; Dam to Dam Dinghy Race
Port Hedland: Spinifex Spree Carnival
Roebourne: Cup

AUGUST

ACT
Canberra: Writers Festival

NSW
Byron Bay: Writers Festival
Louth: Races
Murwillumbah: Tweed Valley Banana Festival and Harvest Week
Narromine: Agricultural Show
Sydney: City2Surf
Taree: Cup

NT
Alice Springs: Henley-on-Todd Regatta
Borroloola: Rodeo, Gymkhana and Campdraft
Darwin: Cup Day; Festival
Gulkula: Garma Festival
Katherine: Ultra Challenge (endurance sports event); Races
Mataranka: Rodeo
Tennant Creek: Cup

Qld
Airlie Beach: Whitsunday Fun Race (sailing)
Anakie: Gemfest
Brisbane: Ekka (Royal Brisbane Show); International Film Festival; Poetry Festival
Cairns: Festival (Aug–Sept)
Camooweal: Drovers Camp Festival
Cloncurry: Curry Merry Muster Festival
Cunnamulla: Cunnumulla Fella Festival
Gympie: Country Music Muster
Hervey Bay: Seafood Festival; Ocean Festival
Ingham: Australian-Italian Festival
Mission Beach: Banana Festival
Mount Isa: Rotary Rodeo
Tara: Festival of Culture & Camel Races (odd-numbered years)
Townsville: Australian Festival of Chamber Music; Cultural Fest
Yungaburra: Tablelands Folk Festival

SA
Adelaide: SALA Festival
Coober Pedy: Races and Gymkhana
Gawler: Agricultural Show
Port Lincoln: Show
Whyalla: Show

Vic.
Leongatha: Daffodil and Floral Show
Melbourne: Writers Festival

WA
Broome: Rodeo; Opera Under the Stars; Shinju Matsuri (Festival of the Pearl)
Derby: Rodeo, Gymkhana and Campdraft
Mullewa: Wildflower Show
Northam: Avon River Festival; Avon Descent (whitewater race)
Port Hedland: Cup
Tom Price: Nameless Jarndunmunha Festival
Wyndham: Cup

Henley-on-Todd Regatta, Alice Springs

SEPTEMBER

ACT
Canberra: Floriade (Sept–Oct)

NSW
Boggabri: Spring Fair
Bowral: Tulip Time Bowral (Sept–Oct)
Broke: Village Fair
Broken Hill: Broken Heel Festival
Forbes: Agricultural Show
Gosford: Australian Springtime Festival
Henty: Machinery Field Days
Hillston: Show
Maitland: Garden Ramble
Narrandera: Agricultural Show and Sheepdog Show
Narromine: Agricultural Show
Wollombi: Music Festival
Wollongong: Spring into Corrimal Festival

NT
Alice Springs: Desert Festival
Pine Creek: Rodeo

Qld
Beenleigh: Show
Birdsville: Races
Brisbane: Brisbane Festival
Cairns: Amateur Racing Carnival
Noosa Heads: Jazz Festival
Tamborine: Springtime on the Mountain Flower Festival
Theodore: River Festival
Toowoomba: Carnival of Flowers
Winton: Outback Festival (odd-numbered years)

SA
Adelaide: Bay to Birdwood Run (vintage vehicles)
Barmera: Riverland Field Days
Ceduna: Oysterfest
Kimba: Agricultural and Horticultural Show
Port Pirie: Blessing of the Fleet
Wudinna: Show

Tas.
Claremont: Daffodil Show

Vic.
Melbourne: ALF Grand Final; Royal Melbourne Show; Underground Film Festival
Mildura: Country Music Festival

WA
Broome: Dragon Boat Regatta
Coolgardie: Day
Dalwallinu: Wattle Week Festival
Esperance: Anglican Wildflower Festival
Geraldton: Sunshine Festival
Kununurra: Kimberley Writers Festival
Perth: Royal Show (Sept–Oct); Kings Park Wildflower Festival; Fashion Festival
Port Hedland: Pilbara Music Festival
Ravensthorpe: Wildflower Show

OCTOBER

NSW
Bathurst: Bathurst 1000
Broken Hill: Silver City Cup
Cessnock: Opera in the Vineyards
Cobar: Festival of the Miner's Ghost
Coffs Harbour: Festival of Golf; Buskers and Comedy Festival
Coonabarabran: Starfest
Gilgandra: Coo-ee Festival
Grafton: Jacaranda Festival (Oct–Nov)
Griffith: Festival of Gardens; Springfest
Kempsey: Slim Dusty Country Music Festival
Leura: Village Fair
Murrumbateman: Field Days
Newcastle: Mattara Festival
Old Bar: Beach Festival
Orange Region: Wine Festival
Parkes: Country Music Spectacular
Uralla: Thunderbolt Festival
Wee Waa: Cotton Capital Country Music Muster
Wollombi: Music Festival

NT
Alice Springs: Masters Games (mature-age athletics, even-numbered years)
Berry Springs: Mango Festival

Qld
Atherton: Taste of the Tablelands
Bowen: Gem of the Coral Coast Festival
Bundaberg: Arts Festival
Condamine: Rodeo
Crows Nest: Festival
Gympie: Gold Rush Festival; International Film Festival
Ingham: Maraka (community festival)
Mission Beach: Aquatic Festival
Rockhampton: Barra Bounty
Townsville: Greek Festival
Warwick: Rodeo
Yeppoon: Oktoberfest; Lions Pinefest
Yungaburra: Tablelands Folk Festival

Kings Park Wildflower Festival, Perth

Melbourne Cup

SA
Kapunda: Kapunda and Light Agricultural Show
Kingston SE: Show
Port Pirie: Country Music Festival
Renmark: Rose Festival; Show

Tas.
Burnie: Skilled Burnie 10 (footrace)
Deloraine: Tasmanian Craft Fair (Oct-Nov)
Longford: Agricultural Show
Wynyard: Bloomin' Tulips Festival

Vic.
Ararat: Golden Gateway Festival
Horsham: Spring Garden Festival
Melbourne: International Arts Festival; Spring Racing Carnival (Oct–Nov)
Sale: Agricultural Show (Oct–Nov)
Wangaratta: Festival of Jazz (Oct–Nov)
Warrnambool: Spring Orchid Show

WA
Dwellingup: Nanga Music Festival
Esperance: Agricultural Show
Fremantle: Blessing of the Fleet; Festival (Oct–Nov)
Kalgoorlie-Boulder: Spring Festival; Kalgoorlie Cup
Kulin: Bush Races
Margaret River: Agricultural Show
Narrogin: Spring Festival
Perth: Royal Show

NOVEMBER

NSW
Albury: Show
Blackheath: Rhododendron Festival
Bulahdelah: Show and Rodeo
Eden: Whale Festival
Queanbeyan: Show
Sydney: Sculptures by the Sea
Wollongong: Viva La Gong

Qld
Gold Coast: Pan Pacific Masters (even-numbered years)

SA
Bordertown: Spring Festival & Show

Tas.
Deloraine: Tasmanian Craft Fair
Hobart: Point to Pinnacle Road, Run and Walk
Scottsdale: Agricultural Show
Sheffield: Agricultural Show

Vic.
Ballarat: Springfest
Melbourne: Cup
Queenscliff: Music Festival
Portland: Upwelling Festival
Stawell: Orchid Society Show

WA
Bridgetown: Blues Festival
Broome: Mango Festival

Darlington: Arts Festival
Fremantle: Festival
Jurien Bay: Indian Ocean Festival
Margaret River: Gourmet Escape
Perth: Leederville Carnival

DECEMBER

NSW
Sydney: Sydney to Hobart Yacht Race: Boxing Day Test (cricket)

Qld
Caloundra: Christmas Art & Craft Fair
Rockhampton: Summer Solstice Light Spectacular (Dec–Jan)
Woodford: Folk Festival (Dec–Jan)

Tas.
Hobart: Sydney to Hobart Yacht Race; Taste Festival
Stanley: Circular Head Show

Vic.
Lorne: Falls Festival
Murray River: Massive Murray Paddle (Yarrawonga to Swan Hill kayak race)
Traralgon: Agricultural Show

1

THE DREAM LAP

Driving along the Great Ocean Road

A lap of Australia is one of the country's greatest travelling experiences, and one that largely follows the National Highway – a 14,000km journey that links capital cities and provincial centres through the five mainland states and the Northern Territory. You can start the journey at any point along the highway and make detours or take shortcuts on many of the connecting inland highways as well. There are almost endless interesting towns, national parks and other attractions to see, and some people spend years trying to see it all.

Although the highway is a major road for most of its length, conditions vary greatly. It ranges from two-lane country roads to eight-lane super highways. There's even a roughly 630km section, between Normanton in Queensland and Borroloola in the Northern Territory, which is largely unsealed, mostly restricted to four-wheel drives and only open in the dry season.

The Dream Lap will take you through the densely populated east coast, over the long and lonely Nullarbor Plain, through mining and outback areas, farming country, fishing towns and into some of Australia's most beautiful environments. You will see forests, deserts, cities and sea. Whether you have a month, to see some of it, or a year to try it all, travelling around the coastal regions of Australia is an unforgettable experience.

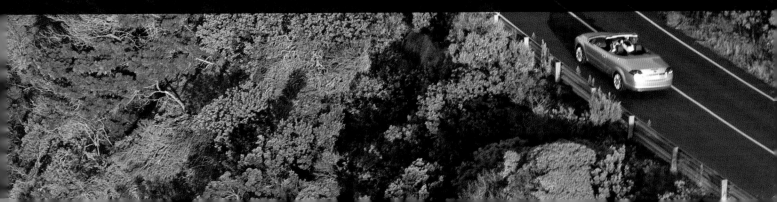

MELBOURNE TO SYDNEY pp. 8–24

Princes Freeway and Princes Highway (1041km)

This scenic coastal section of the Princes Highway links the major cities of Melbourne and Sydney. The route travels down the popular Mornington Peninsula, south of Melbourne, before turning east into the Gippsland Lakes region and through numerous coastal holiday resorts. Never far from the coast, it winds through the dense forest in Victoria's south-east before emerging on the stunning Sapphire Coast over the border in New South Wales. From here it passes numerous coastal hamlets, quiet fishing villages surrounded by lush farming areas, before arriving at the busy industrial city of Wollongong, just an hour south of Sydney. Along the way there are many good art and craft shops in which to browse, coffee shops offering a quiet cappuccino and plenty of places to get in or on the water.

⚑ PLAN YOUR TRIP

Melbourne is a vibrant and multicultural metropolis offering great restaurants, excellent shopping, tree-lined boulevards and magnificent public gardens. Inner-city public transport is top-notch and the best way to explore the CBD.

Rather than following Highway One as it escapes Melbourne's outer suburbs (and its traffic), the Mornington Peninsula Freeway, which is wide and open, carries commuters and holidaymakers south. Leaving the peninsula, the roads are well maintained and modern passing Phillip Island and Wilsons Promontory until meeting Highway One again at Sale. Fuel and services are regularly available.

From Sale the highway winds through the magnificent Gippsland Lakes region, a popular holiday destination. Although the highway is very good, the area is busy during holiday periods, especially in mid-summer when families flock to the beach and lakes.

From Orbost to Genoa the route rolls into the heavily forested hills of East Gippsland, with some lovely rest areas in the roadside forests. It's worth taking a short diversion off the highway to follow the coast near Marlo.

From Genoa to Bega the beautiful forests continue as the highway swings north towards the very popular New South Wales South Coast. The highway travels through this section and there are few towns to stop at, although distances between facilities aren't great.

Near Bega there are two routes north to Batemans Bay – either along Highway One or sticking to the coast. Both routes are good, although the coast road between Tathra and Bermagui is narrow and winding in parts. It's my pick of the two, even though there isn't any phone reception in some sections.

Batemans Bay north to Nowra is an often-busy route that carries year-round tourist traffic due to its proximity to Sydney. Nearly every seaside town is worth stopping in, as are many of the country hamlets like Milton and Burrill Lake. The highway has many opportunities for overtaking and plenty of places to stop.

The highway winds through the countryside between Nowra and Sydney, although recent highway upgrades have seen most of the towns bypassed now. The coastal diversion between Nowra and Gerringong is still popular. Wollongong is worth a detour too as its beachside northern suburbs offer many great things to do.

Sydney is one of the world's most beautiful cities with its sweeping surf beaches, soaring cliffs and the glittering waters of Sydney Harbour. Combined with great restaurants, superb architecture and interesting historic sites, the city is an irresistible destination. However, plan to stay on its outskirts, as there are no caravan parks in its inner suburbs and traffic is always exceptionally busy.

☁ BEST TIME TO GO

This is a great year-round tourist route but the many coastal resorts, always popular during school holidays, reach fever pitch at the height of summer and Easter. During these times, consider sticking to the more inland routes, where family tourism is less popular.

SYDNEY TO BRISBANE
pp. 25–38

Pacific Highway (962km)

The rambling Pacific Highway is a major coastal route linking New South Wales and sunny Queensland. Squeezed between the Great Dividing Range and the sea, the entire coastal strip is a popular year-round tourist destination. The golden beaches of the New South Wales Central Coast, subtropical resorts of northern New South Wales and world class attractions of the Gold Coast are all exciting destinations for holidaymakers.

Kangaroos on Pebbly Beach

Wategos Beach, Byron Bay

📌 PLAN YOUR TRIP

Once you've escaped Sydney's notorious inner suburbs' traffic to join the freeway north to Newcastle and Hexham, the superb multi-lane highway winds through rugged sandstone escarpment and crosses the picturesque Hawkesbury River. From this point you can detour through the Central Coast to take in the beautiful coastline and the magnificent Lake Macquarie, whose shore is dotted with many great caravan parks.

From Hexham, near Newcastle, to Kew, south of Port Macquarie, you will journey through the hills and forests near Bulahdelah, and out to the coast through the Great Lakes region. The coast is a holidaymaker's playground with pristine beaches, still lakes and numerous caravan parks. Along the highway the road surface is great, but through the Lakes Way to the coast, the road can be less than ideal in sections. In parts it's steep, winding and narrow, with few opportunities to overtake.

Some of New South Wales' best coastal regions are found between Kew and Coffs Harbour, with miles of sandy beaches, uncrowded national parks and numerous historical sites to discover. Up on the Dorrigo Plateau is an area of outstanding natural beauty, dense rainforests and numerous waterfalls. While the road condition in the coastal regions is great, up on the plateau it can often be damaged by heavy rainfall.

From Coffs Harbour to Ballina the highway winds its way through forest and passes lush dairy farms as it runs alongside the Clarence River. This is one of the last sections of the Pacific Highway to be upgraded, so roadworks are still common and many towns are being bypassed.

At Ballina, the highway climbs across a rich volcanic range between coffee and macadamia-nut plantations before sweeping down towards the fabulous coastal towns of Lennox Head and Byron Bay. If you're in a hurry then avoid driving through Byron Bay as the traffic is always slow. To the north, the wonderful Tweed Coast is a collection of beautiful beaches and prospering coastal holiday towns.

From Tweed Heads the highway runs inland a little, although you can easily detour along the Gold Coast Highway to experience the coast. This glamourous coastal strip is renowned for great beaches, excellent weather and a resort lifestyle. It's also home to many popular theme parks and colourful tourist attractions.

Brisbane's subtropical climes and river setting are very appealing. Buy a TransLink pass and crisscross the river to explore the many highlights on the city's ferries.

☁ BEST TIME TO GO

The constant mild climate means holidaymakers can make use of the area's natural coastal features practically all year round. October to April has ideal swimming weather on these sections of coast.

BRISBANE TO COOKTOWN pp. 39–60

🅰 Bruce Highway, Captain Cook Highway and Mulligan Highway (2000km)

The Bruce Highway links Brisbane with Cairns in the north, and several large regional cities in between. Beyond Cairns, the incredibly scenic Captain Cook Highway continues north to Port Douglas, while the Mulligan Highway heads inland before arcing back to the coast at Cooktown. This coast is dotted with great holiday destinations, romantic island resorts, lush tropical rainforests and sparkling beaches. The popular Sunshine Coast is just an hour or so north from Brisbane. Further north are the Whitsunday Islands and colourful city of Cairns. Busy cargo ports, fields of lush sugarcane, orchards of tropical fruits, sandy beaches, mountain playgrounds and great accommodation choices ensure the continuing popularity of this section of the Queensland coast.

📌 PLAN YOUR TRIP

To the north of Brisbane, the Bruce Highway sweeps through the Sunshine Coast region to Gympie. Take a detour to the range-top villages of Maleny and Montville, where craftspeople and artisans display their exquisite wares. The pristine beaches of the Sunshine Coast are easily accessible too, with an excellent coastal route running from Caloundra to Noosa Heads.

North from Gympie, leave the highway near Maryborough to travel along the protected waters of Hervey Bay. The bay's calm water offers a fabulous opportunity to view migrating humpback whales Apr–Oct. Further north, there's another worthwhile diversion to Bundaberg – home to the famous rum of the same name. A tour of the distillery is a must and the Mon Repos turtle rookery to the east is equally intriguing.

Although the Gin Gin to Rockhampton section of this drive isn't considered amongst the highlights, detouring via the coast to Agnes

Lake McKenzie, Fraser Island

CAIRNS TO DARWIN pp. 61–78

Kennedy Highway, Gulf Developmental Road, Burketown–Normanton Road, Nardoo-Burketown Road, Carpentaria Highway, Stuart Highway (2405km)

Journey across the top of Australia in this classic section of Highway One, commonly referred to as the Savannah Way. The route climbs steeply from the coastal plain of Cairns to the agricultural Atherton Tableland and then further west to the Barkly Tableland. Kurumba, Normanton and Burketown are sun-drenched winter havens, great for fishing and perfect escapes from the chill of the southern winter. Litchfield and Kakadu national parks and spectacular Nitmiluk (Katherine) Gorge are extremely popular destinations.

⚓ PLAN YOUR TRIP

From the modern city of Cairns, the Atherton Tableland, perched high above the coastal plain, is a fabulous destination with some wonderful attractions. However, the road up to Mareeba is steep and winding, so take your time and enjoy the views. From incredible waterfalls and colourful village markets to idyllic lakes, there is plenty to keep you occupied on the way to Mount Garnet.

From Mount Garnet, the route travels past the amazing Undara Lava Tubes and delightful Cobbold Gorge. Although most of the roads through the region are sealed some are only a single strip of bitumen, so take care around oncoming traffic. Further west, the iconic Gulflander takes you on an interesting train journey from Normanton to Croydon. Karumba, to the north, is an angler's paradise.

The route between Normanton and Borroloola is almost entirely unsealed, and this dry-weather route is best suited for four-wheel drives. If you don't fancy leaving the bitumen there's a fully sealed detour south from Normanton to Cloncurry, then west through Mount Isa to Three Ways Roadhouse on the Stuart Highway.

From Borroloola, the traveller has two options to continue west. The first is along the sealed Carpentaria Highway to join the Stuart Highway at the iconic Daly Waters. The alternative is to go north and then west on the off-road adventure through Limmen National Park, to join the Stuart Highway further north near Mataranka and its famous thermal pools.

From Daly Waters, the Stuart Highway sweeps northwards, passing by Mataranka and Cutta Cutta Caves. Spectacular Nitmiluk (Katherine) Gorge is just a short drive from the major outback centre of Katherine.

On the way to Darwin, stop at the fabulous Litchfield National Park with its wonderful swimming holes and waterfalls, or the historic Pine Creek goldfields and many WWII sites. Kakadu National Park is easily accessible from both ends of the park by sealed routes, and this amazing World Heritage–listed park has so much to offer. From cruising the spectacular Yellow Water Billabong to watching the brilliant sunset from Ubirr, the experience will be unforgettable.

Darwin is a modern cosmopolitan city in the sweltering Top End. It has great restaurants, thanks to its multicultural influences, as well

Water and Seventeen Seventy is a must. Just a short detour from the highway, the industrial city of Gladstone also offers plenty of things to do. It's also notable as the southernmost point in Queensland you're likely to see a wild crocodile.

Now officially in the tropics, having crossed the Tropic of Capricorn on the southern outskirts of Rockhampton, the next section of highway stretches past cane country and cattle properties. Be sure to detour to the Capricorn Coast and the popular holiday town of Yeppoon. Further north is Mackay, undeniably a coal mining town, but one with real class and great things to see. Don't miss the hinterland attractions in Eungella National Park.

Between Mackay and Townsville, the fabulous Whitsunday Islands lie off the coast from the town of Airlie Beach. Several small, secluded resort towns are dotted along the coast and Bowen is one of the highlights. Townsville is a busy coastal city with plenty for the visitor to see and do.

Small beach communities are nestled along the highway from Townsville to Cardwell and quiet, freshwater swimming holes are never far away either. Beyond the sugarcane centre of Ingham, the mountainous silhouette of beautiful Hinchinbrook Island looms into view.

North to Cairns, the highway passes through Australia's areas of highest rainfall with abundant fields of sugarcane below the towering summit of Queensland's highest mountain. In this section visit the wonderful Mission Beach or take a winding detour from Innisfail through the Atherton Tableland. Cairns is a colourful city and the capital of the tropical north. Its location is superb with the Great Barrier Reef to the east, the rainforests of the tableland to the west, and perfect beaches both north and south.

☁ BEST TIME TO GO

The weather ranges from moderate, dry winters in the subtropical south to hot, wet summers in the north. Travellers heading to the northern regions will enjoy more moderate conditions Apr–Nov. Just be aware that some areas are very popular and, where possible, bookings should be made at least a few days out to ensure you will get a spot.

as interesting museums and a range of fabulous tourist activities. Its climate is hot and dry or hot and humid, which just adds to the tropical feel.

☁ BEST TIME TO GO

Travel is popular in the cooler, drier months (Apr–Oct) as the hotter and more humid wet season makes travel uncomfortable. During the wet season, swollen rivers render many roads impassable too, especially the unsealed sections between Normanton and Borroloola.

DARWIN TO PORT HEDLAND
pp. 79–88

> **Stuart Highway, Victoria Highway, Great Northern Highway, Broome Highway (2167km)**

Highway One links Darwin and Katherine before veering south-west towards Broome and Port Hedland on the north-west coast of Western Australia. Across the border, the lush Ord River area, the rugged Kimberley and the long, sweeping beaches of Broome are just some of the attractions. The landscape ranges from rugged, rocky hills and deep gorges to rich, irrigated fields, intersected by the great Victoria, Ord and Fitzroy rivers.

⚓ PLAN YOUR TRIP

From Darwin's interesting museums, great restaurants and fabulous tourist attractions, the Stuart Highway heads steadily south to Katherine giving opportunities to explore beautiful locations like Litchfield and Kakadu national parks.

From Katherine, the Victoria Highway sweeps past a number of the Territory's legendary cattle properties and crosses the great Victoria River before arriving at Timber Creek. Even in this remote part of Australia, most of the roads are sealed, and it's only some tracks, like those in Judbarra (Gregory) National Park, that require four-wheel drive.

From Timber Creek to Kununurra you'll journey past grassy plains and wind through picturesque rocky ranges before crossing from the Northern Territory to Western Australia. Take note that all your fresh fruit and vegetables will have to be surrendered at the border, so if you have a lot consider a few days camping in Keep River National Park to eat it all first. Just after the border, turn off the highway to magnificent Lake Argyle, just 34km south-west.

On your way through the Kimberley to Fitzroy Crossing visit the remarkable beehive-shaped formations of Purnululu National Park. It's an extraordinary destination but only accessible to four-wheel-drive vehicles and single-axle off-road trailers. Other highlights of this section are the historic Old Halls Creek townsite and Geikie Gorge, which is easily reached from Fitzroy Crossing. A cruise is the best way to see the gorge's spectacular sites. The road is wide and well maintained in this section, with numerous rest areas, but beware of flash flooding, which can cut access for short periods following storms.

Between Fitzroy Crossing and Broome, take a diversion to Derby, a frontier port town at the head of King Sound. Further west, the magnificent beaches and relaxing charm make Broome a great place to stay.

The long section of the Great Northern Highway between Broome and Port Hedland runs parallel to the coast, although the sea is rarely in sight. However there are many opportunities to turn off to one of the coastal camping areas, that are popular for fishing, to rest for a few days, or weeks, before heading in to the busy industrial centre of Port Hedland.

☁ BEST TIME TO GO

The temperate dry season, May-Nov, ensures comfortable and usually dry travelling conditions. It is far less comfortable during the hot wet season, and high rainfall can restrict access to many areas too. Remember that of the entire Australian coastline the area between Broome and Exmouth is the most prone to cyclones.

PORT HEDLAND TO PERTH pp. 89–98

> **Great Northern Highway, North West Coastal Highway, Indian Ocean Drive (1752km)**

This fabulous Western Australian coastline is a destination that caters for a diverse range of interests. Skim the waves on a windsurfing board, catch a fish at a deserted beach, swim in the crystal-clear waters or picnic by a carpet of exotic wildflowers – the choices are endless. The Pilbara, a rich mining region that includes Port Hedland and Karratha, is also renowned for its spectacular red gorges – a landscape photographer's dream. There's also excellent access to tropical coral reefs and wonderful beachside holiday towns provide unlimited chances to camp by the water.

Jim Jim Falls, Kakadu National Park

Greens Pool, near Denmark

⚓ PLAN YOUR TRIP

On the way south from Port Hedland to Nanutarra Roadhouse, the coastal towns of Port Hedland, Karratha, Wickham and Dampier are all associated with mining. The historic towns of Point Samson, Cossack and Roebourne have plenty to offer those interested in local history as does the historic port of Onslow. The highway is well maintained, but roadside rest areas are basic, and most of the attractions are well off the main road.

Between Nanutarra and Carnarvon, the Ningaloo Coast is within easy reach of the highway. Just head north to Exmouth, a town humming with activity, to swim with whale sharks, or take a glass-bottom boat tour to see the beautiful coral reef. Further south, Coral Bay is a fabulous coastal resort, while Carnarvon is an important fruit-growing area and busy fishing port.

Between Carnarvon and Geraldton, the Shark Bay World Heritage Area is a lengthy deviation off the main route, but worth every kilometre. The stromatolites, historic telegraph station, shelly beaches and Monkey Mia dolphins make this area extremely popular. Further south, Kalbarri, at the mouth of the Murchison River, has sandy beaches, stunning gorges and colourful wildflowers, while Geraldton itself is a very popular seaside destination.

The Brand Highway carries most of the commercial and transport traffic south to Perth, but most of the tourists stick to the idyllic Indian Ocean Drive along the coast. Holiday resort towns thrive along this popular coast where activities reach fever pitch during the summer break. Fishing, windsurfing, boating and swimming are the main leisure pursuits. Commercial crayfish boats operate from every port, prolific wildflowers attract visitors during the balmy spring weather and grain crops grow throughout this fertile agricultural region.

Perth, with a Mediterranean-type climate and its magnificent coastal and river setting, is ideal for an outdoor lifestyle. Visitors to this city – one of the most isolated in the world – will find clean beaches, tranquil forests and well-kept parklands all within easy reach of the city centre.

☁ BEST TIME TO GO

Of the entire Australian coastline, the area between Broome and Exmouth is the most prone to cyclones. However further south most of the year is great for making the most of coastal, water-based activities, and rainy days are few and far between. South of Shark Bay, the wildflowers are a spectacular drawcard, particularly July–Oct.

PERTH TO ADELAIDE pp. 99–117

Ⓐ Old Coast Road, South Western Highway, South Coast Highway, Coolgardie–Esperance Highway, Eyre Highway, Princes Highway (3208km)

Dotted with vineyards, quality orchards and towering forests, South-West Western Australia is a mecca for travellers. This picturesque area, with numerous beach resorts and large coastal towns is popular during the warmer holiday periods and holds a special place in my heart. Crossing the Nullarbor Plain – that wide, flat, featureless geographical barrier separating west from east – is a long drive that's far from boring, and quite an adventure.

⚓ PLAN YOUR TRIP

From Perth the highway follows the coast south to Bunbury and then runs through a scenic fruit-growing region where fresh produce is readily available.

Rather than continuing to Manjimup, in the heart of timber country, divert from Highway One at Bunbury for a drive through one of Western Australia's most fabulous regions along the Bussell Highway. With great surfing and swimming beaches, quality wineries and a host of activities, this coast really comes alive during the warmer holiday periods.

From Manjimup the South Western Highway winds its way through towering forests on its way to Albany. Along the way experience the remarkable Valley of the Giants Tree Top Walk or spend a day learning about whales and local whaling history at Albany's historic whaling station.

From Albany to Norseman, the South Coast Highway heads inland through Ravensthorpe, a popular wildflower region, on its way to Esperance. Turn off the highway to explore and relax in the smaller coastal communities or to visit the extensive Fitzgerald River National Park near Bremer Bay.

Although Norseman isn't technically the beginning of the Nullarbor Plain, it is the point from which the Eyre Highway heads east, first through the great western woodland before the country opens up and the trees disappear on the 'treeless plain'. Once you cross the border into South Australia, the spectacular Nullarbor Cliffs are a wonderful feature of the Eyre Highway. Several rest areas along the cliff tops are great observation points, particularly for whale-watching. Further on, Penong is famous for its many windmills.

From Ceduna, leave Highway One for a diversion down the western coastline of the Eyre Peninsula. Tracking through the mallee flora, the Flinders Highway hugs the shoreline linking a series of beachside communities. This is quite a popular stretch of coast, renowned for mouth-watering whiting and oysters, great fishing and excellent camping. On the east coast of the peninsula the route follows the protected waters of Spencer Gulf up the Lincoln Highway to Port Augusta. Along the way the small coastal communities and the industrial city of Whyalla are popular tourist destinations.

From Port Augusta the highway continues to hug the coast as it travels south along the Yorke Peninsula – this is the long way to Adelaide, but worth every extra day (or week) it takes. This narrow strip of land, bounded by the Spencer Gulf and Gulf St Vincent, is dotted with sleepy, welcoming coastal villages. It's partly protected by the wonderful Innes National Park and has excellent camping options throughout.

It's less than an hour and a half to Adelaide from the eastern shores of the Yorke Peninsula. Adelaide is a well-planned city, set on the wide curves of the River Torrens and the picturesque beaches of the South Australian mid coast. Its location belies the fact that beyond the rolling hills are great tracts of arid scrubland – Adelaide is the capital of the driest state in Australia.

☁ BEST TIME TO GO

Weather in the south-west can be ideal, although it is often quite windy along the exposed coast, and it can be cold and damp in winter. Conditions across the Nullarbor are changeable, but temperatures soar during summer.

ADELAIDE TO MELBOURNE pp. 118–131

🄰 Anzac Highway, Princes Highway, Great Ocean Road, Princes Freeway (1189km)

The coastal route linking Adelaide with Melbourne is one of Australia's most unforgettable scenic drives. The mystical Blue Lake at Mount Gambier, seaside town of Portland (with some of Victoria's earliest historic buildings), southern right whales off the coast of Warrnambool, spectacular Great Ocean Road and fabulous Otway Ranges ensure there is something for almost everyone.

⚑ PLAN YOUR TRIP

From the well-planned city of Adelaide, detour south along the Fleurieu Peninsula – a long-time favourite with Adelaide holidaymakers. This area includes the coastal town of Victor

Harbor, with its history of whaling, and Goolwa, once a major port for paddlesteamers.

From the Fleurieu Peninsula, follow the route around Lake Alexandria back to the highway. The road travels through farming country and along the sand-swept lagoons of the Coorong, then across the ancient limestone coasts and volcanic lands to Mount Gambier.

From Mount Gambier to Port Fairy, the highway sweeps inland through forests, but the coastal route via Nelson is a great alternative. Portland is a busy regional town, while the historic fishing village of Port Fairy is popular for beachside holidays.

From Port Fairy to Colac, the highway follows the coast until Warrnambool, where it leads inland through rich dairying country, with dramatic remnant volcanoes and endless stone fences.

At Warrnambool, the Great Ocean Road beckons. One of the country's most spectacular drives, it passes exciting surf beaches and popular holiday resorts, and boasts breathtaking scenery. The road winds high above the thundering surf and twists through the dense, green forest of the Otway Ranges.

Melbourne is a vibrant and multicultural metropolis offering great restaurants, excellent shopping, tree-lined boulevards and magnificent gardens.

☁ BEST TIME TO GO

Winter can be cold and blustery in this region, but spring and autumn are fabulous seasons for touring. During the summer-holiday periods, tourists flock to many of the popular beaches.

Fleurieu Peninsula

MELBOURNE TO PHILLIP ISLAND

NEED TO KNOW

- 232km

- Foreshore camping reserves, family caravan resorts

- Spring, summer and autumn

- Beachfront camping, Phillip Island

- Apart from the traffic exiting Melbourne, the roads are great.

- This route travels through a densely populated part of Victoria and all facilities and services are available.

- None apply

Phillip Island penguins

MAKING THE MOST OF MELBOURNE

Melbourne's CBD is one of the easiest cities to explore on foot or by public transport thanks to its extensive tram network and grid-like city plan. If you're visiting and planning on spending a few days or more in Melbourne, get a myki Explorer card, which is the prepaid, reusable ticket to all of Victoria's public transport network. It comes with a ready-to-use card and handy maps to help show you around.

Well known for its great shopping, laneway bars and eateries, it's the sort of place you come to indulge in good food, great art and a little bit of shopping. For the caravan aficionados I suggest making your way to Chuckle Park Bar and Café on Little Collins Street, which is a great little cocktail joint serving from a vintage Franklin caravan.

INTRODUCTION

This diversion includes the extensive foreshore campgrounds of the Mornington Peninsula and the wild beaches, historic fishing villages and spectacular stretches of bushland that typify the Gippsland region and Phillip Island. Just south and east of Melbourne, this stretch of coast, is an area jammed with great things to do, excellent camping and interesting history to explore.

WHERE TO GO

The **Mornington Peninsula**, or just 'the Peninsula' to locals, is an incredibly popular holiday destination, especially in summer. Along the beaches at **Rosebud**, **Rye** and **Sorrento** the shire council manages three great camping areas, but they are almost always entirely booked out between Christmas and when school returns. The middle of the year is quiet though, and it's a great base for exploring the area's many restaurants (my favourite is The Milbri in Rosebud) and the greater peninsula, or just relaxing by the beach.

The peninsula is considered a golfer's paradise, with 14 different courses scattered across it, although the highlight is the course at **Flinders** for its uninterrupted views over the ocean. The peninsula is also increasingly becoming known as a food and wine destination, with an established wine and farmgate trail, and over 50 cellar doors, distillers and breweries.

If you're not interested in battling Melbourne's traffic to head west along the Great Ocean Road (*see* p. 127), the **Sorrento** to **Queenscliff** ferry runs daily across the mouth of Port Phillip, turning what can be a three hour, 200km trip into a pleasant 12km boat ride.

From the peninsula to **Phillip Island**, a trip of about an hour and a half, you'll follow the shores of Western Port. (It is actually to the east of Port Phillip Bay, but was named by George Bass on his 1798 expedition and was the most western point they reached.) The port is designated as a wetland of international importance in the Ramsar convention, so there are plenty of opportunities for boating and birdwatching. There's also the chance of seeing seals and dolphins.

Phillip Island is best known for its penguin colony and the Grand Prix Circuit. Before you get to the island, stop at the Maru Koala and Animal Park where you'll get the chance to meet a koala and feed native animals. Take a break in **San Remo** – it always amazes me how fast the tide rushes through the passage between the mainland and Phillip Island. There's also an excellent fisherman's co-op here, selling seafood that's come off the boat the night before.

Phillip Island is renowned for its wildlife experiences which include the famous little penguin colony, a platform for viewing wild koalas, Victoria's largest fur seal colony, birdwatching and whale-watching between May and October.

During the day, The Nobbies Centre and boardwalk is one of the best places to see Phillip Island in all its glory. Strolling along the boardwalk gives you the opportunity to see an amazing blowhole that's most impressive during large southern swells, or wander through Sea Bird Gardens where it's not uncommon to see penguins.

The nightly penguin parades require pre-booking, but there are a range of experiences available, including an underground viewing where you watch the parade from a bunker with the penguins passing at eye level. More up-close tours are available for smaller groups to private beaches too. Fees apply, and bookings are essential. Book online at www.penguins.org.au or call (03) 5951 2800.

The Grand Prix Circuit is an attraction in itself, even when there's no racing on. It hosts a 760m scale replica go-kart track of the circuit, offers regular hot laps and has a History of Motorsport museum that displays the history of motor racing on the island. Fees apply for all attractions. Call (03) 5952 9400 for details.

DON'T MISS

→ 19 holes – Flinders Golf Club

Whether you're into golf or not, the Flinders Golf Club has some of the most dramatic views over Bass Strait and Western Port. You can drive or walk the perimeter of the course and there are numerous places to stop and admire the view, with access to a few of the beaches too. The 18-hole course is just over 5km long and is open to the public seven days a week. The licensed clubhouse is open Tuesday, Thursday, Saturday and Sunday. Call (03) 5989 0583 for details.

→ A local character – Phillip Island Wines

Phillip Island is increasingly becoming known for its wine and food attractions, and cellar doors like Phillip Island Wines are a great way to meet local characters. Proprietor, Tim O'Brien is a real character who's never short of a story or a laugh. He's also a great source of local information and I've often asked his advice on what's best on the island.

→ A scenic detour – Yarra Valley and Mount Dandenong

The scenic Yarra Valley, about an hour's drive north-east of Melbourne is responsible for some of Australia's best cool-climate wines. It also has some incredible day-use areas, like Badger Weir Picnic Ground which is set amongst a stunning mountain ash forest with the prettiest little creek running through it. Likewise, **Mount Dandenong** is a good day-trip location filled with enchanting European-style gardens and great food stops along the way.

WHERE TO STAY

1 BIG4 Mornington Peninsula Holiday Park

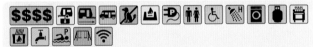

📍 2 Robinsons Rd, Frankston South
📞 (03) 5971 2333
🖥 www.big4mphp.com.au

BIG4 HOLIDAY PARKS

This is a good quality park in the far outer, south-eastern suburbs of Melbourne. It is a great base for those exploring the Mornington Peninsula or those connecting with the Sorrento to Queenscliff ferry. Bookings are required in peak periods.

2 Rosebud Foreshore Reserve camping area

📍 1380 Point Nepean Rd, Rosebud
📞 (03) 5950 1011
🖥 www.mornpen.vic.gov.au

This is the largest part of an extensive area of foreshore camping areas spread across 13km of beachfront in three different sections. Most sites are grassy and large with plenty of shade. The facilities are basic, but kept clean. In summer, this is an exceptionally busy camping area, and people often set up for the whole Christmas period.

3 Point Leo Foreshore camping area

📍 Point Leo Ring Rd, Point Leo
📞 (03) 5989 8333
🖥 www.pointleo.com

Another Mornington Peninsula foreshore camping area, but this one on the eastern shore. It's a smaller area. There are over 160 sites, 45 of which are powered. The facilities here are basic, but clean and well-kept. A ballot system works for peak times.

4 Anchor Belle Holiday Park

📍 272 Church St, Cowes
📞 (03) 5952 2258
🖥 www.anchorbelle.com.au

A great family holiday destination, this park is just 100m from the beach and 2km from the town centre.

PHILLIP ISLAND TO SALE

NEED TO KNOW

🕐 **226km**

🏠 **Beachside caravan parks, country showgrounds**

☁ **The weather is most pleasant between spring and autumn. The water is the warmest early in autumn.**

👁 **Fishing, surfing, beachside camping, Australian mainland's southernmost point**

🅰 **The roads in this part of Victoria are well maintained, although there are limited overtaking opportunities away from the highway.**

🍴 **All of these popular coastal towns have facilities to service the basic needs of tourists.**

⚠ **None apply**

Walhalla Goldfields Railway

INTRODUCTION

Whether you continue to follow the coast along the South Gippsland Highway, or decide to head further inland along Highway One, the Bass Coast between Phillip Island and Sale is Melbourne's playground. Along these routes you can venture to the Australian mainland's southernmost point via stunning coastal drives or explore some of Victoria's colonial and goldmining past.

WHERE TO GO

Coastal towns like **Kilcunda** and **Cape Paterson**, just 20 and 40 minutes from Phillip Island respectively, can be quiet places to relax by the ocean, but still close to many of the attractions of the Bass Coast. A great day out on bikes can be had along the Bass Coast Rail Trail between **Anderson** and **Wonthaggi**, which is Victoria's only coastal rail trail. It runs for 23 easy kilometres with just two moderate hills. Mostly compact gravel, with some boardwalk, it should take around three leisurely hours on a bike.

Cape Paterson is a typical Victorian seaside town just five minutes from the district's main business centre, Wonthaggi. It's vibrant and busy in summer, but quiet the rest of the year. There's a great foreshore walk which takes you 1.4 easy kilometres through native bushland and past the popular rockpool, which was blasted out by miners in the 1960s.

Back in Wonthaggi, you can visit the State Coal Mine Heritage Area, which is managed by Parks Victoria and open daily 10am–4.30pm. Underground mine tours are run daily at 11am and 2.30pm, taking you down into a historical coal mine. It's the only tour of its kind in the southern hemisphere. The area also has a nice cafe as well as extensive gardens to wander through, an old steam locomotive to climb aboard and a great heritage walk.

Wilsons Promontory, another hour to the east, is predominantly national park and an exceptionally wild and beautiful place. The most popular camping is at **Tidal River**, on the western shore of the peninsula – throughout summer you have to enter a ballot to get a spot. Here, the river offers a safe place to swim and play on the sand with good facilities at the camping area. From Tidal River you can embark on the two-day hike to mainland Australia's southernmost point, or you can just take your time to enjoy some of the shorter walks nearby. My favourite is the Squeaky Beach Track, which takes about an hour one way and heads over the headland to the beach.

If you've decided to take the inland Highway One route to Sale, there's a worthwhile diversion to **Walhalla**. The village is set in a steep-sided valley, and its historic buildings, heritage sites and period shops attract large numbers of tourists. I suggest leaving the caravan at a caravan park at Moe and exploring the town by car and foot. Experience the region's colourful mining history on a tour of the Long Tunnel Extended Gold Mine. Operating between 1865 and 1914, it was the richest single mine in Victoria. Tours are run daily into the underground machinery chamber. On weekends tours run at midday, 1.30pm and 3pm and on all other days tours run at 1.30pm. Fees apply, call (03) 5165 6259.

Nearby **Morwell**, which was settled in 1861 and supplied provisions to diggers heading to the Walhalla and Tanjil goldfields, has grown into a major regional city servicing the neighbouring mines and power-generating facilities. Powerworks at Morwell is a major interpretive centre for the region's power industry. It offers interesting guided tours for individuals and groups of the coalmining and power-generating facilities. Open Fri–Sun 10am–3pm. Bookings are essential for tours.

Sale is the main administrative centre in Gippsland and offers excellent shopping and all services. In 1888 the completion of the Sale Canal linked the town with the Thompson River, establishing a busy port for the steamers working the Gippsland Lakes. Today, the city has strong links with the rich offshore oil and gas fields. The RAAF Base East Sale is the home of the awesome Roulettes aerobatic display team.

DON'T MISS

→ **Historic Windsor House – Walhalla**
Picturesque Windsor House, Walhalla's only brick dwelling, was built in 1878 by J. Gloz using 90,000 handmade bricks. It is classified by the National Trust and also listed as being of national significance. Used for many years as a boarding house, the building has been restored and is now a luxury B&B.

WHERE TO STAY

5 Cape Paterson Caravan Park

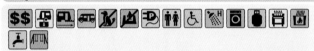

📍 1 Surf Beach Rd, Cape Paterson
📞 (03) 5674 4507
🖥 www.cpcp.com.au

This is a popular, beachside caravan park about 90 minutes from Melbourne. It's got large grassy sites in a natural coastland setting. It's very popular year-round with surfers and for fishing, and very busy in summer, when bookings are required.

6 Venus Bay Caravan Park

📍 113 Jupiter Boulevard, Venus Bay
📞 (03) 5663 7728
🖥 www.venusbaycaravanpark.com.au

An expansive caravan park tucked in between the beach and the river, it's a popular spot for surfing, fishing and beachside holidays. The facilities here are good and well maintained, and there's plenty of space for kids to run around. Dogs are permitted outside of peak times.

7 Tidal River camping area

📍 Wilsons Promontory Rd, Tidal River
🖥 www.parkweb.vic.gov.au

This is one of southern Victoria's favourite camping areas, in fact it is so popular in peak times that a ballot runs to allocate sites. The grounds are grassy and the sites large with good access to the beach and river. The camping area has a well-stocked kiosk and good facilities.

8 Seaspray Caravan Park

📍 1 Futcher St, Seaspray
📞 (03) 5146 4364
🖥 www.seaspraycaravanpark.com

This is a large and popular caravan park just behind the foredune at Seaspray. It has generously sized sites and good facilities. This is a very family friendly park, with a large playground, jumping pillow, camp kitchen and games room. Bookings required in peak periods. Discounts apply for three- and seven-night stays in off peak.

9 Sale Showground Caravan & Motorhome Park

📍 1–5 Maffra Sale Rd, Sale
📞 (03) 5144 6432

Located about 1km north of the town centre, just off the Princes Highway, this is a typical showground campsite that offers basic facilities at a good price. The site is pet friendly with a nice outlook. Discounts apply for CMCA members.

SALE TO ORBOST

Paynesville waterways

INTRODUCTION

This area, incorporating the Gippsland Lakes, Lakes Entrance and the charming town of Bairnsdale, has one of the highest densities of caravan park and camping areas in the state. It's an area where my family spent many summer holidays so I have fond memories of camping trips through here as a child. The Princes Highway offers a good road surface through most of the popular holiday towns, although in busy periods traffic can build up.

WHERE TO GO

From Sale, it's a slight backtrack to get to **Loch Sport**, but well worth it. The beachside resort town is set on a long spit between Lakes Reeve and Victoria. Fishing and watersports are the main attractions. The town has limited shopping and services, but it can still be busy during the holiday periods.

There's also good access to Ninety Mile Beach from town.

Back on the highway, and along the banks of the Avon River, **Stratford** was the site of the first permanent settlement in Gippsland. At the centre of a lush dairying area, the town has limited services, but it's a popular rest stop.

The old lakes port of **Bairnsdale** is an excellent, and popular, base for exploring the Gippsland Lakes region. A great way to get into the middle of the lake is along the Mitchell River silt jetties, which are a long thin landform stretching out into Eagle Point and Jones bays from **Eagle Point**. The narrow promontory has a gravel road almost to the end, with spots to stop to fish or picnic along the way. Don't tow your caravan down there though – it will be hard to turn it around.

Paynesville, a popular resort town, is almost entirely surrounded by water. It has a strong history in shipbuilding and today retains much of the region's boating repair and maintenance industry. Watersports and fishing are the main recreational pursuits. The town has basic shopping and services. Nearby **Raymond Island** is a wildlife sanctuary.

A popular resort town that lies at the eastern extremity of the extensive Gippsland Lakes system, **Lakes Entrance** is a year-round holiday destination. There are approximately 25 holiday parks in town and many have several permanent holiday vans. This is one of the most popular tourist destinations in Victoria. Even though there are many caravan parks, bookings are essential during holiday periods as the town can become extremely busy. The town has a good shopping centre and most services. The amazing carved stumps along the Lakes Entrance foreshore are a spectacular attraction for tourists as each piece has been crafted from a tree stump.

Orbost, the last stop on this section of the route, is located on the fertile flats of the Snowy River. There's a small range of services and a selection of shops – including a great bakery which I always stop at for a pie. In the main street there's a nice park that is ideal for a picnic lunch. The town is just off the highway and the small diversion is worthwhile.

DON'T MISS

→ Access to the High Country – Great Alpine Road (B500)

From Bairnsdale, you can escape the coast and travel the Great Alpine Road all the way to Wangaratta. The journey winds up to Omeo, the state's highest town, then climbs past Mt Hotham on Australia's highest all-weather road, before descending into the lovely town of Bright in north-east Victoria.

→ Australia's fourth longest beach – Ninety Mile Beach

Ninety Mile Beach stretches from Seaspray to Marlo. The pounding surf rolls in from Bass Strait and holidaymakers flock to the area for the great fishing. Although visitors could once drive along this beach, now no Victorian beaches have 4WD access. For those looking for a bit of adventure, a seasonal off-road trail does run behind some of the beach.

→ Lake activities – near Paynesville

The Gippsland Lakes are an extensive lake system separated from Bass Strait by the dunes of Ninety Mile Beach. The lakes surround many small islands and there is a seemingly endless choice of waterways that are navigable by small craft. Fishing, boating, waterskiing, sailing, swimming and canoeing are all popular recreational activities. Eagle Point and Paynesville are both good bases from which to explore the lakes.

WHERE TO STAY

10 Stratford on the River Tourist Park

📍 16 McMillan St, Stratford
📞 (03) 5145 6588
💻 www.stratfordontheriver.com.au

TOP PARKS

This is a good-quality park with a range of accommodation, just a short 600m walk from the centre of the small town. There are good facilities and it is ideally located for overnight stops or longer stays. Bookings are required in peak periods, and a minimum-length stay applies during Christmas, Easter and long weekends.

11 NRMA Bairnsdale Riverside Holiday Park

📍 2 Main St, Bairnsdale
📞 (03) 5152 4654
💻 www.nrmaparksandresorts.com.au/bairnsdale

NRMA Parks + Resorts

This is at the Mitchell River end of the main street (Princes Highway), just 500m from the centre of town. It sits on the bank of the Mitchell River and has beautifully maintained surrounds. Bookings are required in peak periods, and a minimum-length stay applies in all holidays.

12 Silver Sands Tourist Park

📍 33 Myer St, Lakes Entrance
📞 (03) 5155 2343
💻 www.ssands.com.au

Kui Parks
www.kuiparks.com.au

A smaller, owner-operated park close to the centre of town and catering only for tourists, this is a great selection for a stay in Lakes Entrance.

13 Lakes Beachfront Holiday Park

📍 430 Lake Tyers Rd, Lake Tyers Beach
📞 (03) 5156 5582
💻 www.lakesbeachfront.com.au

Just five minutes from Lakes Entrance and located on Victoria's magnificent Ninety Mile Beach, this is an ideal location for a family holiday or maybe a few days away from the hustle of life in a resort-style park.

14 Orbost Caravan Park

📍 2–6 Lochiel St, Orbost
📞 (03) 5154 1097
💻 www.orbostcaravanpark.com.au

Just 500m from the centre of town and off the main highway, this park has large shady trees, good, basic facilities and is convenient for overnight stops.

ORBOST TO GENOA

NEED TO KNOW

🕐	**122km (Highway One) to 140km (Marlo-Conran Rd)**
🏠	**Free, inexpensive, holiday resorts**
☁	**Spring, summer and autumn**
👁	**Fishing, surfing, walking, history**
🛣	**Good to great**
🍴	**This route passes through many small towns and regional areas, so services are limited.**
⚠	**None apply**

Frenchs Narrows, Marlo

INTRODUCTION

The undulating, forested ranges of East Gippsland embrace the highway as it winds inland away from the coast. Roadside rest areas surrounded by forest are ideal for a short break, and there's no shortage of camping options to suit every different traveller. As the eastern coastal extremities of Victoria enjoy a milder climate than Melbourne (about five degrees higher during winter), this region is a popular year round holiday destination. I often stay in the area because of the wide variety of holiday activities available.

Croajingolong National Park

WHERE TO GO

After the Snowy River rises on the slopes of Mount Kosciuszko it travels through the rugged, isolated ranges of East Gippsland before flowing quietly past the small coastal town of **Marlo** at its mouth. There's even a few great little free camping spots alongside it as you roll into town from **Orbost** (*see* p. 12). Sailing boats and paddlesteamers once ferried produce and passengers to and from the port.

Rather than heading back to Highway One from Marlo, follow the coast road to **Cape Conran Coastal Park**, about 19km to the east. There is a range of camping options and beachside cabins along East Cape Beach. Operated by Parks Victoria, this park is a popular holiday destination with lovely beaches and good coastal fishing. For information, call 13 1963.

Back on the Princes Highway, the small hamlet of **Cann River** services the local timber and dairy industries. The town is strategically located at the junction of the Princes and Monaro highways, the latter is a fully sealed route to Canberra (*see* p. 248). The township has limited services, but has a caravan park and is well situated for tourists passing through the area.

About 48km further on, **Genoa** is a small village at the turnoff to Mallacoota. The town has a hotel, camping area and post office, but no other services.

The gem of this section is definitely **Mallacoota**. At the mouth of Mallacoota Inlet, this resort town has a lot of appeal for tourists and lovers of the outdoors. It is surrounded by great bushwalking tracks, lovely beaches and protected waterways. It offers good fishing, boating and easy access to Croajingolong National Park. There is a range of shops and services in town, as well as an amazing caravan park that sprawls along the waterfront.

DON'T MISS

→ **Point Hicks Lighthouse – Cook's first sighting**
Captain Cook's journals, written aboard his ship *Endeavour*, record the first sighting of the Australian coast on 19 Apr 1770. The place was named Point Hicks after Lieutenant Hicks who made the sighting. Accommodation is available at the

lighthouse on this remote stretch of coast. For more information, call (03) 5156 0432.

→ **Drummer Rainforest Walk –
   refresh yourself**

Alongside the Princes Highway, where it crosses the Thurra River, is a walking track that meanders through the beautiful Drummer Rainforest. A stroll through this temperate environment is a relaxing break and a great idea if you need to stretch your legs after a long drive.

→ **Croajingolong National Park –
   a special place**

The 86,000 hectare Croajingolong National Park conserves a large expanse of undisturbed habitat along 100km of coastline. It is classified as a UNESCO World Biosphere Reserve. The park boasts over 300 bird species, including glossy black cockatoos, king parrots and lyrebirds. There are walking trails, camping areas and magnificent views from Genoa Peak. There is also excellent surf fishing. The park can be reached from Mallacoota. Contact 13 1963.

WHERE TO STAY

14 Orbost Caravan Park

See p. 13 – Sale to Orbost.

See p. 13 – Sale to Orbost.

15 Marlo Caravan Park and Motel

⦿ 10 Argyle Pde, Marlo
📞 (03) 5154 8226
🖥 www.marlopark.com

This is only a small caravan park with attached motel, but it offers grassy sites, has well-cared-for facilities, a basic playground and is only a short walk to the shops and local pub. There are also good discounts for longer stays.

16 Banksia Bluff camping area

⦿ Yeerung River Rd, Cape Conran
🖥 www.parkweb.vic.gov.au

This is a basic, but very popular, national park camping area within Cape Conran National Park. Sites are mostly level, dirt and set into the native bushland. A basic, flushing toilet block services the whole campsite, and there is a cold, outside shower. Great access to the beach. To camp in summer peak, a ballot runs, which must be entered before Aug.

17 Bemm River Caravan Park

⦿ 2–14 Sydenham Inlet Rd, Bemm River
📞 (03) 5158 4216 or 0428 557 438
🖥 www.bemmrivercaravanpark.com.au

Bemm River is a quiet coastal fishing village and its caravan park caters well to keen fishers. Its sites are grassy and even, and many of them are shaded by large trees. The facilities are modern and well kept, and it's a short walk to the local pub. There is no fuel available in Bemm River.

18 Cann River Rainforest Caravan Park

⦿ 7536 Princes Hwy, Cann River
📞 (03) 5153 9500

Situated on the banks of the Cann River within lush temperate rainforest, this is a delightful free camp for short stops (maximum 36 hours). It has many of the facilities of a paid caravan park, including toilets, (cold) showers and marked sites, but is currently free. Popular stop, so plan to get here early during busy periods.

19 Mallacoota Foreshore Holiday Park

⦿ Allan Drive, Mallacoota
📞 (03) 5158 0300
🖥 www.eastgippsland.vic.gov.au/Services/Council_Caravan_
   Parks/Mallacoota_Foreshore_Holiday_Park

This amazing, picturesque caravan park sprawls along the water's edge. There are over 650 sites and the reception building is just 150m from the town centre. Some waterfront sites even have their own moorings. This park is a bargain. Bookings are required in busy periods.

20 Wallagaraugh River Retreat

⦿ 73 Peisley Rd, Genoa
📞 (03) 5158 8211
🖥 www.facebook.com/wallagaraugh

This park is located at the end of 8km of good, unsealed road and the turnoff is well signposted on the Princes Highway, around 8km east of Genoa. On the banks of the Wallagaraugh River, this is a secluded spot for fishing, canoeing, and general peace and quiet. Bookings are required in peak periods.

GENOA TO BEGA

NEED TO KNOW

 126km

 Free camps, beachside caravan parks, family-friendly caravan resorts

 There is charm here all year round.

 Whale-watching, surfing, fishing

 This is an often winding, but good, section of Highway One.

 There are very limited services between Genoa and Bega.

 None apply

Whale watching in Merimbula

INTRODUCTION

Between Genoa and Bega, the road mostly travels inland, winding through the tall south-eastern forests. There's not a lot of traffic and it's quite pretty. Nearer to Eden, the highway skirts the coast again before sweeping inland through the dairy farming regions of the Bega River valley. There are numerous rest areas along the roadside, many in peaceful forested areas.

WHERE TO GO

On the shores of Twofold Bay one of the world's deepest natural harbours, and surrounded by lush, rugged forests, **Eden** was once a major whaling port. In more recent times, however, the town's focus has turned to whale-watching, which attracts large numbers of tourists Oct–Nov. A great time to visit is around the Eden Whale Festival, on the first weekend of November. Eden is considered one of the best land-based whale-watching spots in New South Wales.

George Bass, on his epic voyage in an open whale boat from Sydney Cove to Victoria's Western Port, sailed up the Pambula River in 1797. Graziers followed, establishing a rural industry. Today, visitors are attracted to the beauty of the area, especially for its coastal walking trails and charming village feel.

Merimbula is a major holiday centre. The beaches, lakes, bushland and year-round pleasant climate attract visitors to this region, which has been dubbed the Sapphire Coast. The town boasts a resort-style shopping centre with a good selection of cafes and restaurants. There is excellent local swimming, surfing and fishing, with the wharf a popular spot to drop in a line.

Tathra is my favourite seaside village along this stretch of coast. It is a popular beachside resort just south of Mogareeka Inlet and the mouth of the Bega River (which is sometimes closed to the sea). On the escarpment above town there is great mountain-biking. The park adjacent to the main surf beach has great facilities, including a good playground, skateboard ramps and a few cafes along the boulevard. The beach is patrolled and often produces very good surf conditions. The historic Tathra Wharf, classified by the National Trust, is a renowned fishing spot with a very good cafe.

Famous for its locally produced cheeses, **Bega** services a strong dairy industry and is the commercial centre of this region. You can visit the Bega Cheese Heritage Centre daily for cheese tastings, great interpretive displays and to purchase specialty Bega Cheese products. The town is close to the junction of the Princes and Snowy Mountain highways, making it an easy trip to the snowfields of New South Wales from here.

Tathra Oysters

→ Spot a killer whale – Eden

Established in 1931, the Eden Killer Whale Museum focuses on the history of early Eden and houses the skeleton of 'Old Tom', a killer whale renowned for his amazing antics. He, along with other orcas during the whaling period, would alert whalers to nearby whales and often swam around crew members who had gone overboard in an act that was believed to be protecting them from sharks. The museum is fascinating to visit. An entry fee applies and it is open 9.15am–3.45pm Mon–Sat and 11.15am–3.45pm Sun. Call (02) 6496 2094 for details.

→ Boyds Tower – near Kiah

Built at Red Point to serve as a lighthouse during the 1840s, Boyds Tower was never used as intended. Instead, it became a whale-spotting tower for the whaling industry. The tower is now conserved within Ben Boyd National Park and can be accessed via a short walking track. A park entry fee applies.

→ Candelo Markets – near Wolumla

The small historical village of Candelo, with its delightful old-world charm, draws a large crowd when it hosts the biggest markets on the South Coast on the 1st Sunday of each month (8am–1pm). With more than 150 stallholders regularly in attendance, these busy markets are definitely worth a visit.

WHERE TO STAY

21 Genoa rest area

📍 4 Park Rd, Genoa

This quiet, shady camp has plenty of open grass area with well-kept amenities. Perfect for overnight stops. Donations accepted for stays of up to 72 hours.

22 Boydtown Beach Holiday Park

📍 1 Boydtown Park Rd, Boydtown
📞 0405 447 361
💻 www.boydtownbeachholidaypark.com.au

Located close to the beach this park has a nice open camping area with lots of level grassy sites. The amenities are dated but tidy, and dogs are allowed Feb–Nov.

23 Garden of Eden Caravan Park

📍 Corner Princes Hwy and Barclay St, Eden
📞 (02) 6496 1172
💻 www.edengarden.biz

Set amongst shady trees and spacious lawns this family-friendly park has good facilities including modern amenities, fully enclosed camp kitchen and a lagoon-style swimming pool.

24 Eden Beachfront Holiday Park

📍 441 Princes Hwy, Eden
📞 (02) 6496 1651
💻 www.edenbeachfrontholidaypark.com.au

Just a short drive from the town centre, this beachside park has good facilities and a range of site choices available including ensuite, with some fronting onto the beach or creek.

25 NRMA Merimbula Beach Holiday Park

📍 2 Short Point Rd, Merimbula
📞 (02) 6499 8999
💻 www.nrmaparksandresorts.com.au/
merimbula-beach

NRMA
Parks + Resorts

Perched on the edge of the point in the heart of Merimbula this well-appointed park has breathtaking views up and down the sapphire coast. Perfect for whale-watching from May–Nov. The park is very family friendly with lots of activities for children, including a large swimming pool and splash park, and the amenities are modern and tidy.

26 Tathra Beachside

📍 2 Andy Poole Dr, Tathra
📞 (02) 6494 1302

Right on Tathra's beachfront, this popular park is actually owned by television personality Frankie J. Holden. The park has extensive facilities for families and is a short walk to most of Tathra's best attractions. Pets allowed during the quiet seasons.

BEGA TO BATEMANS BAY

NEED TO KNOW

🕐	**146km (Highway One) to 162km (Tathra–Bermagui Road)**
🏠	**Inexpensive camping areas to holiday resorts**
☁	**Spring, summer and autumn**
👁	**Fishing, surfing, walking, history**
🅰	**Good to great**
🍴	**Bega and Batemans Bay have good services.**
⚠	**None apply**

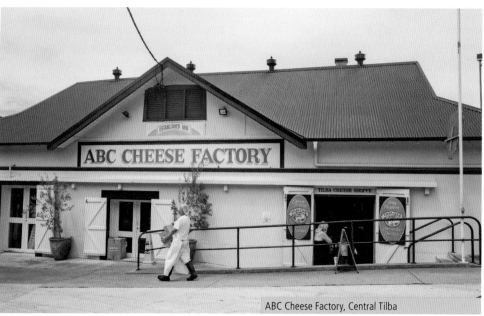

ABC Cheese Factory, Central Tilba

INTRODUCTION

This part of New South Wales is full of sandy beaches, rivers, lakes, fishing villages, rolling hills, rugged escarpments and native forests that have proved remarkably resilient to the excesses of coastal development. The region had its beginnings in whaling, but today sustainable tourism and dairying are the mainstays. The cooler climate makes summer the peak period – though even then, the area has a laidback feel.

WHERE TO GO

For the first half of this trip you have a tough choice to make – keep blasting up the highway, missing all the coast, or follow the Tathra–Bermagui Rd by backtracking to **Tathra**. The coastal route sticks close to the coastline through tiny towns like Wapengo, Barragga Bay and Bermagui before rejoining the Princes Highway again at Tilba Tilba.

The best reason to take the coast road is for the chance to camp in Mimosa Rocks National Park – one of my top ten spots in Australia – particularly Gillards Beach camping area in the park's south. The camping areas here, which are just behind the beach's foredunes, are grassy and large. There's a gravel road in, which is suitable for all vehicles. Spend your time here

fishing, surfing or exploring the distinct rock formations halfway along the beach.

The Tathra–Bermagui Rd continues north through the spotted gum forests of Mimosa Rocks National Park, crossing a few small creeks with terrific old timber bridges. It then follows the coast closely past **Barragga Bay** and **Cuttagee**, both of which have nice beaches.

Bermagui is the largest of the small towns along this stretch, and it's well regarded for its fishing. A number of big-game fishing charter boats moor here during summer, which is one of the main attractions. Bermagui is also well known for its unique horse-head-shaped rock, which is best viewed at sunrise when the light shines under its arch. Follow the Wallaga Lake Rd and park in Camel Rock car park to take the short walk out to Horse Head Rock.

Before rejoining the highway again, just south of Tilba Tilba, you'll cross Wallaga Lake on the narrow, natural weir and over a long single-lane bridge. Vehicles coming from the south must give way.

Although just off the highway, **Central Tilba** is a great place to stop. There's a great little, boutique cheese factory which is one of the town's main attractions. As well there's an almost overwhelming range of great little cafes, bric-a-brac shops and artisans' galleries. Parking can be tight close to town on weekends, especially if you're towing, so it's best to park on the outskirts.

At the mouth of the Wagonga Inlet, **Narooma** is another popular fishing resort town that offers numerous fishing charters. The town has a challenging cliff-top golf course – one fairway is split in two by the ocean and I've lost a number of balls to it. Boat cruises also operate to the famous penguin and seal colonies of Montague Island Nature Reserve. The nearby small town of **Dalmeny** has a very popular camping area, which my family regularly visited when I was a kid. It has barely changed since.

Close to the lush, forest-covered ranges, the small town of **Moruya** is at the heart of a strong dairy-farming region. Many of the town's buildings were built with the same locally quarried granite that was used in the construction of the Sydney Harbour Bridge. Moruya has good shopping and all basic services, as well as local markets at the Riverside Park each Saturday.

Another great town along here is **Mogo** – a town rich in history and full of quirky boutique stores, from an old-style lolly shop to a replica gold-rush colony. Formerly called Old Mogo Town, it's now The Original Gold Rush Colony. It's open daily 10am–4pm. Entry fees apply. Call (02) 4474 2123 for details.

Batemans Bay is the largest town south of Nowra, and a very popular beachside destination. Situated on the sweeping estuary of the magnificent Clyde River, the town is located at the junction of the

Kings and Princes highways. Batemans Bay has beautiful beaches and great restaurants, and is another popular fishing spot.

DON'T MISS

→ Cobargo – rural character

Cobargo is a small country town that retains its rural character. It has interesting buildings, cafes, and art and craft shops. The fabulous leather store, South Coast Leather, is in the old butcher's building, which is over 100 years old. It showcases a wide range of quality outdoor clothing, boots, handbags and leather craft.

→ Mogo Zoo – go wild

Mogo Zoo is a privately owned zoo dedicated to the survival of endangered species. There are several great exhibits, but the Nepalese red pandas, snow leopards and golden lion tamarins are some of the highlights. The zoo offers the opportunity to get up close and personal with many of the animals, including the chance to feed tigers and lions. I've done both and they were scary, humbling and amazing experiences. It's open 9am–5pm daily and entry fees apply. Contact (02) 4474 4930.

→ Exceptional fishing opportunities – everywhere

Fishing is one of the biggest tourist attractions throughout this coastal region. Keen anglers will find jetties and rocky points to cast from, along with quiet lagoons and a seemingly endless number of bays, lakes and rivers. Big-game anglers flock to the region Nov–June in search of a substantial catch, and fishing charters operate from most ports along the coast.

WHERE TO STAY

27 Gillards Beach camping area

♀ Mimosa Rocks National Park, Nelson
🖥 www.nationalparks.nsw.gov.au/camping-and-accommodation/campgrounds/gillards-campground

Nestled between the beach and bush, this camping area is suitable for caravans, motorhomes, tents and camper trailers. Barbecue facilities and pit toilets are available.

28 Reflections Holiday Park Bermagui

♀ 1 Lamont St, Bermagui
📞 (02) 6493 4382
🖥 www.reflectionsholidayparks.com.au/park/bermagui/

Situated opposite the stunning Horseshoe Bay Beach this dog-friendly park has large, flat grassy sites and is within walking distance of the local shopping area.

29 Mystery Bay Camp Ground

♀ 216 Mystery Bay Rd, Mystery Bay
📞 0428 622 357
🖥 www.mysterybaycampground.com.au

Bush camping at its best, this campground is surrounded by lush bushland and has absolute beach frontage. All sites are unpowered with pit toilets and cold showers available. The nearby cliff top provides the perfect spot for whale-watching Sept–Nov.

30 Dalmeny Campground

♀ Noble Pde, Dalmeny
📞 0428 635 641
🖥 www.dalmenycampground.com.au

With the beach on one side and Mummuga Lake on the other, this grassy camping area is perfect for a summer escape. The facilities are basic, but clean, and the local IGA is just across the road. Parts of the park are quite sloped and it can get windy at times.

31 Riverbreeze Tourist Park

♀ 9 Princes Hwy, Moruya
📞 (02) 4474 2370
🖥 www.riverbreeze.com.au

Overlooking the north bank of the Moruya River this well-maintained park is just a short walk over the bridge from the centre of town. Facilities include a swimming pool and recreation room, perfect for young families. This is a pet-friendly park.

32 BIG4 Batemans Bay Beach Resort

♀ 51 Beach Rd, Batehaven
📞 (02) 4472 4541
🖥 www.beachresort.com.au

This great beachfront park is about 3km from the centre of Batemans Bay. It has good facilities with plenty of options for children. Bookings are essential during peak times and a minimum length stay applies during Christmas, Easter and public holidays.

BATEMANS BAY TO NOWRA

NEED TO KNOW

🎨	**118km**
🏠	**Family friendly caravan parks to basic campgrounds**
☁	**Any time**
👁	**Fishing, surfing, walking, history**
🅰	**Good to great**
🍴	**You are never far away from a major regional centre.**
⚠	**None apply**

Lookout on 'One Track for All', Ulladulla

INTRODUCTION

The areas that surround the 118km of highway between Batemans Bay and Nowra is the summer playground of southern Sydney, and this region is so packed with small, coastal holiday towns that it would be almost impossible to do all of them justice in one pass. I've been visiting for over 20 years, and still have more to explore. The roads through here are great, the scenery ever changing and the little villages very welcoming.

WHERE TO GO

A gem of the New South Wales south coast is Murramarang National Park – one of the few places in Australia where spotted gums grow to the ocean's edge. In fact, of all the views in Australia, these through the skinny trunks of spotted gums to the ocean is one of my favourites. The national park hosts some great basic campsites and a few other more developed holiday parks, but all are a great base to explore the park's drives, walks and beaches.

Skirting the northern border of Murramarang National Park are the quiet coastal villages of **Merry Beach**, **Kioloa**, **Racecourse Beach** and **Bawley Point**. Each has its own great caravan park that is serviced by the one small grocery shop. These are really beautiful, family-friendly locations that fill up over summer.

Between here and Ulladulla, the highway doesn't venture far from the coast, although you can never see it, and is dotted with more small coastal holiday villages. **Lake Tabourie** has a very popular caravan park that overlooks Crampton Island, which can be accessed on foot at low tide and is also a local surfing hot spot. There's a quaint museum here, which houses an eclectic collection of artefacts from times past collected over a period of 20 years by a Tabourie local.

Right on the Princes Highway, **Ulladulla** is a busy fishing port that services most of the smaller surrounding towns with a large supermarket complex, library and a main street that's busy with cafes and small shops. Markets are held on the 2nd Sunday of each month at the harbour wharf off Watson St.

Bordering Ulladulla is the historical village of **Milton** where distinguished buildings date back to 1860. Cafes, antique stores, and art and craft shops line the main street, with the Rainbow Bakery renowned for its pies. For something different, head to Pilgrims, on the main street at the zebra crossing, which serves very popular vegetarian burgers. Milton has a small grocery store and basic services.

Sussex Inlet is a resort town located on the shores of the channel connecting St Georges Basin with the sea. Its population is largely made up of retirees and holidaymakers with fishing and boating

enthusiasts particularly attracted to the area. In season, there's a small strawberry farm accessed off Sussex Inlet Rd that is a great place for cheap, fresh-picked berries. Surf brand Ocean and Earth also has a factory outlet store here, which is a great place to pick up bargain beachwear.

Jervis Bay is one of the region's highlights thanks to its stunning clear waters, beautiful natural landmarks and the incredibly white sand of Hyams Beach (which is often, although incorrectly, called the whitest beach in Australia). Boating, watersports and scuba diving are the main attractions here. **Huskisson** (Huski, for short), overlooks the natural harbour and has some great seafood restaurants and fish and chip shops, as well as a small shopping centre and basic services. The Jervis Bay Maritime Museum on Woollamia Road chronicles the area's early ship-building history.

Located on the banks of the Shoalhaven River, **Nowra** is the key regional centre with a good shopping centre and all services. The bustling town services the numerous small communities dotted along the adjacent coast, as well as the nearby naval airbase and a strong farming community.

DON'T MISS

→ **Dolphin Point – a leisurely float down the creek**
At Burrill Lake, I recommend timing your visit for a sunny day on an outgoing tide

when you can join everyone rafting or tyre tubing out of the lake's opening to the sea. As the water drains, it reveals a pleasant sandy channel that winds its way to the main beach. Kids and adults alike can spend hours floating down, then walking back to the start to do it all again.

→ Pigeon House Mountain

Morton National Park's 720m high Pigeon House Mountain was named by Captain Cook in 1770. The rewarding climb to the top, including steel ladders, takes about four hours (return) from the carpark (accessible by conventional cars along an unsealed road).

From the top you can see as far Jervis Bay or Bermagui. A reasonable level of fitness is required. Morton National Park also encompasses the spectacular Fitzroy Falls (*see* p. 219).

→ Bendalong

I have soft spot for Bendalong because it's the location of our annual summer family holiday. The small town which is only serviced by a fish and chip shop, general store and caravan park, is on a small promontory with an exposed surf beach to the south, and sheltered bay to the north. The campsite is open and friendly, and due to

the surrounding native pines, protected from most of the main bad weather.

→ Something for aviation enthusiasts – near Nowra

Australia's Fleet Air Arm Museum is located just outside the gates of the naval air station HMAS Albatross. The museum has a fine collection of military aircraft, memorabilia, weapons and aviation equipment. Fly-in days and airshows are held regularly. It is open 10am–4pm daily and entry fees apply. Contact (02) 4424 1920 for details.

WHERE TO STAY

33 NRMA Murramarang Beachfront Holiday Resort

📍 Banyandah St, South Durras
📞 (02) 4478 6355
🖥 www.murramarangresort.com.au

NRMA Parks + Resorts

This beachside park is part of a large resort complex surrounded by beautiful bushland. There are plenty of activities onsite or you could head out exploring on any one of the many bush tracks surrounding the complex.

34 Pebbly Beach camping area

📍 Pebbly Beach, Murramarang National Park
📞 (02) 4478 6582
🖥 www.nationalparks.nsw.gov.au/camping-and-accommodation/campgrounds/pebbly-beach-campground-murramarang-national-park

This slightly remote campsite is nestled amongst the trees in the Murramarang National Park and is famous for the large number of kangaroos that enjoy lounging around. It is walking distance to the beach and there are numerous bush tracks nearby for exploring.

35 Merry Beach Caravan Resort

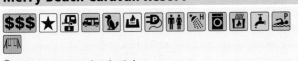

📍 46 Merry Beach Rd, Kioloa
📞 (02) 4557 1065
🖥 www.merrybeach.com

A wonderful, beachfront caravan park surrounded by pretty bushland. Many sites are absolute beachfront and

kangaroos often pay a visit. A quiet spot that's not too far from the region's attractions, but far enough to have no mobile reception.

36 Bendalong Point Holiday Park

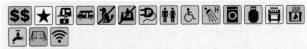

📍 1 Waratah St, Bendalong
📞 1300 733 025
🖥 https://bendalongpoint.holidayhaven.com.au

Located on Red Point Headland, Bendalong Point Holiday Park is ideal for a family holiday and perfect for those interested in fishing, boating and surfing.

37 Honeymoon Bay camping area

📍 Honeymoon Bay R, Beecroft Peninsula
📞 (02) 4448 3411
🖥 www.navy.gov.au/sites/default/files/documents/Honeymoon_Bay_Camping_flyer.pdf

This is a quaint, leafy campsite on the Beecroft Peninsula, on the northern shore of Jervis Bay. The facilities are good, although basic, but the wonderful, sheltered bay and small beach is the biggest attraction. Much of the Peninsula is used by the military as a weapons training range, so access is regularly cut while training operations are underway.

NOWRA TO SYDNEY

NEED TO KNOW

141km (Highway One) to 197km (Laurence Hargrave Dr)

Bush campsites, caravan parks and holiday resorts

Throughout the year, outside of school holidays

Hiking and walking, cafes and boutique stores, surfing, wineries

Good to great

There are three major centres between Nowra and Sydney, so all major and minor facilities can be accessed.

The highway between Wollongong and Heathcote is often affected by thick fog. Very strong westerly winds are also common throughout winter, especially under the escarpment.

Sea Cliff Bridge

INTRODUCTION

Set under the Illawarra escarpment, this leisurely stretch from Nowra to Sydney takes in the stunning coastline affectionately known as the Coal Coast. Along this route you'll find some of Australia's earliest colonial history, walk some of the country's best coastal hikes and enjoy a wide choice of camping options. It's a testament to how great the area is for caravanning and camping that I live along this stretch, but still regularly camp at various places along this section.

WHERE TO GO

Whether you're into coastal or hinterland experiences, there's little shortage of either as you head north from **Nowra**. First up, head to the bustling town of **Berry**, which is alive with excellent cafes and small restaurants, and boutique craft shops and antiques dealers. It's also home to the Berry Butchery, arguably one of the best in Australia.

From Berry you can head east to the small coastal towns of **Gerroa** and **Gerringong** where you'll find some of the route's best fishing and surfing. The two holiday parks either side of the Crooked River are popular family destinations throughout the holidays, but are generally quiet over the cooler months.

Heading west from Berry will take you up the prettily winding road to **Kangaroo Valley**. There's a great free camping site here with waterfront access to the Kangaroo River, which is popular for canoeing, kayaking and fishing. There's also an inexpensive caravan park with great facilities. The small town is a delightful mix of old-world charm and modern cafes.

From Kangaroo Valley continue north to the Southern Highlands towns of **Fitzroy Falls** and **Robertson**. The area is renowned for its local pie makers, and you can even follow a 'Pie Trail'. My favourite's the Robertson Pie Shop. Worth some of your time too are the walks around Fitzroy Falls.

Two easy options follow the rim of this 80m waterfall, rewarding you with some stunning views.

Whether you went along the coast, or into the highlands, head next to **Kiama**. From Robertson, you'll come down Macquarie Pass, which is steep, narrow and has two particularly sharp hairpins. If you are towing, take it very cautiously and use the lay bys to let other motorists past.

Kiama is a lively coastal town most famous for its blowhole. A naturally occurring shoot through the coastal cliffs, when the swell's running from the south-east, it shoots plumes of water up to 60m into the air. From here there's also a great 8.5km walk (one way), north to the Minnamurra River, taking in some of the region's most stunning coastline. There's a train station at each end, so you can jump on one to head back.

Continuing north, stick to the coast and head through the northern suburbs of Wollongong, including **Corrimal**, **Bulli** and

Coledale, which all have campgrounds right on the beach. From any of these it's an easy trip to Royal National Park, the world's second oldest, for some stunning walks or picnics. Highlights of the park include Wattamolla and Bonnie Vale, the latter which also has a camping area.

Sydney itself is reasonably light on good camping options, but it's well serviced by public transport if you wish to set up camp in Wollongong or Bonnie Vale to the south, or the NRMA Sydney Lakeside Holiday Park on Sydney's northern beaches. All are serviced by public transport and can get you into the CBD in less than 90 minutes.

DON'T MISS

→ The Big Potato – Robertson
It would be remiss of us not to mention one of Australia's most controversial 'big things'.

Celebrating the town's potato-growing heritage, a 10m long, 4m tall potato was constructed in the 1970s, although it looks far less like a potato and more like, how do we say it politely … a large poo in a field. Anyway, make up your own mind when you visit.

→ Food, craft and foragers markets – Wollongong
Wollongong and its northern suburbs are increasingly embracing local markets. Eat Street Markets, each Thursday night on Crown Street in Wollongong is the highlight, bringing together some of the region's best food trucks and restaurants in a lively marketta-style event. Through summer it also runs Saturday nights at the Bulli greyhound track. Other markets happen regularly at Coledale, Bulli and Helensburgh.

→ Minnamurra Rainforest Walk – Budderoo National Park
Minnamurra Rainforest in Budderoo National Park is a rare tract of subtropical rainforest adjoining Minnamurra Falls. There are elevated timber boardwalks (some with disabled access), as well as the Minnamurra Rainforest Centre and Lyrebird Cafe.

WHERE TO STAY

38 Coolendel camping area

$$$ ★

Grassy Gully Rd, Buangla
(02) 4421 4586
www.coolendel.com.au

Coolendel is a quiet bush campground on private property about half an hour west of Nowra. Almost entirely surrounded by a curve of the Shoalhaven River, it is one of the few places you can reliably get a spot at over Christmas if you're booking last minute. Facilities are basic and there is no power, but its natural setting and river playground make it exceptionally popular.

39 Mountain View Resort

$$

14 Shoalhaven Heads Rd, Shoalhaven Heads
(02) 4448 7281
www.mtview.com.au

This is a large, quality park with great amenities and very good facilities, including tennis courts, minigolf and a very popular 500m walking track with eight gym stations. Ask about the courtesy bus which runs from the park to Shoalhaven Heads Bowls Club. Bookings are essential in peak periods, and a minimum-length stay applies during Christmas, Easter and long weekends.

40 Seven Mile Beach Holiday Park

$$$

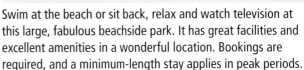

200 Crooked River Rd, Gerroa
(02) 4234 1340
www.kiamacoast.com.au/seven-mile-beach-holiday-park

Swim at the beach or sit back, relax and watch television at this large, fabulous beachside park. It has great facilities and excellent amenities in a wonderful location. Bookings are required, and a minimum-length stay applies in peak periods.

41 BIG4 Easts Beach Holiday Park

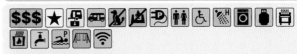

$$$ ★

30 Ocean St, Kiama
(02) 4232 2124
www.eastsbeach.com.au

This is a fabulous, large and well laid out beachfront park with very good amenities and facilities. The East family is a prominent owner of several New South Wales caravan parks and this is a fine example of one of their establishments. Bookings are required at peak times, and a minimum-length stay applies then also.

42 Coledale Beach camping area

$$ ★ 🏕️ 🚴 🏔️ 🎣 ⚡ 👫 ♿ 🚿ᴴ 🧺 📷 🔥 🚰

📍 677 Lawrence Hargrave Dr, Coledale
📞 (02) 4267 4302
💻 www.coledalebeach.com.au

A simple but popular campsite on a narrow strip of land between Lawrence Hargrave Drive and the beach, this is possibly the best camping area close to Sydney. The amenities are only basic, but the outlook is spectacular. It's very popular in summer, mostly filled by locals camping down the road from home.

43 Bonnie Vale camping area

$$$ ★ 🚴 🏔️ 👫 🚿ᴴ 📷 🔥 🚰

📍 Sea Breeze Lane, Bundeena
📞 1300 072 757
💻 www.nationalparks.nsw.gov.au/camping-and-accommodation/campgrounds/bonnie-vale-campground

This is a great national park camping area close to Sydney within Royal National Park. Adjacent to the isolated beachside suburb of Bundeena, there are a limited number of powered sites, good facilities and enviable proximity to Port Hacking estuary. It's a short ferry ride to Cronulla.

44 NRMA Sydney Lakeside Holiday Park

$$$$ 🏕️ 🚐 🚗 🚴 🏔️ 🎣 ⚡ 👫 ♿ 🚿ᴴ 📷 🛢️ 🚽 🔥 🚰 🏊 ⛺ 📶

📍 38 Lake Park Rd, North Narrabeen
📞 1800 008 845
💻 www.nrmaparksandresorts.com.au/sydney-lakeside

NRMA
Parks + Resorts

This is the pick of the Sydney caravan parks – of which there aren't many. It is a large, grassy park on the banks of Narrabeen Lake and just a short stroll from the beach. It is located in a quiet area on the north shore, away from the city humdrum. Excellent facilities complete the picture, including television cables to ensuite sites. Access is good along main roads.

Fitzroy Falls

SYDNEY TO NEWCASTLE

Wangi Point, Lake Macquarie

INTRODUCTION

The Sydney–Newcastle Freeway between Hornsby and Hexham is a spectacular multi-lane motorway, winding through the rugged sandstone escarpments and crossing the picturesque Hawkesbury River. The Old Pacific Highway gives better access to the caravan parks, mostly located by the beaches. Exit at Gosford and take the coastal route to Newcastle for the best places to stay and see.

WHERE TO GO

It's a little out of the way, but **Wisemans Ferry** is a very quiet, laidback rural town right on the edge of metropolitan Sydney. At the bottom of the deep valley carved out by the Hawkesbury River, the rustic town is full of Australia's colonial history, and the local pub, a grand sandstone building from 1827, is allegedly haunted. There's some good camping nearby and the area is also popular with hikers and mountain-bikers.

Back on the freeway, heading north, **Gosford** is the major commercial centre on the Central Coast and lies at the northern end of Brisbane Water. The region is a popular beachside tourist destination and has a steadily growing population, with many residents commuting daily to Sydney.

One of the area's main attractions is the award-winning Australian Reptile Park which has a fascinating display of snakes and lizards, and an incredible range of other wildlife. The park also milks Sydney funnel-web-spider venom for use in antivenoms and runs daily shows about the process. It's open 9am–5pm daily and entry fees apply. Call (02) 4340 1022 for details.

Following the coast, **The Entrance** is another popular beachside tourist town located on a narrow isthmus squeezed between the ocean and Tuggerah Lake. Fishing, sailing, windsurfing, surfing and swimming are all popular. There's also a great and very easy bike trail that follows the shores of the lake to Tuggerah. The whole thing is 28km return, but shorter if you don't go all the way to Tuggerah.

Further north, the landscape is dominated by Lake Macquarie, Australia's largest coastal saltwater lake. Its shores are dotted with a dozen or so delightful little caravan parks, most of them with views of the water in nearly every direction. Lake Macquarie is very popular for fishing, sailing and watersports, and its waters are warm nearly year round thanks to a number of power stations that use its waters for cooling.

On the northern shores of Lake Macquarie is **Swansea**, bordered on its other edge by the ocean. There is excellent access to the lake, and the town is close to great surfing beaches too. Just north, Nine Mile Beach can be accessed by four-wheel drives (permit required). To the south, Caves Beach has ocean-side caves which make it one of the prettiest beaches in New South Wales.

The freeway bypasses the major industrial centre and port of **Newcastle**. However, excellent surfing and swimming beaches close to the city draw many holidaymakers. Newcastle has excellent shopping and all services. The nearby Hunter Valley is one of Australia's premium wine-producing regions, and many wineries welcome visitors. Tours run daily from Newcastle.

WHERE TO STAY

45 NRMA Ocean Beach Holiday Park

📍 Sydney Ave, Umina Beach
📞 1800 611 522
🖥 www.nrmaparksandresorts.com.au/ocean-beach

NRMA Parks + Resorts

Just 2km from the centre of Umina, and set in a fabulous beachfront position, this quality park is a favourite of mine. There is a wide range of facilities, and children's activities are held most weekends and during the school holidays. It's a little more than an hour from Sydney.

46 Dunleith Tourist Park

📍 2 Hutton Rd, The Entrance North
📞 (02) 4332 2172
🖥 www.dunleithtouristpark.com.au

This park has a picture-postcard location on the waterfront where Tuggerah Lake meets the sea. It has good tourist facilities and is in walking distance of town. Pets are allowed, but not in school holidays. Bookings are required in peak periods and a minimum-length stay applies during holidays.

47 Norah Head Holiday Park

📍 22–30 Victoria St, Norah Head
📞 (02) 4396 3935
🖥 www.norahheadhp.com.au

TOP PARKS

This large, council-operated beachside park is a popular holiday destination. Bookings are required in peak seasons.

48 Belmont Pines Lakeside Holiday Park

📍 24 Paley Cres, Belmont
📞 (02) 4945 4750
🖥 www.lakemacholidayparks.com.au

Not far south of the city of Newcastle, this park is in a superb position on the shores of Lake Macquarie, in a quiet location, off the highway. It faces north, with great views across the water. It is a good family park and an ideal base for watersports enthusiasts.

49 Stockton Beach Holiday Park

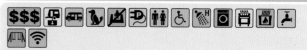

📍 3 Pitt St, Stockton
📞 (02) 4928 1393
🖥 www.stocktonbeach.com

TOP PARKS

This park is located on the beachfront, just north of the port of Newcastle. Stroll along the beach, join in with the fishing on the breakwater, or just watch the large ships come and go. The park has large, grassy areas and very good amenities. Bookings are required in peak periods, and a minimum-length stay applies at these times.

NEWCASTLE TO KEW

NEED TO KNOW

🚗	**307km**
🏠	**Beachside caravan parks, family holiday resorts, inexpensive caravan parks**
☁	**The NSW mid-north coast has a mild climate and is pleasant all year.**
👁	**Surfing, national parks, four-wheel driving**
A	**Highway One is excellent, and very new in some places. The Lakes Way is narrow, winding and bumpy in sections.**
🍴	**Forster, Tuncurry and Taree are large centres with all services, but locations like Seal Rocks have only a general store and no fuel.**
⚠	**None apply**

Kayak, Two Mile Lake, Myall Lakes NP

INTRODUCTION

Following the highway between Newcastle and Kew you'll be travelling along some of Australia's newest road, thanks to years and years of roadworks designed to bypass many smaller towns, improve road safety and decrease congestion during peak holiday times. It's a section best explored by being prepared to venture off the highway as often as possible. It's dual lane the entire way along Highway One, but most of the diversions are winding single-lane roads with turnouts to allow faster vehicles to pass.

WHERE TO GO

Found on the end of Tomaree Peninsula, **Nelson Bay** is one of New South Wales' premier tourist destinations and the district is awash with caravan parks. Popular for fishing, boating, sailing, surfing and four-wheel driving this is a well-developed tourist town with good shopping and great restaurants.

Bulahdelah is a popular town for overnight stays, especially now the highway (and trucks) bypass it. There's also a great, free camping area overlooking the Myall River, just across the bridge from the town's main shopping district. Situated at the foot of the Great Dividing Range, Bulahdelah is surrounded by bush reserves and the last chance to stock up on supplies before heading into Myall Lakes National Park and its camping opportunities.

Rather than continue along the highway, the Lakes Way is a magnificent scenic drive that winds past three lakes systems, often the road is just metres from the water's edge. It also passes more than 20 beaches, three national parks and several state forests. The route is dotted with pretty picnic spots and vantage points overlooking stunning vistas before emerging at Forster and Tuncurry.

Seal Rocks is one of the more popular diversions from the Lakes Way. A small fishing and tourist village overlooking Sugarloaf Bay, it has a good caravan park and small general store, the view from which is amazing. Here you can visit Sugarloaf Point

Lighthouse, built in 1875 and one of only two lighthouses in Australia with an external staircase. It's open daily and entry to the park and around the tower is free.

The popular family and fishing holiday centres of **Forster** and **Tuncurry** grace the entrance of picturesque **Wallis Lake**. This shallow tidal waterway is a boating and recreational playground. Along with cruises and magnificent coastal scenery, the galleries, cinemas, fun parks and restaurants provide interest and entertainment for holidaymakers of all ages.

The culturally diverse town of **Taree** is the hub of the Manning Valley and features excellent sporting and shopping facilities with roads leading to quaint craft villages, beautiful seaside sports and mountainous national parks. Riverfront parklands in the centre of town provide space to relax.

Continue further west from Taree to visit **Wingham**, a town full of character with its National Trust–listed buildings and manicured gardens. Wingham Brush Nature Reserve, close to the town centre, has giant Moreton Bay figs and interesting wildlife.

Log bridge over Manning River, Barrington Tops State Forests

It's the largest remaining riverine rainforest in New South Wales.

Kew is a small, tidy town on the Pacific Highway most famous for its 'big axe'. The town also makes clever use of its name in catchy, and often slightly 'abrasive' phrases – Far Kew bumper stickers are exceptionally popular. The iKew Information and Community Centre has an interesting display on aviation pioneer Nancy Bird Walton, who was born in the town, as well as good motorhome parking and a public dump point.

DON'T MISS

→ Climb the tower – Cape Hawke Lookout

Forster and Tuncurry are awash with great lookouts, which during whale-migration season, are usually packed with people. My favourite, because it's a little further out of town, is the Cape Hawke Lookout. From the carpark, there are around 400 stairs to climb before you get to an 8.4m high tower that rises through the canopy and offers 360 degree views over the region. It's a great place to watch the sunset.

→ Barrington Tops

The town of Gloucester calls itself the base camp for Barrington Tops National Park. This green and peaceful town is known for its top quality produce including Barrington beer and perch. The Tops is a subalpine rainforest area with great walking, four-wheel driving and fishing opportunities.

→ New South Wales' tallest tree – the Grandis

Just a short detour from the Lakes Way follow the unsealed Stony Creek Rd to the 400-year-old flooded gum that's over 76m tall with a circumference of 11.5m. Although the area was heavily logged in the 1970s, this tree was spared. Today, the National Parks and Wildlife Service maintains a nice picnic area under the tree. Park entry fees apply.

Pelicans, Tuncurry, Great Lakes

WHERE TO STAY

50 Ingenia Holidays One Mile Beach

$$$

📍 426 Gan Gan Rd, One Mile Beach
📞 (02) 4982 1112
💻 www.ingeniaholidays.com.au

This quality, award-winning caravan park is located in the popular Port Stephens region, just a few kilometres south of Nelson Bay. Set alongside a popular surf beach it has excellent amenities and great recreational facilities. I always enjoy staying here. Bookings are required in peak periods.

51 NRMA Myall Shores Holiday Park

$$$

📍 Resort Rd, Bombah Point
📞 1300 769 566
💻 www.nrmaparksandresorts.com.au/myall-shores

This park is situated on the shores of Myall Lake. Access is from Bulahdelah and 10km of the road in is unsealed. Located in a picture-postcard position close to the vehicle ferry crossing, it has good facilities and a cafe. Bushwalking, canoeing, fishing, sailing, swimming and waterskiing are all popular activities. It is very easy to spend a few days here lazing on the shores of the lake. Bookings are required in peak periods.

52 Reflections Holiday Parks Seal Rocks

$$$$

📍 Kinka Rd, Seal Rocks
📞 (02) 4997 6164
💻 www.reflectionsholidayparks.com.au

It's located in an idyllic position overlooking a popular beach, so the park's powered sites are very in demand. There is little more than a shop at Seal Rocks. Bookings are required, especially in peak seasons, and a minimum-length stay is imposed.

53 The Ruins camping area

$$ ★

📍 The Lakes Way, Booti Booti National Park
💻 www.nationalparks.nsw.gov.au/camping-and-accommodation/campgrounds/the-ruins-campground-and-picnic-area

An open grassy campsite in between the Lakes Way and the beach, it's a popular family spot in school holidays with a locally renowned surf break out the front of the beach. Facilites are well maintained but basic, typical of most national park campsites. Not all the sites are level, so don't forget your ramps.

54 BIG4 Forster Tuncurry Great Lakes Holiday Park

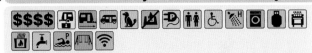

$$$$

📍 1 Baird St, Tuncurry
📞 (02) 6554 6827
💻 www.greatlakes.com.au

A quality park on the water's edge. It is in a quieter area of town, but just a short distance from the centre. There is a good range of facilities and bookings are required in peak periods – a minimum-length stay applies during all holidays.

55 Diamond Waters Caravan Park

$$$

📍 152 Diamond Head Rd, Dunbogan
📞 (02) 6559 9334
💻 www.diamondwaterscaravanpark.com.au

On the peaceful banks of the Camden Haven River and bordered by Crowdy Head National Park, this is a picturesque camping area with good facilities and off the general tourist route. Sites are grassy and flat, and the park is pet friendly.

KEW TO COFFS HARBOUR

NEED TO KNOW

🎨	**173km**
🏠	**Beachside caravan parks, family caravan resorts**
☁	**This is a beautiful area all year round.**
👁	**Fishing, surfing, beachside holidays, boating**
🅰	**The highway between Kew and Coffs is great, although traffic through Coffs Harbour can be slow.**
🍴	**There are all major services and facilities along this section of Highway One.**
⚠	**None apply**

Yarriabini National Park

INTRODUCTION

Taking in the popular coastal resort towns of Port Macquarie, Crescent Head, Nambucca Heads and Coffs Harbour this section drifts through forests, past coastal towns and along stunning rivers. This section of highway is comfortable to drive, especially now that the majority of roadworks have been completed.

WHERE TO GO

First settled as a convict outpost in 1821, **Port Macquarie** is one of the state's oldest towns. It is a busy regional centre at the mouth of the Hastings River and a very popular holiday destination with great waterfront pubs, a vibrant restaurant scene and plenty of water activities to keep holidaymakers entertained.

If your rig can handle a little bit of off-road towing, take the ferry across the river and head along the narrow and often rough Point Plomer Rd which runs parallel to the beaches between Port Mac and Crescent Head. There are great places to camp along here, including **Point Plomer**, **Delicate Nobby** and **Racecourse Head**. The road is not suitable for two-wheel-drive vehicles

that are towing and should be avoided entirely after heavy rain.

The sealed route up the highway will take you past **Kempsey** – from where you can drive out to Crescent Head. Kempsey is the centre of a diverse agricultural area and also home to the Akubra Hats Factory. There's also an excellent native food reserve in Wigay Aboriginal Cultural Park. It's open year round and is a great place to try local bush tucker.

Crescent Head is a worthwhile detour to take in the surfing town's relaxed beachside atmosphere. It's classified as a National Surfing Reserve and is also popular with beach anglers. The town also has a golf course and an excellent caravan park. From Crescent Head you can travel all the way to South West Rocks without rejoining Highway One.

South West Rocks is a popular destination for camping, bushwalking, fishing and boating. It has a small shopping centre and basic services. The biggest attraction in the area is Trial Bay Gaol, which was first occupied in 1886 by 'good conduct' prisoners. It then became an internment camp for German nationals during WWI. Today you can wander through the re-created cells and adjoining grounds.

The gaol and attached museum are in Arakoon National Park, east of South West Rocks, and an entry fee applies. It's open 9am–4pm daily. Contact (02) 6566 6168 for details.

Now bypassed by the new highway, **Nambucca Heads**, at the picturesque mouth of the Nambucca River, is a holiday destination where fishing, surfing and windsurfing are popular. I often stop in town for lunch when doing the Sydney to Brisbane trip in a day and enjoy a break in Bellwood Park (off Riverside Dr) or a walk along the Nambucca V-Wall to admire all the painted rocks. Nambucca Heads has good country-town shopping and all services for travellers.

Coffs Harbour began as a port for cedar cutters in the 1840s but has developed into a key regional town and holiday destination. A fishing fleet operates from the harbour and bananas flourish on nearby hillsides. In fact, the Big Banana was one of Australia's first 'big' attractions. Today visitors can amuse themselves at the growing theme park that's being constantly developed on the site. Attractions include a large water-slide park, toboggan rides, a magic show and minigolf. Coffs is a major regional town and has all facilities.

→ Crocodile pies – Frederickton

The small town of Frederickton, north of Kempsey, is home to the famous Fredo Pies. Here you will discover a seemingly endless choice of sumptuous pies made on the premises, including the famous crocodile pie. Look for the small shop on Macleay St after taking either of the Kempsey exits. It's open 7.30am–5pm daily. Contact (02) 6566 8567.

→ Timbertown – near Wauchope

At Timbertown, many buildings delightfully re-create a timber town of the 1880s. Attractions include a blacksmith, sawmill and steam train. See demonstrations of sleeper cutting and shingle splitting, then eat damper and roast meat at the town's inn. Timbertown also has a nice little campsite, while the Bago Tavern across the road is a delightful country pub. Open daily 10am–3pm. Contact (02) 6586 1940.

→ Performing dolphins – Coffs Harbour

Dolphin Marine Magic at Coffs Harbour is terrific entertainment for the whole family. It is home to rescued dolphins, seals and penguins and offers the chance to feed penguins or be kissed by a seal (they taste like fish). Entry fees apply; check the website for show times (www.dolphinmarinemagic.com.au). It's open 9am–4pm daily. Contact (02) 6659 1900.

WHERE TO STAY

56 Reflections Holiday Parks Bonny Hills

- 920 Ocean Dr, Bonny Hills
- (02) 6585 5276
- www.reflectionsholidayparks.com.au/park/bonny-hills

This beachside holiday park has a range of accommodation options including premium ocean-view sites. It has good, modern amenities and is just a short walk down to the beach. Bookings are required during peak periods.

57 NRMA Port Macquarie Breakwall Holiday Park

- 2 Munster St, Port Macquarie
- (02) 6583 2755
- www.nrmaparksandresorts.com.au/port-macquarie

NRMA
Parks + Resorts

Located just a short distance from the heart of Port Macquarie this is a large, good-quality park right on the waterfront. It has spacious grassy sites and excellent amenities. Bookings are required during peak periods and a minimum-length stay applies over Christmas, Easter and public holidays.

58 Point Plomer camping area

- Point Plomer Rd, Limeburners Creek
- www.nationalparks.nsw.gov.au/camping-and-accommodation/campgrounds/point-plomer-campground

This campsite is right on the beachfront in the picturesque Limeburners Creek National Park. It has plenty of shade and mostly level campsites, with basic but clean amenities. There is no power available and no marked sites.

59 Crescent Head Holiday Park

- Reserve Rd, Crescent Head
- (02) 6566 0261
- www.macleayvalleycoastholidayparks.com.au/crescent-head

Popular with the surfing crowd, this beachside holiday park offers a choice of beach- or creek-side accommodation with dated but clean amenities. Local shops and cafes are just a short walk down the road, as are the bowling and golf clubs. Bookings are required in peak periods and a minimum-length stay applies over Christmas, Easter and public holidays.

60 BIG4 Sunshine Resort South West Rocks

- 161–171 Phillip Dr, South West Rocks
- (02) 6566 6142
- www.big4southwestrocks.com.au

BIG4
HOLIDAY PARKS

This family-friendly park is close to the historic Trial Bay Gaol and has an excellent range of facilities including a large swimming pool with a separate toddler area and pirate-ship water park. Bookings are required in peak periods and minimum-length stay applies during holidays.

61 Park Beach Holiday Park

- 1 Ocean Pde, Coffs Harbour
- 1800 200 555
- www.parkbeachholidaypark.com.au

BIG4
HOLIDAY PARKS

This lovely beachfront park has excellent drive-through sites and a range of great facilities including a resort-style swimming pool and splash park. It is centrally located in walking distance of the beach and just a short drive to all of Coffs Harbour's wonderful attractions including the Big Banana and Dolphin Marine Magic.

COFFS HARBOUR TO BALLINA

	214km
	Beachside family caravan parks, basic camping areas, national parks
	This region has a great climate all year.
	Surfing, fishing, beach holidays, four-wheel driving
	Good to great
	Most facilities are readily available.
	None apply

Evans Head

INTRODUCTION

Winding through pretty countryside and alongside majestic rivers the highway is close to many great seaside and rural towns that make welcome stopovers. Yuraygir National Park, stretching from north of Coffs Harbour all the way to Angourie, is some of the least-developed stretches of coastline in eastern Australia. There are several key centres and numerous small resort towns, plus kilometres of sandy beaches, national parks, wild river estuaries and nearby mountain ranges all set in a terrific subtropical climate.

WHERE TO GO

The short stretch between **Coffs Harbour** and **Arrawarra** is dotted with quiet beachside towns, often with little more than a general store and caravan park. They are a nice contrast to the busyness of Coffs itself. I really like **Red Rock** (whose name comes from a tragic part of European-Aboriginal relations in Australia) for its wonderful estuary, usually quiet caravan park and nice nearby walks. **Woolgoolga**, which is a far larger town, is also great for its sheltered beach and good fishing. Across the road from the caravan park is Bluebottles Brasserie, which is in my opinion, the best cafe between Sydney and Brisbane.

Yuraygir National Park offers an untold number of experiences and contains some out-of-the-way camping areas that are often cited as the best in Australia, although many can only be reached after driving along a beach or two. My family really enjoy staying at **Illaroo**, just north of **Minnie Water**. Here you camp amongst the gum trees, overlooking Sandon Beach. It's popular with fishermen, surfers and four-wheel drivers who can access the beach around the low tide. The small town of Minnie Water has a general store which sells reasonably priced fuel and great fish and chips.

Further north, **Grafton** is a large inland regional centre on the mighty Clarence River famous for its graceful buildings, many that are classified by the National Trust. It is also known for its magnificent jacarandas. There is very good regional shopping and a fine art

Darlington Beach Holiday Park

Big Banana, Coffs Harbour

gallery if you venture past the service centres on the highway. As a side note, if you want to bypass Grafton's service centres, turn onto Centenary Dr, which bypasses town from either direction and shaves five minutes off the north-south route.

You'll follow the Clarence River from here all the way to Yamba. On the way, **Maclean**, with its proud Scottish heritage is well worth a stop. Many of its signs even carry Gaelic translations and an annual Maclean Highland Gathering, a Scottish festival, is held here each year around the last weekend in March.

Yamba is one of my favourite towns in Australia for its laidback beach atmosphere and culture that revolves around life on the water. It overlooks the estuary of the Clarence River and has good rock, beach and deep-sea fishing. There's an active sailing community and it's just minutes from some legendary surfing spots too. A particular highlight is to spend a summer evening at the dining lounge of the historical Pacific Hotel which sits above Main Beach.

Across the Clarence is **Iluka** – a daily passenger ferry runs between the two communities. Iluka is a much smaller coastal town on the edge of World Heritage–listed Iluka Nature Reserve which contains the largest remnants of beachside rainforest in New South Wales. Easy walking paths

through the lilly pillies in this compact reserve are popular with birdwatchers, while endangered animals and birds, such as the black-necked stork, little tern and squirrel glider, make their home here.

Evans Head is another popular holiday destination, with safe swimming beaches, surf beaches and a quiet estuary. It nestles between Broadwater and Bundjalung national parks and is home to one of New South Wales' largest caravan parks. Beach fisherman can explore over 40km of beach in four-wheel drives north of here, all the way to South Ballina.

At the mouth of the Richmond River, **Ballina** is an ideal base from which to explore the Northern Rivers region. The beaches and estuary are popular with anglers and surfers. Ballina is also the centre of Australia's tea-tree oil industry and has a growing restaurant and cafe scene along the main street. It has a number of large supermarkets and all facilities.

DON'T MISS

→ Inland alternative – Grafton to Brisbane
The Summerland Way is a picturesque alternative route linking Grafton and Brisbane. It is about the same distance as the route along the Pacific Highway, but the winding, fully sealed road takes in Casino, Kyogle and Beaudesert, climbing through the ranges close to the Queensland border.

→ Medicinal oil – near Ballina
Tea-tree oil is reputed to have extraordinary medicinal applications, being antiseptic and fungicidal. Thursday Plantation pioneered the development of the tea-tree oil industry and now exports its products around the world. Visitors can see the oil being produced, walk through herb gardens and find their way through a tea-tree maze. It's open 9am–5pm weekdays, 10am–4pm weekends. Contact (02) 6620 5150 for details.

→ Rafting across the Pacific – Ballina
See an unusual boat in Ballina's Naval and Maritime Museum. The famous Las Balsas raft (made from balsa wood) successfully made the epic journey from Ecuador in South America to Ballina in 1973. Admission is by donation and it's open 9am-4pm daily. Contact (02) 6681 1002 for details.

WHERE TO STAY

62 NRMA Darlington Beach Holiday Park

$$$$ ★ ...

104–134 Eggins Dr, Arrawarra
(02) 6640 7400
www.nrmaparksandresorts.com.au/
darlington-beach

NRMA
Parks + Resorts

This popular beachfront park has flat grassy sites and excellent facilities. It is extremely family friendly with plenty to entertain the kids including a large swimming pool complete with spa and waterslide, jumping pillows, BMX bike track and bowling green. Bookings are required during peak periods and a minimum-length stay applies.

63 Reflections Holiday Parks Red Rock

$$$ ...

2 Lawson St, Red Rock
(02) 6649 2730
www.reflectionsholidayparks.com.au/park/red-rock/

This quiet, back-to-basics park offers open grassy spaces with basic, clean amenities. It's very popular with fishermen and young families.

64 Illaroo camping area

$ ★ ...

Sandon Rd, Minnie Water
www.nationalparks.nsw.gov.au/camping-and-accommodation/campgrounds/illaroo-campground

This out-of-the-way camping area has a large grassy site with absolute beach frontage. There is four-wheel drive access to the beach nearby and a lovely little cafe in the town, just a short drive down the road. Good quality pit toilets are available onsite. Pre-booking is not available so early arrival is recommended.

65 Gateway Lifestyle Holiday Park

$$ ...

598 Summerland Way, Grafton
(02) 6642 4225
www.glhp.com.au/parks/grafton

This well-maintained park offers large grassy sites with space for your car and awning. It has good facilities including a tennis court, pool and modern amenities.

66 Nymboida Canoe Centre

$$$ ★ ...

Armidale Rd, Nymboida
(02) 6649 4155
www.nymboidacanoecentre.com

This is a lovely, quiet, riverside camping area which offers peaceful bush camping on mostly flat grassy sites. Amenities are basic but clean and there is limited power available.

67 Reflections Holiday Parks Evans Head

$$$ ...

18 Park St, Evans Head
(02) 6682 4212
www.reflectionsholidayparks.com.au/park/evans-head

A popular coastal destination, this dog-friendly park is conveniently located just a short walk into town for easy access to shops and facilities. Bookings are required during peak season and a minimum-length stay applies during Christmas, Easter and public holidays.

68 Flat Rock Tent Park

$$$$ ...

38 Flat Rock Rd, Ballina
(02) 6686 4848
www.flatrockcamping.com.au

This great little bush camping area has spacious grassy sites with good clean amenities. There is plenty of shade and it is just a short walk to the beach which is popular for fishing and swimming.

BALLINA TO TWEED HEADS

Lyrebird track, Mt Warning

INTRODUCTION

Exquisite beaches, wide rivers, World Heritage rainforest and a laidback lifestyle are some of the features of this tropical paradise in the north-east of the state. An area always known for its alternative-lifestyle offerings, it's increasingly becoming a sought-after area to live and holiday for those seeking an escape from mainstream ideals. Popular activities include fishing, surfing, diving, hiking and whale-watching. For the more laidback travellers, there are markets, festivals, scenic drives and excellent local restaurants.

WHERE TO GO

Bangalow is a small town now bypassed by the highway. (As an interesting side note, I once pulled into the service station here and ran out of fuel as I rolled up to the bowser – lucky!) It has become quite trendy with craft shops, eateries (many with a focus on healthy and organic produce) and galleries attracting visitors.

The coastal strip between **Skennars Head** and Byron Bay, taking in Lennox Head and Broken Head, is incredibly popular for its world class surfing spots, in particular Lennox Head point break and the Pass, at the southern end of Clarkes Beach in Byron Bay.

Lennox Head has a nice, grassy caravan park adjacent to Lake Ainsworth. The main street is popular for its numerous cafes, restaurants and boutique shops.

Byron Bay is an incredibly popular resort town with restaurants, accommodation, extensive resort-style shopping and most services. Despite its image as a laidback town with a slower lifestyle, traffic through it often comes to a standstill and the town is often in news headlines for its stance on free camping. Even so, its beaches are stunning and there is no shortage of boutique shops to visit, local produce to buy and great restaurants to try out.

North-west of Byron Bay and into the hinterland, **Mullumbimby** is known for its fabulous woodwork and has good, country-town shopping. Markets are held on the 3rd Sunday of each month and each Friday 7–11am, offering great opportunities to engage with the local community and growers.

Further north, on the banks of the Tweed River, **Murwillumbah** is at the centre of the rich Tweed Valley. It has restaurants, hotels, clubs and a good regional shopping centre. The nearby Tweed Regional Art Gallery has an ever-changing display of excellent local art and a great restaurant.

Tweed Heads lies on the New South Wales' side of the border with Queensland, adjoining **Coolangatta** and occupying both banks of the Tweed River. Many parks and reserves along the foreshore are really popular for picnics and pleasant walks, while boating, fishing and surfing are other favoured pastimes. Numerous boats operate in the estuary and there are fishing and diving charters available, as well as cruises up the Tweed River. The town is known for its great clubs and has extensive shopping and all services.

DON'T MISS

→ **Mount Warning – near Murwillumbah**
Although there are plenty of places to take a break, a stop at Wollumbin (Mt Warning) is a must. Named by Captain Cook, to warn passing ships of the reef nearby, it is the first spot on the Australian mainland to be hit by the sun each morning. It also plays a significant role in the initiation of Bundjalung men. Although its Summit Walk is very popular with tourists, in Aboriginal culture the uninitiated are forbidden to climb it. At the base of the Summit Walk is the Lyrebird picnic area and walk, which is a short, easy stroll through lush Gondwana rainforest. At the base of the mountain there's a small, grassy camping area that is popular in warmer weather, but pretty quiet the rest of the year.

Australia's easternmost point – Byron Bay

For those interested in setting foot on Australia's cardinal points, Cape Byron is the most accessible. The 3.7km Cape Byron walk, which also takes in Cape Byron Lighthouse and Watergos Beach, leads out to the Australian mainland's easternmost point.

Fresh seafood – Brunswick Heads

At Brunswick Heads, the Brunswick-Byron Fisherman's Co-op, located on the river's edge adjoining the marina, has a large retail outlet with a delicious selection of fresh and cooked seafood. Buy fresh fish to take away or enjoy freshly cooked fish and chips in the adjoining park. The shop is open daily.

WHERE TO STAY

69 BIG4 Ballina Headlands Holiday Park

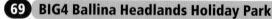
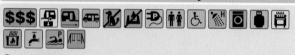

📍 35 Skennars Head Rd, Skennars Head
📞 (02) 6687 7450
💻 www.ballinaheadlands.com.au

Located in a quiet area between Lennox Head and Ballina, this park has some excellent facilities including a solar-heated pool and spa, beach volleyball court and flat grassy sites. Perfect for a long or short stay.

70 Reflections Holiday Parks Lennox Head

📍 Corner Ross St and Pacific Pde, Lennox Head
📞 (02) 6687 7249
💻 www.reflectionsholidayparks.com.au/park/lennox-head

With the beach on one side and Lake Ainsworth on the other this is the perfect spot for water lovers. There are some nice cafes within walking distance, as well as the local surf club.

71 Broken Head Holiday Park

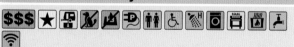

📍 184 Beach Rd, Broken Head
📞 (02) 6685 3245
💻 www.brokenheadholidaypark.com.au

Broken Head Holiday Park is ideally situated right on the beach and is popular with surfers and people looking to escape the crowds of Byron Bay.

72 Tweed Coast Holiday Parks Pottsville South

📍 Tweed Coast Rd, Pottsville
📞 (02) 6676 1050
💻 www.tchp.com.au/tweed-coast-holiday-parks-pottsville-south

This tidy riverfront caravan park has good facilities and is a short walk to the local shops. However, sites do get busy during peak times and larger rigs may have trouble manoeuvring between the crowds.

73 BIG4 Tweed Billabong Holiday Park

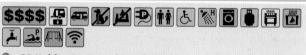

📍 30 Holden St, Tweed Heads South
📞 (07) 5524 2444
💻 www.tweedbillabong.com.au

This large, award-winning caravan park is perfect for families and boasts its own tidal billabong and a large water park with heated pools and multiple water slides. Bookings are essential during peak periods.

TWEED HEADS TO BRISBANE – THE GOLD COAST

Aerial view of Surfers Paradise

INTRODUCTION

From the long, near-perfect beaches and bustling coastal cities like Surfers Paradise, to the heavily developed theme parks south of Brisbane, nearly everything about the Gold Coast is intended to entertain and delight visitors. The Pacific Motorway links the Gold Coast to Brisbane, and in places carries eight lanes of traffic. The old road, now the Gold Coast Highway, meanders along the coast, but it can often be heavily congested. Those bypassing the Gold Coast should stick to the M1.

WHERE TO GO

Despite Surfers Paradise carrying the name, **Coolangatta**, right on the Queensland–New South Wales border, is the Gold Coast's surfing centre. Constant flow from the mouth of the Tweed River has created a build-up of sand to the north, resulting in what's generally considered as one of the world's best surfing waves at Snapper Rocks. It's a sight to see on a good swell, even if you're not a surfer. Watch the action from the balcony of the Rainbow Bay Surf Lifesaving Club. Coolangatta shares great shopping and

services with the bordering New South Wales town of Tweed Heads (*see* p. 35).

Parklands on either side of Currumbin Creek are popular spots for picnickers and offer access to the beach. From Palm Beach Parklands, on the northern shore, there's a great walk following the creek through Tarrabora Reserve and Beree-Badalla Reserve. At points the boardwalk takes you out over the creek.

Surfers Paradise, with its high-rise buildings and extensive shopping complexes, is only minutes from some of south-east Queensland's most popular caravan parks. The light rail that was developed for the 2018 Commonwealth Games makes travel around the area easier too. Beachfront markets run Wed, Fri and Sun nights 4–9pm, while nearby Cavill Avenue is the precinct's main shopping and entertainment hotspot.

For a quieter Gold Coast experience, head away from the beaches. Currumbin Rock Pools, up in the Currumbin Valley, is a natural swimming hole in the upper reaches of Currumbin Creek that also offers good picnic grounds. A small cafe and gallery operate across the road.

There are also some great drives across the Gold Coast hinterland which take in

charming little towns like **Canungra** (with nearby campsite Sharp Park River Bend Bush Camping) as well as **Mount Tamborine** and its stunning waterfall walks and swimming holes, and even a glow-worm tunnel. The Tamborine Rainforest Skywalk is another popular attraction, with steel bridges up to 30m high amongst the rainforest canopy.

Brisbane is located on the banks of the picturesque Brisbane River, and is a central base from which to tour nearby coastal areas. Paddlesteamers, yachts, floating restaurants, ferries and cruise boats play a pivotal role in the life of this vibrant city. Visitors will discover it is both modern and relaxed.

DON'T MISS.

→ **Highland quiet – Gold Coast hinterland**

World Heritage–listed Lamington National Park is an area of rugged ranges and deep valleys covered in subtropical rainforest. There are two sections to explore, both with access to stunning walks along burbling creeks or past roaring waterfalls with hikes for all levels of ability. Green Mountains section, via Canungra, contact (07) 5544 0634; Binna Burra section, via Nerang, contact (07) 5533 3584.

→ Parrot paradise – Currumbin

Currumbin Wildlife Sanctuary is one of the best attractions in this area. The sanctuary is home to the world's largest collection of Australian native animals, spread over 27 hectares of landscaped grounds. The park is especially famous for the magnificent rainbow lorikeets that visit each day to be fed. Entry fees apply and it's open daily 8am–5pm.

→ The theme parks

The Gold Coast is internationally renowned for its string of big theme parks which includes Dreamworld, Movie World, Sea World, Wet'n'Wild and WhiteWater World. The five parks (and a number of smaller theme parks) are owned by two companies, which each offer combo passes to their establishments – if you're planning on visiting more than one, this is the best way to book. Each park also has reciprocal deals with the nation's large motoring clubs like NRMA and RACQ, so discounts are often available.

WHERE TO STAY

74 Tallebudgera Creek Tourist Park

📍 1544 Gold Coast Hwy, Palm Beach
📞 (07) 5667 2700
🖥 www.goldcoasttouristparks.com.au

A favourite of ours, this caravan park fronts onto Tallebudgera Creek and is just a short walk from the beach. It is among the Gold Coast's best parks, centrally located with good amenities and a wide range of facilities, including a tennis court and heated pool. Bookings are required in peak periods and a minimum-length stay applies at Christmas, Easter and on long weekends.

75 NRMA Treasure Island Holiday Park

📍 117 Brisbane Rd, Biggera Waters
📞 (07) 5500 8666
🖥 www.nrmaparksandresorts.com.au/treasure-island

NRMA
Parks + Resorts

This is a good-quality park owned by the NRMA. It has a licensed family bistro and a range of great facilities, including a resort pool, jumping pillow, spas and minigolf. The park is a short stroll from Harbourtown shopping complex, a movie theatre and a number of good restaurants.

76 Broadwater Tourist Park

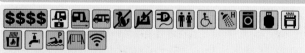

📍 169 Marine Pde, Southport
📞 (07) 5667 2730
🖥 www.goldcoasttouristparks.com.au

Position is everything and this spacious council-owned park fronts the Gold Coast's Broadwater. It has very good facilities and outstanding views across to Marina Mirage and the Palazzo Versace. There are several restaurants within walking distance and the main Southport business and shopping centre is about 1.5km away. A minimum-length stay applies at Christmas and school holidays.

77 Brisbane Holiday Village

📍 10 Holmead Rd, Eight Mile Plains
📞 (07) 3341 6133
🖥 www.brisbaneholidayvillage.com.au

TOP PARKS

Easily accessed from the Pacific Highway, this large, quality park is on the south side of the city. Facilities include minigolf, a tennis court, convenience store, cafe and lovely grassy sites. For the children, there is a novelty swimming pool and playground. The park is a good base for exploring Brisbane. Bookings are required in peak periods.

78 Brisbane Gateway Resort

📍 200 School Rd, Rochedale
📞 (07) 3341 6333
🖥 www.brisbanegateway.com.au

Situated 16km from the city centre, this is a good-quality park with easy access to all the major highways, including the Pacific Motorway. Its excellent facilities include a resort pool and tennis court. Bookings are required in peak periods.

BRISBANE TO GYMPIE

NEED TO KNOW

167km

Beachfront caravan parks, full-featured caravan parks, basic camping areas

This is a great year-round route

Australia Zoo, fishing, four-wheel driving, beaches

Good to great

It passes through many large centres so all services are available.

None apply

Noosa North Shore camping

INTRODUCTION

From Bribie Island in the south and Rainbow Beach to the north, the Sunshine Coast offers far more than just stunning beaches and bustling coastal towns. Inland, the forested ranges and ridges of the hinterland hide quaint villages and hamlets where visitors can enjoy waterfalls, walks, scenic drives and superb views. The Bruce Highway, which travels through the middle of it all is a busy, multi-lane highway with good overtaking opportunities.

WHERE TO GO

Caboolture is a fast-growing satellite city of Brisbane that's in the heart of pineapple-growing country. To the east is **Bribie Island**, which is the only one of south-east Queensland's islands that's accessible by bridge. The island has a rich history as a tourist destination and was a WWII army base protecting the northern entrances to Moreton Bay. It's popular for fishing, boating, golfing and four-wheel driving on the long beach north of **Woorim** (permits apply). It also has a great museum at **Bongaree** that details the island's natural, Indigenous and colonial histories. Open daily with free entry.

The Glass House Mountains were named by Captain Cook when he sailed north along the coast in 1770 as he thought their jagged peaks resembled the giant furnaces of his homeland. The two best places to view them are from the Glass House Mountains Lookout on Glass House Woodford Rd, or over Pumicestone Passage from White Patch (Bribie Island) at sunset.

Caloundra is situated at the north end of Pumicestone Passage and in sight of Bribie Island. It's got great beaches, good restaurants and is just minutes from attractions like the Eumundi Markets which run each Wednesday. Caloundra is also near great surfing beaches, has good shopping and is popular for fishing and boating. Our family loves spending our evenings walking the Bulcock Beach foreshore boardwalk.

The scenic route along the top of the Sunshine Coast hinterland through **Maleny** and **Montville** is almost another world. Craft stores, cafes, restaurants, artisans at work and fabulous views of the coast make this a magnificent trip. The views over the Glass House Mountains from Mary Cairncross Park are awesome on a clear day. The route up and down the range is steep, but the road is very good.

Maroochydore is the commercial centre of the Sunshine Coast and has all services, excellent shopping and good restaurants.

The Maroochy River is popular for fishing, but the patrolled beaches are the major tourist attraction.

Despite being bypassed by the highway, **Nambour** remains a key service centre on the Sunshine Coast and has a major public hospital. Nambour is most famous as the home of the Big Pineapple, just 10 minutes south. Markets run every Sat, 6.30am–1pm, while a heritage train and small zoo are open every day. Contact (07) 5442 3102 for details.

Noosa Heads is the most famous of the Sunshine Coast's destinations, and for good reason as the holiday town has stunning beaches and excellent surf. The whiting fishing from the beach is so good you can often see them swimming in the shallows. The town has lots of accommodation, numerous great restaurants and its famous north-facing beach is spectacular at sunset. To escape the crowds, though, head across the river on the ferry and stay on the Noosa North Shore.

Gympie was originally a gold-rush town after the metal was discovered in 1867. Queensland's largest nugget, the 37kg Curtis Nugget, was found here. The Gympie Gold Mining and Heritage Museum is a great spot to learn more about it. Gympie has most services and good shopping and is a gateway to both the Cooloola Coast and Fraser Island.

Australia Zoo

→ **Australia Zoo – near Beerwah**

Australia Zoo was home to television's popular 'Crocodile Hunter' the late Steve Irwin who tragically died in 2006. His legacy lives on under the guidance of his wife, Terri, and their children Bindi and Robert. The zoo has a large display of crocodiles, birds, snakes and African animals, although the daily wildlife shows by Bindi and Robert are my kids' favourite things to see. It's open 9am–5pm daily and entry fees apply. Contact (07) 5436 2000 for details.

→ **Massive markets – Eumundi**

Locals and visitors alike flock to the Eumundi Markets in search of crafts, great gifts, fresh produce or an elusive bargain. Spend a delightful morning strolling around the hundreds of stalls. The selection is huge – leatherwork, pottery, clothing, toys, ironwork, candles, soaps and much more. Operates Wed 8am–1.30pm and Sat 7am–2pm.

→ **The Ginger Factory – Yandina**

More than just a venue to show off the region's ginger-growing prowess, the Ginger Factory is a great place to discover much of the Sunshine Coast's best features. At the factory, you can take tasting and making tours, ride the Ginger Train, shop for local treats, let the kids play in the great playground and wander through the tropical gardens. Fees apply for some attractions. Contact 1800 067 686 for details.

WHERE TO STAY

79 Bribie Island Caravan Park

⚲ 40 Jacana Ave, Woorim
☎ (07) 3408 1134
🖥 www.bribieislandcaravanpark.com.au

Located on the ocean side of Bribie Island, this tidy little caravan park is just a stone's throw from the beach and local shops. There are plenty of onsite activities for families including a shaded swimming pool and minigolf course. Minimum-length stay applies during peak periods.

80 Toorbul Caravan Park

⚲ 119 Esplanade, Toorbul
☎ (07) 5498 8701
🖥 www.moretonbay.qld.gov.au/toorbul-caravan-park

This quiet seaside caravan park, just 10 minutes off the Bruce Highway, is perfect for boating and fishing with a boat ramp just 400m away. Sites are flat and grassy with room for an awning.

81 Cotton Tree Holiday Park

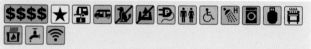

⚲ Cotton Tree Pde, Maroochydore
☎ (07) 5459 9070
🖥 www.sunshinecoastholidayparks.com.au/holiday_parks/cotton_tree_holiday_park

This large council-run caravan park has a great location right on the water's edge with views over the Maroochy River. There are shops conveniently located directly across from the park and it is just a short walk in to Maroochydore central. Bookings are required during peak times and minimum-length stay applies during Christmas, Easter and public holidays.

82 Maroochy River Park

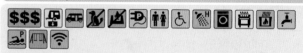

⚲ 1 Diura St, Maroochydore
☎ (07) 5443 3033
🖥 www.maroochyriverpark.com.au

This great little park has nice, updated amenities and is just a short stroll to the Maroochy River. Local facilities, including shops and a medical centre, are also just a short walk down the road. Nice grassy sites with eco mats and extra room for a boat trailer on some.

83 Landsborough Pines Caravan Park

- Steve Irwin Way, 1 Eudlo St, Landsborough
- (07) 5494 1207
- www.landsboroughpines.com.au

Nestled amongst nine acres of parkland, this site is in a great central location for many of the Sunshine Coast's tourist attractions. The main one being Australia Zoo, which is just over 3km down the road. The park has a pool and good, clean amenities.

84 Noosa North Shore Beach Campground

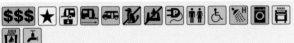

- 240 Wilderness Track, Noosa North Shore
- (07) 5449 881
- www.noosaholidayparks.com.au/noosa-north-shore

This out-of-the-way, camping area has absolute beach frontage and is perfect for escaping the hustle and bustle of town. It has simple amenities with coin-operated showers and laundry. There is plenty of space about but only eight sites have power so booking ahead is recommended for those that want it.

85 Gympie Caravan Park

- 1 Jane St, Gympie
- (07) 5483 6800
- www.gympiecaravanpark.com

Easily accessible off the Bruce Highway, this site has good, clean amenities, is pet friendly and has a pool onsite. A great overnight stop or to use as a base for exploring the surrounding area.

Eumundi Markets

GYMPIE TO GIN GIN

Eli Creek, Fraser Island

INTRODUCTION

With highlights like Fraser Island, sensational whale-watching, incredible camping and some of Australia's best beach fishing, the wider Hervey Bay region is amongst my favourites in Australia. There are plenty of small beachside towns where you can relax free from the crowds, but never far away from larger towns with more services and attractions. While the Bruce Highway services coastal and regional towns, many of the roads linking other smaller towns are popular tourist routes you can meander along at your own pace.

WHERE TO GO

Following the Bruce Highway between Gympie and Maryborough is best done only if you're in a hurry. Far better to detour through Rainbow Beach, Tin Can Bay and Poona, all of which have great camping options. **Rainbow Beach** is the last mainland town to stock up for people travelling to Fraser Island, so has most basic services. The fuel can be a bit expensive though, so, if you can, fill up in Gympie and

just top up here. It's very popular with four-wheel drivers, and many travel direct from Noosa via the beach (permit required). The camping along Inskip Peninsula is excellent.

Tin Can Bay is a quieter town with a big interest in fishing and many charters leave daily from its marina. Each day at about 7am, a pod of nine dolphins turns up at Barnacles Cafe to be fed by volunteers and curious onlookers. For a small donation, and the cost of the fish, you can feed wild dolphins. Find out more at www.barnaclesdolphins.com.au.

One of Queensland's oldest cities, **Maryborough** has many historic buildings, including many old Queenslanders. As it has most major services, it's a good place to restock. Without rejoining the highway, head to **Hervey Bay**, especially if it's whale-watching season as many charters run from here into one of Australia's busiest whale nurseries.

Following the highway north, each of the small beach towns like **Burrum Heads** and **Woodgate** are worthy detours. There's excellent whiting fishing off each of these beaches – dig for blood worms in the sand on low tide to use for bait and you can't go wrong. I really enjoy staying on **Kinkuna**

Beach in Burrum Coast National Park. A 4WD is needed for access, but this quiet, sand-bottomed camping area is peaceful and inexpensive. Nearby, Woodgate has a great caravan park, good RSL and basic services.

Another worthwhile diversion is to **Bundaberg** – famous for its rum distillery, Bundaberg Rum. The distillery has become a very popular tourist attraction and guided tours, which take you through the process of making rum and end with tastings, run daily. Many small-batch varieties can only be bought here. As well as a large port that attracts international yachts the city's subtropical climate and extensive natural and man-made tourist attractions make Bundaberg a very popular stop.

Back on the highway north, **Gin Gin** is a town originally settled by Gregory Blaxland – one of the party that crossed the Blue Mountains in 1813. It's at the centre of a strong pastoral industry, but many farms are turning to grapes and are part of a developing wine industry in the north Burnett. Gin Gin has country-town shopping and all services.

→ The world's biggest sand island – Fraser Island

The most northern of south-east Queensland's sand islands, World Heritage–listed Fraser Island is also the world's biggest. A four-wheel drive is needed to explore the island and anything less than a week spent here is cutting it too short. From its expansive beaches and excellent fishing, to the sandy inland tracks that take in the many stunning freshwater lakes and subtropical rainforest, everything about the island is wonderful. Caravans are often brought onto Fraser Island, although care and experience are needed to negotiate the often-soft sand. Highlights include floating down the crystal-clear Eli Creek as it flows to the ocean, or cooling down in the stunning waters of Lake McKenzie. Regular barge services operate from Inskip Point and River Heads, while several tour companies offer day trips.

→ Humpback whales – Hervey Bay

The protected waters of Hervey Bay become a haven for whales during the season which lasts from Aug–Oct. As well as many commercial cruises, it's not uncommon to see whales from land-based locations along the coast. For a really distinct experience, some operators are even licensed to take you swimming with the giant and beautiful creatures.

→ Turtles – near Bargara

Mon Repos Conservation Park is an important turtle breeding area. Flatback, green and endangered loggerhead turtles come ashore to lay eggs between Nov–Jan, and the hatchlings emerge between Jan–Mar. Fees apply for night viewing. Contact (07) 4159 1652 for details.

Whale-watching Hervey Bay

WHERE TO STAY

86 MV Sarawak camping area

- Inskip Rd, Inskip Peninsula
- 13 7468
- www.npsr.qld.gov.au/parks/inskip-peninsula/camping.html

One of the more popular camping areas on Inskip Peninsula as all its sites are two-wheel-drive accessible. Most are shaded by the coastal trees and a number of sites look out over Tin Can Bay or over to Fraser Island. Facilities are limited, though, so come prepared.

87 Tin Can Bay Tourist Park

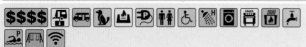

- 54–74 Trevally St, Tin Can Bay
- (07) 5486 4411
- www.tincanbaytouristpark.com.au

TOP PARKS

This updated caravan park has grassy, level sites with ensuites available. Amenities are modern and tidy and there is a pool onsite. Dolphin feeding happens each day at the nearby beach. Dogs are welcome during off-peak times only.

88 Discovery Parks Fraser Coast

- 20 Fraser St, Torquay (Hervey Bay)
- (07) 4124 9999
- www.discoveryholidayparks.com.au/qld/fraser_coast/fraser_coast

Discovery HOLIDAY PARKS

This popular family-friendly caravan park is conveniently located just a short walk to the beach and close to the main esplanade with access to shops and cafes. Sites are level and grassy with good, clean amenities.

89 Iron Ridge Park

- 1472 Goodwood Rd, Redridge (Childers)
- (07) 4126 8410
- www.ironridgepark.com.au

This peaceful caravan park offers generous sites and very well-maintained amenities. There is a small undercover camp kitchen and fire pits are provided. The park is pet friendly and there is even an off-leash area for dogs.

90 Elliott Heads Holiday Park

- 1 Lihs St, Elliott Heads
- (07) 4159 6193
- www.bundabergholidayparks.com.au/elliott-heads-holiday-park

Popular for fishing and snorkelling, this beachfront caravan park, located just 15 minutes from Bundaberg, is the perfect location to stop and explore the surrounding area. Sites are level and grassy with ensuites also available.

91 Bundaberg East Cabin & Tourist Park

- 83 Princess St, Bundaberg East
- (07) 4152 8899
- www.bundabergtouristpark.com.au

family parks

Conveniently located close to many local attractions, including the famous distillery, this caravan park has large double-slab sites available as well as open grass areas. Amenities are well kept and there is a nice swimming pool onsite.

92 Binnowee Bush Camp

- 305 Bucca Rd, Bundaberg
- 0432 024 725

This lovely quiet camping area set beside the dam offers spacious grassy sites in an absolutely stunning location. Visitors must be fully self-contained and bring their own water.

Burrum Coast National Park

GIN GIN TO ROCKHAMPTON

Kayaking in Deepwater National Park

INTRODUCTION

Although the stretch between Gin Gin and 'Rocky' isn't usually considered amongst the most desirable touring locations, along it you'll tick off quite a few significant points. This section crosses the Tropic of Capricorn, passes the east coast's northernmost surf beach, meets the Great Barrier Reef and offers the first chances to catch a big barramundi or spot a crocodile in the wild. The Bruce Highway is very good and many of the roadside rest areas are popular overnight stops for people in caravans and motorhomes, especially the one at the Calliope River.

WHERE TO GO

A short drive north of **Gin Gin** is Lake Monduran, which was formed when the Kolan River was dammed. Near **Calliope** is Lake Awoonga, formed when the Boyne River was dammed. Both lakes are stocked with barramundi and have very good caravan parks, so are extremely popular with keen fishers. I've stayed at Lake Awoonga,

but due to some recent cold weather and heavy rains, all the barra had spooked and were allegedly sitting on the bottom waiting for things to get back to normal. My wife and I caught plenty of big catfish, though.

Between the two lakes, and back on the coast, are **Agnes Water** and **Seventeen Seventy** – the towns where I intend to retire. Early. Agnes Water is typically recognised as Queensland's northernmost surf beach (although Nine Mile Beach in Byfield National Park, north of Rockhampton, does get an occasional wave, it also gets an occasional crocodile!). The adjacent Deepwater National Park has some great beaches to explore and good four-wheel-drive tracks and camping areas, although it rained for three days straight when I stayed there! There's good fishing off all the beaches. Seventeen Seventy is a popular fishing town named for the year Captain Cook and his crew landed at what was then called Round Hill Inlet. Both towns have big caravan parks, basic services and limited facilities.

After returning to the highway and heading north, the best option is to exit

again at **Benaraby** and head for **Gladstone**, which is a busy industrial port that's officially the southernmost point you'll see crocodiles in the wild. (Although in 2016 there were 21 sightings south of here, in fact as far south as the Mary River, just north of Fraser Island!) Gladstone is at the southern end of the Great Barrier Reef and sightseeing trips depart regularly from the marina, as well as charter boats for sport fishing.

Just north of the Tropic of Capricorn, **Rockhampton** is one of Queensland's major cities. 'Rocky', which began its life as a river port, is now known for its beef with more than one third of Australia's cattle raised on central Queensland properties. The Fitzroy River divides the city, and the Capricorn Coast is just a 30 minute drive away.

DON'T MISS

→ **Free camping – near Calliope**
Free camping has become very popular with travellers and the spacious free camps on both banks of the Calliope River often have dozens of campers spread across the large areas. Located between the Calliope township turn-off and Mount Larcom it is

suitable for all vehicle types, and has toilets and bins and is pet friendly. A 48 hour limit applies to stays.

→ Heritage-listed gardens – Rockhampton

The Rockhampton Botanic Gardens were heritage listed in 1999 and consist of 38 hectares of spectacular tropical and subtropical gardens. They contain many species of palms, ferns and cycads, and there is a delightful Japanese garden too. Stop for refreshments at the tearooms or use the barbecues. These fabulous gardens are alongside the main highway and open daily from 6am to sunset. Contact 1300 225 577.

→ Historic street – Rockhampton

On the banks of the Fitzroy River, Rockhampton has many fine 19th-century buildings that you can admire as you wander down Quay St, which has been listed as a historic streetscape. In particular, visit the sandstone Customs House with its impressive copper dome and semicircular Corinthian colonnade (it now houses the visitor information centre). Other buildings of note are the Criterion Hotel and 1864 ANZ bank.

Rockhampton

Lake Awoonga

WHERE TO STAY

93 Lake Monduran Holiday Park

$$ ★

📍 Monduran Dam Rd, Monduran
📞 (07) 4157 3881
🖥 www.lakem.com.au

Popular for fishing and boating, this lakeside caravan park offers spacious grassy sites with good, clean amenities. Facilities include an onsite store and tackle shop.

94 Agnes Water Beach Caravan Park

$$$$

📍 55 Jeffrey Crt, Agnes Water
📞 (07) 4974 7279
🖥 www.agneswaterbeach.com.au

This busy, beachfront caravan park is extremely popular with surfers seeking the perfect ride. There is an excellent cafe onsite or it is just a short walk to the town centre. Bookings are required during peak periods.

95 1770 Camping Ground

$$$$

📞 (07) 4974 9286
🖥 www.1770campingground.com.au

Situated in a secluded bay, this camping area is in an idyllic location with absolute beach frontage and level, shady sites. A great spot for reef fishing and beautiful sunsets.

96 Discovery Parks Tannum Sands

$$$$

📍 Millennium Espl, Tannum Sands
📞 (07) 4973 7201
🖥 www.discoveryholidayparks.com.au/ qld/gladstone/tannum_sands

Conveniently located just a short walk to the beach and a 2 min drive to the town centre, this neat and tidy caravan park offers well-sized, grassy sites suited to most travellers' needs.

97 Gladstone Showground

$$

📍 70 Tank St, Gladstone Central
📞 0407 792 861

Perfect for an overnight stop, the camping area is spacious and grassy with simple amenities. It is just a short stroll into town and there is an aquatic centre next door.

98 Gracemere Caravan Park

$$$

📍 118 Old Capricorn Hwy, Gracemere, Rockhampton
📞 (07) 4933 1310

Situated just 5 minutes west of Rockhampton, this caravan park has large, shady, drive-thru sites and tidy amenities suitable for most travellers' needs. There is a nice swimming pool and undercover camp kitchen which is neat and tidy.

99 Discovery Parks Rockhampton

$$$

📍 394 Yaamba Rd, North Rockhampton
📞 (07) 4926 3822
🖥 www.discoveryholidayparks.com.au/caravan-parks/queensland/capricorn-rockhampton

This is a good, family-friendly caravan park on the northern side of the city. It has a great range of facilities including tennis courts, swimming pool, gymnasium and onsite cafe. Sites are level and grassy with concrete slabs for annexes.

ROCKHAMPTON TO MACKAY

Keswick Island, off Mackay

INTRODUCTION

Although, Rockhampton, Yeppoon and Mackay are large regional centres, much of this route is dotted with small towns that were once important, but are now only relics of their former glory. The Bruce Highway carries a lot of traffic and passes through cane country and cattle-grazing properties but there are plenty of opportunities to overtake (or be overtaken). You can drive between 'Rocky' and Mackay in a day, but there are plenty of choices for stops along the way.

WHERE TO GO

Yeppoon, the largest town on the Capricorn Coast, and Emu Park are both very popular holiday destinations. So popular in fact, that last time my family passed through, there were no vacancies at any of the caravan parks – so be warned, it's wise to book ahead in peak seasons. Both spots are popular for the abundant fishing

opportunities, and fresh, high quality seafood is easy to obtain. Often fish like Spanish mackerel is the 'fish of the day' at the local fish and chip shops.

Yeppoon is the gateway to Byfield National Park, popular for its four-wheel-drive tracks and beach camping. For those not interested in heading off-road, the graded gravel road in to Upper Stony Creek leads to a pristine, safe, wild swimming hole with a great picnic area and nearby Red Rock camping area. You could spend a lot of time in this part of the Capricorn Coast.

The small towns that dot the Bruce Highway all have their little charms. Marlborough, now off the highway, was once an important stop when the old route had few stops between here and Sarina. In 1993, a local farmer created the Principality of Marlborough in an attempt to prevent the bank seizing his property. It didn't work though, as 11 days later his property was entered by police and he and his family were removed.

Saint Lawrence, 80km north, is on the north-south railway line and many trains run through it. The town was an important port in the 1800s, but today only remnants of the wharf remain. Nearby Carmila is a small community where cattle and sugarcane are the main industries. It has basic services and a very popular beachfront, free camping area.

Sarina and Mackay are at the centre of the region's sugarcane and mining industries. Mackay is often bypassed by travellers, who think it's just a sugar and mining town (I'm guilty of that), but recently a big focus on tourism and community has seen Mackay's restaurant scene develop, markets establish and farm gates open. Mackay is also a popular spot for whale-watching and has good access to the reef, without the busyness of Airlie Beach.

Nearby Eungella National Park can't be missed – it's about 45 minutes west of Mackay, in the hinterland. The park has some incredible short walks through tropical rainforest to roaring waterfalls, as well as

Singing Ship monument

quiet brooks where you'll likely spot a playful platypus. My wife and I always plan some time here when we visit.

DON'T MISS

→ A singing ship – Emu Park
On the headland at Emu Park is a fabulous white sculpture – the Singing Ship. It was built as a bicentenary memorial to Captain Cook in 1980, a date that also happened to

mark Emu Park's centenary. The ship really does sing! Hidden organ pipes are activated by the onshore breezes, causing the sculpture to whistle eerily.

→ Sweet day out – near Sarina
A short drive south of Sarina, the Sugar Shed is a great way to learn about the sugar-making process. From start to finish, the tour gives an interesting insight into the sugar

industry, and the sight of a warehouse full of sugar is mind-blowing. Taste tests of local products, like the locally distilled rum, are a highlight. Field of Dream Parkway, Entry fees apply and it's open daily 9am–4pm. Contact (07) 4943 2801.

→ Capricorn Caves – the Caves
The privately owned Capricorn Caves is an award-winning tourist attraction. The limestone caves are above ground and the highlight is the huge, domed Cathedral Cavern, which has special acoustic properties. The caves have been a tourist attraction since 1884! You can choose between exciting adventure caving or more relaxed guided tours. There is a caravan park here too. Entry fees apply and it's open daily 9am–5pm with last tours starting at 4pm. Contact (07) 4934 2883.

Rhino Passage Cathedral Caves, Capricorn Caves

WHERE TO STAY

100 Beachside Caravan Park Yeppoon

📍 45–51 Farnborough Rd, Yeppoon
📞 (07) 4939 3738
🖥 www.beachsidecaravanparkyeppoon.com.au

This is a popular beachside caravan park with good, basic facilities located on the shores of Keppel Bay. Bookings are required in peak periods.

101 Byfield Campstay

📍 53 Castle Rock Rd, Byfield
📞 (07) 4935 1002

A tranquil, private camping area amongst tropical forest and woodland with basic facilities for campers who don't need to plug into power. Plenty of wildlife and tropical fruit orchards on the property.

102 St Lawrence Recreational Reserve

📍 624 St Lawrence Connection Rd, St Lawrence
📞 1300 472 227

A simple, inexpensive camping area on the edge of town that offers toilets, showers, barbecues, fireplaces and a dump point. It's pet friendly. Bookings required in advance.

103 Carmila Beach camping area

📍 29 Esplanade, Carmila

This is a very popular budget camping area right on the beach. Facilities are simple, and often in heavy usage, but the outlook is worth it for those who can camp self-contained.

104 Cape Palmerston Holiday Park

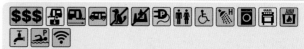

📍 989 Greenhill Rd, Ilbilbie
📞 (07) 4950 3987
🖥 www.capepalmerston.com

Set on 63 acres, this is an expansive and popular caravan park on the Isaac Coast, near Cape Palmerston National Park. There are over 70 drive-thru sites and more basic camping in an undeveloped area in a stunning bush setting.

105 Sarina Palms Caravan Village

📍 31 Anzac St, Sarina
📞 (07) 4956 1892
🖥 www.sarinapalms.com.au

Located in a quiet area of town, this caravan park will suit the needs of most short-term travellers. It has powered and drive-thru sites, a laundry and barbecues.

106 Andergrove Van Park

📍 40–68 Beaconsfield Rd East, North Mackay
📞 (07) 4942 4922
🖥 www.andergrovevanpark.com

Sweeping lawns are visible as you enter this excellent caravan park, set in a quiet, off-road position with easy access from the Bruce Highway. It has good features at a reasonable price and is an ideal base for exploring the Mackay region. Bookings are required in peak periods and a minimum stay might apply.

MACKAY TO TOWNSVILLE

Whitehaven Beach, Whitsunday Island

INTRODUCTION

The Bruce Highway between Mackay and Townsville traverses a rich plain where sugarcane is the predominant crop. Expect to see slow-moving harvesting equipment and cane trains Jun–Nov. There are plenty of opportunities to escape to vibrant coastal towns which have good access to the reef and plenty of options for travellers.

WHERE TO GO

To the north of Mackay, the laidback town of **Seaforth** is very popular with travellers for its simple, if dated, camping area right on the foreshore. Many people set up for months at a time, and plenty have been coming to the same spot for years so have created lasting friendships. Fishing is popular along the beach, or by boat.

The nearby Cape Hillsborough Nature Reserve is famous for its daily gathering of kangaroos on the beach at sunrise. If early mornings aren't your thing, the reserve's teahouse puts on a very good Devonshire tea. It's open daily 9am–3.30pm. Contact (07) 4959 0528.

If you can drag yourself away from Seaforth (my family and I went for a week but stayed three, the first time), the next good stop is **Midge Point**, a quiet coastal town just south of the failed Laguna Quays Resort. With an excellent caravan park and semi-deserted beach, that was ravaged by cyclone Debbie, it's a great place to stop before the busyness of Airlie Beach.

After turning off at **Proserpine**, a sugar town on the highway which has an airport and most services, **Airlie Beach** quickly comes into view. Airlie overlooks the Whitsunday Passage and is a great holiday destination, with a great sense of timelessness. The town is an incredibly popular port for yachties sailing the reef and islands, and has extensive resort-style attractions and an excellent stinger-free swimming area.

On the shores of McCanes Bay, further north, **Bowen** is the centre of a diverse region. Fruit and vegetables grow in the rich river delta, cattle-grazing properties lie inland, a fishing fleet operates from the harbour, coal is mined near Collinsville, and the Bowen Saltworks is situated south of town (you cannot miss the saltpans from the highway). There are also beautiful beaches where snorkelling is popular. Bowen is known as the 'mural capital of the mainland' with 22 murals, each by a Queensland artist, clearly depicting the area's history.

Really popular with both birdwatchers and windsurfers, **Ayr** is a small town that sits on the banks of the Burdekin River. Surrounded by extensive wetlands, it's an important bird reserve.

Not far north is one of Queensland's major cities. **Townsville** is an administrative, commercial and educational centre with historic buildings and a fabulous redeveloped waterfront precinct – the Strand. The Strand has everything from boutique burger joints to a free water park. Due to its geographical position, Townsville's annual rainfall is lower than most of this coast, so it enjoys typically warm, clear days throughout winter. Head up Castle Hill, the pink granite mountain above town, where you can enjoy views over to Magnetic Island.

DON'T MISS

➔ **The wonderful Whitsundays**
Forming part of the Great Barrier Reef Marine Park (a World Heritage area), the Whitsunday Passage is a remarkable waterway, naturally protected by some

74 islands. Fabulous beaches, clear-blue water and a range of resorts make this an international, year-round holiday destination.

→ Animal encounters – near Alligator Creek

Dedicated to the preservation of native animals, Billabong Sanctuary is involved in a captive-breeding program for the endangered southern cassowary. Numerous 'animal encounters' are available, including opportunities to hold a koala or python, and see dingoes or wedge-tailed eagles

being fed. It's about 17km south of Townsville and entry fees apply. Open daily 9am–5pm. Contact (07) 4778 8344.

→ Discover the Great Barrier Reef – Townsville

Reef HQ is the educational centre for the Great Barrier Reef Marine Park Authority. See a living coral reef and its surrounding ecosystem in an aquarium environment with fish, crustaceans, turtles, sharks and sea stars. Reef HQ is a great attraction and I recommend a visit. It's open daily

9.30am–5pm and entry fees apply. Contact (07) 4750 0800, www.reefhq.com.au.

DID YOU KNOW

The Whitsundays were named by Captain Cook as he travelled through them on what he thought was Whitsun, or Pentecost, the 8th Sunday after Easter. It was in fact, a Monday, though nobody has ever considered changing the name – Sundays being far better than Mondays after all…

WHERE TO STAY

107 Cape Hillsborough Nature Resort

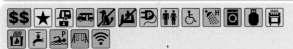

📍 Cape Hillsborough Rd, Cape Hillsborough
📞 (07) 4959 0152
🖥 www.capehillsboroughresort.com.au

This caravan park within Cape Hillsborough National Park offers camping and caravan sites and is a great spot for a break. Bookings are required in peak periods.

108 Seaforth camping area

📍 22 Palm Ave, Seaforth
📞 (07) 4966 4359
🖥 www.mackay.qld.gov.au/community/council_facilities2/council_facilities/camping

This is a popular, open camping area right on the beachfront in the heart of this small town. It's my favourite place to camp around the Mackay region.

109 Travellers Rest Caravan and Camping Park

📍 29 Jackson St, Midge Point
📞 (07) 4947 6120

There are no more sandflies or midges at Midge Point than elsewhere, but there is a lovely beachside caravan park with lawns, shady trees and a host of other great features.

110 Flametree Tourist Village

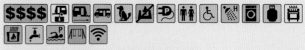

📍 2955 Shute Harbour Rd, Airlie Beach
📞 (07) 4946 9388
🖥 www.flametreevillage.com.au

This is a well-known caravan park in the heart of a popular holiday destination. Enjoy the pool, covered barbecues, and other features. This is a good place at a reasonable price in a busy coastal strip.

111 Queens Beach Tourist Village

📍 160 Mount Nutt Rd, Bowen
📞 (07) 4785 1313
🖥 www.qbtvbowen.com.au

This wonderful caravan park in historic Bowen has fabulous garden-like sites. Located within walking distance of many attractions and amenities, it's ideal for a few days or a longer holiday.

112 BIG4 Townsville Woodlands Holiday Park

📍 548 Bruce Hwy, Deeragun
📞 (07) 4751 6955
🖥 www.big4.com.au/caravan-parks/qld/townsville-surrounds/townsville-woodlands-holiday-park

This is a spacious caravan park located about 15km north of the city alongside the Bruce Hwy. It's a convenient, friendly place to stop, especially if you just want to stay here overnight. Bookings are required in peak periods.

TOWNSVILLE TO CARDWELL

NEED TO KNOW

 165km

 National parks, coastal caravan parks

 Although Townsville experiences lower summer rainfall than the rest of the coast, this is still a dry-season-only route.

 Fishing, birdwatching, tropical island hiking

 Although this is a busy section, the roads are well maintained.

 As this is a popular and populated area, there are good facilities and services in the larger towns.

 Crocodiles inhabit most waterways. Heavy seasonal rain can cause road closures and flooding. During summer, dangerous stingers inhabit coastal waters.

View to Hinchinbrook Island

INTRODUCTION

The Bruce Highway follows the coastal plain, but along here the mountains are taller than they were further south and the road runs closer to the foot of the range. It winds through waving cane fields and throughout the cane-harvesting season (July–Nov) there may be slow-moving agricultural machinery and cane trains operating. The highway is generally well maintained, but the surface can break up and potholes can develop during the wet season.

WHERE TO GO

Heading north from Townsville, the next major stop is the sugar town of Ingham, but there's plenty to see on the way. The two small towns of **Bluewater** and **Rollingstone** both have popular free camping areas that are very important to the local communities that otherwise have limited services. On the coast, **Rollingstone Beach** has a popular caravan park with absolute foreshore frontage overlooking Palm and Havannah islands.

Don't pass up a chance to stay at Jourama Falls in Paluma Range National Park. The camping area is along 2.8km of unsealed road that is accessible for caravans and motorhomes of almost any size. The area is forested and popular with birdwatchers – you may see beautiful azure kingfishers flitting around Waterview Creek. A 1.5km walking track leads to the lookout over the cascading falls. The waterfall plunges over salmon granite down into the crystal-clear creek which has two amazing pools – the Little and Big Crystal Creek swimming holes. The lower hole is underneath a historical 1930s stone-arch bridge.

The sweetest part of this trip, though, is **Ingham**, which supplies much of Australia, and a significant proportion of the world, with sugar. Ingham's Victoria Mill, which opened in 1883, is the largest sugar mill in the southern hemisphere. Ingham developed to support the local sugarcane industry and from the late 1800s to the mid-1900s, many Europeans, especially Italians, flooded in to work on the burgeoning cane fields. In the 2016 census, 23 per cent of Ingham's respondents claimed Italian ancestry, compared to just two per cent for Queensland as a whole. Each year in Aug the town hosts the Australian Italian Festival celebrating that heritage.

From Ingham, it's worth diverting from the highway out to **Lucinda**, which is situated on the coast at the southern entrance to the Hinchinbrook Channel. The surrounding waters encompass some of Queensland's most well known fishing spots – even Lucinda's wharf is popular. Spectacular, rugged Hinchinbrook Island lies just to the north. Lucinda is a major sugar port with a bulk-sugar loading jetty stretching nearly 6km out to sea. The town has basic services and a small number of shops with its seafood outlets being particularly popular.

Back on the highway, **Cardwell**, the oldest town in north Queensland, fronts the beach overlooking Rockingham Bay to the north-east. It is a very popular tourist centre with excellent fishing and a regular ferry service to Hinchinbrook Island. The region supports a strong timber industry, most services are available and there is a good selection of shops.

DON'T MISS

→ TYTO Wetlands – Ingham

This 90-hectare wetland reserve is named for the endangered eastern grass owl (*Tyto capensis*) that can best be seen on dusk. The reserve is home to over 230 bird species, and has extensive walking trails, excellent parklands and visitor centre with a regional art gallery. The parklands and wetlands are accessible all the time, but the visitor centre and gallery open daily 9am–4pm.

→ Picnic beside a pool – near Cardwell

Cardwell Forest Drive is a well-signposted, 9km drive through pine plantations and native forests. The drive takes in a lookout, the Spa Creek pool, picnic areas and a range of forest information stations. There are easily accessible swimming holes at many of the stops along the way. This is a pleasant drive along a maintained gravel forestry road; it is, however, also frequented by logging trucks.

→ Hinchinbrook Island National Park – near Cardwell

Hinchinbrook Island is one of Australia's largest island national parks. Mangrove shores, pristine beaches and dense rainforest are features of this rugged isle that's dominated by the towering peak of Mt Bowen (1121m). Bushwalking is popular, with several marked walking tracks, including the four- to seven-day Thorsborne Trail. A ferry operates from Cardwell or Lucinda; for times and bookings call (07) 4066 8601.

WHERE TO STAY

113 BIG4 Rollingstone Beach Front Resort

- 2 Hencamp Creek Rd, Rollingstone
- (07) 4770 7277
- www.big4.com.au/caravan-parks/qld/townsville-surrounds/rollingstone-beach-front-resort

BIG4 HOLIDAY PARKS

This is a modern resort caravan park with a fabulous beachfront outlook. It has a wide range of facilities, a selection of sites and a big camping area. It does lack shade, but it would be a great wintertime destination.

114 Big Crystal Creek camping area

- www.nprsr.qld.gov.au/parks/paluma-mount-spec/camping.html

This is a great national park camping area right next to one of north Queensland's best freshwater swimming holes. Lots of space and shade, although camping areas must be booked online in advance. Facilities include toilets, showers, water and fireplaces. Bring mosquito repellent.

115 Taylors Beach Holiday Park

- 91 John Dory St, Taylors Beach
- (07) 4777 8560
- www.taylorsbeach.net

Situated on the beautiful Victoria Inlet, this caravan park has developed from a small fishing village into a popular beachside destination. The pet-friendly park has great facilities, including a saltwater swimming pool, camp kitchen and separate fish-cleaning benches. It is very well managed.

116 Cardwell Beachcomber Motel & Tourist Park

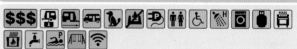

- 43a Marine Pde, Cardwell
- (07) 4066 8550
- www.cardwellbeachcomber.com.au

This caravan park is centrally located, just a short distance from the centre of town and across the road from the beach (ideal for fishing). It has good facilities and a licensed restaurant/cafe in the attached motel. Bookings are required in peak periods.

CARDWELL TO CAIRNS

NEED TO KNOW

🧭 **182km**

🏠 **Basic, beachfront caravan parks; full-featured caravan parks; holiday resorts**

☁ **These areas have Australia's highest rainfall through summer. It's best to come Apr–Sept.**

👁 **Fishing, Paronella Park**

⚠ **Heavy rainfall often damages roads. Take care.**

🍴 **All facilities and services are available in Cairns, and basic services everywhere else.**

⚠ **Crocodiles inhabit most waterways. Seasonal flooding can close roads and block access.**

Josephine Falls

INTRODUCTION

Some of Australia's prettiest scenery is found along this tropical and mountainous coastline – rugged mountains, lush rainforest, waterfalls, Great Barrier Reef islands, holiday resorts and a lot more. This section of coast, which winds through vast areas of sugarcane as it skirts the Bellenden Ker Range is Australia's highest rainfall area, so conditions can often be wet. Even in Sept and Oct, expect around 80mm of rainfall each month.

WHERE TO GO

Sugarcane dominates the landscape and industries of this region, and **Tully** is a great place to take it all in – the atmosphere, not the sugar, mind you. Tully has a large mill that produces about two million tonnes of sugar a year. It runs tours daily so tourists can see what it takes to sweeten their coffees. For a healthier experience, Fruit Forest Farm, near Mission Beach runs great tours of its tropical-fruit farm (www.fruitforestfarm.com.au). The

Tully River is also an exciting whitewater rafting destination.

Less adrenalin inducing are the postcard-perfect beaches of **Mission Beach**, one of Australia's most popular holiday destinations. With its magnificent, white, sandy beaches, swaying palms and tropical rainforests, it's little wonder people come here year after year never really bothering to go further north. Day cruises to **Dunk Island** operate from the jetty.

A unique Australian tourist attraction is just north of here, too. Paronella Park is the ruins of a Spanish-style castle and garden set in the tropical north Queensland hinterland. Turn off the highway near Silkwood to the south and head for Mena Creek. Built by a Spanish immigrant between 1929 and 1935, it features the ruins of magnificent stairways, buildings and gardens set around a waterfall. Its hydro-electric generator supplies power to the adjacent caravan park, where your first night's accommodation is included in the cost of entry to the park.

After the wonder of Paronella Park, **Innisfail** might seem dull, but it is a major town with good shopping and major

services. As well as sugar, fishing plays a key part in the town's economy and a large fishing fleet operates from here. The Australian Sugar Industry Museum in **Mourilyan**, just south of Innisfail, showcases the multicultural heritage of this strong industry and houses a permanent display of historical and innovative equipment.

Continuing north, you'll pass through **Babinda**, squeezed between the Bellenden Ker Range and the coast. The town regularly wins the Golden Gumboot Award for the highest rainfall per year – averaging over 4.5m. Just 6km from town, Babinda Boulders, with its large water-worn granite boulders, has walking tracks, camping and a popular swimming hole.

Another impressive sight, just south of Cairns, is Walshs Pyramid, a lonely mountain that rises to 922m above Gordonvale. There's a popular walk to the top, and even an annual race. The record stands at 1 hr 15 min, but set aside at least 3 hrs.

Cairns is the capital of the tropical north and gateway to the Great Barrier Reef, Cape York and Savannah Way. The city is modern and progressive, with good nightlife and

Cairns

plenty of free attractions, plus all major services. Don't miss the chance for a dip at sunset in the Cairns Lagoon, a 4800sq m saltwater pool that offers year round swimming safe from stingers and crocs.

DON'T MISS

→ Queensland's highest peak – Mt Bartle Frere

Mt Bartle Frere is Queensland's highest mountain (1622m). A 15km return walking track winds through rainforest to the summit. It begins from Josephine Falls, which is a worthwhile stop in itself, reached via a turnoff from the highway 2km south of Mirriwinni. The track is steep, and suitable for experienced, fit walkers only.

→ The Big Gumboot – Tully

Although Tully usually loses the Golden Gumboot Award to nearby Babinda, a 7.9m tall golden gumboot has been built in the town – representing the highest recorded rainfall, in 1950! Inside, a spiral staircase takes visitors to the top, showing a pictorial history of various floods along the way. A viewing platform from the top overlooks town.

A FORK IN THE ROAD

You've got some tough choices when leaving Cairns. Heading west across the Great Dividing Range will eventually set you on to the Savannah Way, or back south to Townsville via the tropical north's hinterland. To the north of Cairns, you can continue to the stunning Port Douglas, the Daintree and Cape Tribulation. Alternatively, you can skirt Cape Tribulation from Port Douglas and keep heading north to Cooktown, or even further to the northernmost point of Australia, at the top of Cape York. Turn the page and we're going to Cape Tribulation and Cooktown. To plan your trip across the Savannah Way, flick to page (63) or page (61) to travel the hinterland route back to Townsville. The only bad choice is to go back the way you came…

WHERE TO STAY

117 Beachcomber Coconut Holiday Park

📍 122–132 Kennedy Espl, South Mission Beach
📞 (07) 4068 8129
💻 www.beachcombercoconut.com.au

BIG4 HOLIDAY PARKS

This is a wonderful, resort style caravan park that borders tropical rainforest and is frequently visited by the resident cassowaries. Right on the beach, it's got a licensed cafe, large swimming pool and extensive camp kitchen.

118 Kurrimine Beach camping area

📍 Robert Johnstone Pde, Kurrimine Beach
📞 (07) 4030 2222
💻 www.cassowarycoast.qld.gov.au/camping-facilities

This council-run camping area offers flat, grassy sites with absolute beach frontage. The beach has excellent fishing and there is a boat ramp at one end of the park. Facilities are basic but well maintained.

119 August Moon Caravan Park

📍 64174 Bruce Hwy, Innisfail
📞 (07) 4063 2211
💻 www.augustmoon.com.au

Located about five minutes from Innisfail CBD this pet-friendly caravan park is the perfect base for exploring the surrounding area. Facilities are dated but tidy. There is a pool onsite and a large, well-equipped camp kitchen.

120 Flying Fish Point Tourist Park

📍 39 Elizabeth St, Flying Fish Point, Innisfail
📞 (07) 4061 3131
💻 www.ffpvanpark.com.au

This seaside camping area is a fishing enthusiast's delight with river, estuary and reef fishing all available. Sites are flat and grassy with basic amenities.

121 BIG4 Cairns Coconut Holiday Resort

📍 23–51 Anderson Rd, Woree, Cairns
📞 (07) 4054 6644
💻 www.coconut.com.au

BIG4 HOLIDAY PARKS

This award-winning caravan park, located on the southern side of the city, is extremely family friendly, boasting numerous activities for children, multiple pool areas and a free minigolf course to name a few. There are multiple options for camping including grass, concrete slab and ensuite sites. Bookings are required in peak periods and a minimum-length stay applies.

Babinda Boulders

CAIRNS TO COOKTOWN

NEED TO KNOW

🕐	**334km**
🏠	**Full-featured caravan parks, beachside camping areas**
☁	**During the dry season – Apr–Oct**
👁	**Fishing, warm winter weather, national parks**
⚠	**The highway conditions north to Cooktown are good. Taking the shortcut from Cape Tribulation, through Bloomfield, is unsealed and not suitable for towing.**
🍴	**Basic facilities and services are available north of Cairns.**
⚠	**Crocodiles inhabit most waterways. Check with local guides for safe swimming areas. During summer, dangerous stingers inhabit coastal waters.**

Palm Cove

INTRODUCTION

This is an area of spectacular coastal drives, that in my opinion trumps the Great Ocean Road for edge-of-the-ocean driving. The Captain Cook Highway is the most spectacular road in Queensland, while Cape Tribulation Rd through the Daintree is another kind of beautiful. And whether you stick to the sealed Mulligan Highway to Cooktown or shortcut along the steep (and not caravan friendly) Bloomfield Track, you'll be rewarded with outstanding scenery and great camping.

WHERE TO GO

While **Cairns** is nice and central, **Palm Cove**, around half an hour north, is a relaxed resort town. Everybody here, except the caravanners and campers, is paying through the nose to stay, and they aren't as close to the water either. Palm Cove Caravan Park is a popular spot for those

wintering in the north, as well as anyone getting ready to continue up, or take stock after returning from, Cape York Peninsula. The town has a croc-safe swimming area, an excellent restaurant strip, and a very relaxed atmosphere. I always plan to stop in here when I'm in the north.

Following the Captain Cook Highway north from Palm Cove, you'll pass through the idyllic tropical beach town of **Ellis Beach**, where the Macalister Range is only kept from the ocean by the road you're driving on. For almost the entire drive to Port Douglas, there's steep rainforest to one side and a spectacular drop to the turquoise ocean on the other.

Port Douglas is a relatively recent tourist hub, largely due to Christopher Skase's development of the Sheraton Mirage resort which has put this location on the map. It was established as a mining town and involved in the timber industry, but slowly lost relevance due to its isolation. In 1960, the town reportedly had a population of just

100. Today, people flock here from all over the world to visit the Great Barrier Reef or indulge in the tropical climate.

About 40km north is the ferry trip across the Daintree River (*see* www.douglas.qld.gov.au/daintree-ferry for prices). The narrow, sealed road that winds through the northern section of the Daintree is stunning at every bend, passing great lookouts like Mt Alexandra Lookout and crossing burbling creeks with crystal-clear water. Another worthwhile stop is the Daintree Discovery Centre and aerial walkway. **Cape Tribulation** is a very sleepy township with bungalows and camping areas set in the rainforest that runs all the way to the beach. There are some great walks, following the many creeks into the Daintree rainforest, and cassowary sightings are very common along the roads. Phone reception is limited in the Daintree, and Cape Tribulation has very limited shopping and services.

From Port Douglas, the Mulligan Highway to Cooktown is dotted with small towns that are little more than roadhouses serving this or that famous food. **Mount Carbine** has Janine's Pies, **Palmer River** has got steak sambos and **Lakeland** has its burgers. The highway passes the mysterious Black Mountain on the way in to Cooktown.

For anyone who's come this far north, **Cooktown** is the last big town before Weipa for anyone heading to Cape York. It is popular for its pleasant winter climate and excellent fishing. It's also a good base from which to explore the surrounding tropics, visit the botanic gardens or James Cook Museum, which even displays the anchor from the **Endeavour**.

DON'T MISS

→ A reef experience – near Port Douglas

Port Douglas is an excellent spot to book a reef experience from. Low Isles Reef is just a 15 min boat ride from town, which means more time in the water – or less chance of getting sea sick for anyone so afflicted. Several charters run daily.

→ Follow Cook's weary footsteps – near Cooktown

Grassy Hill, although a little more forested now, was named by Cook, who often trudged up it to help find a passage out of the Endeavour River. Today, the Grassy Hill Lighthouse is a major attraction, and many make the climb at sunrise or sunset to see a view that's barely changed since Cook first looked down from the rise.

→ An off-road shortcut

Between Cape Tribulation and Bloomfield, the once-controversial Bloomfield Track is a well-maintained but exceptionally steep shortcut to Cooktown. The road is restricted to those in four-wheel drives and towing a caravan is not recommended due to the steep inclines and declines in sections, and other narrow parts. It passes through Wujal Wujal and Bloomfield and skirts the Bloomfield River for a way before passing the famous Lions Den Hotel. Controversy surrounded the construction of the track in 1984 as bulldozers crashed through 33km of pristine rainforest to create it.

Daintree Rainforest boardwalk

WHERE TO STAY

122 Palm Cove Holiday Park

$$$$ ★ icons...

- 149 Williams Espl, Palm Cove, Cairns
- (07) 4055 3824
- www.escape2holidayparks.com.au/palm-cove

This neat little holiday park is in a great location, right on the beachfront just a short drive from central Cairns. Local shops and activities are just a stroll down the road. Some sites are shorter and more sloped than others so larger rigs should check prior to arrival.

123 Cape Tribulation Camping

$$$$ ★ icons...

- 3812 Cape Tribulation Rd, Cape Tribulation
- (07) 4098 0077
- www.capetribcamping.com.au

This lush green camping area is surrounded by dense rainforest on one side and fronted by Myall Beach on the other. The amenities are clean and tidy, and there is a shop and bar onsite where you can order wood-fired pizza. The camping area is closed seasonally from Nov until Easter school holidays.

124 Tropic Breeze Caravan Park

$$$$ icons...

- 24 Davidson St, Port Douglas
- (07) 4099 5299
- www.tropicbreeze.com.au

Perfectly positioned between the beach and the river, with the main town in between, at this park you won't even need to unhitch. This well-maintained caravan park has good amenities, a pool and a choice between grass or slab sites.

125 Mount Carbine Caravan Park

$$$ icons...

- 6806 Mulligan Hwy, Mount Carbine
- (07) 4094 3160
- www.mtcarbine.com

This quiet, shady caravan park, nestled amongst the bush, is an excellent spot to stop on the way to and from the Tip. Amenities are simple, but clean, and sites are nice and spacious with plenty of opportunity for wildlife spotting and birdwatching. With prior arrangement you can even store your van here while you tackle the Telegraph Track up the Cape.

126 Cooktown Caravan Park

$$$ ★ icons...

- 14–16 Hope St, Cooktown
- (07) 4069 5536
- www.cooktowncaravanpark.com

Situated on five acres of bushland, at the base of Mt Cook, this nice, shady caravan park has good, clean amenities and mostly flat, grassy campsites. It can get windy at times, so be sure to pull down awnings at night and before heading out to explore.

View from Grassy Hill Lookout at Cooktown

CAIRNS TO MOUNT GARNET

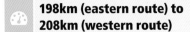
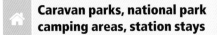
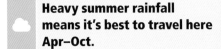
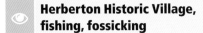
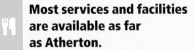

Millaa Millaa Falls

INTRODUCTION

As you travel up to the Atherton Tableland above Cairns, the changes in scenery are quite remarkable. Leaving the palm-fringed wet tropics, you climb steeply into the thick rainforest around Kuranda before the land gradually becomes dominated by open eucalypt forest and a landscape shaped by volcanic activity. For the most part we say goodbye to multi-lane highways, but the road between Cairns and Mount Garnet is good, and at least two lanes the whole way.

WHERE TO GO

High above **Cairns**, and surrounded by rainforest, **Kuranda** is a magnet for visitors. The Kuranda Scenic Railway and Skyrail Rainforest Cableway both terminate in this vibrant village. Many choose to travel here in one and return on the other to visit both the town, and nearby Barron Falls. A free shuttle operates between the two carparks at the bottom, which are 7km apart. Kuranda is a vibrant village populated by artists and people seeking an alternative lifestyle, and the Kuranda Markets, held every day of the year, are a major attraction.

While **Mareeba** isn't considered a must-stop destination by many, it's a major town in the region, with good shopping available. The town services the local agricultural industry which grows tea tree, nuts, tropical fruits and coffee, but was formerly the centre of a large tobacco-growing area. The nearby Granite Gorge Nature Park is the best place to stay, with its large camping area, swimming holes and great walking tracks through Granite Gorge.

For more croc-free swimming, and excellent camping, head to Lake Tinaroo from **Tolga**. It's the main dam servicing irrigation needs in the Atherton Tableland, but is also very popular for waterskiing, sailing and canoeing – when water levels permit. Barramundi is also in season year-round, and black bream is abundant, as is redclaw crayfish. There are several good camping areas dotting the lake's shore, including full-featured caravan parks, and plenty of more simple sites.

Further on, **Atherton** is the hub of the Tableland with supermarkets and plenty of shops. It's also the last place to get cheap fuel before heading west to Normanton. You have two options leaving Atherton – the first turns east off the highway along Gillies Range Rd to enjoy sights like **Yungaburra**, a historical town with 28 heritage-listed buildings and Peterson Creek, where there is a platypus viewing area. A network of roads in the area pass numerous waterfalls, including Malanda Falls and the stunning Millaa Millaa Falls, which are easily accessed via a 250m walk from the carpark.

Taking the western route from Atherton (Atherton Herberton Rd) takes you through the **Herberton** Historic Village, which is a collection of historically significant buildings collected from all over the Herberton region to showcase what life was like in North Queensland from the 1880s onwards. It's easily one of the best open-air museums in Australia, and I love spending time there.

Whichever way you go, you'll rejoin Highway One before **Ravenshoe**. Nestled in the Great Dividing Range, at 920m above sea level, this former timber community is Queensland's highest town. Waterfalls are nearby and the barramundi-stocked Koombooloomba Dam is just 38km south. Although there's a campsite here, it's not suitable for caravans or motorhomes, but worth a day trip if you have a four-wheel-drive vehicle.

Both **Innot Hot Springs** and **Mount Garnet** have rich mining histories – Innot for tin, and Mount Garnet in, you guessed it, garnet as well as tin, copper and zinc. Both towns have basic facilities but you can relax in the mineral rich hot springs at Innot Hot Springs, or try your luck at the public fossicking areas near Mount Garnet.

DON'T MISS

→ Stunning Woodwork – Tolga

Tolga Woodworks is renowned for high-quality woodwork, much of which is handmade in the adjoining workshop. Stop in to view work in the gallery or sit down for a simple meal and coffee at the adjoining cafe. The town has a long history in the timber industry, and cedar and maple still grow in the region. It's open daily 9am–4pm. Contact (07) 4225 0686.

→ Spectacular waterfalls

North Queensland has an abundance of great waterfalls, and some of the most spectacular are very easy to access. There's even an official Waterfall Circuit – a drive that takes in Malanda, Millaa Millaa and Millstream falls, as well as seven others. Barron Falls, near Kuranda, is easily seen from different viewing areas along a stunning walk through tropical rainforest. Millstream Falls, south-west of Ravenshoe, is another spectacular fall which can be seen after taking a 300m walk from the carpark. Millstream is reputedly Australia's widest single-drop fall.

→ Mt Hypipamee Crater – Near Atherton

Located in a small pocket of dense rainforest that forms Mount Hypipamee National Park, this eerie, narrow, extinct volcanic crater can be reached along a short sealed road from the Kennedy Highway. From the carpark it is an easy 250m walk to this extraordinary sight.

WHERE TO STAY

127 Trinity Plains Tourist Park

$$$

- 186 Tinaroo Creek Rd, Mareeba
- 1300 221 888
- www.trinityplains.com.au

Kui Parks
www.kuiparks.com.au

This pet-friendly caravan park has large, grassy camping areas with some drive-thru spots available. The park is relatively new so amenities are very clean and modern.

128 BIG4 Atherton Woodlands Tourist Park

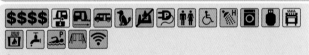

$$$$

- 141 Herberton Rd, Atherton
- (07) 4091 1407
- www.woodlandscp.com.au

BIG4
HOLIDAY PARKS

Located in the heart of the stunning Atherton Tableland, this caravan park has lovely grassy sites and good clean amenities. Some sites are pet friendly with prior approval. There is an internet kiosk onsite and many walking trails and mountain-bike tracks in the surrounding woodland to be enjoyed.

129 Ravenshoe Railway Caravan Park

$ ★

- 63–65 Grigg St, Ravenshoe
- (07) 4097 6005
- www.ravenshoesteamrailway.webs.com

This is a fantastic volunteer-run camping area in a nice shady spot with room for up to 50 caravans. Amenities are clean and tidy, and May–Oct a campfire is lit each night during happy hour.

130 Woodleigh Station

$$$

- Ravenshoe
- (07) 4097 0204
- www.woodleighstation.com.au

This relaxed farm camping area has a variety of powered and unpowered sites available with a few right by the riverbed. Toilets and showers are provided, although they are not easily accessible from all sites.

131 Mount Garnet Travellers Park

$$

- Lot 2, Nymbool Rd, Mount Garnet
- (07) 4097 9335
- www.mount-garnet-travellers-park.com

This is a nice, quiet caravan park with open spaces, clean amenities and a good-sized camp kitchen. Powered sites are available, and fires are permitted in pits. Timber is provided free of charge.

MOUNT GARNET TO KARUMBA

588km

National parks; station stays; free campsites; basic, outback caravan parks

Apr–Sept, although Undara is stunning during the wet season (if you can get there).

Undara Lava Tubes, Cobbold Gorge, barramundi fishing

This route is sealed, except to Cobbold Gorge, which has well-formed gravel roads that are usually suitable for two-wheel drive vehicles.

This is a remote area of northern Queensland, so facilities are limited and services basic.

Saltwater crocodiles inhabit many of the waterways in this area. Be especially cautious around them and if in doubt, assume they are there and don't enter the water.

Cobbold Gorge

INTRODUCTION

From Mount Garnet, the road generally heads west, the typical open bushland of the Gulf Savannah becoming almost monotonous, as you near Normanton. Several geological wonders should entice you to stop along the way. Although the road to Normanton is sealed all the way, in some places it's only a single lane of bitumen and some of the side trips are on unsealed roads.

WHERE TO GO

I made the mistake of bypassing **Undara Lava Tubes** on my first trip through this region, but not the second time, and I won't make it again. These mammoth caves are the nearly-200,000-year-old remains of significant volcanic activity on the Atherton Tableland. Various tours into the caves run

daily, including a sunset bat cave tour during which you'll see up to half-a-million bats leave the cave for their nightly feast. In the wet season, snakes hang from the trees trying to catch a flying morsel as it flaps past and it's an amazing sight! The adjacent caravan park, which also features renovated train carriages as accommodation, is simple yet popular, while the licensed restaurant serves what I'd consider the best sausages in the country. Each morning, the park also puts on a billy-tea breakfast, which is very popular.

The nearby town of **Mount Surprise** is a small community on the edge of the immense Undara lava field. It's a centre for gem fossicking and you can try your luck hunting for topaz, quartz, aquamarine and garnet at the Mt Surprise Gem Den – or just buy something from the gift shop. Russell Dennis, proprietor of Planet Earth

Adventures Caravan Park, puts on daily snake shows out the front of the park which are incredibly entertaining and informative. His shows are a genuine highlight of the Savannah Way and the park has sites from as little as $12 per night too.

Before getting to Georgetown, leave the Savannah Way for **Cobbold Gorge** on Robin Hood Station. Although the station has been running cattle since 1901, it wasn't until 1992 that the Terry family discovered the gorge and decided to develop it as a tourist site. Today the family run walking and boat tours of the gorge with its stunning 30m high sheer walls and water so still it's hard to tell reality from reflection. The property also offers camping facilities, a licensed bar and an infinity pool.

Georgetown was once the heart of a promising goldfield on the Etheridge River,

Karumba sunset

but is now the administrative centre for the region. **Einasleigh** and **Forsyth** lie to the south and ghost towns are scattered around the old diggings. Fossicking is popular in this diverse geological region and permits can be obtained from the local mine warden's office.

Much of the region's goldmining and pioneering history is preserved in **Croydon**, which was once the gold capital of the north. Gold was discovered here in 1885 and the town boomed, but by 1925 it was all over and the population had dwindled to 400. The Croydon General Store, which has traded continuously since 1894, has an interesting collection of relics on display, while the Visitor Information Centre provides a map of the Croydon Heritage Precinct, which consists of the police sergeant's residence (c. 1898), police station and gaol (c. 1896), and Croydon Town Hall (c. 1890). The precinct is open daily and free to enter.

With gold discoveries along the Etheridge River, and copper being mined in Cloncurry, **Normanton** became, for a time, an important inland river port. The railway to Croydon was completed in 1891, and many original buildings, including the railway station and council offices are good examples of early architecture. Possibly the most identifiable landmark in town is the famous Purple Pub. Normanton has basic

services, and a good caravan park, but if you've come all this way, you're best to continue on to Karumba.

Karumba is the only town on the southern coast of the Gulf of Carpentaria and exceptionally popular for the excellent fishing on the Norman River. There are five caravan parks in town, and all of them regularly book out during peak season, which is around June–Sept. The Karumba Tavern, with its sunset-viewing area is a very popular place to congregate of an afternoon, and many people come not only to watch the sunset and enjoy a drink, but to share travelling tales and advice.

DON'T MISS

→ A trip back in time – Normanton
A ride on the *Gulflander* is a fascinating train trip. The railway has operated continuously since 1891 and the diesel railmotor departs year-round from Normanton each Wednesday at 8.30am for the 152km journey to Croydon, returning Thursday. For a shorter trip, book a ride on the Gulflander RM60, a 45hp petrol railmotor that operated between 1960 and 1964.

→ Clouds of glory – near Karumba
The Morning Glory is a unique cloud formation that can be seen around the Gulf of Carpentaria Sept–Nov. The spectacular tubular formations spread from horizon to horizon, stretching for hundreds of kilometres, usually rolling in from the Gulf in banks of three or four, and are accompanied by strong winds.

→ Krys – Normanton
At almost 9m long, 'Krys the Savannah King' was reputedly the largest estuarine crocodile ever caught. A lifesize replica of this monster sits in the park next to the council offices in Haig St, Normanton.

WHERE TO STAY

132 Undara Experience

$$$ ★ ...

⦿ Undara Volcanic Park, Savannah Way
☎ (07) 4097 1900
🖥 www.undara.com.au

This caravan park, part of Undara Lava Lodge, is 40km east of Mount Surprise. Nestled at the edge of Undara Volcanic National Park, the complex has a range of accommodation and a well-stocked shop, plus an excellent restaurant. There are guided tours to nearby caves.

133 Cobbold Gorge Caravan Park

$$$$ ...

⦿ Agate Creek Rd, Forsayth
☎ (07) 4062 5470
🖥 www.cobboldgorge.com.au

This caravan park is very popular and has good facilities, including a restaurant, bar and infinity pool. The main attraction here is the guided gorge tours by electric boat, although the walking tours are also excellent.

134 Cumberland Mine rest area

⦿ Gulf Developmental Rd, 20km west of Georgetown

A popular, free camping area at the site of the old Cumberland town. Basic facilities are provided, including a toilet, bins and picnic tables. There are plenty of birds in the area, if you look out for that sort of thing.

135 Croydon Caravan Park

$$ ...

⦿ 52 Brown St, Croydon
☎ (07) 4745 6238
🖥 www.croydon.qld.gov.au

This well-maintained, council-owned caravan park is close to the centre of town. It has lots of green grass, large shady trees and cable television. It is within walking distance of everything in town.

136 Normanton Tourist Park

$$$ ...

⦿ 14 Brown St, Normanton
☎ (07) 4745 1121
🖥 www.normantontouristpark.com.au

Located in the centre of town, this caravan park has good amenities, some large shady trees and the town's swimming pool within its bounds. The ground can be very hard to drive pegs into though – I had to revert to screwdrivers.

137 Karumba Point Sunset Caravan Park

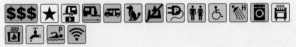

$$$ ★ ...

⦿ 53 Palmer St, Karumba
☎ (07) 4745 9277
🖥 www.sunsetcp.com.au

Karumba is an extremely popular winter destination and reservations are needed for much of this season. This is a good-quality caravan park close to the boat ramp and very popular with those tourists who flock to the area in the cooler winter months. Some stay for the whole winter.

Undara Lava Tubes

NORMANTON TO BORROLOOLA

NEED TO KNOW

	733km
	Free; basic caravan parks; roadhouse camping areas
	Come during the dry season or you are likely get flooded in.
	The Savannah Way, barramundi fishing, outback camping
	This is mostly unsealed and four-wheel drives are recommended. Expect rough roads, occasional bulldust sections and seasonal flooding.
	Normanton, Burketown, Doomadgee and Borroloola have basic facilities, but this is a remote area, so come prepared.
	Crocodiles – everywhere! Remember Queensland and the Northern Territory operate on two different time zones – AEST is a half an hour different to ACST. Put your clocks forward if you're heading west or back if you're travelling east.

Northern Territory border

INTRODUCTION

Between Normanton and Borroloola, the Savannah Way is mainly unsealed and although it's generally well maintained it's only passable in the dry season. There are several river crossings, few of which have bridges, and frequent stretches of rough corrugation or patches of bulldust and potholes. While many do traverse it in regular cars, caravans and motorhomes, it's much better suited to those with four-wheel drives and semi- or off-road-versions of caravans, camper trailers and motorhomes. An alternate route, south to Cloncurry, west via Mount Isa to Three Ways Roadhouse and north along the Stuart Highway, is fully sealed.

WHERE TO GO

Leaving **Normanton**, its more than 200km to Burketown, your next fuel stop, but despite the seeming isolation, there are a few places to stop along the way. Burke and Wills, who were the first explorers to cross the continent from south to north on their ill-fated 1860–61 expedition, reached the coast near the mouth of the Bynoe River. Their most northerly campsite (Camp 119), can be found on the banks of the river 37km west of Normanton – it is clearly signposted.

Further on, the Savannah Way crosses the Leichhardt River, a major Gulf tributary which winds its way north from the ranges south of Mount Isa. Between Normanton and Burketown, the main road crosses the river at Floraville, 74km south-east of Burketown and just above Leichhardt Falls. A short stroll takes you to the top of the falls where there's also a monument to Fred Walker, the Commandant of the Queensland Native Police. This is also a popular free camping spot, although access can be difficult for vehicles with low ground clearance.

Burketown is the oldest town on the Gulf of Carpentaria, with a history dating back more than 150 years. Burketown is now a centre for the regional cattle industry and is about 25km from the Gulf by boat. As the town has no all-weather access roads, it can quickly become isolated and even a small amount of rain can close the black-soil roads. There is great barramundi fishing in the Gulf tributaries, though, so it's a popular stop throughout the dry season. Changes to camping access in the area in 2016 saw an introduction of camping fees at many of the previously free sites, although the cost is still modest.

Although it's not on the Savannah Way, taking the detour from Burketown to **Gregory Downs**, and then Boodjamulla (Lawn Hill) l National Park is well worth it. The park is a true oasis, complete with palm-fringed rivers and lily-covered billabongs. Nearby **Adels Grove** was once a botanical garden created by French botanist Albert De Lestang which supplied seedlings and tropical plants to gardens all over the world. His work was undone by suspected arson in the early 1950s, yet some of his legacy lives on in the form of a spectacular caravan park with attached bar and restaurant.

The nearby Riversleigh D Site is worlds away in landscape – a barren, rocky desert – but it's one of the richest fossil sites in the world. Daily tours can be booked from Adels Grove.

After taking the Lawn Hill detour, you'll rejoin the Savannah Way between Doomadgee and Hells Gate Roadhouse. **Doomadgee** is an Aboriginal community on the Nicholson River which has a roadhouse open to travellers seven days. Alcohol restrictions apply in Doomadgee, and penalties for taking alcohol past the roadhouse can be severe. **Hells Gate Roadhouse**, about 50km before the Northern Territory–Queensland border, serves hot food and fuel, and has an international, all-weather airstrip. Hells Gate is the last chance to get fuel before Borroloola, around 320km away.

Borroloola was once a frontier town with a tough and colourful past, although fishing is the area's main attraction now. To the south, the giant McArthur River Mine extracts a complex silver-lead-zinc ore, which is road-freighted to the nearby port of Bing Bong. There are numerous fishing camps along the coastal rivers with King Ash Bay by far the most well known. Camping is permitted at the King Ash Bay Fishing Club.

DON'T MISS

→ Station stays – near Borroloola
Although there used to be a lot more, a number of the remote cattle stations surrounding the Savannah Way welcome caravanners and campers, often offering incredibly remote and private camping areas. Seven Emu Station, owned by three generations of the Indigenous Shadforth family, offers camping areas overlooking the Robinson River. Four-wheel drives are needed to access the sites. Contact (08) 8975 9904 or (08) 8975 8307, www.sevenemustation.com.au.

→ A lock-up museum – Borroloola
Borroloola was once a tough frontier town filled with wild characters. However, its police station is no longer needed for its original purpose and is now a regional museum managed by the National Trust. It houses a special display dedicated to the police presence in Borroloola in the late 1800s, as well as exhibits covering the area's Aboriginal heritage, Macassan visitations and early European exploration. Grab a key from the caravan park or service station to check it out. Contact (08) 8983 4222.

Adels Grove

WHERE TO STAY

138 Little Bynoe River camping area

- Savannah Way, 37km west of Normanton

This is a quiet, free camping area on the banks of the Little Bynoe River. There are no facilities, but a great outlook over the river. Beware of crocodiles.

139 Leichhardt River Falls camping area

- Nardoo Burketown Rd, Gregory

A stunning, free camping area at the crossing of the Leichhardt River. With a sandy cover over a firm base, this is a popular stop. It's no good for tents, though – it's too hard to drive a peg into the ground. No facilities, so campers must be fully self-sufficient. Beware of crocodiles.

140 Burketown Caravan Park

- 23 Sloman St, Burketown
- (07) 4745 5118
- www.burketowncaravanpark.net.au

This is a tidy caravan park with all the usual facilities. In addition to a well-stocked kiosk, there is a separate takeaway food outlet at the front gate (which sells cooked local barramundi). The park is in the heart of Burketown, so you can walk everywhere. Bookings are required Mar–Nov.

141 Tirranna Springs Roadhouse

- Savannah Way, 26km west of Burketown
- (07) 4748 3998
- www.tirrannasprings.com.au

A welcoming roadhouse stopover with a basic camping area behind the main building, or more private sites on the banks of the Gregory River.

142 Hells Gate Roadhouse

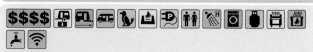

- Savannah Way, Hells Gate
- (07) 4745 8258
- www.hellsgateroadhouse.com.au

Named for the small gap in the ranges that the first pioneers passed through to take up land in the Northern Territory, this is an important roadhouse with a basic camping area out the back. Powered and unpowered sites are available, although as power is generated locally, powered sites are reasonably expensive.

143 McArthur River Caravan Park

- 781 Robinson Rd, Borroloola
- (08) 8975 8734
- www.mcarthurcaravanpark.com.au

This is a grassy, evenly laid out camping area within Borroloola. The facilities are basic, but the manager is nice and welcoming. There's good barramundi fishing nearby, on the McArthur River.

Boodjamulla Gorge

BORROLOOLA TO STUART HIGHWAY

NEED TO KNOW

- **390km via Cape Crawford to 558km via Limmen National Park**
- **National parks, station stays, free camping areas**
- **During the dry season – Apr–Nov**
- **Outback camping, fishing**
- **The Carpentaria Highway is sealed, but rough. The track through Limmen National Park is four-wheel drive only.**
- **This is a very remote area and basic services are not always available.**
- **Most of the waterways through here have crocodiles. Be careful around riverbanks and don't go swimming.**

Towns River

INTRODUCTION

From Borroloola there are two great routes that finally meet the Stuart Highway. One travels largely off-road and is the longest section detailed in this book without a fuel stop on the direct route. There's no fuel between Borroloola and Roper Bar, and Roper Bar will be closed on a Sunday, so you may not get fuel until Mataranka. Highway One sticks to the bitumen, but glides through some stunning territory. If you're taking the easier route, along the all-weather Carpentaria Highway, be wary of road trains hauling ore from the McArthur River Mine to Bing Bong.

WHERE TO GO

Sticking to the Carpentaria Highway you'll pass by the Caranbirini Conservation Reserve, just 46km west of Borroloola. Protected within the reserve are sandstone pillars up to 25m tall. A really well-marked, 60 min walk zigzags through the pillars allowing you to explore the maze of fascinating geological structures.

Cape Crawford, the location of the Heartbreak Hotel, is at the junction of the Carpentaria and Tablelands highways. The hotel complex provides basic accommodation, fuel and meals, as well as a caravan park. The rich Barkly Tableland stretches to the south and there are several 'lost city' escarpment rock formations in the area. Taking the Tablelands Highway will deliver you to the Barkly Highway (see p. 188).

It's 270km to the famous Daly Waters Pub. **Daly Waters** was a refuelling point for Qantas international flights during the 1930s. Today a few houses and the pub are all that remain. About 1km north of Daly Waters is a tree with a barely discernable carved letter 's' on its trunk. It's believed to have been marked by explorer John McDouall Stuart as he struggled to cross the continent in the 1860s (which is how the Stuart Highway got its name).

If it wasn't for the pub, though, no one would stop here. It was built in the 1930s to service crew and passengers of international aircraft. Today, it still caters for travellers.

Like many outback pubs, it has its quirks – brassieres and ladies' underwear hang from the ceiling, and stickers and photographs adorn every wall. Many stop here to enjoy the jovial atmosphere of the adjoining caravan park and the pub's famous Beef and Barra Barbecue that happens nightly Apr–Oct.

If you take the northern, off-road route, you'll pass through Limmen National Park and Roper Bar before rejoining the highway at Mataranka, 106km south of Katherine and 167km north of Daly Waters. Limmen is one of the Territory's youngest national parks, having only been officially established in 2012, but it is quickly becoming a bucket-list destination for its rugged beauty, amazing waterholes and great fishing.

The road is rough and dusty, but not challenging, although it's only suitable for four-wheel drives and off-road- caravans or motorhomes. Last time I passed through, it shook a driving light from my bull bar, which I never managed to find. The park is very remote so visitors must be self-sufficient.

Roper Bar is a very small community on the banks of the Roper River. It has a police station, motel and store – the Roper Bar Store, which also has a basic caravan park. You can get fuel and basic supplies here before camping at the very popular Munbililla (Tomato Island) to the east, or continuing on to Mataranka in the west (*see* p. 71).

(*see* p. 71)

DON'T MISS

→ Butterfly Falls – Limmen National Park

Just a short walk from the camping area of the same name in Limmen National Park, Butterfly Falls has a stunning, croc-free waterhole underneath that's home to thousands of common crow butterflies and friendly archer fish.

→ Lorella Springs Wilderness Park – near Limmen National Park

Lorella Springs Wilderness Park is a one-million-acre cattle station that's widely regarded as one of the best places in Australia to camp. With a large main camping area and many smaller remote campsites dotted across the park, its facilities include a bar, fuel and general store, as well as accommodation options. It's open throughout the dry season, and access is usually possible for most vehicles. Call ahead for conditions (08) 8975 9917. Campsite fees apply, but bookings aren't required.

WHERE TO STAY

144 King Ash Bay Fishing Club

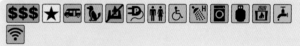

$$

📍 Batten Point Rd, Borroloola
📞 (08) 8975 9800
💻 www.kingashbay.com.au

This informal camping area is located right on the riverbank and is a popular destination for keen fishers. Powered sites are available year-round, however their unpowered sites, that are right down at the river's edge, are closed during the wet season.

145 Heartbreak Hotel Caravan Park

$$

📍 Corner Carpentaria and Tablelands hwys, Cape Crawford
📞 (08) 8975 9928
💻 www.heartbreakhotel.com.au

This outback camping area behind the Heartbreak Hotel offers grassy sites with some shade and basic facilities. There is a pool onsite. The hotel provides some excellent meal options and you can book a helicopter flight from there to take you over the Lost City.

146 Goanna Creek rest area

📍 Carpentaria Hwy, 40km west of Cape Crawford

A great spot for overnight stops with magic views at sunrise and sunset. No facilities available so it's more suitable for self-contained vans.

147 Daly Waters Pub Caravan Park

$$$

📍 Stuart St, Daly Waters
📞 (08) 8975 9927
💻 www.dalywaterspub.com

This is an extremely popular caravan park, especially during the peak season Apr–Oct when the pub puts on its famous Beef & Barra BBQ every night. The site does not take bookings so it's best to arrive early. Powered and unpowered sites are available with basic facilities.

Butterfly Falls

DALY WATERS TO KATHERINE

NEED TO KNOW

- **276km**
- **Basic outback caravan parks, free camping areas**
- **These areas are affected by wet-season rains so visit Apr–Oct.**
- **Nitmiluk (Katherine) Gorge, Mataranka Hot Springs**
- **The highway between Daly Waters and Katherine is wide and sealed.**
- **Facilities are limited to roadhouses and small stores until Katherine.**
- **Crocodiles inhabit many waterways.**

Swimming at Bitter Springs, Mataranka

INTRODUCTION

One of the more interesting sections of the Stuart Highway – the scenery becomes less featureless as it passes through groves of pandanus and over some of the Territory's rivers. There is no speed limit on parts of this road, but if you are towing it's certainly not safe to maintain speeds over 110km/hr. Many vehicles will be travelling much faster though, so take care when overtaking slower vehicles, as it can be hard to judge the speed of vehicles when you're looking at them in your mirrors.

WHERE TO GO

The blink-and-you'll-miss-it town of **Larrimah** is home to about a dozen people and the 'Big Stubby'. Many stop here for the photo opportunity with it and the resident Pink Panther statue. Larrimah also has a small museum showcasing the town's war efforts throughout WWII. It's always open, so just head in. Larrimah's service station burnt down in 2009 and hasn't been rebuilt, but the town has a small caravan park.

Mataranka, where you'll join the highway if you've come through Limmen

National Park (see p. 69), is best known for its crystal-clear hot springs. It was also the setting for Jeannie Gunn's autobiographical account, *We of the Never Never*, which describes her experiences around Elsey Station in 1902. The historic Elsey Cemetery is an interesting place to stop and visit the graves of some of the larger-than-life characters from her novel, including that of her husband. (Copies of the novel are usually available at shops in Mataranka, although it can be downloaded for free on a Kindle, if you're interested in reading it.) The cemetery is well signposted from the Stuart Highway and only about 6km along a sealed road.

Mataranka has a good range of basic services including fuel, and plenty of good camping options. The newest of these is the Little Roper Stockcamp, set up in 2017 by an ex-ringer named Des and his wife, Telka. There are only limited spots available, which usually fill up daily. Des, who's a genuine Territory character, regularly puts on campfire dinner nights and runs daily stockyard demonstrations. The property is only a few minutes' walk from the hot springs.

Katherine, just over 100km north at the junction of the Stuart and Victoria highways,

is a major centre in the heart of the Northern Territory. It has a selection of caravan parks, both near the town centre and within easy distance, plus a wide range of other accommodation options. Katherine's visitor information centre, at the southern entrance to town, has a large parking area specially for caravans (day-use only). It also has a drinking water tap that for $2 will run for five minutes, allowing travellers to fill up water tanks. Conveniently, it's located adjacent to a service station and across the road from a large shopping centre which has a supermarket, bottle shop and bakery. The Katherine Community Markets run just behind here every Saturday through the dry season 8am–1pm.

Of course, Katherine's biggest attraction, is the spectacular Nitmiluk (Katherine) Gorge, which is 29km north-east of town. Get the latest information on tours and free activities from the visitor centre.

DON'T MISS

→ **Palms by the pool – Mataranka**
Mataranka Thermal Pool was proclaimed as a reserve in 1967 to preserve the pool and surrounding palm forest. The water is a constant 34°C and flows at an amazing

30.5 million litres per day. The adjoining camping area is very popular with travellers, who stop for a dip in the rock-paved thermal pool.

→ Rare bats – near Katherine
The Cutta Cutta Caves, close to the Stuart Highway 27km south-east of Katherine, are the only caves open to the public in the Territory. The limestone caves have spectacular stalactites and stalagmites, and are home to rare orange horseshoe bats and ghost bats. Entry fees apply and cave tours run daily during the dry season at 9am, 10am, 11am, 1pm, 2pm and 3pm.

→ Amazing gorges – near Katherine
Nitmiluk (Katherine Gorge) contains a series of 13 gorges that cut through the landscape by the Katherine River. The gorges can be explored by foot, on the water or in the air and several tours and experiences operate every day during the dry season. With more than 100km of walking tracks, bushwalkers are well catered for with walks that range in length from about an hour to five days. Boat cruises and canoeing tours are popular, and can be booked from the gorge's visitor information centre which is open daily and has a cafe and display centre.

WHERE TO STAY

148 Larrimah Wayside Inn Caravan Park

📍 5 Mahoney St, Larrimah
📞 (08) 8975 9931

This outback caravan park has level, shady sites with basic facilities to suit most travellers' needs. The pub is interesting and great for a cold drink.

149 Little Roper Stock Camp

📍 547 Homestead Rd, Mataranka
📞 0427 880 819
💻 www.littleroperstockcamp.com.au

A great little caravan park with spacious, level sites and modest amenities. During the dry season a three-course camp oven dinner is offered on Mon, Wed and Fri nights. Bookings are essential.

150 Bitter Springs Cabins and Camping

📍 255 Martin Rd, Mataranka
📞 (08) 8975 4838
💻 www.bitterspringscabins.com.au

Located just 500m from Bitter Springs Thermal Pools this rustic caravan park offers both powered and unpowered options on large shady sites with basic amenities to meet most travellers' needs.

151 Shady Lane Tourist Park
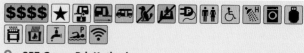

📍 257 Gorge Rd, Katherine
📞 (08) 8971 0491
💻 www.shadylanetouristpark.com.au

Set amongst the shady trees and palms this great little caravan park offers good-sized sites, some with concrete slabs. Amenities are well maintained and there is a large swimming pool onsite.

Katherine Outback Experience

KATHERINE TO DARWIN

NEED TO KNOW

🎨 **317km**

🏠 **National park camping areas, full-featured caravan parks, station stays, family caravan resorts**

☁ **During the dry season – Apr–Oct**

👁 **Edith Falls, Darwin, Mindil Beach markets**

⚠ **This is a well-travelled highway that's usually in good shape.**

🍴 **Once you hit Darwin, all services and facilities are available.**

⚠ **Crocodiles inhabit most waterways and coastal waters.**

Leliyn (Edith Falls), Nitmiluk National Park

INTRODUCTION

There is almost too much to see on the trek from Katherine to Darwin, especially when compared to the remote-area driving you've done to get this far. Darwin itself is a hive of activity and entertainment, and there are also the wonders of Kakadu and Litchfield national parks, and plenty of WWII history to take in along the way. The well-maintained Stuart Highway traverses low, undulating hills north of Pine Creek. There are few overtaking areas and almost no rest stops along this section though, so plan to stop in some of the small towns if you need a break.

WHERE TO GO

One of the Northern Territory's most stunning and accessible camping areas is at Leliyn (Edith Falls), on the western edge of Nitmiluk National Park. The falls are a three-tiered cascade with three separate pools that are very popular swimming holes. A steep, short but rewarding walk circumnavigates the three pools offering great views over the valley. The well-managed camping area adjacent to the lowest and largest pool is very popular June–Sept. It often fills up nightly, so get in early if you can as camping is on a 'first in, best dressed' basis.

The next stop is the 1870s gold-rush town of **Pine Creek** which has a general store, basic services and a very pleasant picnic area in the middle of town that's a popular stop for lunch. There are many interesting relics of the town's goldmining days, including the Ah Toys Bakery building, which still has the ant-bed mortar ovens that were used to bake the town's bread until the beginning of WWII. The Pine Creek Railway Station, which was built in 1888 as part of the grand plan to connect South Australia and Darwin by rail, is now a National Trust museum displaying rail memorabilia and an 1877 steam locomotive. The town is also the southern launching point for visits to Kakadu National Park (*see* p. 76).

Further north, **Adelaide River** was a base for servicemen during WWII and in 1947 was chosen by the Commonwealth War Graves Commission as the site for the War Cemetery. The Adelaide River War Cemetery is the resting place for the 434 British, Canadian and Australian servicemen who died in this region during WWII. In the adjoining Civil Cemetery, the 63 civilians are buried, including the nine post office workers who were killed as a result of a direct hit on the Darwin Post office by Japanese bombs in 1942.

Although Mataranka gets all the glory for its thermal pools, the natural pools at **Berry Springs**, 50km south of Darwin, are just as good, partly because they aren't hot on a hot day. Three separate pools form three separate swimming areas with crystal-clear water where you can see turtles and archer fish. There's also a shady picnic area, which is welcome on a hot Top End day.

Darwin is regarded as Australia's northern outpost, and its proximity to Asia and immersion in Aboriginal culture make it one of the world's most interesting cities. This diversity stretches back to the early days of Darwin's development when Aboriginal, European and Chinese people worked side-by-side. One of my favourite accounts of early Darwin life is in the

Crocosaurus Cove, Darwin

regular shows from eMDee – a didgeridoo-based band playing the Indigenous instrument like you never imagined possible. Open 4–10pm Thurs and 4–9pm Sun between the last Thurs in Apr and Oct. BYO alcohol for responsible consumption.

→ Leanyer Recreation Park – Darwin
Part of the raft of government initiatives to make living in the Top End heat bearable, the Leanyer Recreation Park is a free outdoor swimming pool and water park with three large water slides. With the adjacent parklands and picnic areas, this is a very popular spot for people of all ages to keep cool. It's where I take the kids on the hottest days to keep cool.

→ Museum and Art Gallery of the Northern Territory – Bullocky Point
Darwin's main museum is a great place to visit, and not just because it's blessedly air-conditioned. Along with an ever-changing variety of exhibits, on permanent display is Sweetheart, the 5m long croc which was caught nearby; an excellent timeline of evolutionary progress; and the cyclone Tracy exhibition, which details the devastating effects of one of Australia's worst natural disasters. Entry is free and it's open daily 10am–5pm. Contact (08) 8999 8264.

autobiographical account of Tom Cole – *Hell West and Crooked* – which is worth looking up. There are endless things to do in and around town, so don't plan a short stay here. (*See* p. 76 for information on visiting Kakadu National Park.)

DON'T MISS

→ Litchfield National Park – Near Batchelor
In spectacular Litchfield National Park you will see numerous waterfalls cascading from a sandstone plateau. There are also intriguing magnetic termite mounds, a small 'lost city' formation and some relics of early pastoral interest. There are several camping areas in the park, although Wangi Falls is the only one suitable for caravans. Arrive early if you want a site, especially a caravan site, as there is no reservation system. An all-weather sealed road links many of the popular sites. The only sealed entry to the park is from Bachelor, which was originally a town servicing Australia's first uranium mine at the interestingly named Rum Jungle.

→ Mindil Beach Sunset Markets – Darwin
Possibly Australia's most famous bazaar, the Mindil Beach Sunset Markets live up to the hype. It's the place to come for an eclectic mix of international food vendors, quirky fashions and crafts while watching one of the prettiest sunsets in the north. Don't miss the

Mindil Beach Sunset Markets

WHERE TO STAY

152 Nitmiluk Centre Campground

📍 Gorge Rd, Nitmiluk National Park
📞 (08) 8972 1886

Set in the striking Nitmiluk National Park this camping area has very good facilities, including a beautiful pool and kiosk. Both gravel powered and grass unpowered sites are available. Advance bookings are recommended.

153 Leliyn (Edith Falls) camping area

📍 Nitmiluk National Park
🖥 www.nt.gov.au/leisure/parks-reserves/find-a-park-to-visit/nitmiluk-national-park

Located just a short walk from the stunning Leliyn (Edith Falls) with a beautiful clear swimming hole just below, this busy camping area has good level sites and clean, modern amenities. Early arrival is recommended as bookings are not taken.

154 Pine Creek Railway Resort

📍 1 Railway Tce, Pine Creek
📞 (08) 8876 1001
🖥 www.pinecreekrailwayresort.com.au

This small, tidy caravan park has very good facilities including a pool and seasonal licensed restaurant open Apr–Oct. Caravan sites are limited so booking ahead is advised.

155 Mount Bundy Station camping area

📍 315 Haynes Rd, Adelaide River
📞 (08) 8976 7009
🖥 www.mtbundy.com.au

Located on a working station, this is a unique riverfront farmstay with basic, but good, amenities and well-shaded, grassy sites. You can pay to take a guided tour of the station in the evening with drinks and nibbles provided at sunset.

156 Coolalinga Caravan Park

📍 418 Stuart Hwy, Coolalinga
📞 (08) 8983 1026
🖥 www.coolalingacaravanpark.com.au

Centrally located between Darwin and the popular Berry Springs, this basic, pet-friendly park makes for a good base to explore the greater Darwin region. Ensuite sites are reasonably priced and amenities are dated but tidy.

157 Darwin FreeSpirit Resort

📍 901 Stuart Hwy, Holtze
📞 (08) 8935 0888
🖥 www.darwinfreespiritresort.com.au

Located just 15km south of Darwin this is a large, family-friendly caravan park with good facilities including a quality licensed restaurant, and multiple pools. This is a busy park and bookings are required during peak season.

Florence Falls, Litchfield National Park

KAKADU NATIONAL PARK

NEED TO KNOW

465km

🏠 National park camping areas, full-featured caravan parks, remote campsites

☁ Come Apr–Sept – it's a little too hot after this.

👁 Birdwatching, fishing, Aboriginal culture and heritage, amazing scenery and walks

🚗 The Kakadu and Arnhem highways are both sealed, although many access roads to popular attractions aren't. A four-wheel drive is recommended on most of these roads.

🍴 Facilities are limited, although there is good shopping at Jabiru.

⚠ Crocodiles can be found in all Kakadu waterways and swimming is not officially condoned.

Boat cruise on the Yellow Water Billabong

INTRODUCTION

Kakadu National Park is one of Australia's iconic destinations because with relative ease you can camp by tropical, lily-covered billabongs, take part in Indigenous art classes with tribal elders, compete with massive crocodiles for giant barramundi, and overlook some of the Northern Territory's most spectacular landscapes. There is a wide range of camping on offer, from remote free camps designed for the totally self-sufficient, to developed caravan parks with resort-like facilities.

The Arnhem and Kakadu highways are wide, sealed roads with good visibility and ample opportunities for overtaking, although be wary of slow-moving tourist traffic. During the dry season regenerative burning often takes place in the park, so be wary when that's happening as the smoke can impair visibility.

WHERE TO GO

If you've been in Darwin first, you'll enter Kakadu National Park from **Humpty Doo**, which is the site of a failed rice-growing area from the 1950s. Today the town has developed into an intensive market-gardening area where mango and other fruit plantations are common.

The first major landmark is the Adelaide River, which you also crossed on your way to Darwin, as the Stuart Highway passed over it at the small town of the same name. This crossing is also the boarding location for the famous jumping-crocodile cruises that take place every day during the dry season. (There are two separate operators.)

Soon after, you'll cross the Mary River, which has the highest concentration of crocodiles in the Northern Territory. Mary River National Park has a number of remote camping areas and is a popular destination for birdwatchers, four-wheel drivers and keen fishers chasing barramundi. Steer clear of the water's edge, though.

Between the park boundary and Jabiru a number of four-wheel-drive-only tracks veer off the Arnhem Highway. To the south are the idyllic Red Lily, Bucket and Alligator billabongs, all of which have basic camping areas on the shores and are popular, out-of-the-way fishing spots.

Jabiru, almost on the border of Kakadu and Arnhem Land was originally constructed for workers at the Ranger Uranium Mine, and their families. Completed in 1982, the town has since become a major tourist centre serving visitors to the park.

Maguk

Jabiru offers most services including a supermarket, service station and a good bakery. The Bowali Visitor Centre, the main one for the park, is only a short drive away and it's a great place to visit to find out everything about Kakadu. It also has a nice little restaurant.

About 40km north-west from Jabiru, and on the floodplains of the East Alligator River, Merl Campground is a popular spot with great short walks from the campsite, and one of the most extensive Indigenous rock-art galleries in Australia. Nearby **Ubirr**, which many climb for its out-of-this-world sunset views, is also a popular photographic opportunity. There's a great rainforest walk along the banks of the East Alligator, which starts and finishes at Cahills Crossing – the entrance to Arnhem Land. Whatever you do, don't walk onto the weir, as people have been taken by crocodiles, even in the ankle-deep water. I have never seen so many crocodiles in one place, and even lost a big barra to them while fishing nearby.

Following the Kakadu Highway back to Pine Creek will take you past many of the stunning waterholes and waterfalls that are popular for swimming – although Kakadu's official stance on swimming is that it's not safe anywhere in the park. Jim Jim Falls, Gunlom and Maguk are all accessed via four-wheel-drive tracks, which can often be rough and aren't suitable for caravans.

The Gagudju Lodge resort complex at **Cooinda** is situated close to the fabulous Yellow Water (Ngurrungurrudjba) Billabong. The lodge offers most basic services, including fuel, accommodation, camping and a small resort-style shop. Bus transfers to the Yellow Water cruise boats leave from the front of the resort and the Warradjan Aboriginal Cultural Centre (known as 'the turtle') is only a short walk away along a bush path.

DON'T MISS

→ Waterbird haven – near Humpty Doo

The Fogg Dam Conservation Reserve lies outside Kakadu, but is an excellent place to view birds, as the they congregate here to feed. Boardwalks wind around the reserve through a variety of fascinating habitats.

→ Amazing rock art – Nourlangie Rock Walk (Burrungkuy)

About 35km south of Jabiru, this 1.5km walk takes you through some of Australia's oldest rock-art sites which span a period from around 20,000 years ago to the Indigenous people's first encounters with Europeans. The walk is wheelchair accessible and ranger-guided tours operate during the dry season.

→ Window on Kakadu – near Cooinda

Yellow Water (Ngurrungurrudjba) Billabong is one of the most accessible windows to the Kakadu wetland. There is a boardwalk, but the billabong is best viewed on a boat tour. A large number of bird species, abundant wetland flora and some estuarine crocodiles are usually seen. Tours depart six times a day, although the sunset tours are widely considered the best. Fees apply. Contact (08) 8979 1500.

Ubirr

TRAVEL TIP

Kakadu National Park is a wetland where mosquitoes are usually present. Apart from being a nuisance, they can also carry debilitating diseases, so pack tropical-strength personal insect repellent and around dawn and dusk, cover up in long-sleeved clothing and trousers. I don't travel anywhere without BushMan's DEET-based insect repellent and use mosquito coils to keep them away too.

STAY CROC WISE

Estuarine crocodiles inhabit every waterway within Kakadu National Park and the official word from park management is "We don't recommend that people swim in Kakadu's waterways, but some people choose to do so at their own risk." Under absolutely no circumstances should you enter the waters of the larger creeks or billabongs, however some of the waterholes on the escarpment in the south of the park are less likely to be accessed by crocodiles.

PARK PASSES

Kakadu is Aboriginal land, so an entry pass is needed for travel through the park, and stays are restricted to a maximum of 14 days. The passes can be bought online, at the Kakadu Visitor Information Centre, and from several places around Darwin, Katherine and Kakadu – find out more at www.parksaustralia.gov.au.

WHERE TO STAY

158 Mary River Wilderness Retreat & Caravan Park

$$$$

📍 Mary River Crossing, Arnhem Hwy, Annaburroo
📞 (08) 8978 8877
🖥 www.maryriverpark.com.au

This beautiful shady caravan park has lush green sites and good, clean amenities. There is a lovely pool onsite and a restaurant which provides delicious hot meats for lunch and dinner.

159 Anbinik Kakadu Resort

$$$$

📍 83 Jabiru Dr, Jabiru
📞 (08) 8979 3144
🖥 www.anbinik.com.au

Surrounded by beautiful bushland this caravan park has level, grass sites with some ensuites available. There is a nice pool onsite and you can walk across the road to hear interesting talks by the local park rangers. Bookings are recommended as sites are limited.

160 Merl camping area

$$$

📍 Oenpelli Rd, Kakadu National Park
📞 (08) 8938 1120
🖥 www.parksaustralia.gov.au/kakadu/stay/camping/merl-campground

This is a great camping area with simple amenities and large, shady sites. There are a number of walking tracks that lead out from the campground and it is a short distance to the stunning rock paintings in Ubirr. Beautiful sunset viewing.

161 Mardugal One camping area

$$$

📍 Kakadu Hwy, Kakadu
🖥 www.parksaustralia.gov.au/kakadu

A beautiful camping area located close to Jim Jim Creek and a boat ramp. The site has plenty of open space and shade as well as good hot showers and toilets. It's a good base from which to explore some of the four-wheel-drive tracks and billabongs in the area.

KATHERINE TO TIMBER CREEK

NEED TO KNOW

🕐 **289km**

🏠 **Free camps, station stays**

☁ **Through the dry season – Apr–Oct**

👁 **Fishing, national parks, outback hospitality**

🛣 **This is a fully sealed route, although most side roads are unsealed and four-wheel drives are recommended for those.**

🍴 **Once you have left Katherine, services are limited to roadhouses and small stores.**

⚠ **Crocodiles inhabit most waterways in this part of the Northern Territory.**

River crossing, Buchanan Highway

INTRODUCTION

The Victoria Highway between Katherine and Timber Creek is a wide, sealed road with views across numerous interesting hill formations around Victoria River Roadhouse and Timber Creek – the only service points along this section. Judbarra (Gregory) National Park is accessible from the Victoria Highway, or from the unsealed Buchanan Highway. While many of the tracks are only suitable for four-wheel drives, there are some that are accessible by two-wheel-drive vehicles, although towing caravans and trailers is not recommended.

WHERE TO GO

On the way out of **Katherine** stop in at the Katherine Hot Springs, which has a developed swimming area, picnic grounds and a small cafe set up in a converted shipping container.

Between here and the **Victoria River Roadhouse**, there are few landmarks apart from a rest area at the junction of the Buntine and Victoria highways. The roadhouse complex is almost completely surrounded by the Victoria River section of Judbarra (Gregory) National Park. The fully licensed roadhouse has accommodation, fuel, food and a caravan park, and is a popular stopover for travellers. It's an excellent base for fishing during the season.

The surrounding national park features spectacular limestone gorges, sandstone formations and rugged ranges. Follow one of the marked walking tracks in the Victoria River section, such as Joe Creek Walk, which starts alongside the highway, 10km west of the roadhouse.

In the western section of the park, there are several camping areas, but facilities and vehicle access are mainly limited to four-wheel-drive vehicles. It is possible to leave your caravan at Timber Creek and visit a lot of the highlights in a single, long day's drive. This will give access to the historic Bullita Homestead, as well as billabongs, good barramundi fishing and even some fossil sites.

Timber Creek is rich in Territory history – drovers, stockmen and early settlers all used this historic river port – and today it is a busy service centre for travellers along the Victoria Highway. The old police station is now a National Trust museum with displays of historical artefacts (open Apr–Aug). There is a historical reserve approximately 15km north-west of town that includes Gregory's Tree, an old boab tree inscribed by the explorer Augustus Gregory in the 1850s.

DON'T MISS

→ **Victoria River tours – Timber Creek**
Take a tour on a Victoria River cruise. Operating from Timber Creek, a 3.5hr tour plies 35km of the Victoria River. This is a great opportunity to view the local wildlife, including estuarine crocodiles, birds and wallabies, along with the spectacular sunset over the river. Fees apply and tours depart daily at 4pm. Contact 0427 750 731 or 0428 588 960.

→ **Riverside camping – near Jasper Gorge**
About 40km south of its intersection with the Victoria Highway, the unsealed Buchanan Highway winds through Jasper Gorge for several kilometres. The scenery is spectacular and south of the Jasper Creek crossing there is a popular camping spot. Charlies Crossing is a bush camp with no facilities.

WHERE TO STAY

Victoria Highway

163 Victoria River Roadhouse Caravan Park

$$

📍 Victoria Hwy
📞 (08) 8975 0744

Located on the grounds behind the roadhouse, this caravan park offers large, shady sites with plenty of room and basic, clean amenities. The roadhouse serves hot meals and cold beers. Perfect for overnight stops to break up the driving.

164 Wirib Tourism Park

$$

📍 Victoria Hwy, Timber Creek
📞 (08) 8975 0602
🖥 www.wirib.com.au

Located in the centre of Timber Creek township, this is a good-quality caravan park with lush green lawns and large drive-thru sites. It has good facilities, including a well-stocked store and a swimming pool.

165 Bullita Homestead camping area

$

📍 Judbarra (Gregory) National Park, Timber Creek
📞 (08) 8975 0888
🖥 www. nt.gov.au/leisure/parks-reserves/find-a-park-to-visit/judbarra-gregory-national-park

This is a small bush camping area on the East Baines River. It is suitable for off-road caravans only as the road in can be quite rough. There is a drop toilet and rainwater tank onsite.

162 Manbulloo Homestead Caravan Park

$$$

📍 275 Murnburlu Rd, Katherine
📞 (08) 8972 1559
🖥 www.manbulloohomesteadcaravanpark.com.au

This pet-friendly caravan park, located on a working cattle station beside the Katherine River, has good facilities and large, level camping areas set on a wide, open, green, grassy expanse. There is ample opportunity for birdwatching, bushwalking and fishing.

TIMBER CREEK TO KUNUNURRA

NEED TO KNOW

- 225km

- National parks, full-featured caravan parks

- The dry season is the best time to visit (Apr–Oct), although the waterfalls are amazing during the wet.

- Outback scenery, walking, fossicking, history

- The road between Timber Creek and Kununurra is sealed, although the road into Keep River National Park is not, and is often rough.

- Kununurra is a busy regional centre with most facilities and services, although there is nothing between Timber Creek and Lake Argyle resort.

- Crocodiles inhabit most waterways. In Keep River National Park, especially, seasonal flooding can mean crocodiles are even near walking tracks. Remember the Northern Territory and Western Australia operate on two different time zones – ACST is 1.5 hours different to AWST. Put your clocks forward if you're heading west or back if you're travelling east.

Mirima National Park, Kununurra

INTRODUCTION

From Timber Creek you start moving into Kimberley country. Already you will have seen a few distinctive boabs lurking by the side of the road, but these will become more common the closer you get to Kununurra. The Victoria Highway continues sealed and wide all the way and is easy going. There are actually only two sealed roads that enter Western Australia, and this is one of them. Before you get that far, though, there's more opportunity to explore Judbarra (Gregory) National Park, or continue on to Keep River National Park, just this side of the border.

WHERE TO GO

Just 10km west of **Timber Creek** is the popular Big Horse Creek Campground. It has a sealed boat ramp that offers the best access to the creek and the Victoria River's best barramundi fishing.

There's a quarantine station on the Northern Territory–Western Australia border where you have to give up fresh fruit, vegetables, plants, flowers, seeds, nuts, honey and used fruit and vegetable containers, so plenty of travellers stop off in Keep River National Park for a few days to make sure as much as possible gets eaten, rather than thrown out.

The park, which juts up against the border, north of the highway, offers visitors excellent opportunities for bushwalking, photography and camping. There are short and long walks, and two camping areas. Rugged sandstone formations and Aboriginal art sites are special features of the park. Although access is via a gravel road, it's suitable for two-wheel-drive vehicles.

Once through the quarantine station at the border, it's only 43km to Kununurra, however it's well worth the detour to **Lake Argyle**. The tourist village on the northern banks of the man-made lake is mainly associated with tourism so is busiest Apr–Oct. However, people are increasingly planning visits for late in the wet season to see the stunning waterfalls at their best.

One of the major attractions here is the Durack family's historic Argyle Downs homestead, which was reconstructed from the original before the lake was flooded. Divers can still see the ruins of the original homestead on the lake floor.

The village has basic but improving services, accommodation, fuel and a caravan park.

Kununurra sprouted with the damming of the mighty Ord River and is located downstream from the dam wall on the banks of Lake Kununurra. The diversion dam, completed in 1963, channels water to an enormous irrigation area where crops of sugarcane, melons, bananas and a whole range of other produce thrive. As a result, locally grown fruit and vegetables are available straight from the farm. The town has all facilities and caters well for tourists – for example, the local butcher will be pleased to cryovac meat orders, which is a great boon for caravanners and campers.

DON'T MISS

→ **Ord River Dam – near Kununurra**
Completed in 1971, this enormous engineering feat resulted in Lake Argyle, which encompasses an area of 2000 sq km and can hold enough water (at flood level) to fill Sydney Harbour 54 times over. The vast Argyle Downs Station, once owned by the pioneering Durack family, sadly lies totally submerged beneath the lake. The reconstructed Argyle Downs Homestead, which is close to the dam wall, is open daily Apr–Sept. Entry fees apply.

→ **Zebra rock – near Kununurra**
Thought to be unique to a small area near Kununurra, this type of sedimentary stone has unusual contrasting striped and spotted patterns, hence its name. Local craftspeople at the Zebra Rock Gallery shape and polish the stone into items ranging from jewellery to wine racks. Zebra rock can be found in most shops in Kununurra or at the Zebra Rock Gallery in Packsaddle Rd. Entry fees apply.

WHERE TO STAY

166 Goorrandalng camping area

$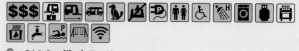

⚲ **Keep River National Park**
💻 www.nt.gov.au/leisure/parks-reserves/find-a-park-to-visit/keep-river-national-park

This is a basic Northern Territory national park camping area with good facilities that are limited to toilets, barbecues and fire pits. The view from camp at sunset is stunning. There's a great walk from the camping area, as well as others in the park. The road in can be rough.

167 Lake Argyle Caravan Park

$$$$

⚲ Lake Argyle Rd, Lake Argyle
📞 (08) 9168 7777
💻 www.lakeargyle.com

Set on the shores of the stunning Lake Argyle, this caravan park has one of the best outlooks in the Kimberley. It has an onsite restaurant and bar, and a well-stocked shop with basic groceries. Its highlight however, is the amazing infinity pool which overlooks the lake.

168 Ivanhoe Village Caravan Resort

$$$

⚲ 214 Coolibah Dr, Kununurra
📞 (08) 9169 1995
💻 www.ivanhoevillageresort.com

This is a high-quality caravan park just 600m from the town centre. It has excellent amenities and a wide range of facilities, including a resort-style pool with a spa. Bookings are required in peak periods.

Lake Argyle

KUNUNURRA TO FITZROY CROSSING

NEED TO KNOW

649km

Station stays, national park camping areas, roadhouse campsites

The Kimberley is at its best early in the dry season (Apr) through to Oct.

National parks

The roads are good through here, although unsealed and rough to many attractions

Services are limited outside of Kununurra.

Crocodiles inhabit many Kimberley waterways.

Purnululu National Park

INTRODUCTION

Rather than taking the often-rough Gibb River Road, that's only suitable for four-wheel drives and off-road recreational vehicles, you'll keep the Durack Range to the west as you drive the Victoria and Great Northern highways between Kununurra and Halls Creek, passing isolated cattle stations along the way. The road is subject to flash flooding and can be cut following storms. Between Halls Creek and Fitzroy Crossing the highway is wide and well maintained with numerous rest areas.

WHERE TO GO

Detouring north to **Wyndham** will take you to the northernmost town in Western Australia. It sits on the banks of Cambridge Gulf, into which flow the five mighty rivers of the Kimberley – the Durack, King, Pentecost, Forrest and Ord. They can all be clearly identified from the panoramic Five Rivers Lookout at the top of the Bastion Range, 335m above sea level.

Thousands of fortune seekers landed at Wyndham during the 1886 Halls Creek gold rush. It became a small centre serving the

area's pastoralists, including the Duracks. Today, the port exports cattle from the Kimberley and produce from the Ord irrigation area, but in town you'll only find basic facilities.

From Wyndham, it's not far to one of the Kimberley's famous boab prison trees. This one actually has the most credible evidence to suggest it was ever used as a lock-up for Indigenous men and women. Follow the unsealed King River Rd for 23km to find it.

By far the biggest attraction along the Great Northern Highway south to Halls Creek is the distinct domes of the Bungle Bungle Range in Purnululu National Park. Horizontal bands of orange and grey colour the striking sandstone domes. Visitors from all over the world come to admire sites like Cathedral Gorge, a natural amphitheatre with world-class acoustics – even a Sydney Symphony Orchestra quintet have played there. The 53km access road from the Great Northern Highway is only suitable for four-wheel-drive vehicles with good ground clearance, and single-axle off-road trailers. Many people set up camp at the Warmun (Turkey Creek) Roadhouse or Bungle Bungle Caravan Park and plan a big day trip to see the sights.

Halls Creek was established when gold was found at the Elvire River in 1885 and

thousands flocked to the new field, but the rush was short-lived, lasting just four years. In 1910, the Canning Stock Route was completed, enabling east Kimberley cattle to be driven 2000km from Old Halls Creek to Wiluna and the southern goldfields' markets. The modern town was relocated 15km to the west in the 1950s when the Great Northern Highway was completed, and now most services are available there.

On your way in to town, take a short drive to the China Wall, a vertical quartz formation that winds its way across the countryside for many kilometres.

It's another 290km from Halls Creek to Fitzroy Crossing, but there are numerous roadside rest areas which are popular overnight stops. It's not unusual for 30 or 40 caravans and motorhomes to roll into these camping areas each night during the cooler winter months, so don't arrive late in the day expecting to find the best site still available.

Fitzroy Crossing developed to service travellers fording the mighty Fitzroy River at this point. A low bridge was constructed in 1935 but was closed for months during the wet season each year. The current high-level bridge was built in 1974. The Crossing Inn, located near the old ford, dates back to the 1890s.

Picturesque waterholes that are a haven for wildlife and fish are found close to the town which has most basic services.

DON'T MISS.

→ Old Halls Creek – near Halls Creek

Old Halls Creek was the site of Western Australia's first gold rush when Charlie Hall and John Slattery struck it rich in 1885. Today fossickers still search the area, dreaming of a nugget. Crumbling remnants of the old post office and cemetery can still be seen, while nearby are delightful springs and waterholes – refreshing picnic spots on hot days. To get there, follow Duncan Rd from Halls Creek, past China Wall.

→ Geikie Gorge National Park – near Fitzroy Crossing

The spectacular Geikie Gorge was carved by the mighty Fitzroy River through the limestone of a 350-million-year-old Devonian reef. The Parks and Wildlife Service runs cruises through the gorge, but departure times vary, so check with the Fitzroy Crossing Visitor Centre. Camping is not permitted in the Geikie Gorge National Park, but it's open 6.30am–6.30pm during the dry season.

WHERE TO STAY

169 Parry Creek Farm Tourist Resort and Caravan Park

🅟 Parry Creek Rd, Wyndham
📞 (08) 9161 1139
🖥 www.parrycreekfarm.com.au

Set in a quiet, rural area on the banks of Parry Lagoon, this caravan park offers powered and unpowered sites spread across three acres of well-maintained lawns. There is also the option of private self-contained campsites depending on your personal set up. The onsite restaurant is open Apr–Sept serving breakfast, lunch and dinner.

170 Bungle Bungle Caravan Park

$$$$ 🅟🅟🅟🅟🅟🅟🅟🅟🅟🅟🅟🅟🅟🅟🅟

🅟 Great Northern Hwy, Purnululu National Park access rd
📞 (08) 9168 7220
🖥 www.bunglebunglecaravanpark.com.au

An excellent choice for those wishing to spend some time exploring the Bungle Bungle and surrounds, this caravan park offers ample unpowered camping with a few powered sites and basic, but clean, facilities.

171 Fitzroy River Lodge

🅟 277 Great Northern Hwy, Fitzroy Crossing
📞 (08) 9191 5141
🖥 www.fitzroyriverlodge.com.au

This good-quality caravan park has decent amenities with a tennis court and comfortable campsites. A great spot for overnight stops or to stay a while and explore Geikie Gorge. Advance bookings are not accepted.

China Wall, near Halls Creek

FITZROY CROSSING TO BROOME

Cable Beach, Broome

INTRODUCTION

From the near stereotypical 'outback experience' to the bustling multicultural metropolis of Broome, the great north-west is a popular and exciting place for caravanners and campers. Broome is one of the most remote settlements in Australia, and visitors come for the tropical climate, amazing scenery and excellent fishing. As it is so popular, the Great Northern Highway between Fitzroy Crossing and Roebuck Plains Roadhouse is well-maintained and wide, as are the Derby and Broome highways.

WHERE TO GO

Although there aren't any towns or services between Fitzroy Crossing and Derby, there are plenty of options for great camping and things to see. It's an interesting diversion to head north not far out of town and stop at Tunnel Creek National Park, Western Australia's oldest cave system, where water has eroded a tunnel beneath the Napier Range. Also along the same road is Windjana Gorge National Park, which has some spectacular scenery and camping areas with toilets and water. The gorge itself is

3.5km long and cuts through the limestone of the Napier Range, part of an ancient reef.

If you stay on the highway though, many travellers take their time on this journey of nearly 300km to spend a few days camped by Ellendale Lake, on **Ellendale Station**. The owners have opened up a small parcel of land for travellers to camp on for free, but they do ask that it's left in good condition. As this is a working cattle station, dogs are not permitted.

After some rest and relaxation along the road, a diversion to **Derby** calls. Located on King Sound, Derby experiences the highest tidal range in Australia – the record high tide is 11.8m. The town's main jetty, where ships load ore from nearby mines, can be left high and dry at low tide. The main industries in the area are pastoral pursuits and mining. The port was used by pearl luggers in the 1880s after fine pearl shell was found in King Sound in 1883. A handful of pearl farms still operate in the area today. Two supermarkets and a selection of other shops provide most necessities.

The second of the Kimberley's purported boab prison trees can also be found nearby. As the story goes, the bulbous trunks of the trees grow to such enormous widths

that police patrols during the 19th and early 20th centuries used the hollows as lock-ups for troublemakers. However there's very little evidence to suggest this tree was ever used for such a purpose.

Between Derby and Broome, the **Willare Bridge** and **Roebuck Plains** roadhouses offer travellers fuel, decent food and good camping. Willare Bridge has a fully licensed restaurant specialising in barramundi and steaks of local beef. It attracts a lot of people willing to throw a line in the Fitzroy and catch their own dinner too. Roebuck Plains is strategically located at the intersection of the Great Northern and Broome highways with a more typical pub fare and huge servings.

Broome itself is a fascinating town with a tropical climate, rich history and distinctive style of architecture. It has grown rapidly in the past decade due to tourism, and wonderful Cable Beach, historic Chinatown and the tempting pearl shops are just a few of the great attractions. It's a large resort town and all services are available, including a number of caravan repairers. It does get exceptionally busy for such a remote outpost though, and bookings for caravan parks can be hard to come by during the busiest periods. The PCYC runs an overflow camping area between 1 June and 31 August each year, although camping in June is restricted if you have a pet dog or cat. From July onwards, bookings are open to anyone.

DON'T MISS

→ Crocodile feeding – near Broome

The Malcolm Douglas Crocodile Park and Animal Refuge runs daily crocodile feeding tours and is home to numerous large crocodiles and a range of other wildlife. Feeding takes place at 3pm. The park is located 15 min from Broome, on the Broome Highway. Entry fees apply and it's open daily 2–5pm. Contact (08) 9193 6580, www.malcolmdouglas.com.au.

→ Pearling history – Broome

The Pearl Luggers Museum in Broome provides a fascinating insight into the history of the pearling industry. There are two original luggers, fully restored, and a host of memorabilia from the early pearling days. The museum also offers guided tours. (Visit www.pearlluggers.com.au for more information.) You can also discover a little of the multicultural heritage of Broome with a visit to the Japanese Cemetery in Port Rd. Large, roughly hewn headstones mark the graves of more than 900 Japanese divers who died during the early days of the pearling industry.

→ The mighty Gibb River Road

The Gibb River Road tracks east from Derby, winding through the heart of the Kimberley to Kununurra. It's best suited to four-wheel-drive vehicles, and even though the road has been greatly improved over the years it is still considered a challenge by many travellers. Find out more in *Explore Australia by Camper Trailer*, by Lee Atkinson.

WHERE TO STAY

172 Willare Bridge Roadhouse and Caravan Park

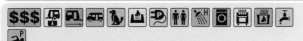

📍 Great Northern Hwy, Willare Bridge
📞 (08) 9191 4775
🖥 www.willareroadhouse.com

Located in the grounds behind the roadhouse, this caravan park has large, grassy sites with simple amenities. There is a pool for your convenience and the roadhouse has a small store and serves good hot meals.

173 Kimberley Entrance Caravan Park

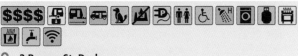

📍 2 Rowan St, Derby
📞 (08) 9193 1055
🖥 www.kimberleyentrancecaravanpark.com

Located just 100m from the town centre, this conveniently located caravan park offers shady sites and good-quality amenities. Short-term storage options are available on enquiry for those wishing to explore the region sans van.

174 Broome Caravan Park

📍 14 Wattle Dr, Broome
📞 (08) 9192 1776
🖥 www.broomecaravanpark.com

This beautiful, shady caravan park has a choice of grassed, double-slab or gravel-base sites. The facilities are excellent with modern amenities and an amazing lagoon-style pool. Short-term storage options are also available.

175 Broome's Gateway Pet Friendly Holiday Park

📍 3000 Broome Rd, Roebuck Plains
📞 0437 525 485
🖥 www.broomesgateway.com

This great outback caravan park has large, spacious campsites with basic, clean amenities but no powered sites. Generators are permitted during daylight hours.

BROOME TO PORT HEDLAND

Eighty Mile Beach

INTRODUCTION

This is a long section of road with little to see, but there is access to the coast from various points with camping and accommodation available at several locations. If you have the time and don't mind the unsealed access roads, break your trip up with stays at Eighty Mile Beach Caravan Park and Barn Hill Beachside Station Stay. If you are sticking to the highway, there are plenty of rest areas and a popular free camping area at De Grey River, about halfway to Port Hedland.

WHERE TO GO

For many, the 600km trip between Broome and Port Hedland is one of the least interesting on the big lap as it straddles the edge of the Great Sandy Desert, but never ventures far from the rugged west coast.

Fishing is really popular along the coast and people do flock to the few coastal caravan parks in the drier months. The coast is subject to large tidal movements, though, so check the tide charts before heading out onto the tidal flats. Also note that poisonous stonefish inhabit the coastal waters, so wear strong footwear if walking on rocky reefs.

The first landmark of note is **Sandfire Roadhouse**, a complex midway between Port Hedland and Broome. Over the years it has been devastated by cyclones and burned down, but it still continues to serve the public fuel, food and basic accommodation every day of the year.

Pardoo Roadhouse is located 152km north of Port Hedland providing fuel, meals, accommodation and a caravan park.

From here there is access to several great campsites near the beach at **Cape Keraudren**, just 10km away. It's a great spot for walking, crabbing and fishing.

On the way in to **Port Hedland** from the Red Bank Bridge you'll see Rio Tinto's massive stockpiles of salt awaiting export to world markets. The salt is recovered by the natural dehydration of sea water from large evaporative ponds and the area also provides a habitat for vast numbers of beautiful birds.

Home to one of the world's busiest bulk-export ports, Port Hedland sees off around 500 million tonnes of iron ore each year. Iron ore is delivered, by the BHP-owned rail network, to Port Hedland from mines as far afield as Newman. As Port Hedland is a busy mining and port town, it has most facilities and services.

Several guided and self-guided tours are the best way to see the sights of Port Hedland, and the most popular is the 45 min tour of BHP's Nelson Point facility, which shows visitors through the various stages of iron ore production. Tours run Mon, Tue and Thurs; book through the visitor centre. Another great tour is the Port Hedland Local Tour run by historian Julie Arif, which takes people through the town's heritage and history. Again, make bookings at the visitor centre.

When the iron-ore boom began in the 1960s, it quickly became obvious that Port Hedland did not have sufficient land suitable to develop housing and infrastructure for the planned explosion in the population. This led to the development of South Hedland, 20km to the south, and today this is the primary residential area and has a large shopping complex and two caravan parks.

DON'T MISS

→ Wildlife wonders – Port Hedland

Almost year-round, Port Hedland is an important marine habitat for various threatened and endangered species. Humpback whales are regular visitors June–Oct on their migration to warmer waters, and they can often be seen playing off the coast from a number of land-based viewing spots. Guided tours are run Oct–Mar to view and monitor flatback turtle nesting and hatching. (Contact Care for Hedland – www.careforhedland.org.au.)

→ Hedland history – Port Hedland

Charming Dalgety House Museum dates back to 1903 and is one of the few remaining examples of early-20th-century architecture in the region. The various displays cover the early history and development of Port Hedland. It's open weekdays 9am–1pm. Contact (08) 9173 4100.

WHERE TO STAY

176 Eighty Mile Beach Caravan Park

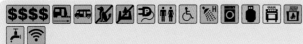

$$$$

📍 Great Northern Hwy, Eighty Mile Beach
📞 (08) 9176 5941
🖥 www.eightymilebeach.com.au

This quality beachside caravan park is located just 9km off the Great Northern Highway. It's popular for fishing and crabbing, and there are over 100 shady powered sites available with modest amenities.

177 Pardoo Station Caravan Park

$$$ ★

📍 Great Northern Hwy, Pardoo
📞 (08) 9176 4930
🖥 www.pardoostation.com.au

This caravan park is perfect for those wanting a real outback experience with a few homely comforts. There is an onsite store and swimming pool and plenty of opportunity for barramundi fishing and birdwatching. If you visit Mar–Sept, you may be able to experience the annual cattle muster. The park is closed for the wet season each year Dec–Mar.

178 Blackrock Tourist Park

$$$

📍 2115 North Circular Rd, South Hedland
📞 (08) 9172 3444
🖥 www.blackrocktouristpark.com.au

This tidy little caravan park is a great base for visiting the Port Hedland area. The amenities are basic, but clean, and there is a small pool onsite.

179 Discovery Parks Port Hedland

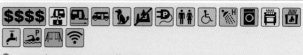

$$$$

📍 2 Taylor St, Port Hedland
📞 (08) 9173 1271
🖥 www.discoveryholidayparks.com.au/caravan-parks/western-australia/pilbara-port-hedland

This pet-friendly caravan park has good facilities and is surrounded by the beautiful waters of the port. It's the perfect spot for fishing and exploring nature. You can experience the amazing 'staircase to the moon' phenomenon if you stay Apr–Oct.

PORT HEDLAND TO ONSLOW

Pyramid Hill, Millstream Chichester National Park

INTRODUCTION

Whether you stick to the coast and Highway One or take the inland route through Newman, Tom Price and Karijini National Park, you're guaranteed a great time in the Pilbara. It's one of the most iron-rich landscapes in the world, and the deep reds permeate nearly everything. The North West Coastal Highway is a well-maintained, wide, sealed road though, so the going is easy and there are plenty of reasons to stop often.

WHERE TO GO

As the oldest gazetted town in Western Australia's north-west, **Roebourne** has a fascinating history that involves almost complete destruction on two separate occasions by cyclones. Its population peaked in the 1890s thanks to gold discovered nearby in 1878, although today its population is only around 1000 people. Many heritage-listed buildings constructed after the first devastating cyclone in 1872 are still standing. You can find out more about them by visiting the information centre on Roe St.

To the east of Wickham, the historic town of **Cossack** is a great tourist destination. Originally the first landing point for pastoralists on Western Australia's north-west coast in 1863, the port developed rapidly, later becoming the first pearling site in the state. The town flourished in the 19th century, but by WWI pearling had moved north to Broome and only a few inhabitants remained. A 3km heritage trail takes visitors past the most significant sites including the old courthouse, which is now a museum.

Nearby, the mining town of **Wickham**, which was established in the 1970s is primarily visited by large ore carriers, which dock at a jetty that is one of the longest (2.7km) and tallest (17.8m above the high-water mark) in Australia. Further on, **Point Samson** is a small, but rapidly growing community just 20km north of Roebourne and an attractive place to stay. Fishing is popular on the beaches and in the estuaries of this region.

Karratha is the major hub of the Pilbara region, but it's more than just a mining service town. The North West Shelf Project Visitor Centre, in nearby **Dampier**, details the important offshore gas stations, and is worthy of a few hours' time. **Hearsons Cove** is a stunning beach, and one of the few places to witness the famous 'staircase to the moon' phenomenon. There are also over 10,000 Aboriginal rock-art paintings on the Burrup Peninsula, making it Australia's largest rock-art site.

Further down the coast, the small town of **Onslow** is 80km north of the highway. Keep a lookout for the giant termite mounds along the highway near here. These prolific features are the work of the spinifex termite, which eats grass, not wood. Many mounds are more than 100 years old and incorporate a network of tunnels reaching down to underground water. Onslow was originally settled at the mouth of the Ashburton River in 1885, but moved to its present-day site in 1925. Many buildings were relocated, but the brick-and-stone police quarters and a cemetery still remain. History buffs should visit the Goods Shed Museum, at the visitor centre.

DON'T MISS

→ **Millstream Chichester National Park – near Karratha**

Around 2hr south of Karratha, Millstream Chichester National Park protects an amazing red landscape and wonderful swimming holes fed by underground aquifers and provides excellent off-grid camping areas. There are a number of great walks throughout the park which range from a few hundred metres to 18km long.

WHERE TO STAY

180 The Cove Caravan Park

📍 259 Macleod St, Point Samson
📞 (08) 9187 0199
🖥 www.thecoveholidayvillage.com.au

A sparkling, newer caravan park by the coast, this place is proving very popular as a tourist destination in the quiet seaside community of Point Samson. There are good amenities and these are still expanding.

181 Discovery Parks Pilbara

📍 70 Rosemary Rd, Karratha
📞 (08) 9185 1855
🖥 www.discoveryholidayparks.com.au/ caravan-parks/western-australia/ pilbara-pilbara-karratha

Discovery
HOLIDAY PARKS

This is one of the better-quality caravan parks in the heart of the Pilbara mining region. It has extensive facilities to ensure your stay is enjoyable.

182 Dampier Transit Caravan Park

📍 The Esplanade, Dampier
📞 (08) 9183 1109

A small caravan park with about 20 sites, this place is operated by the Dampier community and there is a three-night maximum stay. The park is across the road from the water and within sight of Hamersley Iron's Park Point loading facility. Bookings are required in peak periods.

183 Forty Mile-Gnoorea Point camping area

📍 Forty Mile Beach Rd, Gnoorea
🖥 www.karratha.wa.gov.au/camping

This is a council-run basic camping area that's popular for fishing. Facilities are restricted to toilets and bins, but it's got a great outlook. Camping fees apply 1 May – 30 Sept, but not for the rest of the year. Campers must be reasonably self sufficient.

184 Ocean View Caravan Park

📍 6 Second Ave, Onslow
📞 (08) 9184 6053
🖥 www.ashburton.wa.gov.au

Situated on the beachfront, this caravan park is ideal for fishing enthusiasts. It is also a good place for a rest, with clean, basic facilities. In the busy season the park holds sausage sizzles once a week. Bookings are required July–Aug.

Fishing on the Mackerel Islands, off Onslow

ONSLOW TO CARNARVON

NEED TO KNOW

🚗 **812km**

🏠 **Station stays, national parks, beachside caravan parks, roadhouse campsites**

☁ **Although it can get hot in summer, this is a good year-round route.**

👁 **Snorkelling, diving, fishing**

🅰 **Most of the roads are generally in good condition, although some national parks and stations only have unsealed access.**

🍴 **Until Carnarvon, services are limited to basic tourist needs.**

⚠ **None apply**

North West Coastal Highway, Exmouth

INTRODUCTION

One of the most enviable coastlines in the world, this section of the big lap takes in the stunning resort town of Exmouth, the beaches and rugged beauty of Cape Range National Park, and the unparalleled reef access, fishing and snorkelling of the Ningaloo Coast. Leave the North West Coastal Highway as soon as you can to get closer to the ocean and enjoy the best this region has to offer.

WHERE TO GO

Onslow and Exmouth are only 105km from each other as the crow flies, but it is a significant drive between the two. **Exmouth** was established as a support town for the Harold E. Holt US Naval Communication Station during the Cold War, so it wasn't uncommon for many of the local businesses to trade in US currency and during the 1960s and '70s, cars even drove on the right (wrong) side of the road. It was devastated by a cyclone in 1999, but is now a significant resort town that's an ideal base from which to explore the North West Cape region. It has excellent surfing, fishing, snorkelling,

diving, boating, windsurfing, kiteboarding, bushwalking, birdwatching and photographic opportunities. Yep, there's a lot to do here.

Cape Range National Park, which is just 50km away by road (half that by crow), has some outstanding camping areas, if you can cope without any facilities. The best way to experience the park's spectacular gorges and picturesque coastline is by following any of the many walking trails. Don't miss the panoramic views from Charles Knife Canyon, or the spectacular crystal-clear blue waters of Yardie Creek Gorge.

Access to the national park is by sealed roads suitable for a two-wheel drive, except for the four-wheel-drive-only Yardie Creek crossing. This crossing, which gives access to the beaches further south, is notorious for bogging vehicles and drivers that aren't careful. Entry fees apply in the park.

The Ningaloo Marine Park protects the state's largest fringing coral reef, and diving over the exquisitely coloured corals is one of the many popular activities around here. Divers can swim with whale sharks (Mar–June) and migrating manta rays and humpback whales (Aug–Nov), activities which are major drawcards to the area because it's one of the few places in the

world where either can be done. Charter-boat operators can also take you big-game fishing, which can be just as exciting.

About 150km south, **Coral Bay** is breathtakingly beautiful. The coral reef stretches 2km into the bay to form a magnificent natural lagoon rimmed by white, sandy beaches. Boating, snorkelling and swimming are popular, and coral-viewing boats operate off the beach. There are two caravan parks in town, and a range of basic services and shops.

Back on the highway, after visiting Coral Bay, **Minilya Bridge Roadhouse** offers the normal roadhouse services, including good food, fuel and local information. There's also a small caravan park, convenient for overnight stays. It is strategically located on the North West Coastal Highway near the junction with the Minilya–Exmouth Rd.

Another 140km south is **Carnarvon**, which as well as being the commercial capital of the Gascoyne region, supports flourishing fruit and vegetable plantations; irrigated from the Gascoyne River. Fresh tropical fruit is available from farm gates along the South River and North River roads. On Babbage Island, connected to the town by a causeway, the Heritage Maritime

Coral Bay

Whaleshark on Ningaloo Reef

Yardie Creek Gorge

Precinct encompasses the original port, One Mile Jetty, a lighthouse and a historical steam train. Most services are available in town and there is good shopping, as well as a growers' market which runs at 21 Robinson St each Saturday May–Oct.

DON'T MISS

→ The not-secret US intelligence base – near Exmouth
The Harold E. Holt Communication Station is still in active use today, just 15km north of Exmouth. The base is a relay station that communicates with ships and submarines in the Indian and south-western Pacific oceans.

At the main antenna field, the central mast stands 388m high. It's possible to walk around some of the non-restricted areas to learn a little of the role the station plays in naval communications.

→ Turquoise Bay – near Coral Bay
One of the easiest and prettiest places to go snorkelling on the Ningaloo Reef is at Turquoise Bay. The current runs from the southern end of the beach, so it's as simple as wading in, putting your head underwater and drifting over the reef. It can get strong, so check with locals about the best place to hop back out.

WHERE TO STAY

185 Nanutarra Roadhouse Caravan Park

$$$

📍 North West Coastal Hwy, Nanutarra
📞 (08) 9943 0521
💻 www.nanutarra.com.au

On the northern bank of the Ashburton River, this is a simple roadhouse caravan park with powered and unpowered sites. It's a nice overnight stop.

186 RAC Exmouth Cape Holiday Park

$$$$

📍 3 Truscott Cres, Exmouth
📞 1800 871 570
💻 www.parksandresorts.rac.com.au/exmouth

BIG4 HOLIDAY PARKS

Located close to the centre of town, and alongside the main road, this is a good quality caravan park near the tourist centre and not too far from the shops. It is a good base for exploring the region. Bookings are required in peak periods. Motoring club members get a discount.

187 Kurrajong Campground

$$ ★

📍 Yardie Creek Rd, Cape Range National Park
📞 (08) 9949 2808
💻 www.parks.dpaw.wa.gov.au/site/kurrajong-campground-cape-range

A very basic camping area within Cape Range National Park, its highlight is the stunning red sands contrasting with the vibrant blues of the ocean. There are toilets here and nothing else, but the road in is suitable for two-wheel drives.

188 South Lefroy Bay, Ningaloo Station

$

📍 Off Yardie Creek Rd, Ningaloo
📞 (08) 9942 5936
💻 www.ningaloostation.com.au

Ningaloo Station is a working sheep and goat station which manages several beachfront camping areas on its property. All are limited to a patch of grass to camp on and total self-sufficiency is required, but the outlook is spectacular, the fees are very modest (currently $35 per week) and numbers are restricted, so it's never crowded.

189 Peoples Park Coral Bay

$$$$

📍 13 Robinson St, Coral Bay
📞 (08) 9942 5933
💻 www.peoplesparkcoralbay.com.au

Set in a wonderful location across the road from the fabulous beach and close to the coral reef, this caravan park is a great holiday spot. Diving and fishing are popular, along with coral viewing in glass-bottom boats. Coral Bay is very busy during the holidays and bookings are essential. The park adjoins a cafe and well-stocked general store.

190 Minilya Bridge Roadhouse

$$

📍 North West Coastal Hwy, Minilya
📞 (08) 9942 5922
💻 www.minilyabridgeroadhouse.com.au

This is a popular roadhouse camping area with grassy sites, good facilities and free use of the washing machines during your stay. The roadhouse serves good meals, making it a popular spot for travellers to treat themselves.

191 Capricorn Holiday Park

$$

📍 1042 North West Coastal Hwy, Carnarvon
📞 (08) 9941 8153
💻 www.capricornholidaypark.com.au

Capricorn is conveniently located at the junction of Highway One and Robinson St, the main access road to town. This is a convenient caravan park for an overnight stop or an extended stay to explore the area. Bookings are required July–Aug.

CARNARVON TO GERALDTON

476km

Full-featured caravan parks, station stays

This is a good, year-round destination, with wildflowers best seen late winter to early spring.

Fishing, surfing, dolphin feeding, walking, history

The roads are quite good and well maintained.

Kalbarri and Geraldton are both busy centres with most facilities available.

None apply

Stromatolites at Shark Bay

INTRODUCTION

One of the prettiest stretches of coastline for travellers north of Perth, this section takes you past million-year-old fossils to the Australian mainland's westernmost point, and gives you the chance to feed a wild dolphin and drive through some of Western Australia's best wildflower country. All of the main roads are sealed and the going is easy, thanks to the almost uniform flatness of the landscape.

WHERE TO GO

It's a long drive from Carnarvon to **Denham**, the pretty town on the Peron Peninsula, in the middle of Shark Bay, but definitely worth it. The area is popular with holidaymakers, with many coming to see the famous Monkey Mia dolphins, or visit Francois Peron National Park. Fishing is a major industry and pastime here, and on a clear day you can see the mounds of salt at the Useless Loop saltworks across the bay.

Monkey Mia is just 25km to the east, on the other side of the peninsula to Denham. Each day a pod of bottlenose dolphins visits, some time between 7.30am and noon,

for an easy feed. Although a large family pod turns up, only five of the females will accept the food offered. The Shark Bay World Heritage Area is more than just a buffet for five dolphins, though, as it also protects a large dugong population and is a turtle-nesting ground.

To the north, Francois Peron National Park is largely restricted to high-clearance four-wheel drives, although the road in is sealed to the original Peron Homestead. Here you can take a self-guided tour of the shearing sheds and shearers' quarters following the interpretive signs which give a remarkable insight into life on a remote Western Australian sheep station.

As you'll have to backtrack to continue south, take the time to stop along Shark Bay Road. Shell Beach, with tiny white shells stacked meters deep, and the historic Hamelin Pool Telegraph Station (incorporating a museum and tearooms) are both close to the road. Near the telegraph station you will find the stromatolites of Hamelin Pool. These sedimentary rocks are made up of fossilised blue-green algae – the largest of these fossils in the world.

Further south, the picturesque holiday town of **Kalbarri** is almost completely surrounded by the national park of the

same name. The climate, spectacular cliffs, rugged gorges and windswept beaches all add to the beauty of the town and surrounding area.

The park, which is located on the lower reaches of the Murchison River, has a fascinating geological history, coastal cliffs and spectacular gorges carved by the Murchison over millions of years. Come between July–Oct to see the best of the west's stunning wildflowers. Here you'll be able to spot countless grevilleas, banksias, star flowers, featherflowers, smokebushes, kangaroo paws and rare orchids. Also keep an eye out for emus, kangaroos and thorny devils.

South of Kalbarri, following Gregory Grey Dr, you'll pass Hutt Lagoon – better known as Pink Lake. It's turned that colour by a carotenoid-producing algae (carotenoid is one of the things that makes carrots orange) that gets caught in the salt crystals.

Gregory, with its huge white sand dunes, good swimming beaches and interesting convict ruins is well worth visiting. Set on a natural, reef-protected harbour, it has operated as a port since 1853. The town name was officially changed from Port Gregory to Gregory in 1967, but many locals still call it by its original name.

The Loop, Kalbarri National Park

Back on the North West Coastal Highway, **Northampton** is a town rich in history. One of the oldest settlements outside of Perth, it is listed by the National Trust as a historic town. Basic services are available. North-west of Northampton, and still welcoming tourists, is the Principality of **Hutt River**, an 'independent land' since its owner seceded from the Commonwealth of Australia in 1970. Entry requires presentation of a passport for stamping, or purchase of a visa. Both cost $4 and must be paid in cash.

A key port on the Western Australian coastline, **Geraldton** is the self-proclaimed lobster capital of the world – a highly contentious issue if you ask the people of Kingston SE in South Australia or New Brunswick in Canada, both of which have 'big lobsters' on display to prove their mettle. The Geraldton Fisherman's Co-operative (on Ocean St), has a live-lobster-processing factory and runs 90 min guided tours. (Call (08) 9965 9000 for the latest times and bookings.) The Western Australian Museum in town has an excellent shipwrecks display. Geraldton is also one of Australia's top windsurfing and kiteboarding destinations, with the best winds occurring Nov–Apr.

DON'T MISS

→ Treasures of the deep – Shark Bay

The Shark Bay World Heritage Discovery and Visitor Centre in Denham explores, through interactive technology, the natural wonders of Shark Bay, the maritime and pastoral history of the area, and relics from Dutch, English and French sailing vessels dating back to 1616. The centre takes you on an amazing journey through time and around Shark Bay. Contact (08) 9948 1590.

→ Australia's westernmost point – near Shark Bay

Steep Point, the Australian mainland's westernmost point, is a popular remote camping and fishing location that is only accessible by people with high-clearance four-wheel drives and off-road caravans or camper trailers. A permit is needed before visiting, so it's best to plan well ahead, as the camping areas on the Edel Peninsula are known to book out. Contact (08) 9948 3993 or visit www.steeppoint.com.au.

St Francis Xavier Cathedral, Geraldton

WHERE TO STAY

192 Wintersun Caravan & Tourist Park

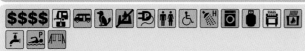

- 546 Robinson St, Carnarvon
- (08) 9941 8150
- www.wintersuncaravanpark.com.au

This quality, pet-friendly caravan park offers a wide range of facilities, including a bowling green and swimming pool. Sites are flat and grassy with eco mats on most. Unpowered sites are not offered at this park.

193 Denham Seaside Tourist Village

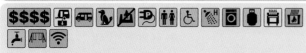

- 1 Stella Rowley Dr, Denham
- (08) 9948 1242
- www.sharkbayfun.com

This great caravan park is conveniently located just a few minutes from the centre of town overlooking the stunning clear waters of Shark Bay. Perfect for those keen on fishing, there is easy access to the boat ramp down the road. The entire park is paved in shell grit, so a drill is recommended for those requiring pegs. Bookings are essential during peak periods.

194 RAC Monkey Mia Dolphin Resort

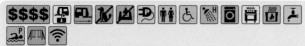

- Monkey Mia Rd, Money Mia
- 1800 871 570
- www.parksandresorts.rac.com.au/monkey-mia

Come for the dolphins and stay for the scenery, or the fish, or the sunshine in winter – whatever your reason, this newly refurbished caravan park is a great place to stop and experience one of the west coast's most famous attractions. The upgrade has almost tripled the size of the camping area and it now offers powered ensuite sites and up to 120 standard powered sites, some of which are beach sites. Bookings are required during peak times and national parks fees may apply on top of accommodation costs.

195 Kalbarri Tudor Holiday Park

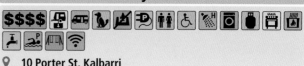

- 10 Porter St, Kalbarri
- (08) 9937 1077
- www.kalbarritudor.com.au

This caravan park is surrounded by beautiful beaches, breathtaking gorges and excellent fishing. There are also stunning wildflowers seasonally Aug–Oct. Sites are flat and shady with some ensuites available. Dogs will only be considered during off-peak season.

196 Northbrook Farmstay

- 5800 North West Coastal Hwy, Alma
- (08) 9934 1222
- www.northbrookfarmstay.com.au

This laidback camping area set on picturesque farmland is perfect for those seeking peace and quiet. With beautiful views of the surrounding countryside and basic, but clean, amenities, bring a book and enjoy the serenity. There is a large camp kitchen available and a nice big grassy area for camping, however some powered sites are uneven and require a bit of manoeuvring.

197 BIG4 Sunset Beach Holiday Park

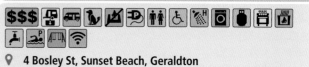

- 4 Bosley St, Sunset Beach, Geraldton
- (08) 9938 1655
- www.sunsetbeachpark.com.au

Located just 6km from the city, right on the beachfront, this well-appointed caravan park is an excellent option for those wishing to explore the surrounding area. There is a range of site options including large-motorhome-friendly, drive-thru, concrete slab and grassed. Bookings are required during peak times and a minimum-length stay applies at Easter.

GERALDTON TO PERTH

NEED TO KNOW

 442km

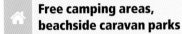 **Free camping areas, beachside caravan parks**

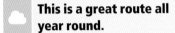 **This is a great route all year round.**

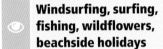 **Windsurfing, surfing, fishing, wildflowers, beachside holidays**

 **The Indian Ocean Drive is an excellent tourist route – largely free of heavy transports.**

 **Most small-town facilities are available.**

 **None apply**

Indian Ocean Drive

INTRODUCTION

The Brand Highway (Highway One) is the most direct route from Geraldton to Perth, but it suffers from heavy transport traffic so you'll want to get off it as soon as possible. Completed in 2010, the Indian Ocean Drive provides just the chance to do that with a beautiful scenic route along the coast from south of Dongara, through Lancelin and on to Perth. The road passes through several small communities and lobster fishing ports, and is resplendent with wildflowers July–Oct.

WHERE TO GO

The first in a string of popular, seaside fishing towns, **Port Denison** and **Dongara**, which sit either side of the Irwin River, are popular, year-round holiday destinations. A 'big lobster', sits at the corner of the Brand Hwy and Moreton Tce. A pleasant 1.6km heritage trail through town shows off some of the most notable historical buildings.

About 30km south of Dongara, the Indian Ocean Dr leaves the Brand Hwy and almost immediately rewards travellers with three free camping areas around **Cliff Head**. The grassy beachfront camping areas underneath impressive limestone cliffs have recently been improved with updated amenities. Stays of up to three nights are permitted.

The largest town on Indian Ocean Drive, **Jurien Bay** is situated on a sheltered bay with long, sandy beaches. The town has most services and is also the best place from which to explore the Jurien Bay Marine Park – a sanctuary for around 800 sea lions with extensive seagrass meadows. It's popular for boating, snorkelling and windsurfing too.

The most recognisable attraction in the area, though, is the Pinnacles Desert. When Dutch sailors first saw the Pinnacles from the sea in the 1650s they mistook them for ancient ruins. In fact they are thousands of limestone pillars, some up to 5m tall. When the wildflowers are in bloom, July–Sept, is arguably the most stunning time to visit. The Pinnacles Desert is in the Nambung National Park, and an entry fee applies.

As there are no camping options in the national park, the best place to stay nearby is **Cervantes**, which is a popular holiday town where fishing and windsurfing are the main pursuits.

Further south, the busy holiday town of **Lancelin**, and smaller **Yanchep**, are two of Perth's residents' favourite locations – so steer clear on summer weekends or school holidays if you want to avoid the crowds. With a stunning beach, protected by nearshore reefs that are responsible for 14 shipwrecks (and a resultant world class dive trail), it's very popular for fishing. The nearby Lancelin sand dunes area is one of the most popular four-wheel-driving locations close to Perth.

One of the most isolated capital cities in the world, **Perth** is closer to Singapore than it is to Sydney – amazingly, it's cheaper to fly to too. On the banks of the Swan River, and founded in 1829, it's a scenic and sophisticated city with a Mediterranean climate, plenty of sunshine and a relaxed atmosphere. It's often claimed to be the sunniest state capital in Australia.

DON'T MISS

→ **Lake Indoon – near Jurien Bay**
With a great free camping area on its banks, Lake Indoon is a waterskier's paradise after the winter rains when it's full of water. It's also an important wetland for birds on their north-south migratory route. During summer and autumn, the lake is usually dry, with a vast saltpan and nice walks through the woodlands of banksia and flooded gums.

Sea lion in Jurien Bay Marine Park

→ **Wildflower caravan park – near Eneabba**

In spring consider a visit to the Western Flora Caravan Park. Situated on the Brand Highway, 22km north of Eneabba, its 65 hectares contain a diverse range of plants. The owners are passionate about the wildflowers and conduct walks each day at about 4pm. Their well-stocked shop has a good selection of souvenirs and wildflower books.

WHERE TO STAY

198 BIG4 Dongara Denison Beach Holiday Park

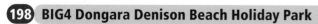

9 250 Ocean Dr, Dongara
📞 (08) 9927 1131
🖥 www.ddbeachholidaypark.com

BIG4 HOLIDAY PARKS

This lovely grassy caravan park has water views and is located just a short walk to the local boat harbour. There is a range of sites to choose from with various sizes to suit most travellers' needs. Bookings are required during peak times as it gets very busy.

199 Jurien Bay Tourist Park

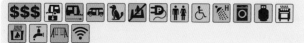

9 1 Roberts St, Jurien Bay
📞 (08) 9652 1595
🖥 www.jurienbaytouristpark.com.au

TOP PARKS

Conveniently located in the heart of town, this beachside caravan park has good facilities including a nice little takeaway shop. Amenities are well managed and sites are varied with a choice between grassed and gravel.

200 RAC Cervantes Holiday Park

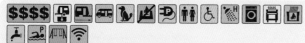

9 35 Aragon St, Cervantes
📞 (08) 9652 7060
🖥 www.parksandresorts.rac.com.au/cervantes

This recently renovated caravan park has excellent modern facilities with nice level shady sites. There is an onsite cafe and shop and a large, resort-style swimming pool. This is a popular location for fishing.

201 Guilderton Caravan Park

9 2 Dewar St, Guilderton
📞 (08) 9577 1021
🖥 www.guildertoncaravanpark.com.au

Situated at the mouth of the Moore River, and beside the picturesque white sandy beach, this popular caravan park has shady, level sites and good, clean amenities.

202 Discovery Parks – Perth Airport

9 186 Hale Rd, Forrestfield
📞 (08) 9453 6677
🖥 www.discoveryholidayparks.com.au/
caravan-parks/western-australia/
south-east-perth-airport

Discovery HOLIDAY PARKS

This is a good-quality caravan park in a central location with excellent amenities. Sites range in size and are available as drive-thru, grassed or concrete-slab base. Bookings are required during peak periods.

PERTH TO MANJIMUP

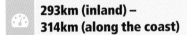
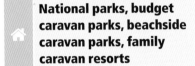
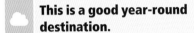

Bunbury

INTRODUCTION

Sticking to Highway One through this section guarantees you miss out on some of the best parts south of Western Australia's capital city. Between Perth and Bunbury, you'll rarely venture very far from the coast and get to enjoy some of the state's most popular waterways. Once you start to head inland, you'll pass through some of Western Australia's richest fruit-growing areas and tallest forests.

WHERE TO GO

Fremantle, just 30 min from Perth, is the perfect small city to walk around enjoying good cafes or wandering between the well-preserved sites of its colonial history, all before sitting down on the beach to watch the sunset. Particularly good is the Fremantle Prison which housed convicts and prisoners from the 1850s through to 1991. (Book a tour at www.fremantleprison.com.au.) Another highlight is the Western Australian Maritime Museum, which has the America's Cup winning *Australia II* on permanent display. Entry is just $7.50 for a concession.

Both **Rockingham** and **Mandurah** are popular beachside towns. Rocky, as the locals call it, is a protected bay popular for sailing and snorkelling. Mandurah's coast is littered with 17 shipwrecks, which although unfortunate for the mariners involved, have created a very pleasant foreshore walk to spot as many as possible. Ironically, the Peel Inlet, an estuary system four times the size of Sydney Harbour is now one of the South-West's safest places to boat.

About 35km south of Mandurah you can stop in at **Lake Clifton** to see a colony of thrombolites – rock-like formations of microorganisms that are actually alive. Thrombolites were the first organisms to produce oxygen, dating back some 3500 million years, well before plants or animals. Take care as the sign to the turn-off is easy to miss. Overnight camping is permitted in the carpark but there are regular reports of thefts here, though, so be careful.

Bunbury is the last place in the world you'll find a native stand of tuart forest (*Eucalyptus gamphocephala*). Tuart forest once covered much of the coastal strip from Dunsborough to Jurien Bay, growing in a band about 10km wide, but little remains now. The old-growth forest at the end of Ocean Dr is well worth a visit to take the easy 1.2km walk. Or if you prefer to stick near the ocean, the foreshore walk along Ocean Dr is very pleasant during the evenings. Or head to the Marlston Hill Lookout Tower for a bird's-eye view of the coast.

Donnybrook, to the south-east, is in a rich agricultural area and famous as the 'home of the Granny Smith apple', which has been grown here since the year 1900. With so much local produce in the area, there are countless roadside fruit and produce stalls. As the quality is so good, this is the best way to stock up on fresh fruit.

Manjimup made its name through the timber industry and is surrounded by karri and jarrah forests. I suggest heading to the Diamond Tree, 9km out of town, which is 52m high and has a fire-lookout cabin perched on top with a ladder spiralling the

Thrombolites at Lake Clifton

tree all the way to the top. It was built in 1939 and refurbished in 1991. You can climb it, if you're game. I tried, but only got about 10m up before I decided I'm not that brave.

DON'T MISS

→ Dwellingup – Lane Poole Reserve.

Not quite on the southerly route, Lane Poole Reserve, just south of Dwellingup is one of the region's most popular camping destinations. Perched on the edge of the Murray River, it's a popular summer destination because of the safe swimming and paddling, good walking and great camping amongst the jarrah forest.

→ Boyup Brook – this is 'country' country

About 31km north-east of Bridgetown, and off Highway One, the small town of Boyup Brook is unofficially Western Australia's country music capital. The town hosts a huge country music festival on the third week in February each year.

→ What's in a name?

Many of the towns throughout this part of Western Australia end in 'up' – Wattleup, Binningup, Boyanup, Kirup, Mullalyup, Balingup and Manjimup, as well as more than 90 more throughout the South-West. In this case, 'up' simply means 'place of' and is derived from the Indigenous dialect. Now you've just got to work out what 'Manjim' and 'Baling' and 'Mullaly' mean …

Swimming with dolphins at Rockingham

WHERE TO STAY

203 Cee & See Caravan Park

- 2 Governor Rd, East Rockingham
- (08) 9527 1297

This is a pleasant caravan park, typical of parks in the area. It has large, grassy sites, wide avenues and is less than 1km from the heart of town. This is a popular park, especially during the warmer months.

204 Mandurah Caravan & Tourist Park

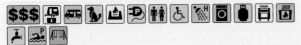

- 522 Pinjarra Rd, Mandurah
- (08) 9535 1171
- www.mandurahcaravanpark.com.au

A great family caravan park with a pool and playground, and all the other facilities you would expect. Come for a weekend, a few days' break or a longer holiday.

205 Estuary Hideaway Holiday Park

- 2151 Old Coast Rd, Bouvard
- 0407 838 061
- www.estuaryhideaway.com.au

A pleasant and shady caravan park that's nestled against Collins Pool estuary south of Dawesville. Most sites have views to the water and access to the camp kitchen. It has good, clean amenities.

206 Chuditch camping area – Lane Poole Reserve

- Nanga Road, Nanga Brook
- www.parks.dpaw.wa.gov.au/site/chuditch-campground

This is a small camping area of 24 sites set in shady jarrah forest a little way back from the river. Not all of the sites are suitable for caravans, but most smaller camping vehicles will fit without a drama. Facilities are basic, limited to picnic tables, pit toilets and communal barbecues under a shelter.

207 Discovery Parks – Bunbury Foreshore

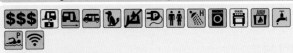

- Koombana Dr, Bunbury
- (08) 9791 3900
- www.discoveryholidayparks.com.au/ caravan-parks/western-australia/ bunbury-bunbury-foreshore

Right in the heart of Bunbury, this quality caravan park offers discerning caravanners a range of excellent facilities including a coffee shop and tennis court. Bookings are required in peak periods, and there is a minimum-stay period during peak periods.

208 Bridgetown Caravan Park

- South Western Hwy, Bridgetown
- (08) 9761 1900
- www.bridgetowncaravanpark.com.au

Set on the banks of the Blackwood River this is a leafy caravan park with both developed and undeveloped camping areas. There is access to the river for canoes and kayaks. It's pet friendly.

209 Manjimup Central Caravan Park

- 561 Mottram St, Manjimup
- (08) 9777 2355
- www.manjimupcentralcaravanpark.com.au

This well-appointed caravan-park in Manjimup has plenty of space – 'no rig is too big' as they say here. It makes a fine base for exploring the South-West.

BUNBURY TO MANJIMUP – SOUTH-WEST CAPES DIVERSION

Cape Leeuwin Lighthouse

INTRODUCTION

Rather than heading inland at Bunbury, sticking to the coast will take you through the stunning regions of Busselton and Margaret River and past Australia's most south-westerly point. The coastline through here is wild and dramatic, but also offers some of the west's best surfing, wineries and the southern hemisphere's longest timber jetty.

WHERE TO GO

Following the gentle curve of Geographe Bay takes you to **Busselton**, which is an idyllic coastal town where the population swells in the summer months. Its most famous attraction is the 1.8km long jetty, which was built in 1865 and serviced the shipping industry until 1978. These days it's only used by tourists who come to walk its length (or catch the train), fish or swim off its sides, or visit the underwater observatory at the end. A $4 fee applies for entry to the jetty during the Interpretive Centre's opening hours

(8am–6pm in summer, 9am–5pm in winter), otherwise it's free. Allow at least 1.5hr, just for the walk.

Cape Naturaliste Lighthouse, which is 20m tall, was first turned on in 1904 and is one of the most accessible in the South-West. Tours run daily and you can even book a two-lighthouse pass, which credits you with a tour at Cape Leeuwin Lighthouse as well (*see* below). It's also the beginning (or end) of the Cape to Cape Track, a walk which runs for 135km between the two capes.

Nearby, Sugarloaf Rock is one of the most spectacular places on the coast to watch the sunset. A 3.7km long, wheelchair-accessible section of the Cape to Cape Track joins the two sites.

The two biggest attractions of **Margaret River** are also amongst my two favourite things – wine and surfing (best not enjoyed together, though). The region has long been home to some of Australia's best wineries, and is developing into a world class destination for lovers of fine dining, too. My tip is to book into tours of some of the limestone caves which dot this section of

coast – the best are Ngilgi, Jewel, Lake and Mammoth caves. They're open daily 9am–5pm (longer in holidays) and entry fees apply.

For those interested in surfing or whale-watching, head to Prevelly, where the aptly named Surfers Point looks over the main surf break and provides the best vantage spot to see migrating whales.

Continuing south, **Cape Leeuwin** is Australia's most south-westerly point and the spot where an imaginary line divides the Indian and Southern oceans. Daily tours of the Cape Leeuwin Lighthouse can be booked online or at the gate (9am–5pm). It's the tallest lighthouse on mainland Australia at 39m.

DON'T MISS

→ **Pemberton – trams and treadlies**
Another timber town set amongst towering karri forests, Pemberton is home to a historical tramway which runs trips through the local woodlands. At the station there's also a collection of historical trains and carriages. It's also a hub for mountain-bikers, who flock here on weekends to ride the many and varied trails that wind through

the bush. A word of warning, the BP service station's canopy is only 3m high, so don't try to park your caravan or motorhome under it, or you might lose your air conditioner.

→ Gloucester Tree – scare yourself
Another one of the eight fire-tower lookouts perched atop giant karri trees, the Gloucester Tree is the highest of them all. The lookout tower is 58m above the ground and reached by climbing 153 pegs spiralling around its trunk.

WHERE TO STAY

210 RAC Busselton Holiday Park

📍 97 Caves Rd, Busselton
📞 (08) 9755 4241
🖥 www.parksandresorts.rac.com.au/busselton

BIG4 HOLIDAY PARKS

This is one of the neatest caravan parks I have visited in recent times, and the camp kitchen has to be one of the best I've seen – even in a part of Australia that is renowned for its quality parks. Bookings are required in peak times, and a minimum-stay period applies during Christmas, Easter and long weekends.

211 BIG4 Taunton Farm Holiday Park Margaret River

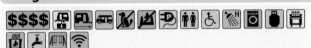

📍 8113 Bussell Hwy, Cowaramup
📞 (08) 9755 5334
🖥 www.big4.com.au/caravan-parks/wa/south-west/taunton-farm-margaret-river

BIG4 HOLIDAY PARKS

This is possibly the best base for exploring the wonderful Margaret River region. It is a quality caravan park in a great farm setting. Bookings are required in peak periods.

212 Prevelly Caravan Park

📍 99 Mitchell Dr, Prevelly
📞 (08) 9757 2374
🖥 www.prevellycaravanpark.com.au

This is the closest caravan park to the famed beaches and surfing locations in the Margaret River region. It's a popular spot during summer, and will also book out around the time of the Margaret River Drug Aware Pro, an international surfing competition usually held in April.

213 RAC Margaret River Nature Park

📍 Carters Rd, Margaret River
📞 (08) 9758 8227
🖥 www.parksandresorts.rac.com.au/margaret-river

Offering a range of camping and eco-style accommodation options in a stunning bush setting, this is a great alternative to the run-of-the-mill caravan park stay. Just minutes from the best attractions of Margaret River in Wooditjup National Park (formerly Bramley).

214 Hamelin Bay Holiday Park

📍 Hamelin Bay Rd, Hamelin Bay
📞 (08) 9758 5540
🖥 www.hamelinbayholidaypark.com.au

Located within Leeuwin–Naturaliste National Park, this caravan park has great facilities for caravans and motorhomes. It is right alongside the beach and has a kiosk that sells basic necessities. There is a minimum-stay period during busy times.

215 Flinders Bay Caravan Park

📍 1 Albany Tce, Augusta
📞 (08) 9780 5636
🖥 www.flindersbaypark.amrshire.wa.gov.au

The only beachfront caravan park in Augusta, it's in a lovely natural setting with good access to the beach and town nearby. It's closed during the winter months – June–Aug.

216 Pemberton Caravan Park

📍 1 Pump Hill Rd, Pemberton
📞 (08) 9776 1300
🖥 www.pembertonpark.com.au

This is a spacious place with lots of shade and trees, just 1km from the town centre. The budget-priced caravan park has basic amenities, and a natural-style pool right next door. Bookings are required in peak periods.

MANJIMUP TO ALBANY

Elephant Bay

INTRODUCTION

Through this section of country, it's easy to underestimate how long it will take to get from A to B – I certainly did the first time. Leaving Manjimup or Pemberton, you'll travel through winding forest roads for over 100km before meeting the coast at Walpole. From here, you're never far away from what is arguably Australia's most striking section of coastline.

WHERE TO GO

Once you've sampled the attractions around **Manjimup** (see p. 99) and **Pemberton** (see p. 102), you won't strike another town until **Walpole**, around 120km south-east. Walpole was developed in the 1930s following the Depression as part of a scheme to give unemployed city men and their families the chance to carve farms out of the virgin bush. It's remained quiet to this day. The drive is quite pleasant though, and I encourage you to stop at one of the roadside picnic areas in the karri forests. The air in here is rich with scents of the karri and wildlife is often seen.

On the way, stop in at the Valley of the Giants which features a 600m long, 38m high tree-top walk through the canopy of giant red tingle trees. It's wheelchair-accessible and suitable for all levels of fitness. Fees apply, but for those less comfortable with heights, there's a ground-level boardwalk that snakes through the forest, which is free to enjoy. It's open daily and there is space in the carpark for cars with caravans. Contact (08) 9840 8263.

About 15km before Denmark, I highly recommend taking the turnoff to **Greens Pool** in William Bay National Park. The sign is only small, however Greens Pool and the adjacent Elephant Rocks are two of the local's favourite swimming spots. Greens Pool is a sheltered beach that's ringed by giant granite boulders creating a stunning, natural, ocean swimming pool. The sand is white and the water a very inviting turquoise. I only turned in here by chance, and am very glad I did. A short walk over the granite boulders heading east takes you to Elephant Rocks, a smaller beach protected by towering, elephant-shaped boulders of granite. If you've come from Greens Pool, you get to the beach through a narrow gap in two boulders, so it's like stepping from a cave into paradise.

Denmark itself is a thriving coastal tourist town with plenty to do. It's got all the major services you'll need, so makes a good place to stock up. Four times a year, the town runs a large art and craft market. Contact the visitor centre (08) 9848 2055.

Albany is the site of Western Australia's first settlement, after the brig *Amity* arrived in Princess Royal Harbour in 1826. The first Anzac soldiers destined to fight in WWI also left from here in 1914. Today, it's one of the best places in the south-west for land- or water-based whale-watching (Aug–Nov) with whales often making their way into the harbours and bays to the delight of everyone.

Whales have always played a big part of the regional centre's fortunes and Albany's Historic Whaling Station, which is inside the old Cheynes Beach Whaling Station, displays the factory as it was when it was actively processing whales. There's also a fully restored whaling ship to explore for a very real look into Australia's whaling past. It's well worth the admission fee.

→ **Stirling Range National Park – near Mount Barker**

About 100km north of Albany, the Stirling Range is the only major mountain range in the South-West. The highest peak, Bluff Knoll, is 1095m above sea level.

The range is awash with wildflowers, with over 1500 species on display, Aug–Nov – which is, conveniently, the same period as the whale-watching season. There are great walking trails to many of the range's peaks. Mount Barker, the largest town to the south, is renowned for its wineries – the riesling in particular.

→ **Honey wine and ice-cream – near Denmark**

Bartholomews Meadery, about 16km west of Denmark and near the turnoff to Greens Pool, produces organic honeys and excellent ice-creams as well as the mead. Treat yourself. It's open daily 9.30am–4.30pm. Contact (08) 9840 9349.

WHERE TO STAY

217 Coalmine Beach Holiday Park

📍 2525 Coalmine Beach Rd, Walpole
📞 (08) 9840 1026
💻 www.coalminebeach.com.au

This is a large tourist caravan park, situated near an inlet, with good amenities and a range of facilities. The Valley of the Giants is nearby, as are some good fishing spots. Bookings are required in peak periods.

218 Ayr Sailean

📍 21 Tindale Rd, Bow Bridge
📞 (08) 9840 8098
💻 www.ayrsaileancamping.com.au

A wonderfully quiet property offering camping areas and charming bush cottages in a natural setting. All facilities are provided and doggy day care is offered for a modest fee. Pet friendly.

219 BIG4 Denmark Ocean Beach Holiday Park

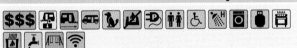

📍 770 Ocean Beach Rd, Denmark
📞 (08) 9848 1105
💻 www.big4.com.au/caravan-parks/wa/
south-west/denmark-ocean-beach-holiday-park

This great caravan park is set in bushland just a short walk from the beach. It is comfortable and has modern facilities. Bookings are required in peak seasons.

220 Denmark Rivermouth Caravan Park

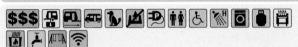

📍 Inlet Dr, Denmark
📞 (08) 9848 1262
💻 www.denmarkrivermouthcaravanpark.com.au

This popular caravan park is located right on the water, a short 1km walk from the town. It's a basic caravan park at a competitive price. A boat ramp adjoins the park. Bookings are required in peak seasons.

221 BIG4 Middleton Beach Holiday Park

📍 28 Flinders Pde, Middleton Beach
📞 (08) 9841 3593
💻 www.big4.com.au/caravan-parks/wa/
south-west/middleton-beach-holiday-park

A great place for a holiday, this quality caravan park has a fabulous position fronting onto 500m of popular swimming beach. Just 3km from the Albany post office, it has good amenities and a range of facilities, including a theatre and spa. Albany is a popular holiday destination and bookings are necessary in peak periods.

Valley of the Giants Tree Top Walk

ALBANY TO NORSEMAN

NEED TO KNOW

🎨	**650km to 661km with detours**
🏠	**Free camping areas, inexpensive caravan parks, holiday resorts**
☁	**Spring, summer and autumn**
👁	**Fishing, surfing, walking, wildflowers, whale-watching**
🅰	**Good to great**
🍴	**Albany and Esperance have great facilities, but if you are heading across the Nullarbor, Norseman is the last spot until Ceduna that does.**
⚠	**None apply**

Twilight Beach, Esperance

INTRODUCTION

Spanning nearly 700km, this is one of the longest sections tackled by this book. From Albany the South Coast Highway sweeps inland through vast tracts of hardwood plantations before giving way to wheat and sheep country. The road is well maintained but lacks passing opportunities up until Esperance, so be mindful of others behind you and pull over to let them past if possible.

WHERE TO GO

Although Esperance and Cape Le Grand National Park are the highlights of this trek, there's plenty to stop and see before you get there. Beachside towns like **Cheyne Beach** and **Bremer Bay** with their white, sandy, protected beaches attract plenty of caravanners content to fish away the days.

About 70km off the coast, the Bremer Bay canyon hosts the highest concentration of orcas on the West Australian coast, and tours run daily Jan–Apr. Southern right whales often calve in the sheltered waters July–Oct and can often be seen just metres from the shore.

Nearby Fitzgerald River National Park is another of the South-West's wildflower hotspots, at its most spectacular in spring. Over 1800 varieties grow in the park. There are some bush camping areas with limited facilities, but there are only a few for big rigs so check ahead by calling (08) 9838 1967. The park is best accessed by taking Hamersley Dr from the highway, or from Hopetoun, which is a mostly sealed route, however many roads through the park are unsealed and not all are suitable for caravans or large motorhomes.

Esperance has been everything from a whaling station and gold-rush town to an agricultural and tourism centre. Today, its port handles over 200 ships a year, taking lithium, copper, iron and nickel ores, gold, grain and woodchip to the world.

Of all the South-West's coastal towns, Esperance stole my heart. Its stunning beaches of pearly white sand, seascape littered with picture-perfect granite islands, and the laidback town right on the foreshore make it understandably popular. I also regularly found myself at the Brown Sugar Cafe too, which is clearly the best in town, and much of its food uses native ingredients.

It's full of quirky attractions, too. Just north-east of town there's a life-size replica of Stonehenge. Made from local pink granite, its station stones line up with the winter and summer solstice, so the rays shine onto the altar stone at sunset. Entry fees apply (cash only) and it's open Thu–Mon 8.30am–5pm. Contact (08) 9075 9003.

Another one-of-a-kind attraction is the Mermaid Leather factory, which uses discarded fish skins to make a high-quality leather product used in handbags, wallets and stationery. Contact (08) 9071 5248.

Just 60km west, Cape Le Grand National Park is popular for its incredible waterfront camping and the range of four-wheel driving options. Its beaches are consistently voted as the best in Australia. Lucky Bay is the most popular destination, although the camping is also excellent at Cape Le Grand campground. Both have water and toilets, a camp kitchen and barbecues, although no showers. Bookings can't be made as it's on a 'first come, first served' basis. Contact (08) 9083 2100.

From Esperance to Norseman is a 3hr drive due north through open mallee country that's typical of the south-western outback. **Norseman** reputedly gets its name from a horse, Hardy Norseman, which pawed a large nugget of gold out of the ground, much to the delight of his owner. A statue of the horse is in the middle of town. As the last major town before the Nullarbor, this is the place to stock up before heading east.

Wonderful wetlands – near Esperance

A series of lakes surround Esperance, all of which are an internationally significant wetland habitat for up to 20,000 waterbirds. A wetland walk with bird hides has been set up at Woody Lake, which is a great alternative to the Pink Lake – that's rarely pink any more. It's pink colour was the result of algae producing beta carotene (yep, the same stuff in carrots), which give the algae a high light tolerance, but it's so rarely colourful these days there's talk of changing the name back to its original name, Spencer Lake.

Cape Le Grand Coastal Trail

This 15km trail following the coast between Le Grand Beach and Rossiter Bay is broken up into four sections, so can be tackled in shorter chunks. A popular section is from Thistle Cove to Lucky Bay, because it's the easiest and shortest section and only takes around 1hr (one way). The other sections are considered difficult and will need two to three hours each (one way).

Why is the sand so white?

Lucky Bay, in Cape Le Grand National Park has the whitest sand in Australia – a fact proven by science on two separate occasions. But why is that so? Whiter sands are often made of very pure fine grains of quartz. In contrast, the white sands of Hawaii's beaches are the ground up coral eaten and then pooped out by parrot fish.

WHERE TO STAY

222 Cheynes Beach Caravan Park

$$$

- 12 Bald Island Rd, Cheyne Beach
- (08) 9846 1247
- www.cheynesbeachcaravanpark.com.au

Located in an extremely picturesque coastal village this large caravan park is just a short walk to the beach in a well-protected area. Due to its popularity, bookings are essential during peak times such as Christmas and Easter.

223 Bremer Bay Beaches Resort and Tourist Park

$$$

- 33 Wellstead Rd, Bremer Bay
- (08) 9837 4290
- www.bremerbaybeaches.com.au

This pet-friendly caravan park has a lovely outdoor alfresco area and onsite pool. It is also only a short drive to the local beaches and boat ramp.

224 Hamersley Inlet camping area

$

- Fitzgerald River National Park
- www.ravensthorpe.wa.gov.au

Located in Fitzgerald River National Park, but run by the Shire of Ravensthorpe, this camping area has basic facilities. However, it is surrounded by one of the most diverse botanical regions in Australia, if not the world. There are numerous tracks for bushwalking and the rocky headlands provide the perfect location for fishing. Whale-watching is popular Aug–Nov.

225 Bathers Paradise Caravan Park

$$$ ★

- 45 Westmacott St, Esperance
- (08) 9071 1014
- www.batherscpark.com.au

A very well-maintained, little caravan park within walking distance to the beach, it has level grassy sites and clean amenities to suit most travellers' needs.

226 Esperance Seafront Caravan Park

$$$

- Corner Goldfields and Norseman rds, Esperance
- (08) 9071 1251
- www.esperanceseafrontcp.com

This grassy, relaxed caravan park overlooks the beautiful Esperance Bay and is just 2km from the town centre. When the tide is right, it is possible to walk to town along the shoreline.

227 Acclaim Gateway Caravan Park

$$$

- 1175 Prinsep St, Norseman
- (08) 9039 1500
- www.acclaimparks.com.au/locations/norseman

This tidy little caravan park is perfect for a stopover before heading across the Nullarbor. It has level gravel sites with some drive-thru spots available, and basic, but clean, amenities.

THE NULLARBOR

The Nullarbor

INTRODUCTION

Crossing the Nullarbor is one of Australia's great bucket-list roadtrips. Unlike many other trips, for example the Savannah Way or Great Ocean Road, many seem to want to cross the Nullarbor to say they've endured it, rather than enjoyed it. It's easy to do either, it depends on your attitude. I loved crossing the Nullarbor and found that even though there are long stretches of open plain to cover, there is lots to see and do if you're not in a rush.

WHERE TO GO

Top up on fuel before leaving **Norseman**, as the roadhouses along the Nullarbor are often up to 30c a litre more expensive than here. It's 1200km until Penong and Ceduna, when prices become more reasonable again, so you'll likely have to top up, but if you do, my suggestion is to only get enough to safely make the distance.

It's 225km from Norseman to the western end of the 90-mile straight – Australia's longest section of straight road – but there are a few worthy stops along the way. Interestingly, before you reach the 'treeless plain' you'll pass through the world's largest

hardwood forest – the Great Western Woodlands – which is home to Fraser Range Station. This sheep station offers camping and caravanning accommodation, plus home-cooked meals each night 6–7pm. The aptly named Nullabar also serves drinks.

Balladonia, which is little more than a hotel, roadhouse and caravan park, became famous in 1979 when the NASA space station *Skylab* crashed to earth around it. Pieces of the wreckage are on display at the hotel's small museum, which also details the history of the Eyre Highway's construction.

After you've stopped for a picture at the western end of the long straight, you won't see a bend in the road until you reach **Caiguna**, a small roadhouse and caravan park. Just 5km west of here is the Caiguna Blowhole, an air-intake point for the limestone cave system beneath – if you stand close to it, you can feel it 'breathe' as air is pushed out of, or pulled into, the hole. Wind speeds of up to 72km/hr have been recorded from it. There's also a nice little rest area here, where you can camp.

Take the opportunity to stop at Madura Pass, which is one of the highest points on the Nullarbor and has a terrific view over the plain, looking south and east. The escarpment, which begins as sea cliffs east of Nuytsland Nature Reserve, eventually meets the sea again at **Eucla**, becoming the extensive sea cliffs of the Great Australian Bight.

There's a quarantine station near **Border Village** where anyone heading west from South Australia will have to surrender their fruit and vegetables. Although for those heading east, you can hold onto it until you get to Ceduna, where there's another quarantine station.

Once in South Australia, you'll travel through Nullarbor National Park, skirting the sea cliffs of the Great Australian Bight for around 130km before veering away from the coast again. There are great lookouts along this stretch and some popular free overnight camps. It can be very windy atop the cliffs, though, so it's not always pleasant. There's also a good chance you'll see southern right whales from any of these spots June–Oct.

The long straight

For the best place to spot whales, though, turn off at the sign to Head of Bight, 14km east of the **Nullarbor Roadhouse**. It's considered one of the best land-based whale-watching locations in Australia, and May–Sept up to 100 whales, including mothers and calves, can be seen from the lookout. Get there by following an 11km sealed road into Yalata Aboriginal Land. A fee applies for entry.

The final stop on the Nullarbor, **Ceduna** is the biggest town you've seen since Esperance. Shelly Beach Caravan Park is my favourite place to stay. Now, on the edge of the Eyre Peninsula, turn your focus to oysters and King George whiting. There's a great fresh oyster outlet on the northern side of town – the Ceduna Oyster Bar – so stop in to get your fill.

DON'T MISS

→ Nullarbor Links – the world's longest golf course

Stretching from its official start in Kalgoorlie through 18 varied holes across the Nullarbor all the way to Ceduna, along this route you'll be able to join the course from the fourth hole – a 463m par five at the Norseman Golf Club. You can grab a score card from the Norseman Visitor Centre (68 Roberts St). Most of the holes are at roadhouses or golf courses along the way and clubs are available for hire at each hole for $5. More information at www.nullarborlinks.com.

→ Abundant birdlife – near Cocklebiddy

Eyre Bird Observatory is housed in the former Eyre Telegraph Station, a lovely old stone building erected in 1897 close to the beach. The observatory, which has permanent wardens, is in Nuytsland Nature Reserve, 29km south of the Eyre Highway – the final 12km section of track is suitable for four-wheel drives only and not suitable for towing. Over 240 species of birds may be seen in the area. Day visitors are welcome and entry fees apply. Contact (08) 9039 3450.

Cliff-top lookouts

WHERE TO STAY

228 Fraser Range Caravan Park

- Eyre Hwy, 100km east of Norseman
- (08) 9039 3210
- www.fraserrangestation.com.au

This is a great find. Approximately 89km north-west of Balladonia Roadhouse and some 100km east of Norseman, the station caravan park is 2km off the highway on a well-signposted, good dirt road. The park has a number of interesting buildings and colourful bougainvillea adds to the scene. The owners are very proud of this convenient park.

229 Balladonia Hotel Motel

- Eyre Hwy, Balladonia
- (08) 9039 3453
- www.balladoniahotelmotel.com.au

A basic camping area on the edge of the Nullarbor that offers powered and unpowered sites, and simple amenities. It is pet friendly, sells fuel and has a bar and space-themed museum.

230 Caiguna Roadhouse

- Eyre Hwy, Caiguna
- (08) 9039 3459

This is another simple camping area, behind Caiguna's 24hr service station. Facilities include powered sites, good showers, toilets and a laundry, plus it is pet friendly.

231 Madura Roadhouse

- Eyre Hwy, Madura
- (08) 9039 3464

A shady camping area behind the roadhouse which offers powered and unpowered sites, showers, toilets, fuel, a swimming pool and meals. It's pet friendly.

232 Mundrabilla Roadhouse and Motel

- Eyre Hwy, Mundrabilla
- (08) 9039 3465

This is a great spot for an overnight stop with clean, basic facilities and a licensed bar. The site is pet friendly, and there are powered and unpowered sites are on offer, with clean amenities.

233 Eucla Caravan Park

- Eyre Hwy, Eucla
- (08) 9039 3468

One of the better caravan parks along the Nullarbor, this establishment is laid out on gravel on top of a ridge with views over the sand dunes to the south. It's a short stroll from the caravan park to the roadhouse, where there is good takeaway food, as well as a bar and a more formal dining area.

234 Border Village Roadhouse

- Eyre Hwy, Border Village
- (08) 9039 3474
- www.bordervillageroadhouse.com.au

Right on the border, on the South Australian side, this pet friendly place is a popular stop with an expansive caravan park without formal sites marked out. The adjacent roadhouse has a licensed bar and serves good meals.

235 Nullarbor Roadhouse

- Eyre Hwy, Nullarbor
- (08) 8625 6271
- www.nullarborroadhouse.com.au

Another popular stop for an overnighter with powered and unpowered sites, and coin-operated showers. There's interesting artwork depicting local history in the roadhouse.

236 Shelly Beach Caravan Park

- 178 Decres Bay Rd, Ceduna
- (08) 8625 2012
- www.cedunacaravanpark.com.au

Situated on the beach, just 3km from the town centre, this place offers easy access to good snorkelling, swimming and fishing. The caravan park has developed over recent years and it's the best in the area. It offers budget $10-a-night sites for the self-contained, or my favourite, the powered sites atop the foredune overlooking Denial Bay.

EYRE PENINSULA

NEED TO KNOW

 748km

🏠 Free camping areas, inexpensive caravan parks, waterfront caravan parks, beachside campsites

☁ Spring, summer and autumn – it's too cold in winter.

👁 Fishing, surfing, diving with sharks, whale-watching

🛣 The roads are generally very good, especially on the eastern side of the peninsula.

🍴 Towns like Whyalla and Port Lincoln are very well serviced, but the smaller fishing villages have only basic, but good, services.

⚠ If you eat too many oysters, you might turn into one... Well, maybe...

Port Lincoln

INTRODUCTION

The Eyre Peninsula isn't on the way to anywhere – not to Adelaide, not to Western Australia, or even to Darwin. It doesn't matter where you are coming from, if you are not specifically going to somewhere on the Eyre Peninsula, there is absolutely no reason to go there. That said, there are plenty of places on the Eyre Peninsula that you should specifically go to. And considering there is not really much of note between Ceduna and Port Augusta along Highway One, you'll be doing yourself a favour by taking the long way.

WHERE TO GO

The west coast of the Eyre Peninsula is by far the most stunning, so you've done yourself a favour coming this way from the Nullarbor. **Smoky Bay**, the first coastal town you come to, sits on the shores of the protected Laura Bay. The historic jetty is a popular place to fish for squid, while there's also a boat ramp.

Smoky Bay oysters are also highly regarded – Angel Oysters, which farms in the area, is one of the pioneers of organic-certified oyster farming.

Streaky Bay is the largest town between Ceduna and Port Lincoln and is home to a couple of good caravan parks. You can also access the Point Labatt sea-lion colony, which is the only place on mainland Australia where the pups can be seen learning to swim.

Further south, about 40km from Streaky Bay, Murphys Haystacks are ancient, wind-worn, pink granite inselbergs standing sentinel on a hilltop around 2km from the highway. A small access fee is payable and there are picnic facilities and toilets at the site.

Just north of **Elliston**, slow down long enough to drive the Anxious Bay cliff-top drive, which rivals any part of the Great Ocean Road for stunning seascapes. The drive is gravel, but easily negotiated in any vehicle with numerous places to stop and admire the view. There are a few small campsites on the beach to the north. Elliston

is popular for surfing, bushwalking and fishing with many drawn to its 423m long jetty to cast a line.

My favourite camping area along this stretch is down on Sheringa Beach. For just $10 a night (pay in advance at the Sheringa Roadhouse on the highway), you can camp in the central campsite, or further north right above the beach. It is popular with both surfers and keen fishers, plus you can drive further north along the beach to really get away from the very small crowds that settle here.

Coffin Bay is a destination in itself. In fact, the first thing I did the first time I visited was check out the real-estate boards. It's an incredibly popular holiday destination – famous for its oysters and popular for boating in the large protected bay.

Coffin Bay National Park is also a bucket-list destination for many four-wheel drivers, although much of the park is accessible in two-wheel-drive vehicles. Sealed roads will take you as far as Point Avoid and Yangie Bay, the latter which has

Swimming with sea lions

a great camping area with nine designated caravan sites.

Port Lincoln is the peninsula's largest centre and worth more than a few days of your time. From here you can join a number of great adventure tours, including boat trips to swim with Australian sea-lions. There are a number of operators to choose from, but I recommend the Adventure Bay Tours swim with the sea-lions trip (www.adventurebaycharters.com.au, 08 8682 2979). It is amazing how close the sea lions are happy to come to you, and on a few occasions I felt the rush of water as one raced past. Port Lincoln is also the shark diving capital of Australia. The region's maritime history is significant, and the Axel Stenross Maritime Museum, just north of Port Lincoln, has an excellent display of wooden boats and information (www. axelstenross.com.au, 08 8682 3624). Run by volunteers, the museum is constantly rebuilding timber boats from the area. Entry fees apply.

Cowell, around halfway between Port Lincoln and Whyalla, is easily bypassed because its township is off the highway, but it's well worth the short detour. Cowell is one of the breeding grounds for the famed Coffin Bay oysters. It's worth noting that as not all oysters grow into the ideal shape to be presented on an expensive restaurant's menu, many of the Cowell farms sell off 'oyster seconds' for a fraction of the usual price. The shells look weird, but the oysters are still the best in the world. Cowell also has one of the largest and oldest jade deposits in the world. The majority of it is green, although a limited amount of black jade is mined and this commands the best prices.

You can see and buy local jade from the Cowell Jade Motel.

Further north, the **Whyalla** Maritime Museum preserves the naval- and ship-building history of the region. The prime exhibit is the 1941 WWII corvette, **Whyalla**, one of the four corvettes built at the Whyalla shipyards. Also on display is the 1814 edition of Matthew Flinders' charts and journals. Entry fees apply.

Port Augusta is one of the most significant crossroads in Australia, situated at the junction of two of the country's most important road-transit routes – the Eyre and Stuart highways. It's a big town with every modern convenience and large shopping centre complexes. The visitor information centre is one of the best in Australia, too. The Wadlata Outback Centre has an excellent display called the Tunnel of Time. In this very interactive timeline, you'll wander through prehistoric Australia, explore Indigenous culture and eventually walk through more

recent colonial history. Allow at least 1.5hr. Entry fees apply.

About 3km north of Port Augusta, on the Stuart Highway, the Australian Arid Lands Botanic Gardens covers over 250 hectares and has 12km of walking trails. You can pick up a map from the visitor centre to see the themed routes through the park. My favourite was the bush tucker discovery walk. The visitor centre also has some great interpretive displays, a cafe and gift shop. Entry is free, although there are regular guided tours available for a small fee. The gardens are open 7.30am until sunset, while the visitor centre is open 9am–5pm. Contact (08) 8641 9117.

DON'T MISS

→ **Fred's marina tours – Port Lincoln**
A great, if obscure, tour is Fred's Marina Cruise on his small electric boat, the *Tesla*. Fred will take you on a very pleasant tour around the marina, explaining how all the fisheries work and filling you in on plenty of local history. Make a booking through Adventure Bay Charters (www.adventurebaycharters.com.au, 08 8682 2979).

→ **Oyster farm tours – Coffin Bay**
If you can line it up with the tides, tours are available of the oyster farms, which will see you in a pair of gumboots and waders trudging through the mud at low-tide exploring the oyster leases. Visit www.oysterfarmtours.com.au for more information.

Coffin Bay oysters

WHERE TO STAY

237 Smoky Bay Caravan Park

$$

- 64 South Tce, Smoky Bay
- (08) 8625 7030
- www.smokybaycaravanpark.com.au

This is a quiet caravan park in a peaceful fishing town on the north-west side of Eyre Peninsula. It's close to the wharf and has basic, but well-looked-after facilities.

238 Discovery Parks – Streaky Bay Foreshore

- 82 Wells St, Streaky Bay
- (08) 8626 1666
- www.discoveryholidayparks.com.au/
  caravan-parks/south-australia/
  eyre-peninsula-streaky-bay-foreshore

Discovery HOLIDAY PARKS

Located on the north-facing shallow waters of Streaky Bay, this caravan park has numerous waterfront sites where tinnies can be launched from the beach. There are several fish-cleaning stations along the foreshore and a well-stocked shop that serves takeaway food, including local whiting.

239 Waterloo Bay Tourist Park

- 2 Beach Tce, Elliston
- (08) 8687 9076
- www.visitelliston.net

TOP PARKS

Elliston is a quiet holiday location and this is a neat and tidy park adjacent to the beach. Bookings are required in peak periods and a minimum-stay applies at Christmas and Easter.

240 Sheringa Beach camping area

- Sheringa Beach Rd, Sheringa
- (08) 8687 8761
- www.sheringaroadhouse.com.au

Pay for your camping area at the roadhouse, then follow Sheringa Beach Rd to the ocean. There's a developed camping area with drop toilets at the sheltered north end of the beach, or camping right above the ocean available over the next headland. Good surfing and beach fishing here.

241 Coffin Bay Caravan Park

- 91 Esplanade, Coffin Bay
- (08) 8685 4170
- www.coffinbaycaravanpark.com.au

Coffin Bay township is located on a beautiful shoreline and the caravan park, at the centre of town, is just across the road from the water. Bookings are required during Christmas and Easter holidays and a minimum-stay period applies at these times.

242 Port Lincoln Tourist Park

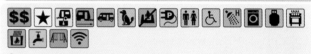

- 11 Hindmarsh St, Port Lincoln
- (08) 8621 4444
- www.portlincolntouristpark.com.au

TOP PARKS

This caravan park with nicely terraced sites is just 3km from the centre of town in a quiet waterfront location. You can watch the fishing boats stream across Boston Bay from your van window. There are huge sites for the largest motorhomes and excellent squid fishing off the groyne at the bottom of the park.

243 Tumby Bay Caravan Park

- 47 Tumby Tce, Tumby Bay
- (08) 8688 2208
- www.tumbybaycaravanpark.com

TOP PARKS

This is a well-presented caravan park on a protected stretch of coast. Bookings are essential during the peak periods of Dec–Jan and Easter.

244 Arno Bay Tourist Park

- 10 Park La, Arno Bay
- (08) 8628 0157
- www.arnobaycaravanpark.com

Close to the water, with good facilities, this is an attractive caravan park that makes a great holiday destination, particularly for those interested in a little fishing. Bookings are necessary for the summer and Easter holiday periods.

245 Cowell Foreshore Caravan Park

📍 70 The Esplanade, Cowell
📞 (08) 8629 2307

Located on the foreshore, at the end of the main street, this caravan park is ideally situated for anyone who enjoys walking everywhere. Fresh Cowell oysters are on sale at reception too. Bookings are required Jan–Apr and a minimum-stay period applies over Easter and long weekends.

246 Discovery Parks Whyalla Foreshore

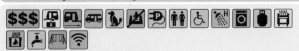

📍 53 Broadbent Tce, Whyalla
📞 (08) 8645 7474
🖥 www.discoveryparks.com.au/caravan-parks/
south-australia/spencer-gulf-whyalla-foreshore

This large caravan park close to town has most amenities for tourists. Bookings are required at Easter.

247 Discovery Parks Port Augusta

📍 31 Stokes Tce, Port Augusta West
📞 (08) 8642 2974
🖥 www.discoveryholidayparks.com.au/
workforce-parks/south-australia/
spencer-gulf-port-augusta

With very good facilities, this caravan park is strategically based at the junction of the Eyre, Princes and Stuart highways. It can get quite busy here, even in the low season. The park is about 1.5km from the town centre. Bookings are required in the peak seasons.

Locks Well Beach, Elliston

YORKE PENINSULA

NEED TO KNOW

703km

Freedom camping, inexpensive caravan parks, national park camping areas

Spring, summer and autumn

Fishing, surfing, walking, history

Good

Most of the peninsula is made up of small coastal towns, but all basic services, including a hospital with emergency centre, are available, just not in every town.

Some areas of the Yorke Peninsula still don't have mobile phone coverage.

Stenhouse Bay Jetty, Inneston

INTRODUCTION

After touring the fabulous Eyre Peninsula, the Yorke may seem a little dull, when looked at from a distance. But this boot-shaped outcrop covering more than 6000 square kilometres is truly an underrated gem of the South Australian coastline. It offers an incredible amount of choice for campers, thanks to the local council's acknowledgment that bush camping is an important aspect of local culture. The drive is a series of small towns where the locals are extremely friendly, the fishing is excellent and those that like to explore at a slow pace can take on plenty of great walks that explore the region's natural wonders and history.

WHERE TO GO

Port Pirie, the first major centre as you travel down the Spencer Gulf, is a vibrant coastal town that sprung up in the 1800s to service the mining industry, especially processing the silver and zinc from Broken Hill. There's a caravan park here that's a great launching spot for fishing expeditions or for a paddle on Samuels Creek. The Port Pirie National Trust Museum is excellent too.

From here, make your way to **Moonta Bay** to explore the peninsula's copper-mining history. The most popular attraction here is the Moonta Mines Railway – an open-topped miniature train that takes you through the old copper mine. It's not open every day, so call ahead. Moonta Bay Caravan Park is clean, basic and right on the water and once there, it's hard to think of a reason to leave. For a treat, head to the Patio restaurant, above the caravan park – it's the best restaurant in town.

Many of the beaches along this stretch, and especially further north, are renowned for their abundance of blue swimmer crab. Through summer especially, some of the most satisfying crabbing you'll ever do is raking for them. This involves walking out onto the tidal shallows with a wire rake, looking for irregularities in the sand created by buried crabs and raking them into a bucket. There's a bag limit of 20 per person, so you'll be eating like kings that night.

Continuing on, the towns only get sleepier and the roads far less busy. I broke down in my motorhome and no one passed me for over an hour. Glad I did, though, as I ended up limping into **Point Turton** to stay at the small caravan park there, which is truly a gem of the area. Mal, who runs it, believes in good old-fashioned service and operates a clean, popular park overlooking the gulf. Fish for squid off the wharf till dark, and in the unlikely event that you don't catch any then walk up the hill to the tavern for dinner.

The real highlight is Innes National Park, which covers the south-western 'foot' of the peninsula. It's the fishing, camping, surfing and walking that bring people here – I visit for all four and don't leave disappointed. Walks range from 600m to long enough to take a day, although the most popular is the shortest – out to Cape Spencer Lighthouse, usually to watch the sunset. A stroll through Inneston Historic Township is also very interesting. There are also five shipwrecks off the coast, although the easiest to see is the *SS Ethel* that's partly buried in the sands of the beach that carries its name.

On your way out of the park, stop in at the Studio Surf Art Gallery at **Marion Bay** to see (or buy) some of the artwork by owner Jason Swales and other local artists.

Port Vincent foreshore

Jason's a really interesting storyteller, so don't rush through.

Heading back up the east coast don't hurry through **Port Vincent** either. It's home to an incredible caravan park right on the foreshore of the Gulf St Vincent – and I mean right on it as the water almost laps at the bottom of your caravan.

DON'T MISS

→ Raking for blue swimmer crabs – Port Broughton

This small village of fishing shacks is the best place to rake for crabs, although it isn't technically on the peninsula. But it's on the way to Adelaide, and there's a free camping area.

→ The Yorke's bush camping – freedom of choice

There are 19 designated bush camping areas on the Yorke Peninsula, all well managed by the local council. Permits start at $10 a night, but get significantly cheaper per night the longer you stay. One permit covers all the campsites, which you can choose between at your leisure – no bookings are required. Gleesons Landing is my favourite, but most of them are stunning.

→ Walk the Yorke – a 500km round trip

The entire peninsula is joined by a continuous walking track, although there's no need to commit to the whole thing – and at this point only one couple has so far. There are great sections that can be tackled in an hour, or a day. There's details of the local section in nearly every town, or ask at the caravan parks for a map.

Innes National Park

WHERE TO STAY

248 Rangeview Caravan & Cabin Park

📍 Lot 513, A1 Highway, Port Pirie
📞 (08) 8634 4221
🖥 www.rangeviewcaravanpark.com.au

Situated on the highway, just five minutes from Port Pirie, and overlooking the southern Flinders Ranges, this is a good base to explore both north into the ranges or south into the peninsula.

249 Moonta Bay Caravan Park

📍 5 Tossell St, Moonta Bay
📞 (08) 8825 2406
🖥 www.moontabaycaravanpark.com.au

Set on two levels overlooking Moonta Bay, this caravan park is clean and well managed. Most sites have slabs and the amenities are kept clean. Very quiet at night and across the road from the local bistro.

250 Point Turton Caravan Park

📍 Bayview Rd, Point Turton
📞 (08) 8854 5222
🖥 www.pointturtoncp.com.au

A small but very friendly caravan park catering for travellers who only need basic facilities. Overlooks Hardwicke Bay with good access to a boat ramp and jetty for fishing.

251 Gleesons Landing camping area

📍 Gleesons Road, White Hut
🖥 www.visityorkepeninsula.com.au/camping

One of the best bush camping areas on the Yorke Peninsula, overlooking the sea. Popular for surfing and fishing, facilities are limited to drop toilets and rubbish bins. Permit must be purchased in advance, as there's no phone reception out there. Gravel road in is suitable for two-wheel-drive vehicles.

252 Pondalowie Bay Campground

📍 Pondalowie Bay Rd, Inneston, Innes National Park
📞 1800 202 445
🖥 www.environment.sa.gov.au

The best of the six camping areas in Innes National Park, it's closest to the park's boat ramp and protected from much of the wind. It's not suitable for bigger rigs. All campsites need to be booked prior to arrival now.

253 Port Vincent Foreshore Caravan Park

📍 12 Marine Pde, Port Vincent
📞 (08) 8853 7073
🖥 www.portvincentfcp.com.au

A very pretty caravan park, right on the foreshore of Port Vincent, it's grassy and open with very good facilities for every level of traveller. Some sites are so close to the water you can almost fish from under your awning.

254 Crystal Brook Caravan Park

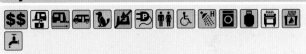

📍 330 Goyder Hwy, Crystal Brook
📞 (08) 8636 2640
🖥 www.crystalbrookcaravanparksa.com

This is a small, neat, council-owned caravan park just on the edge of town. It is a very pretty park with large red gums, a creek alongside and lawn sites. It is very good value.

255 Port Wakefield Caravan Park

📍 Corner of Wakefield and Burra sts, Port Wakefield
📞 (08) 8867 1151

On the water's edge and close to the town centre, this caravan park is located in a quiet, off-highway position and is just 100km from Adelaide. It's great for a couple of nights.

ADELAIDE TO VICTOR HARBOR – FLEURIEU PENINSULA

Glenelg Beach, Adelaide

INTRODUCTION

The first time my family and I visited the Fleurieu Peninsula, we intended to stay a week, but left six later. I even worked one of them in a caravan park cleaning the toilets, we wanted to stay that much. The relaxed city life of Adelaide, the stunning coastline, incredible wineries and stopping everything to watch the sunset over the Gulf St Vincent each night are the things that keep us coming back.

WHERE TO GO

A day or two exploring Adelaide's CBD is well worth the trip. The city of churches is just as well known for its giant schnitzels – the best in my opinion being available at the Coopers Alehouse on Putney St. There are plenty of excellent small bars around Leigh St, Peel St and Gilbert Pl if you're looking to discover local craft beers. The Adelaide Zoo is also well regarded, and you shouldn't pass up a visit to the Art Gallery of South Australia.

Every time we visit Adelaide we stay at the Christies Beach Caravan Park. **Christies Beach**, the town, doesn't have a great reputation around Adelaide, but we love how relaxed it is at the park. In fact, all the parks

along the mid-coast are great, although the one at Brighton is the most popular, and for good reason.

Using any of the mid-coast caravan parks as a base, venture into the McLaren Vale wine region. There are over 40 cellar doors in the region known for its shiraz, cabernet sauvignon and grenache. For an indulgent experience, head to d'Arenberg Wines for one of their blending bench sessions, where you'll get to design your own wine, and take home a bottle of it. (Mine's called the Editor's Payrise – a dry shiraz with subtle elements of blackcurrant and oak …)

Sticking to the coast, **Port Noarlunga** is the best spot to spend a day by the water and the beach and jetty are incredibly popular throughout summer. The highlight though is Port Noarlunga Reef, which can be accessed via the jetty and offers excellent snorkelling, even featuring a self-guided tour following 12 underwater glass plaques. Over 200 marine plants and 60 fish varieties call the reef home.

There are two ways to travel south to Victor Harbor, although the quickest is a waste of time. Follow the B23 along the coast through quaint little villages like **Myponga** and **Yankalilla**, heading for **Cape Jervis**, where you can board the ferry for Kangaroo Island. Don't miss the walk to

Second Valley Beach or a visit to the Nan Hai Pu Tuo Temple.

Victor Harbor is a wonderful coastal playground. Nearby are some of the region's best surfing beaches, while closer to town are some great walks to do, like over to Granite Island. It has very good shopping and a number of great cafes and restaurants.

DON'T MISS

→ **Kangaroo Island – Australia's third largest**

Just a 45 min ferry ride from Cape Jervis, it's surrounded by sandy beaches and sheer cliffs that withstand giant waves year-round. About 30 per cent of the island is covered by national park which are havens for native flora and fauna. Local produce includes cheese, wine, marron, fish and honey from Ligurian bees. It's expensive to take a caravan over, so consider just taking the car and staying in B&Bs or cabins for a few days.

→ **Victor Harbor – Close encounters**

The site of Matthew Flinders and Nicolas Baudin's famous encounter in 1802, a visit here will ensure you encounter whales (in season), Australian fur seals and common dolphins, all of which inhabit the inshore islands. The walk around Granite Island at

Sculptures, d'Arenberg Wines

sunrise is stunning. Another 'must do' is catching the historic horse-drawn tram out along the 800m wooden causeway. Penguins used to be commonly seen here, but local predators have nearly wiped them out.

WHERE TO STAY

256 Christies Beach Tourist Park

📍 39 Sydney Cres, Christies Beach
📞 (08) 8326 0311
🖥 www.christiesbeachtouristpark.com.au

TOP PARKS

One of the smaller caravan parks on Adelaide's mid coast, Christies has a range of sites suitable for big and small rigs with great views over the gulf. There's a great camp kitchen and good amenities.

257 Brighton Caravan Park

📍 4 Burnham Rd, Kingston Park
📞 (08) 8377 0833
🖥 www.brightoncaravanpark.com.au

Right on the foreshore, Brighton is a very ordered caravan park with great facilities that include a camp kitchen, dump point and designated fish-cleaning area. It's popular with keen fishers as it's close to the local boat ramp.

258 NRMA Victor Harbor Beachfront Holiday Park

📍 114 Victoria St, Victor Harbor
📞 (08) 8552 1111
🖥 www.nrmaparksandresorts.com.au/victor-harbor

NRMA Parks + Resorts

One of the caravan parks that caters for families as well as it does for grey nomads, it has powered sites from $38. Other facilities include a water park, including water slide, laundry, free WiFi and two camp kitchens.

259 BIG4 Port Elliot Holiday Park

📍 Port Elliot Rd, Port Elliot
📞 (08) 8554 2134
🖥 www.big4.com.au/caravan-parks/sa/fleurieu-peninsula/port-elliot-holiday-park

BIG4 HOLIDAY PARKS

Another caravan park right on the water with large, grassy and flat sites. Being right on the water does mean it can be quite windy though, but further in offers more protection. The managers here are friendly and there's a very casual atmosphere. There's a great kids' playground too.

Granite Island, Victor Harbor

VICTOR HARBOR TO MOUNT GAMBIER

NEED TO KNOW

🎨	**439km (via Langhorne Creek Rd and Prince Hwy) to 454km (via Murray Bridge)**
🏠	**National park camping areas, inexpensive campsites, holiday resorts**
☁	**Spring, summer and autumn**
👁	**Fishing, four-wheel driving, birdwatching, wineries, history**
🛣	**Good to great**
🍴	**The Limestone Coast is a major tourist region and all services are available. However, there isn't much between Goolwa and Kingston SE.**
⚠	**None apply**

Long Beach, Robe

INTRODUCTION

Taking in the mouth of the Murray, parts of South Australia's Riverland and following South Australia's Limestone Coast before eventually finishing in the volcanic regions around Mount Gambier, this section is spectacularly diverse.

WHERE TO GO

The lovely seaside town of **Port Elliot** is home to one of Australia's best pie shops – the Port Elliot Bakery – so stop here first. Nearby **Goolwa** is one of the sites of three barrages that control the flow of the Murray into the Coorong. The Coorong is an internationally significant coastal lagoon that stretches for 130km, only separated from the Southern Ocean by a narrow peninsula of sand dunes – which is also Australia's longest beach. At Goolwa you can walk out onto the barrage where you'll likely see seals waiting for an easy feed as fish find their way through the open gates.

To continue to Mount Gambier, you have to skirt Lake Alexandria. By giving it an extra

wide birth, and passing through **Murray Bridge**, you'll be a stone's throw from the Monarto Open Plain Zoo. In fact, it's so big the best way to enjoy it is on the free shuttle buses that continually circuit the grounds. You'll pass through lions' enclosures, come face to face with giraffes, rhinos and many animals from the African savannah. There's plenty of space to park a caravan, too.

Following the coastal route along the Princes Highway (B1), you'll hug the side of the Coorong. There are often glimpses across the shallow wetlands, although there's little else to see between **Meningie** and Kingston SE unless you're prepared to head off-road, through the wetlands and onto the beach. However, that's not an excursion for the fainted hearted!

At the southern end of the Coorong, the beachside towns of **Kingston SE**, **Robe** and **Beachport** are all charming. Each offers great services for caravanners and campers, so don't rush through them. Kingston SE is home to one of Australia's 'big things' – a lobster named Larry that celebrates the local lobster industry. Most of the beaches through here can be driven on, although

the prettiest is Robe Long Beach with its firm, white sand, sparking blue water and excellent fishing.

From here I recommend tearing yourself away from the coast and heading north-east into the Coonawarra – one of Australia's best cab sav producing wine regions. Australia's first patron saint, Mary MacKillop was governess for a family in this region, where she met the Reverend Julian Wood, who became her mentor over many years. The story of her life as told in the Mary MacKillop Penola Centre, in **Penola**, is genuinely captivating and well worth the hour or two it will take to explore.

Mount Gambier is the largest centre along this route, and it's most famous for its various holes in the ground. To the south is the Mount Schank volcanic crater, which has a great walk around its rim, although it's a bit of a climb to the top. The Umpherston Sinkhole, also known as the Sunken Garden, requires less energy, but is just as amazing. The highlight though is Blue Lake, which turns a stunning turquoise blue Nov–Mar.

Goolwa beach free camp

➔ **Naracoorte Caves National Park –
Victoria Fossil Cave tour**

To understand why this is called the
Limestone Coast, visit Naracoorte Caves
National Park and join a guided tour into
the Victoria Fossil Cave – a limestone
cave formed when this was an off-shore
part of Australia. In it, there's one of the
world's most significant fossil deposits,
the result of animals falling into a hole
and becoming trapped over hundreds of
thousands of years.

➔ **Mayura Station – the Tasting Room**

For a unique, and very indulgent, dining
experience, book into a tasting experience
where the onsite chef prepares the
station's own chocolate- and lolly-fed
wagyu in a variety of mouth-watering
ways. Bookings essential. Contact
(08) 8733 4333, www.mayurastation.com.

➔ **Famous faces of the
Limestone Coast**

David Unaipon – the Indigenous elder
and inventor on our $50 note and the first
Aboriginal child born in an Australian mission

Mary MacKillop – Australia's first patron
saint, officially St Mary of the Cross
MacKillop, patron saint of Australia

John Riddoch Rymill – Led the 1934 British
Graham Land Expedition, mapping 1000km
of the Antarctic Peninsula

Reverend Julian E. T. Woods – A priest
and a highly regarded scientist who
theorised the Limestone Coast was actually
a series of coasts that had developed over
millions of years

Blue Lake, Mount Gambier

WHERE TO STAY

260 Strathalbyn Caravan Park

- 4 Ashbourne Rd, Strathalbyn
- (08) 8536 3681
- www.strathalbyncaravanpark.com.au

This is a modestly priced caravan park with simple, but clean, facilities for caravanners and campers. Right on the edge of town, walking distance to the shops, it's pet friendly and has level, grassy sites suitable for big rigs.

261 Lake Albert Caravan Park

- 25 Narrung Rd, Meningie
- (08) 8575 1411
- www.lakealbertcaravanpark.com.au

Located on the shore of Lake Albert, about 1km from the town centre, this is a budget-priced caravan park with a great expanse of lawn and shady trees. It is a well-laid-out and well-managed park, with good facilities and a great outlook. Bookings are required in peak periods, with minimum-length stays at Christmas, Easter and long weekends.

262 Kingston SE RV Park

- Marine Parade, Kingston SE

This is the community-managed free camping area at the north end of town which allows 48hr parking for self-contained travellers. Bookings aren't required, but you must pay for your stay at the self-service machine. It's a flat fee (currently $10) for up to 48 hours.

263 Kingston Caravan Park

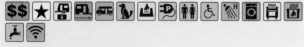

- 34 Marine Pde, Kingston SE
- (08) 8767 2050
- www.kingstonforeshorecaravanpark.com.au

A popular caravan park just across the road from the beach, in a township where fishing is popular. The park is competitively priced and located 1.5km south of the town centre. There is a well-stocked kiosk. Bookings are required in peak periods.

264 Discovery Parks Robe

- 70–80 Esplanade, Robe
- (08) 8768 2237
- www.discoveryparks.com.au/sa/ limestone_coast/robe

This good-quality caravan park is an easy walk across the road from a popular beach, about 2km from the centre of the coastal resort town. This is a great place to stay. Bookings are required at Christmas, Easter and long weekends, with a minimum-stay period at Christmas and Easter.

265 Coonawarra Bush Holiday Park

- 242 Comaum School Rd, Comaum
- 0455 146 647
- www.cbhp.com.au

A terrific and grassy caravan park in the heart of the Coonawarra wine region. As well as powered and unpowered sites, the park has 200 acres of bushland with walking tracks throughout and a dam stocked with marron you are allowed to catch.

266 BIG4 Blue Lake Holiday Park

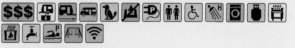

- Bay Rd, Mount Gambier
- 1800 676 028
- www.bluelake.com.au

Just across the road from Mount Gambier's amazing Blue Lake, this is a sprawling, full-featured caravan park that's popular year-round. With a large children's playground, tennis courts and a dog-friendly section, there is something here for everyone.

MOUNT GAMBIER TO PORT FAIRY

Port Fairy

INTRODUCTION

The Princes Highway between Mount Gambier and Port Fairy is well maintained and mostly carries local traffic, including trucks loaded with timber. Numerous heavy transports use the road between Mount Gambier and Portland, so be aware of their presence and note that there are limited overtaking opportunities. A popular alternative is the coastal route through Nelson, which is fully sealed.

WHERE TO GO

Port MacDonnell is one of my favourite places along this stretch of coast. There's a spectacular coastal drive that heads back west to **Carpenter Rocks**, and on the way you can visit the Cape Northumberland Lighthouse ruins and the fairy-penguin colony in the same location. Most people come here to fish, though, and the narrow beach, just inside the harbour's breakwall, is lined with four-wheel drives and empty trailers throughout summer. Nearby Orwell Rocks beach is the most popular swimming spot, and the beach can be driven on to set up picnics or launch boats.

Experienced divers and snorkellers also visit the area to explore the crystal-clear,

spring-fed fresh waters of Ewens Ponds and Piccaninnie Ponds, which are both located in conservation parks.

Just over the border, on the Victorian side, **Nelson** is a picturesque town that was named after the *Lady Nelson* – the first ship to sail west to east through the Bass Strait and which charted much of this coastline during that voyage in 1800. Nelson is in the estuary of the Glenelg River and near the Lower Glenelg National Park, which makes the town a popular tourist destination.

Portland, where you meet the Princes Highway again, was Victoria's first permanent European settlement, having been first farmed by Edward Henty in 1834. The town was named by the commander of the *Lady Nelson*. The town is popular with four-wheel drivers, as the nearby Portland Buggy Club's land is the only place in Victoria that the coastal dunes can be driven on. Portland's history is steeped in whaling and there's a complete sperm-whale skeleton on display at the Maritime Discovery Centre. Saint Mary MacKillop also taught in the town in the 1860s.

Port Fairy has a proud seafaring history and commercial abalone, squid and lobster boats still operate out of the picturesque port. Like so many places along this coast, fishing is the biggest attraction. Bag and size

limits apply, especially to rock lobster and abalone, and most caravan parks and visitor information centres will have the latest details. The town has numerous historical buildings, but is probably best known for the Port Fairy Folk Festival which is held in March each year.

DON'T MISS

→ **Cave adventures – near Nelson**
Princess Margaret Rose Cave, in Lower Glenelg National Park, is 18km off the highway (or accessible along an unsealed road from Nelson). The old cave is adorned with wonderful stalactites, stalagmites and helictites, which can be viewed on a guided tour. Tours are conducted daily 10am–4.30pm. Entry fees apply and there is also a camping area in the park. Contact (03) 8738 4171.

→ **Chainsaw sculptures – Dartmoor**
At Dartmoor, the Atlantic cedar trees planted to commemorate WWI servicemen from the district have avoided complete removal by having the stumps spectacularly carved by chainsaw sculptor Kevin Gilders as a memorial.

Portland

WHERE TO STAY

267 Port MacDonnell Foreshore Tourist Park

📍 **12 Eight Mile Creek Rd, Port MacDonnell**

A good value, budget-priced caravan park situated on the beachfront about 1.5km from the centre of Port MacDonnell. The park has good facilities and is an ideal location from which to explore the region. There is a free laundry and special rate for singles.

268 Kywong Caravan Park

📍 **92 Nelson North Rd, Nelson**
📞 **(08) 8738 4174**
🖥 **www.kywongcp.com**

Located on the northern side of town, this large, budget-priced caravan park has good facilities. It is about 1.5km from the centre of the small township.

269 Swan Lake camping area

📍 **Discovery Bay Coastal Park**
🖥 **www.parkweb.vic.gov.au/explore/parks/discovery-bay-coastal-park/things-to-do/swan-lake-camp**

Adjacent to the only coastal area in Victoria where driving on the coastal sand dunes is still permitted, this is a basic camping area on grass and sand with facilities limited to toilets and picnic tables. Advance bookings and payment are required, and minimum stays apply for Labour Day weekend, Easter and Melbourne Cup weekend.

270 NRMA Portland Bay Holiday Park

📍 **184 Bentinck St, Portland**
📞 **(03) 5523 1487**
🖥 **www.nrmaparksandresorts.com.au/portland-bay**

NRMA Parks + Resorts

This is a neat and tidy caravan park, recently bought by the NRMA. It has all the modern facilities and is well managed. Koalas can be spotted in trees in the park, and the tourist tram stops out the front.

271 Port Fairy Holiday Park

📍 **139 Princes Hwy, Port Fairy**
📞 **(03) 5568 1816**
🖥 **www.portfairyholidaypark.com.au**

TOP PARKS

This is a lovely boutique caravan park with magnificent gardens. It has very good facilities, including a tennis court and boat-parking area. Bookings are required at Christmas.

PORT FAIRY TO GEELONG

NEED TO KNOW

- 209km
- Holiday resorts; inexpensive, council-run caravan parks
- This is a year-round beauty, but it can be cold in winter.
- Fishing, surfing, local history
- Highway One is great through here.
- Both Warrnambool and Geelong are major regional cities, so services are great. In between, most basic facilities can be found.
- None apply

Flagstaff Hill Maritime Village, Warrnambool

INTRODUCTION

Although most holidaymakers travel the Great Ocean Road between Port Fairy and Geelong, the more northerly, inland route is quieter, rolls through ancient volcanic ranges and has plenty of quaint attractions to make it more than worthwhile.

WHERE TO GO

The volcanic plains of western Victoria extend from Mount Gambier through to Colac. There are many volcanic lakes and craters throughout the region, including the stunning Tower Hill Lake near Warrnambool. However, the last volcanic activity here was roughly 5400 years ago.

Warrnambool itself is a key regional centre and popular beachside destination. Over 100 shipwrecks are scattered along the coast to the east and west of town, and the Flagstaff Hill Maritime Museum showcases much of this history. Logans Beach, just east of town, is a southern right whale nursery. Whales come here to calve June–Sept each year. They often swim and frolic close to the beach and can easily be viewed from the shoreline or a specially constructed platform. The area can be extremely busy during peak holiday periods, so bookings

at any caravan park you intend to stay in are essential.

Warrnambool is also the generally accepted beginning, or end, of the Great Ocean Road, which is one of Australia's most spectacular drives and a great alternative to the country route that follows the Princes Highway. (*See* p. 127)

Terang, 45km east of Warrnambool, is a small town servicing the local agricultural industry. Some of the town's beautiful avenues of deciduous trees have been listed on the National Trust. The visitor centre, in the old courthouse, is the best place to learn more about the town's history. Contact (03) 5592 1984.

Camperdown, another 30km east, is located on the edge of Mount Leura, a volcanic cone. Nearby, Lakes Gnotuk and Bullen Merri are two spectacular crater lakes where fishing for trout and Chinook salmon is popular. Camperdown has most services and good shopping, with a craft market held 1st Sun of each month.

Another local landmark of note is the hundreds of kilometres of dry stone wall, most of which were built by skilled craftsmen between the 1860s and '70s, although some date back to the 1840s. Known locally as the Stony Rises, they serve as boundaries and paddock fences.

Colac is a service centre for the surrounding, closely populated agricultural area and the local timber industry. The town lies on the eastern edge of the volcanic plain that covers most of western Victoria and into South Australia. Lake Colac, to the north of town, is a large freshwater lake popular for boating and fishing. The Colac Botanic Gardens on Gellibrand St, are on the banks of the lake. More than 1000 specimens are displayed in the gardens, which were listed by the National Trust in 1990.

Winchelsea is a small community on the Princes Highway, mainly servicing the surrounding farming area. It has a couple of lovely galleries and the historic Barwon Bridge with its graceful stone arches that opened in 1867. The town also has basic services and a small selection of shops.

DON'T MISS

→ **Re-created maritime village – Warrnambool**
The unique Flagstaff Hill Maritime Museum complex in Warrnambool is an excellent attraction that showcases the area's early maritime history, including the numerous shipwrecks along the rugged south-west Victorian coastline. There are replicas of 19th-century buildings, including a town hall,

bank and church. It's open daily and entry fees apply. Contact (03) 5559 4600.

→ **Peace and quiet – Gellibrand**
If you're really looking to escape the crowds, set up in Gellibrand, a small rural town halfway between Colac and the Great Ocean Road. The town is located near the Gellibrand River, and is a good base from which to discover the Great Otway National Park and the Otway Fly Treetop Walk.

WHERE TO STAY

272 Surfside Holiday Park Warrnambool

⌖ 120 Pertobe Rd, Warrnambool
☎ (03) 5559 4700
🖥 www.surfsidepark.com.au   **family parks**

This is a large, very good-quality, council-owned caravan park right on the beachfront. Great for family beachside holidays, it has good facilities and is just 1km from the city centre and close to Flagstaff Hill. Bookings are required at Christmas and a minimum booking of one week applies during Christmas and in January.

273 Terang Community Caravan Park

⌖ 14 Warrnambool Rd, Terang
☎ (03) 5592 1687

One of those delightful, small-town caravan parks where the amenities are clean, the sites are good and the fees are very modest. A great spot to spend a few days while exploring.

274 Lake Colac Caravan Park

⌖ 51 Fyans St, Colac
☎ (03) 5231 5971
🖥 www.lakecolaccaravanpark.com.au

This caravan park is located on the water's edge, within easy walking distance of town. Facilities are basic, but well maintained.

275 Winchelsea Caravan Park

⌖ 24 Willis St, Winchelsea
☎ 0422 365 652

This is a small, private caravan park with only a limited number of sites. The grounds are grassy, have plenty of shade and amenities are basic, but well kept.

Lake Bullen Merri

THE GREAT OCEAN ROAD

The Great Ocean Road

INTRODUCTION

Generally considered one of Australia's most highly desired roadtrips, the Great Ocean Road is also Australia's longest war memorial, having been built by over 3000 returned servicemen from WWI. It was officially opened on 26 Nov 1932. Today its coastal towns and villages thrive on tourism and there's barely a point along the trip that isn't worth stopping at for a closer look.

WHERE TO GO

Port Campbell is a great place to set up if you're planning on spending a few days exploring the Twelve Apostles, Loch Ard Gorge, London Bridge and Bay of Islands. The Twelve Apostles are best viewed at sunset. There are only eight remaining – originally, they were called the Sow and the Piglets, there were only ever nine. There's a

huge parking area here and a well-trodden boardwalk to the best viewing locations.

If you're looking to kill some time before sunset, there is some great history surrounding much of the 'rocky' lookouts along this stretch. One is the tale of poor Dave Darrington who was stranded on London Bridge when its connection to the mainland collapsed in 1990. Another is the story of the *Loch Ard*, a three-mast clipper which was wrecked off the coast of Port Campbell and gives its name to Loch Ard Gorge. The full story, including that of the two survivors, is told along a signposted walk above the gorge.

The detour onto Cape Otway provides one of the most reliable places to see koalas in the wild, with many of them inhabiting the coastal manna gums right beside the narrow, winding road. You genuinely need to be careful driving along here as it's not uncommon for tourists to be parked precariously on the side of the

road, or to suddenly come to a stop to take photographs. **Cape Otway** is the northern landfall on the treacherous entry to Bass Strait, and throughout the 19th century around 160 ships foundered along this dangerous coast. Cape Otway Lighthouse began operation in 1848 and is now open to the public daily 9am–5pm.

The Great Otway National Park, best accessed from Apollo Bay or Lorne, is a spectacular change from the relentless coastal scenery of the B100. There are many walks through the park, some good opportunities to free camp and nearly a dozen waterfalls to visit. If you're seeking some adrenaline-fuelled adventures, explore the mountain-bike tracks, or visit the Otway Fly, a zipline tour through the canopy of the forest, up to 30m off the ground.

From Apollo Bay onwards, the Great Ocean Road scarcely leaves the ocean and it's between here and Lorne you'll find those stretches that seemingly hover on the edge

The Twelve Apostles

who would disguise himself and hide out in the pub trying to catch him. The pub is also allegedly haunted, so head on in for the full story.

→ Aireys Inlet

Aireys Inlet is ideal for a relaxing holiday. The main landmark, Split Point Lighthouse, was built in 1891 and still operates. There is a 3.5km cliff-top walk between the lighthouse and Sunnymead Beach, with fabulous views. The nearby coastal heathland has abundant wildflowers in spring.

of a sea cliff or skirt a near-deserted beach. Apollo Bay is a thriving little coastal town. Worth a look are the large woodcarvings that adorn the foreshore park alongside the visitor centre. Carved from local wood, each piece depicts an aspect of the region's relationship with the sea.

Between **Lorne** and Torquay is the undisputed surfing capital of Victoria. The water's rarely warmer than 19°C though, so understandably that's not for everyone. Lorne is another great base for exploring the Otways and the town is well stocked with cafes along the great foreshore walk.

Torquay, which is either the beginning or end of the trip, is a well-developed coastal town that's also the hometown of two of the world's biggest surfing brands – Rip Curl and Quicksilver – both started in 1969. The Australian National Surfing Museum traces the history of the sport and culture in the area, and Australia, and is well worth a visit. Nearby, **Bells Beach** is also one of the world's most famous surfing destinations.

DON'T MISS

→ Boggy Creek Pub – Curdie Vale

Pubs are usually the last stop on a good roadtrip, but the Boggy Creek Pub in Curdie Vale, about 35km from Warrnambool, is a 'must visit' country watering hole. Built in 1853, it was the haunt of Thomas Delany who ran a moonshine operation and was for years chased by Detective John Christie

Triplet Falls, Great Otway National Park

WHERE TO STAY

276 Port Campbell Holiday Park

📍 30 Morris St, Port Campbell
📞 (03) 5598 6492
🖥 www.pchp.com.au

Set in a beautiful scenic location, close to the centre of town and just a short walk to the beach, this caravan park offers level, grassy sites with clean and tidy amenities.

277 Johanna Beach camping area

📍 Old Coach Rd, Great Otway National Park
🖥 www.parkweb.vic.gov.au/explore/parks/great-otway-national-park/things-to-do/johanna-beach2

This national park camping area has wide, open, grassy sites and clean drop toilets. It is beside the beach which has good fishing. Advance bookings and payment are required.

278 BIG4 Apollo Bay Pisces Holiday Park

📍 311 Great Ocean Rd, Apollo Bay VIC
📞 (03) 5237 6749
🖥 www.piscespark.com.au

BIG4
HOLIDAY PARKS

Located directly opposite Apollo Bay's main beach this family-friendly caravan park enjoys spectacular ocean views. There is a wide range of facilities available including a heated swimming pool and indoor games room as well as a choice of ensuite, concrete-slab and full-grass sites.

279 Cumberland River Holiday Park

📍 2680 Great Ocean Rd, Cumberland River
📞 (03) 5289 1790
🖥 www.cumberlandriver.com.au

This picturesque caravan park is situated on the banks of the Cumberland River and offers wide, open, grassy spaces and beautiful scenery. Amenities are basic, but tidy, and there are only six powered sites available. Bookings are recommended.

280 Barwon Heads Caravan Park

📍 1 Ewing Blyth Dr, Barwon Heads
📞 (03) 5254 1115
🖥 www.barwonheadscaravanpark.com.au

Ideally located, just a short walk from the town centre and fronting the beautiful Barwon River, this large caravan park offers spacious grassy sites and modern facilities. Ocean views come at an extra cost. Bookings are required during Christmas, Easter and public holidays.

TORQUAY TO MELBOURNE

NEED TO KNOW

🚗	**105km (Princes Fwy) to 174km (via Bellarine Peninsula)**
🏠	**Beachside caravan parks, holiday resorts**
☁	**This beachside location is best visited during the warmer months, although it is very busy over the Christmas holidays.**
👁	**Fishing, surfing, boating, beaches**
🛣	**The roads on the Bellarine Peninsula are great.**
🍴	**This is a large satellite city of Melbourne so has all facilities and services.**
⚠	**None apply**

Lifeguard bollards at Eastern Beach Reserve, Geelong

INTRODUCTION

It would be easy to bypass everything between Torquay and Melbourne, but this coastal strip which includes Geelong, the Bellarine Peninsula and Barwon Heads is both charming and varied in its attractions.

WHERE TO GO

Located on the western shore of Corio Bay, **Geelong** is Victoria's largest provincial city. An industrial centre with a large shipping and export grain terminal, it was home to the Ford Motor Company's engine plant which operated between 1925 and 2016 and built over 4.5 million engines. Today, the Geelong foreshore is vibrant and busy with plenty of things to do, including a visit to the National Wool Museum or the Geelong Gallery which was built in 1886. (Entry fees apply for both.)

Rather than rejoining the highway north, the alternative scenic route through the Bellarine Peninsula takes you to the seaside towns of Barwon Heads, Ocean Grove, Queenscliff and Portarlington. **Barwon Heads** is a laidback town popular with surfers and coffee drinkers and has a great caravan park right on the Barwon River.

Nearby **Queenscliff** hosts the historic Queenscliff Fort, which was built in 1882 to protect the entrance to Port Phillip. Today, it contains a great museum and guided tours are offered daily (11am Mon–Fri, 1pm and 3pm on weekends; fees apply).

From Queenscliff you can also take the Queenscliff to Sorrento Ferry to avoid travelling through Melbourne. The 180km trip from Geelong to Sorrento can take up to three hours thanks to heavy congestion, and will cost between $7.50 and $13 in tolls. By contrast, the vehicle ferry that operates daily 7am–6pm takes around 50 min. Contact (03) 5257 4500.

Portarlington is a popular tourist destination during the summer and Easter holidays. The bayside beach is a safe family spot and popular fishing area. The local caravan park is one of the largest around.

Midway between Melbourne and Geelong, the satellite city of **Werribee** is bypassed by the freeway. It has a large shopping centre and all community services. South of the city, extensive market gardens grow a range of fresh vegetables with numerous farm gates where you can buy fresh in-season produce before enjoying

them at a nice picnic spot along the picturesque shores of Port Phillip.

DON'T MISS

Historic mansion – near Werribee
In Werribee Park is a historical 60-room mansion built in the 1870s. It's been opulently furnished in the style and time of the original occupants as a fascinating museum. The Victorian State Rose Garden is also part of the property. Both are open daily and entry fees apply. Contact 13 1963.

Open range zoo – near Werribee
Werribee Open Range Zoo showcases a range of animals, including rhinoceros, giraffes, zebras, monkeys, antelopes, cheetahs and lions, on 200 acres of parkland. Join a guided tour to view these marvellous creatures up close. It's open daily and fees apply. Contact 1300 966 784.

WHERE TO STAY

280 Barwon Heads Caravan Park

See p. 129 – Great Ocean Road.

281 BIG4 Beacon Resort

📍 78 Bellarine Hwy, Queenscliff
📞 (03) 5258 1133
🖥 www.beaconresort.com.au

BIG4 HOLIDAY PARKS

This award-winning establishment has all the trimmings you would expect of a caravan park of this quality, including a heated indoor swimming pool and tennis courts. It's just a short walk to the beach. Bookings are required at Christmas, with a minimum-length stay at Christmas, Easter, long weekends and during school holidays.

282 Discovery Parks Geelong

📍 59 Barrabool Rd, Belmont
📞 (03) 5243 6225
🖥 www.discoveryholidayparks.com.au/
   caravan-parks/victoria/geelong-geelong

Discovery HOLIDAY PARKS

This is a great caravan park on the south side of the Barwon River, just 2km from the centre of Geelong. Bookings are required at Christmas, Easter and long weekends.

Portarlington

2

GREAT OUTBACK ADVENTURES

Kata Tjuṯa

Even though Australia's population centres are all on the coastal extremities of the country, our national identity is tied to the outback. Some of Australia's greatest heroes and our utmost national achievements have happened within the interior, and much of our wealth has been dug from it, grown on it, or driven over it, hard kilometre by hard kilometre. From the enduring explorers – Stuart, Giles, Leichhardt, Sturt, Burke, Wills, Mitchell – men who give our inland highways their names, to the humble characters immortalised in the poetry of Banjo Paterson – the jolly swagman, Clancy of the Overflow, the Man from Snowy River – we are as much in love with the harsh desert as we are with the lush coast.

These ten great touring routes each cross an amazing part of the interior and many of them closely follow the routes carved out by the very person who gave the lonely stretch of highway its name. These are the great north–south routes from Adelaide to Darwin or Melbourne to Karumba, or the 'short cuts' like those that cross from northern Queensland to southern Western Australia or through the vast mining regions of outback New South Wales and Western Australia, or the fossil-rich areas of central Queensland.

And far from being rugged and daunting, each one is totally achievable for any travellers who are able to handle a bit of dirt-road driving or spend a few nights away from the comforts of a coastal caravan park. This is in no way more real than any other part of Australia, but when you're out there, it certainly feels like it is. Which is why you'll keep going back.

MELBOURNE TO KARUMBA

pp. 140–151

 Hume Freeway, Goulburn Valley Freeway, Newell Highway, Kidman Way, Mitchell (Matilda) Highway, Landsborough (Matilda) Highway, Capricorn Highway, Burke Developmental Road (Matilda Highway) (2909km)

Sweeping northwards from Melbourne, this network of highways has become popular due to the strong marketing of the Kidman Way and Matilda Hwy tourist routes. The fully sealed route crosses three states and many tourists travel north to escape the cold southern winters for the balmy tropics. The wineries of the Murrumbidgee Irrigation Area, Tambo's famous teddy bears and the Australian Stockman's Hall of Fame at Longreach are all 'must-see' attractions for travellers visiting this area.

⚓ PLAN YOUR TRIP

The busy Hume Freeway heads northwards bypassing all towns, in the style of busy east coast main roads. As it reaches the regional areas of Victoria, the route joins the Goulburn Valley Freeway and passes by notable vineyards before reaching Shepparton in the fertile Goulburn Valley.

From Shepparton it crosses the Murray River and the highway changes names to become the Newell. This is a large rice-producing area and the edge of Kelly Gang country until it reaches the small town of Jerilderie, made famous by Ned and his associates.

Just north of Jerilderie, the route leaves the Newell Hwy at the beginning of the Kidman Way. It travels past rice paddies and crosses the Murrumbidgee River, south of Griffith, into a fertile, irrigated area where vineyards and orchards flourish before the real outback begins at Cobar.

From Cobar, a rich mining area, the Kidman runs straight north to Bourke, that iconic outback town. Make sure you stop to soak up the town's heritage and explore its surrounding areas. The Kidman continues out the back 'o town, into the outback in full swing. It stretches north past grazing communities spread to the horizon and arrives at Barringun, a tiny community on the New South Wales/Queensland border.

Now the Mitchell Hwy, the road stretches north across the plains to Augathella. Along the way take some time in Charleville to learn more about the Royal Flying Doctor Service at its excellent visitor centre.

From Augathella, the highway changes name again, now the Landsborough, which passes through Tambo with its delightful hand-crafted teddies, historic Blackall and Barcaldine, the town where the Australian Labor Party was founded.

After Barcaldine, Longreach's famous Australian Stockman's Hall of Fame and historic Qantas hangar, are worth taking the time to visit. As is Winton's spectacular Waltzing Matilda Centre.

From Winton the highway runs past the famous Blue Heeler Hotel at Kynuna – which claims to be the location where Banjo Paterson first performed 'Waltzing Matilda'. Further north is the Walkabout Creek Hotel at McKinlay, made famous by *Crocodile Dundee*.

At Cloncurry the highways end, and the route follows the Burke Developmental Rd to Karumba. This is a great drive past the grazing properties that sprawl across this area. Karumba is a popular spot to wait out the cold southern winters, and catch a barra or two while you're at it.

☁ BEST TIME TO GO

Western Queensland and the Gulf Country are best experienced in the balmy winter months, while the Murray River is a popular summer playground.

ADELAIDE TO DARWIN pp. 152–163

 Augusta Highway, Stuart Highway (3033km)

Bisecting Australia's dry Red Centre, the Stuart Hwy sweeps across vast plains, weaves through the rugged MacDonnell Ranges, passes by lonely roadhouses and runs close to some of Australia's most iconic landmarks and areas – Uluru, Kata

Uluru

Kata Tjuṯa

Tjuṯa, Nitmiluk (Katherine) Gorge and Kakadu. The route is the country's premier south–north inland route, offering easy access to awesome scenery, remote deserts and the fabulous gorges close to Alice Springs.

⚓ PLAN YOUR TRIP

North of Adelaide the highway skirts the western foot of the southern Flinders Ranges bypassing the wonderful Yorke Peninsula, then reaches Port Augusta, a point where the outback meets the sea and the red landscape dominates.

From Port Augusta the highway climbs steadily, passing by large, usually dry salt lakes, through a rocket-testing range to the opal-mining capital of the world – Coober Pedy. Along the way, visit Woomera's rocket museum.

From Coober Pedy to the Northern Territory border, the route passes dry creek beds, rocky hills and creeks that seldom flow. Once in the Territory, rich red sand dunes appear, becoming small ranges before the awe-inspiring MacDonnell Ranges rise above the horizon on the approach to Alice Springs.

Detour 200km south of Alice Springs, at Erldunda Roadhouse to take in the majesty, spectacle and ancient culture at Uluṟu, the most spectacular monolith in the desert, and Kings Canyon with its dramatic sheer walls.

In Alice Springs, a busy but isolated town more than 1500km from the nearest capital city, enjoy the fine array of galleries which focus mainly on Indigenous art, excellent museums and a terrific wildlife park, all set in the centre of the scenic MacDonnell Ranges.

The Stuart Hwy continues to climb north to historic Tennant Creek, the site of Australia's last gold rush, and Three Ways Roadhouse, where two great highways meet.

From Three Ways, the route drifts past large cattle properties, including the mighty Newcastle Waters Station, as well as others which have opened their gates to campers and caravanners. At Daly Waters, that iconic pub in the north, travellers can find one of the most jovial camping areas and welcoming pubs in the country.

From Daly Waters, the Stuart Hwy sweeps northwards, passing by Mataranka Thermal Pool and Cutta Cutta Caves. Spectacular Nitmiluk (Katherine) Gorge is just a short drive from Katherine, a major outback centre.

On the way to Darwin, stop at the fabulous Litchfield National Park with its wonderful swimming holes and waterfalls, the historic Pine Creek goldfields or the many WWII sites. Kakadu National Park is easily accessible by two fully sealed routes, and this amazing World Heritage–listed park has so much to offer. From cruising the spectacular Yellow Water Billabong to watching the brilliant sunset from Ubirr Rock, the experience will be unforgettable.

Darwin is a modern cosmopolitan city in the steaming Top End. It has great restaurants thanks to its multicultural influences, interesting museums and a fabulous range of tourist activities, many of which are free. Its climate is hot and dry, or hot and humid, which just adds to the tropical feel.

☁ BEST TIME TO GO

The most popular time to travel through the Red Centre is during the cooler months, Apr–Oct – although it is starting to get very hot by early Oct. The days are usually warm and sunny and rain is less likely during this period.

PERTH TO PORT HEDLAND pp. 164–169

🛣 Great Northern Highway (1649km)

The Great Northern Hwy is an important, direct inland route linking Perth with the far north of Western Australia. It crosses the rich grain-growing area of the south, the sheep properties in the centre of the state and the larger cattle properties in the north. Many of the frontier towns along this route are steeped in mining history, and mining continues at several large sites alongside the highway, including the iron-ore operations at Newman. The spectacular, rugged, red Pilbara gorges are easily reached from this route before the highway rolls in to busy Port Hedland.

⚓ PLAN YOUR TRIP

The Great Northern Hwy winds through small rural towns as it heads north into a thriving grain-growing region. Australia's only monastic town, New Norcia, attracts tourists who come to enjoy a guided tour or just buy a freshly baked loaf from the monastery's renowned bakery. As the highway continues north to Mount Magnet it passes through extensive wildflower country, and past historic goldmining towns.

The long section of highway from Mount Magnet to Newman travels through the heart of the state's mining country. The highway links the goldmining towns in the south with the iron-ore mining towns in the north. Make time to take a tour of the impressive BHP Billiton Mt Whaleback mining operations at Newman. Road trains and wildlife frequent this stretch of road, so be wary of both.

North of Newman, Karijini National Park is a highlight of this route. Its spectacular red Pilbara gorges are easily reached from the highway, which winds through scenic ranges before approaching the coastal plain. The section through Munjina Gorge, south of the Auski Roadhouse, is quite stunning.

Port Hedland is a busy industrial centre with plenty to see and do, and it's close to great coastal areas for fishing.

☁ BEST TIME TO GO

The best time to travel in the far north of Western Australia is in the cooler, drier months (Apr–Oct). In the south of the state, year-round travel is possible.

Louth free camp

SYDNEY TO ADELAIDE pp. 174–185

 Great Western Highway, Mitchell Highway, Barrier Highway (1685km)

The Great Western Hwy climbs west through the spectacular Blue Mountains, a formidable barrier shielding inland New South Wales from the coast. The busy tourist centres of Leura and Katoomba soon give way to numerous large towns and small villages, like Orange, Dubbo, Nyngan, Cobar and Wilcannia. Broken Hill is a destination with character – the historic mining town is now home to a strong artistic community. Silverton, a ghost town to the north-west, has also attracted some excellent artists. The highway drifts westward into South Australia across boundless plains before swinging south to Burra, a historic copper-mining centre. Gawler is the northern gateway to Adelaide, and just a short drive from the famous Barossa Valley.

⚓ PLAN YOUR TRIP

From the bustling coastal capital, Sydney, the highway winds steeply into the Blue Mountains, passing by Leura, where lush manicured gardens thrive, and on to Katoomba, near one of Australia's most photographed geographic features – the Three Sisters.

Down the short and steep Victoria Pass and past Lithgow, the route passes through Bathurst, where it's possible to drive around the public roads that make up Mount Panorama – the famous motor-racing circuit. Watch the speed limit, though.

Between Orange and Dubbo, the limestone caves at Wellington are worth a stop, while in Dubbo the superb Old Gaol and the fascinating Taronga Western Plains Zoo are great attractions.

West of Dubbo the highway gradually enters the real outback, passing through the large town of Narromine, a popular gliding centre. Beyond it continues through the cotton fields near Nevertire and on to the historic mining town of Cobar.

Between Cobar and Broken Hill, the towns are few and far between, and the best spots are visited by zigzagging west, only meeting the highway when you need to cross it to get to the next great spot before finally settling into the wonderful outback town of Broken Hill.

From Broken Hill to Adelaide, the Barrier Hwy sweeps into South Australia across vast saltbush plains. The town of Burra is steeped in history dating back to its early copper mining activities and the Clare Valley is an important wine region.

Adelaide is the country's most laidback capital city, set on the wide curves of the River Torrens and the wonderful beaches of South Australia's mid-coast. It's a place easily explored where each day is finished watching the sun set over the Gulf St Vincent.

☁ BEST TIME TO GO

The far west of New South Wales (and even Adelaide) can be extremely hot during summer, while the Blue Mountains can be savagely cold in winter – it sometimes snows. I find spring and autumn ideal times to travel these regions.

GUNDAGAI TO MILDURA pp. 170–173

 Hume Highway, Sturt Highway (636km)

The Hume and Sturt highways combination is a great tourist route linking Sydney to Adelaide. This section between Gundagai and Mildura crosses the barren Hay Plains, on the edge of the New South Wales outback, and skirts highly intensive rice-growing regions. The highway loosely follows first the Murrumbidgee River then the Murray River beyond Balranald. While major centres along this route are interesting destinations, it's one of the most remote detours, into Mungo National Park, that is the obvious highlight.

⚓ PLAN YOUR TRIP

The Sturt Hwy is mostly a well-maintained, two-lane road, passing through grain-growing and grazing land along the Murrumbidgee River. Wagga Wagga is a large regional centre, while Narrandera and Hay service local communities. The rich Murrumbidgee Irrigation Area, the town of Griffith and its surrounding wine-producing areas lie to the north of Darlington Point.

West of Hay, the highway crosses a large expanse of flat, featureless countryside known as the Hay Plains. Westbound travellers often experience much higher than normal fuel consumption along this section, especially when the prevailing south-westerly wind blows. From Balranald, off-road capable travellers can head north to the ancient Mungo National Park, where some of the oldest human remains in the world have been found.

Closer to Mildura, the road follows the Murray River through undulating, sandy country where vineyards and fruit orchards predominate.

☁ BEST TIME TO GO

Autumn and spring are the best for travel as summer temperatures are high and can soar to over 40°C on the hottest days. Winters are cool and the majority of rain falls during these months.

ROCKHAMPTON TO THREE WAYS ROADHOUSE pp. 186–189

Capricorn Highway, Landsborough (Matilda Highway), Barkly Highway (1955km)

Explore Central Queensland on the highways that link Rockhampton on the east coast to the Stuart Hwy in the heart of the Northern Territory. This popular tourist route passes through the heart of Australia's cattle country, the Central Queensland coalfields and the cosmopolitan mining centre of Mount Isa. Further west, the highway crosses the stark Mitchell-grass plains of the Barkly Tableland before joining the Stuart Hwy at Three Ways Roadhouse, north of the historic goldmining centre of Tennant Creek. Major tourist attractions in this area include Longreach's Australian Stockman's Hall of Fame and the Waltzing Matilda Centre in Winton.

⚓ PLAN YOUR TRIP

This route stays just south of the Tropic of Capricorn until Longreach. Along the way it carries travellers west past expansive cattle stations and follows the major rail line between the coastal ports and central Queensland coal mines. Travellers can try their hand at fossicking for precious gems in the rewarding gem fields around Emerald and Rubyvale.

From Barcaldine and its famous Tree of Knowledge the Landsborough Hwy carries travellers further west to Longreach's famous Australian Stockman's Hall of Fame. Further west is Winton, where you can race chickens, find dinosaurs and relive the history of Banjo Paterson's poem 'Waltzing Matilda'.

Rockhampton

Leaving Winton, the highway continues north-west to Cloncurry. This interesting stretch of highway, with some photogenic mesa formations, is probably best known for the famous Blue Heeler Hotel at Kynuna and McKinlay's Walkabout Creek Hotel, which featured in *Crocodile Dundee*. Cloncurry was the site of the first Royal Flying Doctor Service flight and it's a great place to learn of the iconic service's history.

West of Cloncurry, the highway passes through the mining metropolis of Mount Isa, with its great museums and mining experiences, then on to the historic border town of Camooweal. In the Northern Territory, the Barkly Hwy climbs over the tableland it's named for on the way to Australia's great central, north–south road – the Stuart Hwy.

☁ BEST TIME TO GO

During the winter months, the weather is pleasant, however, temperatures and humidity rise during the build-up to the wet season towards the end of the year. The best time to travel is Apr–Nov.

TOWNSVILLE TO CLONCURRY
pp. 190–193

Flinders Highway (774km)

Travel deep into the Queensland outback down the Flinders Highway, a strategic route linking the major coastal city of Townsville with inland industrial centres. Although the highway deteriorates west of Torrens Creek, the attractions along this route are great. The historic mining centre of Charters Towers is an exciting town to explore and the fascinating dinosaur trail through Hughenden and Richmond certainly makes the journey worthwhile.

⚓ PLAN YOUR TRIP

The Flinders Hwy, also known as the Overlander's Way, leads inland to busy Charters Towers then to the smaller gold-rush town of Pentland, which was an important town for Australia's war efforts during WWII. Next it passes through Prairie, from where you can detour to Kooroorinya Falls, popular for birdwatching, before reaching Hughenden and the beginning of dinosaur country.

From Hughenden, the route continues west into the heart of Queensland's outback and deeper into dinosaur country, where palaeontological digs have uncovered some of the most significant prehistoric fossil examples in the world. Check them out at Kronosaurus Korner. The road then continues through Julia Creek, many regular travellers' favourite outback Queensland town, before finishing at Cloncurry. This important mining and cattle centre, at the intersection with the Landsborough Hwy, is the home of the Royal Flying Doctor Service.

☁ BEST TIME TO GO

Summer is hot and humid in this region, so the warm days and cool nights of the temperate months are the best times to travel – May–Oct.

The Outback Way

KALGOORLIE TO GERALDTON

pp. 194–197

🛣 **Goldfields Highway, Sandstone-Leinster Road, Mount Magnet-Sandstone Road, Geraldton-Mount Magnet Road (1020km)**

The route from Kalgoorlie to the Great Northern Hwy at Mount Magnet and on to the North West Coastal Hwy at Geraldton is a viable alternative to travelling through the outer suburbs of Perth. The roads are good, the scenery is interesting, and services are available. History buffs will be enthralled by the goldmining heritage of the region, and can even choose to follow the Monsignor Hawes Heritage Trail. Wildlife is also evident and numerous wedge-tailed eagles are often seen feeding along the roadsides.

⚑ PLAN YOUR TRIP

Commencing at Kalgoorlie-Boulder, now the prosperous key city in the goldfields, the Goldfields Hwy is a wide sealed road that carries large volumes of traffic associated with the mining industry. It passes a string of historic mining settlements and ghost towns, and takes in one of the most captivating wide-scale artistic installations in Australia on the desolate, dry Lake Ballard. The Leinster to Mount Magnet section is wide and easy driving, with plenty of rest areas – the last part is sealed too.

West of Mount Magnet, the road is still good, as it passes many mine workings that dot the plains as the road continues south-west. Through here, the famous architect-priest, Monsignor Hawes left his mark on the landscape, having designed 15 classic church buildings. All of them can be seen on the heritage trail that bears his name.

As the road approaches the coast it winds through hills and across the coastal plain, sharing the way with road trains delivering ore to Geraldton's ports.

☁ BEST TIME TO GO

Winter and spring attract multitudes of tourists to this region, all hoping to explore the vast fields of wildflowers. It's a good time to visit, but while the days may be warm and dry, the nights can be clear and cold, so just be aware of plummeting temperatures. Summer is very hot, so is best avoided.

THE OUTBACK WAY – HUGHENDEN TO KALGOORLIE pp. 198–202

🛣 **Kennedy Developmental Road, Winton Road, Donohue Highway, Plenty Highway, Stuart Highway, Lasseter Highway, Tjukaruru Road, Great Central Road, Goldfields Highway (3290km)**

The Outback Way officially links the remote central Queensland town of Winton with the remote Western Australian outback town of Laverton, but practically it links Hughenden with Kalgoorlie – or even Cairns and Perth! At 3300km it's dubbed Australia's longest shortcut. Along the way it mixes lonely sealed highways with remote gravel ones to cross three states, passing through the MacDonnell Ranges and past Uluru before venturing through the barren desert regions in the centre of Western Australia. There are plans to fully seal the route, and each season the trip gets easier, so even if you're not up for it now, this is an epic cross-country trip to pencil in for the future.

⚑ PLAN YOUR TRIP

Although the Outback Way doesn't officially start until Winton, if it's truly being used as a 'shortcut' most will join it from tropical north Queensland. It passes through Hughenden, the major pastoral centre on the banks of the Flinders River, before taking the easy, but long trip south-west to Winton and its fascinating dinosaur fossil sites.

From Winton, the Outback Way tracks through Middleton, site of one of Queensland's most isolated pubs, to Boulia, home of the famed and feared Min Min lights. Heading west from Boulia, the road is unsealed but generally good until the Northern Territory border.

Here it becomes the famous Plenty Hwy, and a number of great cattle station owners have opened up their properties to travellers along this route, offering modest outback campsites and essentials, like fuel.

When the Plenty meets the Stuart Hwy, here's your chance to explore the wildly beautiful MacDonnell Ranges, the vibrant city of Alice Springs and the sacred wonders of Uluṟu and Kata Tjuṯa.

West of these amazing formations, the road is again unsealed and a transit permit is required. It crosses the Western Australian border passing by small Aboriginal communities where wonderful artwork is often on display. You can also learn about famous outback road builder Len Beadell. This is a remote area, with varying opening times, so be sure to call ahead to your next stops to ensure fuel is available.

Eventually, the Great Central Rd emerges into Western Australia's goldfields, where historic and bustling mining towns have all sorts of attractions to offer. Don't miss taking a diversion to the amazing artistic installation of Antony Gormley's Inside Australia at Lake Ballard, as you head south to Kalgoorlie.

☁ BEST TIME TO GO

The arid outback regions of Australia are incredibly hot during summer and many remote services will have limited facilities available due to reduced tourist traffic. Plan to travel between autumn and spring to make the most of the cooler weather.

THE FLINDERS RANGES pp. 203–205

 Flinders Ranges Way (335km)

On the driest continent in the world, in the driest state in Australia, the Flinders Ranges is one of the driest mountain areas in the state, and are all the more stunning for it.

Rising dramatically out of the seemingly flat plains before it, the Flinders Ranges is one of the most accessible outback regions that's easily explored on a mixture of good sealed roads, well-maintained gravel roads or adventurous off-road tracks. Within its bounds you'll discover wonderful hospitality, amazing mountains and a history that spans billions of years.

📌 PLAN YOUR TRIP

The Flinders Ranges are easily accessed from Adelaide, or further north at Port Augusta. From the relative lushness around the Gulf St Vincent, the landscape very quickly gives way to outback scrubland, dry rivers and endless plains as it climbs into the southern Flinders, where sheep share the land with wineries.

From Hawker, the unofficial gateway to the Flinders Ranges, the rugged mountains rise up almost suddenly from the flat landscape. This is dry and barren country, often seeing no rain in a calendar year – last time I was there it hadn't rained for 300 days. However, many historic sheep stations welcome travellers to their properties, which are open for exploration. Don't miss Rawnsley Park Station, Willow Springs and Wilpena Pound. If you have a four-wheel drive, take the long road north to the former sheep-station turned wilderness sanctuary at Arkaroola.

Visit the historic copper-mining town of Blinman before heading to the western side of the ranges where camel, kangaroo and emu are on the menu at the famous Prairie Hotel. Choose where to continue north, further into the interior, past Leigh Creek and Maree, or back south to Hawker, completing a wonderful loop of an amazing landscape.

☁ BEST TIME TO GO

Most of the year the days are sunny, but throughout summer the temperatures can be extreme, often over 40°C. Plan your travel between autumn and spring to make the most of the region.

Skytrek, Willow Springs

JERILDERIE TO COBAR

NEED TO KNOW

 497km

🏠 Free sites, inexpensive camping areas, holiday resorts

☁ Spring is the best time to visit Griffith, when its gardens and orchards are all in bloom.

👁 Griffith and its gardens and wineries, Cobar's mining heritage

🛣 This is a good, well-maintained stretch of road.

🍴 The best facilities are found in Griffith.

⚠ None apply

Cobar Railway Station

INTRODUCTION

The Kidman Way heads north from Jerilderie, across the edge of the Hay Plains, through the incredibly rich farming land and wine regions of Griffith, before stepping into the edge of the real outback on the way to Cobar. Although the terrain can often seem featureless, there are some great towns to stop in, as well as good camping areas and caravan parks along the way. Be wary of slow-moving tractors on the highway, especially during the rice harvest. Also, expect the best, and worst, of highway conditions.

WHERE TO GO

Heading north from **Jerilderie**, you have two options. One eventually takes you to the central Queensland coast, via the New South Wales central west. The other goes straight up into the outback, eventually arriving at the Gulf of Carpentaria.

First off you'll pass through New South Wales' youngest town, **Coleambally**, which was established in 1968 to support the local irrigators. Services are limited to the pleasant picnic area and basic amenities.

Further north, on the Murrumbidgee River, the old town of **Darlington Point** was established as a river crossing point. The first bridge, built in 1905 and replaced in 1979, now forms the entrance to the caravan park. I once accidentally booked myself in there – thinking I was booking into Darlington Beach, 1200km away. After I didn't show up, the owners called to make sure I was safe, having waited for me until 10.30pm.

That sort of hospitality continues further north, as you head to **Griffith**. A town designed by Walter Burley Griffin, it's something of an oasis on the edge of the outback that surprises many people. Griffith is one of the premier wine-growing regions in Australia, and has a significant Italian heritage, as many Italian migrants flocked here after WWII. As such, there is very good dining and coffee in town, and exceptional gardens scattered throughout the region, especially at many of the wineries. During spring, Griffith puts on the annual Springfest, which is well known for its orange sculptures, open gardens and large community street party.

One of the more morbid pieces of Australian heritage can be found in the small town of **Merriwagga**, an area which is often referred to as the 'Black Stump District'.

As the story goes, the name arose from the unfortunate death of Barbara Baine, a bullocky's wife, who was burned to death in a campfire in 1886. Her remains, according to her husband when he found them, resembled a black stump. A monument to the event is found in the middle of town.

First described by the explorer John Oxley as 'useless for all purposes of civilised man', **Hillston** is now an agricultural centre with most services and basic shopping. Plus it's the last place for fuel before Cobar, over 250km north.

Cobar has a long mining history and several fine buildings. One of my favourites is the Great Western Hotel, which has the longest verandah of any pub in New South Wales. Copper was discovered at Cobar in 1869 and the area became a magnet for Cornish miners. In fact, the CSA (Cornish, Scottish and Australian) Mine is still the largest producer of copper in the country. Since 1991, gold has also been mined at Cobar, and from the Fort Bourke Hill Lookout, just east of town, you can look down into the New Cobar Open Cut Goldmine. Actually it's not new, but was in fact Cobar's first mine. There are good camping options around Cobar, some of them free.

DON'T MISS

→ Award-winning whites – Near Griffith

There are several significant wineries in the Griffith area, including the McWilliam's cellar door at Hanwood, which was established in 1913. This winery is close to the Kidman Way and has a unique, barrel-shaped wine-tasting centre, as well as a museum of vineyard memorabilia. Nearby, De Bortoli Wines has acres and acres of landscaped gardens, the pleasure project of owner Emeri De Bortoli. It's a very simple pleasure to wander her gardens after a good wine-tasting session.

→ A rich copper lode – Cobar

Copper was discovered here in 1869, and the ore, which is said to be called 'gubar' in the local Indigenous tongue, even gives the town its name. With the development of mines, there was an influx of Cornish migrants, and many local surnames are Cornish in origin. Visit the Great Cobar Heritage Centre, a terrific museum, for a glimpse into Cobar's history.

TRAVEL TIP

Some caravan parks in the area may, from time to time, be home to seasonal workers. Cotton chippers, fruit pickers and processing-plant workers follow the work across Australia and many stay in caravan parks for the affordable accommodation on offer. To be sure of a site it's wise to phone ahead and book, or at least check availability. Most caravan parks, do, however, retain some sites for tourists, even during the busiest times.

WHERE TO STAY

283 Jerilderie Motel and Caravan Park

$$

📍 121 Newell Hwy, Jerilderie
📞 (03) 5886 1366

Situated just off the Newell Hwy, this flat grassy caravan park has very good amenities and well-sized sites to suit most travellers' needs.

284 Darlington Point Riverside Caravan Park

$$

📍 Kidman Way, Darlington Point
📞 (02) 6968 4237
💻 www.darlingtonpointcaravanpark.com

This small, quiet caravan park offers large grassy sites and good clean amenities. There is a boat ramp and excellent fishing offered on the nearby Murrumbidgee River.

285 Griffith Caravan Village

$$$

📍 MacKay Ave and Gardiner Rd, Griffith
📞 (02) 6962 3785
💻 www.griffithcaravanvillage.com.au

In a city known for its gardens, this simple, but inviting caravan park does itself proud. It has nice grassy sites, some with drive-thru access and plenty of shade. There is also a children's playground, pool and it is close to the city's attractions.

286 Hillston Caravan Park

$$

📍 101 High St, Hillston
📞 (02) 6967 2575

This caravan park is conveniently located within walking distance of town and the local RSL club, which offers good hot meals. Sites are level and grassy, and amenities are dated but clean and well kept. A good overnight stop after a long drive.

287 Billabourie Riverside Tourist Park

$$

📍 Mt Grace Rd, Hillston
📞 0427 674 131

A birdwatcher's paradise in a beautiful riverside setting, this caravan park has good, modern facilities and nice level grassy sites.

288 Cornish rest area

$

📍 Corner of Barrier Hwy and Kidman Way, Cobar

A simple free camping area under the iconic Cobar sign on the outskirts of town. Facilities are limited and there's a 24-hour limit on stays.

COBAR TO BARRINGUN

NEED TO KNOW

🕐	**315km**
🏠	**Free camping areas; full-featured, outback caravan parks**
☁	**Winter, spring and autumn**
👁	**Bourke and its surrounds**
🛣	**Long and flat with plenty of opportunities to overtake.**
🍴	**This is a remote part of the New South Wales outback and only basic services are available.**
⚠	**None apply**

PV *Jandra*

INTRODUCTION

Between Cobar and Barringun, on the Queensland/New South Wales border, you'll pass through remote outback areas, but without sugarcoating it, only the town of Bourke is really worth spending a lot of time in. '"Bourke is not a town," they said, "but a city whose borders are hundreds of miles apart."' This classic line from Mary Durack's amazing account of pioneering life, *Kings in Grass Castles*, still accurately sums up the town. Colloquially it's seen as the second most remote place in Australia, followed only by places out the back of it. It's one of my favourite outback locations, and I love going back.

WHERE TO GO

Spend any time in **Bourke** and you quickly come to understand that there's more to it than just red dirt, gidgee trees and big skies. The best place to camp is at Kidman's Camp, north of town. It's by far the favourite of travellers, so empties and fills like the tide as its transient population slowly fill it each afternoon, then empty it each morning.

As well as Kidman Camp, there are two popular free camping areas on the banks of the Darling River. Mays Bend, to the north of town, a little way past Kidman Camp is not signposted, however a short, red-dirt track leads to the river where there's space to set up camp. Give it a miss if there's any rain forecast though, or you'll never get out.

On the other side of town, the Fisheries is a series of bends in the river with a number of camping areas spread out along them. Facilities are restricted to a few barbecues and fireplaces, but it has a very pretty view over the river.

Up until the 1930s, Bourke was a port at the head of the Darling River and paddlesteamers carried the local wool clip from here to market. Today, the replica paddlesteamer, the *PV Jandra*, runs daily tours from Kidman Camp, which include a commentary on the region's history over the hour-long ride.

Bourke has a long agricultural history and cotton, introduced in 1966, is now an important local crop. Citrus fruit, grapes and a range of horticultural crops also contribute greatly to the local economy. The cotton plants reach maturity in late summer and harvesting usually takes place during March.

One of the town's highest profile attractions is the Back O' Bourke Exhibition Centre, which recounts the legends of the back country, the history of the Darling and the growth of Bourke. Opened at the beginning of 2008, the seven million dollar centre on the north side of town is alongside the Kidman Way. It's well worth taking the time to stop and explore.

From Bourke, there's a great circuit you can do that takes in two excellent camping areas and one quirky outback pub. Mt Oxley, a large granite outcrop, is as alien to the surrounding landscape as Uluru is to Yulara. While it's not as big, or as famous, it's part of the Ngemba people's creation story, and very significant. It is on private property, but permission can be obtained to camp at the top. You'll need to organise access through the visitor centre before you head out as the gate at the entrance is locked. From Oxley, take the unsealed, and very red, Oxley Rd to the Tarcoon–Byrock Rd and turn right. Once you meet the Mitchell Hwy, you'll be at the Mulga Creek Hotel at Byrock, which is always friendly, likes to entertain late, and has a great camping area out the back. Behind the campground are Aboriginal rock holes, which have a short, signposted bush-tucker walk around them. Avoid this detour if it's been raining, though.

Between Bourke and Barringun, 140km to the north, the only town you'll pass through is **Enngonia**, a small residential community with a pub. A mobile coffee trailer regularly sets up to fuel travellers, if not their vehicles. Barringun is similarly small, although its roadhouse has a camping area behind it.

As fuel isn't available at Barringun anymore, you won't be able to fuel up again until Cunnamulla – 250km north of Bourke.

DON'T MISS

**→ Poetry on a plate –
   Kidman Camp, Bourke**
Each Tue, Thurs and Sat night, Kidmans Camp hosts a bush poetry night, with a very hearty campfire dinner. As of 2018, Frank Povah, a local musician, poet and publisher has taken the reins. A Bourke local, he was the managing editor of the *Western Herald* – Bourke's now defunct local paper, whose most famous employee was Henry Lawson. It's easily one of the highlights of Bourke. Admission fees apply; book in at the camp's reception.

→ The Bourke cemetery – Bourke
I can never resist a stroll through the Bourke cemetery. It's older than the town itself and provides a fascinating history lesson about the town and the outback in general. Among the more interesting and heartbreaking headstones are those of three children killed in 1888 at a children's picnic, and that of Sergeant John McCabe, shot dead by bushranger Captain Starlight. Fred Hollows is also buried here. Nearly everyone old enough to remember him has a story of the selfless humanitarian. Bourke Indigenous elder Phil Sullivan remembers him as a hard man to work with, who loved the Indigenous people of Bourke as much as they loved him. The cemetery is easily one of the most fascinating places around Bourke.

**→ The Outback Show – Back
   O' Bourke Exhibition Centre**
I highly recommend the Outback Show, where horseman Luke Thomas shows what it was like in the outback's pioneering days. Combining cleverly trained animals and stock, the highly choreographed and often (crudely) funny show is very entertaining. It's on every day Apr–Oct and entry fees apply.

WHERE TO STAY

289 Kidmans Camp

$$$ ★

⬡ **Mitchell Hwy, North Bourke**
📞 **(02) 6872 1612**
🖥 **www.kidmanscamp.com.au**

Located just 8km from the heart of town, on the banks of the mighty Darling River, this caravan park has large grassy spaces with good clean amenities. Every Tue, Thurs and Sun you can treat yourself to a delicious slow-cooked meal, dessert and show, all served around the campfire at the park's 'poetry on a plate' dinner. Fees apply.

290 Mays Bend camping area

⬡ **Bullamunta Rd, North Bourke**

This beautiful bush camping area is located right beside the river and is home to an abundance of native wildlife. There are no amenities or drinking water available and the dirt roads become very slippery mud after rain.

291 Bush Tucker Inn Caravan Park

$$
⬡ **Mitchell Hwy, Barringun**
📞 **(02) 6874 7584**

Tucked away behind the roadhouse this camping area is a great overnighter for those doing the long haul to Queensland. Power outlets are limited but there is plenty of unpowered room. Amenities are basic, but clean, and the roadhouse offers delicious hot meals and coffee.

Sheep at the Outback Show, Bourke

BARRINGUN TO AUGATHELLA

Charleville Cosmos Centre

INTRODUCTION

The Mitchell Highway follows, roughly, the course of the Warrego River to the north, all the way to Augathella, 400km north. Along the way it runs through a region dominated by large leasehold properties and open plains of mulga and eucalypt forest. It's barren, but beautiful. The road passes through some typical Queensland outback towns along the way, with plenty of opportunities to camp on the river.

WHERE TO GO

Each of the four outback towns along this section of the Mitchell Highway are found on the banks of the Warrego River. **Cunnamulla** is a service centre for the local pastoral industry and a crossroads for traffic heading west to Innamincka or the south-west Queensland oil and gas fields. The town has a large number of historic buildings which can be seen along the heritage trail. There are a number of popular caravan parks in town too.

Further north, **Wyandra** is a tiny township with many unoccupied buildings. The old gaol, which has actually been moved from its original location to the nearby caravan park, is an interesting stopover.

On the river is a small free camping area with a limited number of spots and basic toilet and shower facilities. The town also has a hotel and small store, but relies heavily on passing tourists for income.

Further upstream, **Charleville** is a major regional centre and an important service centre for a large sheep and cattle industry. The town has numerous historical buildings, including the grand Corones Hotel. Cobb & Co. also operated a coach-building factory here for 34 years before closing in 1920, when motorised vehicles replaced the coaches. In the past two decades, the town has been twice ravaged by flooding of the Warrego River.

Charleville is also an important railway terminal on the Brisbane to Quilpie line. It's the terminus of the *Westlander* which has been running between Brisbane and Charleville since 1954.

One of the town's most popular attractions is the Royal Flying Doctor Service Visitor Centre. It has a small cinema which shows a film depicting everyday life in this important service. It also has a display of past and present equipment and a shop stocked with a range of RFDS merchandise. Entry fees apply and it's open 8.30am–4.30pm weekdays and 10am–4.30pm weekends. Contact (07) 4654 7771.

Further north, **Augathella**, most of which is set back from the highway, is a small town with facilities limited to the roadhouse, motel and caravan park. The Ellangowan Hotel is a popular stopover for travellers thanks to its inexpensive meals and free camping area out the back.

DON'T MISS

→ **A grand old hotel – Charleville**
The luxurious Corones Hotel in Charleville was an illustrious social meeting place in the 1930s and '40s. Take a guided tour of this grand establishment and hear the interesting tales of its famous guests and days gone by. Tours begin at 2pm most days and the tour fee includes afternoon tea. Contact (07) 4654 1022.

→ **Look to the heavens – Charleville**
Charleville Cosmos Centre is a fascinating astronomy institution with powerful Meade telescopes that make the most of the clear, light-pollution-free skies of the outback. Gaze at the skies with the help of an expert guide and learn about Indigenous cosmology. Entry fees apply and it's open every day except Sun. Bookings are essential for night-time observatory sessions. Contact (07) 4654 7771.

EXPLORE AUSTRALIA BY CARAVAN & MOTORHOME

WHERE TO STAY

292 Cunnamulla Tourist Park

📍 65 Watson St, Cunnamulla
📞 (07) 4655 1421
💻 www.cunnamullapark.com

TOP PARKS

Set amongst the trees in a quiet, peaceful little country town this caravan park has good, clean facilities, allows pets and is walking distance from the town proper.

293 Wyandra Caravan Park and Store

📍 35–37 Railway St, Wyandra
📞 (07) 4654 9212

This caravan park has good, clean amenities and level sites. There is a store attached to the park which has a selection of hot foods available including burgers and fish and chips.

294 Bailey Bar Caravan Park

📍 196 King St, Charleville
📞 (07) 4654 1744
💻 www.charlevillebaileybar.com.au

TOP PARKS

This is a very good caravan park in a quiet position off the main drag. The lawns are well maintained and the facilities nice and clean. Bookings are essential during peak periods.

Bilby in Charleville

Sheep-shearing in Cunnamulla

Wyandra

AUGATHELLA TO BARCALDINE

Blackall Woolscour

INTRODUCTION

Passing through wide open grazing country either side of the Landsborough Highway, we're on our way beyond the Black Stump. The highway runs through some of outback Queensland's oldest towns and into regions whose populations have shaped the political climate for over a century. The road is fully sealed, in good condition and well maintained, plus there are plenty of opportunities to overtake, or be overtaken.

WHERE TO GO

At just over an hour's drive north of Augathella, **Tambo** is the oldest town in central western Queensland, with its settlement dating back to 1863. Lying to the west of the rugged limestone country of the Carnarvon Range, it is a rural service town for the surrounding sheep and cattle stations. There are basic services for travellers, as well as one of the most adored teddy bear shops in all of Australia. Tambo Teddies, in the main street, has an amazing range of teddy bears made from sheepskin. A number of local women handcraft each one. If you visit, you'll have trouble resisting the urge to buy at least one.

Further north and west, and on the banks of the Barcoo River, **Blackall** is at the centre of a large merino sheep farming area with many large stations nearby. Jackie Howe, the famous shearer, lived in Blackall and made both blade and mechanical shearing records on local stations. Blackall is also another location claiming to be the origin of the phrase 'black stump'. Locals say it derives from a surveyor's reference point from 1880 that was dubbed 'the black stump'. A replica of the original can be found on Thistle St.

Although there are plenty of great places to get a feed along the Matilda Way, one of the best is the simple camp-oven roast dinners put on nightly at the Blackall Caravan Park May–Aug. Everyone is welcome, but bookings are essential.

It's another 100km north to **Barcaldine**, although along the way there's a nice little free camping area at Douglas Ponds Creek. It extends much farther past the entrance sign, so continue away from the highway for the best spots.

Barcaldine lies at the junction of the Capricorn and Landsborough highways and the town was founded in 1886 when the railway pushed west from Rockhampton. Soon after, Barcaldine became famous as the centre of the shearers strike of 1891, and the Australian Labor Party was formed as a result of the strike meetings. The tree under which the strike meetings took place became known as the Tree of Knowledge and stood in Barcaldine for another 115 years before it was mysteriously poisoned in an act of vandalism in 2006. So significant is the tree that the original trunk has been preserved and is on display in town as part of a spectacular memorial which is best viewed at night. Saplings from cuttings have been preserved (and some grow in Barcaldine) while the tree was also cloned – one clone is growing healthily in Brisbane.

DON'T MISS

→ **Legendary shearer – Blackall**
On Alice Downs Station in 1892, Jackie Howie, a gun shearer, managed to shear 321 sheep in 7 hrs and 40 min with blade shears. Jackie lived and died in Blackall and is buried in the town cemetery. His incredible record stood until electric shears were introduced in the 1950s! A memorial to Jackie's achievement stands outside the visitor centre in Short St.

→ **How they toiled – Barcaldine**
The Australian Workers Heritage Centre at Barcaldine showcases the experiences of workers and the difficult conditions in which they often laboured in days gone by. This popular tribute is in the centre of town on two hectares of landscaped gardens. It's open daily 10am–4pm and entry fees apply. Contact (07) 4651 2422.

→ **An old woolscour – near Blackall**
The historic woolscour at Blackall operated until 1978 and is the last remaining example of a steam-powered plant in Australia.

The scour is located next to a natural artesian bore and there is also a 20-stand shearing shed attached to the plant. Tours are available daily on the hour 9am–4pm.

WHERE TO STAY

295 **Tambo Mill Motel and Caravan Park**

$$$

📍 34 Arthur St, Tambo
📞 (07) 4621 7000
🖥 www.tambomotel.com.au

Located right in the centre of town, this clean and grassy caravan park is within walking distance of local cafes and there is a beautiful saltwater pool onsite.

296 **Blackall Caravan Park**

$$$

📍 53 Garden St, Blackall
📞 (07) 4657 4816
🖥 www.blackallcaravanpark.com.au

Set back from the highway, this quiet, shady caravan park offers flat, grassy sites. It is within walking distance of the main shops and May–Aug you can enjoy a camp-oven roast dinner onsite complete with damper and syrup.

297 **Barcaldine Tourist Park**

$$

📍 51–65 Box St, Barcaldine
📞 (07) 4651 6066
🖥 www.barcaldinetouristandcaravanpark.com.au

Easily accessible off the Matilda Hwy, this caravan park offers flat, grassy sites and May–Sept you can enjoy free damper and billy tea in the afternoons.

Barcaldine Tree of Knowledge

BARCALDINE TO WINTON

Australian Age of Dinosaurs

INTRODUCTION

Well and truly into Queensland's outback, this area is particularly rich in unique Australian tourist attractions, which can make it hard to choose which to see and what to miss. From dinosaur footprints to songs about shearers, there's plenty to do, so consider allowing a little extra spending money and time when passing through. The quality of the road has also greatly improved over the years. It runs alongside the railway line for most of the way, so trainloads of cattle heading to market are a common sight.

WHERE TO GO

If you travel between Barcaldine and Ilfracombe Aug–Sept, there's a good chance winter rains have blanketed the area in wildflowers and attracted multitudes of birds to the area, so the drive can be very pretty.

Ilfracombe was once the transport centre for Wellshot Station, one of the most productive sheep stations in the country and the location of Australia's first motorised mail service. Today this small town provides basic services for travellers. There is an interesting machinery display that stretches along the roadside for the length of the town, affectionately called the Ilfracombe Machinery Mile. Some of the items are very rare, so I recommend stopping for a walk through them.

Only a short drive further west, is **Longreach**, which has a number of excellent tourist attractions, including the Australian Stockman's Hall of Fame and Outback Heritage Centre. Many people travel here specifically to visit this spectacular tribute to stockmen and the outback. Qantas relocated its operations to Longreach early in its history and the company's original hangar is now the Qantas Founders Museum. The town is also an important regional centre for a large sheep and cattle area, and home to a large agricultural college. It's really popular during the cooler months when the caravan parks are often very busy. Even the well-known free camping area at Longreach Waterhole, 35km north-west of town, is often full to the brim.

Two hours north of Longreach, **Winton** abounds with outback history. The township claims the first public performance of Banjo Paterson's 'Waltzing Matilda' took place here in 1895 at the North Gregory Hotel (which is still there today). The Waltzing Matilda Centre in the main street now pays tribute to this famous song. Winton was also the home of Qantas' first registered office, which opened in 1920. The remarkable dinosaur 'stampede' prints in Lark Quarry Conservation Park are about 110km south of town. Like Longreach, Winton is a very popular town through winter, with a number of great camping options and good services.

DON'T MISS

→ **The first home of Qantas – Longreach**

The Qantas Founders Museum is in the company's original hangar at Longreach. Discover some of the early history of one of the world's great airlines. There is a full-size replica of an Avro Space 504K, the first type of aircraft operated by Qantas. Standing proudly alongside the museum is a Boeing 747, a landmark on the horizon as you approach Longreach from the east. A number of other historic aircraft are also on display, including a Boeing 707 and Douglas DC3. It's open daily 9am–5pm and entry fees apply. Contact (07) 4658 3737.

Qantas Founders Museum, Longreach

→ **Racing rainbow chickens – Winton**

In the same pub that hosted the first performance of one of Australia's most classic tunes is the quirkiest spectacle in Queensland. Each night at the North Gregory Hotel, Ben's Rainbow Chickens race around a pen following a remote-controlled car full of feed. Each chicken is auctioned off, and the winning chicken's owner gets half the takings, with the other half going to charity. It's a really incredible night out.

TAKE THE SHORT CUT

Winton is the official beginning of the Outback Way (*see* p. 198), a cross-country touring route that passes through Queensland, the Northern Territory and Western Australia to finish in Laverton. It's dubbed 'Australia's longest short cut'.

WHERE TO STAY

298 Ilfracombe Caravan Park

📍 **10 Main Ave, Ilfracombe**
📞 **(07) 4658 1510**

This small but popular caravan park is in an excellent location right next door to the Wellshot Hotel. Flat, grassy sites and slabs are available. A great spot to stop for a few days and explore the surrounding country.

299 Longreach Tourist Park

📍 **12 Thrush Rd, Longreach**
📞 **(07) 4658 1781**
🖥 **www.longreachtouristpark.com.au**

Just 2km from the town centre, this caravan park is in walking distance of the Australian Stockman's Hall of Fame. It has good facilities, including a pool and onsite restaurant with live entertainment most nights during peak season (Apr–Oct).

300 North Gregory Hotel

📍 **Elderslie St, Winton**
📞 **(07) 4657 0647**
🖥 **www.northgregoryhotel.com**

Located in the grounds behind the hotel, the space is cosy but comfortable, with room for just 18 vans at capacity. Although all sites are unpowered, the fee is modest and you have access to the hotel's facilities, including the laundromat, showers and WiFi.

WINTON TO KARUMBA

NEED TO KNOW

🕐	**801km**
🏠	**Free camping areas, roadhouses, caravan parks, beachside camping areas**
☁	**Late autumn to spring**
👁	**Prehistoric exhibits, Australian history, iconic pubs, fishing**
🛣	**Mainly good, with some degraded areas.**
🍴	**The southern regions have good facilities, as do Normanton and Karumba. The smaller communities only have basic services.**
⚠	**Crocodiles inhabit many waterways in these areas. Be careful around the water's edge.**

Karumba

INTRODUCTION

Although this stretch forms part of the main road-train thoroughfare between Brisbane and Darwin, it's also a popular tourist route with some great attractions and distinctive outback pubs. Before finally reaching the Gulf of Carpentaria, the terrain varies from open floodplain to woodland and the savannah of the Gulf country. Be sure to take adequate breaks, as the distances between each town are significant.

WHERE TO GO

If you look hard enough, there is plenty of evidence of dinosaurs, even outside the tourist hotspots of Winton. It's not unusual to turn over a rock you'd planned on using to ring your campfire and find the fossilised remains of some prehistoric lifeform underneath it. Especially at some of the more out-of-the-way free camping areas north-west of Winton.

The first town you come across is **Kynuna** which was originally an important staging post for Cobb & Co., but now caters for travellers at the iconic Blue Heeler Hotel. One of those quirky outback pubs, it's got a friendly atmosphere with messages and notes scrawled all over the walls. It's believed by the locals here – much to the chagrin of the locals at the North Gregory Hotel in Winton – that this was the location of Banjo Paterson's first public performance of 'Waltzing Matilda'. Either way, it's believed that events at the nearby Combo Waterhole on the Diamantina River involving the shearer Samuel Hoffmeister inspired the ballad. The turnoff to the waterhole is signposted 16km east of Kynuna, after which there is an 8km unsealed track and a short walk.

Another Australian icon is immortalised in **McKinlay**, which is best known for the Walkabout Creek Hotel. It, along with other buildings in town, featured in the hit movie *Crocodile Dundee*, although the whole thing was relocated to front the highway in 1990. The pub is still a welcoming place to have a beer and see some of the movie memorabilia. The owners do ask that you either buy a drink or make a donation to the Royal Flying Doctor Service if you visit. Camping is also available out the back.

Just over 100km further on, at the junction of the Flinders and Landsborough highways, is the frontier town of **Cloncurry** which turned 150 in 2017. Copper mining played a major role in the town's early history, but mining waned after WWI until uranium was discovered nearby in the 1950s. In 1922 Qantas operated its first regular air service between Cloncurry and Charleville, and the Royal Flying Doctor Service was launched here in 1928 using a Qantas aircraft.

There's a great museum dedicated to Reverend John Flynn and the founders of the Royal Flying Doctor Service. The John Flynn Place Museum includes exhibits of the first pedal wireless and a scale model of the *Victory*, the first plane that took off with a doctor on board in 1928. Entry fees apply and it's open 9am–4pm weekdays and 9am–3pm weekends.

From Cloncurry, the Burke Developmental Road passes through the tiny settlement of **Quamby**. It was once a Cobb & Co. staging point, although now not even the pub remains open. A little further on, and off the highway, it's a similar story at **Kajabbi** which was once the railhead for cattle being sent to eastern markets. A train hasn't come through town in years now. The town's Kalkadoon Hotel was another of those fascinating outback pubs, moved here from the nearby mining fields, but it too has closed down.

Which means the best watering hole in the region is the **Burke and Wills Roadhouse**, about 200km south of Normanton. Amid Gulf Savannah cattle country, it is strategically located on the crossroad with the Wills Developmental Rd to Julia Creek in the south-east and Gregory Downs in the north-west. Here you can get fuel, accommodation and meals – the roadhouse is renowned for its pies.

Although it's a long drive north to Normanton, the roadside is dotted with good free overnight rest areas. The best is 62km south of Normanton on the southern bank of the Flinders River.

With gold discoveries along the Etheridge River and copper being mined in Cloncurry, for a time **Normanton** became an important

inland river port. The railway to Croydon was completed back in 1891, and many original buildings, including the railway station and council offices are good examples of early architecture. Possibly the most identifiable landmark in town is the famous Purple Pub. Normanton has basic services, and a good caravan park, but if you've come all this way, you're best to continue on to Karumba.

Karumba is the only town on the southern coast of the Gulf of Carpentaria and is exceptionally popular for the excellent fishing on the Norman River. There are five caravan parks in town, and all of them regularly book out during peak season – around June–Sept. The Karumba Tavern, with its sunset-viewing area is a very popular place to congregate of an afternoon, and many people come not only to watch the sunset and enjoy a drink, but to share travelling tales and advice too.

DON'T MISS

→ **Sunset views – Cloncurry**
Sunset Hill is a short walk from Cloncurry's Discovery Parks' caravan park. The hill offers superb 360° views of the town and is an ideal spot to relax at the day's end to watch or photograph the vivid winter sunsets.

→ **Fabulous fishing – Normanton and Karumba**
The quality of the sports fishing in this region's river estuaries and in the Gulf of Carpentaria is one of the great attractions. Barramundi are the prize catch. There are boats for hire in both towns as well as several charter fishing boats. If you are not so keen on catching it yourself, fresh seafood is readily available in both places too.

WHERE TO FROM HERE

Normanton is on the Savannah Way. Turning east will take you back to Cairns and tropical north Queensland (see Mount Garnet to Karumba, p. 63). Heading west will take you all the way to Darwin and Broome (see Normanton to Borroloola, p. 66).

At Cloncurry heading east will take you to Townsville (see Townsville to Cloncurry, p. 190) or west to the Stuart Highway via Mount Isa, joining it at the Three Ways Roadhouse (see Cloncurry to Three Ways Roadhouse, p. 188).

From Winton you can take a route that leads all the way to Perth across the centre of Australia (see the Outback Way, p. 198).

WHERE TO STAY

301 Walkabout Creek Motel

$$

📍 Corner of Landsborough Hwy and Middleton St, McKinlay
📞 (07) 4746 8424

The small camping area at the back of the pub is a flat open area with basic facilities and a little bit of shade. You're probably here more for a drink in Crocodile Dundee's pub than for the camping facilities, but it's a good stopover on the way north.

302 Discovery Parks Cloncurry

$$$

📍 Flinders Hwy, Cloncurry
📞 (07) 4742 2300
💻 www.discoveryholidayparks.com.au/qld/outback_queensland/cloncurry

Discovery
HOLIDAY PARKS

This is a quality caravan park located 2km east of the town centre on the main highway. Relax in the pool and spa, or

enjoy a meal in the undercover barbecue area. There is a good range of facilities and the park adjoins a small rocky rise known as Sunset Hill. Bookings are required in peak periods.

303 Burke and Wills Roadhouse

$$

📍 Burke Developmental Road, Four Ways
📞 (07) 4742 5909

This is a basic camping area with a number of powered sites that is attached to a busy roadhouse. Life can be chaotic here, but it's okay for an overnight stay. The roadhouse offers good meals and other supplies.

136 Normanton Tourist Park

See p. 65 – Mount Garnet to Karumba.

137 Karumba Point Sunset Caravan Park

See p. 65 – Mount Garnet to Karumba.

PORT AUGUSTA TO COOBER PEDY

Rockets on display in Woomera

INTRODUCTION

Almost as soon as you leave the waters of Port Augusta you're undeniably in desert country. The land from here to Coober Pedy is dry, dotted with the occasional whites (and sometimes pinks) of dried lakes and endless desert scrub as far as the eye can see. It's a very pretty drive, but its attractions are long distances apart, so plan your fuel stops and breaks.

WHERE TO GO

The Australian Arid Lands Botanic Gardens, about 1.5km north of the beginning of the Stuart Highway, is well worth the break – it's been a long drive so far, you deserve it … The park has an incredible display of the plants that thrive in Australia's arid regions, and some great walking paths through it. There's a good cafe in the main centre and as it's a long drive to the next roadhouse at Pimba it's a good opportunity to get a coffee for the road.

Just 20km before Pimba is a rise looking over the impressive Island Lagoon.

Camping is permitted here, although the facilities are basic and the trucks noisy overnight. It's worth stopping just to take in the view of the large salt lake.

From the Spud Roadhouse at **Pimba** it's worth the detour to **Woomera**, a facility established in 1947 as a rocket-launching site. Until 2003 it was also the site of a controversial immigration detention centre. Woomera is still run by the Department of Defence and is mostly closed off to civilians, but the Woomera Village is open to the public with a caravan park, supermarket and a rocket museum.

You can find the museum in the centre of town within the Oasis Community Centre. The Woomera Heritage and Visitor Information Centre has an outdoor display of rockets and missiles and is complimented by substantial displays and information inside. An entry fee applies.

Back on the Stuart Highway, after the detour, it's a long run up to Coober Pedy, with only **Glendambo** to break up the drive. It's a small settlement with a roadhouse and basic accommodation and is the last place to get fuel before the 255km drive into Coober Pedy.

There really isn't anywhere like **Coober Pedy**. You know you're getting close when you start driving through fields filled with piles of rubble, the diggings from the random holes dug by miners hoping to strike it rich. Found in the arid centre of South Australia, this is a busy, cosmopolitan opal-mining town whose closest neighbour is over 160km away down a rough dirt road. About 85 per cent of Australia's opals are found in the diggings around the town and almost every business and attraction somehow incorporates them into their offerings.

Many residents live underground in dugouts to escape the searing heat, and the town has several underground buildings including a hotel, galleries, churches and even a camping area. I've stayed in the hotel and found it incredibly dark! Coober Pedy has a good selection of shops and restaurants too.

DON'T MISS

→ **Dingo Fence – near Coober Pedy**
Did you know Australia has the longest fence in the world? It stretches from south-east Queensland, along part of the border

New South Wales shares with Queensland and South Australia, and then on to the South Australian coastline past Ceduna. It's over 5300km long. Near Coober Pedy you can drive along part of it, and follow interpretive signs telling of its history and continual maintenance. The road is unsealed, but generally well maintained and suitable for two-wheel drives. Grab a map from the information centre.

→ Breakaways – near Coober Pedy
Just 30km north of Coober Pedy, the Breakaways are remarkable flat-topped mesas that are the remnants of a vast inland sea that covered the area over 70 million years ago. There are spectacular views over the gibber deserts surrounding them from a number of lookouts. Follow the unsealed Oodnadatta Rd.

TAKE A SHORT CUT

If you're travelling south from central Australia and intend heading west, consider taking the unsealed road that leaves the Stuart Highway 53km north of Glendambo and heads south-west to Wirrulla on the Eyre Highway. At 290km this route is more than 350km shorter than following the bitumen through Port Augusta, but it is only suitable for four-wheel drives with off-road caravans or camper trailers.

WHERE TO STAY

247 Discovery Parks Port Augusta

See p. 114 – The Eyre Peninsula.

304 Discovery Parks Roxby Downs

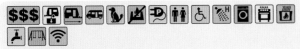

$$$

📍 56–94 Burgoyne St, Roxby Downs
📞 (08) 8671 1991
💻 www.discoveryholidayparks.com.au/caravan-parks/south-australia/central-corridor-roxby-downs

Discovery
HOLIDAY PARKS

In the little town of Roxby Downs, this is a quality caravan park with good facilities, and an ideal base for exploring the area. However, as is the case with many parks in mining areas, it is expensive.

305 BIG4 Stuart Range Outback Resort

$$$

📍 Hutchison St, Coober Pedy
📞 (08) 8672 5179
💻 www.stuartrangeoutbackresort.com.au

BIG4
HOLIDAY PARKS

Located close to the Stuart Hwy, this spacious caravan park has good facilities and a range of accommodation. The shower blocks now boast granite benchtops. I recommend the park's pizza bar for those who enjoy pizza.

306 Riba's Underground Tent Camping

$$ ★

📍 1811 William Creek Rd, Coober Pedy
📞 (08) 8672 5614
💻 www.camp-underground.com.au

If you travel with a spare tent, then a night or two in the underground camping area at Riba's is a unique experience. If you don't have a tent, basic rooms with a bed are available. Above ground, traditional campsites are also available.

The Breakaways

COOBER PEDY TO ALICE SPRINGS

NEED TO KNOW

🕐	**688km**
🏠	**Roadhouse caravan parks, full-featured caravan parks, free camping areas, station stays**
☁	**For the best weather, come during spring or autumn.**
👁	**Outback scenery, the MacDonnell Ranges**
🅰	**The Stuart Highway is long, flat and featureless, with plenty of opportunities to overtake. A 130km/hr speed limit applies in parts.**
🍴	**There are limited facilities and fuel stops between Coober Pedy and Alice Springs.**
⚠	**130km/hr is far too fast to tow a caravan. Keep to more reasonable speeds.**

Camping near Alice Springs

INTRODUCTION

There is no need to stick to the Stuart Highway on the long burn up to Alice Springs, especially if you've got a four-wheel drive and off-road-capable caravan or camper. A number of outlying towns are worth a visit, to see some stunning desert areas. If you do stick to the bitumen, the drive is still filled with great things to see as the road sweeps across wide plains and through cattle-grazing country, although distances between each sight are often significant.

WHERE TO GO

The highway continues north to **Cadney Park Homestead**, a roadhouse and service point strategically located at the turn-off to the Painted Desert.

However, if you've got a four-wheel drive, you can pass through the Painted Desert on the way out to Oodnadatta from Coober Pedy before returning to Marla on the Stuart Highway. To follow this diversion, take the unsealed Kempe Rd (Oodnadatta Rd) and follow the signs to Arckaringa Homestead (which has basic camping). From there the road passes though the strikingly vibrant hills which change colour during the day as the light varies.

The Pink Roadhouse at **Oodnadatta** is one of the most recognisable buildings in Australia and a popular stop for people travelling from Adelaide to the Simpson Desert or Flinders Ranges. It's a post office, general store, food stop and bistro all in one. The Oodnadatta Track back to Marla is unsealed and often rough, but not too challenging.

Over the border in the Northern Territory, the first stop is **Kulgera**, which has a roadhouse and accommodation. From here you can take a detour along the unsealed road to Finke and along the way visit the Lambert Centre – which is the gravitational centre of Australia.

Compared to the distances you've already travelled, it's only a short 75km drive to the **Erldunda Roadhouse** at the junctions of the Stuart and Lasseter highways. It's the turn-off to Yulara, Uluṟu and Kings Canyon (*see* p. 157), but is also a popular stop with various styles of accommodation, a caravan park and restaurant.

About 70km north of Erldunda the unsealed, but two-wheel-drive suitable, Ernest Giles Rd leads to the Henbury Craters which were formed when a meteor slammed into Earth about 4700 years ago. There are 12 craters and the largest is 180m across and 15m deep. A self-guided walk through them takes around 45 min. There's a basic camping area here too.

Continuing north on the highway, there's a worthwhile stop at **Stuarts Well Roadhouse** which has a caravan park, free camping area and licensed inn. Next door is a camel farm which offers camel rides that vary from a few minutes to five-day safaris through the heart of Australia.

Just north of Stuarts Well is the stunning sandstone formation known as Rainbow

Stuarts Well Roadhouse

Valley, part of the James Ranges. The much-photographed location is a sandstone cliff face with bands of rock that resemble a rainbow. The brilliant colours are most spectacular late in the afternoon, and sometimes, after good rains, the cliff face is beautifully reflected in the water-filled claypan in front of it. There are several camping areas and free gas barbecues.

Alice Springs is a destination in itself, and somewhere I could easily spend weeks. There are multiple Aboriginal art galleries and cultural sites to explore in and around town including the National Road Transport Hall of Fame and the Araluen Cultural Precinct where you will find the Museum of Central Australia. There is also the Alice Springs Desert Park and the Old Ghan Museum, which preserves the history of the legendary narrow-gauge train that once operated between Marree and Alice Springs.

The town is also the best place to take advantage of the East and West MacDonnell ranges, which offer stunning walking trails, access to amazing Indigenous rock-art galleries and excellent camping. Some of the best sights in the East MacDonnell Ranges are easily accessible via sealed roads. Both Emily and Jessie gaps – stunning art sites sacred to the Arrernte people – have great walking tracks through them, while Trephina Gorge's Panorama Track is an energetic, hour-long walk that overlooks the gorge as it winds north into Mordor Pound. There's also

a great camping area here that's suitable for all sorts of rigs.

DON'T MISS

→ Painted Desert

The Painted Desert, so called because of the striking, different-coloured rocks that dominate the landscape as far as the eye can see, was created by a process of erosion and weathering that spanned 80 million years. Once an ancient seabed, the cycle of irregular erosion and reforming of rock has created strata of rich reds, browns and yellows. Even if you can't tow your caravan through it, a day trip in your four-wheel drive is well worth it.

Rainbow Valley

WHERE TO STAY

307 Cadney Park Homestead

📍 Stuart Hwy, Marla
📞 (08) 8670 7994

This outback camping area offers shady, gravel sites and basic amenities. There is a pool onsite and the roadhouse offers hot meals and fuel. It's a good stopover for people wishing to visit the Painted Desert.

308 Marla Travellers Rest

📍 Plover St, Marla
📞 (08) 8670 7001
💻 www.marla.com.au

This camping area has spacious gravel sites with some grassy areas and shade. There is a pool onsite and the roadhouse has a small store attached. You can also get a hot meal and fuel.

309 Kulgera Roadhouse and Caravan Park

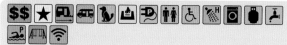

📍 Kulgera Cres, Kulgera
📞 (08) 8956 0973

This roadside camping area offers shady gravel sites with basic amenities. The roadhouse has good pub-style food and a small gallery of Aboriginal artworks which may also be purchased.

310 Erldunda Roadhouse Desert Oaks

📍 Corner Stuart and Lasseter hwys, Erldunda
📞 (08) 8956 0984
💻 www.erldundaroadhouse.com

Strategically located at the junction of the Stuart and Lasseter highways, this caravan park has excellent facilities, including a licensed restaurant, emu enclosure and kangaroo farm. Perfect for overnight stops.

311 Stuarts Well Roadhouse and Caravan Park

📍 Stuart Hwy, Stuarts Well
📞 (08) 8956 0808
💻 www.stuartswellroadhouse.com.au

A great stopover with good, hot meals available from the roadhouse, this camping area has the option of paid sites or free camping. Paid sites have a choice of drive-thru or flat grassy areas and access to basic amenities. There are no amenities in the free camping area but for a small fee you can obtain access to the powered-site facilities.

312 BIG4 MacDonnell Range Holiday Park

📍 25 Palm Pl, Alice Springs
📞 (08) 8952 6111
💻 www.macrange.com.au

This family-friendly caravan park has a great range of facilities including a gymnasium, heated swimming pool and basketball court. Sites are spacious and shady, and the amenities are modern and tidy.

313 Wintersun Cabin & Caravan Park

📍 Cnr North Stuart Hwy & Head St, Alice Springs
📞 (08) 8952 4080
💻 wintersun.com.au

Conveniently located just 2km from the city centre, this caravan park has good-sized, shady camping areas with a large undercover camp kitchen and a nice swimming pool onsite.

314 Ross River Resort

📍 Ross Hwy, Ross River
📞 (08) 8956 9711
💻 www.rossriverresort.com.au

Surrounded by the majestic scenery of the MacDonnell Ranges, this camping area has good flat, grassy sites and basic amenities to suit most needs. The historic homestead has a bar, serves hot meals and is full of interesting pieces from days past.

KINGS CANYON, ULURU AND KATA TJUTA

NEED TO KNOW

- 1171km

- Free camping areas, inexpensive caravan parks, holiday resorts

- Avoid Uluru in summer if you plan on doing some walking, as many of the walks are closed due to the heat.

- Indigenous heritage, walking tracks, amazing scenery

- Most is sealed highway, but some areas require a high-clearance four-wheel drive.

- Alice Springs is a major centre and Yulara has a large resort, but otherwise facilities are very basic. If you need more than fuel or basic groceries, you might be left wanting.

- If driving early in the morning, or after sunset, beware of wildlife, including camels.

Rim Walk at Kings Canyon

INTRODUCTION

Alongside the Sydney Opera House and Sydney Harbour Bridge, there is not a more iconic Australian landmark than Uluru. Steeped in Indigenous cultural significance, home to its fair share of controversy, and consistently one of the most popular tourist attractions in Australia, Uluru is one place that lives up to the hype, no matter how often you visit. It's not the only rock out there worth looking at, though, as both Kata Tjuta and Kings Canyon are exceptional locations in their own rights.

WHERE TO GO

A lot of people don't quite realise how remote Uluru actually is. It's over four hours'

drive from Alice Springs if you're coming from the east, and Kata Tjuta is only about 170km from the Western Australian border in a straight line. The most direct route to the area is by turning onto the Lasseter Hwy, 200km south of Alice Springs at **Erldunda Roadhouse**, but this is only one of two interesting routes to the giant inselberg of sandstone that rises 348m above the surrounding plain.

From the highway it's about 250km to Yulara and now the Mount Ebenezer Roadhouse has closed again, the only place to get fuel is **Curtin Springs**, 160km from Erldunda. Curtin Springs is the ideal place to stop if you're looking for the facilities of a caravan park, but don't want to pay the premiums charged at the Ayers Rock Resort. At just a 40 min drive to the entrance of Uluru–Kata Tjuta National Park, it's an easy

drive, even if you're hoping to be there early for a sunrise viewing. Curtin Springs has fuel, a licensed bar and restaurant.

If you have the time, take a tour of Curtin Springs' old abattoir, which has been transformed into a small paper mill. Here owner Lyndee Severin and her daughter create beautiful, one-of-a-kind papers out of native Australian grasses. Every piece has its own colour and texture, some with added extras such as flowers, bangtails or even treated cow manure.

From a few vantage points before and after Curtin Springs, you'll catch glimpses of Mt Conner, a striking flat-topped mountain south of the Lasseter Highway. Given its shape and the lack of surrounding landforms, many tourists (me included) have mistaken it for Uluru. Some locals even refer to it as 'Fooluru', the occurrence is so common.

Field of Light, Uluru

It's on private land, but tours can be arranged at Curtin Springs.

About 85km further on, past a few free overnight rest areas, which have some of the most exceptional views over Uluru, is **Yulara**, the major service point for visitors to the Rock. Here you'll find an extensive array of accommodation, a good caravan park, a shopping centre and a handful of very good restaurants. Everything is expensive, though, from the fuel to the food to the tyres – if you're unlucky enough to need one while here.

The most convenient way to visit Uluru and Kata Tjuta is by booking a couple of nights at the Ayers Rock Resort. However, I suggest setting up camp before sunset, as after the sunset viewing of Uluru, crowds of backpackers, caravanners and campers flock into the park hoping to get a spot and the lines into reception stream out the door and down the driveway. Once you're settled in, pack a picnic, some refreshing drinks and head to the sunset-viewing area to take in the spectacular colour changes of the Rock as the sun slowly sinks below the horizon. After the show has finished you'll be able to drive leisurely back to camp past everyone who was less organised.

If you thought sunset over Uluru was amazing, then you'll be just as impressed with it at sunrise as the brightening day reveals the many colours of the sandstone monolith. Once the sun is up, the best way to explore Uluru is on foot. There's a 9km circuit walk around the base, which takes most people about three hours to complete and is best done earlier in the morning before the day gets too hot. If it's a shorter walk you'd prefer, the Mutitjulu Waterhole Walk is an easy 20 min to the waterhole of the same name – it's one of Uluru's lesser-known beauties.

The Cultural Centre is best visited around the middle of the day, when it is hottest outside. Here you'll learn about the history and significance of Uluru to the Indigenous owners, book tours or grab a bite to eat in the cafeteria. On most days local Anangu women run art workshops in the shade of the trees surrounding the centre.

If you've still got time before heading back to camp, drive over to Kata Tjuta (the Olgas). Far fewer people and tour groups visit here, so it's not uncommon to have the place to yourself. The sunset viewing of Kata Tjuta (which means 'many heads') is arguably even more spectacular than the one over Uluru. There are a number of walks of varying length and difficulty, although I recommend the Walpa Gorge Walk to experience the immense size and wonder up close and personal. This is a short, easy walk which could be done with small children, no problems.

It's about three hours' drive from Uluru to Kings Canyon, which has been carved out of the rugged George Gill Range by Kings Creek. The canyon has two walks: one along the canyon floor and the more arduous, but more spectacular Rim Walk. The rich, stunning colours of the canyon walls, the weathered domes and the lush Garden of Eden along the creek make this a beautiful destination.

Kings Canyon Resort, about 7km away is a full-featured resort with accommodation that ranges from deluxe five-star suites to basic unpowered camping areas. It has a range of dining options too, befitting the various styles of accommodation available.

There's no need to backtrack all the way from Kings Canyon to the Lasseter Highway and out to Erldunda to return to Alice Springs. From here, the popular Red Centre Way winds its way up to the top of the range before continuing deep and red until the road forks – the southern route to Hermannsburg and the northern route through the West MacDonnell Ranges. Four-wheel drives are recommended, and caravans are not, however when I travelled it, the road was easy going, flat and dare I say it, boring. A permit is required, which can be purchased from Kings Canyon Resort.

DON'T MISS

→ Field of Light – Uluru
The Field of Light is an internationally acclaimed art installation by Bruce Munro, which transforms an area in front of the pop-up restaurant that overlooks Uluru. Over 50,000 tiny lights spread across a space as big as seven football fields transform the scenery into a colourful, sparkling wonderland. Bookings are essential, and a range of different experiences are offered. Bookings are taken at the reception areas of most accommodation options in Ayers Rock Resort, including at the caravan park.

→ Palm Valley – near Alice Springs
Accessed via Larapinta Dr, Palm Valley is a spectacularly remote camping area about 135km west of Alice Springs on a section of the Finke River. A high-clearance four-wheel drive and off-road caravan are required, as at one point the road runs down the middle of the Finke River, which is exceptionally rocky and rough. Once there, the camping area has excellent walks and is the only place in the world where the red cabbage palm grows. Contact (08) 8999 4555.

WHERE TO STAY

315 Curtin Springs Station camping area

📍 Lasseter Hwy, Petermann
📞 (08) 89562906
💻 www.curtinsprings.com

This is a great roadhouse camping area where camping is free if you don't use power and there is almost endless space to spread out. There are four powered sites. Basic facilities are available, although there is a charge for the showers, due to the remote location. It has a licensed bar and a great beer garden.

316 Ayers Rock Resort Campground

📍 213 Yulara Dr, Yulara
📞 (08) 8957 7001
💻 www.ayersrockresort.com.au

As this is the closest and most obvious caravan park to Uluru, it is incredibly busy and reasonably expensive. Check in early to beat the post-sunset rush. Its facilities are top notch, however.

317 Kings Creek Station

📍 Kings Creek Caravan Rd, Petermann
📞 (08) 8956 7474
💻 www.kingscreekstation.com.au

Located 39km from Kings Canyon, this large camping area on a cattle station caters solely for tourists and has a restaurant and many sites in bush settings. There are numerous activities including camel rides, helicopter flights, and quad bike and Harley Davidson rides. Bookings are required in peak periods.

318 Kings Canyon Resort

📍 20049 Larapinta Dr, Petermann
📞 (08) 8956 7442
💻 www.kingscanyonresort.com.au

This is a very good resort and caravan park, located about 7km from Kings Canyon. The resort has a range of accommodation, a restaurant and well-stocked roadhouse. Bookings are required in peak periods.

Palm Valley, Central Australia

ALICE SPRINGS TO THREE WAYS ROADHOUSE

NEED TO KNOW

🕐 **531km**

🏠 **Free camping areas, national park camping areas, basic caravan parks**

☁ **Spring, summer and autumn**

👁 **Aboriginal sites, outback camping, mining history**

🛣 **Two-lane highway with adequate overtaking opportunities**

🍴 **Only basic services are available north of Alice Springs.**

⚠ **The Stuart Highway doesn't have a speed limit in places, so be wary of faster-moving vehicles.**

A mine at dusk at Tennant Creek at Battery Hill

INTRODUCTION

Taking in one of the world's oldest religious sites, the UFO capital of Australia and the site of our country's last gold rush, the drive between Alice Springs and Three Ways Roadhouse might be long, flat and often featureless, but it isn't boring. The route follows almost exactly the same one laid out by explorer John McDouall Stuart, back in the early 1860s, although now the Stuart Highway is wide, well maintained and sealed.

WHERE TO GO

Not far north of **Alice Springs** there's a perfect photo opportunity where the Tropic of Capricorn crosses the Stuart Highway. There's an overnight rest area, with information and a large sculpture. The **Aileron Roadhouse** is the first major stop, though, 134km north of Alice. It's a popular caravan park and roadhouse, and two impressive statues dominate the skyline as you get closer. The Anmatjere Woman and Child, and accompanying Anmatjere Man, are 17m high depictions of traditional people

from the local Anmatjere tribe that are striking in their detail.

Just 60km north, **Ti Tree** is a small township where the roadhouse is the main service centre for travellers. In the middle of red, dusty and dry Australia, the nearby Red Centre Mango Farm is also a pleasant stop to try a variety of mango-inspired delicacies. John McDouall Stuart calculated that the nearby Mt Stuart was the geographical centre of Australia.

After Ti Tree, **Wycliffe Well Roadhouse** and the adjoining UFO museum are one of the more bizarre attractions on the Stuart Highway. The location is said to be the site of most UFO sightings in Australia and the small museum is filled with newspaper clippings and paraphernalia supporting the argument. The roadhouse also has a small shop and a caravan park. It's quirky, but certainly interesting for kids.

The closest town to Karlu Karlu (Devils Marbles) is **Wauchope**, which has a hotel, roadhouse and caravan park that's popular with people wanting to explore the granite rock formations, but prefer more than the basic facilities at the reserve's camping area.

According to Aboriginal Dreamtime stories, the **Karlu Karlu (Devils Marbles)** are the fossilised eggs of the rainbow serpent. They've been formed over many millions of years by wind and sand eroding away the edges of what were once large rectangular boulders of granite. The site is a favourite of photographers, and very popular with tourists, with many staying at the adjacent camping area.

Tennant Creek was the location of Australia's last gold rush in 1932. Today gold is still mined on the rich Tennant Creek fields and fossickers also come to try their luck. Just 1.5km east of town there's a very interesting gold-mining museum. The town is busy for one so remote, with most basic services available to travellers, including a couple of reasonable caravan parks.

The **Three Ways Roadhouse** sits at one of Australia's most well-known intersections, at the junction of the Barkly and Stuart highways. (The Barkly Hwy will take you to Townsville. The roadhouse provides fuel, meals and accommodation for travellers.

DON'T MISS

→ **Overland Telegraph Line –
   near Alice Springs**

Completed in 1872, the Overland Telegraph Line was a major technological feat for its time. The 1800km single overhead wire, together with an undersea cable that ran to Java in Indonesia, linked Australia to the rest of the world for the first time. Although the line has been long surpassed by new technology, many remnants still remain, including the repeater stations at Alice Springs, Barrow Creek and Tennant Creek.

→ **Battery Hill Mining Centre –
   near Tennant Creek**

This impressive complex, 1.5km east of Tennant Creek, showcases the rich mining history of the area. It boasts a working underground mine, one of only three 10-stamp batteries still operational in Australia, and a host of historical mining equipment. The Battery Hill Mineral Museum is part of the centre and houses some fascinating specimens. The complex adjoins the visitor information centre in Peko Rd. Entry fees apply and it's open daily 9am–5.30pm. Contact (08) 8962 1281.

WHERE TO STAY

319 Wycliffe Well Holiday Park

📍 Stuart Hwy, Davenport
📞 (08) 8964 1966

A short drive from one of the Northern Territory's most amazing natural landscapes, Karlu Karlu (Devils Marbles) this is a great spot for an overnight stay.

320 Devils Marbles camping area

📍 Karlu Karlu (Devils Marbles) Conservation Reserve, Davenport
📞 (08) 8962 4599
🖥 www.nt.gov.au/leisure/parks-reserves/find-a-park-to-visit/karlu-karlu-devils-marbles-conservation-reserve

This basic camping area is located right in the middle of Karlu Karlu (Devils Marbles) Conservation Reserve. Small fires are permitted only in fireplaces and visitors are advised to bring their own firewood and water. No generators are allowed within the reserve.

321 Tennant Creek Caravan Park

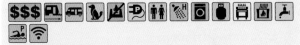

📍 208 Stuart Hwy, Tennant Creek
📞 (08) 8962 2325
🖥 www.tennantcreekcaravanpark.com.au

This is a nice little spot with a shaded pool and drive-thru sites available. There's plenty of grass and shade, and the amenities are basic but clean.

Karlu Karlu (Devils Marbles)

THREE WAYS ROADHOUSE TO DALY WATERS

Playing Bowls, Daly Waters Pub

INTRODUCTION

As the Stuart Highway forges further north into the tropics, the scenery slowly greens. It never quite leaves behind the harsh tones of the Red Centre – but as it moves into areas of more regular rainfall and past towns with water in their names, the change is subtle but welcome. The highway continues wide and well maintained, with plenty of roadside stops, free camping options and interesting little towns to visit.

WHERE TO GO

About 60km north of **Three Ways Roadhouse**, just after a memorial to one of Stuart's most significant camps at Attack Creek, is the turn-off to Churchills Head. This unusual rock formation is said to resemble Winston Churchill's features. By Northern Territory standards, it's not a very impressive rock to look at, but the drive, which parallels the highway for about 14km is a nice detour.

A little way further north is the historical **Banka Banka Station**, which offers informal camping and is a great alternative to the more commercial caravan parks. Situated 101km north of Tennent Creek (or

60km south of Renner Springs), it has lovely grassy caravan sites, hot showers, a kiosk, a dump point and a laundry. It has proven to be one of the more popular stops along this section, thanks to its modest prices and friendly service.

In the tiny highway town of **Renner Springs**, life revolves around the roadhouse complex. The town is named after Frederick Renner, who was the doctor to the workers on the Overland Telegraph Line. Dr Renner discovered springs in the area when he observed flocks of birds gathering there. The service station, motel and caravan park offer a convenient service point for travellers. Meals, fuel and accommodation are available although facilities are basic.

The basic community of **Elliott** was named after Captain Snow Elliott, the officer in charge of a nearby camp for troops during WWII. It has basic services for travellers, including a caravan park, fuel, basic meals and limited supplies. I've stayed at the caravan park before, but probably wouldn't again. To the south of town is an interesting little war memorial.

Just north of Elliott is the historical, but deserted town of **Newcastle Waters**, situated on the edge of Newcastle Waters Station. A couple of the buildings, including

the Jones Store and old hotel can still be visited and explored, although camping isn't permitted at the site. A larger-than-life tribute to the drovers, who often met here because it was the busy junction of the Barkly and Murranji stock routes, makes the town an interesting deviation.

Dunmarra has a good caravan park, which, with the service station and motel, forms the centre of this small town. Many travellers stop here, feeling it's the best place since Banka Banka Station when heading north.

Only another 50km north is **Daly Waters**, formerly a refuelling point for Qantas international flights during the 1930s. Today a few houses and the pub are all that remain but it still caters for travellers. About 1km north of Daly Waters is a tree with a barely discernable carved letter 's' on its trunk. This is believed to have been marked by explorer John McDouall Stuart as he struggled to cross the continent in the 1860s.

If it wasn't for the pub, though, no-one would stop here. Like many outback pubs, it has its quirks – brassieres and ladies' underwear hang from the ceiling, and stickers and photographs adorn every wall. Many stop to enjoy the jovial atmosphere of the adjoining caravan park (which allows

Renner Springs Roadhouse

pets, but not elephants) and the pub's famous Beef and Barra Barbecue that happens nightly Apr–Oct.

DON'T MISS

→ **The Overland Telegraph Line monument – near Dunmarra**
Less than 30km south of Dunmarra is the Sir Charles Todd Memorial. This monument marks the place where the last historic join occurred in the single-wire Overland Telegraph Line on 22 Aug 1872. A few remaining telegraph poles are also visible immediately alongside the highway.

WHERE TO STAY

322 Banka Banka Outstation

$$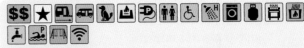

📍 Stuart Hwy – 76km north of Three Ways Roadhouse
📞 (08) 8964 4511

Banka Banka is a popular stopover on the Stuart Highway for its wide open, grassy sites, great outback hospitality and good, clean facilities which include toilets, showers, laundry, fireplaces and a camp kitchen. It's pet friendly too.

323 Dunmarra Roadhouse Caravan Park

$$ ★

📍 Stuart Hwy, Dunmarra
📞 (08) 8975 9922

Part of a roadhouse complex, this caravan park is fine for an overnight stop. The roadhouse has a good restaurant and licensed bar.

147 Daly Waters Pub Caravan Park

See p. 70 – Borroloola to Daly Waters.

Jones Store, Newcastle Waters

PERTH TO MOUNT MAGNET

NEED TO KNOW

🎨	**513km to 580km**
🏠	**Basic, inexpensive caravan parks; station stays**
☁	**Wildflowers start to bloom around July and continue until about November.**
👁	**Historic towns, gold-mining heritage, wildflowers**
🅷	**The roads here are good, but you'll share them with road trains.**
🍴	**Dalwallinu and Mount Magnet are both large regional centres with all services available.**
⚠	**None apply**

Splendid Everlasting near Mount Magnet

INTRODUCTION

Passing through Australia's only monastic town, broadacre grain-farming lands and sheep runs, this is prime wildflower country Sept–Nov. Along the way it also passes through historic gold-mining towns and offers excellent camping opportunities.

WHERE TO GO

Just an hour and a half from the cosmopolitan streets and beaches of **Perth** is Australia's only monastic town and a visit is an unforgettable experience. The settlement of **New Norcia** was founded on the Victoria Plains in 1846 in an attempt to 'help' the local Aboriginal people. Today it is still owned and operated by the Benedictine monastic community. The whole town is registered on the National Estate and 27 of its buildings are classified by the National Trust. In recent years the monastery has opened its doors to visitors and tours depart twice a day from the museum gift shop. The fascinating New Norcia Museum and Art Gallery houses a fine collection of heritage material, while a roadhouse and general store cater for travellers.

A little further north, **Dalwallinu** is a regional centre for wheat and sheep farming and the shire is the largest wheat-producing area in Western Australia. This area can be ablaze with wildflowers July–Nov. Wattles are the dominant plant in the region, with more than 80 varieties found. Depending on the rains, you may also see stunning displays of white, yellow and pink everlasting daisies.

Moving into some of Western Australia's historic gold-mining regions, **Paynes Find** is a great example of an old fossickers' settlement. The Gold Battery and Museum is worth a visit, but not much else remains apart from the hotel, which has meals, fuel, basic accommodation and cold beers. There is a small caravan park too.

Mount Magnet is the oldest operating gold settlement in Western Australia – gold was discovered here in 1891. Mining still continues close to town, and a tourist trail map is available. The town also has a museum displaying pioneering and mining artefacts, and there are many buildings of historical significance.

If you come in spring then expect to see the landscape covered in wildflowers. Head north of town any time to find the Granites, an Aboriginal rock art-site with a nice picnic spot nearby. Another interesting site is the ghost town of **Lennonville**, just to the north. A former gold-rush town, it fell into decline in the early 1900s and has been empty ever since. Take care, as there are dangerous old mine shafts in the area.

DON'T MISS

→ **New Norcia produce – New Norcia**
The Benedictine monks of New Norcia make a range of wonderful products, including olive oil, table wine and their famous long-life nut cake. A variety of fresh bread is also baked each day in the monastery's 130-year-old wood-fired oven. The produce is available from the museum gift shop or roadhouse.

→ **Stay at a station – Great Northern Highway**
Several station properties along the Great Northern Highway offer camping during the year, and are popular when the wildflowers are in bloom. These include Narndee, Nallan, Nalbarra, Kirkalocka and Ninghan stations. Some of these turn-offs are well signposted with caravan-park symbols. While some stations are close to the highway, others are many kilometres off it.

WHERE TO STAY

324 Moora Caravan Park

📍 52 Roberts St, Moora
📞 0409 511 400

A small but pleasant caravan park with good access, wide avenues and grassy, landscaped sites. The facilities here are simple but well cared for. It also has a free laundry.

325 Dalwallinu Caravan Park

📍 10 Dowie St, Dalwallinu
📞 (08) 9661 1253

A council caravan park that has been redeveloped in recent years, this a very neat and tidy place. It is easily accessible from the Great Northern Hwy.

326 Kirkalocka Station

📍 Great Northern Hwy, Mount Magnet
📞 (08) 9963 5827
🖥 www.kirkalocka.com

This is a rustic station stay in a terrific part of Western Australia. The facilities are basic, but the hospitality is welcoming. It's a great place to stay to explore the wildflower regions during late spring and winter.

327 Mount Magnet Caravan Park

📍 100 Hepburn St, Mount Magnet
📞 (08) 9963 4198
🖥 www.mtmagnet.wa.gov.au

A good-quality, council-run caravan park, which has all basic facilities. There are shady trees, a patch of lawn for tents and clean amenities.

St Gertrude's College, New Norcia

MOUNT MAGNET TO NEWMAN

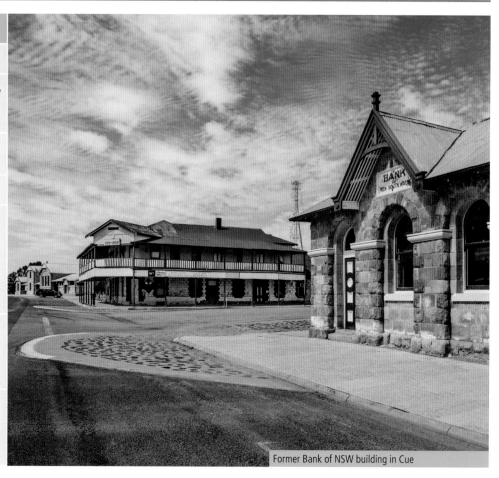

Former Bank of NSW building in Cue

INTRODUCTION

Well into the western desert regions now, the Great Northern Highway crosses the Murchison, Gascoyne and Pilbara regions between Mount Magnet and Tom Price. All these areas are dominated by low mulga woodlands, immense sheep and cattle runs and large iron-ore mines. However, there are very few population centres, except what mining money can sustain. The wide open spaces do offer some exceptional camping opportunities though, and it's the remoteness that attracts many people to the area.

WHERE TO GO

Cross the vast salt Lake Austin and catch a glimpse of the goldmining ghost town of **Austin**, both named after explorer Robert Austin. Further north, **Cue** is another small historic goldmining town that has basic services for travellers. The town boasts several historical buildings, some dating back to the late 19th century, with many classified by the National Trust. Just some to look out for are the old hospital ruins, Great Fingal Mine Office and Masonic Lodge in Dowley St (built largely of corrugated iron). Details of the Cue Heritage Trail can be obtained from the Cue Visitor Information Centre.

Be sure to visit the abandoned town of **Big Bell**, whose bar was reputedly the longest in Australia. Although there are only a few buildings left, the townsite is still very distinguishable, and a few information boards help paint a picture of life in the town. There's a basic free camping area too.

Settled by prospectors in 1896, **Meekatharra** has a rich goldmining history and mining is still a major industry today. It's also an important base for the Royal Flying Doctor Service and has a School of the Air too. A park on Main St has a selection of mining relics on display, including an old battery. The three heritage walks are the best way to explore the town and its surrounds. From here it's over 400km to Newman, with only one stop for fuel over 260km away at the Kumarina Roadhouse, so leave prepared.

Opened only in 2013, the Karalundi College Caravan Park has been impressing travellers passing through. Although it's nothing special, the owners have managed that perfect mix of friendly hospitality, big sites and clean amenities set amid a beautiful landscape. Dogs are allowed, and a small cafe serves meals and coffee.

The drive to Newman is long, but can easily be broken up with a stay at one of the many overnight rest areas that dot the edge of the highway.

Newman was built to house the workers at BHP Billiton's Mt Whaleback Mine, the largest open-cut iron-ore mine in the world – it turned 50 in 2017. There are several other ore deposits also being mined nearby and all of the ore is transported by train to Port Hedland on BHP Billiton's own rail network.

The town has good facilities, including a shopping centre with a supermarket, and there are two good caravan parks south of town.

DON'T MISS

→ Heritage trails – Meekatharra

The local council has established three heritage walking trails around town. The Meeka Town Heritage Walk is a 2km walk around the town, featuring interpretive panels about the landmark buildings. The Meeka Creek Trail is a 3km loop trail following the creek past 17 interpretive panels about Meekatharra and the surrounding rangelands. The Meeka Lookout Trail is a 900m walk to a lookout with stunning views over the rangelands and town. All three walks commence from the tourist information bay.

→ Mt Whaleback Mine – Newman

Tours of BHP Billiton's Mt Whaleback mining operations depart daily from the Newman Visitor Information Centre. The tour takes about 90 min and includes a video presentation. Bookings are required, and don't forget full-cover clothing and enclosed shoes.

→ Ophthalmia Dam – near Newman

An integral part of Newman's water supply, the dam is a popular recreational area for the locals. About 17km from Newman, it's a good spot for a swim or a picnic, especially on those hot Pilbara days.

WHERE TO STAY

328 Cue Tourist Park

$$

📍 1 Austin St, Cue
📞 (08) 9963 1107
🖥 www.cue.wa.gov.au

A council caravan park in the main street of Cue, this establishment has undergone development and expansion. It is popular with amateur prospectors, who arrive in large numbers during the cooler months. The park has attractive discounts for pensioners and seniors.

329 Peace Gorge camping area

📍 Meekatharra

This camping area has been used as a picnic spot since the 1920s. Today it is a well-managed and tidy camping area run by the Meekatharra Shire. There are no facilities, but it is very pretty, and close to town and some walks.

330 Karalundi Community Caravan Park

$$$

📍 Great Northern Hwy, Meekatharra
📞 (08) 9981 2937
🖥 www.karalundi.wa.edu.au

Set on the grounds of the temporarily closed Karalundi College (formerly a boarding school for Indigenous kids from the region) it is a spacious, green area amongst a sea of red dirt. The facilities are modern, yet basic, and serve the traveller well.

331 Oasis @ Newman caravan park

$$

📍 44 Great Northern Hwy, Newman
📞 (08) 9328 1100
🖥 www.oasisnewman.com.au

This is Newman's newest caravan park, offering a range of accommodation options and attached to a top-quality restaurant. Development is ongoing.

Mt Whaleback Mine, Newman

NEWMAN TO PORT HEDLAND

NEED TO KNOW

🕐	**454km**
⌂	**National park camping areas, basic caravan parks**
☁	**Karijini National Park is at its best early in the dry season.**
👁	**Karijini National Park**
A	**Great because all roads are sealed and well maintained to make sure the mining transports have no dramas.**
🍴	**While Newman and Port Hedland are major centres with most services available, there is often a long wait for basic facilities due to the high demand.**
⚠	**None apply**

View to Mt Bruce

INTRODUCTION

Newman to Port Hedland takes in the best of the Pilbara, including the stunning oasis that is Karijini National Park, Western Australia's second largest. The Great Northern Highway passes through some very scenic range country and you'll get the most from it if you take your time.

WHERE TO GO

From **Newman**, Karijini National Park is the first major attraction. This great national park would be overrun by tourists if it wasn't so far from everything. The place is a walker's paradise, renowned for its extraordinary gorges with multicoloured walls, hidden pools and waterfalls.

There are seven different gorges in the park that can be explored along self-guided trails. Most end at, or even pass through, an enchanting outback waterhole or pretty burbling creek. A few of the park's best walks require a reasonable level of fitness, and involve climbing down wet gorges to find amazing swimming holes. Both Weano and Hancock gorges are tough

work, but worth it for the rewards at the end.

Dales Gorge is one of the most popular camping areas in the park, thanks to its proximity to the stunning Fortescue Falls waterhole which can be accessed by following a 15- to 20-min walk. For those after more facilities, the Karijini Eco Retreat has unpowered camping areas, all amenities and even an alfresco restaurant.

Throughout spring, Karijini's hills are covered in brilliant wildflowers. The challenging, but very rewarding, walk to the top of Mt Bruce, at 1234m above sea level, gives stunning views over the wildflower gardens. Allow five hours for this 9km, Class 4, hike that includes a chain-assisted climb to the summit.

Returning to the Great Northern Highway, **Auski Roadhouse** is a short drive north, nestled at the base of the Hamersley Range. It provides fuel, meals, accommodation and a camping area. During the cooler months of the tourist season, a helicopter based at the roadhouse offers scenic flights over the spectacular Karijini gorges. This is also the last place to get fuel before the 270km drive to South Hedland.

Home to one of the world's busiest bulk-export ports, **Port Hedland** sees off around 500 million tonnes of iron ore each year. Iron ore is delivered, by the BHP Billiton-owned rail network, to Port Hedland from mines as far afield as Newman. As Port Hedland is a busy mining and port town, it has most facilities and services.

A number of guided and self-guided tours are the best way to see the sights of Port Hedland. The most popular is the 45 min tour of BHP Billiton's Nelson Point facility, which shows visitors through the various stages of iron-ore production. Tours run Mon, Tues and Thurs – book through the visitor centre. Another great tour is the Port Hedland Local Tour run by historian Julie Arif. Again, make bookings at the visitor centre.

When the iron-ore boom began in the 1960s, it quickly became obvious that Port Hedland did not have sufficient land suitable to develop housing and infrastructure for the expected explosion in the population. This led to the development of **South Hedland**, 20km to the south, and today this is the area's primary residential area. It has a large shopping complex and two caravan parks.

→ **Great fishing – near Port Hedland**

Fishing is very popular along the north-west coast of the state and in the cooler dry months people flock to the caravan parks and resorts between Port Hedland and Broome just to cast a line each day. Fishing charters based in Port Hedland are a great way to see the sights off the coast while landing a big one. If shore-based fishing, be aware that this coast is subject to large tidal movements so check tide charts or apps before venturing onto the tidal flats.

Fishing on Eighty Mile Beach

WHERE TO STAY

332 Tom Price Tourist Park

$$$$

⊙ Nameless Valley Dr, Tom Price
📞 (08) 9189 1515
🖥 www.tompricetouristpark.com.au

This caravan park is one of the few developed options in the Pilbara region. It is a good park with space for big rigs.

333 Auski Tourist Village

$$

⊙ Great Northern Hwy, Karijini
📞 (08) 9176 6988
🖥 www.auskitouristvillage.com

Part of the Auski Roadhouse complex, this is a convenient base from which to explore the gorges in Karijini National Park. It is a good, basic park and accessible along bitumen roads, whereas access to some of the nearby national park camping areas is often via badly corrugated roads.

178 Black Rock Tourist Park

See p. 88 – Broome to Port Hedland.

179 Discovery Parks Port Hedland

See p. 88 – Broome to Port Hedland.

334 Karijini Eco Retreat

$$

⊙ Weano Rd, Karijini National Park
📞 (08) 9425 5591
🖥 www.karijiniecoretreat.com.au

Karijini Eco Retreat has unpowered camping areas, all amenities and an alfresco restaurant. It's a good option for those who want to stay in the park, but don't want to rough it too much.

Karijini National Park

GUNDAGAI TO HAY

Historic Monte Cristo Homestead, Junee

INTRODUCTION

The Riverina stretches across the flat, fertile plains of south central New South Wales. It is one of Australia's richest agricultural regions, watered by the Murrumbidgee River through a vast irrigation system. The open landscape, brilliant clear skies and warm weather make touring through the wide district a pleasure.

WHERE TO GO

Most people who travel out across the Sturt Highway head south from **Gundagai** along the Hume Highway to meet the westbound road near Wagga Wagga. However, it's a far better drive if you head due west from Gundagai to the charming little town of **Junee**. Rich in history, it has a couple of good museums, an excellent liquorice and chocolate factory, as well as what's considered Australia's most haunted house – Monte Cristo Homestead. Junee has a range of good camping options, including a free camping area in nearby Old Junee.

From Junee it's an easy drive south to **Wagga Wagga**, inland New South Wales'

third largest city – so good they named it twice, according to the locals. It lies on the banks of the Murrumbidgee River and supports nearby air force and army bases, as well as a large rural area. Numerous sporting greats were born here, including golfer Steve Elkington, cricketer Mark Taylor and tennis player Tony Roche. With all major services, Wagga Wagga is a good place to stock up, although go easy on the fruit, as a fruit-fly exclusion zone begins between here and Narrandera.

As the country continues to open up into the central western plains, you're almost on the edge of the outback, and the small town of **Narrandera** is typical of the regional towns as you continue west. On the banks of the Murrumbidgee River, the town has a tidy free camping area on its outskirts. My kids always remember it as the halfway point to South Australia, because that's where we stop if we do the two-day drive from the east coast. There's good regional shopping in town, and a quaint op shop where I bought the wine glasses that are still in our caravan.

Still on the Murrumbidgee River, the old town of **Darlington Point** was established as a river-crossing point. The first bridge,

built in 1905 and replaced in 1979, now forms the entrance to the caravan park. The Sturt Highway intersects with the Kidman Way (*see* p. 140) near Darlington Point.

It's worth a detour north to **Griffith** – a town designed by Walter Burley Griffin. It's somewhat of an oasis on the edge of the outback that surprises many people. Griffith is one of the premier wine-growing regions in Australia, and has a significant Italian heritage, as many Italian migrants flocked here after WWII. As such, there is very good dining and coffee in town, and exceptional gardens scattered through the region, especially at many of the wineries. During spring, Griffith puts on the annual Springfest, which is well-known for its orange sculptures, open gardens and large community street party.

Back on the Sturt, heading west, there are plenty of great little camping areas tucked into river bends. The most popular of these is at Sandy Point Reserve in Hay, which has a large open area, some toilets and is close to town.

Hay is surrounded by a flat treeless and featureless landscape – the Hay Plain. It services the surrounding sheep and grain farms, so I often stop here on trips west as the main shopping strip provides most services, has a good bakery and a small selection of retail outlets. There are also two excellent museums worth visiting – the Dunera Museum and Shear Outback.

DON'T MISS

→ Dunera Museum – Hay

The Dunera Museum is a centre preserving the history of the prisoner-of-war camp where the 'Dunera Boys' (Austrian and German internees) and Japanese POWs were held during WWII. It is housed in restored railway carriages at Hay Railway Station on Murray St. Entry fees apply and it's open daily 9am–6pm. Contact (02) 6993 2161.

→ Shear Outback – Hay

The Australian Shearers Hall of Fame at Shear Outback is an incredible tribute to the men and women who toiled in the wool industry when it was a major part of Australia's economy. There's an extensive collection of shears, very energetic demonstrations and information on some of Australia's most famous shearers. Find it on the Sturt Hwy, just west of town. It's open daily 9am–5pm and entry fees apply. Contact (02) 6993 4000.

WHERE TO STAY

335 Gundagai Tourist Park

$$$

📍 1 Nangus Rd, Gundagai
📞 (02) 6944 4440
💻 www.gundagaitouristpark.com.au

Situated just a short 2 min walk into historic Gundagai, this caravan park offers unique undercover drive-thru ensuite sites. A great spot to stop overnight or stay longer to explore the surrounding area.

336 BIG4 Wagga Wagga Holiday Park

$$$ ★

📍 93 Hammond Ave, Wagga Wagga
📞 (02) 6921 4287
💻 www.big4wagga.com.au

BIG4 HOLIDAY PARKS

Nestled on the banks of the Murrumbidgee River, right in the heart of Wagga Wagga, this family-friendly caravan park offers a great range of facilities including a swimming pool, games room and camp kitchen. It has level gravel sites with ensuite options, including some that are suitable for larger motorhomes.

284 Darlington Point Riverside Caravan Park

See p. 141 – Jerilderie to Cobar.

285 Griffith Caravan Village

See p. 141 – Jerilderie to Cobar.

337 BIG4 Hay Plains Holiday Park

$$$$ ★

📍 4 Nailor St, Hay South
📞 (02) 6993 1875
💻 www.haybig4.com.au

BIG4 HOLIDAY PARKS

Ideally located a short walk from the river and town centre this little country caravan park offers a good range of site options including drive-thru, slab-base and grassed. The amenities are basic but clean and there is a small pool onsite.

Junee Liquorice and Chocolate Factory

HAY TO MILDURA

NEED TO KNOW

🕐	**296km**
🏠	**National parks, riverside caravan parks, riverside free camping areas**
☁	**This area is great all year, but temperatures soar over summer.**
👁	**Mungo National Park**
🅰	**The highway is sealed and well maintained. Access to Mungo National Park is unsealed, but usually suitable for two-wheel drives coming from Mildura.**
🍴	**There are only basic shopping and facilities until Mildura.**
⚠	**The roads out here can be bumpy or poorly maintained, and even covered in water after heavy rains.**

Roadside fruit stand near Mildura, The Murray

INTRODUCTION

From Hay the Sturt Highway continues across the wide-open plains of south-western New South Wales before briefly meeting the Murray River at Euston then again at Mildura. It touches the edge of some of New South Wales' driest regions and significant Indigenous heritage sites. There is great camping and lots of open space to enjoy.

WHERE TO GO

It is a long drive along the Sturt Highway from Hay to Balranald, but it can be broken up by taking the Maude Rd west from Hay on the northern side of the Murrumbidgee River. About 12km west of town, stop to look at the Hay Weir, one of seven on the river that help control its flow. It's a great place to fish, or just stop for a picnic before continuing on to **Maude**. The very small town has a basic caravan park and a friendly pub.

From Maude, follow Maude Rd back to the highway and continue west

to **Balranald**. This lively riverside town is the oldest settlement on the lower Murrumbidgee, with records dating back to 1850. The ill-fated Burke and Wills expedition crossed the river here in 1860, while attempting to cross the continent from south to north. Today the town is a centre for a large pastoral area and has a popular bakery and grassy riverside caravan park. It's also one of the best towns from which to access Mungo National Park, 147km north. However, the road is unsealed and often rough from this direction and access is usually better from Mildura.

Two of my favourite towns on the Murray are **Robinvale** and **Euston**, if only because I've had some great times there camped with friends. Robinvale is a popular tourist destination, particularly during the Christmas and Easter holidays when many people camp along the river. The town is central to the local fruit industry and abounds with table-grape farms and orchards. The Robinvale caravan park, right on the riverbank, is a top spot for a happy hour, watching the sun set

over the river. Across the river, the Euston Club is a great place for a good feed.

From Robinvale it's only a short drive to **Mildura**, a key citrus and grape-growing area with a warm Mediterranean climate. In addition to its numerous vineyards and orchards, Mildura is the regional home of Australia's dried-fruit industry. That's why the region's name – Sunraysia – sounds familiar. Many small producers grow then sun-dry their fruit on racks. The city offers a diverse selection of accommodation, including houseboat hire, and has an abundance of caravan parks. It has an incredible food scene too, especially for somewhere so remote. It's been led by celebrity chef Stefano de Pieri, who has been running his Italian restaurant here since 1991.

DON'T MISS

→ **Window to the past – near Mildura**
The World Heritage–listed Mungo National Park encircles an ancient dry lake bed that preserves a record of human life dating back some 50,000 years. Access roads to the

park are all unsealed but they are suitable for two-wheel drive vehicles, caravans and campers that are well fitted to withstand long stretches of gravel. The park is about 150km from Balranald and 110km from Mildura. There are two camping areas in the park, but both have limited facilities.

WHERE TO STAY

338 Balranald Caravan Park

- 60 Court St, Balranald
- (03) 5020 1321
- www.balranaldcaravanpark.com.au

Set in a shady, open area right on the river this caravan park offers green, grassy sites within walking distance of the town centre. Amenities are dated but clean and there is a saltwater pool onsite.

339 Robinvale Riverside Caravan Park

- 25 McLennan Dr, Robinvale
- (03) 5026 4646
- www.robinvaleaccommodation.com.au Family Parks Holiday Parks & Campgrounds

Conveniently located just 1km from the town centre, this riverfront caravan park offers large shady sites on level green lawn with a good number of waterfront sites available. Amenities are spacious and clean, and there is a boat ramp onsite.

340 Apex Riverbeach Holiday Park

- 435 Cureton Ave, Mildura
- (03) 5023 6879
- www.apexriverbeach.com.au Family Parks Holiday Parks & Campgrounds

This large pet-friendly caravan park has a range of accommodation options including riverfront, concrete-slab and drive-thru sites. The amenities are dated but well kept, and the river beach across the road is excellent for swimming.

Mungo National Park

SYDNEY TO LITHGOW

Lake Lyell

INTRODUCTION

The explorers Blaxland, Wentworth and Lawson crossed the Blue Mountains in May 1813 and by December 1814 the first road through the range had been completed. Today, the multi-lane Great Western Highway follows remarkably close to the route marked out by the three men. It's an easy drive through elegant mountain villages and towns. The steepest section is at Victoria Pass, but modern vehicles handle it with relative ease.

WHERE TO GO

After you escape the urban sprawl of Sydney's west, the Great Dividing Range is almost as much of a significant barrier to development now as it was in the 19th century. **Glenbrook** is the first community west of the M4 – the main motorway carrying traffic west. There are a number of shops here as well as lovely parklands perfect for picnics. Glenbrook provides access to the southern section of Blue Mountains National Park and the popular bike ride along Woodford-Oaks fire trail.

Further up the mountain, some of Australia's most beautiful and private gardens thrive in **Leura**. The main shopping strip is a trendy place to be on most weekends with quaint cafes, boutiques and restaurants. Leura's Village Fair, on the second weekend in Oct, attracts people from all around the country.

The neighbouring town, **Katoomba**, is at the heart of the Blue Mountains and the largest of its centres. Some of the area's most recognisable natural features are just minutes away from its bustling main street. The Blue Mountains' most famous attraction – the Three Sisters – towers majestically above the Jamison Valley. The Queen Elizabeth Lookout at Echo Point offers an excellent view of this eroded sandstone rock formation which is also floodlit at night. The name comes from an Aboriginal legend that three sisters were turned to stone by a witch doctor to protect them, but the witch doctor was killed before he could restore life to their bodies.

This area is an extremely popular tourist destination and offers activities like bushwalking, abseiling, canyoning and rock climbing. The town has a wide range of accommodation, several art galleries, great restaurants and good shops.

From Katoomba the highway continues to climb, past the grand old Hydro Majestic Inn to **Blackheath**, the highest town in the Blue Mountains. Local attractions include Govetts Leap, Evans Lookout and Walls Cave, although I rarely pass through without stopping for a burger at the Blackheath Fish and Chip Shop. Blackheath is renowned for its fabulous Campbell Rhododendron Gardens.

EXPLORE AUSTRALIA BY CARAVAN & MOTORHOME

From Blackheath the road swiftly loses elevation down Victoria Pass and winds through farming land early 19th century Australians could only dream of before coming to Lithgow. Rich in heritage, **Lithgow** has a history in coal and steel, while Lithgow Arms is unique in Australia for the fact it has manufactured both sporting and military weapons. The Lithgow Small Arms Museum showcases a comprehensive collection of small arms from around the world, including many manufactured at the nearby factory. Lithgow has most services and good shopping, as well as a nice caravan park.

DON'T MISS

→ **Awe-inspiring views – Wentworth Falls**

In 1836, naturalist Charles Darwin arrived at the tiny settlement of Weatherboard and followed a path towards the edge of the plateau. There, atop a cascade now known as Wentworth Falls, he came upon 'a most magnificent astounding and unique view … certainly [the] most stupendous cliffs I have ever seen.' The scene is just as awe-inspiring today. What's more, excellent walking trails lead along the cliffs to other viewpoints and to the base of the waterfall.

→ **Soar over the Jamison Valley – near Katoomba**

At Katoomba's Scenic World, the glass-floored Scenic Skyway crosses a deep gorge 270m above the valley floor, while the Scenic Cableway is Australia's steepest cable-car ride and the Scenic Railway is the world's steepest incline railway. All three provide wonderful views of the Jamison Valley and the Three Sisters. Fees apply and it's open daily 9am-5pm. Contact (02) 4780 0200.

→ **Year-round trout fishing – near Lithgow**

On the banks of Lake Lyell, a man-made reservoir for the Mt Piper and Wallerawang power stations, it is stocked with brown and rainbow trout and can be fished all year round. There is an excellent camping area on its shores, and the waterway is also popular for waterskiing in summer.

WHERE TO STAY

44 NRMA Sydney Lakeside Holiday Park

See p. 24 – Nowra to Sydney.

341 Katoomba Falls Caravan Park

📍 100 Katoomba Falls Rd, Katoomba
📞 (02) 4782 1835
🖥 www.bmtp.com.au

Located in a quiet, off-the-highway setting, this well-appointed caravan park is very close to Katoomba's cable car and scenic railway. It is an ideal park for a few days stay to explore the area. Bookings are required in all holiday periods.

342 Blackheath Glen Tourist Park

📍 67 Prince Edwards S, Blackheath
📞 (02) 4787 8101
🖥 www.bmtp.com.au

In the heart of the Blue Mountains, this caravan park is situated in pretty parkland near the Campbell Rhododendron Gardens, and within easy walking distance of the town centre and Govetts Leap lookout area. There are good, basic facilities and just over the road is a playground. Bookings are required at Christmas, Easter and long weekends.

343 Lake Lyell Recreation Park

📍 Magpie Hollow Rd, Lithgow
📞 (02) 6355 6347
🖥 www.lakelyellrecreationpark.com.au

Right on the banks of Lake Lyell with a range of powered and unpowered sites, this is a Blue Mountains summer playground popular for boating, swimming and trout fishing. I love visiting in winter, when it's usually much quieter, the trout are still biting and fires at night keep us warm.

The Three Sisters

LITHGOW TO ORANGE

NEED TO KNOW

🎨	**118km**
🏠	**Full-featured caravan parks, basic caravan parks**
☁	**Spring, summer and autumn**
👁	**Motor racing, Jenolan Caves, wineries**
🅰	**The Great Western Highway is very good, but some back roads can be in need of maintenance.**
🍴	**Bathurst is a major regional city and has all facilities.**
⚠	**Extreme winter weather, with occasional snow and ice, can cause hazardous driving conditions, and fog is quite common, so take care.**

Emirates One&Only Wolgan Valley

INTRODUCTION

Although this section leaves the Great Dividing Range behind, the Great Western and Mitchell highways still pass over marvellous hill country and farming land. If you are prepared to detour, there's plenty to see and do, great places to camp and good history to be found. Plus, there's the chance to drive Australia's most famous racetrack.

WHERE TO GO

Instead of heading due west, straight out of **Lithgow**, consider spending some time at the historic town of **Newnes**. It's right at the end of the Wolgan Valley – take Wolgan Rd off the Castlereagh Highway and follow it until it ends. On the way in you might catch a glimpse of one of Australia's most exclusive resorts, the Emirates One&Only Wolgan Valley – where rooms start at around $2000 a night! The immense sandstone amphitheatre at the end of the road contains the historic shale-mining town of Newnes and its large free camping area. It's one of my family's favourite places close to Sydney.

After backtracking to Lithgow and rejoining the Great Western Highway, it's worth leaving it again at the turn-off to **Jenolan Caves**, a spectacular attraction that's been luring Sydneysiders west since the 1880s. The grand Caves House is listed on the New South Wales Heritage Register and has been serving tourists for over 115 years.

On the way back to the highway, you pass through **Oberon**, which is a little piece of England tucked into the mountains. There are spectacular gardens, great trout fishing and it's a popular place for horseriders who explore the many wandering trails year-round. As there is no camping near Jenolan Caves, the Jenolan Caravan Park at Oberon, 30 min away is the best base for caravanners to stay.

From Oberon you can simply follow the winding O'Connell Rd through rolling farmland and dense mountain forest all the way to **Kelso**, an outer suburb of Bathurst.

Bathurst, proclaimed in 1815, is Australia's oldest inland settlement. Gold was discovered in the area in 1823, but it was not until discoveries at Ophir and Sofala in the 1850s that the town boomed. In 1862

Bathurst supported 50 hotels. Past Prime Minister Ben Chifley was born and lived in Bathurst and the city council maintains the Chifley Home at 10 Busby St, just like it was when the Chifleys lived there. The Mt Panorama motor-racing circuit hosts one of Australia's most popular motor-racing events, the Bathurst 1000 on the 1st weekend in October. Keep this in mind when travelling because accommodation can be booked out for 100km in any direction, so prepare early, or avoid the area at this time.

Another interesting goldmining town further west is **Lucknow**, just outside of Orange. It is the site of the Wentworth Goldfields which were distinctive in two respects – the quality of gold found here was good, and it was on private land, so public prospecting was not permitted. Gold was mined here until 1938 and several relics still remain.

Orange, known as Australia's Colour City, experiences very distinct seasons and the city's trees change through the spectrum of greens to reds and oranges. In 1951 Australia's first major seam of gold was discovered at Ophir, 30km north. Since 1983 grapevines have been planted in the area and now more than 50 vineyards dot the landscape. As a result, Orange has developed a reputation for producing quality food and wine. The town has all services, excellent shopping and some very good restaurants.

DON'T MISS

→ Racing fever – Bathurst

The famous Mt Panorama race circuit is a public road and can be driven on most times of the year – I've done a lap or two towing caravans. There is a strict speed limit of 60km/hr around the 6.213km circuit, though – so if your best lap is faster than 6 minutes and 13 seconds, you'll likely be booked for speeding. Under race conditions, the current fastest lap is just over 2 min,

an average speed of around 180km/hr. Race enthusiasts might also like to visit the National Motor Racing Museum which houses a wide selection of racing cars and bikes, including some that have won the Bathurst 1000. Entry fees apply and it's open daily 9am–4.30pm. Contact (02) 6332 1872.

→ The man from … – Orange

Orange is the birthplace of the great Australian poet A. B. (Banjo) Paterson, author of *The Man from Snowy River*, who spent his early years in Yeoval (80km north-west). Each February his birthday is celebrated in Orange with the Banjo Paterson Festival.

→ Golden history – Hill End

It's well off the tourist trail, but the historic goldmining town of Hill End is one of the most delightful in New South Wales. Best accessed from Bathurst via Sofala, most of its buildings have historic significance. Many of the buildings are open to the public for free, although donations are welcome. Tours of the nearby mines run regularly, and there's a pleasant camping area on the village green with only very modest fees for powered or unpowered sites.

WHERE TO STAY

344 NRMA Bathurst Panorama Holiday Park

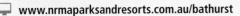

- 250 Sydney Rd, Kelso
- (02) 6331 8286
- www.nrmaparksandresorts.com.au/bathurst

NRMA Parks + Resorts

This is a quality caravan park on the Great Western Highway, 5km east of the centre of Bathurst. It offers a range of accommodation and great facilities including games and entertainment rooms. Bookings are required for peak times, particularly Christmas, Easter and around Bathurst 1000.

345 Colour City Caravan Park

- 203 Margaret St, Orange
- (02) 6393 8980
- www.orange.nsw.gov.au

This is a council-run caravan park with good, basic facilities, It's in a quiet, off-highway position, about 2km north of the city centre, adjoining the showgrounds. It is good value at a budget price. Bookings are recommended all year round.

Union Bank Wine Bar, Orange

ORANGE TO DUBBO

Taronga Western Plains Zoo, Dubbo

INTRODUCTION

From Orange to Dubbo the highway meanders across open farming country, passing through several smaller towns and the larger community of Wellington. There's plenty of early pioneering history to uncover, as well as some of New South Wales' most popular attractions to explore.

WHERE TO GO

Less than half an hour north-west of **Orange**, **Molong** is a charming rural town on the Mitchell Highway. Cobb & Co. coaches once ran through Molong, and in later years moved their passengers onto the railway. Sadly, the train no longer stops at Molong. About 2km east of town is the grave of Yuranigh, the Aboriginal guide for explorer Sir Thomas Mitchell. The town has basic facilities and limited shopping, but there are some good craft- and gift-shops.

Rather than following the Mitchell Highway to Wellington, a better route is along Euchareena Rd and Burrendong Way to the picturesque Lake Burrendong. This large water storage of the Macquarie River is popular for watersports, fishing

Old Dubbo Gaol

and camping. As well as two caravan parks on different parts of its shores, there is a major botanical garden with over 500,000 plants from more than 2000 native species. The gardens will delight naturalists and gardeners, especially from late winter to early summer when many plants are in bloom.

Further downstream, and set at the junction of the Macquarie and Bell rivers, **Wellington** is the second oldest town west of the Blue Mountains. There is a museum in the old bank, built in 1883. But the town is perhaps best known for its spectacular caves. The Wellington Caves, Phosphate Mine and many fossils are found at the holiday complex. Guided tours visit Cathedral Cave, which boasts the world's largest stalagmite; the Gaden Cave, renowned for its cave 'coral'; and the Phosphate Mine. The mine is a chance to see how miners worked during WWI. Entry fees apply

and it's open daily 9am–4.30pm. Contact (02) 6845 2970.

Dubbo, which is about halfway between Brisbane and Melbourne is a popular hub of central New South Wales. Indeed it's so popular April–Oct that it's a good idea to call ahead the day before to book your site. The most popular attraction is the Taronga Western Plains Zoo, which is home to over a thousand animals from across the world. Most people take two days to see it all. It's well worth a visit, and because it's so big, cars can be driven around the grounds, or bikes hired at the entrance.

DON'T MISS

→ **Stone cells and convicts' chains – Dubbo**

The Old Dubbo Gaol offers a fascinating self-guided tour through an 1870s gaol that operated until 1966. See the original gallows, stop a moment in the solitary-confinement

cell, and listen while animatronic models tell the convicts' stories. Entry fees apply and it's open daily 9am–4pm. Contact (02) 6801 4460.

→ **Taronga Western Plains Zoo – Dubbo**

Home to over a thousand animals from across the world in more than 300 hectares of bushland, the Taronga Western Plains Zoo is justifiably one of the state's most popular attractions. My experience has been that many animals are more active in the cooler morning, and tend to lie in the shade during the middle of the day. If possible, plan your visit early and make sure you allow adequate time. I feel a minimum of four hours is required, although passes are for two-day entry. There are some welcome picnic areas in the zoo, so pack a lunch. Entry fees apply and it's open daily 9am–4pm. Contact (02) 6881 1488.

WHERE TO STAY

346 Wellington Caves Holiday Complex

📍 Caves Rd, Wellington
📞 (02) 6845 2970
💻 www.wellingtoncaves.com.au

Relax and let a few days slip by at this spacious caravan park, located 6km south of the town centre alongside Wellington Caves – a popular tourist attraction. It is a quality park and makes an ideal stopover. Bookings are required at Easter and for long weekends.

347 Wellington Riverside Caravan Park

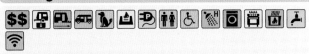

📍 1 Federal St, Wellington
📞 (02) 6845 1370
💻 www.wellingtonriversidepark.com.au

This is a well-maintained caravan park on the banks of the Macquarie River, close to the highway and just a short walk from the centre of town. The park has good facilities at a budget price. Bookings are required at Easter and for long weekends.

348 Dubbo City Holiday Park

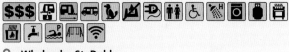

📍 Whylandra St, Dubbo
📞 (02) 6801 4530
💻 www.dubbocityholidaypark.com.au

Enjoy the sights of Dubbo from this centrally located caravan park. It is conveniently located on the Newell Hwy about 2km from the city centre and just a short drive from the Taronga Western Plains Zoo. This park has a selection of accommodation and good facilities, including a car-washing bay. Bookings are required at peak times.

DUBBO TO COBAR

NEED TO KNOW

🕐	**301km**
🏠	**Roadhouse caravan parks, free camping areas, outback caravan parks**
☁	**Avoid the region during the heat of summer.**
👁	**Mining history, outback camping**
🛡	**This is a fully sealed route.**
🍴	**After Dubbo, most services are available, but they are often basic.**
⚠	**None apply**

Great Western Hotel, Cobar

INTRODUCTION

West of Dubbo, and particularly west of Nyngan, is considered outback Australia – complete with red dirt, ephemeral waterways, immense pastoral leases and wide-open skies. Here the roads are long and straight, the camping good and the locals friendly.

WHERE TO GO

Further downstream from **Dubbo**, on the banks of the Macquarie River, **Narromine** is a small outback town that services the surrounding farmland. Grazing and grain growing have been a way of life here for more than a century. Narromine is known worldwide as an excellent centre for gliding. Its advantages are many – there are few airspace restrictions, the terrain is flat, the hot, dry climate is excellent for soaring and there are plenty of safe places to land in the surrounding area. Narromine is also a popular ultralight centre. For those not prepared to take to the sky in an aircraft without a motor, there is an aviation museum at the Narromine airport, 1.8km north-west of town. It tells the history of the airport – once one of Australia's most significant regional air centres. Entry fees apply and

it's open Wed–Mon 10am–4pm. Contact (02) 6889 7131.

Nearby, **Trangie** has most basic services and is at the centre of a rich irrigation area where cotton is the predominant crop. The weir at nearby **Gin Gin** on the Macquarie River is popular for boating, fishing and swimming.

A sign at the entrance to **Nyngan** greets you boldly informing you you're finally in the 'Great Outback'. (Interestingly, a similar sign farewells you as you leave Dubbo too.) Situated on the banks of the Bogan River, at the junction of the Mitchell and Barrier highways, Nyngan is an important centre for a large mixed-farming district. In 1990 heavy rains contributed to devastating flooding which required the whole town to be evacuated from the railway station by helicopter. A museum, the only building to escape the flood, highlights the town's history, including that fateful event. Nyngan has most basic services and a small section of shops.

The Barrier Highway travels almost due west from Nyngan to Cobar, and late in the afternoon on a sunny day it's a nightmare to drive on because the sun can be blinding. It's a trip best done in the morning, with the sun behind you.

Cobar has a long mining history and several fine buildings. One of the favourites

is the Great Western Hotel, which has the longest verandah of any pub in New South Wales. Copper was discovered here in 1869 and the area became a magnet for Cornish miners. In fact, the CSA (Cornish, Scottish and Australian) Mine is still the largest producer of copper in the country. Since 1991, gold has also been mined at Cobar, and from the Fort Bourke Hill Lookout, just east of town, you can look down into the New Cobar Open Cut Goldmine. Actually it's not new, but was in fact Cobar's first mine. There are good camping options around Cobar, some of them free.

DON'T MISS

→ **A rich copper lode – Cobar**
Copper was discovered here in 1869, and the ore, which is said to be called 'gubar' in the local Indigenous tongue, even gives the town its name. With the development of mines, there was an influx of Cornish migrants, and many local surnames are Cornish in origin. Visit the Great Cobar Heritage Centre, a terrific museum, for a glimpse into Cobar's history.

WHERE TO STAY

349 Narromine Tourist Park & Motel

$$ ★

- ⦿ Aerodrome, Mitchell Hwy, Narromine
- 📞 (02) 6889 2129
- 🖥 www.narrominetouristpark.com.au

Located in a popular gliding area this caravan park is conveniently located next to the airfield and just a short walk from the Narromine Aviation Museum. With flat, grassy sites and clean, well-kept amenities this park is suited to most travellers.

350 Nyngan Riverside Caravan Park

$$ ★

- ⦿ Barrier Hwy, Nyngan
- 📞 (02) 6832 1729
- 🖥 www.nynganriverside.com.au

This lovely riverfront caravan park has a range of accommodation options including flat, grassy, unpowered, powered and drive-thru ensuite sites. It is a popular spot to enjoy fishing and watersports.

351 Mulga Creek Hotel and Caravan Park

$$ ★

- ⦿ Mitchell Hwy, Byrock
- 📞 (02) 6874 7311

This rustic bush camping area located behind the hotel has large, level sites and basic but clean amenities. The pub provides a good hot meal and cold brew. Perfect overnight stop.

288 Cornish rest area

See p. 141 – Jerilderie to Cobar.

Ultralight at Narromine

COBAR TO BROKEN HILL

Silverton

INTRODUCTION

The Barrier Highway between Cobar and Broken Hill is a long, flat road broken only by Wilcannia. Although the surface is generally good, and there are ample opportunities to overtake, it's a road only for people who are in a hurry. If you've got the time, and can handle a decent amount of time on graded dirt roads, venturing both north and south of the highway will see you in iconic outback towns like Louth, Tilpa and Menindee.

WHERE TO GO

About 132km north-west of **Cobar** the tiny town of **Louth** sits on the banks of the Darling River. Settled when a pub was built as a stopover for the river trade carting wool down the Murray it's still just a one-pub town. Its most notable attraction

is the 8m high Celtic cross, a monument to Mary Mathews, the young wife of the town's founder who died at just 42. Each night as the sun sets, the cross' reflection blazes spectacularly for three minutes. From Cobar, the first 32km are sealed, although the last 100km is dirt, it is usually very well maintained and suitable for two-wheel drives.

From Louth, the all-dirt Darling River Rd follows the course of the river until it reaches **Tilpa**. Tilpa's another tiny town which claims to have the shortest heritage walk in Australia – it starts and ends on either side of the main road in front of the pub. The cemetery is unique because there isn't anyone buried in it.

The road from Tilpa continues unsealed to **Wilcannia**. Once a key Darling River paddlesteamer port the town grew into a strong regional administrative centre for the grazing industry. Today, many of the

classic sandstone buildings remain and a self-guided heritage trail gives a hint of the town's former glory, when it was Australia's third largest port carrying wool from north-western New South Wales to market.

From Wilcannia, the Barrier Highway continues its straight run to Broken Hill, but 155km south-west are the expansive Menindee Lakes. When full these lakes hold three times more water than Sydney Harbour. Some of the most satisfying outback camping I have ever done is on their banks when they're full. Burke and Wills camped here on their 1860 journey north too. **Menindee** itself is small, mostly servicing tourists passing through and has a friendly pub, service station and caravan park. Nearby Kinchega National Park maintains the historic Kinchega Woolshed.

It's 116km from Menindee to **Broken Hill** via the sealed, but wandering, Menindee Rd. In 1883 the rich Broken Hill silver, lead and zinc deposits were discovered and by 1885 the Broken Hill Proprietary Company had been formed to mine ore there. Over more than a century, the infrastructure, highways, roads and water supply have improved to transform this once-remote frontier mining town into a modern city, well connected with the larger coastal cities. As mining has declined over the recent decades, tourism has grown and Broken Hill is now a busy tourist centre noted for its red sandy surrounds and talented arts community. The city has many galleries, including those of Pro Hart, Jack Absalom and Roxanne Minchin. It also has all services, good shopping and some excellent restaurants.

North-west of Broken Hill is **Silverton**, a significant commercial centre for silver-mining operations at the end of the 19th century. The town's fortunes soon withered when Broken Hill became the mining centre, and many houses in Broken Hill are actually originally from here. It's probably most famous as the filming location for the movie *Mad Max 2*, starring Mel Gibson. Each day hundreds of tourists make the 30 min trek out to have a beer in the pub, take in the extensive collection of Mad Max memorabilia at the Mad Max 2 Museum

(entry fee applies, cash only) or to visit the stunning and varied galleries of the talented artists that reside here. Just outside of town, a rise above the Mundi Mundi forms an excellent lookout. It's one of the few land-based places on earth flat enough to show the curvature of the earth. Apart from the pub, there are no services.

DON'T MISS

→ Louth Races – Louth

The Louth Races is one of the best outback racing carnivals in Australia and each year attracts up to 5000 people to the tiny town which has a population of just 43. It's always held on the weekend following the August bank holiday, and is an incredibly jovial event which sees the campground full and the pub overflowing.

→ An historic woolshed – Kinchega National Park

Many people who visit the Kinchega woolshed marvel that they can still smell the scent left by the millions of sheep which were shorn here between 1875 and 1967. In actual fact, the rangers in charge of its upkeep actually treat the wooden structure with lanolin, to preserve it. It was once the largest

shearing shed in the southern hemisphere, but only about half of it remains. It is still fascinating to see though and guided tours are available during the Easter, winter and spring school holidays.

→ Flying doctors – Broken Hill

Australia's world famous Royal Flying Doctor Service has a base and visitor centre at the Broken Hill airport, to the south of the city. You can take a tour through the base and see the organisation at work. The centre has a theatre, museum and gift shop. Entry fees apply and it's open 9am–5pm weekdays and 10am–3pm weekends. Contact (08) 8080 3714.

TRAVEL TIP

Broken Hill, although in New South Wales, operates on Australian Central Standard Time, the same as South Australia, 50km to the west. It also uses the South Australian area code for its phone numbers. The city's business dealings are generally with South Australia, so this is more convenient. Broken Hill's ore is shipped to Port Pirie for refining and most general supplies are sourced from South Australia.

WHERE TO STAY

352 Trilby Station

$$$

📍 Toorale Rd, Louth
📞 (02) 6874 7420
💻 www.trilbystation.com.au

A basic camping area on a working station, this is a very welcoming location in the heart of black-soil country. Both powered and remote, unpowered sites are offered, on the banks of the Darling River.

353 Warrawong on the Darling

$$$

📍 Barrier Hwy, Wilcannia
📞 1300 688 225
💻 www.warrawongonthedarling.com.au

Another beautiful riverfront caravan park with excellent modern amenities and flat grassy sites. A perfect spot to enjoy the scenery and wildlife or explore the surrounding region. Campfire dinners are available seasonally.

354 Broken Hill Tourist Park

$$$$

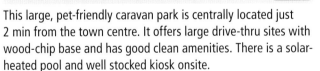

📍 142 Rakow St, Broken Hill
📞 1800 803 842
💻 www.brokenhilltouristpark.com.au

This large, pet-friendly caravan park is centrally located just 2 min from the town centre. It offers large drive-thru sites with wood-chip base and has good clean amenities. There is a solar-heated pool and well stocked kiosk onsite.

Trilby Station

BROKEN HILL TO ADELAIDE

Escapegoat Adventures Bike Wine Tour, Adelaide Hills

INTRODUCTION

The Barrier Highway sweeps into South Australia across vast saltbush plains, roughly following the same route the Broken Hill to Port Pirie railway once did. It passes through the historic town of Burra, comes close to Peterborough and then runs through the fabulous Clare Valley, an important wine region.

WHERE TO GO

Between **Broken Hill** and Port Pirie, the narrow-gauge railway was once one of the busiest and most profitable railways in the world. The towns along the line sprang up simply to service it and the trains that came through. The border town of **Cockburn**, for example, was once an important rail terminal where freight was transferred from trains to camels carrying supplies north to outback settlements.

Yunta, now a small town servicing the local pastoral community and highway traffic, was established when gold was discovered nearby in the late 1880s. By the 1890s it was a significant rail town servicing the line. Today, an unsealed route north is a popular access point to the Flinders Ranges (*see* p. 203).

Of all the railway towns in the area, though, **Peterborough** was the most significant. So many steam trains were serviced at the town's rail works, it's said the climate actually warmed in the local area. It has a very popular rail museum, as well as motorcycle, farming and miniatures museums. The town is not on the highway, but a popular diversion with a few good accommodation options in and out of the town.

The route from Peterborough to Port Augusta, via Orroroo and Wilmington, is a popular shortcut for travellers heading west. The road is fully sealed, in good condition and passes along what I consider to be one of the prettiest sections of highway in Australia at Horrocks Pass.

Continuing on the Barrier Highway to Adelaide, it passes through the historic town of **Burra**, a former coppermining centre 158km north of Adelaide. It is one of the country's best preserved mining towns with numerous historic buildings and significant mining infrastructure still in place to show visitors what life and work were like in a 19th-century copper mine.

From Burra it's only a small diversion to the wonderful Clare Valley. There are over 30 cellar doors in the region, which is best known for its riesling. From the Clare Caravan Park, the most central place to stay,

you can hire bikes to ride the Riesling Trail. The 35km long walking and cycling track passes by some of the region's best wineries and there aren't many hills.

It's only a little over an hour from the Clare Valley to **Adelaide**, one of Australia's most relaxed capital cities. Every time my family visits Adelaide we stay at the Christies Beach Caravan Park. Christies Beach, the town, doesn't have a great reputation around Adelaide, but we love how relaxed it is at the park. In fact, all the parks along the mid-coast are great, although the one at Brighton is the most popular, and for good reason.

Using any of the mid-coast caravan parks as a base, venture into the McLaren Vale wine region. (*See* Fleurieu Peninsula p. 118.)

DON'T MISS

➔ **Rail heritage – Peterborough**
Peterborough was once an important railway centre and Steamtown is an operating museum maintaining a working link with Peterborough's narrow-gauge railway heritage. The attractions include Australia's only triple-gauge turntable and an excellent 'Sound and Light' show, which is a feature-length documentary watched from restored 19th-century rail carriages. I loved it and so did the kids.

→ A key to the past – Burra

The Burra Heritage Passport, on sale at the Burra Visitor Centre, comes with a key that allows entry to eight locked historic sites. The heritage trail is 11km in length and can be walked, cycled or driven. Stops include the Burra Mine Site, 1847 lock-up, 1956 gaol, brewery cellars and miners' dugouts. It's one of the best things to do in the area.

TRAVEL TIP

The Barrier Highway is a popular route between Sydney and Adelaide. It passes through relatively dry, saltbush sheep-grazing country. Large kangaroos are often a problem in this area and they are most common around dawn and dusk. They are also difficult to see at night. A collision with a kangaroo can cause extensive damage to vehicles, so it is very important to take care when driving this route.

WHERE TO STAY

355 Peterborough Caravan Park

📍 36 Grove St, Peterborough
📞 (08) 8651 2545

This tidy little caravan park is in a lovely heritage town and is close to the excellent Steamtown heritage rail museum. It has good-sized gravel sites with nice clean amenities.

356 Burra Caravan Park

📍 12 Bridge Tce, Burra
📞 (08) 8892 2442

Situated on the banks of the picturesque Burra Creek, just a short walk from the centre of the old mining town, this caravan park has good basic facilities and plenty of shade. Bookings are required from Easter to Oct.

357 Discovery Parks Clare

📍 Lot 136 Main North Rd, Clare
📞 (08) 8842 2724
🖥 www.discoveryholidayparks.com.au

Discovery
HOLIDAY PARKS

Just two hours from Adelaide, in the middle of wine country, this is a great caravan park to base yourself in to spend a few days exploring the Clare Valley. Nice grassy sites with good clean amenities and just a short drive in to the main town.

358 Barossa Tourist Park

📍 Penrice Rd, Nuriootpa
📞 (08) 8562 1404
🖥 www.barossatouristpark.com.au

BIG4
HOLIDAY PARKS

This large caravan park is within walking distance of the town centre and has a number of excellent onsite facilities including a swimming pool and outdoor chess set. Nice shady area with a choice of grass or gravel sites. Bookings required during peak times and minimum-length stays apply during Christmas, Easter and public holidays.

359 Levi Park Caravan Park

📍 1a Harris Rd, Vale Park, Adelaide
📞 (08) 8344 2209
🖥 www.levipark.com.au

TOP PARKS

Just 5km from the city this caravan park is an excellent base for exploring central Adelaide. Nestled on the banks of the River Torrens there is plenty of shade and the amenities are good and clean. A nice spot, close to the Adelaide CBD.

256 Christies Beach Tourist Park

See p. 119 – Fleurieu Peninsula.

257 Brighton Caravan Park

See p. 119 – Fleurieu Peninsula.

ROCKHAMPTON TO BARCALDINE

Fairbairn Dam

INTRODUCTION

The Capricorn Highway surges westward through the cattle region west of Rockhampton, alongside enormous coal trains which thunder along the major rail link between the Central Queensland coalfields and the export ports. It passes through coalfields, rich agricultural land, gem fields and cattle country, before arriving at the birthplace of the Australian Labor party in Barcaldine.

WHERE TO GO

On the Tropic of Capricorn, **Rockhampton** is one of Queensland's major cities. 'Rocky', which began its life as a river port, is known for its beef – more than one third of Australia's cattle are raised on central Queensland properties. As the highway tracks west, it passes by many of them. The Mount Hay Gemstone Tourist Park is a popular first stop heading this way. It's an internationally renowned area to fossick for thunder eggs – crystalline rock formations caused by cooling gas bubbles in molten lava.

Another natural rarity can be found in the small town of **Duaringa**. The Duaringa stringy bark, once of great significance to the local Aboriginal people, is now only found, locally, at Mackenzie Park. Overnight camping is also permitted (for a donation) at this convenient rest area alongside the highway that has showers, toilets, free WiFi and barbecues.

After passing through **Dingo** and **Bluff**, both of which have basic caravan parks near or behind the pubs, the highway comes to **Blackwater**, which lies in the Bowen Basin and is considered the Coal Capital of Australia. Approximately 15 million tonnes of coal are transported annually from local mines to the terminal at Gladstone. There are several mines around Blackwater, some of which offer tours – check with the information centre, which is located in the Blackwater Coal Centre, adjoining the Japanese Gardens on the Capricorn Highway.

Between Blackwater and **Emerald**, the Capricorn Highway runs side-by-side with the railway line through land that varies between open grazing country and small stands of eucalypt forest. Emerald is the major centre in this area and has good shopping and services. Gem fields lie to the west, while around town there is agricultural land growing cotton, sorghum and citrus. Nearby Fairbairn Dam (Lake Maraboon) is a popular recreational area that's stocked with eight different species of fish, including barramundi and red claw crayfish. Lake Maraboon Holiday Village has a boat ramp, offering access to the lake for boating, fishing and waterskiing.

To the west, the towns of **Rubyvale**, **Sapphire**, **Willows Gemfields** and **Anakie** are at the heart of the central Queensland gem fields. The fields produce a wide range of attractively coloured sapphires, most notably in yellow and variegated colours. You can try your luck fossicking or buy stones and finished jewellery from various shops in the area. Rubyvale's hotel in town is built from local 'billy boulders' a popular construction method in the area.

Barcaldine lies at the junction of the Capricorn and Landsborough highways and the town was founded in 1886 when the railway pushed west from Rockhampton. Soon after, Barcaldine became famous as the centre of the shearers strike of 1891, and the Australian Labor Party was formed as a result of the strike meetings. The tree under which the strike meetings took place became known as the Tree of Knowledge and stood in Barcaldine for another 115 years before it was mysteriously poisoned in an act of vandalism in 2006. So significant is the tree that the original trunk has been preserved and is on display in town as part of a spectacular memorial which is best viewed at night. Saplings from cuttings have been preserved (and some grow in Barcaldine) while the tree was also cloned – one is growing healthily in Brisbane.

DON'T MISS

→ **A sea of white cotton – near Emerald**

Cotton is a major crop in the Emerald agricultural area, which produces 25 per cent of Queensland's cotton. The crops reach maturity late in summer, covering the fields with white, fluffy bolls. Harvesting usually begins in Mar, the crop being processed at local cotton gins.

→ **How they toiled – Barcaldine**

The Australian Workers Heritage Centre at Barcaldine showcases the experiences of workers and the difficult conditions in which they often laboured in days gone by. This popular tribute is in the centre of town on two hectares of landscaped gardens. It's open daily 10am–4pm and entry fees apply. Contact (07) 4651 2422.

WHERE TO STAY

99 **Discovery Parks Rockhampton**

See p. 47 – Gin Gin to Rockhampton.

360 **Silver Wattle Caravan Park**

📍 50691 Burnett Hwy, Mount Morgan
📞 (07) 4938 1550
🖥 www.silverwattlecaravanpark.com.au

This basic caravan park is suitable for a couple of days' stay to check out this historic mining town. Large sites are available for big rigs and it's pet friendly.

361 **Lake Maraboon Holiday Village**

📍 Corner of Fairbairn Dam Rd and Selma Rd, Emerald
📞 (07) 4982 3677
🖥 www.lakemaraboonholidayvillage.com.au

This caravan park is located 18km south-west of Emerald on the shores of Lake Maraboon, a popular spot for watersports and fishing. Red claw crayfish are a major attraction. There is a restaurant that opens daily for lunch and dinner and the park offers boat hire too. Bookings are required in peak periods and a minimum-length stay applies at Christmas and Easter.

297 **Barcaldine Tourist Park**

See p. 147 – Augathella to Barcaldine.

Cotton, near Emerald

CLONCURRY TO THREE WAYS ROADHOUSE

NEED TO KNOW

🕐	756km
🏠	Free camping areas, basic outback caravan parks
☁	Autumn to early spring
👁	History, dinosaur fossils, mine tours, free camping
🅰	Good to great
🍴	Mount Isa is a busy mining centre and has most services.
⚠	The highway carries a lot of heavy transports and has long stretches without fuel stops.

O'Shannassy River near Boodjamulla National Park

INTRODUCTION

The Barkly Highway winds slowly through the picturesque ranges as it approaches Mount Isa, a busy mining centre and residential city. Take some time and enjoy a tour of the mine, or visit the Riversleigh Fossil Centre. Further west, the highway stretches across the black-soil plains of the Barkly Tableland, a major cattle-grazing region.

WHERE TO GO

It is just over an hour's drive from the former coppermining centre of **Cloncurry** to the coppermining capital of Australia – **Mount Isa**. Isa, as it's locally known, is the largest industrial and commercial centre in north-west Queensland so it has very good shopping, all services and plenty of accommodation. It owes its interesting history to copper, silver, lead and zinc.

Mount Isa Mines is Australia's largest underground mine and all its features can be experienced at the Hard Times Mine, adjoining the Riversleigh Fossil Centre. There are 1.2km of tunnels, where you will encounter all the sights, sounds and sensations of a working underground mine.

The unique Riversleigh Fossil Centre in Mount Isa gives you a great insight into the World Heritage-listed fossils excavated during 1976 at Riversleigh Station, about 190km north of Camooweal. The centre provides a rare glimpse of exotic animals that lived in the area 25 million years ago. There are many displays, a theatrette and fossil material.

The only town between Mount Isa and the Northern Territory border, **Camooweal** was proclaimed a town in 1887 and was an important pre-Federation customs outpost at the Queensland border. Today it is a popular tourist stop, especially during the cooler winter months. Most basic services are available, and this is the last fuel stop before Barkly Homestead, 263km west. Many travellers stop to look at the Freckleton's Store building or visit Camooweal Caves National Park, 24km south along the unsealed Urandangi Rd. Only properly equipped and experienced cavers should enter this complex dolomite labyrinth, and it is recommended that caving be restricted to the dry season.

The Barkly Tableland covers a large area of the midlands of the Northern Territory, and rich Mitchell-grass plains stretch to the horizon both north and south of the Barkly Highway. The **Barkly Homestead Roadhouse** is a key service centre in this remote area, with fuel as well as a bar, restaurant, motel and extensive caravan park, with predominantly drive-thru, powered sites. It is not the cheapest, or even the best, caravan park you'll ever find but it is an oasis on the Tableland. Remember, it's the sort of place that is worth supporting so that it can continue to operate for travellers like us.

It's another 190km from Barkly Homestead to the Stuart Highway, and one of Australia's best known intersections. The **Three Ways Roadhouse** provides fuel, meals and accommodation for travellers, and is only 24km north of Tennant Creek.

Tennant Creek was the location of Australia's last gold rush in 1932. Today gold is still mined on the rich Tennant Creek fields and fossickers also come to try their luck. The town is busy for one so remote, with most basic services available for travellers, including a couple of reasonable caravan parks. There's a very interesting goldmining museum just 1.5km east of town.

DON'T MISS

→ **Flying doctor dedication – Cloncurry**
There's a great museum dedicated to Reverend John Flynn and the founders of the Royal Flying Doctor Service. The John Flynn Place Museum includes exhibits of the first pedal wireless and a scale model of the *Victory*, the first plane that took off

with a doctor on board in 1928. Entry fees apply and it's open 9am–4pm weekdays and 9am–3pm weekends.

→ **A remote oasis – north of Camooweal**

Discover stunning Boodjamulla (Lawn Hill) National Park, 245km north of Camooweal.

Lawn Hill Gorge has colourful cliffs rising 60m to the surrounding plateau. On the gorge walls are Aboriginal rock paintings, and middens also remain. Visitors can see these from the boardwalk and viewing platforms. The creek has permanent water and offers a habitat for tropical vegetation. The water attracts various bird species and

reptiles including freshwater crocodiles, tortoises and water monitors. There are several walking tracks in the park and canoeing and kayaking are popular ways to explore the gorge system. The road into Lawn Hill can be rough in places, so a four-wheel drive is recommended.

WHERE TO STAY

302 Discovery Parks Cloncurry

See p. 151 – Winton to Karumba.

362 Discovery Parks Mount Isa

⚲ 185 Little West St, Mount Isa
📞 (07) 4743 4676
🖥 www.discoveryholidayparks.com.au/ qld/outback_queensland/mount_isa

Discovery HOLIDAY PARKS

This pet-friendly caravan park has a range of accommodation options including grassy-unpowered, concrete-slab and powered-ensuite sites. The amenities are well kept and there is a swimming pool and restaurant onsite.

363 Camooweal Roadhouse Caravan Park

⚲ Barkly Hwy, Camooweal
📞 (07) 4748 2155
🖥 www.camoowealroadhouse.net.au

This roadside camping area offers large, flat and grassy sites with power. Fuel and gas refills are available from the roadhouse as well as hot meals. Perfect for overnight stops before crossing the NT border.

364 Barkly Homestead Caravan Park

⚲ Barkly Hwy, Barkly Tableland
📞 (08) 8964 4549
🖥 barklyhomestead.com.au

A perfect little oasis in what appears to be the middle of nowhere, this lovely outback homestead offers large drive-thru sites with good amenities and a pool. The Bar and Grill is very popular, especially at happy hour. Fuel is available from the roadhouse.

321 Tennant Creek Caravan Park

See p. 161 – Alice Springs to Three Ways Roadhouse.

Lawn Hill Gorge

TOWNSVILLE TO HUGHENDEN

NEED TO KNOW

🕐 **380km**

🏠 **Inexpensive caravan parks, holiday resorts**

☁ **Townsville's climate and rainfall is much milder than the rest of north Queensland, so it can be visited year-round. Further west, summer is hot, so it's best to visit Apr–Sept.**

👁 **Goldmining history, dinosaur exhibits, fossicking**

🛣 **These are good regional roads. Beware of large trucks.**

🍴 **Townsville and Hughenden have good services, but there's little in between.**

⚠ **Crocodiles inhabit many north Queensland waterways.**

Blacksmith/Ironmonger, Charters Towers

INTRODUCTION

The Flinders Highway leads inland to busy Charters Towers, a historic mining town with many magnificent buildings from the 1880s and 1890s. Further west, the highway passes through several small communities before arriving in the town of Hughenden, an important regional centre which also has a strong prehistoric history.

WHERE TO GO

From the idyllic coastal city of **Townsville** (*see* p. 51) with its long sunny days, cosmopolitan CBD and great caravan parks, it's about an hour's drive west to **Charters Towers**. Gold was discovered here in 1871 and by the 1890s Charters Towers was a prosperous city – the second largest in Queensland. Many monuments paying tribute to the goldmining heritage can be seen in gardens around the city. More than 100 years on, it's the heart of a busy cattle-raising industry with all services needed by travellers.

The central business area of Charters Towers is a historic area retaining many wonderfully preserved buildings from the 1880s and '90s. The old-world architecture is prominent with prime examples the Stock Exchange, City Hall and Australian Bank of Commerce buildings.

Between Charters Towers and Pentland the highway follows the train line, passing **Balfes Creek**. The only business here, a pub which had a small caravan park out the back, closed in 2016. **Pentland**, 77km west of Charters, grew out of the Cape River Goldfields with the arrival of the railway in 1884. It was once a cattle centre but today is a small settlement providing basic services to travellers including a caravan park. There's also camping behind the pub, which has a great history wall in its main bistro outlining the town's past.

Those who are experienced and self-sufficient bushwalkers should explore White Mountains National Park. For those well prepared, this wilderness area is full of spectacular scenery and many varieties of wildflowers bloom in late winter and spring. Bushwalkers should register with the ranger,

and bookings are required to camp in the park, although the camping area is only suitable for tents.

West of the park, **Torrens Creek** is a blink-and-you'll-miss-it town that was once an important staging post for Cobb & Co., and an ammunition dump during WWII. Today its pub welcomes travellers with camping out the back and fuel out the front.

Another 45km west along the train line, **Prairie** is an even smaller town, with a windmill to welcome you as you enter. Its hotel was built in the 1860s. Koorooorinya Falls, approximately 60km south of town, is a popular nearby attraction, offering birdwatching, fishing and swimming. The road to the falls can be rough though, especially in the wet season, so a four-wheel drive is recommended.

At the junction of the Flinders Highway and Kennedy Development Rd, **Hughenden** is a major pastoral centre on the banks of the Flinders River – Queensland's longest. The area was once home to dinosaurs and marine species, while the surrounds are still rich in gemstones. A lifesize replica of a *Muttaburrasaurus langdoni* stands on

EXPLORE AUSTRALIA BY CARAVAN & MOTORHOME

the median strip in the town centre. As it services such a wide community, it has most services and good, but basic, shopping.

DON'T MISS

→ Gold fever – Charters Towers

The Venus Battery in Charters Towers operated for 100 years until 1972 and processed more than 500,000 ounces of gold. Now fully restored by the National Trust, it can be seen in action on guided tours giving an insight into 19th-century gold-processing techniques. Entry fees apply and it's open daily June–Sept, but limited days the rest of the year. Contact (07) 4761 5533.

→ Dinosaur country – Hughenden

The Flinders Discovery Centre houses a lifesize replica skeleton of the 7m long, bird-footed dinosaur *Muttaburrasaurus langdoni*, and several other fascinating fossils collected from the region. Entry fees apply and it's open daily 9am–5pm. Contact (07) 4741 2970.

WHERE TO STAY

112 BIG4 Townsville Woodlands Holiday Park

See p. 52 – Mackay to Townsville.

365 BIG4 Aussie Outback Oasis Charters Towers

$$$$

📍 76 Dr George Ellis Dr, Charters Towers
📞 (07) 4787 8722
💻 www.big4.com.au/caravan-parks/qld/townsville-surrounds/aussie-outback-oasis-holiday-park

BIG4 HOLIDAY PARKS

This owner-operated caravan park is located on the eastern side of town and has excellent facilities in a bush setting. It isn't very old (by caravan park standards) and has developed well. Bookings are required in peak periods.

366 Pentland Caravan Park

$$

📍 Flinders Hwy, Pentland
📞 (07) 4788 1148

Halfway between Charters Towers and Hughenden, this small caravan park is suitable for an overnight stay with clean facilities and very modest prices.

367 Allan Terry Caravan Park

$$

📍 2 Resolution St, Hughenden
📞 (07) 4741 1190
💻 www.hughendenvanpark.com.au

Around 1.5km from the centre of Hughenden, this is a good, basic caravan park adjoining the town's swimming pool. Porcupine Gorge is nearby.

Fishing by the Burdekin River

Flinders Discovery Centre, Hughenden

HUGHENDEN TO CLONCURRY

Along the highway near Julia Creek

INTRODUCTION

After crossing large pastoral leaseholds, the highway passes through the small towns of Richmond and Julia Creek. Once part of an ancient inland sea, Richmond is home to Kronosaurus Korner, where some of Australia's best examples of vertebrate fossils are exhibited. The route intersects with the Landsborough (Matilda) Highway at Cloncurry, an important mining and cattle centre.

WHERE TO GO

Hughenden, Richmond and Winton, to the south, form a local tourist route known as Australia's Dinosaur Trail and each of the three towns proudly displays its prehistoric significance in excellent museums. **Richmond**, despite now being 500km from the ocean, was in the middle of a giant inland sea, and the major marine fossil finds in the vicinity are some of the most notable examples in the world. Kronosaurus Korner houses an amazing display of local fossils. Located on the banks of Queensland's longest river, the Flinders, the town is a service centre for many large cattle properties and has most

basic services and supplies. The rich Mitchell and Flinders grass plains, and a reliable artesian water supply, ensure this is some of the north's most productive cattle country.

From Richmond the highway tracks almost due west, past the tiny towns of **Maxwelton** and **Nelia**, which are little more than rail sidings. Then it arrives at the regional service centre of **Julia Creek**, near the junction of the Flinders Highway and Wills Developmental Rd. A favourite of nomads who champion freedom camping, Julia Creek has one of outback Queensland's most adored caravan parks, as well as a free camping area on the banks of the river. The caravan park hosts amazing bush dinner nights each Mon, Apr–Sept, which anyone, even people camping at the free site, are welcome to join. Julia Creek has a long history in outback Queensland, having been settled by pastoralists just a year after Burke and Wills passed through in 1861. The town still has strong ties with the pastoral industry and has most basic services.

At the junction of the Flinders and Landsborough highways is the frontier town of **Cloncurry** which turned 150 in 2017. Coppermining played a major role in the town's early history, but mining waned after

WWI until uranium was discovered nearby in the 1950s. In 1922 Qantas operated its first regular air service between Cloncurry and Charleville, and the Royal Flying Doctor Service was launched here in 1928 using a Qantas aircraft.

There's a great museum dedicated to Reverend John Flynn and the founders of the Royal Flying Doctor Service. The John Flynn Place Museum includes exhibits of the first pedal wireless and a scale model of the *Victory*, the first plane that took off with a doctor on board in 1928. Entry fees apply and it's open 9am–4pm weekdays and 9am–3pm weekends.

DON'T MISS

➔ **Kronosaurus Korner – Richmond**
Kronosaurus Korner in Richmond houses the amazing Richmond Marine Fossil Display. A 5m long pliosaur and the armoured minmi, both on display, are two of the most complete and well-preserved fossils of their type in the world. Be sure to come in and see why such great prehistoric discoveries were made in the middle of Queensland's outback. Entry fees apply and it's open weekdays 8.30am–4pm and weekends 8.30am–3pm. Contact 1300 576 665.

→ Australian uranium – Cloncurry

The Mary Kathleen Uranium Mine was opened by Prime Minister Robert Menzies in 1958. The mine, between Cloncurry and Mount Isa, was abandoned and is now a ghost town situated on private property. Visitors are welcome, and can travel a further 5km to see the open cut mine. The mine has been immortalised in Cloncurry's Mary Kathleen Park and Museum. Four buildings re-erected in the park house much of the mine's history, including an 18,000-piece mineral display. Entry fees apply and it's open daily. Contact (07) 4742 1361.

Julia Creek

WHERE TO STAY

368 Lakeview Caravan Park

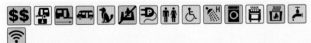

- 109 Goldring St, Richmond
- (07) 4741 3772
- www.richmondlakeviewcaravanpark.com.au

This is a tidy caravan park with good facilities, where every site is a drive-thru one. The park is on the eastern approach to town overlooking Lake Fred Tritton. Bookings are required in peak periods.

369 Julia Creek Caravan Park

- Julia St, Julia Creek
- (07) 4746 7108
- www.jccaravanpark.com.au

This neat and tidy caravan park offers great bang for your buck with large drive-thru sites, grassy unpowered sites and excellent amenities. They have added four luxurious private bathhouses, perfect for washing the dust away.

302 Discovery Parks Cloncurry

See p. 151 – Winton to Cloncurry.

KALGOORLIE TO SANDSTONE

NEED TO KNOW

🕐	**996km**
🏠	**Simple outback caravan parks, roadside free camping areas**
☁	**Avoid travelling in summer, when the weather is dangerously hot. Wildflowers are best seen late in winter or early in spring.**
👁	**Wildflowers, mining history**
🅰	**This is a major road linking big mines so it's well maintained.**
🍴	**Kalgoorlie-Boulder has great facilities, although specialty services can be in high demand. Further north, services are more limited.**
⚠	**Large and wide transports regularly move mining equipment between mines. Give them all the room they need.**

Inside Australia sculptures

INTRODUCTION

Commencing at Kalgoorlie-Boulder, now the prosperous key city in the goldfields region, the Goldfields Highway leads north past a string of mining settlements and ghost towns. Near Leinster, which is just off the highway, it turns westwards, through a landscape of impressive breakaways and rock formations to the aptly named town of Sandstone.

WHERE TO GO

In their heyday, **Kalgoorlie** and **Boulder** boasted eight breweries and 93 hotels, and while there aren't that many now they are still at the centre of the region's goldmining industry. Large mining operations regularly come into view as you drive this route and large ore-carrying trucks are continually on the move. So take care on the roads.

One of the first towns the highway passes is **Menzies**. Originating from a mining lease, the settlement had to endure heat, flies, lack of water and poor transportation, often with little reward. Typical of many mining towns, it once boasted 13 hotels, three banks and its own brewery. Today, mining activity continues throughout this region and the town proudly boasts numerous historic buildings. The region's most famous attraction, however, is the artistic installation called Inside Australia, by award-winning artist Antony Gormley. Found on the remote Lake Ballard, 50km along an unsealed red-dirt road these 51 captivating sculptures bring people from all over the world to a dry saltpan in the middle of nowhere.

Another 100km past Menzies is the third largest town on the north-eastern goldfields. **Leonora** was established when gold was found in 1896 and numerous buildings from the gold-rush era remain. Mining has continued to the present day with gold, and now nickel, being produced in large quantities. Leonora has limited facilities for tourists, but does have a caravan park, service station and basic shopping. The most interesting site nearby is **Gwalia**. At this mining 'ghost town' the old State Hotel, historic buildings and the abandoned open-cut mine and a small museum can all be explored.

As the highway tracks north to Leinster, several basic rest areas dot the side of the road, some far better than others. Along here, and the rest of the Goldfields Highway, expect to encounter numerous wide-load transports as mining equipment moves in and out of the area. While the roads are wide, allow these over-sized trucks all the road, and pull over in a safe place where possible. All extremely wide loads have escort vehicles to warn oncoming traffic of their approach.

Just 3km off the highway, **Leinster** is a modern mining town which services one of BHP Billiton's nickel operations. Although it's not specifically a tourist town, it has struck a chord with many travellers who appreciate the outback hospitality and good caravan park (with free washers and dryers). The Village Mess, a buffet-style diner that does cheap dinners most nights of the week, is also popular.

Now heading west, Agnew–Sandstone Rd travels through the undulating woodlands of the mid-west. **Sandstone**, like most other towns in the region, was settled after gold was discovered in 1894. It was named for the surrounding rust-coloured sandstone landscape. By 1920 the intense gold-rush activity had petered out, but the town survived to service the surrounding pastoral properties. The people of Sandstone proudly preserve their history and have designed a self-guided heritage trail. This 18km drive, which takes in the spectacular sandstone formation dubbed London Bridge, can be done in a leisurely half day.

DON'T MISS

→ Australia's longest shortcut – near Leonora

From Laverton, near Leonora, it's possible to travel all the way to Winton in central Queensland, taking in wonderful outback towns and sights like Uluru and Kata Tjuta, Alice Springs and Boulia. The Outback Way route traverses 2700km of varied road, but is more than achievable with a four-wheel drive and caravan set up for a lot of gravel-road towing. (*See* p. 198)

→ Pan for gold – Kalgoorlie

Hannans North Tourist Mine, which incorporates the Super Pit Shop, is a fascinating facility that shows visitors through the gold-rush history of the area, and the intricacies of modern goldmining. Here you can pan for gold, take the self-guided tour or climb aboard a massive mining haul truck. Tour fees apply and it's open Sun–Fri 9am–4pm. Contact (08) 9022 1664.

WHERE TO STAY

370 Prospector Holiday Park

- 📍 11 Ochiltree St, Somerville, Kalgoorlie
- 📞 (08) 9021 2524
- 🖥 www.acclaimparks.com.au/locations/kalgoorlie/prospector-holiday-park/

Easily accessible from the Great Eastern Highway, this is a spacious caravan park with good amenities and gravel-base sites. It is a good base from which to explore the historic region. Bookings are required Aug–Sept.

371 Laverton Caravan Park

- 📍 211 Weld Dr, Laverton
- 📞 (08) 9031 1072
- 🖥 www.opl.net.au/accommodation/laverton-caravan-park

A popular stopover for people travelling along the Great Central Rd this caravan park has tidy amenities. It is just a short walk to the town centre and the Great Beyond Visitor Centre which has an excellent historical museum and cafe.

372 Leinster Caravan Park

- 📍 Mansbridge St, Leinster WA
- 📞 0436661725

This is a shady outback campsite in a picturesque bush setting close to local shops and facilities. The local supermarket is well stocked and the amenities are basic but clean.

373 Alice Atkinson Sandstone Caravan Park

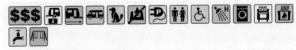

- 📍 59 Irvine St, Sandstone
- 📞 (08) 9963 5859

An excellent little outback caravan park with green grassy common areas, well-cared-for modern amenities and a good-sized camp kitchen.

SANDSTONE TO GERALDTON

NEED TO KNOW

🕐	**494km**
🏠	**Inexpensive, council-owned caravan parks; family holiday resorts**
☁	**Spring, for the wildflowers**
👁	**Wildflowers, history, beach activities**
Ⓐ	**The roads through here are reasonable and can carry heavy traffic and road trains.**
🍴	**Most of the settlements are small outback communities with limited services. Geraldton, a major coastal city, has everything you'll need.**
⚠	**None apply**

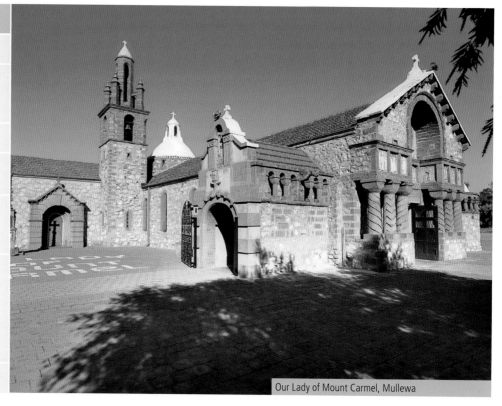

Our Lady of Mount Carmel, Mullewa

INTRODUCTION

Mine workings dot the plains as the road makes its way south-west through Mount Magnet and Yalgoo. About 100km short of Geraldton is Mullewa, the site of the Our Lady of Mount Carmel church. This building is testament to the skill of architect-priest Monsignor John Hawes, and a highlight of the Monsignor Hawes Heritage Trail.

WHERE TO GO

From **Sandstone**, the road is wide and sealed with plenty of good rest areas on the way to **Mount Magnet**, the oldest operating gold settlement in Western Australia. Gold was discovered here in 1891 and mining still continues close to town. A tourist trail map is available that guides you around the local mining sites, both past and present. The town has a museum displaying pioneering and mining artefacts and there are many buildings of historic significance.

If you come in spring expect to see the landscape covered in wildflowers. Head north of town any time to find the Granites,

an Aboriginal rock-art site with a nice picnic spot nearby. Another interesting site is the ghost town of **Lennonville**. A former gold-rush town, it fell into decline in the early 1900s and has been empty ever since. Take care, as there are dangerous old mine shafts in the area.

West of town the road continues nice and wide, but its surface can be a little damaged so take care. Eventually the road passes through the delightful little town of **Yalgoo**. The small community has a rich goldmining history and operating mines still dot the landscape nearby. Road trains of rich iron ore trundle through the town day and night heading to the port of Geraldton. There are many old buildings in town and a small museum in the old Court House.

Before the road approaches the coast, and starts to wind through the hilly country near Geraldton, it passes through the ghost town of **Pindar** and the rural service centre of **Mullewa**. Surrounded by land dedicated to grazing and cropping, this is a spectacular wildflower region, with the amazing wreath flower being the local star attraction. The town has basic shopping and a very tidy caravan park. Around the town there are

several buildings that were the amazing work of architect-priest Monsignor John Hawes including the church of Our Lady of Mount Carmel and the Holy Apostles St Peter and St Paul. Hawes spent just 24 years in Australia, but certainly left a mark on this region of Western Australia. The Monsignor Hawes Heritage Trail takes in some 15 classic buildings.

A key port on the West Australian coastline, **Geraldton** is the self-proclaimed lobster capital of the world – a highly contentious issue if you ask the people of Kingston SE in South Australia or New Brunswick in Canada, both of which have 'big lobsters' on display to prove their mettle. The Geraldton Fisherman's Co-operative (on Ocean St), has a live-lobster-processing factory and runs 90 min guided tours. (Call (08) 9965 9000 for the latest times and bookings.) The Western Australian Museum in town has an excellent shipwrecks display. Geraldton is also one of Australia's top windsurfing and kiteboarding destinations, with the best winds occurring Nov–Apr.

→ **Windows on the past – near Yalgoo**

The rich mining history of Sandstone, Mount Magnet, Paynes Find and Yalgoo tells a colourful story of hard lives, riches won and lost, and amazing experiences, some far-fetched and some true. There are numerous sites to explore. Yalgoo also has the Chapel of St Hyacinth, designed by Monsignor Hawes in 1819. South of Yalgoo on the Paynes Find Rd is the Jokers Tunnel – signposted – carved through solid rock by the workers of an early goldmining syndicate.

→ **Wildflowers – near Mullewa**

This region of Western Australia offers an amazing display of wildflowers in spring, with fields of everlastings, distinctive wreath flowers, wild pomegranate, orchids, acacias, grevilleas, blue cornflowers, yellow bells and many more. There are thousands of flowering plants, so stop to take a wander and look. The region's visitor centres provide information on flower trails and the annual Mullewa Wildflower Show is usually held during the last week of Aug and the first week of Sept.

Geraldton Marina

WHERE TO STAY

327 **Mount Magnet Caravan Park**

See p. 165 – Perth to Mount Magnet.

374 **Yalgoo Caravan Park**

$$

⌖ **Geraldton–Mt Magnet Rd, Yalgoo**
☎ **(08) 9962 8472**
🖥 **www.yalgoo.wa.gov.au**

This attractive caravan park in the main street of Yalgoo is a good example of what a small community can achieve. The layout is simple and the amenities are basic, but the result is good. There is a visitor information centre at the park.

375 **Mullewa Caravan Park**

$$

⌖ **5 Lovers La, Mullewa**
☎ **(08) 9956 6643**

On the highest hill in town, this council-operated caravan park is as neat as a pin, with kerbed roadways, green grass and most amenities. Mullewa is a great base for exploring this spectacular wildflower region in springtime.

197 **BIG4 Sunset Beach Holiday Park**

See p. 96 – Carnarvon to Geraldton.

Wildflowers

HUGHENDEN TO ALICE SPRINGS

🕐	**1390km**
🏠	**Basic outback caravan parks, roadhouse camping areas, free roadside rest areas, station stays**
☁	**This is a trip best done Mar–Nov.**
👁	**Outback pubs, bush camping, cross-country driving**
Ⓐ	**Conditions vary with many unsealed sections. Between Boulia and the Stuart Highway is often corrugated and bumpy.**
🍴	**This is an extremely remote route and facilities are very limited. The smaller Aboriginal communities in WA may be closed on weekends.**
⚠	**There are long distances between stops and fuel may not be available between Winton and Boulia – a distance of 365km.**

Arnos Wall, Winton

INTRODUCTION

Passing through some of outback Queensland's most interesting country that's still accessible on bitumen roads, this area has significant sites of prehistoric discovery and dinosaur fossils. Some of Australia's most significant historical moments have also played out along this route. Follow the drive to enjoy the hospitality of outback pubs and excellent camping. After Boulia and into the Northern Territory, the road is unsealed, and often rough, but nothing a four-wheel drive and caravan well set up for gravel-road driving can't handle.

WHERE TO GO

The Outback Way officially starts at Winton, 216km to the south-west, but most people will pick it up from **Hughenden** if making the journey south from far north Queensland. At the junction of the Flinders Highway and Kennedy Development Rd, **Hughenden** is a major pastoral centre on the banks of the Flinders River – Queensland's longest. The area was once home to dinosaurs and marine species, while the surrounds are still rich in gemstones. A lifesize replica of a *Muttaburrasaurus langdoni* stands on the median strip in the town centre. As it services such a wide community, it has most services and good, but basic, shopping.

Two hours down the Kennedy Developmental Rd, **Winton** abounds with outback history. The township claims the first public performance of Banjo Paterson's 'Waltzing Matilda' was here in 1895 at the North Gregory Hotel (which is still there today). The Waltzing Matilda Centre in the main street now pays tribute to this famous song. Winton was also the home of Qantas' first registered office, which opened in 1920. The remarkable dinosaur 'stampede' prints in Lark Quarry Conservation Park are about 110km south of town. Winton is a very popular town through winter, with a number of great camping options and good services.

From Winton, the Outback Way follows the Kennedy Developmental Rd east to Boulia, past the small community of **Middleton**. Middleton is one of Queensland's most isolated pubs – the only one within 200km in any direction. The publican, Lester Cain, a former camel driver, has endless tales to tell, of the history of the pub, which was a staging location for Cobb & Co., and of his own life in the outback.

Boulia, another 200km west, is a small outback community in the heart of Channel Country on the banks of the Burke River. It services the surrounding cattle properties

NT/QLD border

and tourists who pass through on their way to the outback. Each year the town hosts the Boulia Camel Races which bring thousands of people to the tiny town. It is also famous for the Min Min Lights – a mysterious ball of light which is said to follow travellers at night with claims of sightings going back over a century. The Min Min Encounter at the Boulia Visitor Centre is a popular 45 min show explaining the curious (and unproven) phenomenon. Boulia has limited services, which include fuel, basic shopping, a hotel and caravan park. There are also a few opportunities to camp nearby on the banks of the Burke River.

The Donohue and Plenty highways sections, between Boulia and about 100km east of the Stuart Hwy, are unsealed and recommended for four-wheel drives. It's a long drive that can be broken up with stays on outback properties like **Tobermorey** and **Jervois** stations. Both offer grassy camping areas and basic facilities like fuel and simple groceries.

Gemtree Caravan Park, which is 140km north-east of Alice Springs, has powered and non-powered camping areas, and also offers guided fossicking tours. A highlight of a stay here is the twice-weekly campfire dinner night (Wed and Sat) prepared in the park's custom-built and award-winning camp-oven kitchen. Bookings are essential, but the servings are generous and the price modest.

Alice Springs is a destination in itself, and somewhere I could easily spend weeks. There are multiple Aboriginal art galleries and cultural sites to explore in and around town including the National Road Transport Hall of Fame and the Araluen Cultural Precinct where you will find the Museum of Central Australia. There is also the Alice Springs Desert Park and the Old Ghan Museum, which preserves the history of the legendary narrow-gauge train that once operated between Marree and Alice Springs.

The town is also the best place to take advantage of the East and West MacDonnell ranges, which offer stunning walking trails, access to amazing Indigenous rock-art galleries and excellent camping. Some of the best sights in the East MacDonnell Ranges are easily accessible via sealed roads. Both Emily and Jessie gaps – stunning art sites sacred to the Arrernte people – have great walking tracks through them, while Trephina Gorge's Panorama Track is an energetic, hour-long walk that overlooks the gorge as it winds north into Mordor Pound. There's also a great camping area here that's suitable for all sorts of rigs.

DON'T MISS

→ Dinosaur country – Hughenden
The Flinders Discovery Centre houses a lifesize replica skeleton of the 7m long, bird-footed dinosaur *Muttaburrasaurus*

langdoni, and several other fascinating fossils collected from the region. Entry fees apply and it's open daily 9am–5pm. Contact (07) 4741 2970.

→ Racing rainbow chickens – Winton
In the same pub that hosted the first performance of one of Australia's most classic tunes is the quirkiest spectacle in Queensland. Each night at the North Gregory Hotel, Ben's Rainbow Chickens race around a pen following a remote-controlled car full of feed. Each chicken is auctioned off, and the winning chicken's owner gets half the takings, with the other half going to charity. It's a really incredible night out.

→ Min Min Lights – Boulia
The first recorded sighting of the Min Min Lights was in 1890 – at the site of the old Boulia Hotel, which burnt down not long after. These strange lights are often said to float in the area, or move erratically, and are most often seen early in the night. A number of theories have been presented, but as yet none have been proven to completely explain the spectacle. The site of the first sighting can still be visited, although little remains. Amongst the wilder theories is that the light is the ghost of the hotel's maid come to take you to your room.

WHERE TO STAY

376 Boulia Caravan Park

$$ ★ 🚐 🐕 🏕 ♿ 👥 ♿ 🚿ᴴ 🔲 🚰

📍 Diamantina Developmental Rd, Boulia
📞 (07) 4746 3320

This busy little caravan park is the perfect place to stop and search for the Min Min Lights with the fun and quirky Min Min Encounter – a unique show that mixes theatre, animatronics and fibre optics – just a short walk down the road. Sites are flat and grassy with simple clean amenities.

377 Jervois Station

$ 🏕 🚐 🚐 🐕 🏕 👥 🚿ᴴ 🔥 🚰

📍 Plenty Hwy, Anatye
📞 (08) 8956 6307

This basic bush camping area is a good place to stop and escape the corrugations for a night. It has simple amenities and a small kiosk with basic supplies.

378 Gemtree Caravan Park

$$$ ★ 🏕 🚐 🚐 🚐 🐕 🏕 ♿ 👥 ♿ 🚿ᴴ 🔲 🚰 🏊 🎱 📶

📍 Plenty Hwy, Gemtree
📞 (08) 8956 9855
🖥 www.gemtree.com.au

This is a good quality outback caravan park with shady, private sites and basic but well-kept amenities to suit most campers' needs. Facilities include a swimming pool, small general store and gem shop. For a bit of fun, you can book a fossicking tour and try your luck at gem hunting or stay on a Wed or Sat evening to experience the award-winning camp oven dinner. Bookings are essential at all times.

379 Rainbow Valley Conservation Reserve camping area

$ 🚫 🏕 ♿ 👥

📍 Rainbow Valley Access Rd, Hugh
🖥 www.nt.gov.au/leisure/parks-reserves/find-a-park-to-visit/rainbow-valley-conservation-reserve

This peaceful bush camping area has good level sites with fire pits provided and well-maintained drop toilets. There is a sunset viewing platform which looks out over the spectacular rock formations that surround the area. The road in is dirt and graded regularly, but it can become quite corrugated. Check conditions if using a 2WD.

The Outback Way

ULURU TO LEONORA

NEED TO KNOW

🕐 **1224km**

🏠 **Free rest areas, outback roadhouse camping areas, basic caravan parks**

☁ **Spring, summer and autumn**

👁 **Outback scenery, remote camping, Aboriginal art**

🅰 **Largely unsealed and variable. 4WD recommended.**

🍴 **Outback roadhouses with limited fuel and basic supplies**

⚠ **Although there are plans to seal more of the Outback Way, large sections currently remain unsealed so it is best suited to four-wheel drive vehicles. Temperatures can soar, and water and fuel are scarce, so travel prepared. Transit permits are required and alcohol restrictions apply – inquire at the visitor centres for details.**

Night sky over old Laverton water tower

INTRODUCTION

Taking in some of the most scenic parts of the Western Australian desert regions, this rather long shortcut covers vast distances through incredibly remote communities, but remains very accessible for those who are prepared. Attractions include historic sites, wonderful Indigenous art galleries, wildlife encounters and interesting outback towns.

WHERE TO GO

After the wonders of Uluṟu and Kata Tjuṯa, the Outback Way continues to the Northern Territory/Western Australia border where it becomes the Great Central Road. Although it's still unsealed, this section is usually in far better condition than the unsealed section between Boulia and Alice Springs.

Along the way there are countless opportunities to remote camp in areas off the side of the road, some of which were used by outback road engineer Len Beadell. The first developed stop is at **Warakurna Roadhouse**. The roadhouse at this small Aboriginal community provides basic accommodation, meals, fuel and a caravan park. The Warakurna Art Gallery displays and sells artwork by local artists, and you may even see some painting in the shade of trees nearby. This is also the site of the Giles Weather Station which plays a significant role in long-range rainfall forecasts for the desert regions. It was surveyed by Len Beadell, whose yellow grader, retired in the 1960s, is on display out the front.

The next settlement, 230km south-west is **Warburton**, established as an Aboriginal ministry site in the 1970s. It's about halfway between Alice Springs and Laverton and has a roadhouse with fuel, food, accommodation and a caravan park. The Tjulyuru Cultural and Civic Centre has some great examples of local art on display and for sale. I actually have an item from the gallery in my living room.

Between Warburton and Laverton you can spot all sorts of wildlife, including kangaroos, dingoes, camels and emus. If there has been any rain recently, the land can be awash with wildflowers too, especially the Sturt desert pea. The **Tjukayirla Roadhouse** and **Cosmo Newberry** Aboriginal community have fuel available but opening hours vary so call ahead to make sure they will be open, as otherwise it's a long way without fuel.

Laverton, officially the last town on the Outback Way, was settled at the end of the 19th century to service the goldmining interests in the area. Today its visitor centre has an excellent museum, the Great Beyond Explorers Hall of Fame that displays the history of the local area, from goldmining to pastoral pursuits. The old gaol can also be inspected and there's an old, Cobb & Co. coach house too. The town has basic groceries, fuel and various accommodation options. Take a detour to the Windarra Mine Lookout for spectacular views across the desert landscape.

From Laverton the road is sealed and continues to **Leonora** which was established when gold was found in 1896. Mining has continued to the present day with gold, and now nickel, being produced in large quantities. Leonora has limited facilities for tourists, but does have a caravan park, service station and basic shopping. (*See* p. 194.)

(*See* p. 194.)

DON'T MISS

→ **Outback Way App**

The Outback Way has developed a clever app that guides travellers through the whole trip. If set up correctly it will give you notifications of points of interest as you approach them, providing information, facts and stories from the various areas along the way. Download it from the relevant app store.

→ **Inside Australia – near Leonora**

Near Leonora is the artistic installation called Inside Australia, by award-winning artist Antony Gormley. Found on the remote Lake Ballard, 50km along an unsealed red-dirt road these 51 captivating sculptures bring people from all over the world to a dry saltpan in the middle of nowhere.

WHERE TO STAY

380 Warakurna Roadhouse

$$

📍 Great Central Rd, Warakurna
📞 (08) 8956 7344
🖥 www.warakurnaroadhouse.com.au

One of the few lonely roadhouses on the Great Central Rd, there is a modest camping area out back with a good camp kitchen and clean facilities. Dingoes frequent the campsite, so keep food and rubbish well concealed. This is one of the few reliable fuel stops, too, so fill up here to ensure you can get to Laverton, or Yulara depending which direction you are heading.

381 Warburton Roadhouse

$$

📍 Great Central Rd, Warburton
📞 (08) 8956 7656
🖥 www.warburtonroadhouse.com.au

A remote camping area on the edge of the local Aboriginal community with large sites that are grassy when there's enough water around to manage it. Good meals in the roadhouse and basic supplies, including fuel. Campfires are permitted, but bring wood as there's not much in the vicinity.

382 Tjukayirla Roadhouse

$$$

📍 Great Central Rd, Tjukayirla
📞 (08) 9037 1108
🖥 www.tjukayirlaroadhouse.com.au

A red-dirt camping area with basic roadhouse facilities. The campground has tapped water, powered sites, a camp kitchen and laundry plus a communal fire area.

371 Laverton Caravan Park

See p. 195 – Kalgoorlie to Sandstone.

See p. 195 – Kalgoorlie to Sandstone.

383 Leonora Caravan Park

$$$

📍 42 Rochester St, Leonora
📞 (08) 9037 6568
🖥 www.opl.net.au/accommodation/leonora-caravan-park

A typical outback caravan park with big sites, clean facilities and modest prices. It's close to nearby attractions like Gwalia Historic Site.

Uluru

THE FLINDERS RANGES

NEED TO KNOW

335km

Station stays, national park camping areas, remote free camps, roadhouse caravan parks

The Flinders Ranges gets very hot in summer, so it's best experienced in the cooler seasons.

Four-wheel driving, walking, scenic drives

Some attractions can be reached via sealed roads, although the section between Blinman and Parachilna is unsealed, as is the road to Arkaroola. Many attractions can only be reached via unsealed roads.

The services within the Flinders Ranges are basic and limited.

There is limited fuel available in the Flinders Ranges. Hawker, Rawnsley Park Station, Wilpena Pound and Arkaroola all sell fuel, but with side trips and scenic drives it can be a significant distance between fills. Water is scarce and temperatures in summer can exceed 40°C.

Bunyeroo Valley Scenic Drive

INTRODUCTION

The Flinders Ranges is one of the most striking natural landscapes in Australia – at once barren, rugged and rich in beauty. It is one of Australia's oldest landscapes. North of Goyder's Line, the arbitrary boundary where South Australia's arable land ends, it receives very low annual rainfall and endless sunny days. It's the perfect outback experience for those testing the waters, as well as seasoned campaigners.

WHERE TO GO

The Flinders Ranges actually stretches south to encompass historic rail towns like Peterborough and Yatina in the undulating country that forms part of the Southern Flinders. Still, the most striking visions of the rugged range are further north as the Flinders Ranges Way approaches **Hawker**, where the ranges seem to rise abruptly out of a flat plain dominated by saltbush, open woodland and dry riverbeds.

Hawker was settled in 1880 and until 1956 was a thriving town servicing the mighty Ghan railway line, until it was upgraded and moved further west. Today it services the needs of travellers heading into the Flinders, and has a pub, a small shop with basic supplies, fuel and a good caravan park. A small museum documents the history of the Ghan, although it is only open some days.

North of Hawker the road forks with each arm heading roughly either side of the range. This route will take us north-east first and circle back to Hawker, but either direction can be followed. The Flinders Ranges Way

Brachina Gorge

continues north into sheep country. Along the way crumbling buildings are remnants of a failed attempt to grow wheat in the area – there's just not enough rain. **Rawnsley Park Station** is one of the oldest sheep properties in the region, but it does a fair trade in tourism too. The station has an excellent caravan park, and is one of the best bases to explore park highlights like Brachina Gorge or Razorback Lookout. Station owner, Tony Smith, runs guided four-wheel-drive tours of the property, which I highly recommend. Its onsite restaurant is not just the best in the region, but one of the best in the outback.

Another station offering camping and excellent facilities is **Willow Springs**. Its famous Skytrek 4WD track is one of the most scenic off-road drives in Australia and suitable for any four-wheel drive with decent ground clearance. It crosses stunning ridgetops and passes ancient Aboriginal sites over the mountain range. A fee applies per vehicle, but it's a great day out.

Just north of Rawnsley Park Station is the area protected by Ikara–Flinders Ranges National Park. A vehicle entry permit is required. The park's most notable feature is Wilpena Pound. Its two narrow, curving ridgelines which meet each other to form a natural amphitheatre are most spectacular when seen from a scenic flight.

The closest accommodation to this natural wonder, **Wilpena Pound Resort** has a range of accommodation varying from unpowered sites to five-star glamping cabins.

The resort's facilities include a swimming pool, bar and bistro. (Although I found the bistro underwhelming and expensive.) There are a number of walks within the pound itself, some of which explore the ruins of an old sheep station, or run around the ridge. Guides are available from the resort.

The drive north of Wilpena Pound remains sealed until **Blinman**, which was named after the shepherd who first discovered copper in the region. Established as a coppermining town in the 1860s, it struggled through years of drought and hardship, but was one of the most profitable mining communities in the area. Today it has some interesting old buildings to explore and relics of the coppermine. The fabulous North Blinman Hotel, and a store with basic supplies, makes it is a popular stop for those continuing on to Arkaroola.

From Blinman the roads are unsealed to the north and west, but are generally suitable for vehicles set up for extended gravel-road driving. About 175km north-east, via the North Flinders Rd, is the remote wilderness sanctuary at **Arkaroola**. While east along Parachilna Gorge Rd heads for the sleepy outback town of **Parachilna**, 37km away on the eastern side of the range. The town was established to support Blinman due to its proximity to groundwater, and later was the site of the railway station which carried ore south to Port Augusta. Never a large town, its only buildings today include the Prairie Hotel,

some old rail buildings and about two permanent residences. Most people visit for the Prairie Hotel (formerly the Parachilna Hotel), which serves a delicious assortment of 'feral' animal dishes, like kangaroo, emu and camel. Its signature is the 'Feral Mixed Grill' which is a combination of all three. There is a basic caravan park at the hotel, although the best camping is back along Parachilna Gorge Rd for those who are self-sufficient. There is no fuel at Parachilna, the closest being at Leigh Creek, 70km north, or Hawker, 90km south.

DON'T MISS

→ Brachina Gorge – near Rawnsley Park Station

Although the drive through Brachina Gorge is only 20km, it travels through 130 million years of geology, displaying various rock formations that have been exposed over time. It's best suited to four-wheel-drive vehicles, although is never difficult. Ideally it should be driven late in the afternoon as the late daylight brings out the best colours of the gorge as well as the rare yellow-footed rock wallabies. Signage along the way details the different ages of the geology.

→ Arkaroola Wilderness Sanctuary – Arkaroola

On the northern edge of the Flinders Ranges, Arkaroola is a former sheep station turned private wilderness reserve with excellent camping, accommodation, walking and four-wheel-drive tracks. While the scenery is stunning, as are some of the guided tours available on the property, any chance for a chat with owner Doug Sprigg will be a highlight – he's one of the true characters of outback Australia. Arkaroola's skies are also amongst the clearest in the world, and the sanctuary has its own observatory.

→ Scenic flight – Wilpena Pound

The best way to see the grandeur of Wilpena Pound, and the greater Flinders Ranges, is from the air. Scenic flights operate on demand from Wilpena Pound Resort and last about 30 min, which is enough time to do a lap of the pound, fly over Brachina Gorge and swing past a number of other significant landforms in the region. Find out more at the Wilpena Pound Resort reception.

WHERE TO STAY

384 Hawker Caravan Park

- 44 Chace View Tce, Hawker
- (08) 8648 4006
- www.hawkercaravanpark.com.au

With the Flinders Ranges providing a breathtaking backdrop for your stay, this tidy little caravan park provides a range of accommodation options with lovely bushy surrounds. Sites are spacious and include drive-thru, grass and ensuite options.

385 Rawnsley Park Station

- Rawnsley Park Rd, Flinders Ranges
- (08) 8648 0008
- www.rawnsleypark.com.au

Nestled at the foot of Wilpena Pound this caravan park is perfect for exploring the Flinders Ranges. It has very good facilities including a pool, licensed restaurant and shop.

386 Wilpena Pound Campground

- Wilpena Rd, Flinders Ranges
- (08) 8648 0048
- www.wilpenapound.com.au

This is a bush-style caravan park surrounded by the stunning walls of Wilpena Pound. Sites come in a range of sizes and amenities are neat and tidy. It is just a short walk to the resort complex where you can access many great facilities, including a licensed restaurant and pool. There is also a general store which has fuel available.

387 Prairie Hotel – The Overflow

- Corner High St and West Tce, Parachilna
- 1800 331 473
- www.prairiehotel.com.au

This wide-open camping area offers level, unpowered sites with basic amenities. The hotel is filled with interesting memorabilia and has good hot meals available.

Arkaroola Astronomical Observatory

3

GREAT
RURAL
DRIVES

Kosciuszko National Park

Long or short, travel through Australia's rural areas is exceptionally rewarding. While none of these trips have the grandeur of a lap of the continent or the romance of endless red-dirt surroundings, more often than not the small towns that dot the routes contained in this book are charming little havens of history, wonderful scenery and great camping. These trips take you through the beating heart of Australian agriculture, pass by exceptional country pubs, wind up and down mountains or wistfully follow Australia's great rivers as they wind their ways to the coast.

And although these trips don't cross deserts or lap a country, they are no less significant. Treading the nearly 2000km between Melbourne and Rockhampton, you'll cross three states, a handful of Australia's great rivers and pass through some of Australia's most spectacular landscapes. Between Newcastle and Gympie, you'll travel along the top of Australia, visiting some of the country's highest towns. Meanwhile the trip between Gundagai and Adelaide closely follows the track of the mighty Murray, from its heights in the Great Dividing Range, to its confluence at Lake Alexandrina.

These are trips you can cut your teeth on, if you've just decided the caravanning or motorhome life is for you, or enjoy slowly taking in the richness of each area. These are all trips filled with great things to do and amazing sights to see.

MELBOURNE TO SYDNEY pp. 212–219

🛣 Hume Freeway, Hume Highway (882km)

Linking Melbourne and Sydney, the Hume Highway is a major route, mostly freeway, carrying a diverse range of traffic, including large interstate transports, local delivery vehicles, farm produce trucks, and tourist cars and vans. The major cities of Albury, Wodonga and Goulburn are linked by this highway, while other cities, including Canberra, the national capital, are close by and depend on the highway for access to Melbourne and Sydney. Many tourists use the Hume Highway to reach destinations that are further afield, but there are interesting places along the route itself, so take a break and enjoy places and towns that are often bypassed.

🛏 PLAN YOUR TRIP

From the vibrant, multicultural metropolis of Melbourne, the busy Hume Freeway heads northwards in the style of most busy main roads, bypassing all towns. As it reaches the regional areas of Victoria from Seymour onwards it passes rich growing and grazing land where local produce is easy to come by if you leave the highway to explore. North-eastern Victoria is largely farming area, but it's also home to some of the nation's older and better-known wineries, especially those around Rutherglen.

At the Murray River, also the New South Wales–Victoria border through here, the highway connects several small townships and intersects with the Sturt Highway. The inland town of Holbrook is an unusual place to find a submarine, while Tarcutta has an impressive memorial to truck drivers.

Tyrell's Wines, Hunter Valley

Near Gundagai, the route bypasses all the major townships in this rich wool-growing area but regional communities like Yass and Gunning are well worth the detours. The Federal Highway to Canberra joins the highway just south of the riverside town of Goulburn. Canberra is a model metropolis, set gracefully on the shores of Lake Burley Griffin. The city boasts a magnificent art gallery and a spectacular war museum.

Between Goulburn and Sydney, the highway is dual carriageway and bypasses all towns. It climbs over the Great Dividing Range and some of the quaint highland towns close to Sydney are well worth detouring to explore.

☁ BEST TIME TO GO

A temperate spring and autumn climate, excellent access to the snowfields during winter and the hotter dry weather in summer make this route a popular year-round travel option.

NEWCASTLE TO GYMPIE pp. 220–229

🛣 New England Highway (1074km)

This spectacular inland route is an alternative to following Highway One along the coast. The route winds through the Hunter Valley, a picturesque wine region with lush, manicured horse studs, before reaching Tamworth, the country music capital of Australia. Several major centres lie along this highway, including Armidale, Glen Innes, Tenterfield, Warwick and Toowoomba. Each town has a diverse range of attractions to engage the traveller – it might be the Hunter Valley and Stanthorpe wineries, Tenterfield Saddler or colourful flowers of Toowoomba that catch your interest.

🛏 PLAN YOUR TRIP

From Newcastle, the 'Steel City' which has been reinventing itself into an artistic and creative hub on the New South Wales' Central Coast, the New England Highway dissects the Hunter Valley, a premier wine region that produces some of Australia's great wines. This soon gives way to coalmining activities and, as the highway climbs towards the headwaters of the Hunter River, spectacular horse studs. The highway also passes through the large towns of Singleton and Muswellbrook.

Horse studs continue into the Scone and Aberdeen areas but the agricultural emphasis changes to grazing. In between the two towns, Lake Glenbawn is a popular recreational area. Further north, Tamworth is a key regional centre, but is also synonymous with the country-music industry.

To the north of Tamworth, the highway climbs abruptly and, consequently, the communities of Armidale, Guyra and Glenn Innes experience a cooler climate with occasional snowfalls. While grazing is the main rural pursuit in this region, potatoes are grown around Guyra.

Between Glen Innes in New South Wales and Warwick in Queensland, the New England Highway remains at high altitudes as it leads north, passing through the fertile Stanthorpe region. This area is renowned for fruit production and its concentration of wineries. Stanthorpe is a popular weekend-getaway destination for residents of Brisbane and the Gold Coast.

Northwards from Warwick the highway passes through the large regional city of Toowoomba. In spring, the spectacular colours of the city's Carnival of Flowers attract plenty of tourists. The road north from Toowoomba is a simple route that joins the Bruce Highway just 14km from Gympie. If you've got a desire to continue on, Gympie offers easy access to Fraser Island and the popular Hervey Bay area.

☁ BEST TIME TO GO

The cool-to-cold winters and hotter summers make autumn and spring ideal in this region. However, the Southern Downs and Granite Belt regions do offer 'Brass Monkey Season' specials to attract visitors in the cooler months. South of the Queensland border the rainfall is mostly in the winter months, but further north there is more likelihood of summer rains.

MELBOURNE TO ROCKHAMPTON

pp. 230–241

> ⛟ **Hume Freeway, Goulburn Valley Highway, Newell Highway, Leichhardt Highway, Burnett Highway (1964km)**

If you are heading north from Melbourne, one of your choices is to travel on Route 39, a major inland highway network linking Melbourne and the central Queensland coast. The route spans three states, crosses some of Australia's important rivers and links many of our great agricultural regions. Along the way you will pass dairy farms and fruit orchards in the Goulburn Valley, extensive rice fields in the Riverina, manicured cotton fields in northern New South Wales and Queensland, and some of Australia's most productive cattle country.

⚑ PLAN YOUR TRIP

As the highway reaches the regional areas of Victoria, the route joins the Goulburn Valley Freeway and passes notable vineyards before reaching Shepparton in the fertile Goulburn Valley.

From Shepparton, where it crosses the Murray River and crosses into New South Wales, the highway changes name to the Newell. This is a large rice-producing area and the edge of Kelly Gang country until it reaches the small town of Jerilderie, made famous by Ned and his associates.

North of Jerilderie, the Newell Highway links Narrandera, West Wyalong, Forbes, Parkes and Dubbo, all of which are important regional centres servicing the surrounding grazing and cropping regions. The Taronga Western Plains Zoo at Dubbo and Parkes Observatory are highlights of this section.

North of Dubbo, the Warrumbungle Range rises starkly on the approach to Coonabarabran. Warrumbungle National Park, and the two nearby observatories, are popular stops for travellers.

Boroka Lookout over Halls Gap, Grampians

North of town, the highway sweeps through the enormous Pilliga Nature Reserve on its way to Narrabri and Moree.

Moree is surrounded by fertile, black-soil plains supporting thriving cotton fields where the crops reach the highway's edge. Further north, across the Queensland border, the route drifts through broadacre farms and large cattle properties around Miles.

The Leichhardt Highway winds north from Miles, skirting the central Queensland coalfields, and linking the historic mining town of Mount Morgan with Rockhampton on the coastal plain. 'Rocky', as the locals and regular visitors call it, is a major Queensland coastal city and at the centre of Australia's cattle industry.

☁ BEST TIME TO GO

While this is a busy route year-round, traffic increases Apr–Nov as travellers drift north to escape the southern winter. The temperatures climb during summer, making the southern reaches more desirable during that time.

MELBOURNE TO ADELAIDE

pp. 242–247

> ⛟ **Western Freeway, Western Highway, Dukes Highway, South East Freeway (737km)**

Explore the grand old mining city of Ballarat or go bushwalking in the magnificent Grampians as you head west on Route 8, a busy interstate highway linking the capital cities of Melbourne and Adelaide. It skirts the northernmost fringe of Grampians National Park near Dadswells Bridge, passes some of the oldest properties in the wine industry and descends through the picturesque Adelaide Hills to the festival city of Adelaide. And that is if you don't detour around Lake Alexandrina to the mouth of the Murray River and explore the Fleurieu Peninsula first.

⚑ PLAN YOUR TRIP

Leaving the vibrant, multicultural metropolis of Melbourne, the highway sweeps towards Ballarat. A rich goldmining centre in the 1850s Ballarat was the site of the Eureka uprising. Sovereign Hill, one of the city's major attractions, recreates the excitement and events of that era and should not be missed.

Beyond Ballarat the highway passes through fertile grazing country and by flourishing vineyards at Ararat and Great Western. A highlight

Oakey

on the way to Horsham is the rugged Grampians National Park, rising abruptly in the west, with walking trails, captivating views and native wildlife to discover.

West of Horsham, the Wimmera, a major grain-growing region, slips slowly by as the highway crosses into South Australia. Stop off at Little Desert National Park near Dimboola to see its beautiful show of spring wildflowers. Mixed farming country, interrupted by patches of mallee eucalypts, fringes the highway to Tailem Bend.

From Tailem Bend you can pass through the stunning Adelaide Hills, detour slightly to the wonderful McLaren Vale wine region, or continue even further south to Goolwa and Victor Harbor to make your way slowly back to Adelaide up the stunning Fleurieu Peninsula.

☁ BEST TIME TO GO

This is a popular route year-round, but most beautiful during spring and autumn. Visit Ballarat in March to catch the city's fabulous annual Begonia Festival.

BATEMANS BAY TO ADELAIDE
pp. 248–259

🅰 **Kings Highway, Monaro Highway, Snowy Mountains Highway, Tooma Road, Murray Valley Highway, Sturt Highway (1591km)**

The interconnecting highways in this section climb from the New South Wales south coast, pass by the national capital and cross the Snowy Mountains to the headwaters of the Murray River. The route then follows the lush Murray Valley through dairy farms, extensive vineyards, rich fruit-growing land and on to the famous wine-producing region of the Barossa Valley. There are snowfields in the Alpine areas, spectacular mountain scenes, superb golf courses, miles of shady river bends to camp on and wineries galore.

⚑ PLAN YOUR TRIP

From Batemans Bay the Kings Highway climbs from the Clyde Valley through abundant forests to the higher farming country and then Canberra. Along the way, soak up some local history in Braidwood, or stroll around the superb craft shops of Bungendore.

Canberra, Australia's capital, is a model city set out charmingly on the shores of Lake Burley Griffin. This small city boasts a magnificent art gallery and one of the best war museums in the world.

Beyond the Australian Capital Territory, as you climb through the Snowy Mountains, the scenery is breathtaking. Admire the engineering feats of the Snowy Mountains Scheme or stop for a few

days and fish for trout, before continuing through the lush farmland on the way to Albury.

At Albury. the route follows the sun-drenched region of the Murray Valley to Echuca, a popular holiday playground. There are excellent golf courses, large lakes, river beaches and the fabulous Rutherglen wine region.

From the historic paddlesteamer port town of Echuca, where you can still ride the river on a historic transport, the highway follows the Murray Valley to Mildura, through thriving dairying country, picturesque orchards and beautiful vineyards. The warm climate, numerous wineries, manicured golf courses and rich history attract travellers year-round.

From Mildura to Berri the route winds through the orchards and olive groves of this irrigated Riverland region. Hire a houseboat to cruise the Murray River, or follow its course to the mouth of that mighty river.

Once through the Riverland, the highway climbs before dropping into the Barossa Valley – one of Australia's best known wine regions. Visitors flock to the Barossa to enjoy the magnificent wineries, dine in excellent restaurants and soak up the region's fascinating Germanic history.

Adelaide is set on the wide curves of the River Torrens, belying the fact that beyond the rolling hills are great tracts of arid scrubland. Indeed Adelaide is the capital of the driest state in Australia.

☁ BEST TIME TO GO

The warm, sunny summer and balmy spring and autumn are features of the Murray Valley and Riverland regions. Expect cooler summers and cold, snowy winters in the alpine areas.

BRISBANE TO GOONDIWINDI
pp. 260–261

🅰 **Cunningham Highway (369km)**

High above the coastal plain west of the ranges lies the fertile Darling Downs, a rich farming area where grain crops thrive. The rugged volcanic rim that stretches northwards from New South Wales was a great barrier to early settlers trying to transport produce to and from the coast. Today, the Cunningham Highway is one of the main routes across the range, providing a major access to Brisbane from the western centres such as Warwick and Goondiwindi. Although it's much easier to drive than it once was, the range is still a steep climb or descent.

Brisbane's subtropical clime and river setting are very appealing. Explore the city's highlights including the heritage architecture and marvellous South Bank precinct. A ride on a river ferry or a visit to one of the major suburban shopping precincts are other popular options. There are fabulous beaches just 90 minutes away, on the Gold Coast to the south and the Sunshine Coast to the north. To the east is the stunning, and four-wheel-drive-only, Moreton Island.

Beyond Brisbane's urban sprawl, market gardens flourish along the coastal plain in the subtropical sunshine. The highway sweeps across the plain, ascending the once daunting Great Dividing Range then descends into broadacre farming country with rich, black volcanic soil. The Cunningham Highway intersects with the New England Highway at Warwick, then continues westwards through the grain-growing and grazing areas around Inglewood and on to Goondiwindi. Olive groves are a relatively new feature of the region and some extensive plantations can be seen west of Inglewood.

☁ BEST TIME TO GO

This region enjoys cool, mild winters and warm-to-hot summers. Rainfall can occur year-round, but during the summer months there is a greater likelihood of storms or rain depressions.

BRISBANE TO AUGATHELLA

pp. 262–267

🚗 Warrego Highway, Landsborough Highway (747km)

Enjoy the friendly country hospitality on offer as you travel along the Warrego Highway, the major westerly route from Brisbane. It crosses the fertile Lockyer Valley and travels through market gardens before abruptly climbing the Great Dividing Range to the picturesque city of Toowoomba. Travellers flock to Toowoomba for its impressive parks and gardens and wonderful show of flowers during spring. Further west, the highway narrows as it traverses the Darling Downs, an intensive farming region where crops of wheat, corn and sorghum grow along the road's edge. The towns of Dalby, Miles, Roma and Mitchell all service busy farming regions.

⚓ PLAN YOUR TRIP

Sweeping westward, the Warrego Highway passes market gardens and roadside stalls which are great places to stop and buy fresh produce. The road climbs steeply up into the range to the main regional centre of Toowoomba and then through rich farming land further west.

Between Dalby and Roma, cotton crops are harvested around Dalby during late autumn and the cotton is transported to a local gin for processing. The highway travels through dry grazing country as it passes through Chinchilla and Miles en route to Roma, a town at the heart of Queensland's early oil industry.

West of Roma, stop and take a break in Mitchell and have a dip in the artesian pools off the main street, or learn about the region's

bushrangers, the Kenniff brothers. The highway passes through cropping and grazing country before sweeping northward to meet the Mitchell Highway south of Augathella.

☁ BEST TIME TO GO

The winter months attract large numbers of tourists to this area. While the days may be warm and dry at this time, the nights can be clear and cold, with temperatures plummeting below zero.

NORSEMAN TO PERTH pp. 268–271

Coolgardie–Esperance Highway, Great Eastern Highway (726km)

Travel to Perth through historic goldmining towns and golden wheat fields on Route 94 – the most direct road linking the eastern states with the cosmopolitan coastal city. The Coolgardie–Esperance Highway intersects Highway One at the historic goldmining town of Norseman on the western end of the Nullarbor Plain crossing. Visit the intriguing Kalgoorlie and Coolgardie goldfields or watch the sun slip below the horizon over vast fields of wheat in the Merredin region.

⚓ PLAN YOUR TRIP

After the expansive emptiness of the Nullarbor Plain, the Coolgardie–Esperance Highway swings north from Norseman across kilometres of mallee country and salt lakes before ending in the once-thriving historic goldmining city of Coolgardie. Kalgoorlie-Boulder, now the prosperous key city in the goldfields, is a short and worthwhile detour from the main route.

Southern Cross marks the unofficial border between Western Australia's goldfields and golden wheat-belt regions. The Great Eastern Highway travels along the pipeline of the historic Goldfields Water Supply Scheme for much of the route. Along the way it passes through Merredin, the heart of the state's wheat industry, and Meckering, the site of a devastating earthquake in 1968. The small historic towns of Northam and York are worth a stop before the highway begins the climb over the hills to Perth.

With a Mediterranean-type climate and magnificent coastal and river setting, Perth is ideal for an outdoor lifestyle. Visitors to this city will find clean surf beaches, tranquil forests and well-kept parklands – all within easy reach of the city centre.

☁ BEST TIME TO GO

In this region, the temperatures climb dramatically during summer, so the best time to travel is during the cooler months Apr–Oct. However, just be aware that most rainfall occurs in the winter period.

SEYMOUR TO ALBURY

NEED TO KNOW

🕐	**215km**
🏠	**Family resorts, basic caravan parks**
☁	**This is a popular route year-round, on the main drag between Melbourne and Sydney.**
👁	**Ned Kelly history, wine and cheese, watersports**
🅰	**Excellent, although the highway bypasses all towns.**
🍴	**Albury and Wodonga are major regional cities, so have all facilities and services.**
⚠	**None apply**

Ned Kelly gear at Bailey's of Glenrowan winery

INTRODUCTION

Although the Hume Freeway between Melbourne and Albury is an excellent dual carriageway that bypasses all of the towns along it, there is plenty to see and do in the north-east of Victoria if you leave the freeway often. Glenrowan and Chiltern will appeal to history buffs, while wine and food aficionados will love the Rutherglen area and King Valley. Don't miss Bright, Beechworth or Yackandandah, either, so allow a few days, if you can.

WHERE TO GO

Moving north from **Seymour**, much of the area's most celebrated history is tied up in the exploits of Ned Kelly and his gang. There's a very intriguing history trail that begins in Avenel, taking in significant Kelly locations in Euroa, Benalla, Glenrowan, Wangaratta and Chiltern.

Avenel was Ned Kelly's boyhood home town and his father's grave is marked in the town's cemetery. Today it's a very quiet town, with basic facilities, although once it was a popular stopover for the mail coaches between Sydney and Melbourne, and fossickers travelling to the Beechworth goldfields.

The location of Kelly's daring bank robbery, **Euroa** was once a busy service point. Today the township mostly provides services to the local primary producers and has a good small-town shopping strip and a great caravan park. Euroa Apex Park, on the banks of Seven Creeks, is a picnic stop with an interesting walk along the creek banks.

Benalla has most services, good shopping and a busy main street that's filled with little cafes and boutique shops. It's popular for its proximity to the Winton Motor Raceway and is home to the Benalla Regional Art Gallery – one of the most visited regional galleries in Australia. Permanent displays include Sidney Nolan's tapestry *Siege of Glenrowan* which illustrates the Kelly legend, and Albert Tucker's painting of Kelly gang member Joe Byrne. It's open Wed–Mon 10am–5pm. Contact (03) 5762 3927.

The centre of Kelly history is Glenrowan, at the southern end of the Warby Range. This is the famous site of the Kelly Gang's last stand where they were captured after a 12-hour siege in 1880. The town is oriented to Kelly aficionados, with a Ned Kelly museum, walks and a larger-than-life statue.

Shopping in town is limited to souvenirs and takeaway food.

The city of **Wangaratta** is a major centre for the region, and a great place to base yourself to explore many of the surrounding regions without towing a caravan. The wine regions of Rutherglen to the west, or Milawa to the east, are both close by, as are the Ovens, King and Buffalo River valleys. Wangaratta is also the beginning (or end) of the Great Alpine Way, which passes through Bright, Mount Hotham and the Victorian High Country before ending at Bairnsdale near the Gippsland Lakes. (See p. 12.)

The historical town of **Chiltern** is a great detour from the highway with 21 buildings registered or owned by the National Trust. A highlight is Linden, which was the birthplace of former prime minister John McEwen. Another building of note is Lakeview, the childhood home of the author known as Henry Handel Richardson – famous for her novel, *The Getting of Wisdom*. Chiltern was also a goldrush town after the precious metal was found here in 1858 and at one point had a population of 20,000 people. Head to the visitor centre for a walking guide to the most significant historical sites.

Albury and **Wodonga** are sister cities, divided by the Murray River and

Victoria–New South Wales border. They are a major service centre on the busy Murray Valley and Hume highways generally being treated as the halfway point between Sydney and Melbourne even though that isn't geographically correct. Nearby attractions like Lake Hume are also popular.

DON'T MISS

→ **Milawa Cheese Factory – Milawa**
What started as a desire for a tree change has led to one of the country's premier boutique cheesemakers. The Milawa Cheese Factory, which was started in 1988 in the town's old butter factory, now boasts a great restaurant and cellar door that's a very popular lunchtime destination. Open daily 9am–5pm. Contact (03) 5727 3589.

WHERE TO STAY

388 BIG4 Seymour Holiday Park

⚲ 30 Trevan St, Seymour
☎ (03) 5792 1530
🖥 www.big4seymourholidaypark.com.au

 BIG4 HOLIDAY PARKS

This caravan park is located about 1km from the town centre in a quiet off-highway location on the banks of the Goulburn River. The park offers good, clean facilities and is easily accessible. There are canoes for hire.

389 Nagambie Lakes Leisure Park

⚲ 69 Loddings La, Nagambie
☎ (03) 5794 2373
🖥 www.nagambielakespark.com.au

 TOP PARKS

Just a 1.5-hour drive from Melbourne, this lakeside caravan park is ideal for a short break for the whole family. It has a pool, jumping pillow and games room. It is owned by Gerry Ryan, the founder and owner of Jayco Caravans in Australia.

390 Euroa Caravan Park

⚲ 73–103 Kirkland Ave, Euroa
☎ (03) 5795 2160
🖥 www.euroacaravanpark.com.au

Just a short walk from the centre of town, this caravan park stretches along the banks of the creek. It is a good spot in a lovely setting and has many tourist sites. Bookings are required in peak periods.

391 Discovery Parks Lake Hume

⚲ 33 Boathaven Rd, Ebden 3691
☎ (02) 6020 6130
🖥 www.discoveryholidayparks.com.au/caravan-parks/victoria/albury-wodonga-lake-hume

 Discovery HOLIDAY PARKS

Located about 12km east of Wodonga, this four hectare park is set on the shores of Lake Hume. It offers a range of recreational facilities, a large kiosk and several pleasant shaded sites. Bookings are required in peak periods, and a minimum-length stay applies during Christmas, Easter and long weekends.

Cheese board at Milawa

ALBURY TO GUNDAGAI

NEED TO KNOW

🕑	**178km**
🏠	**Free camping areas, inexpensive caravan parks, holiday resorts**
☁	**Winter, spring, and autumn**
👁	**Holbrook submarine park, Dog on the Tuckerbox monument**
🛣	**The Hume Highway is excellent.**
🍴	**Most basic services are available after leaving Albury.**
⚠	**Southbound travellers should note that it is not permitted to transport fruit and vegetables across the border from New South Wales to Victoria. Nor is it permitted to carry fruit along the Sturt Highway into the Murrumbidgee fruit-growing area. While there are no permanent inspection stations, fines do apply.**

Lake Hume, Albury

INTRODUCTION

I have very fond memories of this part of the Melbourne to Sydney route, having travelled it at least twice a year, every year to visit family in Melbourne. It travels through rolling farmland and past many interesting small towns as well as being the gateway to the NSW snowfields, Wagga Wagga and Lake Hume. Now the Hume upgrade is completed, all of the small towns are bypassed and the road is an excellent four-lane dual carriageway.

WHERE TO GO

The Murray River, which forms the border between Victoria and New South Wales, has been the lifeblood of the southern region. Major water storages on the river have been designed to hold and divert water along canals to irrigate large areas of farming land. Many of these storage areas have become great recreational destinations. Lake Hume is one of these – it's best accessed from the popular Great Aussie Holiday Park in **Bowna**. The Hume Weir, which dams the Murray to create the lake, is just 14km east of Albury and much of the lake's 400km of shoreline is accessible to the public.

Of all the things to see in a land-locked regional town, **Holbrook** likely has the most unexpected. After the 1994 decommissioning of the HMAS *Otway*, one of six Oberon class submarines built in Scotland for the Australian Navy, all parts above the waterline were purchased and assembled to create a formidable attraction in Holbrook. More recently, the Holbrook Submarine Museum has been incorporated into the visitor centre. The town has long had an association with submarines, having been renamed in 1914 in honour of the Royal Naval Submarine Commander Lieutenant N.D. Holbrook VC. The town was previously gazetted as Germantown, which was deemed unpatriotic during WWI.

Originally Holbrook was a key staging post between Sydney and Melbourne, until the construction of the railway in 1883. Today, the town is a major regional centre servicing the surrounding regional industries. Notably, there are a couple of bakeries along the main street that are popular with travellers.

Further north, **Tarcutta** is a small town with strong links to the transport industry. It has always been an important stop on the Melbourne to Sydney route and for decades has provided many angle parking spaces for trucks in the centre of town. There are minimal services, but roadhouses provide fuel and food.

Another town steeped in colonial history is **Gundagai** – famous for its Dog on the Tuckerbox statue. It's also known for its mention in the song "Along the Road to Gundagai", originally performed by Peter Dawson in 1924 and used as the introduction to the *Dad and Dave* radio show. The town overlooks the wide floodplain of the Murrumbidgee River and boasts the longest wooden bridge in the country. Classified by the National Trust, the bridge crosses the river and floodplain and served as part of the Hume Highway for 110 years after its completion in 1869. South Gundagai lies south of the river and is an important service centre for interstate transport and travellers.

DON'T MISS

→ **Going potty – Holbrook**
Dedicated solely to 19th and 20th century Australian pottery, the National Museum of Australian Pottery has over 1800 pieces on display from the days of convict settlement through to the end of WWI. It's open Thurs–Tue 9.30am–4.30pm, but call ahead just in case. Contact (08) 6036 3464.

→ **Moving tribute – Tarcutta**
In the main street of Tarcutta, the Australian transport industry has placed a memorial to those who have lost their lives on the job. The Memorial Wall is a moving tribute and I recommend you stop for a few minutes to take a look.

→ **Dog on the Tuckerbox – near Gundagai**
The tale of the Dog on the Tuckerbox from Australian folklore is well told in the parklands and rest area surrounding this statue. It's a popular stop for many interstate travellers with a nearby roadhouse, kiosk and information centre.

WHERE TO STAY

392 Great Aussie Holiday Park

$$$ ★

- 14 Hore Rd, Bowna
- (02) 6020 3236
- www.greataussieholidaypark.com.au

TOP PARKS

Set on the banks of Lake Hume, this family-friendly caravan park has much to offer including pet-friendly camping, a kids' water park and 2km of private foreshore with a boat ramp.

393 Holbrook Motor Village

$$$ ★

- Corner Albury and Bardwell sts, Holbrook
- (02) 6036 3100
- www.holbrookmotorvillage.com.au

Conveniently located just off the Hume Highway, this tidy little caravan park is perfect for overnight stops. Or you can stay a few days and enjoy the local attractions including HMAS *Otway*, the Submarine Museum, National Museum of Australian Pottery and the Woolpack Inn Museum.

335 Gundagai Tourist Park

See p. 171 – Gundagai to Hay.

Dog on the Tuckerbox, Gundagai

GUNDAGAI TO GOULBURN

NEED TO KNOW

🌐	**180km**
🏠	**Full-featured caravan parks**
☁	**This is a great year-round route.**
👁	**Canberra, small country towns**
🛣	**This is a major interstate route and the highway is dual carriageway, bypassing all towns.**
🍴	**Facilities on the highway are limited to service centres, but both Canberra and Goulburn have all services.**
⚠	**None apply**

Long Track Pantry, Jugiong

INTRODUCTION

Although the Hume Highway between Gundagai and Goulburn is mostly a dual carriageway that bypasses all the towns, including Goulburn, the surrounding areas and small towns are a delight to stop in. Many of these diversions offer pleasant parklands, free camping areas, boutique shopping opportunities and great cafes.

WHERE TO GO

Proving my earlier point about pleasant parklands, free camping areas and great cafes – **Jugiong** has become a must-stop destination for my family on regular trips between New South Wales and Victoria. The Jugiong Showground allows camping for up to seven days, for a donation. It's just across the road from the Long Track Pantry – a delightful cafe and larder specialising in meals and condiments from local suppliers.

The township of **Yass** is at the centre of a large agricultural region that produces fine wool, canola, oats, grapes and beef cattle. The town has a nice shopping precinct that attracts those with time to browse in the galleries, craft stores and antique shops, or to stop for coffee in one of the cafes.

There are great camping options in town too, from the free riverside camping area at Joe O'Connor Park to the Yass Caravan Park, which is basic but inexpensive.

The nearby **Lake Burrinjuck** is a major water storage on the Murrumbidgee River, built to control water for the Murrumbidgee Irrigation Area. The lake is a popular spot for a range of aquatic activities, including boating, fishing, swimming and waterskiing. A number of caravan parks and camping areas dot the lake's shores.

I once pulled into **Gunning**, a little further north, knowing I needed fuel, but certainly not believing I was desperate, only to put the exact amount in the tank the manufacturer said would fit. As there's no fuel for 40km in any direction, I've got a soft spot for the town that saved me some embarrassment. Explorers Hume and Hovell began their epic overland journey from this small country town, which has several colonial buildings and a historical courthouse. In my opinion, the Merino Cafe serves the best coffee and cakes on the Hume Highway.

Goulburn is Australia's oldest inland city, and today is a large provincial centre servicing a diverse agricultural region. It's also home to the NSW Police Force's training academy and the state's highest security prison. Before the completion of the railway in 1869, Goulburn was a 16-day journey from Sydney on a Cobb & Co. coach. Explorer William Hovell and members of the pioneering Durack family are buried in the town cemetery.

Goulburn's major attraction is the Big Merino, a 15m tall ram that celebrates Australia's world-leading wool production. With all major services and good shopping, this is a popular stop with a number of regionally famous eateries.

→ Sutton – near the ACT

Sutton is a small village in New South Wales, located near the Federal Highway and bordered by the Australian Capital Territory. Only minutes from Canberra, it is a good base from which to explore all the region has to offer. Capital Country Holiday Park is one of the best places to stay.

→ The nation's capital – Canberra

For travellers wishing to visit Canberra, the Barton Highway exits the Hume near Yass, while the Federal Highway leaves just south of Goulburn. Canberra is a rapidly growing city with an emerging food and craft-beer scene. It's popular with cyclists and mountain-bikers, and has some excellent attractions, including the National Museum of Australia and Questacon. The Australian War Memorial is a must-visit location. (*See* p. 248.)

Goulburn Town Hall

WHERE TO STAY

394 Capital Country Holiday Village

$$$$

📍 47 Bridges Rd, Sutton
📞 (02) 6230 3433
🖥 www.capitalcountryholidaypark.com.au

Situated on 40 acres of grassy parkland this caravan park has large, gravel drive-thru sites and excellent facilities.

395 Alivio Tourist Park Canberra

$$$$

📍 20 Kunzea St, O'Connor, Canberra
📞 (02) 6247 5466
🖥 www.aliviogroup.com.au

Located just 4km from the centre of Canberra this caravan park has level gravel sites, good clean amenities and plenty of facilities including a camp kitchen, playground and swimming pool.

396 Yass Caravan Park

$$

📍 Corner Laidlaw and Gramplan sts, Yass
📞 (02) 6226 1173
🖥 www.yassvalley.com.au

This is a neat and tidy caravan park with several drive-thru sites available. Amenities are dated, but clean, and there is plenty of grass area.

397 BIG4 Governors Hill Carapark

$$$

📍 77 Sydney Rd, Goulburn
📞 (02) 4821 7373
🖥 www.big4.com.au/governors-hill

Located on the north side of Goulburn this small caravan park has good facilities, including a well-equipped indoor camp kitchen. Amenities are dated but clean and tidy. The concrete-base sites are suitable for rigs up to 27ft.

GOULBURN TO SYDNEY

Goulburn storefronts

INTRODUCTION

The Southern Highlands, which dominate much of this section, are a rich agricultural region where many city dwellers have settled for the country lifestyle. Small acreages and magnificent gardens dot the landscape. The area is an easy drive from Sydney so it's a very popular weekend destination. There are four distinct seasons as the climate is much cooler than on the surrounding plains.

WHERE TO GO

It's a little off the main drag up to Sydney, but Bungonia National Park is an underrated wonder, just 30 min from **Goulburn**. Most well known for its extensive cave system that attracts many hard-hatted adventurers with rock-climbing equipment and headlamps who crawl though the underground mazes. Several walks take in the spectacular views over the Bungonia Slot Canyon. The Bungonia camping area has good facilities and plenty of space for caravans.

From Bungonia, you'll pass through **Marulan** on your way back to the freeway, which is the site of a heavy-vehicle checking station with a nearby roadhouse servicing passing travellers. It's a good place to fill up if you're planning on passing through Sydney, and to avoid many of the suburban service stations that do not always have driveways that are easy to negotiate with a caravan.

If you're not going straight to Sydney, then stop in at **Moss Vale**, one of the oldest settlements in the Southern Highlands. Moss Vale services a large agricultural area and has good shopping with a large selection of accommodation, cafes and restaurants. It's a great place to base yourself to explore the nearby national parks and waterfalls. Three significant waterfalls – Fitzroy, Belmore and Carrington – are easily accessed and viewed, with great walking tracks nearby.

We're zigzagging a bit, but nearby **Berrima** is also worth a detour. With more than 170 years of history, Berrima has the oldest continuously operated inn in the land – the Surveyor General, which was built in 1834 and licensed the following year. The town's proximity to Sydney has led to its popularity as a destination for lunch and a meander through craft shops or past impressive colonial buildings, including the former gaol and courthouse.

Bowral is one of the most picturesque towns in the Southern Highlands. During spring the Corbett Gardens are the centerpiece of a fabulous tulip festival, while the popular Bradman Museum is a year-round attraction. The town also has good shopping and most services, with farmers' markets held at the Bowral Public School on the 2nd Sat of the month (except in Jan).

The nearby town of **Mittagong** is renowned for its cooler climate – it snowed here in 2016. Several vineyards close to town produce cool-climate wines and the town has good country-town shopping. It's also a gateway to Wombeyan Caves, via the winding and sometimes narrow Wombeyan Caves Rd.

Tulip Time Festival, Bowral

DON'T MISS

→ The Highland's best pies – Robertson

On the Illawarra Highway, at the top of Macquarie Pass, the famous Robertson Pie Shop is a very popular bakery that attracts people from all over. While its meat pies are great, it's the dessert tarts and baked treats that are exceptional. I rarely pass by without taking home a box of Portuguese tarts.

→ Waterfalls and waterholes – Morton National Park

Morton National Park, which stretches from the Southern Highlands near Robertson to south of Ulladulla, has several high waterfalls in its northern section. Most spectacular is Fitzroy Falls, which is an 81m drop with great walks around the gorge's rim. Nearby Carrington Falls, on the Kangaroo River, has several pleasant swimming holes upstream that are perfect for a dip on a warm day.

→ Limestone wonders – Wombeyan Caves

Wombeyan Caves, within Wombeyan Karst Conservation Reserve, is a series of limestone caves carved out by the slightly acidic water dissolving the rock over hundreds of millions of years. There are seven caves that can be explored as well as good walks nearby, and the reserve has a great camping area too.

WHERE TO STAY

397 BIG 4 Governors Hill Carapark

See p. 217 – Gundagai to Goulburn.

398 Mittagong Caravan Park

📍 1 Old Hume Hwy, Mittagong
📞 (02) 4871 1574
🖥 www.mittagongcaravanpark.com.au

Set amongst the natural bushland of the Southern Highlands this pet-friendly caravan park has good facilities, including a large indoor camp kitchen. With easy access to the Hume Hwy it is great for overnight stops.

399 Poplar Tourist Park

📍 21 Macarthur Rd, Elderslie
📞 (02) 4658 0485
🖥 www.poplartouristparkcamden.com.au

On the outskirts of Sydney, with public transport available at the front door, this pet-friendly caravan park is perfect for exploring the greater Sydney region. The facilities are very good and include an internet cafe and recreation room.

44 NRMA Sydney Lakeside Holiday Park

See p. 24 – Nowra to Sydney.

NEWCASTLE TO MUSWELLBROOK

Ballooning, Hunter Valley

INTRODUCTION

The Hunter Valley is Australia's oldest wine region. The first vines were planted here in the 1830s, and today there are more than 140 vineyards and cellar doors, ranging from small, privately owned boutique wineries, to large corporate entities chasing the world market. More than just a wine destination, though, the Hunter has a range of natural attractions, historic towns, good camping options and mostly quiet roads.

WHERE TO GO

If you've come from Sydney and the Hunter Valley is your destination, there's no need to head into Newcastle first – simply take the Freemans Dr exit to Cessnock off the M1.

If you are coming from **Newcastle**, head to Maitland first, then detour through Kurri Kurri to Cessnock, which was once the heart of coalmining in the Hunter Valley, although the last of the underground mines has now closed. Today, vineyards flourish in this rich grape-growing region and tourism is a key industry. There are cellar doors galore and a vast range of accommodation and restaurants in the surrounding areas.

For those looking for some non-alcoholic entertainment, the Hunter Valley Gardens in **Pokolbin** are sensational. Over 60 finely landscaped acres there are 10 distinctly themed gardens designed by award-winning celebrity gardener Bill Roche. There are more than 8km of paths through and around the gardens, of which the highlights are the Japanese and rose gardens. A small boutique shopping mall adjoining the gardens is a popular place for lunch and trinkets. Entry fees apply and it's open daily 9am–5pm. Contact (02) 4998 4000.

The historical town of **Maitland** is a key one on the Hunter River, surrounded by numerous small rural communities, each with its own identity. One such is **Morpeth**, a National Trust–classified village which has over 30 historical buildings and a great heritage walk. Maitland's attractions include a gaol that until 1998 was a maximum-security prison. Today, a range of tours, including one that's self-guided, are popular ways to do time in the prison that's over 150 years old.

Established on the banks of the Hunter River in the 1820s, **Singleton** has long been a coalmining town, with the first opening in 1860. Today there are 20 coalmines in the area, employing nearly 3000 people.

Even so, the area is at the centre of a rich farming district, with cattle and viticulture the most prominent activities. The nearby army base, which is now the infantry-training centre, has been here for over 60 years. The barracks contains the Australian Army Infantry Museum, with displays from the Australian Army's first deployment to Sudan in 1885 to its current roles and operations. Entry fees apply and it's open Wed–Sun 9am–4pm. Contact (02) 6575 0257.

Travelling between Singleton and Muswellbrook you'll skirt the shores of the man-made Lake Liddell, which was created to cool the Liddell Power Station. It used to be a popular swimming, boating, fishing and paddling spot, but after an amoeba that causes infection of the brain was found in the waters, access to the lake has been closed permanently. On its north-eastern shore is a great camping area which is my preferred base to explore the region.

In the northern part of the Hunter region, **Muswellbrook** is a major centre and has numerous wineries, recently planted olive groves, open-cut coalmines and coal-fired power stations. Although mining began here in the 19th century, it wasn't until 1945 that it really began to expand, with the establishment of the Liddell and Bayswater power stations. Today, the town has most services and good regional shopping. Get along to the markets held at the showground on the 2nd Sun of each month.

DON'T MISS

→ Flying aloft – near Cessnock

The Hunter Valley is just the place to float above the vineyards in the early morning light – an exceptional experience that usually lasts an hour. Balloon Aloft Australia has daily sunrise flights – fees apply. Contact 1300 723 279.

→ Mistletoe Wines – Pokolbin

I always love stopping in at the winery of fellow caravanners Ken and Gwen Sloan, who have been making wine on their property since 1989. They've got a great tasting room and wonderful gardens filled with quirky sculptures. Three generations of the family work in the vineyard, and they are always friendly and welcoming.

WHERE TO STAY

49 Stockton Beach Holiday Park

See p. 26 – Sydney to Newcastle.

400 Ingenia Holidays Hunter Valley

📍 137 Mount View Rd, Cessnock
📞 (02) 4990 2573
💻 www.ingeniaholidays.com.au

BIG4 HOLIDAY PARKS

This is the best located caravan park for exploring the Hunter Valley wineries. Just 3km from the centre of Cessnock, it offers good facilities including a Thai restaurant.

401 Lake Liddell Recreation Area camping area

📍 400 Hebden Road, Muswellbrook
📞 (02) 6541 2010

This is a picturesque camping area on the shores of Lake Liddell. While all access to the water has been restricted due to the presence of a potentially deadly amoeba, the park is actively developing the area to incorporate interesting land-based activities, like mountain-biking, rock climbing and even a fitness boot camp. Fees are modest, and the view is still spectacular.

Hunter Valley Gardens

MUSWELLBROOK TO TAMWORTH

Tamworth Country Music Festival

INTRODUCTION

Taking you from the heart of wine-making country to the country-music capital of Australia, the New England Highway climbs from the Hunter Valley into rich farming land passing numerous horse studs that dot the region. This route takes in a fire that's been burning for 6000 years, a historical pub and plenty of rural charm. It's also the birthplace of the blue heeler dog breed.

WHERE TO GO

Before leaving **Muswellbrook** stop by the Blue Heeler Cattle Dog Statue on Bridge St. The statue commemorates the work of Aberdeen farmer Thomas Hall who in 1840 bred a cross of dingoes and the typical English dogs, which didn't cope well with the Australian conditions. The resultant Australian cattle dog breed, also known as the blue heeler, is now one of Australia's most popular and intelligent working dogs.

From **Aberdeen** there is access to Lake Glenbawn, which is widely regarded as one of the best freshwater fishing destinations in New South Wales. From a boat, or the shore,

anglers can catch bass, yellowbelly, silver perch and rainbow trout. Murray cod are also reputedly landed. A caravan park with good amenities is set up on its shores, which is understandably very popular.

If you can wrestle yourself away from the great fishing at Lake Glenbawn, it's an easy trip to **Scone**, a key regional town in the Upper Hunter. It's surrounded by agricultural land and around 65 horse studs from which millions of dollars' worth of foals are bred each year. Some of these studs are visible from the highway and most are model properties with kilometres of timber fences and hectares of lush green pastures where mares and foals graze.

If you're seeking a little bit of solitude, the Washpools camping area in Towarri National Park, about 15km north of Scone, is just the place. The name is derived from the shallow creek cutting through a sandstone gully where local stations brought their sheep to be washed. Today, it's a quiet, green spot with basic facilities and a few short walks.

The small town of **Wingen** isn't much more than a great rural pub on the highway, but it does get a mention in a poem by Aussie bush poet Col Wilson – 'The Wingen

Pub' – which makes it well worth a stop in my book.

Just north of here is one of the most bizarre geological wonders I have ever come across. For 6000 years an underground fire has been burning its way along a coal seam, and you can trace its path following a 4.6km return walk to the summit of Mt Wingen. Information boards along the way tell of the history and geology.

For more typical Upper Hunter and Liverpool Plains scenery, head to the historic town of **Murrurundi**, which has retained its rural heritage with many of its buildings from the 1850s and '60s. Murrurundi has basic shopping and a good information centre with a park where you can take a break.

Tamworth is just an hour's drive north, and it's a very popular tourist destination, especially in Jan during the Country Music Festival. A major regional centre, the city offers most services and excellent shopping in a tree-lined main strip, with large retail chain stores and trendy alfresco cafes. Of course, there's also the giant Golden Guitar, out the front of the tourist centre on Ringers Rd.

→ Country Music Festival – Tamworth

Tamworth is the country-music capital of Australia and the Country Music Festival in Jan is a major national event for more than just country-music fans. It attracts all the top country-music artists and culminates in the industry awards. Thousands of visitors flock to the town and all accommodation (including caravan parks) within a 75km radius is booked out each year.

If you plan to travel to Tamworth during Jan for the Country Music Festival, caravan and camping sites are at a premium and some parks have a minimum-booking period of up to two weeks. A number of parks in outlying towns run daily commuter bus services into Tamworth throughout the festival.

WHERE TO STAY

402 Reflections Holiday Parks Lake Glenbawn

📍 Glenbawn Rd, Scone
📞 (02) 6543 7193
🖥 www.reflectionsholidayparks.com.au

The caravan park is 14km from Scone and easily accessible from Aberdeen. The powered sites do not front the lake, but there are unpowered camping sites available with lake frontage. This is a popular fishing spot where anglers catch bass, yellowbelly, silver perch and rainbow trout. Murray cod are also reputedly landed.

403 Murrurundi Caravan Park

📍 11 Bernard St, Murrurundi
📞 (02) 6546 6288
🖥 www.murrurundicaravanpark.com.au

www.kuiparks.com.au

On the northern edge of town, this small, neatly maintained caravan park is easily accessible from the New England Hwy and is ideal for an overnight stay at an attractive price.

404 Fossickers Tourist Park

📍 103 Jenkins St, Nundle
📞 (02) 6769 3355
🖥 www.fossickersatnundle.com.au

TOP PARKS

The historical town of Nundle is a popular fossicking area. The caravan park, in a tranquil area on the banks of the Peel River, is a pleasant place for a relaxing break.

405 Paradise Tourist Park

📍 575 Peel St, Tamworth
📞 (02) 6766 3120
🖥 www.paradisetouristpark.com.au

BIG4
HOLIDAY PARKS

This caravan park is within walking distance of the centre of town and is extremely popular in Jan during the Tamworth Country Music Festival. Bookings are required at peak times.

Horseriding in Scone

TAMWORTH TO GLEN INNES

NEED TO KNOW

🕐	**206km**
🏠	**Inexpensive caravan parks**
☁	**Spring and autumn bring out the best of the region. Winter can be bitingly cold.**
👁	**National parks, bush camping, wineries, fossicking**
🅰	**Good, but steep and winding in places.**
🍴	**All major services are available, including a number of hospitals, large shopping complexes, and a university.**
⚠	**None apply**

Australian Standing Stones, Glen Innes

INTRODUCTION

The New England district lies some 200km inland and approximately 1000m above sea level. Chilly winters, golden autumns, heritage buildings and large stretches of farmland contrast with the tropical scenery of the nearby north coast. While this route typically sticks to the highlands, as you drive north you'll encounter the first reaches of rainforest on the eastern side of the ranges. (*See* Dubbo to Moree p. 236 for more about the western reaches.)

WHERE TO GO

North of **Tamworth**, the New England Highway climbs abruptly up the Moonbi Hills. There is less heavy traffic along here and it can be a very enjoyable drive on the way to Uralla.

Having lured gold prospectors to the area since the 1850s, **Uralla** is still a favourite of fossickers with gold and gemstones still found today. In town there are craft shops, galleries and a renowned antiquarian book shop, Burnett's Books. Infamous bushranger Captain Thunderbolt was killed in a shootout with police in Uralla in 1870, and a

gravestone in the local cemetery marks his final resting place.

Nestled a touch lower in the northern tablelands, **Armidale** is a regional centre of learning and culture. The city is home to the University of New England, the state's first regional university, as well as two cathedrals and several museums. As a result, Armidale has a vibrant art and emerging food scene. The surrounding rural regions produce fine wool and prime cattle graze in the mountain country to the east.

From Armidale you'll continue to climb to **Guyra**, which at 1320m above sea level is the highest town in New England, and often deals with snow in winter. Even so, the summers here are warm and sunny and the perfect time to explore the nearby Guy Fawkes River and Cathedral Rock national parks and Styx River State Forest.

Still 1km above sea level, and located at the junction of the New England and Gwydir highways, **Glen Innes** is at the heart of Celtic country. Close by are World Heritage–listed national parks, wineries, rich sapphire fields and quality fishing. Historical buildings and museums record much of the past and are testament to the town's strong traditions and predominantly Scottish heritage.

DON'T MISS

→ **Guy Fawkes River National Park – near Guyra**

Vast tracts of land in the ranges are protected by national parks, although my favourite is Guy Fawkes River National Park. It's home to the stunning Ebor Falls and has a couple of great camping areas along the Boyd River that are very popular for kayak and shore-based fishing.

→ **Celtic stones – near Glen Innes**

Few sights illustrate the town's Celtic heritage more than the Australian version of old standing stones, like those around which the ancient Celts danced. The circle of 24 stones represents the hours of the day. The five cardinal stones – four outside the circle representing north, south, east and west, and a single stone inside the circle – form the Southern Cross and link the old and new worlds.

WHERE TO STAY

406 Kootingal Kourt Van Park

$$\text{\$\$}$$

📍 3 Churchill Dr, Kootingal
📞 (02) 6760 3103

Conveniently located alongside the New England Hwy, this tidy caravan park is ideal for an overnight stop. It is also a good base for those attending the Tamworth Country Music Festival in January, when bookings are essential.

407 Country Road Caravan Park

$$\text{\$\$}$$

📍 New England Hwy, Uralla
📞 (02) 6778 4563
🖥 www.countryroadcp.com.au

A popular stopover on the New England Hwy, this caravan park has good facilities and is an ideal base for exploring the area. Bookings are required in peak seasons.

408 Armidale Tourist Park

$$\text{\$\$\$}$$

📍 39 Waterfall Way, Armidale
📞 (02) 6772 6470
🖥 www.armidaletouristpark.com.au

A lovely spot with shady trees and wide expanses of lawn, this caravan park is only 3km from the town centre. A very pet-friendly park.

409 Glen Rest Tourist Park

$$\text{\$\$}$$

📍 9807 New England Hwy, Glen Innes
📞 (02) 6732 2413
🖥 www.gleninnes.com/glenrestpark

Located 3.5km south of Glen Innes, in a pleasant rural setting, this caravan park is an ideal stopover for travellers passing through the region.

Ebor Falls

New England Brewing Company, Uralla

GLEN INNES TO WARWICK

NEED TO KNOW

🕐	**212km**
🏠	**National park camping areas, full-featured caravan parks**
☁	**It can snow on the tableland in winter, so avoid it then if you don't like the cold.**
👁	**Quiet bush camping, national parks, walking, fishing**
🅰	**Good to great**
🍴	**Facilities are basic between Glen Innes and Warwick.**
⚠	**None apply**

Leslie Dam

INTRODUCTION

The highway winds through the undulating New England region and crosses the state border into the rich fruit and winegrowing region of south-east Queensland's Granite Belt. This trip traverses bushranger country, a handful of distinctly rocky national parks and well-established wine regions that are quickly becoming increasingly popular. The highway is mostly free of heavy vehicles, too, which makes for pleasant days on the road, exploring each area slowly. Even though it's the sunshine state, beware of icy roads if travelling through in winter. It even snows through here about once each year.

WHERE TO GO

It may not be well recognised, but the small rural town of **Tenterfield** played a significant role in the birth of Australia as a nation. In colonial times, one of the first to envisage a united Australia was Sir Henry Parkes, former premier of New South Wales. In October 1889, he presented his famous Federation Speech at the Tenterfield School of Arts, which subsequently led to the Federation of Australia in 1901. The building is still there, although it's not the most popular historical building in town.

That title belongs to the Tenterfield Saddler – the workshop of George Woolnough immortalised in song by his grandson, Peter Allen. Woolnough worked from it for some 52 years, and now the National Trust has classified the 100-year-old building.

Visit in summer for the warm days perfect for enjoying local wineries, nearby national parks and even a bushranger trail (*see* Don't Miss).

Just north of Tenterfield you cross the border to Queensland, and if you stick to the highway, pass by the stunning Girraween National Park or if you take Mount Lindesay Rd, past Bald Rock National Park. The bald rock actually straddles the two states. Years ago we camped there and considered climbing it, but after just a few metres decided it wasn't worth near-certain injuries, so admired it from afar instead. A number of other parks in the region are also well worth visiting, like Boonoo Boonoo and Sundown national parks, all of which have good camping suitable for caravans and motorhomes, and great walking within them.

In the heart of the rich Granite Belt, **Stanthorpe** has an altitude and cool climate that are ideal for horticulture and viticulture. Renowned for fruit, vegetables and fine wines, the area has some 40 cellar doors, numerous roadside fruit and produce vendors, and a host of eateries. Fruit-pickers

descend on the town Dec–Mar and tourists flock to the region on weekends.

Follow the winding highway a little further north, and **Warwick** at the crossroads of the New England and Cunningham highways is a key regional centre for the Granite Belt. Springtime sees the town's fabulous roses at their best.

DON'T MISS

→ Bushranger's hideout – near Tenterfield

Frederick Ward, better known as the notorious bushranger Captain Thunderbolt, roamed the Tenterfield region in the 1860s. About 12km along Mount Lindesay Highway from Tenterfield is a signposted 300m pathway to Thunderbolt's Hideout – which is the sort of bush-cave system that young kids dream about. He was fatally wounded in a shootout with police in Uralla, where his body has been laid to rest (*See* Tamworth to Glen Innes p. 224).

→ Aquatic playground – near Warwick

Leslie Dam, 14km west of Warwick, is popular with watersports enthusiasts and anglers. The dam is stocked with golden and silver perch, and Murray cod. A permit is required to fish, which starts at $10 for a week.

Stanthorpe

WHERE TO STAY

410 Kookaburra Camping and Caravan Park

- Castlerag Rd, Deepwater
- 0429 462 473

This peaceful country caravan park offers large unpowered sites and modern amenities. There is a large campfire set-up and an undercover barbecue area with plenty of seating.

411 Bald Rock camping area

- Bald Rock Rd, Bald Rock National Park
- (02) 6736 4298
- www.nationalparks.nsw.gov.au/visit-a-park/parks/bald-rock-national-park

This picturesque bush camping area has level sites with a gravel base and clean drop toilets. An abundance of wildlife can be spotted in the surrounding area and there are a number of excellent walking trails through the national park. Park-entry and camping fees apply.

412 Top of the Town Tourist Park

- 10 High St, Stanthorpe
- (07) 4681 4888
- www.topoftown.com.au

Ideally located right in town and close to shops and cafes this caravan park has spacious sites and tidy amenities with a nice, well-kept swimming pool. Bookings are required Dec–Mar (fruit-picking season).

413 Warwick Freedom Lifestyle

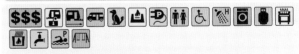

- 98 Wallace St, Warwick
- (07) 4661 2874
- www.warwick.freedomlifestyleparks.com.au

Located on the south side of town this spacious caravan park offers a variety of accommodation options including large motorhome-friendly drive-thru sites. The amenities are clean and tidy and there is a large swimming pool and children's playground onsite.

WARWICK TO GYMPIE

Toowoomba

INTRODUCTION

The New England Highway continues to wind northwards across the patchwork of fertile farmlands that make up the Darling Downs and into wooded country and pine forests. Wineries abound and lots of fresh produce is available along this route, including peanuts from the Kingaroy area. The road surface is good, but overtaking opportunities are not frequent north of Toowoomba, however there are a number of recognised rest areas along the northern part of the journey.

WHERE TO GO

It's not far after leaving the roses and spectacular sandstone buildings that typify **Warwick** that you'll be enticed to stop again. The Glengallan Homestead and Heritage Centre is a magnificent, restored heritage building close to the New England Highway on the way to **Allora**. Stop in for group tours and a quaint coffee shop, or just to enjoy the gardens in an ambience of yesteryear. It's open Wed–Sun 10am–4pm.

It's only a short drive from this lovely garden to the 'Garden City' of **Toowoomba**.

Each spring, visitors flock from all over Australia to partake in the annual Carnival of Flowers which shows off the regional city's magnificent gardens perched high on the range.

Toowoomba's best attraction, though, is the Cobb & Co. Museum, which offers a glimpse into pioneering history and showcases Australia's finest collection of horse-drawn vehicles. There is also a fine cafe on the premises.

A little further on is **Crows Nest**, one of only a few Australian towns named after an Indigenous person. (Bongaree on Bribie Island is another – named after Matthew Flinders' Indigenous guide on the *Investigator*). Jimmy Crow was a well-known tracker in the early 19th century who often helped teamsters who passed by his camp. Eventually the camp became known as Jimmy Crow's Nest. A monument to the man can be found in the middle of town. These days, the town is the centre of a rapidly growing area and tourists are well catered for with cafes, art galleries and craft shops. Nearby Lakes Cressbrook and Perseverance, and Crows Nest National Park are popular with campers, picnickers and bushwalkers.

A popular place to settle in for a few days is the Swinging Bridge Park behind the **Cooyar** Pub. On the banks of Cooyar Creek it is possible to sit quietly at dawn or dusk and watch platypus play in their natural state. After dusk, the pub welcomes travellers for a cold drink, good meals and friendly hospitality. The nearby Muntapa Rail Tunnel, which is listed on the Queensland Heritage Register, is home to a colony of bent-wing microbats and a popular attraction.

Continuing north, the town of **Yarraman** sits at the junction of the New England, Burnett and D'Aguilar highways. The small rural timber and farming community is at the centre of more than 16,000 hectares of hoop-pine forest. Birdlife is prolific, platypus inhabit the streams, wineries dot the area and antique and craft shops are in plentiful supply.

From **Goomeri** follow the Wide Bay Highway and make for the coast via **Gympie**, which is the gateway to Fraser Island, Tin Can Bay and Hervey Bay. Originally a gold-rush town, after the metal was discovered in 1867, Gympie now has most services and good shopping. Queensland's largest nugget, the 37kg Curtis Nugget, was found here and the Gympie Gold Mining and Heritage Museum is a great spot to learn more about it.

→ **Bunya Mountains National Park**

Protected by Queensland's second oldest national park, the Bunya Mountains are a natural wonderland sheltering the world's largest stand of ancient bunya pines. The steep climb to the national park is not for caravans, but is certainly recommended as a day trip from Cooyar or Yarraman while passing through this area.

→ **The Darling Downs**

The Darling Downs is a huge agricultural district spread across 72,000 square kilometres of undulating plains, 900m above sea level. The region's rich volcanic soil yields grapes, oilseeds and wheat, as well as some of the country's most magnificent gardens. Throughout the countryside there are English-style plantings of elms, plane trees and poplars fringing green pastures, neat

grain fields and historical towns. Although the New England Highway only skirts the south-eastern edge of the downs, there are plenty of opportunities to head west

and explore further. Towns like Dalby and Kingaroy aren't too far out of the way and are well worth the visit.

Crows Nest National Park

WHERE TO STAY

414 Spring Creek Caravan Park

📍 616 Spring Creek Rd, Spring Creek
📞 (07) 4697 3397
💻 www.kuiparks.com.au/parks/qld/item/
spring-creek-caravan-park

Kui Parks
www.kuiparks.com.au

A wonderful grassy caravan park halfway between Warwick and Toowoomba on the site of an old Cobb & Co. staging camp. It has broad, grassy sites and clean facilities which include barbecues and laundries. Fires and pets are also permitted.

415 BIG4 Toowoomba Garden City Holiday Park

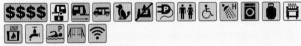

📍 34A Eiser St, Harristown
📞 (07) 4635 1747
💻 www.big4toowoombagchp.com.au

BIG4
HOLIDAY PARKS

Colourful, manicured gardens greet you at the entrance of this high-quality caravan park in a quiet location, about 3km from the city centre. The park has great amenities and is a good base for exploring this wonderful city and the surrounding ranges. Enjoy the cooler temperatures here on top of the Great Dividing Range.

416 Homestead Caravan Park and Village

📍 17 Arthur St, East Nanango
📞 (07) 4163 1733
💻 www.homesteadcaravanpark.com.au

This is a quiet caravan park off the highway where the sites are good value, with each one having its own ensuite. It is a great place for a stopover on the journey north or as a base for exploring the Bunya Mountains.

417 Kingaroy Holiday Park

📍 48 Walter Rd, Kingaroy
📞 (07) 4162 1808
💻 www.kingaroyholidaypark.com.au

A quality caravan park in this regional centre – great for a weekend or a short break in the area. It has big sites for big motorhomes and all modern caravan-park facilities. It's also a good base for exploring the Bunya Mountains.

85 Gympie Caravan Park

See p. 41 – Brisbane to Gympie.

MELBOURNE TO SHEPPARTON

NEED TO KNOW

🕐	190km
🏠	Family holiday resorts, full-featured caravan parks
☁	You'll find this area at its best in spring and autumn.
👁	Nagambie Lakes, wineries, farm gates
🛣	So close to Melbourne and on major transport routes, the roads are great.
🍴	Both Melbourne and Shepparton have all services and facilities.
⚠	None apply

Goulburn River at Mitchelton Wines

INTRODUCTION

While this short part of a much larger journey takes in Victoria's oldest inland town, it's the rich, fertile Goulburn River Valley that's the highlight. Along the way you'll find a great array of camping options, see where Australia's most successful caravan builder spends heaps of his money and pass through some of Australia's most productive fruit-growing land.

WHERE TO GO

In the 1840s, **Kilmore** was the first coach stop on the way to the Victorian goldfields, but today it's an outer suburb of Melbourne with a 40-minute commute for its residents. Settled in 1841, it's inland Victoria's oldest town and the area is well known for horse breeding and training. In town, there are a number of grand old buildings, although the town hall, with its bold Corinthian-style pillars is the most noteworthy.

Nagambie, 70km north, is perched on the edge of Lake Nagambie, which was formed in 1891 with the construction of the Goulburn Weir. Significant investment within the town and into nearby tourist attractions by Jayco Australia's owner, Gerry Ryan, is slowly seeing the town change from

a regional service centre to a chic tourist destination. It's a popular recreation area, particularly for watersports, and regular rowing regattas and waterskiing events are held. In town is a monument to the town's favourite export – the Melbourne Cup–winning Black Caviar.

Nearby is the stunning Mitchelton Wines (also owned by the Ryan family), which has a cellar door and art gallery, while the historic Chateau Tahbilk's winery and vineyard date back to 1860. Tahbilk has developed a significant wetlands area, and there are walking paths, timber boardwalks, docking points for punts and two bird hides. Both venues offer fine restaurants.

Just past Mitchelton Wines is Majors Creek Reserve, a pretty little free camping area overlooking Majors Creek. Facilities are very basic, but I often stay here when passing through for the peace and quiet it offers. From here you can follow a great farmgate trail which crosses the Goulburn River several times before reaching the large, multicultural regional centre of **Shepparton**.

The irrigated surrounds have a reputation for quality fruit and dairy produce, and some of Australia's largest food processors are located in the area. Shepparton has all services, excellent shopping and a good range of accommodation and restaurants.

Victoria Park Lake, close to the centre of the city, is popular for picnics.

DON'T MISS

→ Fine Australian Ceramics – Shepparton

The Shepparton Art Museum is world renowned for its ceramics collections. Here you will see works by the Boyd family, the Bendigo Pottery and many Aboriginal ceramic artists. The gallery's prestigious biennial Sidney Myer Fund Australian Ceramic Award attracts entries from many countries. It's open daily 10am–4pm. Contact (03) 5832 9861.

→ Discount fruit – Shepparton

SPC has a factory sales outlet where you can buy products at considerable discounts. It is a good idea to stop if you're passing through the area to stock up with fruit. It's open weekdays 9am–6pm weekdays and weekends 9am–5pm. Contact (03) 5821 7033.

WHERE TO STAY

418 Melbourne BIG4 Holiday Park

265 Elizabeth St, Coburg
(03) 9353 8222
www.melbournebig4.com.au

This is a tourist caravan park in a quiet area of Melbourne's northern suburbs, just 9km from the CBD. The park has relatively easy access to the Hume Hwy and other northern approaches and is a popular with international campers.

388 BIG4 Seymour Holiday Park

See p. 213 – Seymour to Albury.

419 Nagambie Caravan Park

143 High St, Nagambie
(03) 5794 2681
www.nagambiecaravanpark.com.au

This caravan park has a high proportion of annual and visitor sites but offers good facilities for families over summer and is close to town. It is quiet in the off season.

420 Secura Lifestyle Shepparton East Holiday Park

15 Orrvale Rd, Shepparton
(03) 5829 2396
www.securalifestyle.com.au

On the Midland Hwy, 5km to the east of Shepparton, and close to the Shepparton bypass, this quality caravan park in a rural setting has great amenities and facilities including a tennis court. As with most parks in this area, there can be an influx of seasonal workers during the fruit-picking times.

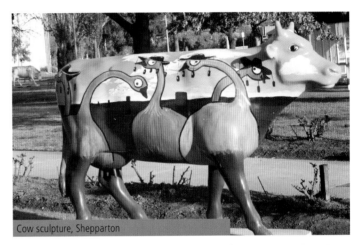
Cow sculpture, Shepparton

Tahbilk Winery

SHEPPARTON TO JERILDERIE

NEED TO KNOW

🕐	**140km**
🏠	**Free camping areas near the Murray, inexpensive caravan parks**
☁	**It's a good area to visit all year round but it can be busy in summer.**
👁	**The Murray River and the opportunity to get on the water are the biggest attractions.**
🛣	**The Goulburn Valley and Newell highways are both very good.**
🍴	**Shepparton has great facilities, and they are still good on the Murray, but thin out as you head north.**
⚠	**None apply**

Gliding, Tocumwal

INTRODUCTION

From the lush fruit-growing districts of the Goulburn Valley and through large tracts of dairy-farming land, this trip crosses the Murray, one of the stretches of water in Australia with the most camping areas. Continuing north through the fertile south-west slopes of New South Wales the highway passes through large rice fields and rich farming areas. As the main interstate route between Melbourne and Brisbane, the highway carries a lot of traffic, including heavy transports. Most towns are only short distances apart though, so there are plenty of places to stop along the way.

WHERE TO GO

North of **Shepparton**, almost all roads lead to the Murray River, across a patchwork of paddocks, orchards and dairy farms. If you stick to the Goulburn Valley Highway, you'll pass through **Numurkah**, which is the centre of an irrigated dairying area that was developed by the Murray River Valley Settlers Scheme – a soldier-settlement scheme after WWI. The Numurkah Rose Gardens, on the banks of Broken Creek are a very pleasant place to stop for a break.

Once you get to the Murray, several riverside towns are great places to start a relaxing time camping by the river. **Tocumwal**, for example, has kilometres of Murray River bends in either direction with a free camping area on nearly every one. In most cases, campers need to be fully self-sufficient, but with so many sites to choose from, you'll often camp alone. For those not interested in self-sufficiency, there are some great, riverside caravan parks up and down the river too.

Tocumwal is home to the largest WWII aerodrome in the southern hemisphere. It was used for training Liberator bomber crews, but today is a popular gliding centre. There's also a 36-hole golf course near town, for those who like to swing a stick at a ball.

If you can drag yourself away from the prime camping and continue north, you'll pass through **Finley**, which is at the centre of a diverse agricultural region with basic services, before coming to **Jerilderie**, on the banks of Billabong Creek. It's another rich farming area where wool, rice, wheat, canola, beans, onions, tomatoes and grapes are all grown locally. It was also the site of the Kelly Gang bank robbery in 1879. From here Ned dictated the famous document known as the 'Jerilderie Letter', in which he outlined how the authorities had mistreated the Kelly family, admitted crimes he had committed and denied others. The Telegraph Station, where the gang cut communications with Melbourne, still stands and is one of the six buildings in town Kelly's gang visited as part of the heist. Pick up a walking guide from the Sticky Fingers Candy Shop.

DON'T MISS

→ Rice paddies – near Finley

You will see fields of rice if you drive through here in spring and summer, as the irrigated region from the Murray River north to Griffith is a major rice-growing area. Seeds are usually spread by aircraft from Oct with harvesting starting in late Feb. Harvested rice is transported by road, back to mills.

→ The Big Cod – Tocumwal

Watersports and other water-based activities are big attractions in towns like Tocumwal on the Murray River. In summer, the waterway is busy with waterskiers, canoes and small fishing boats as well as plenty of people cooling off in the shallows. Tocumwal is also the location of Australia's first 'big thing' the Big Cod – although due to how long it took to make, the Big Banana was finished first. You'll find it on the foreshore in town.

Numurkah Kinnairds Wetlands

WHERE TO STAY

421 Boomerang Way Tourist Park

$$$

📍 65 Murray St, Tocumwal
📞 (03) 5874 2313
💻 www.boomerangwaytouristpark.com.au

TOP PARKS

This well-cared-for, owner-operated caravan park is 500m from the centre of Tocumwal and away from the highway noise. It has a large swimming pool and covered barbecues. Bookings are required in peak periods and a minimum-length stay applies at Christmas, Easter and on long weekends.

422 Oasis Tourist Park

$$$

📍 Corner of Cobram–Koonoomoo and Racecourse rds, Cobram
📞 (03) 5871 2010
💻 www.oasishomes.com.au

This has developed into a great caravan park with unique, multi-sided ensuite amenities a feature. Situated about 4km west of Cobram town centre it is ideal for a few days exploring this great area. Bookings are required in peak periods and a minimum-length stay applies at Christmas, Easter and on long weekends.

423 Finley Lakeside Caravan Park

$$

📍 1 Murray St, Finley
📞 (03) 5883 1170
💻 www.finleycaravanpark.com.au

This caravan park, at the northern end of Finley's main street, is on the shore of a small lake. There are good, basic facilities and the park is a fine space for an overnight stop. It is one of the cheapest parks in the region offering power and water.

283 Jerilderie Motel and Caravan Park

See p. 141 – Jerilderie to Cobar.

JERILDERIE TO DUBBO

Parkes Observatory

INTRODUCTION

The Newell Highway links Narrandera, West Wyalong, Forbes, Parkes and Dubbo, all of which are important regional centres servicing the surrounding grazing and cropping region. Taronga Western Plains Zoo and the Parkes Radio Telescope are major attractions in this section.

WHERE TO GO

As the country continues to open up into the central western plains, you're almost on the edge of the outback, and the small town of **Narrandera** is typical of the regional towns as you continue west. On the banks of the Murrumbidgee River, the town has a tidy free camping area on its outskirts. My kids always remember it as the halfway point to South Australia, because that's where we stop if we do the two-day drive from the east coast. There's good regional shopping in town, and a quaint op shop where I bought the wine glasses that are still in our caravan.

The Newell Highway continues through **West Wyalong**, a former goldmining town. Today it has most services and shops along the famous crooked Main Street, which was formed by the bullock tracks that wound through the diggings.

Further north, **Forbes** is another town built on the back of a gold rush, this one in 1861. The town's historical features include the Albion Hotel, formerly a Cobb & Co. office, plus a network of tunnels used to move gold from local banks to coaches. You can also visit the Forbes Cemetery to see the grave of infamous bushranger Ben Hall. He was leader of one of the most feared gangs of the mid-19th century, frequently holding up mail coaches, plundering hotels and shops, and even holding a police magistrate for ransom. He died, aged only 28, in a shootout with police at Billabong Creek near Forbes in 1865.

Parkes was another town founded on gold, although mining for it and copper still occurs at the Northparkes Mine. It's now at the centre of a rich farming region and has all services, but the town is most famous for its annual festival dedicated to Elvis Presley, and the 64m diameter radio telescope that has been probing outer space for radio emissions since 1961. Over the years the telescope has played an important role in tracking and receiving data from spacecraft, including the Apollo moon landings and the ill-fated Apollo 13 mission. The movie, *The Dish*, portrays the telescope's role in the moon-landing mission.

Further north, the small town of **Peak Hill** was founded on, yep, you guessed it, gold, but it was also the first town in Australia to have a bulk upright wheat silo, installed in 1918. The Peak Hill Goldmine shut down in 2002, although there's now an interesting guided walk around the open-cut pit, with information boards along the way. Peak Hill has two good caravan parks, and a showground that's also popular with travellers.

Dubbo, which is about halfway between Brisbane and Melbourne is a popular hub of central New South Wales. Indeed it's so popular Apr–Oct that it's a good idea to call ahead the day before to book your site. The most popular attraction is the Taronga Western Plains Zoo, which is home to over a thousand animals from across the world. Most people take two days to see it all. It's well worth a visit, and because it's so big, cars can be driven around the grounds, or bikes hired at the entrance.

DON'T MISS

→ **Stone cells and convicts' chains – Dubbo**

The Old Dubbo Gaol offers a fascinating self-guided tour through an 1870s gaol that operated until 1966. See the original gallows, stop a moment in the solitary confinement cell, and listen while animatronic models tell the convicts' stories. Entry fees apply and it's open daily 9am–4pm. Contact (02) 6801 4460.

→ Taronga Western Plains Zoo – Dubbo

Home to over a thousand animals from across the world in more than 300 hectares of bushland, the Taronga Western Plains Zoo is justifiably one of the state's most popular attractions. My experience has been that many animals are more active in the cooler morning, and tend to lie in the shade during the middle of the day. If possible, plan your visit early and make sure you allow adequate time. I feel a minimum of four hours is required, although passes are for two-day entry. There are some welcome picnic areas in the zoo, so pack a lunch. Entry fees apply and it's open daily 9am–4pm. Contact (02) 6881 1488.

→ The dish – near Parkes

The Parkes Observatory, with its famous radio telescope is 25km north of Parkes. Although this is still a working research centre, the adjacent Visitors Discovery Centre is well worth a stop to see the exhibits, videos and a 3D-show that explains radio astronomy. Admission is free, but a fee applies for the theatre presentations. Contact (02) 6861 1777.

WHERE TO STAY

424 Lake Talbot Tourist Park

⦿ 1 Gordon St, Narrandera
☎ (02) 6959 1302
🖥 www.laketalbot.com.au

This is a large lakeside caravan park in a quiet location away from the highway. The park has good amenities and is next to the town's popular swimming complex. There is a range of accommodation options set amongst well-maintained lawns and trees. Bookings are required during peak periods and a minimum-length stay applies during Easter and for the month of March.

425 Coolamon Caravan Park

⦿ 70 Bruce St, Coolamon
☎ 0417 610 946
🖥 www.coolamon.nsw.gov.au

Situated on a grassy field, just a short walk from the historical town of Coolamon, this is a nice tidy little caravan park with good amenities to suit most travellers.

426 West Wyalong Caravan Park

⦿ 60 Main St, West Wyalong
🖥 www.westwyalongcaravanpark.com.au
☎ (02) 6972 3133

This is an excellent overnight stop with convenient large drive-thru sites that do not require unhitching. There is a well-stocked, fully enclosed camp kitchen available as well as simple, clean amenities.

427 BIG4 Forbes Holiday Park

⦿ 141 Flint St, Forbes
☎ (02) 6852 1055
🖥 www.big4forbesholidaypark.com.au

Conveniently located just 2km from the town centre this caravan park predominantly caters for tourists with plenty of shady sites, large open fields of lawn and spotless amenities.

428 Spicer Park Caravan Park

⦿ 37A Albert St, Parkes
☎ (02) 6862 6162

This budget-friendly caravan park has simple amenities to meet most needs. It's located just a short drive from town in a quiet spot off the highway about 16km from 'the Dish'.

429 Double D Caravan Park

⦿ 42 Bogan St, Peak Hill
☎ (02) 6869 1797
🖥 www.kuiparks.com.au/parks/act-nsw/item/peak-hill-double-d-caravan-park-kui-parks

This is a small off-the-highway caravan park with drive-thru sites that can fit larger motorhomes. It is ideal for a one- or two-night stopover.

348 Dubbo City Holiday Park

See p. 179 – Orange to Dubbo.

DUBBO TO MOREE

NEED TO KNOW

 398km

 Basic outback caravan parks

 You'll get the most from this area during spring and autumn.

 Warrumbungle Range, astronomy

 This is a fully sealed route and the roads are generally great.

 Services and facilities are basic, but are suitable for most travellers' needs.

 None apply

Sawn Rocks, Mt Kaputar NP

INTRODUCTION

This land of open spaces straddles the western slopes of the Great Dividing Range and the expanse of the western plains. Cotton crops, vineyards, and sheep and cattle farms draw on the rich volcanic soil and dominate the landscape. Although nature often exerts its presence, as in the case of the Warrumbungle Range and Pilliga Scrub, a half-million-acre tract of mallee-type growth.

WHERE TO GO

After enjoying the wild African-style plains and convict history of **Dubbo**, this drive passes through **Gilgandra**, at the junction of the Newell, Oxley and Castlereagh highways. Sitting on the banks of the Castlereagh River, at the base of the southern end of the Warrumbungle Range, the town is at the centre of a rich farming area producing grain, oilseed, wool and cattle. The whole area is known for its spectacularly clear skies, so it's well worth a visit to the private Gilgandra Observatory where you can get a closer look at the stars. Entry fees apply and it's open from dusk to 10pm Mon–Sat. Gilgandra was known as the town of windmills for the fact the town didn't have a central water supply until 1966, so most people had a windmill in

their yard. At one point there were around 360, dominating the skyline.

It's the next town north, though, which claims to be the astronomy capital of Australia. There are four observatories in and around **Coonabarabran** with about 15 telescopes between them. The Siding Spring Observatory houses the largest optical telescope in Australia. It's capable of seeing stunning astronomical sights – especially considering it's only open during daylight hours! There are also interactive displays, a gift shop and a cafe, so it's even worth visiting on a cloudy day.

Warrumbungle National Park is a very obvious attraction in the area with about 30km of marked walking tracks. Walks range from the 14.5km Grand High Tops, to easy 1km walks on paved paths suitable for wheelchairs. One of the most stunning sights is the Breadknife, a volcanic plug that eroded into a 90m high, thin blade of rock. Belougery Spire is also worth viewing, and you may even see some daredevils rock climbing the 160m high face. There are a few camping areas in the park, with varying facilities.

There are more good walks near Narrabri in Mt Kaputar National Park, which encompasses the dramatic remnants of a once mighty volcano. From the top of Mt Kaputar, you can see a tenth of New

South Wales in a panoramic 360° view. You can drive right to the summit too, or walk 3.5km from the main carpark through beautiful forest. However, the twisty road to the park has unsealed sections and is unsuitable for caravans, although fine for two-wheel-drive vehicles not towing. Camping is permitted in the park and there are good facilities.

Narrabri itself is a busy regional hub for the surrounding farming communities with most services and good shopping. The most powerful radio telescope array in the southern hemisphere is just east of town. An unstaffed visitor centre at the Narrabri Observatory is open daily 8am–6pm, with a barbecue area for public use. Admission is free.

The Newell Highway continues north, passing through the smaller towns of **Edgeroi** (which once had the largest shearing shed in the southern hemisphere), **Bellata** (which once had its own one-pound note), and **Gurley** (whose post office has been running since 1898) before arriving in **Moree**. Surrounded by cotton farms, olive plantations and the massive Trawalla pecan-nut farm, the town has several historical buildings, but is best known for its mineral hot baths. Although there is a well-known commercial centre for the thermal pools, the Gwydir Caravan Park in town has its own artesian-fed hot mineral baths for use by patrons, which is the perfect place for happy hour after a long day on the road.

DON'T MISS

→ **The long coo-ee – Gilgandra**
Ever since 35 men from Gilgandra walked to Sydney in 1915 to volunteer for the war, swelling in numbers as they went until 263 showed up, the town has celebrated the Coo-ee March. The Coo-ee Heritage Centre has exhibitions about the march, as well as local Indigenous heritage and pioneering history. The town also holds an annual Coo-ee Festival in Oct. The Hitchen House Museum was the home of the March's originator and displays war memorabilia. Entry fees apply, and it's open most days by appointment.

→ **Therapeutic waters – Moree**
The invigorating artesian waters at the Moree Artesian Aquatic Centre rise from the ground at a delightful 41°C and are reputed to have therapeutic value. The modern facility has an Olympic pool, gym, water slide, day spa and cafe. Entry fees apply and it's open Mon–Fri 6am–8pm and Sat–Sun 7am–7pm. Contact (02) 6752 2272.

WHERE TO STAY

430 Gilgandra Caravan Park

📍 Newell Hwy, Gilgandra
📞 (02) 6847 2423
🖥 www.gilgandracaravanpark.com.au

Set on a large expanse of lawn, this pet-friendly caravan park has shady, level sites; clean, tidy amenities; and a lovely onsite pool. Discounts are offered for more than one night's stay.

431 John Oxley Caravan Park

📍 Newell Hwy, Coonabarabran
📞 (02) 6842 1635
🖥 www.johnoxleycvn.net

Conveniently located just off the highway this large council-run caravan park has nice, shady, drive-thru sites suitable for most size rigs. Perfect for overnight stops without the need to unhitch. The amenities are dated, but clean and tidy.

432 Narrabri Big Sky Caravan Park

📍 11–35 Tibbereena St, Narrabri
📞 (02) 6792 1294
🖥 www.narrabribigsky.com.au

Conveniently located in the heart of town within walking distance of the local shops and RSL, this caravan park has good facilities with large, level drive-thru sites.

433 Mehi River Van Park

📍 28 Oak St, Moree
📞 (02) 6752 7188
🖥 www.mehirivervanpark.com.au

This pet-friendly caravan park has large, shady sites and good facilities including a pool and thermal spa. Amenities are dated but clean and well maintained.

The Breadknife

MOREE TO MILES

Moonie River

INTRODUCTION

Moree is surrounded by fertile, black-soil plains supporting thriving cotton fields where the crops reach the highway's edge. Further north, across the Queensland border, the route drifts through broadacre farms and large cattle properties. This route takes in a number of Australian firsts, including our first oil wells and first cow bell.

WHERE TO GO

From **Moree** to **Boggabilla**, on the New South Wales–Queensland border, the highway passes through fertile farming land, but no towns mark the scenery. Boggabilla, in New South Wales is the smaller of the two border towns, with **Goondiwindi** offering the best services and most attractions. On the northern banks of the Macintyre River, the town is a large regional centre servicing strong pastoral interests and an intensive cotton industry. The legendary racehorse Gunsynd, often called the Goondiwindi Grey, hailed from here. He won 29 races from 54 starts, finished second on seven occasions, third on eight and was also third in the 1972 Melbourne Cup. A statue of the famous horse has pride of place in Apex Park. It's the second racehorse statue on this trip as Black Caviar is immortalised in Nagambie, Victoria.

It's roughly another 100km along the Leichhardt Highway to the next town, **Moonie**, which was the site of Australia's first oilfield following the discovery of 'black gold' in 1961. The field still operates today but only accounts for a small part of the national production. The town is little more than a crossroads, with the roadhouse being the main provider of services.

From Moonie, there's a worthwhile stop over at **The Gums**, which has an inexpensive camping area at the local nine-hole golf course, but otherwise there's just pretty farming scenery out each window until you roll into Condamine.

Once an important local administrative centre and a changing post on the Cobb & Co. Dalby to Roma route, the importance of **Condamine** decreased when the railway and Warrego Highway bypassed the town to the north. A Condamine blacksmith was credited with making Australia's first cow bell – one specifically designed for use in a country of wide unfenced plains to help drovers locate cattle each morning. A large replica is on display at the Condamine Bell Park, on the main street. Even today, the surrounding farms are mainly cattle-grazing properties or broadacre grain producers.

Originally called Dogwood Crossing, **Miles** was settled in 1844 and still has 15 of its historical buildings from pioneering days on

display, with another 10 replicas. The Miles Historical Village and Museum includes a dairy, church, school and police cells, all relocated from the local area and displayed along a typical pioneer town main street. The modern Miles is at the centre of one of Australia's most active coal-seam-gas mining areas, and has most services and a few good places to camp.

DON'T MISS

→ **Gas fields excursion – near Condamine**

The coal-seam-gas industry is in its infancy in Australia, but the area around Condamine and Miles has been mined for the gas since 2009. A one-day self-drive tour which can be started and finished at Condamine, is a good way to get some insight into the impacts on the local agricultural industries and natural environment. Find out more about the route at www.gasgabtours.com.

TRAVEL TIP

It is often difficult to find somewhere to wash down caravans and motorhomes, especially if you're on the road for a long time travelling Australia's dusty highways. Opposite the large BP roadhouse on the Cunningham Highway in Goondiwindi there is a car wash which is higher than most at about 3.5m. It is a good place to stop in to give the van a rinse.

EXPLORE AUSTRALIA BY CARAVAN & MOTORHOME

WHERE TO STAY

434 Goondiwindi Top Tourist Park

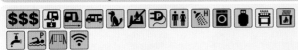

📍 20 Hungerford St, Goondiwindi
📞 (07) 4671 2566
💻 www.goondiwinditouristpark.com.au

TOP PARKS

Set in tranquil bush parkland, with its own private billabong, this caravan park has a range of accommodation options including ensuite sites and large motorhome-friendly spaces. The amenities are clean and tidy and there is a pool onsite for your pleasure.

435 Possum Park Caravan and Camping Park

📍 36865 Leichhardt Hwy, Miles
📞 (07) 4627 1651
💻 www.possumpark.com.au

This unusual caravan park was once a WWII munitions dump and the underground bunkers have been converted into cabins. Owner-operated, it is a great park set in a quiet location alongside the Leichhardt Hwy, 20km north of Miles. It has good facilities and continues to develop.

Macintyre River, Goondiwindi

Miles Historical Village and Museum

MILES TO ROCKHAMPTON

Beef City Statue, Rockhampton

INTRODUCTION

After travelling the long plains of the Riverina, Central West and Darling Downs, the Leichhardt Highway eventually crosses the Great Dividing Range and heads to the coast. It's amazing to think, that although we are so far north of Victoria, we're still in the Murray–Darling basin for much of this trip. Although the highway carries a lot of heavy traffic, it's well maintained and signposted, although as the road winds through the ranges at Mount Morgan it is steep in places, so care needs to be taken.

WHERE TO GO

After the gas fields of **Condamine** and **Miles**, the Leichhardt Highway passes through more farming communities in the Western Downs. One of the first you'll pass through is **Wandoan**, which is a small community developed around a hotel built in the 1890s. A heritage trail tracks through town highlighting its often grim history.

Another point of interest is the stunning mural painted on the water tank.

Further north, the township of **Taroom**, set on the banks of the Dawson River is one of the sites passed through by Ludwig Leichhardt on his epic journey to Port Essington. A tree in the main street was emblazoned with 'LL 1844' but the mark is no longer visible. Taroom serves the local pastoral industry with basic services and a small selection of shops. There are some good free and paid camping options too.

Just north of here, it's worthwhile taking a diversion to Glebe Weir on the banks of Spring Gully (Dawson River), which is a quiet place for a few day's rest. With wide open spaces and an honesty box for your $7-a-night camping fees, there are plenty of pleasant shady spots at the end of the unsealed access road. There are a limited number of powered sites.

There's more good camping near **Theodore**, which urban legend says was designed by Walter Burley Griffin – but that's not based on fact, only that there's a large roundabout in the centre of town (Neville Hewitt Park), like in Canberra. Just past the

small town is Isla Gorge National Park, which is a maze of sandstone gorges and cliffs. The park has no formal walking tracks, though, so only experienced and well-prepared hikers should attempt to explore the gorges. However, there is a lookout close to the highway from where you can gaze down into the extraordinary gorge. The small adjacent camping area is suitable for caravans and motorhomes.

From here the climb over the Great Dividing Range starts, until you reach the great historical mining town of **Mount Morgan**. Over 240 tonnes of gold and 360,000 tonnes of copper were dug from the area in the 109 years until the mine closed in 1991. In the mine's heyday, around 1910, the town supported over 14,000 people and there are many historical relics and buildings from that era.

It's only a short, but steep, drive down the range from here to **Rockhampton**. One of Queensland's major cities 'Rocky' began its life as a river port, but is now known for its beef (*see* p. 45). The Fitzroy River divides the city, and the Capricorn Coast is a 30 min drive away.

DON'T MISS

→ Steam back in time – Mount Morgan

There are two great museums in Mount Morgan showcasing what life was like during its early goldmining days. The Mount Morgan Railway Museum, on the site of the original rail depot, has a range of vintage rolling stock, and a steam engine from 1904. (It's open daily 9am–4pm.) The Mount Morgan Historical Museum has an extensive display of mining equipment and everyday items. Entry fees apply and it's open daily 10am–4pm (closed 20 Dec to 3 Jan).

→ Heritage-listed gardens – Rockhampton

The Rockhampton Botanic Gardens were heritage listed in 1999 and consist of 38 hectares of spectacular tropical and subtropical gardens. They contain many species of palms, ferns and cycads, and there is a delightful Japanese garden too. Stop for refreshments at the tearooms or use the barbecues. These fabulous gardens are alongside the main highway and open daily from 6am to sunset. Contact 1300 225 577.

WHERE TO STAY

436 Taroom Bushside camping area

📍 Polocross Grounds, Injune Rd, Taroom
📞 0447 037 201

This is a simple showground-style camping area on the edge of town with grassy, shady, powered and unpowered sites, and plenty of room to spread out. Facilities include toilets and showers. Pets are welcome.

437 Theodore Recreation Reserve camping area

📍 125 The Boulevard, Theodore
🖥 www.sandstonewonders.com/discover/camping-theodore-showgrounds

An open, ordered showground-style recreation reserve to the north of town, with powered and unpowered campsites for a modest fee. The facilities are basic, but well kept, there's room for big rigs and pets are welcome.

360 Silver Wattle Caravan Park

See p. 187 – Rockhampton to Barcaldine.

99 Discovery Parks Rockhampton

See p. 47 – Gin Gin to Rockhampton.

Mount Morgan Mine

MELBOURNE TO BALLARAT

NEED TO KNOW

117km	
	Family holiday resorts; basic caravan parks
	Spring, summer and autumn
	Sovereign Hill
	This is a busy dual carriageway that bypasses all towns.
	It's so close to metropolitan Melbourne that all facilities are available.
	None apply

Wombat State Forest

INTRODUCTION

Leaving Melbourne, the highway sweeps towards Ballarat, which was a rich goldmining centre in the 1850s and the site of the Eureka uprising. Sovereign Hill, one of the city's major attractions, re-creates the excitement and events of that era and should not be missed.

WHERE TO GO

Although the Western Freeway heads west through some of Melbourne's prettiest outer suburbs, it bypasses them all, encouraging traffic to leave the city as quickly and efficiently as possible. Towns like **Melton** and **Bacchus Marsh** are typified by modern 'rural-living' properties and small acreages where small horse studs, irrigated market gardens and apple orchards flourish. The Werribee Gorge State Park, just west of Bacchus Marsh, is a popular day-use area with great walks and natural swimming holes formed by the Werribee River.

As the road ventures closer to the gold-rush country around Ballarat, it passes through towns built on the back of it. Although it was settled in 1838, **Ballan** developed as people headed from Melbourne to the goldfields in the 1850s. Ballan is now off the freeway, on the upper reaches of the Werribee River, but has basic shopping and a few services.

The Goldfields region of central Victoria is one of the historical jewels of rural Australia. The discovery of gold near **Ballarat** in 1851 transformed a sleepy farming community into a rowdy, anarchic, cosmopolitan and wealthy goldmining frontier town. As a result, Ballarat is now Victoria's largest inland city with many historical buildings. To experience part of Australian history, visit the Eureka Centre (formerly known as the Museum of Australian Democracy at Eureka). On the site of the 1854 uprising, the museum interprets the Eureka Rebellion, when miners angry at license fees being imposed on them raised the flag of the Southern Cross and fought against government troops. The original flag is on display. Entry fees apply and it's open daily 10am–5pm.

Ballarat has many beautiful parks, and the Ballarat Botanical Gardens on the western shores of Lake Wendouree have an outstanding display of magnificent trees and gardens. While in the gardens you can ride a vintage tram and visit the cottage of poet Adam Lindsay. During Mar the tremendous show of begonias in the Conservatory is one of the main attractions of the city's annual Begonia Festival (Labour Day long weekend in Mar).

While in the area, take an 18km diversion north through **Creswick**, which nestles picturesquely amid pine forests and was once another prosperous goldmining centre on one of the world's richest alluvial goldfields, to **Daylesford** and the Mt Macedon Ranges. This is an area establishing itself as a terrific cold-climate wine region, and the famous location for the novel *Picnic at Hanging Rock* by Joan Lindsay. The Hanging Rock Reserve has some excellent walks, including to the summit, and it's also a popular place to fish, as the dam is regularly stocked.

DON'T MISS

→ **Sovereign Hill – Ballarat**
Sovereign Hill is an award-winning museum on a historical mining site close to the centre of Ballarat. For years I kept a piece of quartz I found here while on a school excursion, believing it contained gold. Spread over 25 hectares, it is a re-creation of life during the gold boom and tells the city's story from 1851 to 1861. There is a gold-rush settlement, a fascinating Gold Museum and activities that include panning for gold and touring a goldmine. Entry fees apply and it's open daily 10am–5pm. Contact (03) 5337 1199.

→ Knights and ladies – near Ballarat

There aren't many kids who grew up in Melbourne who don't have a fond memory of Kryal Castle. Just 9km east of Ballarat, it is a replica of a medieval castle, with exhibits of heraldry and medieval displays including jousting, horsemanship demonstrations and even a torture chamber museum. It's open weekends and Victorian school holidays from 10am–4pm. Entry fees apply. Contact (03) 5334 8500.

WHERE TO STAY

418 Melbourne BIG4 Holiday Park

See p. 231 – Melbourne to Shepparton.

1 BIG4 Mornington Peninsula Holiday Park

See p. 9 – Melbourne to Phillip Island.

438 Bacchus Marsh Caravan Park

- 📍 26 Main St, Bacchus Marsh
- 📞 (03) 5367 2775
- 🖥 www.bacchusmarshcp.com.au

Bacchus Marsh is just west of Melbourne and is strategically located between Melbourne, Ballarat, Geelong and Macedon. This is a good caravan park offering a range of facilities and is ideal for a short visit, or even a week's stay.

439 Blackwood Mineral Springs Caravan Park

- 📍 41 Golden Point Rd, Blackwood
- 📞 (03) 5368 6539
- 🖥 www.blackwoodcrownreserves.websyte.com.au

A rustic caravan park surrounded by the Wombat State Forest and above the banks of the Lerderderg River. Sites here are basic, but in a wonderful bush setting. Fireplaces are supplied for each site and there's a large camp kitchen. Mineral springs are a short walk away.

440 BIG4 Ballarat Goldfields Holiday Park

- 📍 108 Clayton St, Ballarat Central
- 📞 (03) 5330 8000
- 🖥 www.ballaratgoldfields.com.au

Located in the historical goldfields, this award-winning caravan park is close to Sovereign Hill. It has all the facilities you would expect of a quality park and is a great base for a Ballarat holiday.

Convent Bar, Daylesford

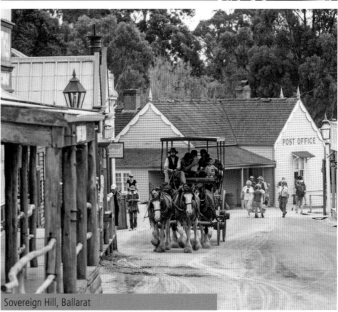
Sovereign Hill, Ballarat

BALLARAT TO HORSHAM

MacKenzie Falls

INTRODUCTION

Beyond Ballarat, the highway passes through fertile grazing country and by flourishing vineyards at Ararat and Great Western. A highlight is the rugged Grampians National Park, rising abruptly in the west, with walking trails, captivating views and native wildlife. It is one of the prettiest places in Australia, with craggy ranges, lakes, waterfalls and stunning scenery.

WHERE TO GO

Beaufort is the first town the Western Freeway doesn't bypass since leaving Melbourne. The small town's main street features a few basic shops, while the nearby Lake Beaufort is popular for waterskiing and fishing, and has a caravan park on its shores.

A few more small towns are bypassed before reaching **Ararat**, which is in an area first explored by Sir Thomas Mitchell in 1836. His glowing report brought early pastoralists, before gold was discovered in the 1850s. Today, Ararat has lovely gardens and historical bluestone buildings, and services a grazing industry and the vineyards of the nearby Pyrenees wine region. A world away from wine and gold (or maybe very related), the former institution for the criminally insane, J Ward, has been restored. It started

life as a prison in 1859 but became a ward of the lunatic asylum in the 1880s. The ward was closed in 1991. Tours now offer a grim history of the bluestone buildings.

One of the region's best-known wineries is in the nearby town of **Great Western**. Seppelt's famous Great Western Winery offers tastings and sales at its cellar door, as well as a grassy picnic and barbecue facility. Guided tours are available of the underground cellars, known as 'The Drives' which stretch for up to 3km and were dug out by unemployed miners over a 60-year period from the 1860s. The cellar door is open daily 10am–5pm and advance bookings are required for tours (fees apply).

Gold was discovered in **Stawell** in 1853 and until fairly recently it was Victoria's largest gold producer – the mine ceased operation in late 2016 before being sold and reopened in late 2017. The town is a strong industrial and pastoral centre, and the home of the Stawell Easter Gift which is one of Australia's best-known professional foot races.

Up in the Grampians, just 20 min up the range, **Halls Gap** is an extremely popular holiday destination and a great base from which to explore Grampians National Park. A major tourist destination, the park offers a range of experiences including bushwalking and adventure activities like rock climbing

and abseiling. Come in spring to witness the landscape carpeted in wildflowers, or visit the many Aboriginal rock-art sites year-round. Be warned, the weather can turn bitterly cold up here without notice, so pack some warm clothing even in summer.

Those not towing a caravan might like to take the long diversion from Halls Gap along Mount Victory Rd. The road is steep, winding and narrow in places, and both the sign at the top, and staff at the Halls Gap Lakeside Tourist Park, discourage caravanners from using it, but motorhomes are fine. It's a fabulous detour, rejoining the highway 17km south-east of Horsham. Stop at MacKenzie Falls, reached by a one-hour return walk (with many steps) from the carpark off Lake Wartook Rd. Zumsteins, a historical picnic area is another interesting stop where you can sometimes have a close encounter with cheeky kangaroos.

Horsham is an important commercial and administration centre for the Wimmera region which has all services and good shopping. The history of the Horsham Botanic Gardens stretches back to the 1870s, and the surrounding area is dotted with quaint wineries and cellar doors.

flow, MacKenzie Falls is one of the Grampians' biggest attractions. An easy wheelchair-accessible 1.9km return walk leads to the Bluff, which overlooks the falls. Or you can take the more difficult 2km one-way walk to the base of the falls, where spray from the cascade creates rainbows above on sunny days.

WHERE TO STAY

441 Acacia Caravan Park

📍 6 Acacia Ave, Ararat
📞 (03) 5352 2994
💻 www.acaciatouristpark.com

Ideally located within walking distance of town and close to the Western Hwy, this is an ideal base for an overnight stop or to explore this wonderful scenic region. It has neat and tidy amenities and a small pool onsite.

442 Halls Gap Caravan Park

📍 Corner School and Grampians rds, Halls Gap
📞 (03) 5356 4251
💻 www.hallsgapcaravanpark.com.au

Located in the centre of town this caravan park is within easy reach of most of the area's attractions. It's a great base for visiting the Grampians.

443 Wimmera Lakes Caravan Resort

📍 9161 Western Hwy, Horsham
📞 (03) 5382 4481
💻 www.wimmeralakes.com

This spacious caravan park on the fringe of Horsham has a range of facilities, including a tennis court and spa. Sites are level with a good amount of shade. Some drive-thru sites are also available for larger vans. It is a good base for exploring the local area.

Underground cellars at Seppelt's Great Western Winery

HORSHAM TO TAILEM BEND

NEED TO KNOW

 332km

🏠 Riverside caravan parks, station stays, remote national park camping areas

☁ This is a nice area year round, although it can get hot in summer.

👁 Riverside camping, four-wheel driving, wildlife

🛣 This is a major interstate transport route and is well maintained. Little Desert National Park's roads are all unsealed, but two-wheel drive access is possible to a point.

🍴 There are most basic facilities available for travellers.

⚠ None apply

Mural in Sheep Hills

INTRODUCTION

The Wimmera, a major grain-growing region, slips slowly by as the highway heads towards South Australia. Stop off at the Little Desert National Park near Dimboola to see its beautiful show of spring wildflowers. Across the border, mixed farming country, interrupted by patches of mallee eucalypts, fringes the highway.

WHERE TO GO

The Wimmera River is the only major watercourse in this dry area. It rises in the hills to the north of Stawell and flows west through Horsham before circling back to Dimboola. It's actually a completely land-locked river system. It drains into Lake Hindmarsh, then further north via Outlet Creek to Lake Albacutya.

Dimboola makes the most of it, though, and has a well-regarded caravan park and basic camping area, both nearby the red gum–lined river banks with walking tracks along the western shore. Fishing, boating and paddling are also popular.

Dimboola is also the access point to Little Desert National Park, which bursts into a colourful carpet of wildflowers during spring. There are numerous nature walks, and you may be lucky enough to see a mallee fowl's nest site – look for a large sandy mound. Conventional vehicles can access day-use and camping areas on the fringes of the park, but the network of tracks throughout are mainly suitable for four-wheel drives only.

The next town along the highway **Nhill** is a wheat belt town that claims to have the largest single-bin wheat silo in the southern hemisphere. It's also one of the closest towns to the ephemeral Lake Hindmarsh, which when full, is Victoria's largest freshwater lake – home to multitudes of birdlife and a popular camping and holiday destination. It can remain dry for years, however Parks Victoria has constant updates of the water level on its website.

On the western edge of the Wimmera region, the small town of **Kaniva** has historical walks and a museum with a large local history collection. On the western outskirts of town, the Rotary Fauna Park has nature walks and a bird hide, which are great ways to break up the drive.

It's not technically on the border, it's 18km west, but **Bordertown** is at the centre of a diverse agricultural region with a vast underground supply of water used for irrigation. It is most famous as the childhood home of former prime minister Bob Hawke – Australia's longest-serving. About 3km south of town, the Clayton Farm Heritage Museum is a volunteer-run site with hand-built examples of historical farm buildings, including the largest thatched-roof shearing shed in the southern hemisphere.

Further northwest, the tiny settlement of **Keith** is often referred to as 'the gateway to the south-east' as the Riddoch Highway leads from here to Naracoorte, Penola and Mount Gambier (see p. 120). Keith's former Congregational Church in Heritage St has leadlight windows that depict the town's history.

Once an important rail town, the significance of **Tailem Bend** has waned

Nhill

over the years, although it's still an important highway service centre. Located on the banks of the Murray it offers great camping, walking, boating and fishing in either direction.

DON'T MISS

→ **Victoria's largest art trail – near Horsham**

From Horsham or Dimboola there's easy access to the Silo Art Trail, which heads north from Rupanyup through Sheep Hills,

Brim, Lascelles and Patchewollock. Each of these towns have invited artists to paint giant murals on the sides of their wheat silos, making spectacular use of otherwise drab parts of the country skyline. Find out more at www.siloarttrail.com.

→ **White kangaroos – near Bordertown**
Bordertown Wildlife Park has a colony of unusual white kangaroos. The park itself is also unusual as it's not staffed and is

maintained by volunteers. Visitors can see the animals in their enclosures from outside the fencing. Seating and canopies are provided so you can be comfortable as you watch the wallabies, emus, ducks, swans, peacocks, native birds, and of course, the white kangaroos wandering around.

WHERE TO STAY

444 Riverside Holiday Park

$$

📍 2 Wimmera St, Dimboola
📞 (03) 5389 1416
🖥 www.riversideholidayparkdimboola.com.au

Nestled under the beautiful river gums beside the Wimmera River this caravan park is conveniently located just a short walk to the local shops and amenities. It has recently refurbished amenities and nice grassy campsites with ten ensuites available.

445 Bordertown Caravan Park

$$$

📍 41 Penny Tce, Bordertown
📞 (08) 8752 1752
🖥 www.bordertowncaravanpark.com

A tidy little caravan park just a short walk from town it has large drive-thru sites and modern amenities to suit most travellers' needs.

446 Cockatoo Downs Farmstay

$$$

📍 82 Eckerts Rd, Keith
📞 (08) 8756 7042
🖥 www.cockatoodownfarmstay.com.au

Popular with families, this camping area on the grounds of a working farm offers good facilities and large grassy sites. There are a number of activities available onsite including daily farm tours and animal feeding.

447 Westbrook Park River Resort

$$

📍 72 Jaensch Rd, Tailem Bend
📞 0427 046 367

Located in a picturesque spot right on the river this caravan park has simple amenities, breathtaking views and excellent fishing.

BATEMANS BAY TO CANBERRA

Holiday park on the Clyde River, Nelligen

INTRODUCTION

The Kings Highway links Batemans Bay and Canberra, the national capital. The highway skirts Budawang National Park, passing through wide, grassy valleys and dense forests on the coastal plain before winding through the Great Dividing Range. Along the highway, the towns of Nelligen, Braidwood and Bungendore are all popular weekend tourist destinations. This is a pretty drive year-round, with ample passing lanes along the steeper ranges.

WHERE TO GO

This could be one of the most underrated tourist drives on the east coast for the simple fact that it only joins two small population centres – no matter how important one of them is to the nation. Turn onto the Kings Highway north of **Batemans Bay** (*see* p. 18) and follow it until it loops back on Clyde River and the charming little riverside town of **Nelligen**. The town was proclaimed in 1854 and its wharf became an important port for the town of Braidwood and the surrounding goldfields. The township has several historic buildings, a picturesque camping area and the popular Steampacket Hotel. The Clyde River is ideal to explore in a canoe or kayak,

and fishing is productive, even close to town. The town is just 10km north-west of Batemans Bay but has limited facilities.

The Kings Highway winds over Clyde Mountain between Nelligen and Braidwood through beautiful forest, offering spectacular views of the ocean through the trees. The climb from the east coast is slow and steep, but there are ample overtaking lanes. If you are towing a caravan, exercise caution when climbing and descending the range.

The entire town of **Braidwood** has the special distinction of being classified by the National Trust. The area was settled in the 1820s and grew steadily until gold was discovered in 1851, when thousands more poured onto the goldfields seeking their fortune. Today, Braidwood services local agriculture and has most services and basic shopping. It is home to several talented artists and craftspeople, plus numerous historical buildings which can be explored on a self-guided walk. For nature lovers, the little-known Monga National Park has some great walking trails through ancient Gondwana forest, which range from just a few hundred metres, to one that will take all day. There is a good range of camping options around Braidwood, to suit any budget.

From Braidwood the highway winds through the pretty farming land of the

tablelands, slowly climbing until it hits **Bungendore**. The town grew out of early settlement in the area during the 1830s and has an abundance of craft and pottery galleries, antique shops and some great restaurants. We highly recommend a visit to the award-winning Bungendore Wood Works Gallery, which showcases fine furniture and other exquisite woodwork by local craftspeople. Across the road is the excellent Leather and Trading, which has been making handmade leather products since 1969. The closest camping area is the showgrounds, just north of town.

The Kings Highway ducks into and back out of the Australian Capital Territory before reaching **Queanbeyan**, which is just 14km east of Canberra. It's a major regional centre servicing a widespread and diverse agricultural industry. There are some excellent mountain-biking tracks in the area, as well as good wineries, so it's a popular weekend destination.

Canberra is a rapidly growing city with an emerging food and craft-beer scene. It's popular with cyclists and mountain-bikers, and has some excellent attractions, including the National Museum of Australia and Questacon. The Australian War Memorial is a must-visit location.

→ Wray Street Oyster Shed – Batemans Bay

Before you leave the coast behind, plan a stop in at the Wray Street Oyster Shed, on the northern shore of the Clyde River. It sells farm-fresh oysters direct to the public either opened (which will keep for about a week, or until lunch, whichever comes first) or unopened, which will stay fresh for two weeks. It's open daily 9am–5pm.

→ Canberra Centenary Trail – Australian Capital Territory

Traversing 145km of urban and rural trails, this walking and cycling loop of the Australian Capital Territory is a great way to discover its heritage. There's no need to do the whole thing at once, and bikes can be hired from most of the caravan parks along its route to tackle as much or as little as you like.

WHERE TO STAY

33 NRMA Murramarang Beachfront Nature Resort

See p. 21 – Batemans Bay to Nowra.

32 BIG4 Batemans Bay Beach Resort

See p. 19 – Bega to Batemans Bay.

448 BIG4 Nelligen Holiday Park

$$$

Kings Hwy, Nelligen
(02) 4478 1076
www.nelligenpark.com.au

BIG4 HOLIDAY PARKS

Nestled on the banks of the Clyde River, this lovely grassy caravan park is just a short walk from Nelligen and only 10km from Batemans Bay. There are plenty of onsite facilities, including a pool and splash zone for the kids. Bookings are essential during peak times and a minimum-length stay applies during Christmas, Easter and public holidays.

449 Queanbeyan Riverside Tourist Park

$$$

41 Morriset St, Queanbeyan
(02) 6297 4749
www.qbnriversidetouristpark.com.au

Sitting on the banks of the Queanbeyan River, and conveniently located just a short walk from town, this lovely shady caravan park is easily accessed off the highway. It gets very busy at times and pre-booking is recommended.

394 Capital Country Holiday Village

See p. 217 – Gundagai to Goulburn.

Australian War Memorial, Canberra

CANBERRA TO ALBURY

NEED TO KNOW

⏱	**435km**
🏠	**Full-featured caravan parks, national park camping areas, free camps**
☁	**There is something for everyone all year, from snow sports in winter to pleasant walks in summer.**
👁	**Skiing, trout fishing, mountain-biking, museums**
🅰	**Although some sections are narrow and winding, the road condition is generally good, except when it is covered in snow or ice.**
🍴	**Good services are available in Cooma and Albury with limited services in between.**
⚠	**Ice and snow can cover roads at any time of the year.**

Jillabenan Cave

INTRODUCTION

At the centre of this region lies Kosciuszko National Park, protecting the continent's highest mountain, its only glacial lakes, some of its rarest natural species and the headwaters of legendary rivers. The Snowy Mountain Highway between Adaminaby and Kiandra climbs across the range, before becoming steep and winding – it's often closed by snow in winter. This is a stunning region though, with excellent camping and natural attractions, and it's largely free from crowds.

WHERE TO GO

The New South Wales' snowfields are Canberra's winter playground, and they all pass through **Cooma** on the way. It is both a busy tourist town and key service centre for the area's large pastoral industry, as well as being the headquarters for Snowy Hydro Limited, which manages the vast water deposits and electricity stations of the Snowy Hydro Scheme. Stop off at the Snowy Hydro Discovery Centre to get an overview of what is one of the world's great engineering feats.

In winter, the town is a major hub for snow-sports enthusiasts looking to hire or buy gear before heading into the mountains. During summer it is quieter, but still a hub for adventure-sports devotees heading to Jindabyne and the mountain resorts.

Jindabyne is a tourist town at the junction of roads to both Perisher and Thredbo mountain resorts. Year-round it's a great base to explore the mountain areas, be that on foot, skis, bike or in a vehicle. In summer I highly recommend the walk from Charlottes Pass to the summit of Mount Kosciuszko, Australia's highest peak. In winter, pair days skiing either of the resorts with a night or two out at any of the excellent restaurants that dot the road to Thredbo.

In the other direction from Cooma, **Adaminaby** is a popular fishing spot where you'll find the world's largest trout – a structure several metres high. The town also has the closest accommodation to the Selwyn snowfield which is ideal for families and beginners. It's also a much cheaper alternative to skiing at Thredbo or Perisher.

Trout fishing is one of the great recreational pursuits in this region, and the many lakes, rivers and streams in the area are home to brown and rainbow trout. State fishing licences are required in New South Wales and the season reaches its peak in summer. You don't need to learn how to fly-fish either, as trout can be taken on more common rigs using lures, specialty trout baits. And if they don't work use the tried and true method of stopping at the shops on the way back to camp…

From Adaminaby, the road winds further into the mountain range, past Mt Selwyn to Australia's 3rd highest town **Cabramurra**. The town's only residents are those who work directly for Snowy Hydro Limited and their families, and there is no accommodation. It's worth a stop to visit the visitor centre's display about the scheme though, and to grab a bite from the bistro.

After winding your way back down the mountain range, and just before you cross the border into Victoria, stop in at **Khancoban**. Just a few minutes away is the Murray 2 Power Station, which has an interesting visitor centre. Those with off-road campers and caravans might also like to take on the Old Geehi Walls Trail, which passes some great old high-country huts and has excellent camping along trout-filled rivers and streams.

Over the border, and located in the Murray River Valley, **Corryong** offers a wide range of leisure pursuits including hang-gliding, whitewater rafting, trail-riding, walking, four-wheel driving and fishing. It's also the resting place of Jack Riley, the man said to be the inspiration for Banjo Paterson's 'The Man from Snowy River'. Riley was buried in the Corryong Cemetery in 1914. The Man from Snowy River Museum features Riley's hut, as well as the era's clothing and ski collections.

The Murray Valley Highway continues to wind its way down the Murray River Valley passing through a number of charming little towns before hugging Lake Hume as it enters the border towns of Albury and Wodonga.

Albury and **Wodonga** are sister cities, divided by the Murray River and Victoria–New South Wales border. They are a major service centre on the busy Murray Valley and Hume highways generally being treated as the halfway point between Sydney and Melbourne even though that isn't geographically correct. Nearby attractions like Lake Hume are also popular.

DON'T MISS

→ **Military memories – near Bandiana**
The Army Museum at Bandiana houses an extensive collection of military memorabilia, equipment and vehicles from several branches of the service. Entry fees apply and it's open Tue, Thurs and Sat 10am–2pm. Contact (02) 6055 2525.

→ **Yarrangobilly Caves and Thermal Pool – refresh yourself**
Set in the northern part of Kosciuszko National Park, the Yarrangobilly section has three stunning caves to explore on guided tours. There's also a natural thermal pool, which maintains a near-constant temperature of 27°C all year round. It's perfect for a dip after taking the short hikes nearby, or for enjoying the warm waters surrounded by snow in winter. The park is open year-round, although the smooth graded gravel road in is not recommended for caravans or vehicles longer than 12.5m. Yarrangobilly Village is just 10 min north.

CHAINED DOWN

During the winter months, many alpine roads in New South Wales can only be travelled if the vehicle is carrying snow chains, although four-wheel-drive vehicles are exempt. The roads can get icy, even in summer and snow isn't uncommon out of season. Take care on the narrow and winding roads, especially if towing a caravan or camper.

Sunset from the summit of Mt Kosciuszko

WHERE TO STAY

450 Cooma Snowy Mountains Tourist Park

$$$

- 286 Sharp St, Cooma
- (02) 6452 1828
- www.coomatouristpark.com.au

Located on the south side of town, this is a popular caravan park during winter with visitors to the snow fields. The sites are flat and well grassed with very good facilities. It is a great base for exploring the surrounding national park area at any time of year.

451 Rainbow Pines Tourist Park

$$

- 11 Lucas Rd, Old Adaminaby
- (02) 6454 2317
- www.rainbowpines.com.au

Located on the shores of Lake Eucumbene, about 7km from the Snowy Mountains Hwy, this is a popular spot where you can enjoy trout fishing, sailing and canoeing. Sites are flat and grassy with the majority of powered sites overlooking the lake. Minimum-length stay applies during holidays and snow season.

452 Tom Groggin camping area

$ ★

- Alpine Way, Kosciuszko National Park
- (02) 6076 9373
- www.nationalparks.nsw.gov.au/camping-and-accommodation/campgrounds/tom-groggin-campground

Set on the banks of the Murray, just off Alpine Way, this relaxed free camping area is the perfect base for people wishing to enjoy some bushwalking, fishing and driving tracks through the high country. Pit toilets are the only amenities available. National park entry fees apply.

453 Jindabyne Holiday Park

$$$$

- 6 Kosciuszko Rd, Jindabyne
- (02) 6456 2249
- www.jindabyneholidaypark.com.au

Conveniently located just 100m from the local shopping centre this caravan park provides a great base for people exploring the Snowy Mountains during summer or winter. Lovely grassy sites overlooking the lake. Very busy during snow season and summer holidays.

454 Kosciuszko Mountain Retreat

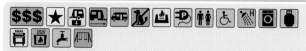

$$$ ★

- Sawpit Creek, Kosciuszko Rd, Kosciuszko National Park
- (02) 6456 2224
- www.kosipark.com.au

Set amongst the snow gums in the picturesque Kosciuszko National Park this caravan park is just 14km from Perisher Valley. Drive-thru powered sites are available for larger vans and there is an excellent indoor camp kitchen with a log fire and lounge area. Perfect for warming up in winter.

455 Khancoban Lakeside Caravan Park

$$$

- 1362 Alpine Way, Khancoban
- (02) 6076 9488
- www.klcp.com.au

This pet-friendly caravan park is situated on five acres of land with magnificent views over the Snowy Mountains. It offers peaceful lakefront sites with modern amenities and a large, fully enclosed camp kitchen and games room.

391 Discovery Parks Lake Hume

See p. 213 – Seymour to Albury.

ALBURY TO ECHUCA

NEED TO KNOW

🕐	229km
🏠	Riverside free camping areas; full-featured caravan parks
☁	This is a popular summer destination to make the most of the sandy river beaches and activities on the river.
👁	Fishing, boating, golf, wineries
🛣	Good to great
🍴	Services vary town to town. Some are only very small and so offer only basic facilities.
⚠	None apply

Lake Mulwala

INTRODUCTION

From Albury to Echuca, north-west along the Murray Valley Highway, there is almost continuous access to the Murray River, much of which has kilometres and kilometres of river bends where camping is permitted. Along the way it passes through rich fruit-growing areas and, in season, produce can be bought direct from the growers at farmgate stalls along the way. Many of the towns have historic significance as river port towns, with plenty to do and see on and off the water.

WHERE TO GO

The Murray Valley Highway leaves **Wodonga** on the Victorian side of the border, but consider crossing the Murray and following the Riverina Highway on the New South Wales side to head through **Howlong** (it's not long, I promise). Howlong has one of the great golf courses along this stretch – the others are at Corowa, Yarrawonga-Mulwala, Cobram–Barooga and Echuca-Moama. Howlong has stunning landscaped gardens that are impressive even if you aren't golfing.

Cross back over the Murray and make for the historical town of **Rutherglen**, at the centre of a legendary wine-producing region. Rutherglen's wineries are renowned for producing top-quality wines, especially full-bodied reds and fortified wines. Many of the vineyards have cellar doors, and most are open daily.

Get used to crossing the Murray by making your way from Rutherglen to **Corowa**, which was where supporters of the Australian Federation first met in 1893. The story of Australia's nationhood is well told at the town's Federation Museum (open Tue, Thurs, Sat and Sun). The excellent golf course and bowling greens are other major attractions in the town.

Continue to follow the Murray downstream to the border towns of **Mulwala** and **Yarrawonga** on the shores of the artificial Lake Mulwala, the lowest major water storage on the Murray River. The towns have most services, good shopping and three large clubs which are popular ways to avoid camp cooking. Throughout summer, especially, the lake is a popular location for waterskiing, sailing, fishing and powerboat racing. Its diversion weir supplies irrigation water to farmers in both New South Wales and Victoria.

Further along the Murray Valley Highway, staying in Victoria for just a little while, is **Cobram**, a Murray River service town that's part of a major fruit-growing and dairy area. Golf, fishing, watersports, bowls and tennis are all popular. Along with nearby **Tocumwal**, which has most services and a small shopping strip, it's in the centre of miles of Murray River bends with a free camping area on nearly every one. In most cases, campers need to be fully self-sufficient, but with so many campsites to choose from, you'll often camp alone. For those not interested in self-sufficiency, there are some great, riverside caravan parks up and down the river too.

Tocumwal is home to the largest WWII aerodrome in the southern hemisphere. It was used for training Liberator bomber crews, but today is a popular gliding centre. There's also a 36-hole golf course near town, for those who like to swing a stick at a ball.

The highway leaves the Murray for a short while until Echuca-Moama. **Echuca** was once Australia's largest inland port and its historic riverside precinct is a bustling tourist attraction. My family really loved taking a cruise on the PS *Emmylou*, one of the many replica paddlesteamers which conduct cruises up and down the river. We also enjoyed visiting the National Holden Museum.

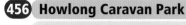

DON'T MISS

→ **The great Murray cod – Murray River**

There is plenty of good fishing in this area and the Murray River is home to the popular, yet elusive, Murray cod. This large freshwater fish can grow to an enormous size with specimens known to exceed 100kg. As well as Murray cod, target species on the border waterway include golden perch, and carp, the latter which is a pest and by law cannot be returned to the water. The waters of the Murray fall within the boundary of New South Wales and a New South Wales fishing permit is required to fish them.

WHERE TO STAY

456 Howlong Caravan Park

⦿ 55 Hume St, Howlong
☏ (02) 6026 5304
▭ www.howlongcaravanpark.com.au

family parks

Situated in the picturesque riverside town of Howlong this caravan park is centrally located between Albury, Corowa and Rutherglen. It offers level, grassy sites and basic amenities. Bookings are required over Christmas, Easter and public holidays.

457 Yarrawonga Holiday Park

⦿ Corner Piper St and Burley Rd, Yarrawonga
☏ (03) 5744 3420
▭ www.yarrawongaholidaypark.com.au

This large, popular caravan park is located right on the banks of the Murray, just below the Yarrawonga Weir. It is close to the town's many sporting facilities, including the public swimming pool and has a recently upgraded playground and splash zone onsite for the children. Bookings are essential during holiday periods.

458 Sandy Beach camping area

⦿ Boomanoomana State Forest

This shady, sandy, free camping area on the banks of the Murray River is suited to self-contained vehicles only. Enjoy the peace and quiet, and excellent fishing.

459 RACV Cobram Resort

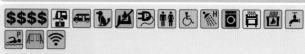

⦿ 154 Campbell Rd, Cobram
☏ (03) 5871 9700
▭ www.racv.com.au/travel-leisure/racv-resorts/
our-destinations/cobram-resort

This is a very highly rated caravan park complex with some 35 powered sites set on sprawling, well-tended lawns. It has a range of accommodation options. Bookings are required during holiday periods.

421 Boomerang Way Tourist Park

See p. 233 – Shepparton to Jerilderie.

460 NRMA Echuca Holiday Park

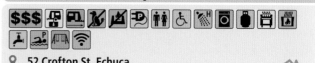

⦿ 52 Crofton St, Echuca
☏ (03) 5482 2157
▭ www.echucacaravanpark.com.au

NRMA
Parks + Resorts

This is a popular, quality riverside caravan park just a short walk from Echuca's historical port precinct on the Murray River. The spacious park has a range of accommodation options with very good facilities. Bookings are required in peak periods and a minimum-length stay applies over Christmas, Easter and public holidays.

ECHUCA TO MILDURA

NEED TO KNOW

🕐	**376km**
🏠	**Riverside free camping areas, full-featured caravan parks**
☁	**This is a great destination all year.**
👁	**Camping on the Murray, playing on the Murray**
🛣	**These are regional roads of varying quality, but the whole route is sealed.**
🍴	**Most basic facilities are available on this route.**
⚠	**None apply**

Paddle steamer docked on the Murray River in Echuca-Moama

INTRODUCTION

As the Murray winds its way further into Australia's interior, the soils become redder and the vegetation opens up. The Murray Valley Highway generally follows the course of the river and most towns are settled serenely on its banks. Like the earlier section, the riverside is full of great camping areas, both free and paid, so there's never a need to drive far to explore the next town or attraction.

WHERE TO GO

Leaving **Echuca**, the highway passes through open farmland dotted with small stands of eucalypts, one of the most typical roadside sights in Australia, before it gets to **Cohuna**. It's located on Gunbower Creek, an anabranch of the Murray River that forms Gunbower Island – Australia's largest inland island. The island is covered in red-gum and box forest and is home to large numbers of waterbirds, kangaroos and emus. Part of the island is protected by Gunbower National Park and Gunbower Island State Forest, which both include forests, marshes and waterways. The island can be accessed via a bridge from town, and there are picnic and barbecue facilities, along with some walking

and four-wheel-drive tracks that usually lead to riverside camping areas.

Continuing downstream, the **Kerang** area is scattered with a vast network of lakes, marshes and streams forming large and significant wetlands. The area is a breeding ground for many waterbirds and Australia's largest ibis rookery is found on Reedy Lake. Kerang has most services and good shopping. Nearby **Murrabit**, 27km north, is home to what is reputedly Australia's largest country market – which has been running continuously on the 1st Sat of the month since 1977.

Kerang is about the furthest you get from the Murray in this section, but the highway charts a course to find it again at **Swan Hill**. The mild weather, river activities and surrounding lakes have made Swan Hill a popular holiday spot for many generations of Victorians who come here to fish, boat and camp by the river. One of its highlight attractions is Pioneer Settlement, a re-created port town of the historic paddlesteamer days. The three-hectare site has a 19th-century main street and numerous artifacts and restored vehicles. There is also an interesting display of local Aboriginal culture. Make sure you take a trip on a horse-drawn carriage, or a cruise on the PS *Pyap*. Entry fees apply and it's open daily 9.30am–4pm.

Two of my favourite towns on the Murray are **Robinvale** and **Euston**, if only because I've had some great times camped there with friends. Robinvale is a popular tourist destination, particularly during the Christmas and Easter holidays when many people camp along the river. The town is central to the local fruit industry and abounds with table-grape farms and orchards. The Robinvale caravan park, right on the riverbank, is a top spot for a happy hour, watching the sun set over the river. Across the river, the Euston Club is a great place for a good feed.

From Robinvale it's only a short drive to **Mildura**, a key citrus- and grape-growing area with a warm Mediterranean climate. In addition to its numerous vineyards and orchards, Mildura is the regional home of Australia's dried-fruit industry. That's why the region's name – Sunraysia – sounds familiar. Many small producers grow then sun-dry their fruit on racks. The city offers a diverse selection of accommodation, including houseboat hire, and has an abundance of caravan parks. It has an incredible food scene too, especially for somewhere so remote. It's been led by celebrity chef Stefano de Pieri, who has been running his Italian restaurant here since 1991.

Swan Hill Pioneer Settlement

DON'T MISS

→ **Murray Sunset National Park – near Mildura**

Located within an area of almost-untouched semi-arid country in the world, the park is popular with bushwalkers, campers and four-wheel drivers. It has a number of pink lakes, historical station buildings and important wetlands which attract all sorts of native birdlife.

WHERE TO STAY

461 Cohuna Waterfront Holiday Park

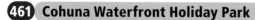

📍 58 Cohuna Island Rd, Cohuna
📞 1800 672 372
💻 www.cwhp.com.au

family parks

This quiet, shady caravan park is popular with anglers and young families. It offers large waterfront sites and has good facilities including a boat ramp, swimming pool and kiosk.

462 Ibis Caravan Park

📍 9399 Murray Valley Hwy, Kerang
📞 (03) 5452 2232
💻 www.ibiscaravanpark.com.au

This pet-friendly park offers nice, shady spots on level grass with clean well-maintained amenities to suit the needs of most travellers.

463 BIG4 Riverside Swan Hill

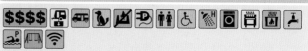

📍 1 Monash Dr, Swan Hill
📞 (03) 5032 1494
💻 www.big4.com.au/caravan-parks/vic/murray/riverside-swanhill-holiday-park

BIG4 HOLIDAY PARKS

Situated on the banks of the mighty Murray River this is a family-friendly park with excellent facilities including a solar-heated pool and onsite cafe. Pets are only allowed on selected sites.

339 Robinvale Riverside Caravan Park

See p. 173 – Hay to Mildura.

340 Apex Riverbeach Holiday Park

See p. 173 – Hay to Mildura.

Farmers Market at Mildura

MILDURA TO ADELAIDE

NEED TO KNOW

🕐	**390km**
🏠	**Riverfront caravan parks, beachside caravan parks**
☁	**Adelaide and the Riverland are wonderful all the time, although through spring is a highlight.**
👁	**Wineries, watersports, Renmark's roses**
🅷	**Good to great**
🍴	**These are well-travelled routes with most services and facilities available.**
⚠	**Most fresh produce can't be carried into South Australia. Eat it or surrender it before you leave Mildura.**

River cruise

INTRODUCTION

We tend to think of the Murray River as the border between New South Wales and Victoria, but the section that runs through South Australia to reach the ocean at Lake Alexandrina is arguably the most interesting part of it. The Riverina is a major fruit-producing centre and as well as vineyards, stone-fruit orchards flourish. This route offers two options, each as good as the other, which finally end up in Adelaide.

WHERE TO GO

From **Mildura**, the Sturt Highway passes through just one tiny settlement on the banks of Lake Cullulleraine, filled from the Murray River, before reaching the rose capital of Australia, just over the South Australian border – **Renmark**.

My son still refers to the Renmark Riverside BIG 4 Caravan Park broadly as 'South Australia' because that was where we stopped after spending two days travelling to the state and where we were when we announced we'd made it.

The riverfront town is renowned for its local produce, especially nuts, fruit and wine. Our favourite place to visit is Ruston's Roses. The garden has Australia's largest collection of roses, an enthralling display of classic Lotus cars (not flowers) and a very decent cafe and restaurant. Even our kids loved wandering through.

Now bypassed by the highway, the Riverland's major centre is **Berri**, which has all services and good shopping. There's a very attractive riverfront parkland that's popular with tourists, plus the town is surrounded by plenty of peaceful fishing and picnic areas, like nearby **Loxton**. It's the hometown of the Berri Fruit Juice Company, even though it's no longer manufactured here. Some might argue the better of the 'fruit juices' is next door at the huge Berry Estate Winery at Glossop.

At the junctions of the former and current Sturt highways, and beside Lake Bonney, is **Barmera**, a small town surrounded by vineyards and orchards. The lakeside town is particularly popular for watersports enthusiasts and has most services, including a naturist caravan park on its western shore.

Although **Waikerie** is bypassed by the highway these days, it's a wonderful place to stop. There is a large parkland on the banks of the Murray River, and some great little cafes in town. My family can't go through without stopping at Havenhand Chocolates where it's hard not to leave without overindulging, especially on the chilli hot chocolate. The Waikerie Bakery (on Peake Tce) is another great local producer, with a huge range of delicious products. It's easy to find and even has a drive-thru service for those in a hurry.

At **Blanchetown**, a holiday town at the Murray River's Lock 1, you can choose to continue following the river south to its mouth near Victor Harbor (see p. 118), or leave the river and travel through the famous wine country of the Barossa Valley.

If you are exploring the Barossa Valley then **Nuriootpa** is the commercial centre of the Barossa Valley. An interesting highlight at the Barossa Valley Tourist Park is Australia's second oldest motorhome, built in 1931 by the inventor Gerhard Kaesler, an Australian born of German parents who taught himself English from a dictionary

Picnic at Maggie's Farm Shop

as a teenager. He also built Australia's first motorhome in 1929, which is on display in Goolwa, just a few hours south at the mouth of the Murray River.

The Barossa Valley is perhaps the best known premium wine–producing area in Australia. This celebrated tourist destination has more than 120 wineries, most with cellar-door sales, a great selection of restaurants and plenty of galleries (often all three are combined). A great place to start a tour of the local wineries is the Barossa Visitor Information Centre (66 Murray St, Tanunda).

Just outside of Nuriootpa is the wonderful Maggie's Farm Shop. Owned by Australian cook and food author Maggie Beer, the shop has a full range of her wonderful gourmet products and a delightful cafe with tables overlooking a large pond that's home to inquisitive turtles and a few fish.

It's only a little over an hour from the Barossa Valley to **Adelaide**, one of Australia's most relaxed capital cities. Every time we visit Adelaide we stay at Christies Beach Caravan Park because my family love how relaxed it is there. In fact, all the parks along the mid-coast are great, although the one at Brighton is the most popular.

Using any of the mid-coast caravan parks as a base, venture into the McLaren Vale wine region. There are over 40 cellar doors in the region known for its shiraz, cabernet sauvignon and grenache. For an indulgent experience, head to d'Arenberg Wines for one of their blending bench sessions, where you'll get to design your own wine, and take home a bottle of it. (Mine's called the Editor's Payrise – a dry shiraz with subtle elements of blackcurrant and oak …)

THE ALTERNATE ROUTE

Because the Barossa is so accessible from Adelaide, a great alternative route is to follow the Murray River as it makes its way to the ocean near Victor Harbor. From **Blanchetown**, head south along Hunter Rd to **Swan Reach**. A very quiet little river town, it has a pleasant caravan park and great access to the Murray. There is no diesel here though, so make sure you have enough to reach Mannum before leaving Blanchetown.

Between Swan Reach and Mannum, the road follows the turns of the river high above it, offering some spectacular views, especially at sunset. If you're lucky you might see the majestic paddlesteamer PS *Murray Princess* taking passengers on seven-night cruises up and down the river.

Near Mannum is the spectacular Monarto Zoo – the largest open-range zoo in the world. In fact it's so big that free buses ferry visitors around all day long. Each bus has a volunteer guide on board to provide information on the animals you pass, including lions, giraffes, African wild dogs, rhinoceros and zebras. There's a giant carpark with plenty of room to navigate a caravan.

From Monarto, follow the river further downstream to **Murray Bridge**, which is a centre for watersports. From here you can choose to return to Adelaide via the Fleurieu Peninsula (*see* p. 118), or east along the Limestone Coast to Mount Gambier (*see* p. 120).

DON'T MISS

→ Bella Lavender Estate – Glossop
Bella Lavender Estate is owned by the Centofanti family. A caravanner himself, Mario was a bouncer and orchid grower until he saw a lavender farm on holidays and came home and planted one himself. The garden is best visited in summer, when the flowers are in bloom, but all year there's no shortage of lavender-infused products for sale in the cafe. If you can, stick around for dinner as Mario's son cooks great wood-fired pizzas.

→ An environmental winery – Banrock Station
Banrock Station Winery and Wetland Centre offers not only wine-tasting and great meals, but also several boardwalks through magnificent wetlands. The entire circuit traverses 8km of very easy walking through these Ramsar-listed wetlands which have amazing birdlife and even support flora that were initially thought to be extinct. The station has rejuvenated the area to the point where it is one of only 20 sites on the lower Murray that enjoys a near-natural flow of water. If you get the chance, don't pass up an opportunity to chat with Wetland Manager Christophe Tourenq or Banrock Station Ranger Tim Field. Both offer exceptionally interesting insights into the significant wetland.

CHECK YOUR FRUIT AND YOUR WATCH

At the Yamba Roadhouse, just a few kilometres over the South Australian border, a quarantine station forces westbound traffic to stop and surrender all fruit and vegetables. Don't make the mistake I did and stock up on oranges at roadside stalls on the way out of Mildura. Westbound travellers should also move their clocks back 30 min at the border, or forward 30 min when travelling east. During the summer months, both states have daylight saving.

WHERE TO STAY

464 Bushmans Rest Caravan Park

- 📍 68 Sturt Hwy, Cullulleraine
- 📞 (03) 5028 2252
- 💻 www.bushmansrest.com.au

This is a wonderful caravan park on the shore of the lake, on the Sturt Hwy west of Mildura. Its good facilities will make your stay enjoyable.

465 Wentworth Willow Bend Caravan Park

- 📍 14–16 Darling St, Wentworth
- 📞 (03) 5027 3213
- 💻 www.willowbendcaravanpark.com

Superbly located on the banks of the Murray River, this is a great place to spend a few days in the area.

466 BIG4 Renmark Riverfront Holiday Park

- 📍 1 Patey Dr, Renmark
- 📞 (08) 8586 8111
- 💻 www.big4renmark.com.au/caravan-parks/sa/riverland/renmark-riverfront-holiday-park

This caravan park makes a perfect holiday destination and I have stayed here many times. It is an ideal base from which to explore the area. Set on the banks of the Murray River, about 2km from the town centre, it has shaded, grassy areas – great for relaxing picnics – and good facilities.

467 Berri Riverside Caravan Park

- 📍 87 Riverview Dr, Berri
- 📞 (08) 8582 3723
- 💻 www.berriholidaypark.com.au

This is a large and very good caravan park about 1km from town and just across the road from the Murray River. It has extensive facilities including a state-of-the-art camp kitchen. This is the best place to stay when passing through Berri.

468 Kingston-on-Murray Caravan Park

- 📍 461 Holmes Rd, Kingston On Murray
- 📞 (08) 8583 0209
- 💻 www.komcaravanpark.com.au

This is a quiet, waterfront, owner-operated caravan park just off the highway and ideal for a few restful days on the riverbank. The park has good, basic facilities and is an enjoyable base for exploring the local area, including the Banrock Station Winery and Wetlands.

469 Waikerie Holiday Park

- 📍 44 Peake Tce, Waikerie
- 📞 (08) 8541 2651
- 💻 www.waikerieholidaypark.com.au

A large council-run caravan park close to the river on the edge of town. This is in a pretty setting, easily located, with good amenities and a range of facilities. Most powered sites are drive-thru.

358 Barossa Tourist Park

See p. 185 – Broken Hill to Adelaide.

359 Levi Park Caravan Park

See p. 185 – Broken Hill to Adelaide.

256 Christies Beach Tourist Park

See p. 119 – Fleurieu Peninsula.

257 Brighton Caravan Park

See p. 119 – Fleurieu Peninsula.

Monarto Zoo

BRISBANE TO GOONDIWINDI

NEED TO KNOW

⏱	**381km**
⌂	**Family holiday resorts; basic, waterside caravan parks**
☁	**This is a great trip all year, although the highlands can be chilly in winter.**
👁	**The Scenic Rim**
⚠	**Mostly good, although there's a steep section climbing the range through Cunninghams Gap. Towards Goondiwindi, the road condition may deteriorate.**
🍴	**This route passes through many regional centres with good services.**
⚠	**None apply**

Warwick

INTRODUCTION

The Cunningham Highway is the major south-western link from Brisbane to the southern states. It joins with the New England Highway at Warwick and the Newell Highway at Goondiwindi, having climbed the Great Dividing Range and crossed the fertile volcanic soils of the Darling Downs. It takes in one of south-east Queensland's fastest developing tourist areas, the Scenic Rim.

WHERE TO GO

Before you leave the urban sprawl of **Brisbane**, the highway passes through the large city of **Ipswich**, which lies on the western fringe of greater Brisbane. It dates back to convict days, but more recently coalmining, railways, foundries and the Amberley RAAF base have been major employers. The city has an emerging food and restaurant scene, and hosts a number of Queensland's high-profile events, so there is almost always something going on. Try to avoid the merger of the Warrego and Cunningham highways into Ipswich Rd during peak hour, though, as commuters from Brisbane create dense traffic most days.

Past Ipswich, the country opens up as the highway makes for **Aratula**, a township at the base of the stunning Scenic Rim. It's surrounded by small rural holdings, including many market gardens that produce a range of vegetables. To the south-east, nestled in the hills, picturesque Lake Moogerah is a popular spot for watersports and has a large camping area on the lake's eastern shore.

The World Heritage–listed Scenic Rim is a semicircular mountain range covered with subtropical rainforest, open forest and mountain heath. The area is a popular bushwalking destination with an extensive network of both short and long walks, some of which start from the highway rest area at the top of Cunninghams Gap.

Over the range, **Warwick** at the crossroads of the New England and Cunningham highways, is a key regional centre for the Granite Belt. Springtime sees the town's fabulous roses at their best. Leslie Dam, 14km west of Warwick, is popular with watersports enthusiasts, including anglers. The dam is stocked with golden and silver perch, and Murray cod. A permit is required to fish, which starts at $10 for a week.

Past Leslie Dam, the highway continues south-west to **Inglewood**, a town which has grown from little more than a lonely hotel along the coach route between Warwick and Goondiwindi. Coolmunda Dam to the east is now a source of irrigation water for local farmers and the town is an emerging centre of Australia's olive industry. Extensive plantations can be seen east of town. With a nice rest area at the eastern end of town, good country-style shopping and ample parking, it's a nice place to stop.

Almost on the border of New South Wales, **Yelarbon** was the site where Australia's first tobacco crops were grown in the 1870s. These are long gone, but remnants of the tobacco-curing sheds can be seen alongside the highway. While the town has minimal services, the sports and recreation ground in the small community has become a popular, low-cost camping area. For a small fee ($15 at last check) you can enjoy powered sites and clean, hot showers.

Goondiwindi, in Queensland, is the larger of the two border towns while

Boggabilla in New South Wales has only basic services. On the northern banks of the Macintyre River, Goondiwindi is a large regional centre servicing strong pastoral interests and an intensive cotton industry. When Queensland separated from New South Wales in 1859, customs collection points were established here and along the border to collect duty and control smuggling. These points were dispensed with after Federation in 1901 and the Goondiwindi Customs House is now a museum.

DON'T MISS

→ An amazing river drive – near Warwick

Just 25 min west of Warwick, in the charming little country town of **Killarney**, is the start of a spectacular, easy off-road drive. The Condamine Gorge Rd passes through an ancient volcanic gorge roughly following the path of the Condamine River. It crosses the river at 14 points along the journey between Killarney and The Heads, and there are a number of nice little spots to stop for a picnic lunch. It's not the place to bring a caravan, though, so leave that in Warwick.

→ Legendary racehorse – Goondiwindi

The legendary racehorse Gunsynd, often called the Goondiwindi Grey, hailed from here. He won 29 races from 54 starts, finished second on seven occasions, third on eight and was also third in the 1972 Melbourne Cup. A statue of the famous horse has pride of place in Apex Park.

WHERE TO STAY

77 Brisbane Holiday Village

See p. 38 – Tweed Heads to Brisbane.

78 Brisbane Gateway Resort

See p. 38 – Tweed Heads to Brisbane.

470 Lake Moogerah Caravan Park

📍 70 Muller Park Rd, Moogerah
📞 (07) 5463 0141
🖥 www.moogerah.com

An expansive, pleasant caravan park on the shores of Lake Moogerah it has open fireplaces and basic, but clean, facilities. There are good options for free-range or powered camping.

413 Warwick Freedom Lifestyle

See p. 227 – Glen Innes to Warwick.

434 Goondiwindi Top Tourist Park

See p. 239 – Moree to Miles.

Goondiwindi Grey statue

BRISBANE TO DALBY

Jimbour House

INTRODUCTION

From Brisbane's appealing subtropical climate and river setting, the Warrego Highway sweeps westward past the market gardens and roadside fruit stalls of the fertile Lockyer Valley. The road climbs steadily up the range to the main regional centre of Toowoomba, and then through rich farming land further west.

WHERE TO GO

As you pass through **Ipswich** on the way out of Brisbane, be sure to check out the city's rich history from convict times to coalmining (*see* p. 260 for more). The city also has an emerging food and restaurant scene and hosts a number of high-profile events, so there is almost always something going on. During peak hours, try to avoid the merger of the Warrego and Cunningham highways into Ipswich Rd, as commuters from Brisbane create dense traffic.

Past Ipswich, the country opens up as the highway makes for **Gatton** at the centre of the rich Lockyer Valley, an intensively irrigated area where potatoes, cabbages, carrots, onions and more thrive. There are usually fresh-produce stands along the highway, and Gatton's township has

good country-town shopping and a range of services.

From Gatton, the highway climbs steeply up the Great Dividing Range to **Toowoomba**, but it is dual carriageway all the way, and there are plenty of opportunities to overtake. Toowoomba is known as the 'Garden City' and each spring visitors flock from all over Australia to partake in the annual Carnival of Flowers which shows off the regional city's magnificent gardens perched high on the range.

In 1853 Freeman Cobb established his coaching business and the name Cobb & Co. became synonymous with transport in rural and outback Australia. Toowoomba's best attraction is the Cobb & Co. Museum, which offers a glimpse into pioneering history and showcases Australia's finest collection of horse-drawn vehicles. There is also a fine cafe on the premises.

Only a short distance west is the small town of **Oakey**, at the heart of the Darling Downs. Although there is limited shopping it is home to the Australian Army Aviation wing. The Australian Army Flying Museum is located at Oakey Airfield in premises adjoining the civil departure lounge. There are numerous aircraft displayed, dating back to a 1914 Bristol boxkite. Guided tours can be booked for groups of five or more.

Halfway between Oakey and **Bowenville**, the small town of **Jondaryan** is little more than a roadhouse and hotel, so is best known for the Jondaryan Woolshed a few kilometres away. Built in 1859, it's the oldest shearing shed in Queensland. Today it is a popular attraction, with fascinating tours and demonstrations of shearing, blacksmithing, working horses and damper making. There are many historical buildings, re-creating a sheep station village. Entry fees apply and it's open daily 8.30am–4.30pm. Contact (07) 4692 2229.

At the centre of the Surat Basin, **Dalby** is one of Australia's richest grain- and cotton-growing regions, and one of only a few places in the world where both summer and winter crops are grown in the same soil. It has Queensland's largest grain depot and holds the largest single-day live-stock market in the country. The neat town has a good selection of shops and all services. Visit the Pioneer Park museum to admire the extensive collection of early model tractors and other agricultural machinery from the area's pioneering days. There are also historical buildings to visit, although the best time to visit is when the working tractor field day is held in May each year. Entry fees apply and it's open daily 8am–5pm. Contact (07) 4662 4760.

→ **The great Bernborough – Oakey**
Bernborough was one of Australia's greatest racehorses. He won 26 of his 38 races, including an amazing 15 in a row in Sydney, Melbourne and Brisbane. He was bought by movie mogul Louis B. Mayer and after breaking down in 1946 retired to stud becoming a very successful sire in Kentucky. A lifesize bronze statue stands outside the council offices in Oakey.

→ **Jimbour House – near Dalby**
One of Queensland's most significant and charming country manors, it was built in 1877 at a cost of £30,000. The centre of a large sheep station, it was one of the most modern homes in the country during the 19th century. Today it remains a private residence, but the gardens can be toured for a donation, while the interior is open for select special events. The gardens are open daily during daylight hours. Contact (07) 5465 3100.

WHERE TO STAY

77 **Brisbane Holiday Village**

See p. 38 – Tweed Heads to Brisbane.

78 **Brisbane Gateway Resort**

See p. 38 – Tweed Heads to Brisbane.

415 **BIG4 Toowoomba Garden City Holiday Park**

See p. 229 – Warwick to Gympie.

471 **Oakridge Motel Tourist Park**

📍 56 Toowoomba Rd, Oakley
📞 (07) 4691 3330
🖥 www.oakridgemoteltouristpark.com.au

Situated on the Warrego Hwy, this is a convenient place for an overnight stay or to use as a base for exploring the Darling Downs area. Sites are large and grassy with plenty of shade in some areas.

472 **Dalby Tourist Park**

📍 32 Myall St, Dalby
📞 (07) 4662 4793
🖥 www.dalbytouristpark.com.au

Easily accessed straight from the highway and centrally located close to local clubs and facilities this caravan park is a great place to stop and wind down for a few days. Sites are large and grassy with drive-thru spots available for larger motorhomes. The amenities are clean and modern.

Jondaryan Woolshed

DALBY TO ROMA

NEED TO KNOW

 271km

 Outback caravan parks

 Temperatures can soar in summer, so plan a trip for the cooler months.

 Warm winter weather, outback history

 Wide, sealed and well maintained

 There are reasonable services along this route.

 None apply

Near Roma

INTRODUCTION

The Darling Downs is a huge agricultural district spread across 72,000 square kilometres of undulating plains, 900m above sea level. The region's rich volcanic soils yield grapes, oilseeds and wheat, as well as some of the country's most magnificent gardens. The highway between Dalby and Roma is wide and well maintained, with great rest areas in small towns like Warra, Dulacca and Wallumbilla.

WHERE TO GO

As the Warrego Highway tracks north-west to Roma, it's the smallest of towns that can be the most interesting. **Warra**, a tiny settlement of around 80 people, has an excellent free camping area across the road from the pub. You'll find the locals are more than happy to chat with travellers over a beer.

Nearby is one of Queensland's most bizarre, but significant, monuments. After prickly pear was imported from the USA as food for the cochineal beetle (which is dried and crushed to make red food dyes) it became a noxious weed. By 1926 over 24 million hectares of Queensland were covered with it, preventing agriculture and grazing. The problem was so severe, many settlers walked off their land. In **Boonarga**,

the Cactoblastis Memorial Hall, listed on the Queensland Heritage Register, was erected in 1936 to commemorate the control of prickly pear by the *Cactoblastis* moth.

Chinchilla, another 18km west, was named after the local Aboriginal name for cypress pines, *jinchilla*, by the explorer Ludwig Leichhardt when he passed through the area in 1844. Today, Chinchilla is a prosperous town, with grain-growing the traditional industry. However, while this area is well known for its cantaloupes, strawberries and grapes, the Chinchilla Melon Festival celebrates the booming local industry in watermelons. Occurring in Feb in odd-numbered years, the festival includes a large parade down the main street. Other activities include a competition for the heaviest melon and the Melon Triathlon.

Originally called Dogwood Crossing, **Miles** was settled in 1844 and still has 15 of its historical buildings from pioneering days on display, with another 10 replicas. The Miles Historical Village and Museum includes a dairy, church, school and police cells, all relocated from the local area and displayed along a typical pioneer-town main street. The modern Miles is at the centre of one of Australia's most active coal-seam-gas mining areas, and has most services and a few good places to camp.

Just over the ambiguous border of the north-western edge of the Darling Downs,

Roma is the administrative centre for the Maranoa region's agricultural and mining operations, and has a range of services and good shops. It was beset by devastating flooding three years in a row from 2010, with recovery efforts costing billions of dollars. Travellers can admire the bottle trees on Heroes Avenue, which were planted to commemorate the local soldiers who died in WWI.

DON'T MISS

→ **Pieces of the past – Chinchilla**
At the Chinchilla Historical Museum, you can see a fully operational vintage steam sawmill, the original town gaol, a pioneer slab hut, a collection of restored steam engines and one of the first two tickets issued by Qantas. It's open Thurs–Mon 9am–4pm. Contact (07) 4662 7014.

→ **A historical night out – Roma**
The Roma Big Rig and Visitor Information Centre is one of those fine examples where the centre is a destination in itself. As well as a comprehensive display of local information, there's an adjacent caravan park, and a three-night-a-week screening of a 35 min documentary outlining the history of oil and gas discovery in the region. Purchase tickets for the show from the centre. It's open daily 9am–5pm. Contact (07) 4622 2325.

WHERE TO STAY

473 Chinchilla Tourist Park

264 Zeller St, Chinchilla

(07) 4669 1465

www.chinchillatouristpark.com.au

This pet-friendly caravan park offers lush green powered sites with modern amenities. Facilities include a swimming pool, camp kitchen and large dining room where hot breakfast and buffet-style dinners are served daily. Additional fees apply.

435 Possum Park Caravan and Camping Park

See p. 239 – Moree to Miles.

474 Villa Holiday Park

67 Northern Rd, Roma

(07) 4622 1309

www.villaholidaypark.com.au

Conveniently located just 2km from the town centre this pet-friendly caravan park has well-maintained facilities and large, grassy camping areas. A good-sized children's playground and pool are onsite.

Roma Big Rig and Visitor Information Centre

Chinchilla Melon Festival

ROMA TO AUGATHELLA

Ellangowan Hotel, Augathella

INTRODUCTION

From the fertile growing regions of the Darling Downs, the Warrego Highway tracks west into the beginnings of Queensland's outback. It's a rural route that passes through a mix of woodland areas, open cultivated farmland and grazing country, where red dirt becomes more common and the towns further apart.

WHERE TO GO

West of **Roma**, **Mitchell** has become very tourist friendly in recent years and there is much to see and do in and around town. A soak in the Great Artesian Spa, a visit to the historical Kenniff Courthouse and a cruise on the Maranoa River are a few such experiences. The town has a lot to offer the traveller, including the facilities at Neil Turner Weir. In an often hot and dusty landscape, this is a lush, green picnic area and a spot for free camping (48-hour limit, donations welcome). Access is along a sealed, signposted road that turns off the Warrego Highway west of town, just beyond the level crossing.

The town of Mitchell was the centre of activity for the Kenniff brothers, habitual horse and cattle rustlers, who were sentenced to death for murdering a policeman and station manager sent to arrest them. In 1903 Patrick Kenniff was the last man hanged in Queensland, while his brother James' sentence was changed to 16 years. Kenniff Courthouse has a collection of historical information. It's open Mon–Fri 8.45am–5pm and Sat 9am–noon.

Midway between Mitchell and Morven is the small community of **Mungallala**. The only businesses in town are the Club Hotel, which also has an inexpensive camping area, and the Mungallala Cafe – a one-stop post office, store and eatery. The Cobb & Co. rest area on the western edge of town was once a changing station for horses, but is now an overnight camping area with barbecues and toilets.

As the land gets redder, the Warrego passes through **Morven**, which is somewhat smaller today than it was in the late 1800s. In those days it was a regular stop for the bullock teams travelling between Mitchell and Charleville, and an overnight stop on the Cobb & Co. coach route. The town has basic facilities, with a large roadhouse 2km to the east.

On the western side of Morven the Landsborough Highway tracks north-west to **Augathella**. Most of the town is set back from the highway, with facilities limited to the roadhouse, motel and caravan park. However, the Ellangowan Hotel is a popular stopover for travellers thanks to its inexpensive meals and camping area out the back.

DON'T MISS

→ Relaxing spas – Mitchell
The Great Artesian Spa forms part of the Mitchell swimming-pool complex. Visitors can enjoy relaxing in the artesian pools – one hot, one cool – that are landscaped with Australian flora. The complex is open daily 6am–6pm, with extended hours to 8pm on Tue and Thurs. Contact (07) 4624 6923.

→ Ooline trees – near Morven
Tregole National Park is 10km south of Morven along a sealed road. This 7500-hectare park preserves a large stand of ooline trees – a species that originated in the rainforest when Australia was a much wetter continent. Ooline trees are noted for their delicate flowers and have been extensively cleared so are vulnerable to extinction. A 2.1km circuit walking track from the day-use area weaves through the ancient forest.

Maranoa River, Mitchell

WHERE TO STAY

475 Major Mitchell Caravan Park

📍 Warrego Hwy, Mitchell
📞 (07) 4623 6600
🖥 www.majormitchellcaravanpark.com.au

Soak away your aches at the artesian spa pools or wander into the centre of town for some sightseeing – both are just a short walk from this modern, popular caravan park. Despite recent expansion, this place gets very busy in the tourist season and space is often scarce. Bookings are required in peak periods.

476 Augathella Riverside camping area

📍 Welch St, Augathella
📞 (07) 4654 5241

A great free camping area behind the Ellangowan Hotel. This is an expansive site with plenty of shade. The pub also does a great meal, and is a hub of activity for locals. There is access to power for those that need it behind the pub. Inquire within.

NORSEMAN TO SOUTHERN CROSS

NEED TO KNOW

 414km

 Council-run caravan parks

 Avoid summer, it's too hot.

 Wildflowers, mine tours, bordello tours

 Good to great

 While Norseman has only basic facilities, Kalgoorlie has everything the traveller needs.

 Road trains and wide-transport vehicles are common in the mining areas.

Golf course, Kalgoorlie

INTRODUCTION

The Great Eastern Highway is the major and most direct route between Perth and the eastern States. This is Western Australia's goldfields region and the landscape is dominated by deep reds and massive goldmines, historic towns and good camping as the highway winds through undulating countryside and across vast plains.

WHERE TO GO

When travelling through this area, Kalgoorlie-Boulder is a must-see so make a diversion north of Norseman through Kambalda then rejoin the highway at Coolgardie. **Kambalda** was a battling goldmining town until the 1960s when nickel was discovered and it boomed. Extensive mining continues in the area. Kambalda actually has two town centres that are divided by 4km of highway – Kambalda East and Kambalda West. If you get the chance to witness the landsailing on nearby Lake Lefroy – a huge salt lake – you certainly should. In the right conditions land sailers can reach speeds of up to 100km/hr! The towns don't have a formal camping area, apart from a 24-hour rest area.

At the heart of the goldfields, and 60km north-west, **Kalgoorlie-Boulder** is home to the second-largest goldmine in Australia – the Super Pit – and the famous Golden Mile, the richest square mile of gold-bearing ore in the world. There is a lot to see and do in this fascinating place including a visit to the famous two-up school that still operates in the original corrugated iron shed each Sun. Tours of Kalgoorlie's famous bordellos are a way to see a different side of the city. The former Langtrees bordello, with its extravagant premises in historic Hay St, has now been turned into an upmarket B&B.

At **Coolgardie**, the Coolgardie–Esperance Highway becomes the Great Eastern Highway to the west. The town was once the 3rd largest settlement in Western Australia when it was a thriving goldmining city. Today tourism sustains the small community and the town's historical buildings serve as a reminder of Coolgardie's boom period. Most of the historical sites in the town are well signed and documented, so walking the town is the best way to see them. The cemetery has the grave of explorer Ernest Giles, who was the first to travel overland from South Australia to Western Australia, although he died in relative poverty while working as a government clerk in the town. It is also filled with many unmarked graves of unidentified children and miners who died as a result of the poor living conditions during the late 19th century – a stark reminder of those harsh times.

Between Coolgardie and Southern Cross, the highway passes through the Great Western Woodlands, which, covering an area larger than England, is the largest undivided area of woodland forest on earth. Part of the woodlands are protected by the Goldfields Woodlands National Park, which is a popular destination offering four-wheel driving opportunities and remote camping areas.

Further west, **Southern Cross** was named after the constellation that the two prospectors used to find their way here when they first discovered the area in 1888. Southern Cross has had its ups and downs, but many goldmines still operate, and there are a few historical sites to visit. After the winter rains wildflowers colour the landscape.

DON'T MISS

→ **Pan for gold – Kalgoorlie**
Hannans North Tourist Mine, which incorporates the Super Pit Shop, is a fascinating facility that shows visitors through the gold-rush history of the area, and the intricacies of modern goldmining. Here you can pan for gold, take the self-guided tour or climb aboard a massive mining haul truck. Tour fees apply and it's open Sun–Fri 9am–4pm. Contact (08) 9022 1664.

→ **Historic architecture – Coolgardie**

The early architecture of the goldfields can be best seen in some of the grand old buildings in Coolgardie. Make sure you see the railway station, courthouse, gaol and the National Trust–restored Warden Finnerty's Residence.

→ **An unusual bottle collection – Coolgardie**

The Goldfields Exhibition Museum is housed in the former Warden's Court Building. Here you will find fascinating displays, including the largest bottle collection in Western Australia, and Aboriginal artefacts. Entry fees apply and it's open daily 9am–4pm. Contact (08) 9026 6090.

WHERE TO STAY

227 **Acclaim Gateway Caravan Park**

See p. 107 – Albany to Norseman.

370 **Prospector Holiday Park**

See p. 195 – Kalgoorlie to Sandstone.

477 **Southern Cross Caravan Park**

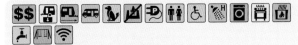

- Coolgardie Rd, Southern Cross
- (08) 9049 1212
- www.yilgarn.wa.gov.au

Alongside the Great Eastern Hwy, at the eastern end of town, this is a neat caravan park with good-quality facilities to meet the travellers' needs. Spacious, level sites are easily accessed and there is room for big rigs.

Coolgardie Courthouse

SOUTHERN CROSS TO PERTH

NEED TO KNOW

 360km

 Inexpensive caravan parks, full-featured caravan parks, holiday resorts

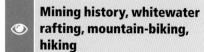 Although it can be a little hot at the eastern end over summer, this route can be travelled year-round. During late winter and spring, the wildflowers are in bloom.

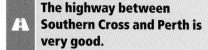 Mining history, whitewater rafting, mountain-biking, hiking

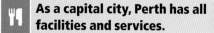 The highway between Southern Cross and Perth is very good.

 As a capital city, Perth has all facilities and services.

None apply

Cottesloe Beach, Perth

INTRODUCTION

From Southern Cross, the highway traverses Western Australia's wheat belt, which is also responsible for a large percentage of Australia's wool production. The highway follows the historical Goldfields Water Supply Scheme pipeline, passing through Merredin and Meckering, which was the site of a devastating earthquake in 1968. The small historical towns of Northam and York are worth a stop too, before the highway begins to climb through the hills to Perth.

WHERE TO GO

While **Southern Cross** is a town divided by two interests – wheat and gold – **Merredin** has but one focus – it's the centre of the region's incredible wheat industry. It lies roughly midway between Perth and the goldfields, and has most facilities, a good caravan park and decent places to eat. Merredin is also home to the Military Museum and the Old Railway Station Museum.

Wave Rock, a 2.7 billion-year-old piece of granite, 15m long and 100m high, is 160km south of here (via Narembeen and Mount Walker). You can then continue on past Lake King to Ravensthorpe, which is a great link if you want to visit the goldfields, but don't want to miss the southern coast either.

On the way to Northam, Western Australia's second largest inland town, the highway passes **Meckering**. On Monday 14 October 1968 the town was struck by an earthquake, which registered 6.9 on the Richter scale – although that number has since been revised to 6.5 that doesn't change its place in history. It was so violent many of the buildings in and around town tumbled down. Information about the earthquake is displayed on an information board in the town's park. There's also a really interesting museum filled with working cameras of all types. It's in the building that looks like a big SLR camera.

Situated on the Avon River, **Northam** is a large agricultural centre. It has an excellent visitor centre on the banks of the Avon

which is also the best place to see the town's famous white swans.

A diversion from the highway south of Northam leads to **York**, a historical town further upstream on the Avon. It was settled in 1831, just two years after the Swan River colony was established. This is a rich agricultural area with an even richer history. Some of its buildings date back as far as the 1840s and the Residency Museum and the Old Gaol and Courthouse should not be missed. The mechanically minded might enjoy a visit to the York Motor Museum. Although the town isn't on the highway, you'll enjoy the detour whether you'd rather explore the historic buildings or enjoy an al fresco lunch in one of its fine cafes.

From Northam, the highway climbs the Darling Range until **Mundaring**, just 34km inland from Perth. Mundaring Weir supplies water to goldfields as far away as Norseman via the pipeline that was completed in 1903. There are several pumping stations along the route to Kalgoorlie-Boulder and Norseman, with the Great Eastern Highway following its route for much of its 563km length.

Mundaring has an evolving art scene and is also a popular destination for nature lovers, with plenty of good walking and bike riding nearby.

One of the most isolated capital cities in the world, **Perth** is closer to Singapore than it is to Sydney – amazingly, it's cheaper to fly to too. On the banks of the Swan River, and founded in 1829, it's a scenic and sophisticated city with a Mediterranean climate, plenty of sunshine and a relaxed atmosphere. It's often claimed to be the sunniest state capital in Australia.

→ **Whitewater adventure – Northam**
The Northam Avon Descent is a classic 124km whitewater event held annually on the 1st weekend in Aug. It's a fabulous event to watch with a highlight the specially designed powerboats with a crew of two that speed down the rapids, bouncing over rocks and obstacles. All sorts of craft compete, though, from kayaks to surf skis.

→ **Swanning around – Northam**
Black swans are the emblem of Western Australia, however, the Avon River at Northam is home to a happy family of European white swans. The birds were introduced in 1896 and have bred successfully since then. Northam's swan warden feeds them each day, but you can also buy some feed at the visitor centre to feed them yourself.

WHERE TO STAY

478 **Merredin Tourist Park**

- 2 Oats St (corner of Great Eastern Hwy), Merredin
- (08) 9041 1535
- www.merredintouristpark.com.au

This caravan park is of a quality rarely found in an inland town the size of Merredin and I highly recommend it. From here it is a comfortable 260km to Perth or 335km to Kalgoorlie so Merredin is an excellent choice for an overnight stop and the adjoining roadhouse serves meals.

479 **Kellerberrin Caravan Park**

- Corner of Moore and George sts, Kellerberrin
- 0428 138 474
- www.kellerberrin.wa.gov.au

This council-owned caravan park offers travellers a budget option just on the edge of town. It has grassy sites in a rural setting with a large camp kitchen.

480 **Toodyay Holiday Parks and Chalets**

- 188 Racecourse Rd, Toodyay
- (08) 9574 2534
- toodyayholidaypark.com.au

This is a great caravan park in a classic West Australian bush setting about 3km from town. Complete with basic, but modern, amenities it's well managed and friendly. It's great for a few days while exploring the area.

202 **Discovery Parks – Perth Airport**

See p. 98 – Geraldton to Perth.

4

TOURING TASMANIA

If travelling from mainland Australia, why not enjoy a relaxing sailing experience across Bass Strait on board the *Spirit of Tasmania*? Once docked in Devonport just drive your caravan or motorhome off the ship and your Tasmanian touring holiday will begin. The picturesque island state is a place where you really can see everything. It is easy to bypass many worthwhile places on the mainland simply because of the sheer immensity of the continent, but in Tasmania you can take your time, so why not make the most of it?

Devonport, on the north coast, is a natural starting point and from here there are basically three routes to follow. The route that cuts through the centre of Tasmania takes you first to Launceston and then down through the Midlands, a farming region dotted with historical places. A trip through the north-west then south-east to Hobart takes you through a vast network of rivers – some of the state's best trout-fishing areas – to Cradle Mountain–Lake St Clair National Park. On the third route, along the east coast, you can explore some of Tasmania's stunning coastal scenery and the historic Port Arthur precinct.

DEVONPORT TO HOBART pp. 276–279

 Bass Highway, Midlands Highway (303km)

Head deep into the fertile undulating plains of Tasmania's Midlands on the Bass and Midland highways, the main route linking the north coast and Devonport with Hobart. The road passes through some major agricultural regions where, in addition to wheat, oats and barley, farmers grow crops such as poppies for medicinal use and pyrethrum for use in insecticides. Tourists flock to many of the delightful historical towns in this part of the state, including Longford, Evandale, Ross and Oatlands. The distances in Tasmania are not great, and driving from Devonport to Hobart takes just a pleasant few hours.

⚑ PLAN YOUR TRIP

From Devonport to Launceston, this section of the route rolls through beautiful coastal hills where cultivated flowers bloom in spring. The road then sweeps inland through regional farming communities to Launceston, the 'Garden City' of the north. Before you head south, take a diversion from Devonport to Port Sorell, a popular coastal holiday resort east of the city.

South from Launceston this area of the state, known as the Midlands, is a drier farming region where sheep and cattle graze contentedly and wheat crops stand tall. Many towns and properties have excellent historical buildings, several of which are regularly open to the public. Do not miss Woolmers Estate near Longford, which dates back to 1817 and is considered Tasmania's most significant colonial property.

Hobart, Australia's second oldest and most southerly city, is situated on the broad estuary of the River Derwent, under the spell of majestic kunanyi/Mt Wellington. A strong maritime flavour and sense of the past give Hobart an almost European air. This feeling is heightened in winter, when daytime temperatures drop to a crisp average of just 12°C.

☁ BEST TIME TO GO

The winters are cold in Tasmania, so spring and autumn are the most popular times to travel. Although warmer, the summers are still very comfortable for touring.

DEVONPORT TO HOBART
via west coast pp. 280–287

 Bass Highway, Murchison Highway, Zeehan Highway, Lyell Highway (639km)

Most tourists who drive around Tasmania will choose to travel on this popular route, especially as there is good, sealed access to both ends of spectacular Cradle Mountain–Lake St Clair National Park. The highway climbs over the famous stark hills surrounding Queenstown and crosses a great trout-fishing region in the centre of the state. The breathtaking west-coast town of Strahan is a very popular tourist destination, where cruise boats ply the tannin-stained waters of the mighty Gordon River.

⚑ PLAN YOUR TRIP

Whether you're straight off the ferry, or returning from an eastern exploration of the island, the moderate climate along the north-west coast of Tasmania, between Devonport and Smithton, makes this a popular tourist region. The highway closely follows the sea and coastal towns along the way all have interesting attractions. The Nut, an unusual rocky formation overlooking the historic township and fishing port of Stanley, has a chairlift from which to take in the wonderful views.

Halfway between Devonport and Smithton, the A10 route climbs south from the coast to lush rainforest, and distant mountain peaks soon become visible. The small, historical mining town of Waratah is a worthwhile diversion to the west. Cradle Mountain–Lake St Clair National Park, with its abundant wildlife and rewarding bushwalks, can be reached from this route.

At Rosebery, the highway veers west to the notorious Macquarie Harbour, site of one of Australia's most remote convict settlements. On its shores, Strahan is an incredibly popular tourist resort, while the historical mining towns of Zeehan and Queenstown each have their own charms. The highway climbs steeply around the bare hills above Queenstown en route to Derwent Bridge, a small community at the southern end of tranquil Lake St Clair.

Winding through the ranges between Derwent Bridge and Hobart, the highway runs along rivers, travels through small rural towns and passes some of the state's best trout-fishing areas. New Norfolk

Cradle Mountain Huts Walk

Port Arthur Historic Site

is an important regional town with many historical buildings – a great place to stop before Hobart, Australia's second oldest city and most southern.

☁ BEST TIME TO GO

The north-west coast has a mild climate – by Tasmanian standards – while the higher country further south has cold and snowy winters. Late spring and early autumn are the best times to travel.

HOBART TO LAUNCESTON pp. 288–293

Tasman Highway (423km)

Experience the popular east coast of Tasmania by travelling north-east from Hobart on the Tasman Highway. From Sorell, take a diversion to the spectacular Tasman Peninsula, one of the most treasured historical areas in the state and the location of Port Arthur Historic Site. The main highway largely follows the coast until St Helens, then turns west to climb through forested ranges before heading towards Launceston, Tasmania's major northern city. The highway also links the picturesque Freycinet Peninsula and several holiday resorts dotted along the coast.

kunanyi/Mt Wellington, Hobart

⚓ PLAN YOUR TRIP

Hobart, as well as being Australia's second oldest and most southerly city, is situated on the broad estuary of the River Derwent. Wedged between the Derwent and the majestic kunanyi/Mt Wellington, Hobart has a strong maritime history and this sense of past gives the city an almost European air.

Hobart is the best place from which to explore the Tasman Peninsula and the Port Arthur Historic Site. The highway twists across the narrow Eaglehawk Neck isthmus towards the eerie penal settlement. The Tasman Arch and the extraordinary Tessellated Pavement are also worth a look along the way.

Heading north from the Tasman Peninsula, the Tasman Highway sweeps along the coast to the small crayfishing town of Bicheno. The Freycinet Peninsula is a short, worthwhile diversion from the main route and is especially popular with bushwalkers, who enjoy exploring its beaches and taking in the magnificent views.

From Bicheno, this stunning drive winds along the coastline and through towering forests. St Helens is a seaside holiday resort with good swimming beaches and excellent access to the amazing Bay of Fires and Binalong Bay. The cascading St Columba Falls are just a short drive north from the highway near Pyengana. Further west is the busy centre of Scottsdale, with a strong farming community.

☁ BEST TIME TO GO

The temperate east coast has beautiful weather during spring and autumn, but is cold in the depths of winter and warm at the height of summer. I love travelling through around February, when the weather and waters are at their chilly warmest.

DEVONPORT TO LAUNCESTON

NEED TO KNOW

	103km
	Full-featured caravan parks
	Spring, summer and autumn
	Beachside holidays, villages with quaint rural charm
	The roads are busy, by Tasmanian standards, but in good condition.
	This is a populated area with all facilities.
	None apply

Wine pairings at Joseph Chromy Wines

INTRODUCTION

The short drive from Devonport to Launceston is often travellers' first-ever glimpse of Tasmania after they've cruised down from Melbourne on the *Spirit of Tasmania*. The area features some incredible natural playgrounds and is dense with history – some of these towns are amongst the oldest in Australia. You could easily get from Devonport to Launceston in a couple of hours, but you're better off spending a couple of days or more.

WHERE TO GO

Tasmania's north-west is rich farming land and the port at **Devonport** is kept busy both exporting local produce and importing excited travellers on the *Spirit of Tasmania*. It's a regional centre with good shopping and most services, making it the ideal base from which to see northern Tasmania. Maritime and water-based pursuits are popular here, and the Bass Strait Maritime Centre is well worth a visit. If boats aren't your thing, the Don River Railway steam train runs 30 min return rides to Coles Beach, which are very popular with families in particular.

About 20km east of Devonport, the former ship-building town of **Port Sorell** is a fast-growing residential area. It's popular as a beachside holiday destination with great beaches, fishing spots and good walks.

South of Devonport, **Latrobe** is rich in history and boasts more than 80 properties classified by the National Trust. Don't miss the Courthouse Museum, which provides an overview of the history of the area's rich farming and foresting pursuits. The town is also home to the Australian Axeman's Hall of Fame as well as the House of Anvers chocolate factory which is a real indulgence just 10 min south of the ferry.

Although it's now bypassed by the highway, **Deloraine** is worth the detour. Established at a crossing over the Meander River, the whole town is National Trust–classified with many Georgian and Victorian buildings. It's also well known for the quality art and craft that is created by its residents. Nearby Mole Creek Karst National Park, is home to King Solomon Cave – one of the prettiest examples of a limestone cave in Australia.

Nearly at Launceston, after a few detours, the rural village of **Westbury** has many old buildings including Pearn's Steam World, which claims to house the best collection of agricultural steam engines in the southern hemisphere. It might not be so bold a claim, as one of Tassie's premier events is the annual Steamfest, held about 20 min away in Sheffield.

Launceston, Tasmania's second largest city, lies at the head of the lush Tamar Valley, which is renowned for its vineyards and fine foods. The city has gracious old buildings,

very good shopping and all services, making it an excellent base from which to explore the region. Do take the time to visit Cataract Gorge Reserve, just a 2 min drive from the CBD. With many walkways, exquisite parklands and the world's longest single-span chairlift, it's not exactly what you expect to find in the middle of a regional city.

The drive north along the banks of the Tamar River takes you through one of Tasmania's premium wine regions. However, the most famous town along here is probably **Beaconsfield**, for the 2006 mining disaster. Today there's a great mining heritage centre which overviews the history of the region, with special attention paid to the incredible mine rescue of Brant Webb and Todd Russell.

Across the river (which can be crossed just south of Beaconsfield) is Australia's third oldest settlement, **George Town**. Steeped in maritime heritage and colonial history, the Old Watch House Museum and Bass and Flinders Centre are both wonderful museums to visit.

DON'T MISS

→ **Horsing around – Beauty Point**
At Beauty Point, near the mouth of the Tamar, the internationally acclaimed Seahorse World allows a spectacular insight into the life and breeding cycle of seahorses. Tours operate every half hour. Entry fees apply and it's open daily 9.30am–4.30pm. Contact (03) 6383 4111.

→ Platypus watching – near Latrobe

Platypus are shy and rarely seen by people. However, the Latrobe Landcare Group operates guided tours daily at dawn and dusk in Warrawee Forest Reserve, along the Mersey River – a chance to see these entrancing creatures in their natural habitat. Fees apply and bookings are essential. Book at the Latrobe Visitor Centre, George Street – contact (03) 6426 2240.

WHERE TO STAY

481 Bay View Holiday Village

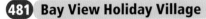

📍 2–12 North Caroline St, East Devonport
📞 (03) 6427 0499

Conveniently located just a stone's throw from the *Spirit of Tasmania* Ferry Terminal this caravan park has basic facilities and all of the sites have an ensuite.

482 Port Sorell Lions Caravan Park

📍 42 Meredith St, Port Sorell
📞 (03) 6428 7267
🖥 www.portsorellcaravanpark.com.au

This riverfront caravan park is conveniently located a short distance from the centre of town and is adjacent to the local boat ramp. It has grassy powered and unpowered sites and is very popular with young families and keen fishers. Bookings are required during peak periods.

483 Deloraine Apex Caravan Park

📍 51 West Pde, Deloraine
📞 (03) 6362 2673

Sitting on the banks of the Meander River this picturesque caravan park has a choice of grass sites or concrete slab with well-managed amenities.

484 Longford Riverside Caravan Park

📍 2a Archer St, Longford
📞 (03) 6391 1470
🖥 www.longfordriversidecaravanpark.com

Another picturesque riverside caravan park, this one has good facilities and is conveniently located within walking distance of the local shops, cafes and restaurants.

485 Old Macs Caravan & Motorhome Farmstay

📍 53 Sandown Rd, Norwood, Launceston
📞 0408 443 696

This farm-stay camping area has a lovely grassy area and is just a short walk to the excellent Stonesthrow cafe where you can get hot coffee and a cooked breakfast. It's better suited to self-contained vehicles as facilities are minimal.

486 BIG4 Kelso Sands Holiday and Native Wildlife Park

📍 86 Paranaple Rd, Kelso
📞 (03) 6383 9130
🖥 www.big4.com.au/caravan-parks/tas/launceston-north-tamar-valley/kelso-sands-holiday-park

This family-friendly caravan park is set on a large grassy area at the top of the Tamar Valley. There are lots of activities for children of all ages including a heated swimming pool, basketball court, volleyball court and go-karts. There is a good range of sites available including room for large motorhomes, and the onsite kiosk is very well stocked.

Cataract Gorge Reserve

LAUNCESTON TO HOBART

NEED TO KNOW

 200km

 Free camping areas, inexpensive caravan parks

 Spring, summer and autumn

 Colonial history and heritage buildings

 Good to great

 While Launceston and Hobart have all facilities, the communities between are small and only have basic services.

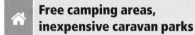 **None apply**

kunanyi/Mt Wellington in Hobart

INTRODUCTION

The Midland Highway winds through Tasmania's Midlands region, an area well known for its prime farming land and much loved for the quaint towns, great free camping areas and concentration of preserved history harking back to the rough colonial times of Tasmania's youth. Although it's the quickest route between Launceston and Hobart, you can take days to complete it if you take your time.

WHERE TO GO

Just 7km off the highway (get used to detours in Tasmania), **Evandale** is a marvellously historical town that is noted for its numerous antiques and craft shops. Every year in February it comes alive for the Penny Farthing National Championships. Many of the buildings are of architectural significance, especially in High St. Clarendon House, a grand Georgian mansion set in formal gardens and scenic parkland, lies 8km south of Evandale. It has been restored by the National Trust, which runs tours through the manor and grounds, including a ghost tour. Entry fees apply and it's open Thurs–Sun 10am–4pm, and by appointment for group bookings. Limited opening hours in winter.

Another 7km along, this time off the western side of the highway, **Longford** is another historic town, settled in 1813. Families will love the immense village green. Another must-visit, just outside town, is Woolmers Estate – Australia's oldest family-owned property. The house was built in about 1817 for the Archer family and consecutive generations of the Archer family lived here until 1994. The property has a remarkable collection of historical farm buildings, including an 1819 woolshed and convicts' chapel, antiques, vintage cars and equipment. It has recently been updated to include a modern visitor centre, gallery, restaurant and function centre. It's open daily 9.30am–4pm with guided tours at 11.15am, 12.30pm and 2pm. Reduced opening hours in winter. Entry fees apply.

Only about 40 min down the road is **Campbell Town** with its stately Red Bridge. Constructed by convicts in 1838 it still features the original stone abutments. The Elizabeth River was actually re-routed underneath the bridge once it was finished. Surrounding are some delightful parks, one of which has a series of carved wooden statues which tell the town's history. Over the river, Blackburn Park offers free 48-hour camping for self-contained travellers.

Just 11km south, and bypassed by the highway, **Ross** is a town I really love

lingering in. Classified by the National Trust, the town's four most famous landmarks stand at the one intersection – each representing what some consider the four cardinal points of life. The buildings are the Ross Female Factory a convict jail for women (damnation), a church (salvation), the Man O' Ross Hotel (temptation) and the town hall (recreation). Just up the road is the Tasmanian Wool Centre museum (free entry) and down the road is one of Australia's oldest and most beautiful bridges which spans the Macquarie River. The convict-built Ross Bridge (c. 1836) displays many fine carvings and earned pardons for two of the stonemasons responsible for the workmanship.

Tunbridge doesn't get much tourism attention, but it has Australia's oldest single-span bridge (c. 1809) and plenty of convict-built manors and buildings. One interesting building is the Blind Chapel, so called because it was built without windows on one side so parishioners couldn't witness the frivolities going on at the local pub.

Press on to **Oatlands**, which has one of the best free camping sites along the highway, in the expansive park overlooking Lake Dulverton. That's also right next door to the historic Callington Mill, which is the oldest wind-operated mill in Australia. Oatlands also has the highest number of pre-1837 buildings in Australia, several of which are prominent in the township.

On your way south to Hobart, make a quick stop in **Jericho**, which was settled in 1816 and does a fine job of imitating a quaint English village, especially the view from the cemetery over the Anglican church. Another notable town is **Bridgewater**, which was established in 1812 around a bridge crossing the Derwent River and as a military outpost to protect travellers who changed coaches here. The crossing was built by convicts in the 1830s and during construction over two million tonnes of clay and rock were moved by wheelbarrow.

Hobart is the crown jewel of Tasmania, at once proud of its pioneering, colonial heritage while revelling in its new-found modern chic. Here you can visit one of the most progressive post-modern art galleries in the world on the same day as sailing on a replica of a 200-year-old tall ship. One of

the best community markets in Australia runs every Sat morning from 8.30am–3pm at Salamanca, across the road from the harbour precinct. Here you can buy everything from the finest local produce to distinctive pieces of artwork and crafts.

Hobart is surrounded by caravan parks, most only a few minutes from the city centre, which makes it a very easy place to explore over a few days or more. I'm always reluctant to leave its charm, attractions and good cafes behind.

DON'T MISS

→ Wind power – Oatlands
The Callington Mill, built in 1837, is the oldest wind-operated mill in the country and is classified by the National Trust. The mill fell into disrepair early in the 20th century but extensive restoration work has taken place since the 1970s, which is ongoing. Although guided tours of the mill aren't available

anymore, visitors are still welcome to walk around the precinct. The Blacksmith's Forge offers 'come and try' sessions every second Sun 1–5pm – bookings essential.

→ Australian Wooden Boat Festival – Hobart
Although it only runs every 2nd Feb (in the odd-numbered years) the Australian Wooden Boat Festival is my absolute favourite thing to do in Tasmania. The event usually attracts the largest collection of wooden boats in the southern hemisphere, including tall ships, some of which sail all the way from America or England to take part. The four-day festival brings over 200,000 people to Hobart for the event and all of the caravan parks, the *Spirit of Tasmania* and much of the accommodation books out, so prepare in advance.

WHERE TO STAY

487 Campbell Town rest area

📍 Franklin St, Campbell Town

This is a popular free-camping area for people with self-contained set-ups. It's little more than a grassy paddock underneath the historic Red Bridge on the banks of the Elizabeth River. A stay of up to 48 hours is permitted.

488 Ross Caravan Park and Heritage Cabins

📍 2 High St, Ross
📞 0437 425 832
🖥 www.rosscaravanpark.com.au

Close to the centre of town on the banks of the Macquarie River and adjoining historical buildings, this small, appealing caravan park is one of the better parks in the Midlands. Bookings are required in peak seasons.

489 Lake Dulverton camping area

📍 The Esplanade, Oatlands

A large free camping area on the shore of Lake Dulverton and adjacent to the Callington Mill. These are basic sites which only provide toilets and fireplaces. A 72-hour camping limit applies.

490 Snug Beach Cabin & Caravan Park

📍 35 Beach Rd, Snug
📞 (03) 6267 9138
🖥 www.snugpark.com.au

This caravan park is located about 30km from Hobart in a small coastal community. It is a great park for a few day's break and also suitable as a base for exploring the area. It is a 10 min drive from here to the Bruny Island ferry terminal.

491 Hobart Airport Tourist Park

📍 Corner 2 Flight St and Back Rd, Cambridge
📞 1800 441 184
🖥 www.hobartairporttouristpark.com.au

A newer caravan park that's only 15 min from the centre of Hobart. It is ordered, has grassy sites with cement driveways and great facilities, which include a heated amenities block and big camp kitchen.

DEVONPORT TO SMITHTON

NEED TO KNOW

 132km

 Beachside caravan parks, free camping areas

 Spring, summer and autumn

 Fishing, beachside holidays, penguins

 Great and it follows closely along the coast.

 All major facilities are available.

 None apply

View from The Nut, Stanley

INTRODUCTION

Taking in the best of Tassie's northern coast, the Bass Highway passes through Stanley's historical buildings, the spectacular Nut, little penguins on Godfreys Beach and excellent caravan parks along the way. The road winds along the coast and Bass Strait is rarely out of sight.

WHERE TO GO

The warmer summers and sandy beaches attract holidaymakers to the bustling town of **Ulverstone** where beach and estuary fishing are popular. The town's most significant landmark is the magnificent clock tower in the centre of town. Built as a monument to the three arms of Australia's military, and on the same site as the town's original ANZAC memorial, it is a striking timepiece.

The next town west, aptly named **Penguin** is a great place to see penguins leave their nests in the morning and return again at dusk after a full day's fishing. Appropriately, the town has a 'big penguin'. Interestingly enough, it's actually the nearby town of **Burnie** which is the best place to view the return at dusk. The Little Penguin Observation Centre has a great boardwalk with bird hides so that the penguins aren't disturbed. Best of all, it's free and free guided tours are run Sep–Mar.

Wynyard is the centre of a large farming area and fishing port, and a popular base for trout fishing, especially in the Inglis and Flowerdale rivers. Trout were first introduced to Tasmanian waterways in 1864 so they now boast some of the best trout fishing in the world. Non-fishers should head to the lookout at Table Cape for exceptional views, visit the lighthouse and take a tour of the Table Cape Tulip Farm (best time is mid to late Oct).

Two things make **Stanley** significant. The Van Diemen's Land Company was established here in 1824 and settled much of the area. The company has operated continuously since then and still runs dairy farms in the area although it is now owned by a Chinese businessman. It is Australia's oldest royally-chartered company, founded during the reign of King George IV. There's also the Nut, a 143m high basalt monolith rising from the sea, which is the area's most obvious attraction. Take a chairlift to the summit (or the walking track for the more energetic) for a terrific view. From the top it is also possible to overlook a rookery for short-tailed shearwaters (muttonbirds) Nov–Apr.

The last stop on this journey is **Smithton**, a regional centre whose economy is largely based on fishing, timber, dairy farming and vegetable production. It is also the gateway to Tasmania's wild Tarkine wilderness and there are countless farm gates and eateries where you can indulge in the local produce.

DON'T MISS

→ **Steam back in time – Don**
The Don River Railway has the largest collection of steam locomotives in Tasmania, dating back to 1879. Steam-train rides operate Wed–Sun along a section of the state's oldest line between Don and Coles Beach, north of Devonport. Fares apply. Contact (03) 6424 6335.

→ **A town of murals – Sheffield**
A quirky town south of Devonport where almost every possible wall has been painted with spectacular murals depicting local scenes and snippets of the area's history. This popular attraction makes a detour to Sheffield an enjoyable experience.

→ **Van Diemen's Land Company – near Stanley**
The historical property of Highfield, north of Stanley, was home to the Van Diemen's Land Company's chief agent from 1834 to 1856. Highfield Historic Site is open to the public daily 9.30am–4.30pm (weekdays only in winter). Entry fees apply. Contact (03) 6458 1100.

WHERE TO STAY

492 BIG4 Ulverstone Holiday Park

📍 57 Water St, Ulverstone
📞 (03) 6425 2624
💻 www.big4ulverstone.com.au

This is a good-quality caravan park ideally situated close to the beach, town centre and nearby wineries. It is just 15 min from the ferry terminal and has well-sized grassy sites and clean amenities.

493 Somerset Beachside Cabin and Caravan Park

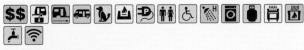

📍 115 Bass Hwy, Somerset
📞 (03) 6435 2322
💻 www.somersetbeachside.com.au

This well-maintained caravan park is the perfect base for those wishing to explore the north-west of Tassie. Sites are nice and flat, and amenities are dated but clean and tidy.

494 Leisure Ville Holiday Centre

📍 145 Old Bass Hwy, Wynyard
📞 (03) 6442 2291
💻 www.leisureville.com.au

This caravan park has nice, flat, grassy sites with good clean amenities. Ensuite sites are also available and there is a wide range of facilities onsite including an excellent cafe and a heated indoor pool.

495 Rocky Cape Tavern and Caravan Park

📍 19375 Bass Hwy, Rocky Cape
📞 (03) 6443 4110

This is a nice, flat, grassy caravan park located behind the tavern with plenty of space. Unpowered sites are free, although a small fee is charged for the use of the amenities. Powered sites are also available at a cost. The tavern provides an excellent spot for a good hot meal.

496 Stanley Cabin and Tourist Park

📍 23 Wharf Rd, Stanley
📞 (03) 6458 1266
💻 www.stanleycabinpark.com.au

Just a short stroll from the centre of town, right on the water's edge, this caravan park has nice, level, grassy sites, some with beach frontage. It has good, clean amenities with a modern camp kitchen and undercover barbecue area.

Highfield Historic Site

SOMERSET TO ROSEBERY

NEED TO KNOW

🕐	**126km**
🏠	**Free camping areas, inexpensive caravan parks, holiday resorts**
☁	**To avoid the cold, come Sept–Apr.**
👁	**Trout fishing, Cradle Mountain–Lake St Clair National Park**
🚗	**The road conditions are good, but there are steep and winding sections.**
🍴	**Once you've left Somerset, there are only basic services on this route.**
⚠	**Roads can be icy in winter.**

Cradle Mountain and Lake Dove

INTRODUCTION

The Murchison Highway winds rapidly from the coastal plain to the mountains, passing great scenery and remote mining sites. It travels close by some of Tasmania's most popular wilderness attractions, like Cradle Mountain and Montezuma Falls, offering lots of opportunities for diversions. There's great heritage to be explored at the historical mining towns along the way too.

WHERE TO GO

It's the small community of **Somerset**, west of Burnie, that has the honour of funnelling tourists onto the Murchison Highway. It's almost enveloped by Burnie's urban sprawl, but there's a popular free camping area at Cooee Point for fully self-contained vehicles which keeps many tourists in the area.

After one of the rare long drives in Tasmania (a whole hour), you'll stumble across the tiny town of **Waratah**, if you divert 7km off the highway amongst heathland and forests. It was once the world's richest tin mine, but it's now closed although the dams that used to service

the mines now provide good trout fishing. Waratah Park, in the middle of town, is a popular place for a picnic or a barbecue. Town facilities are limited, but it does have an excellent budget-price caravan park overlooking the creek that runs through town. Self-guided heritage tours of the town are a great way to take it all in – ask at the caravan park for details.

Only 17km after the intersection to Waratah, the C132 heads east to explore Cradle Mountain–Lake St Clair National Park, which is renowned for its unspoilt beauty and the richness of its plant and animal life. The park has two main focal points – Cradle Mountain in the north and Lake St Clair in the south. There are many walking tracks in the park, with grades to suit all levels of fitness, taking in temperate rainforest, waterfalls and moorland. Perhaps the most famous is the 65km Overland Track, which links the striking Cradle Mountain with the serene Lake St Clair. For those without six days to spare, the Dove Lake Circuit is an enjoyable 5.7km walk.

There is a caravan park on the northern edge of the national park. The park's day-use facilities are good but at times its popularity stretches them. Weather conditions are also

very changeable in this area and it's not uncommon to experience snowfalls in the higher areas in summer. Warm clothing is a necessity and if any walking is planned then suitable footwear is also a must.

Back on the Murchison Highway, and about 40km south of the C132, is the historic goldmining town of **Rosebery**. Gold was discovered in Rosebery Creek in 1893 followed shortly after by lead and zinc. The township developed with the mining activity that followed and mining has continued for more than 100 years. While you're passing through, check out the ghost town of **Williamsford**, about 8km south, which is also the trailhead for the 3km walk to Montezuma Falls – one of Tasmania's highest waterfalls at 104m. The gentle walk follows a disused railway track and passes through lush temperate rainforest.

DON'T MISS

→ **Steam back in time – Tullah**
Hop aboard the 1924 steam locomotive Wee Georgie Wood in the old mining town of Tullah. Until the highway passed through here in the 1960s, the locomotive was the town's connection to the outside world – the only way, apart from on foot

or horse, to reach the mining site. The train operates on the 1st Sun and last weekend of the month Oct–May. Fares apply. See www.weegeorgiewood.com.au for details.

→ **Dove Lake Circuit – Cradle Mountain**

One of the most accessible walks in Cradle Mountain–Lake St Clair National Park, the 5.7km trip circumnavigates the pretty lake which was once fed by glaciers.

Evidence of the ancient ice flow can still be seen on some of the large rocks along the shore. The famous boatshed on its shores was built in 1940 and, apart from some small maintenance in 1983, it remains largely unchanged since.

WHERE TO STAY

497 Hellyer Gorge State Reserve camping area

📍 Murchison Hay, Hellyer Gorge State Reserve, near Waratah
📞 1300 827 727

This is a quiet and unspoilt free camping area, with space on both sides of the highway and basic toilets. There's very little road noise at night due to a lack of regular traffic. Nearby there are a couple of short walks and a trout-filled stream.

Montezuma Falls near Rosebery

498 Waratah camping area

📍 Smith St, Waratah
📞 (03) 6439 7100
🖥 www.warwyn.tas.gov.au

A basic camping area on the banks of a narrow creek. Limited powered spots, but the cost includes free laundry and what's here is good. Plenty of wildlife to be seen, and trout can be caught in the creek.

499 Discovery Parks Cradle Mountain

📍 Cradle Mountain Rd, Cradle Mountain
📞 (03) 6492 1395
🖥 www.discoveryholidayparks.com.au/ caravan-parks/tasmania/cradle-mountain- cradle-mountain

Discovery HOLIDAY PARKS

Set in bushland just outside the World Heritage–listed Cradle Mountain–Lake St Clair National Park, this quality caravan park has good facilities including a large recreation building with open fireplaces. It is a popular camping site for walkers from around the world, who come to walk the renowned Overland Track to Lake St Clair. Bookings are required in peak seasons.

500 Rosebery Caravan Park

📍 1 Park Rd, Rosebery
📞 (03) 6473 1366
🖥 www.westcoastcabins.com.au

This is a small caravan park with basic facilities, but it's good for an overnight stop or a longer stay.

ROSEBERY TO DERWENT BRIDGE

NEED TO KNOW

 196km

🏠 **Free camping areas, beachside caravan parks, roadhouse campsites**

☁ **The temperatures can plummet in winter, so come when it's warmer, and when the trout are biting.**

👁 **Trout fishing, Gordon River cruises, convict history, bushwalking**

🛣 **The roads are good, but very narrow, winding and often wet or icy in winter.**

🍴 **This is a more remote part of Tasmania, so facilities are good, but basic.**

⚠ **The roads can be icy in winter.**

Cruise on Macquarie Harbour

INTRODUCTION

As the road winds through Tasmania's west it takes in remote mining towns, some of the most desolate and dangerous coastlines known to mariners and fragile wildernesses that have some of the most spectacular scenery on the island. This route passes through eucalypt forests in Franklin–Gordon Wild Rivers National Park and crosses the headwaters of the River Derwent at Derwent Bridge.

WHERE TO GO

It's a story that almost repeats itself across a lot of Tasmania – **Zeehan** became a thriving town after the discovery of silver and lead in 1882. Classified by the National Trust, the historical town is named after the ship captained by Abel Tasman on his discovery voyage in 1642. Zeehan's history is well preserved in the West Coast Heritage Centre which has over 30 displays including old trains, a replica mineral mine and courthouse. The Zeehan Bush Camp and Caravan Park is a very popular place to stay in the area with great managers who are constantly improving the facilities.

Further south, out on the coast, **Strahan** was founded in 1877 to service the area's mining settlements on Macquarie Harbour, the only safe anchorage on Tasmania's wild west coast. Huon pine was milled here for many years too. Today the picturesque waterfront village has a wide selection of tourist accommodation and a resort-style shopping centre.

Strahan is also the closest town to the former penal settlement on **Sarah Island**, the harsh conditions of which are well documented in Marcus Clarke's classic novel *For the Term of His Natural Life*. The convict settlement was established on the island in 1822 and operated until 1833. A visit to Sarah Island and its convict ruins – a historic site – is evocative and can be reached from the mainland by various boat cruises.

From Strahan, the road winds its way through the West Coast Range back to **Queenstown**. The historical town nestles at the bottom of a valley surrounded by stark mountains. Copper, silver and gold have been mined here since the 1880s with more than 20,000 kilograms of gold dug out.

It's the unique almost bare mountain landscape surrounding Queenstown that is the town's most notable feature. The hills were stripped of timber to fuel the copper smelters and subsequent erosion left the rock exposed. The naked mountains were quite spectacular, however in recent years the trees have started to regenerate.

From Queenstown to Derwent Bridge the Lyell Highway winds through thick cool-temperate rainforest. About 27km from Queenstown, plan a stop at the trailhead for Nelson Falls – it's very well signposted. One of Tasmania's best short walks takes you to the falls that cascade over a 30m drop. In times of high rainfall they are absolutely breathtaking but even when there's less flow they are serene and beautiful, so you can't lose.

Derwent Bridge is a small community 5km from the Cradle Mountain–Lake St Clair National Park Visitor Centre. The area, surrounded by forests and button-grass plains, is popular with bushwalkers and great for trout fishing. There is a roadhouse and a hotel, but other services are limited.

Sarah Island

DON'T MISS

→ **River cruises – Strahan**

A very popular trip is to cruise from Strahan across Macquarie Harbour and up the dark, tannin-stained waters of the Gordon River. Cool-temperate rainforest hugs the riverbanks where the remaining huon pines still stand majestically in the forest.

→ **Franklin–Gordon Wild Rivers National Park**

This 446,000-hectare national park forms the central portion of Tasmania's World Heritage Area. The Lyell Highway runs through the park and excellent short walks lead off the highway to rainforest, waterfalls and lookouts.

WHERE TO STAY

501 Zeehan Bush Camp and Caravan Park

📍 1 Hurst St, Zeehan
📞 (03) 6471 6633
🖥 www.zeehancaravanpark.com

This caravan park is in a lovely rural setting with lots of trees. The facilities will suit travellers passing through and bookings are required in peak periods. The campground is closed in winter.

502 Strahan Beach Tourist Park

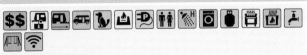

📍 1 Beach St, Strahan
📞 (03) 6471 7468
🖥 www.strahantouristpark.com.au

This is a neat caravan park that's nice and close to the beach, the town and the wharf from where Gordon River boat cruises leave. Bookings are recommended in peak periods over summer.

503 Lake Burbury camping area

📍 Off Lyell Hwy, 2.7km east of Old Royal Hotel

Ideal for self-contained travellers, this is a quiet, out-of-the-way, free camping area on the shores of Lake Burbury. Remember to take out what you take in. The unsealed and unsigned access road is suitable for most vehicles.

504 Derwent Bridge Wilderness Hotel

📍 15573 Lyell Hwy, Derwent Bridge
📞 (03) 6289 1144
🖥 www.derwentbridgewildernesshotel.com.au

This is a simple camping area behind the hotel, which has some of the best meals in the region. Basic but neat facilities are offered, making this a great stop for a night or more.

DERWENT BRIDGE TO HOBART

NEED TO KNOW

🕐	**175km**
🏠	**Free camping areas, inexpensive caravan parks, holiday resorts**
☁	**To avoid the cold, come between spring and autumn. Trout fishing is best Jan–Feb.**
👁	**Trout fishing, colonial history, skiing, hiking**
🅰	**Good to great**
🍴	**Most basic facilities and good shopping are available through here.**
⚠	**There can be ice on the roads in winter.**

Museum of Old and New Art, north of Hobart

INTRODUCTION

Linking Derwent Bridge to Hobart, the Lyell Highway continues to wind by lakes and rivers, passes power stations and visits historical towns. Along the way you can explore Tasmania's oldest national park and its favourite ski field, or do plenty of great freshwater fishing. This central region of Tasmania is steeped in history, having been settled soon after the Hobart area. There is lots to see however, the past doesn't always immediately present itself so it may be necessary to look a little harder.

WHERE TO GO

Tasmania's first hydro-electric power station was constructed in 1916 and in the more than 100 intervening years another 29 hydro-electric power stations have been added across the state network by Tasmania Hydro. Many can be found along this route. Like in **Tarraleah**, a hydro-electricity township which houses electricity commission workers and has a small commercial centre. From town you can see pipes sloping downhill to the nearby power station, where an information board helps visitors understand the magnitude of the scheme.

Another similar town is **Wayatinah**, which is serviced by a small shop, tavern and caravan park. Trout fishing is popular here and wildlife abounds, including platypus, which are a common sight along the river's edge.

Trout fishing – generally for wild brown trout, although there are populations of rainbows – is the major recreational activity in central Tasmania. There are numerous dams and lakes throughout the region and trout are found in almost every permanent stream and river. Fly fishing is extremely popular, and the season reaches its peak in Jan and Feb. You don't need to learn how to fly fish either, as trout can be taken on more common rigs using lures or specialty trout baits. If all else fails you can always use the tried and true method of showing a fishmonger your credit card.

Further on, **Ouse**, on the banks of the River Derwent, has several historical buildings, including St John the Baptist Anglican Church, with its impressive stained-glass windows – consecrated in 1867. Cawood is a two-storey Georgian stone house (1820s) and the Millbrook water mill (c. 1943) in Victoria Valley Rd is also worth a peek.

Another great historical church is St Peters Anglican church in nearby **Hamilton** – it's one of the oldest churches in Australia. It was built in 1834 at a time when Van Diemen's Land was in the Diocese of Calcutta in India. The stone church has only one door for which the popular explanation is that it was to stop any of the convict congregation escaping. The small colonial-era township on the banks of the Clyde River has many other historical buildings too, including Glen Clyde House (c. 1840s) which is now a large craft shop and gallery.

From Hamilton, the Lyell Highway passes through rich farming land – some of which was first cultivated in the early 1800s. About 12km from New Norfolk you can try the local ale and cider at the Two Metre Tall brewery. Their Farm Bar is open Fri and Sun during the season. **New Norfolk**, in the Derwent Valley, has some of Australia's oldest homes, as the town was settled in 1808, just four years after Hobart. This area is a major producer of the hops used by Australian breweries.

From New Norfolk, it's only half an hour to Hobart and all its wonderful attractions (*see* p. 279).

**Mount Field National Park –
near National Park**

Mount Field was the first national park to be declared in Tasmania, back in 1916, and it encompasses one of Tasmania's ski fields – Mt Mawson. The scenery is spectacular, with several waterfalls, including the delightful three-tier Russell Falls. Vegetation ranges from a forest of huge tree ferns and swamp gums to alpine species. The eastern barred bandicoot, nationally listed as vulnerable, is often seen here.

**Plenty of salmon –
near New Norfolk**

North of New Norfolk, take a diversion to Plenty to see the Salmon Ponds Heritage Hatchery and Gardens. This delightful fish hatchery is in a garden setting where rustic bridges cross pools like goldfish ponds amid well-tended lawns. It's a lovely place for a picnic. The hatchery, now run by the Inland Fisheries Commission, began operation in 1864, when trout and salmon ova were imported from England. There is also a fascinating Museum of Trout Fishing here. Entry fees apply and it's open daily 9am–5pm.

WHERE TO STAY

505 **Tarraleah Highland Caravan Park**

Nungina St, Tarraleah
(03) 6289 0111
www.tarraleah.com/tarraleah/tarraleah-highland-caravan-park

Open seasonally 1 Nov – 30 Apr each year this serene little caravan park has large, grassy sites and good amenities. There is a great pub within walking distance that offers hot meals and local wines.

506 **Wayatinah Lakeside Caravan Park**

131 Wayatinah Rd, Wayatinah
(03) 6289 3317
www.wayatinah.net

This lakeside caravan park is popular with keen fishers and young families. Sites are flat and grassy with plenty of space. The pool is open during the summer months and for the colder months there are a limited number of fire pits available.

507 **New Norfolk Caravan Park**

1 The Esplanade, New Norfolk
(03) 6261 1268
www.newnorfolkcp.com

Situated on the picturesque banks of the Derwent River this lovely little caravan park has flat, grassy sites, good facilities and is pet friendly.

Mt Field, Mount Field National Park

HOBART TO BICHENO VIA FREYCINET NATIONAL PARK

NEED TO KNOW

 190km

🏠 Beachside caravan parks, full-featured caravan parks, beachside free camping areas

☁ Spring, summer and autumn

👁 Fishing, surfing, walking, history

🅰 Good to great

🍴 After leaving Sorell, there are only the basic facilities available.

⚠ None apply

Coles Bay, Freycinet Peninsula

INTRODUCTION

Through the undulating hill country east of Hobart that supports picture-perfect farming land and rugged eucalypt forest the highway eventually touches the east coast, which it hugs almost all the way to the Bay of Fires. Along the way it stops in pretty coastal towns where natural, rather than historical, attractions are the highlights.

WHERE TO GO

The drive east out of Hobart is very pretty as it crosses high over the River Derwent, then low over Pitt Water via the convict-built Sorrell Causeway. **Sorell** is the last major town before reaching the east coast and has all modern services as well as a tidy little free camping area. The surrounding areas are heavily involved in fruit growing, and the Sorell Fruit Farm allows visitors to pick their own fruit, especially strawberries around Oct–Apr (seasons vary).

On the way to the coast you'll pass through **Buckland**, which has a wonderful country pub, the Ye Olde Buckland Inn (c. 1843). The historical St John the Baptist church (c. 1846) has a stunning stained-glass window which is believed to date back to the 14th century having been taken from Battle Abbey in Hastings, England. There's a quiet little camping area behind the pub if your counter lunch lasts a little longer than you anticipate.

Orford, on the coast, is a sleepy little holiday town on the estuary of the Prosser River. Scuba diving and fishing are popular with charter boats operating from the river mouth. There are some great walks around town, including to the ruins of the old Probation Station, or along the cliff-top from East Shelly to Spring beaches. The caravan park here is reasonably new, but the owners are friendly and made my family feel very welcome.

On the shores of the next bay north, **Triabunna** is a historical garrison town and whaling port. Today abalone and scallop-fishing boats operate from here, and the marina is a top place to get fresh blue mussels and scallops. According to the locals it also has Tassie's best fish and chips. Old salties might like to take a moment at the Tasmanian Seafarers Memorial, which pays tribute to Tasmanian mariners lost at sea and visiting sailors lost in Tasmanian waters.

Between Triabunna and Coles Bay, the gateway to Freycinet National Park, the road briefly leaves the coast, only to return to its edge, almost touching some of Tasmania's pristine white beaches and stunning blue waters. There's a great free camping area overlooking Mayfield Bay but it can get very busy, so plan to get there early. The exceptionally well-named, convict-built Spiky Bridge is worth a look too. Another popular holiday town through summer, **Swansea** is filled with history, heritage buildings and excellent local oysters.

While you'll have already had a glimpse of Freycinet Peninsula over Great Oyster Bay, it's best discovered by venturing past **Coles Bay**. While the peninsula's most celebrated attractions, like Wineglass Bay and Mt Amos, can only by accessed on multi-hour hikes over steep ranges, I really enjoyed the shorter walks and lesser-celebrated beaches of the park. The walk down to Honeymoon Bay is exceptionally pretty and the stony beach is a hit with kids. The self-guided interpretive boardwalk around Cape Tourville is immensely interesting too. There are a number of great camping areas in the national park, although they can get quite busy. Throughout summer and at Easter a ballot system is in place, which you must enter before Aug. A park-entry fee and camping fees apply.

Bicheno, which was a whaling and sealing port from 1803, is now a crayfishing port and holiday destination with beautiful beaches and great fishing. The town's main attraction is the nightly parade of penguins. Bicheno Penguin Tours get you right up close – my son had one waddle through his legs as he shook with excitement. It is by far one of the best wildlife experiences we've ever paid for. Find out more at www.bichenopenguintours.com.au or call (03) 6375 1333.

DON'T MISS

→ Another historic town – Richmond

The small village of Richmond is Tasmania's most important historical town. The buildings dating from the 1820s and 1830s, the quality art and craft, the quaint shopping and the selection of restaurants and eateries attract large numbers of visitors. I recommend picking up a brochure for a self-guided walk. Be sure to see the picturesque stone bridge (1823), gaol (entry fees apply) and Bridge St, which has numerous historical buildings.

→ Convicts and fossils – Maria Island

Maria Island was the site of the Darlington Penal Settlement which, dating from the 1820s, is smaller and older than Port Arthur. The gaol is the most popular attraction, but the island, now a national park, also has excellent bushwalking, mountain-biking, camping, birdwatching and fishing. There are fossil deposits at the Painted Cliffs. There are no facilities on Maria Island apart from the ferry wharf, drinking water and a public phone at Darlington, but a variety of tours can be organised, including fully catered, multi-day walks.

→ Southern adventures – beyond Hobart

While plenty of the tourist traffic flows south-east to Port Arthur from Hobart, there's some incredible scenery to the south-west too. The Tahune Airwalk is a suspended boardwalk 50m above the ground, overlooking the Huon River and Huon pine forest below. Alternatively, jump on another ferry and spend some time on Bruny Island which is crisscrossed by great bushwalks, and also offers eco-tours and excellent camping.

WHERE TO STAY

508 Sorell Self-Contained RV Stopover

♦ Montagu St, Sorell

Suitable for self-contained vehicles only, this camping area is flat and grassy with plenty of open space. There is an undercover barbecue area and it is close to the local shops and facilities.

509 Ye Olde Buckland Inn

♦ Kent St, Buckland
☏ (03) 6257 5114

This free camping area, located in the grounds behind the inn, has a nice, wide-open, grassy area with a barbecue and clean, well-maintained toilets. It's a great spot for an overnight stop after a few beers at the inn.

510 Orford Beachside Holiday Park

♦ 77 Tasman Hwy, Orford
☏ (03) 6257 1110
🖥 www.orfordholidaypark.com.au

One of Tasmania's newest caravan parks, this is a friendly, family-run site with open, grassy sites, great amenities and a good camp kitchen. It's also right across the road from the beach.

511 Swansea Beach Chalets

♦ 27 Shaw St, Swansea
☏ (03) 6257 8177
🖥 www.swanseachalets.com.au

Sit back and enjoy the peace, quiet and spectacular scenery at this picturesque waterfront site overlooking Coles Bay and Freycinet Peninsula.

512 Freycinet National Park beach camping areas

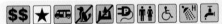

♦ Freycinet Dr, Freycinet National Park
☏ (03) 6256 7000
🖥 www.parks.tas.gov.au

These secluded beachside camping areas offer spectacular scenery, great fishing and simple amenities. A ballot system operates from 18 Dec – 10 Feb and for Easter each year.

513 Bicheno East Coast Holiday Park

♦ 4 Champ St, Bicheno
☏ (03) 6375 1999
🖥 www.bichenoholidaypark.com.au

Centrally located near the beach and shops this caravan park offers a good range of accommodation options to suit most travellers. It is a good base for those wishing to partake in the extremely popular penguin tours.

PORT ARTHUR

NEED TO KNOW

🎨	**150km**
🏠	**Holiday resorts, beachside caravan parks, private bush camping areas**
☁	**The warmer months, Sept–Apr, are the best times to visit.**
👁	**Port Arthur Historic Site, fishing, surfing, walking, history**
🅰	**Good to great**
🍴	**This is an isolated tourist area and services are generally limited to supplying tourists' needs.**
⚠	**None apply**

Cape Raoul, Tasman National Park

INTRODUCTION

Port Arthur was one of the most notorious penal settlements in the Australian colonies, the inspiration for some of Australia's best literature and also the site of one of Australia's most terrible acts of violence. So it seems unfair that it's also one of Tasmania's most stunning areas, with treacherous coastal vistas, untouched wildernesses and some excellent places to camp and explore.

WHERE TO GO

Instead of heading up the Tasman Highway from **Sorell**, head south-east to **Dunalley**, on the north side of Denison Canal which was cut through East Bay Neck in 1905. The canal connects the busy fishing village to Frederick Henry Bay, negating the need to travel all the way south around Cape Raoul and Tasman Island. It's a busy little tourist town with cafes, galleries and craft shops.

Another narrow isthmus along the way is Eaglehawk Neck, a 100m wide strip of land that links the Forestier and Tasman peninsulas. To prevent prisoners from escaping from Port Arthur a 'dog line' of fierce canines once guarded the potential escape route. The notorious bushranger Martin Cash escaped by swimming around it. A garrison was based here and the officers' quarters (1832), which is the oldest timber building in Australia, is now a museum.

It's worth the walk to the north end of Pirates Bay to see the Tessellated Pavement – the closest access is from Pirates Bay Dr. This unusual geological formation looks like a large tiled area of flat stone at the water's edge. Its origins are clearly explained on a nearby information board, just a short walk from the carpark.

At the southern end of Pirates Bay is the unique, much-photographed village of **Doo Town**. Many house names play on the word 'Doo'. The practice was allegedly started by a trio of shack owners who progressively put up signs saying Doo I, Doo Me then Doo Us. The rest is history. Names now include Doo 'n' Time, Love Me Doo and This Will Doo. The town has no shops or services, but a food van (Doolishus) often serves fresh fish and chips from the blowhole carpark.

Most people pass through Doo Town to take in the natural wonders of the Tasman Arch, Devils Kitchen and Tasman Blowhole, which are terrifying sights of the ocean's fury if a large Southern Ocean swell is running.

The legendary penal settlement at **Port Arthur** is one of Tasmania's most popular tourist attractions. It has a fascinating information centre and various cafes, but the highlight is undoubtably the Port Arthur Historic Site. The penal colony operated from 1830 to 1877 and today the old buildings showcase stories of the incredible hardships, cruelty and suffering undergone by an estimated 12,500 prisoners. Allow at least a full day to see it all. The buildings include both ruins and restored period houses. Visit the penitentiary, asylum, church and commandant's house, all set in magnificent gardens. Entry fees apply and it's open daily 9am to dusk, with nightly ghost tours as well. Contact (03) 6251 2310.

West of Port Arthur, on the shores of the picturesque Wedge Bay, **Nubeena** is the largest town on the Tasman Peninsula and lies at the centre of a farming area. It is popular for fishing and surfing at White and Roaring beaches. Coal was once mined nearby and the Coal Mines Historic Site, north of Saltwater River, preserves the ruins of sandstone buildings from the convict mine.

Port Arthur Historic Site

DON'T MISS

→ Little devils – Taranna

The Tasmanian Devil Unzoo has an interesting collection of native animals and is home to recuperating Tasmanian devils. Devils are nocturnal marsupials, voracious feeders on small animals and carrion, that are known for ferocity and aggression, however the species is at risk due to a debilitating facial cancer. The Tasman Peninsula's remote location has quarantined the local population from the disease, though, so conservation efforts here ensure the animals continued existence. Entry fees apply and it's open daily 9am–5pm. Contact 1800 641 641.

→ Giant waves – Tasman Peninsula

Shipstern Bluff is a remote rocky headland on the southern coast of the Tasman Peninsula which is widely regarded as one of the best big-wave surfing locations in the world. It's a relatively easy 8km walk from the end of Stormlea Rd, but you should allow a full day for the hike. On days of large swell, particularly swells from the south to south-south-west, surfers will travel from far and wide to pit their skill against these monsters which rise from the deep. It's an incredible sight, even from the safety of the cliff.

WHERE TO STAY

514 NRMA Port Arthur Holiday Park

📍 1 Garden Point Rd, Port Arthur
📞 (03) 6250 2340
🖥 www.nrmaparksandresorts.com.au/port-arthur

NRMA Parks + Resorts

This is a high-quality caravan park with good facilities, close to the beach. The area is popular for surfing, fishing and bushwalking and is a good base for exploring the Tasman Peninsula. Bookings are required for peak periods and a minimum-length stay applies for Easter and on long weekends.

515 White Beach Tourist Park

📍 128 White Beach Rd, White Beach
📞 (03) 6250 2142
🖥 www.whitebeachtouristpark.com.au

This popular, quality caravan park is only 10 min from Port Arthur. The park has good facilities and large, shady trees. It is very busy during holiday periods and bookings are required at these times.

516 Raoul Bay Retreat

📍 925 Stormlea Rd, Stormlea
📞 (03) 6250 2739
🖥 www.raoulbayretreat.com.au

This is a quiet, primitive camping area on private property in a rural setting. Facilities are basic for the most part, with the exception of the sauna, which is rather indulgent.

BICHENO TO LAUNCESTON

NEED TO KNOW

🎨 **232km**

🏠 **Free camping areas, inexpensive caravan parks, holiday resorts**

☁ **Spring, summer and autumn**

👁 **National parks, Binalong Bay, Bay of Fires**

🅰 **The road surface is generally fine, although it does twist and turn as it climbs the range back to Launceston.**

🍴 **Most small towns only have limited services, although St Helens has good shopping.**

⚠ **None apply**

The highway between Bicheno and St Helens

INTRODUCTION

North of Bicheno, the Tasman Highway hugs the coast, daring you not to leave, even when it eventually turns west to climb the Weldborough Pass. With only small detours you can take in the amazing coastal scenery of Binalong Bay and the Bay of Fires, before exploring the dense cool-temperate rainforests of Tassie's north-east.

WHERE TO GO

As you head north from **Bicheno**, stop in at Douglas Apsley National Park for a swim in Apsley Waterhole. The water is clear, pure and chilly, even in summer. If you've got the time and energy, the three-hour return hike to Apsley Gorge is also nice, and takes you to another of the creek's stunning waterholes. Access via the two-wheel-drive suitable, unsealed Rosedale Rd, 4km north of Bicheno.

Taking a short detour inland will take you through the quaint little town, **St Marys**. Developed when convicts cleared land and built roads during the 1830s, dairy farming and coalmining became the main industries. There's a nice little camping area just out of town, so with interesting little shops to

browse and a stately old pub, it's a pleasant place to spend a few days. Following the road north-east from town will take you across the precipitous, convict-built St Marys Pass.

If you don't veer off the highway (or even if you do, it's not far to backtrack), there's a great free camping area just north of the southern turn-off to St Marys. Lagoons Beach Conservation Area is an ideal place to rest for a few days, at virtually no expense to the fully self-sufficient traveller. Beside the beach and away from town, this is a quiet bushland area, although it is usually busy during peak holiday periods.

On the way north to Binalong Bay and the Bay of Fires, the small holiday villages of **Scamander** and **Beaumaris** are both popular seaside locations with great beaches and good fishing. Interestingly, the farms around Scamander are some of the world's largest producers of poppy flowers for use in making medicinal opiates.

As there are no caravan parks in the very pretty Binalong Bay or north, in Bay of Fires Conservation Park, only free camping areas with very limited facilities, **St Helens** is the best place to camp and still be able to explore the coastal walks and stunning beaches. Once a whaling and sealing port,

it lies on Georges Bay and is now busy with crayfish and abalone boats and popular with recreational sailors. Just north is the Bay of Fires, named for the smoke rising from Aboriginal camps seen by Captain Tobias Furneaux as he sailed past in 1773, rather than the fiery red lichen that decorates the tops of granite boulders which line the beach. The area has superb long and short walks, while the stunningly white beach of **Binalong Bay** is one of the prettiest places I've ever visited, with water that's as clear as it is cold.

The Tasman Highway winds its way back to Launceston via the Weldborough Pass, which, like so many of Tasmania's roads, is well maintained, exceptionally pretty and largely free of traffic. It passes through **Scottsdale** which is at the centre of a busy forestry region and rich farming area. There are plenty of old buildings to look at or even dine in – like Anabel's of Scottsdale. Scottsdale also hosts one of Tasmania's, and Australia's, best mountain-bike parks. The park has a huge network of trails, with rides that are suitable for nearly every level of fitness and ability, so if you travel with a mountain bike, it's worth a stop.

DON'T MISS

→ Saint Columba Falls – near Pyengana

These stunning falls cascade over a granite base and drop nearly 90m into the South George River below. The waterfall can be seen from the carpark, although it is just a short, easy walk to a closer viewing platform.

→ A sea of purple – near Scottsdale

Bridestowe Lavender Estate at Nabowla is the largest lavender farm in the southern hemsiphere, boasting 48 hectares of the exquisite purple flowers. Dec is the best month to walk amongst the vivid, perfumed display, just prior to harvest season in Jan. Visitors can also observe the processing plant and purchase a wide range of lavender products in the farm shop. Entry fees apply and it's open 9am–5pm summer and 10am–4pm winter. Contact (03) 6352 8182.

→ Classic cars – Launceston

The National Automobile Museum of Tasmania showcases a huge collection of superbly restored cars and classic motorcycles. See a 1923 Alpha Romeo, a Ferrari F40, a Bentley S3, a Rolls Royce Silver Wraith and many more. This is a fascinating visit for any car and bike enthusiasts. Entry fees apply and it's open 9am–5pm summer and 10am–4pm winter. Contact (03) 6334 8888.

WHERE TO STAY

517 Lagoons Beach camping area

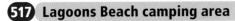

📍 Tasman Hwy, Chain of Lagoons

This large, beachside, free camping area has plenty of open space and level sites. Pit toilets are available but there are no showers or drinking water. Excellent spot for fishing off the beach.

518 Little Beach Conservation Area

📍 21020 Tasman Hwy, Chain of Lagoons

This basic bush camping area is perfect for self-contained vehicles looking to escape the crowds. Sites are nice and shady and there is excellent fishing off the beach.

519 Scamander Sanctuary Holiday Park

📍 Winifred Dr, Scamander
📞 (03) 6372 5311
🖥 www.scamandersanctuary.com.au

Surrounded by picturesque bushland just a short walk from the beach this caravan park has good, modern facilities and well-sized, private sites.

520 BIG4 St Helens Tourist Park

📍 2 Penelope St, St Helens
📞 (03) 6376 1290
🖥 www.big4sthelens.com.au

Conveniently located just 1.5km from the town centre, this well-appointed caravan park is popular with young families and keen fishers. Offering a range of accommodation options, including free-range unpowered, grassy powered and modern ensuite sites.

521 Weldborough Hotel and Campground

📍 Tasman Hwy, Weldborough
📞 (03) 6354 2223
🖥 www.weldborough.com.au

This rustic bush camping area, located behind the hotel, has wide, open, grassy spaces and basic amenities. Treat yourself to a nice hot meal at the pub or choose from the variety of craft beers available.

485 Old Macs Caravan & Motorhome Farmstay

See p. 277 – Devonport to Hobart.

5

MAKING THE MOST OF YOUR TRIP

Thinking about a caravan or motorhome holiday raises a lot of questions – especially if you are still to settle on the right recreational vehicle. Which vehicle type is right for me? Where do we start? How much time can we travel for? How much is it all going to cost? When should we, or when can we, go? If you are planning an extended trip in a caravan you need to add the following questions to your list: is the car up to the job; have we got the right towing equipment; what do we need to pack to be self-sufficient; how do we choose a caravan park that is right for us; how do we stay safe on the road?

This chapter is full of practical information to help you find the right answers to all these questions, and more, and in doing so, ensure that you have the best possible trip.

CHOOSING AND PREPARING YOUR RIG

Working out what you need can take time, research, some trial-and-error, and a bit of legwork. But getting these things right from the outset is important.

→ Which style RV is the best?

When it comes to buying a caravan or motorhome, you are spoilt for choice. There are well over 100 manufacturers of caravans, and dozens of companies that build motorhomes or campervans. Add camper trailers into the mix, and there are more than 200 different companies.

The choice between towed accommodation (caravan or camper trailer) and driven accommodation (motorhome or campervan) is a tough one, though, but if you have a close look at your needs, and the style of travel you do, then the decision

CARAVAN	MOTORHOME
Caravans are generally cheaper than motorhomes, due in part to their popularity, lack of an expensive motor and driveline. Plus, often, you already have a car to tow it with.	Even comparably featured motorhomes usually cost more than a caravan, when you consider the cost of the tow vehicle too.
Caravans and camper trailers don't need to be packed up every time you need to go to the shops or visit an attraction. They can be unhitched, set up and left at camp.	If you want to drive somewhere, you have to pack up your motorhome to do so, or travel with a small vehicle towed behind the motorhome, which adds expense.
Reversing a caravan can be daunting, and it's a skill that needs to be learned.	Motorhomes are easy to reverse, especially if they have reversing cameras.
Towing a caravan or camper precludes you from towing anything else, like a boat.	With a motorhome, you can tow recreational products, like boats, small four-wheel drives or motorbikes. If your motorhome is big enough, you can tow all three.
The articulated hitch of a trailer means the vehicle and caravan can travel out of sync – this is generally referred to as caravan sway, or snaking, and it can get out of control and cause accidents if the right precautions aren't taken	Because motorhomes are generally built on light trucks or light commercial vehicles and vans, they are not as comfortable to drive for long distances as a modern four-wheel drive or car of the same age.
Caravans can only be so big before they are too heavy for modern cars and caravans to tow.	There is almost no limit on how big a motorhome can be, provided you have the money and the licence to drive it.
Fuel economy is heavily affected by the weight and bulk (wind resistance) of a caravan.	Most modern motorhomes are very good on fuel, and use less than an equivalent-sized four-wheel drive towing a caravan.
In many cases it's not very expensive to register and insure a caravan.	Motorhome registration can be expensive, especially for larger examples.
There is a lot of work in hitching up a caravan to get ready to leave camp, when compared to a motorhome, and most of it is outside, which can be a pain in the rain.	In most motorhomes, you can walk from the driver's cabin to the living area without going outside. So in many cases you can pack-up and set up without leaving the motorhome.
If you have a breakdown, usually only one vehicle is affected, so you don't lose the use of both your transport and accommodation.	If the motorhome breaks down and has to be repaired or towed, you've lost your accommodation and transport.
You're spoilt for choice as it's a crowded market place.	The choice is more limited as there aren't as many motorhome manufacturers in Australia.
The resale value of caravans is generally very good.	Motorhomes keep excellent resale value, but not as good as caravans, as the vehicle part of the motorhome devalues faster than the accommodation part.

shouldn't be too onerous. Below are some pros and cons of 'towables' versus 'drivables'.

The biggest difference between the two is the ability to leave a caravan set up at camp while you go explore the surrounding region. It is one of the biggest reasons towables make up more than 90 per cent of recreational-vehicle purchases.

In general, caravan and motorhome manufacturers do a fine job of building a product that is well suited to a big caravan trip. However, the boom in caravan manufacturing over the last decade has seen a few opportunistic people enter the industry without understanding the product as well as they should. In my experience, these are the exception to the rule. My advice is usually to buy what's popular and what suits your budget and needs. Take your time on the decision and avoid being pressured into signing a sales contract, especially at a caravan show.

UNDERSTANDING AND EQUIPPING

Once you've chosen the right RV, remember caravans and camper trailers have to be registered separately to your vehicle, and serviced regularly. Before you set off on your trip, spend some time getting familiar with your unit and its components.

→ Servicing
Wheel bearings and brakes need regular attention on caravans. We have our wheel bearings checked every 20,000 kilometres, or annually. We carry a spare set of wheel bearings. You should also regularly check wheel-nuts, as these are prone to coming undone. Brakes are a little more complex. We have them checked for wear by our garage, but occasionally we find it necessary to visit a brake specialist. Most other service items on caravans are related to checking function and operations.

→ Power supply
Caravans are usually wired to operate on 12 volts and 240 volts. The 240-volt supply must be a plug-in-supply such as that obtained from a powered campsite or home power point. They generally require 15-amp plugs, which are not normally fitted in homes. If you do need to plug into a home

power point, you must either upgrade the socket or use an approved adaptor.

Most caravans have a 12-volt house battery fitted within them to operate the electrics. These days, most caravans are fitted with a smart charging system which can identify the best power source to charge the batteries.

Many modern motorhomes, especially the larger models, are built with on-board generators. There are also portable 240-volt generators available.

Any caravan that utilises the towing vehicle's alternator to charge house batteries should be fitted with an isolation device to ensure that the batteries can be separated when the vehicle is not running.

→ Refrigeration
The choices are the 12-volt and 240-volt compressor-style fridges or the three-way fridge, which can operate on 12 volts, 240 volts or gas. The newer models of three-way fridges are far more effective. With the improvement of battery and solar technology, more and more 12/240-volt fridges are being used in caravans.

→ Gas supply
Most RVs have gas-operated fridges, stoves, ovens and, if fitted, hot-water services. Gas is efficient, clean and quite safe and can be replenished almost anywhere. For safety always stand bottles in a vertical position.

→ Lifestyle extras
Televisions and DVD players are popular items to travel with and, for those who want reliable reception, there is the option of installing a satellite dish, or carrying a portable version. Many new caravans are being fitted with smart televisions too.

A full annex may seem like a desirable item, but if you are moving around a lot you may find that it all gets used very rarely. Awnings tend to be more useful, as they are much easier and quicker to set up.

An outdoor table setting and a couple of comfortable chairs are useful too.

Another fairly indispensable item is an outdoor stove or barbecue. It means not having to live with cooking smells.

Portable chemical toilets are used by those travelling in smaller campervans or caravans that don't have a built-in facility.

Not every caravan site is going to be perfectly flat, so you will need to carry

levelling blocks. They come in the form of shaped wedges (or you can use thick, flat board).

A pair of shaped wheel chocks is very handy for stabilising. They should be placed on the downhill side of the caravan's wheels.

TOWING EQUIPMENT AND MODIFICATIONS

Fitting towing equipment and modifying towing vehicles are specialist activities that should only be done by professionals.

→ Towing equipment
All commercially manufactured tow bars in Australia are built to a standard and should perform well. Each tow bar has a specified maximum trailer mass and a maximum static ball weight. All tow bars are restricted to the maximum recommended capacity of the towing vehicle, or the maximum capacity of the specific bar, whichever is lower. To ensure you aren't towing more than you should be, get your caravan weighed when it is fully loaded. Exceeding towing limits is dangerous, illegal and can result in fines, accidents and non-payment of insurance claims.

Tow bars can be fitted with a choice of towing hitches. Most standard caravans and trailers get by with a 50mm ball hitch, while off-road models may require a more complex off-road hitch.

All caravans and trailers must be fitted with safety chains and these must be securely attached to the towing vehicle. Although it is best practice to use rated shackles, they are not the only legal option.

→ Mirrors
Most caravans are wider than the towing vehicle, so extension mirrors should be regarded as safety equipment. If you travel a lot, avoid ones that just clip onto the existing wing mirror, as they tend to be blown back by the wind of passing trucks. Look for mirrors with an additional stabilising arm.

→ Weight distribution
Weight distribution hitches can be used to maintain a more level profile of the car and van. Distributing weight to the front wheels of the car improves braking and steering performance.

Bush camping

A weight distribution hitch is just one solution, though. It is important to keep some weight on your caravan's hitch so it pushes down on the car's tow ball; but too much or too little can be dangerous. Load your caravan so the heaviest items are near the axles and as low to the ground as possible, while medium-weight items should be forward of this point. Pack light things at the back or up high. Never tow a caravan that has no weight over the tow ball.

PLANNING YOUR TRIP

Plan carefully to make sure your holiday is as stress-free as possible, but some decisions, such as where to go next and how long to stay, are sometimes best left for the road.

TRAVELLING WITH PETS

Around 14 per cent of the population take their dogs on regular holidays. It means you don't have to worry about costly kennels, or the wellbeing of your animal while you are gone, but you will be restricted to staying at pet-friendly sites.

Travelling with a pet you will also need to consider where the animal will sleep, what it will eat and how it will cope with long periods in the car. Remember you'll have to give up activities like visits to national parks because you cannot take your animal with you and they should never be left alone in caravans or cars.

→ When to travel
Whether you are taking a week's leave or embarking on an extended tour of the continent, your first decision is when to travel. The weather, the timing of holidays and the events in the areas you visit will all influence your decision. Each touring section in this book outlines the best time to travel.

→ School and public holidays
For those without children, travelling during school holidays is best avoided, particularly during Easter, Christmas and New Year.

While the holiday periods from state to state do not align exactly, they do tend to overlap. Long weekends are a popular time to get away too.

→ Roadside assistance
Covering yourself in the event of an accident or breakdown is crucial when you will be a long way from home on a holiday and completely dependent upon your car and van or motorhome for transport and accommodation.

Many new motor vehicles, and even some caravans and motorhomes, are sold with a manufacturer's warranty that includes roadside assistance.

Such 'free' packages, though, are often limited in the service they provide. Consider taking out a premium roadside assistance service from one of the major auto clubs.

→ Insurance
The benefits of comprehensive insurance on your vehicle and caravan are obvious: the loss of some personal items from within the vehicle is covered, as is damage to the vehicle through theft, vandalism or accident. Understanding what your insurance covers is important, particularly if travelling off road.

→ Packing
Packing for a holiday is a fine art, even more so when you are contemplating several months on the road. The old adage 'less is more' is generally useful advice.

- **Food** – Do not attempt to carry enough food to last the whole trip: shop as you go. Restrictions on availability, particularly in remote areas, can force prices of fresh produce to fluctuate. One way around this is to look out for produce at roadside stalls. Remember there are restrictions on the movement of fruit and vegetables across some state borders. Cryovac packaging helps keep meat fresh for longer.

- **Cooking equipment** – Most caravans and motorhomes are equipped with a microwave oven, so a selection of microwave-safe bowls is a good investment. A few pots and pans are essential as are a kettle and toaster. Kitchen utensils should include tongs, an egg slice, a breadboard, bottle and can openers, one or two good-quality knives, a wooden spoon and an ovenproof holder. An all-purpose barbecue tool is essential. We use unbreakable crockery and drinking vessels.

- Inexpensive plastic storage containers with secure lids will come in handy.

- **Clothing** – Pack to suit your destination/s and always have something lightweight with long sleeves to wear

Off-road touring in Arnhemland

around dusk when the mosquitoes arrive. If you are planning to do any bushwalking, check out the extremely light, but very warm, clothes available at specialist outdoors stores. Sensible footwear is important too.

- **Health and safety items** – A good first-aid kit is a high priority and don't forget sunscreen and insect repellent. If you take prescription medicine, ask a doctor for enough prescriptions to last the trip.
- **Other necessary and useful items** – You will need some cleaning products and utensils as well as garbage bags, a dustpan and brush, a broom, and a universal sink plug. Don't forget all the usual toiletries and some toilet paper.
- **Hobby equipment** – I love being around the water, so I always travel with fishing rods, surfboards and often a canoe. Bikes are a great way to have fun too.

→ Communications

Whether you are on a short holiday or an extended trip, being able to contact people, and be contacted by them, may be important, or even crucial in remote areas. Mobile-phone coverage has improved significantly, and although Telstra is still the preferred option of long-term travellers many of the smaller providers are improving. With good access to the internet, the sharing of information between travellers has never been better.

Satellite phones are available for use outside the mobile networks. Although units are still expensive, prices have come down significantly, and phone plans are far more flexible. Many devices these days are just add-ons to your everyday mobile phone.

Other devices use the satellite network to send simple messages, a location breadcrumb or even a short text message.

A Citizen Band (CB) radio is a useful device for people travelling in convoys of two or more vehicles. The range is limited to around 30km or so in flat areas.

Ultra-High Frequency (UHF) CB radios, are the preferred communication method of many nomads and truck drivers on the roads. They come in handy when trying to overtake, or being overtaken by long trucks.

ON THE ROAD

Once you set out there are still plenty of things to attend to as you travel. You will have to make sure your rig is well maintained and that you're are well versed in the driving techniques needed for a safe strip. Remember that towing is more tiring than regular driving so watch out for fatigue.

→ Towing skills

If you have not towed a caravan before, you need to practise before leaving home.

- **Learn to reverse** – You will regularly need to reverse your caravan 90 degrees into a space, and often across a kerb.
- **Overtaking** – Allow adequate distance for the reduced acceleration of your rig and make allowances when veering back into your lane. When being overtaken, slow down and move left a little.
- **Avoid trailer sway** – All caravans sway and a number of things contribute. Crosswinds can be a problem and the combination of high speed and crosswinds can dangerously destabilise both vehicle and caravan. The best solution is to slow the caravan down by applying the manual override on your trailer brakes, or by having an anti-sway device fitted.
- **Be courteous to other drivers** – If you desire to travel at a slower speed, you should regularly let the traffic pass.
- **Allow for extra weight** – Towing a van will make the acceleration and braking of your vehicle much slower.

→ Fuel

In remote regions you will have to consider the distances between the lonely highway roadhouses, smaller townships and

Aboriginal communities. More than once we have turned up expecting to get fuel, only to find it's closed or out of fuel.

Fuel should only be carried in an approved fuel container, which must never be stored inside the vehicle.

Remember, your vehicle will use a lot more fuel when towing.

→ Daily checks and chores
Daily checks, regular maintenance, careful packing and ensuring you are informed on the conditions ahead can prevent unwelcome incidents. Limit the items carried in the passenger compartment to necessities and secure heavier items in the boot. A safety barrier or net will protect passengers from flying luggage in an accident.

→ Checklist
Organise a checklist of what to do when packing up and taking off.

→ Roadside maintenance
If you take your vehicle and caravan to a mechanic for a full service on a regular basis, you will probably be able to carry out basic maintenance on your rig yourself. These basic tasks should keep things in order:
- Check the oil level
- Check the coolant level
- Clean the windscreen and fill the washer bottle
- Ensure the lights are working after the van is hitched
- In diesel vehicles, look for sediment or water in glass-bowl type filters
- Examine the tow hitch after a short distance

Once a week you will need to check:
- Brakes and brake operation on both the van and vehicle
- For damp spots, leaks or loose fittings beneath the vehicle
- Brake and clutch (or automatic transmission) fluids
- Tyre pressure when cold

Every 5000km or so you should also check the tread on your tyres for uneven or unusual wear and the tyre walls for damage.

→ Tyre pressure
When it comes to basic vehicle maintenance, tyre pressure is one thing that causes particular confusion. The tyre placard on your vehicle is for normal loading however, the amount of pressure should be calculated according to the amount of weight being borne by that tyre. The manufacturer of your tyre should be able to provide you with a chart (usually on its website). Generally the greater the load on the tyre, the greater the tyre pressure required.

Similarly, recommended tyre pressures are stamped on your caravan's VIN plate but you have to take into account the laden weight.

If you are travelling on gravel roads it is a good idea to let some air out of your tyres. Doing this improves the cushioning effect of the tyre, which reduces the stress rough roads put on your caravan and may reduce the likelihood of punctures.

Reducing tyre pressure can also help improve traction on low-traction surfaces like sand, mud, wet grass, snow or even up steep, gravelly hills. If you become bogged, your first port of call should be to reduce the pressure in all your tyres. Carry a tyre gauge and a portable compressor to inflate them again once you are on firmer ground.

→ Free camping
Many people choose to stay in caravan parks, but there is an increasing trend to freedom camping. This has been a contentious issue for the caravan-park industry, which feels it's losing business when campers stay for free in nearby reserves.

I always camp in the best spot. Sometimes that's an expensive holiday resort, other times a national park campsite, or a flat patch of gravel on the side of the road. I have included a number of really great free campsites in this book where I believe they are the best place to camp in the region.

If you can free camp, ensure you do so in a responsible manner, and only in areas where it is permitted.

Camping in the Snowy Mountains

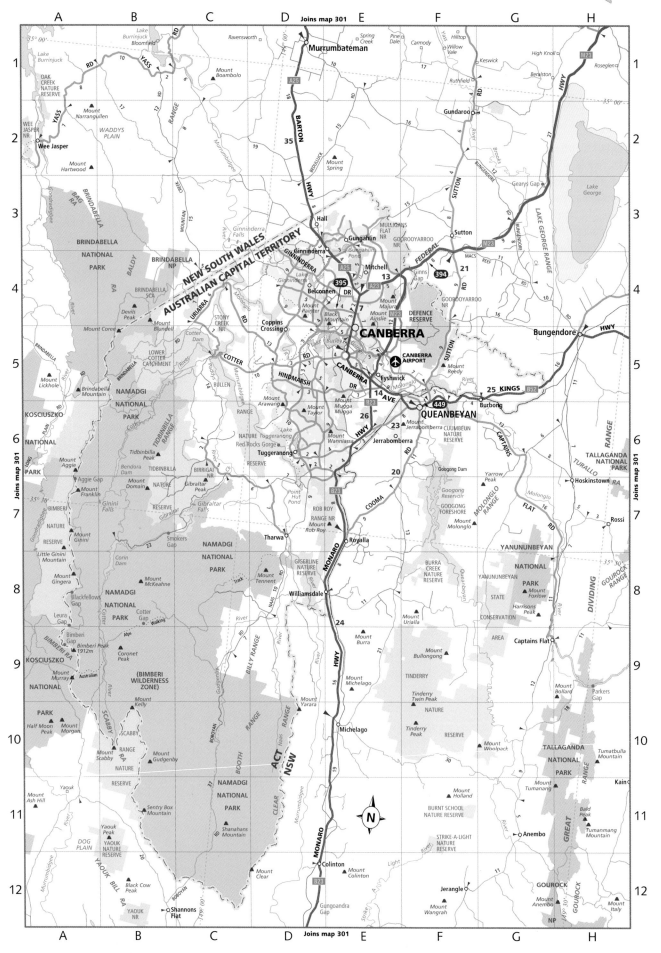

Joins map 301

Joins map 301

Joins map 301

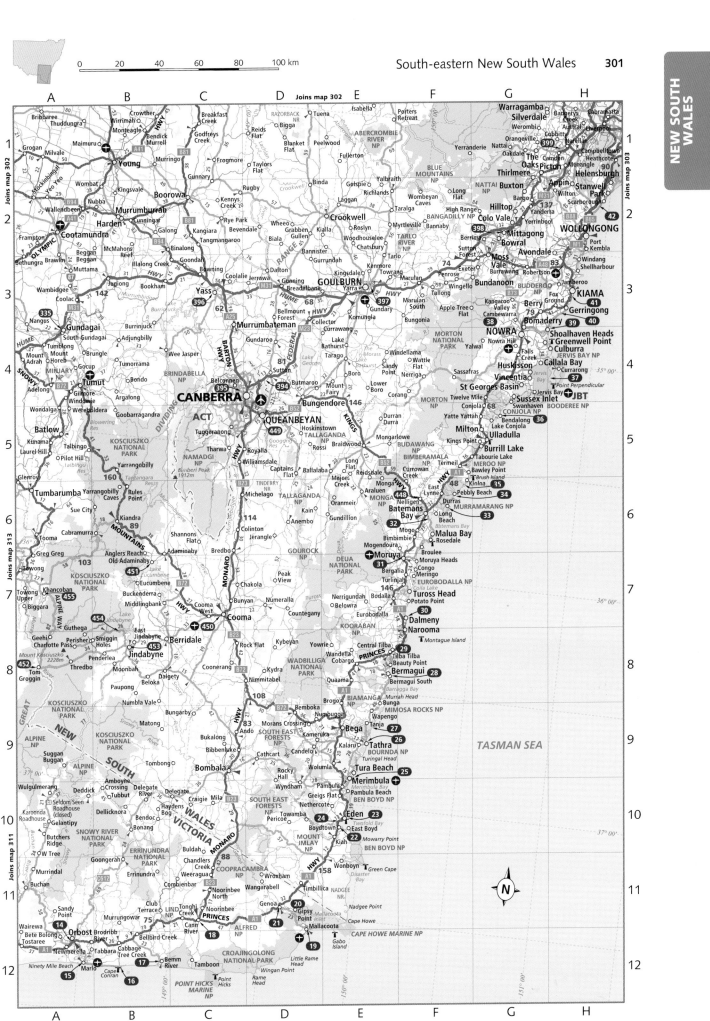

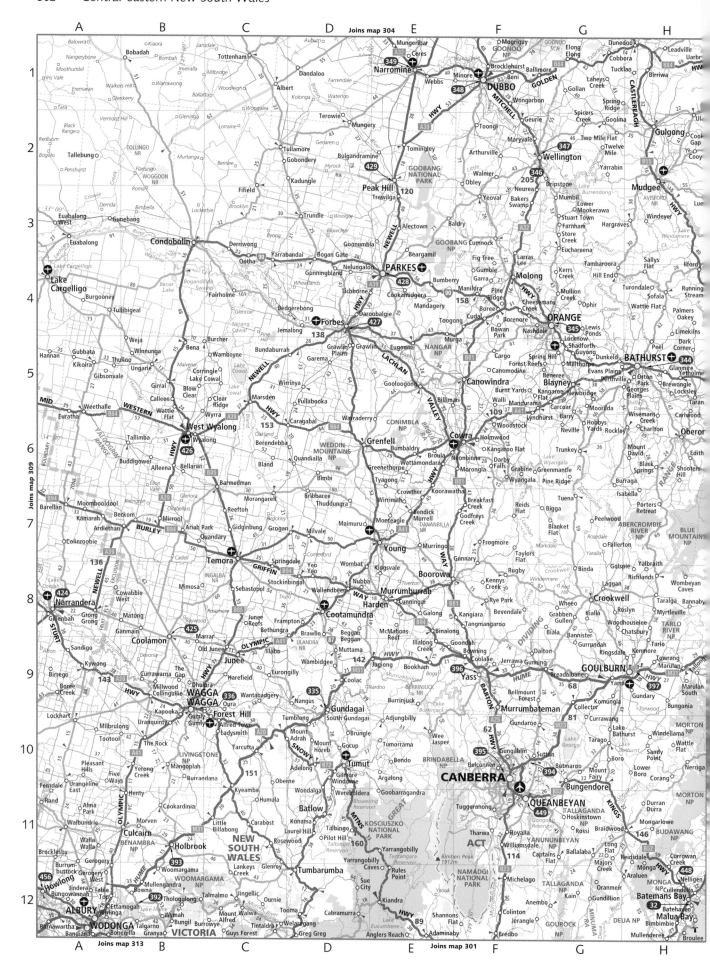

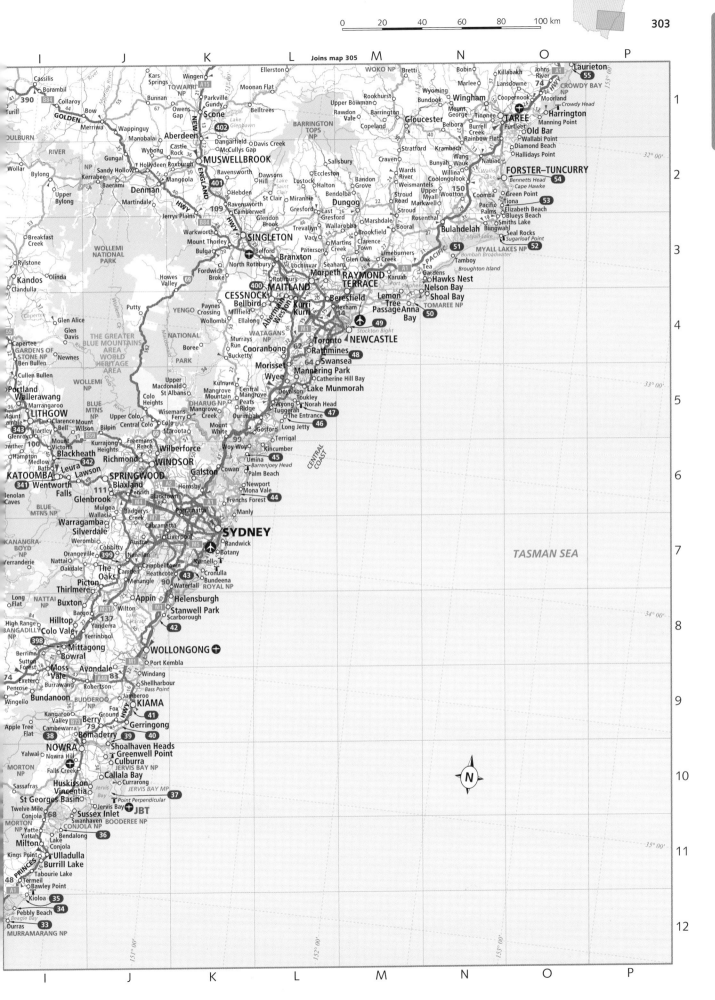

0   20   40   60   80   100 km

Joins map 305

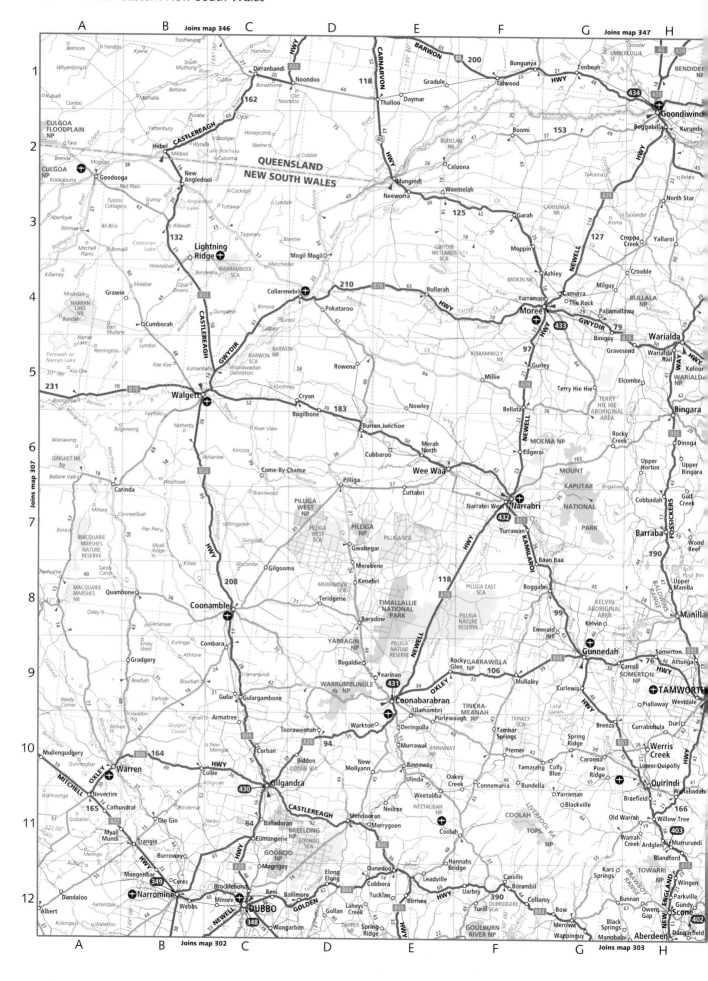

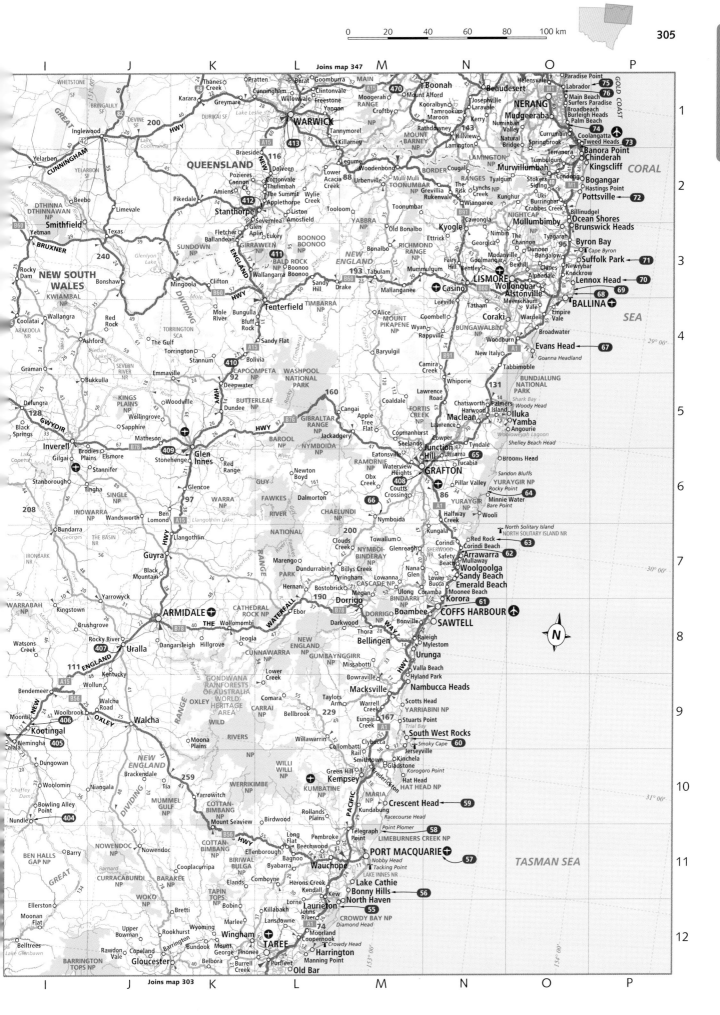

Joins map 347

Joins map 303

0 20 40 60 80 100 km

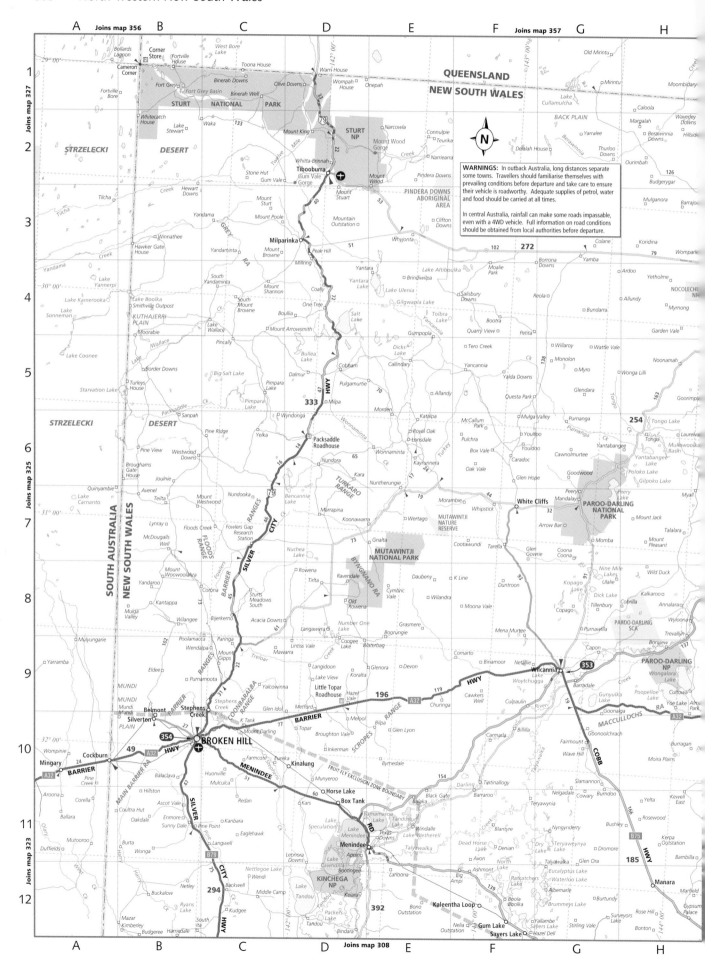

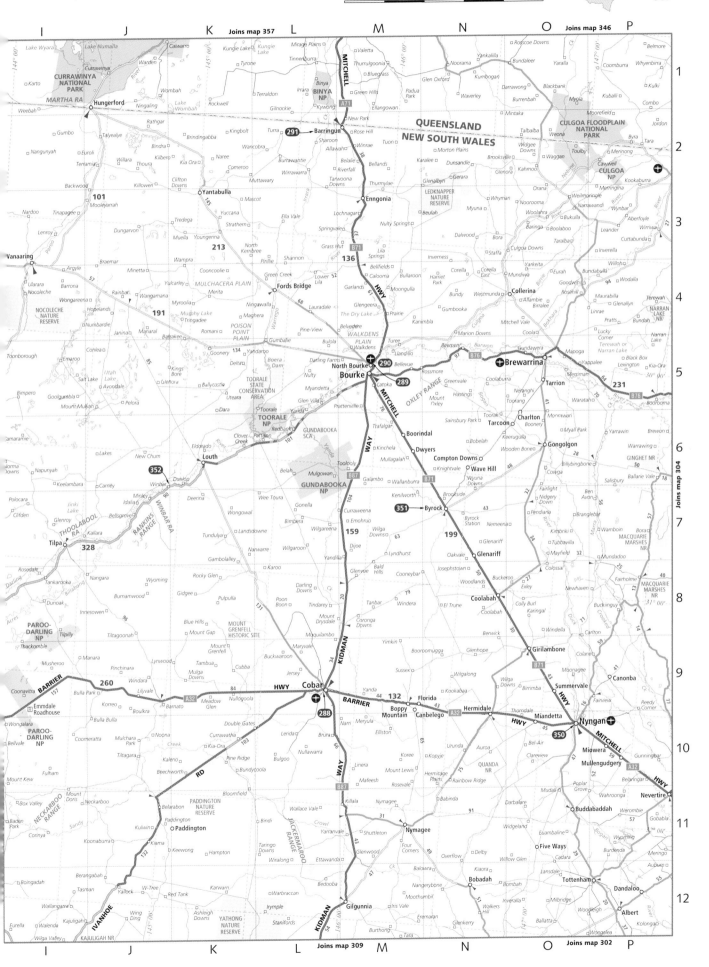

0 20 40 60 80 100 km

Joins map 357
Joins map 346
Joins map 304
Joins map 309
Joins map 302

I J K L M N O P

1
2
3
4
5
6
7
8
9
10
11
12

QUEENSLAND
NEW SOUTH WALES

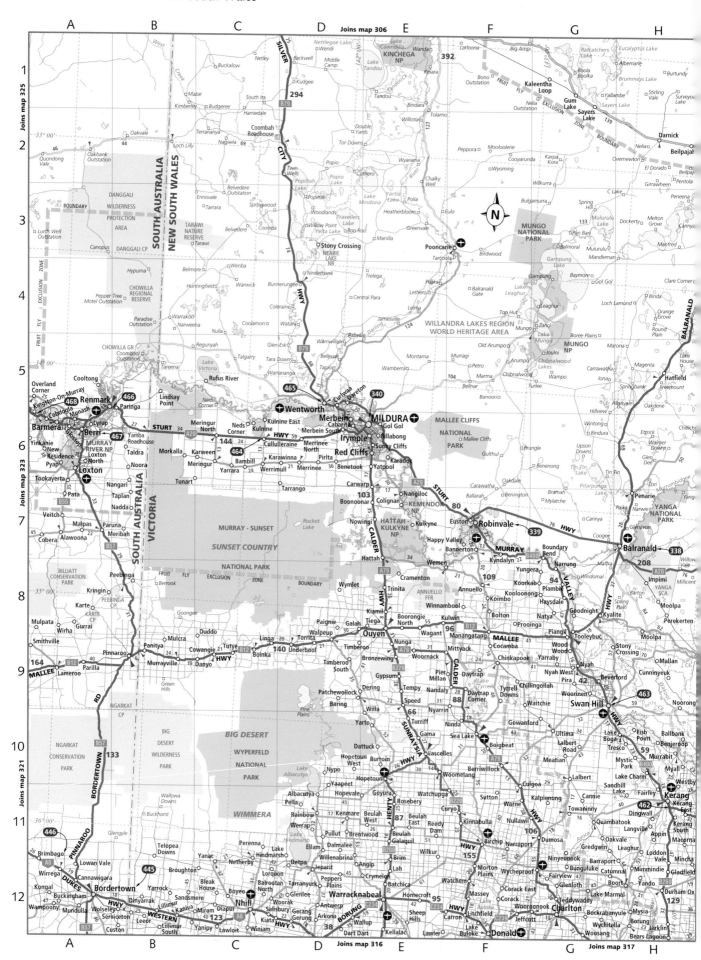

Joins map 306
Joins map 325
Joins map 323
Joins map 321
Joins map 316
Joins map 317

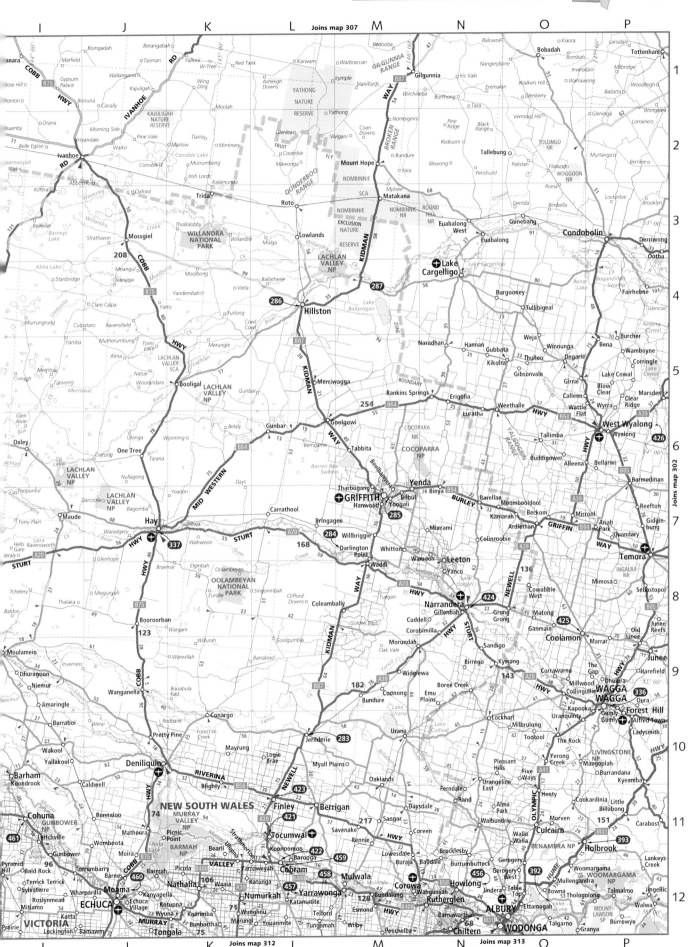

Joins map 307

Joins map 312

Joins map 313

Joins map 302

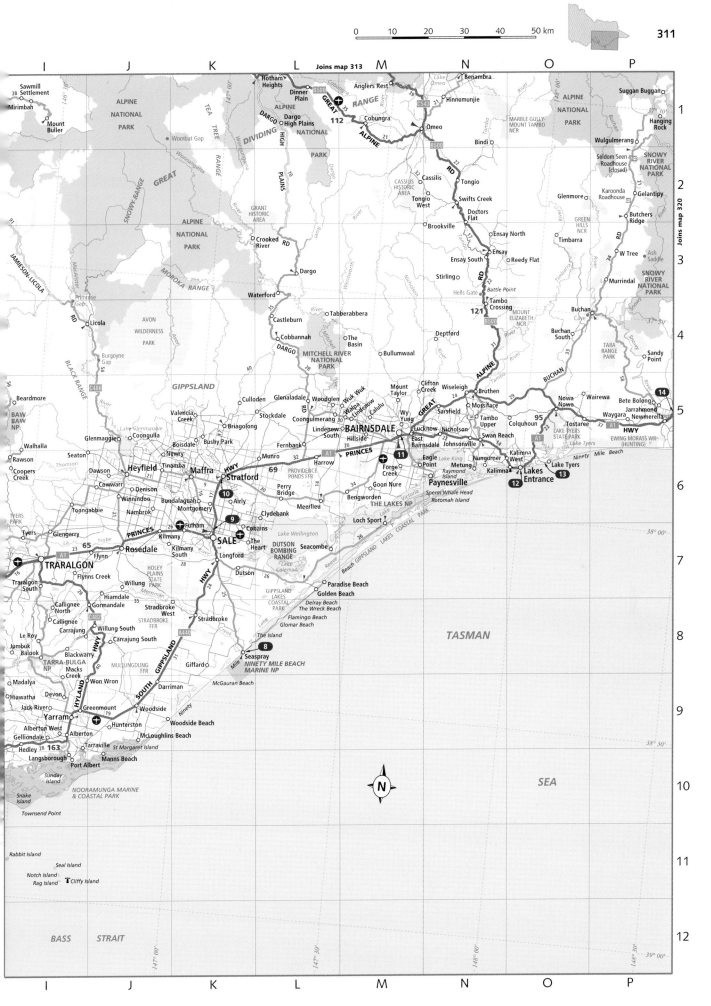

VICTORIA

Map labels

Grid reference 1 (I–P)

Sawmill Settlement 28 · Mirimbah · Mount Buller · ALPINE NATIONAL PARK · Wombat Gap · GREAT DIVIDING RANGE · TEA TREE RANGE · Hotham Heights · Dinner Plain · B500 · Dargo High Plains · DARGO HIGH PLAINS · ALPINE NATIONAL PARK · Anglers Rest · RANGE · 35 · 112 · GREAT · ALPINE · 39 · Cobungra · Lake Omeo · Benambra · C543 · 21 · Hinnomunjie · Omeo · B500 · ALPINE NATIONAL PARK · Suggan Buggan · Hanging Rock · Wulgulmerang · SNOWY RIVER NATIONAL PARK · 37° 30'

Grid reference 2

SNOWY RANGE · GREAT RANGE · ALPINE NATIONAL PARK · GRANT HISTORIC AREA · Wonnangatta · Wongungarra · PLAINS · 70 · Dargo · CASSIUS HISTORIC AREA · RD · Cassilis · Tongio West · Tongio · Swifts Creek · Doctors Flat · MARBLE GULLY-MOUNT TAMBO NCR · Glenmore · Karoonda Roadhouse · Timbarra · Gelantipy · 21 · Seldom Seen Roadhouse (closed) · Butchers Ridge · RD · 34 · W Tree · Ash Saddle

Grid reference 3

91 · JAMIESON-LICOLA · RD · Primrose Gap · MOROKA RANGE · AVON WILDERNESS PARK · Crooked River · RD · Brookville · Ensay North · Ensay · Ensay South · Reedy Flat · Stirling · RD · 72 · Battle Point · Murrindal · SNOWY RIVER NATIONAL PARK · 37° 30'

Grid reference 4

Licola · Burgoyne Gap 54 · BLACK RANGE · River · Waterford · Castleburn · 35 · Cobbannah · DARGO · The Basin · River · Tabberabbera · MITCHELL RIVER NATIONAL PARK · 28 · Bullumwaal · Deptford · Hells Gate · 121 · B500 · Tambo Crossing · MOUNT ELIZABETH NCR · Buchan · Buchan Caves · Buchan South · TARA RANGE PARK · Sandy Point · 23

Grid reference 5

56 · Beardmore · BAW BAW NP · C486 · River · GIPPSLAND · Culloden · Glenaladale · RD · Woodglen · Wuk Wuk · Walpa · Lindenow · Calulu · Mount Taylor · Clifton Creek · Wiseleigh · Sarsfield · Mossiface · Bruthen · 24 · GREAT · Tambo Upper · 29 · 95 · Colquhoun · Nowa Nowa · Wairewa · Tostaree · 37 · A1 · HWY · Bete Bolong · Jarrahmond · Waygara · Newmerella · 14 · Stockdale · Valencia Creek · Briagolong · Lindenow South · BAIRNSDALE · Wy Yung · Lucknow · East Bairnsdale · Nicholson · Johnsonville · Swan Reach · LAKE TYERS STATE PARK · A1 · Lake Tyers · Ninety Mile Beach · EWING MORASS WR (HUNTING)

Grid reference 6

Walhalla · Rawson · Coopers Creek · Glenmaggie · Lake Glenmaggie · Coongulla · Boisdale · Bushy Park · Newry · Tinamba · Maffra · Stratford · HWY · 69 · Fernbank · Munro · 32 · A1 · Harrow · PRINCES · Hillside · 20 · Providence Ponds FFR · Perry Bridge · Goon Nure · Forge Creek · PAYNESVILLE · Eagle Point · Metung · Raymond Island · Nungurner · Kalimna West · Kalimna · Lakes Entrance · 12 · 13 · Seaton · Heyfield · 21 · Dawson · Cowwarr · Denison · Winnindoo · Nambrok · Bundalaguah · Montgomery · 9 · Fulham · 26 · SALE · Airly · 10 · Clydebank · Meerlieu · Bengworden · THE LAKES NP · Lake King · Sperm Whale Head · Rotomah Island · 11 · Thomson · La · Trobe · River

Grid reference 7

Tyers · Glengarry · 65 · A1 · TRARALGON · Traralgon South · 28 · Flynns Creek · Hiamdale · Willung · HOLEY PLAINS STATE PARK · Merriman Creek · PRINCES · Rosedale · Flynn · Kilmany · Kilmany South · Fulham · 26 · Longford · The Heart · Dutson · 28 · HWY · 24 · DUTSON BOMBING RANGE · Lake Coleman · Seacombe · Reeve · Beach · Lake Wellington · 26 · Lake Victoria · 38° 00'

Grid reference 8

Callignee North · Gormandale · Callignee · C482 · Carrajung · Willung South · Stradbroke West · Carrajung South · Stradbroke · STRADBROKE FFR · A440 · 31 · MULLUNGDUNG FFR · Giffard · Seaspray · 8 · The Island · Glomar Beach · The Wreck Beach · Flamingo Beach · Delray Beach · Paradise Beach · Golden Beach · GIPPSLAND LAKES COASTAL PARK · NINETY MILE BEACH MARINE NP · TASMAN

Grid reference 9

Le Roy · Jumbuk · Balook · Blackwarry · TARRA-BULGA NP · HYLAND · HWY · Macks Creek · Madalya · Devon · Won Wron · Hiawatha · Jack River · Darriman · McGauran Beach · Ninety · Mile · Woodside · SOUTH · GIPPSLAND · 40 · Greenmount · 19 · Yarram · Hunterston · Woodside Beach · McLoughlins Beach · 38° 30'

Grid reference 10

Alberton West · Gelliondale · Hedley · 28 · 163 · Langsborough · Tarraville · Alberton · St Margaret Island · Manns Beach · Port Albert · Sunday Island · NOORAMUNGA MARINE & COASTAL PARK · Snake Island · Townsend Point · N · SEA

Grid reference 11

Rabbit Island · Seal Island · Notch Island · Rag Island · Cliffy Island

Grid reference 12

BASS STRAIT · 39° 00'

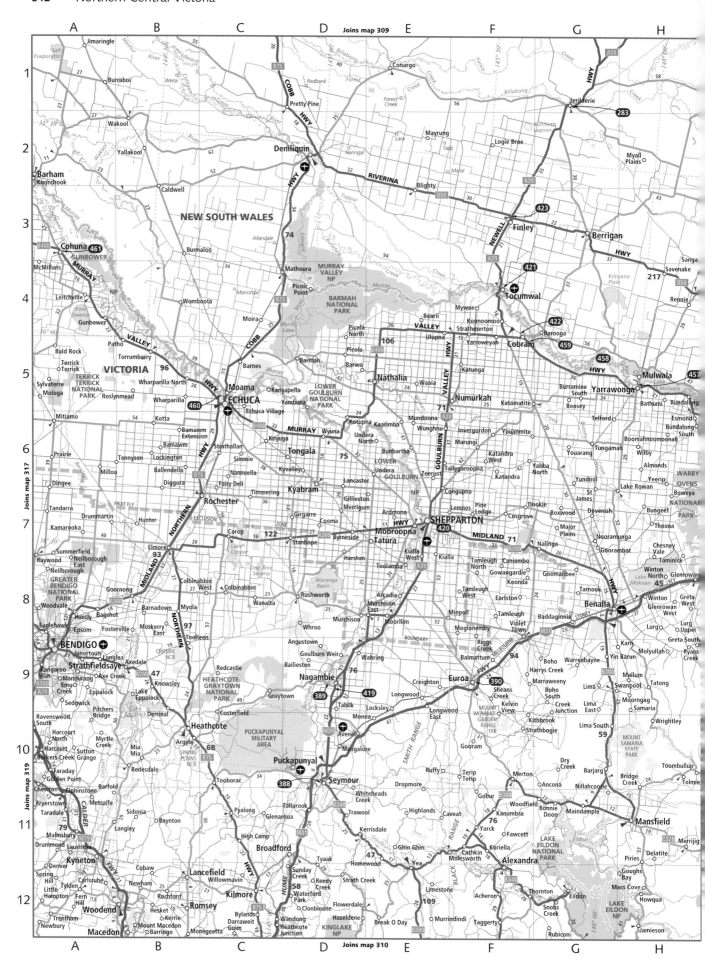

Joins map 309
Joins map 310
Joins map 317
Joins map 319

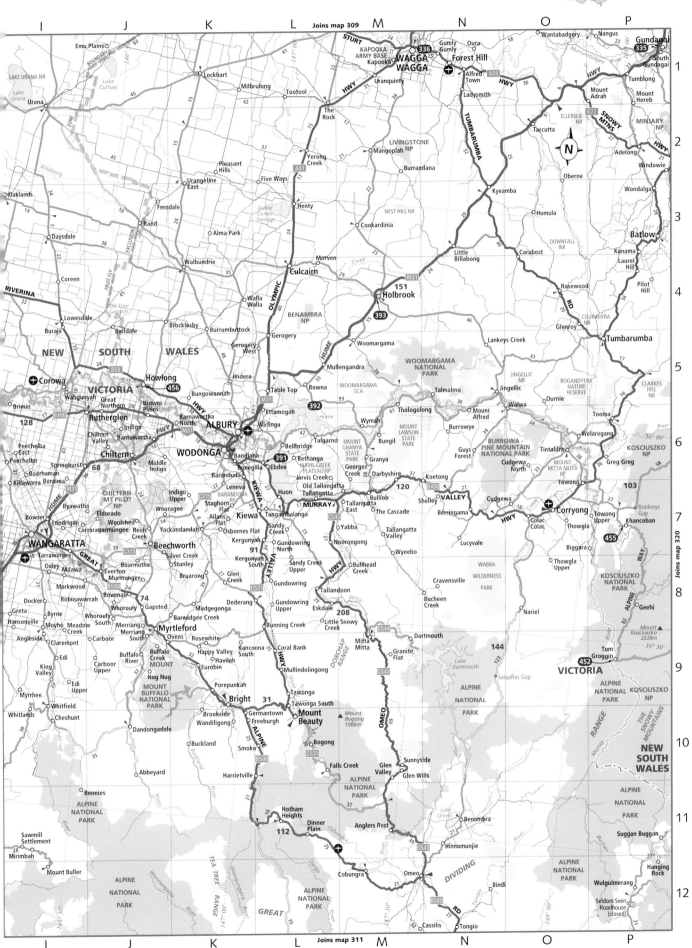

VICTORIA

Joins map 320

NEW SOUTH WALES

VICTORIA

0   10   20   30   40   50 km

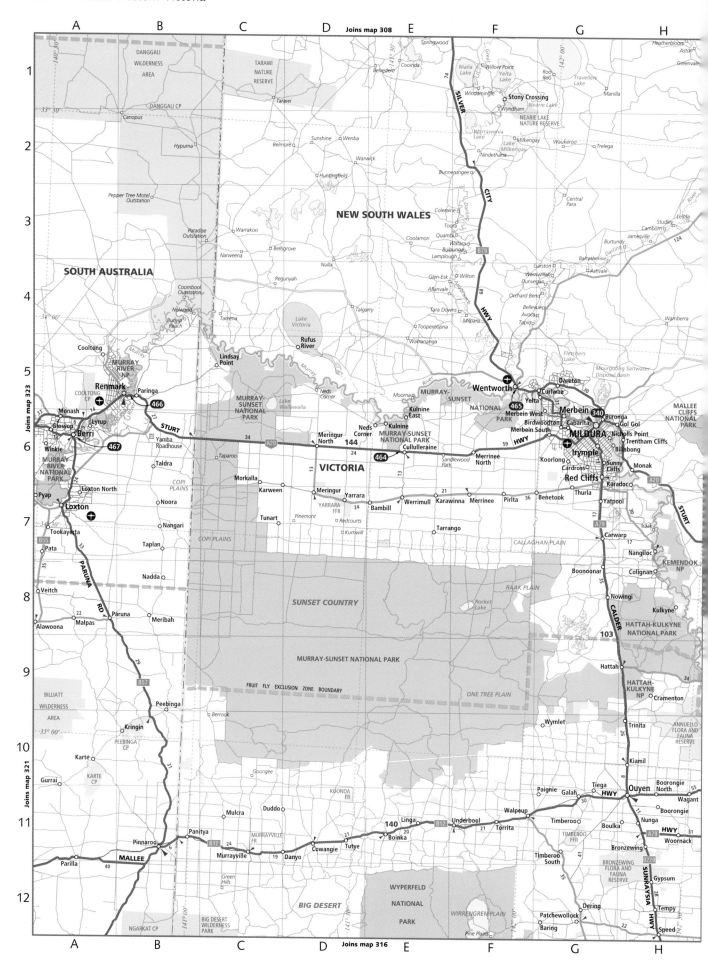

Joins map 308

Joins map 323

Joins map 321

Joins map 316

NEW SOUTH WALES

SOUTH AUSTRALIA

VICTORIA

MALLEE

BIG DESERT

SUNSET COUNTRY

MURRAY-SUNSET NATIONAL PARK

WYPERFELD NATIONAL PARK

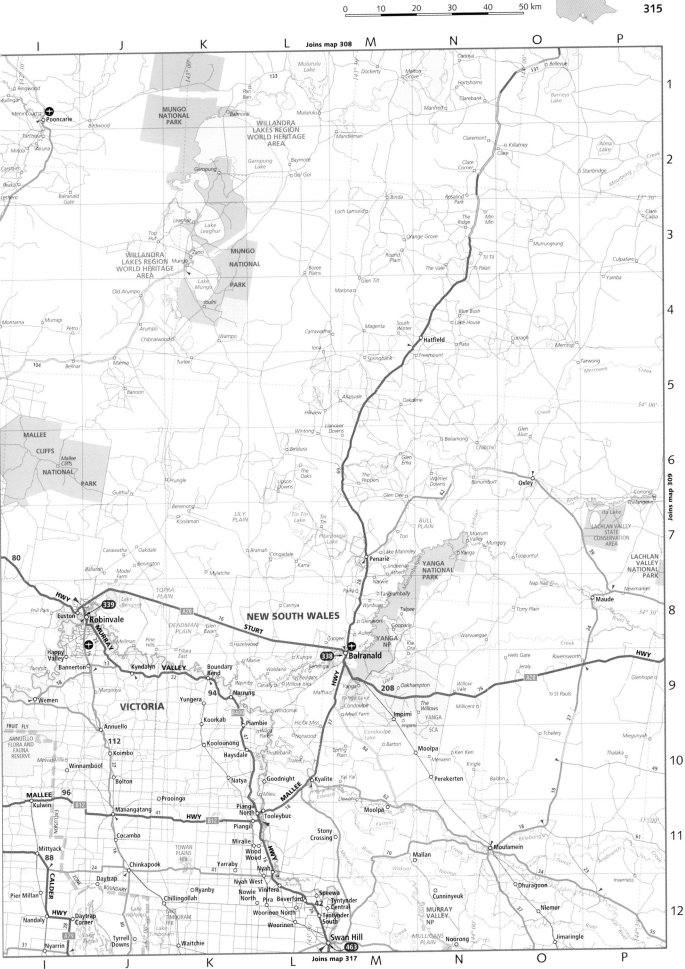

VICTORIA

0 10 20 30 40 50 km

I J K L M N O P

1

Ringwood
Pooncarie
Mehintourt
Tarcoola
Akuna
Minda
Carstairs
Peaka
Lethero
Balranald Gate

MUNGO NATIONAL PARK
Birdwood
Balmoral

WILLANDRA LAKES REGION WORLD HERITAGE AREA

Mulurulu Lake
133
Pan Ban
Mulurulu
Dockerty
Carinya
Malton Grove
Bellevue
131

Hartshorns
Clarebank
Manfred
Barneys Lake

2

Garnpung Lake
Garnpung
Baymore
Gol Gol
Binda
Rosaling Park
Claremont
Clare
Killatney
Stanbridge
Alma Lake
Creek

3

Leaghur
Lake Leaghur
Top Hut
Zanci
Mungo

WILLANDRA LAKES REGION WORLD HERITAGE AREA

MUNGO NATIONAL PARK

Lake Mungo
Joulni
Old Arumpo

Loch Lamond
Orange Grove
Round Plain
The Vale
Glen Tilt

Clare Corner
The Ridge
Min Min
Til Til
Palari
Murrungrung
Culpataro
Yamba

4

Montarna
Murragi
Petro
Arumpo
Chibnalwood
Wampo
Turlee

Carrawatha
Iona
Magenta
South Winter
Springbank

Hatfield
Riata
Freemount
Blue Bush
Lake House
Curragh
Merritop
Tarwong
Merrowie
Creek

5

104
Bellnar
Marma
Banoon

Alianvale
Hilview
Oakdene

Creek

6

MALLEE CLIFFS
Mallee Cliffs
NATIONAL PARK

Prungle
Benenong
Gulthul

Wintong
Llanover Downs
Bindura
The Oaks
Upson Downs
Glen Dee
Glen Emu
The Peppers
Bok
Walmer Downs
Beliamong
Chillichil
Bunumburt
Glen Alvic
Oxley
Corrong
Thelangerin
River
Ita Lake

7

Carawatha
Oakdale
Benington
Koolaman
Ballarah
Model Farm

LILY PLAIN
Tin Tin Lake
Pitarribonga Lake
Bramah
Cringadale
Karra

BULL PLAIN
Tori
Murrum Valley
Mungery
Toopuntul
Nap Nap

LACHLAN VALLEY STATE CONSERVATION AREA

LACHLAN VALLEY NATIONAL PARK
Newmarket

80

HWY
339
A20
Euston
Robinvale
Prill Park

TOPRA PLAIN
Lake Benanee
DEADMAN PLAIN
Glen Ewan
76
STURT

NEW SOUTH WALES

Lake Marimley
Penarie
Jindeena
Athern
Yanga

YANGA NATIONAL PARK

Maude
8

Happy Valley
Tammit
Bannerton
MURRAY
16
13
VALLEY
Kyndalyn
22
Boundary Bend
Narwie
Paika
Tangarambally
Wynburn
Talpee
Torry Plain
Warwaegae
River
HWY

Meilman
Pine Hills
Tillara East
Hazelwood
Googeel
Auler

YANGA NP
Kia Ora
Hells Gate
Ravensworth
Jeraly
Glenhope
A20
9

Murray
18
Margooya
Wemen
94
Yungera
Narrung
Weimby
Manie
Waldaira
Canally
Willow Isles
Reddate
Bendingal
Balranald
338
208
Yanga
Oakhampton
Willow Vale
76
St Pauls
27

VICTORIA
Annuello
112
Koimbo
Winnambool
Bolton
8400
Koorkab
Piambie
Wilga Park
Norwood
Kooloonong
Haysdale
47
Thistlebank
Tralee
Hit Or Miss
Windomal
Maffra
37
Yanga Lake
Condoulpe
Myall Farm
Spring Plain
Barton
The Willows
Millicent
YANGA SCA
Moolpa
Merwein
Keri Keri
Kingle
Baldon
Tchelery
Miegunyah
Thalaka
10

FRUIT FLY
ANNUELLO FLORA AND FAUNA RESERVE

Natya
Goodnight
Kyalite
Yal Yal
Perekerten

Condoulpe Lake

Llewah

Mileu
MALLEE
Moolpa
Edward
62
River
Yarrein

11

MALLEE
96
Kulwin
812
EXCLUSION
ZONE
Mittyack
88
CALDER
Prooinga
Manangatang
41
HWY
B12
Piangil North
Tooleybuc
Piangil
Miralie
Stony Crossing
Mallan
Moulamein
Inverness
18
34
61
23
Biliabong
Forest

12

HWY
Pier Millan
Nandaly
Daytrap Corner
A79
28
31
Nyarrin

TOWAN PLAINS FFR
Cocamba
Chinkapook
Daytrap
ZONE BOUNDARY
Yarraby
Wood Wood
Nyah
Nyah West
Vinifera
Nowie North
Pira
Beverford
Speewa
Tyntynder Central
Tyntynder South
42
Woorinen North
Woorinen
Woorinen South

Ryanby
Chillingollah
Murrabit
River
MURRAY VALLEY NP

Dhuragoon
Niemur
Cunninyeuk
Noorong
Jimaringle
55

Pier Millan
Tyrrell Downs
Waitchie
Lake Timboram FFR

Swan Hill
463

MULLIGANS PLAIN
River

Joins map 309

I J K L M N O P

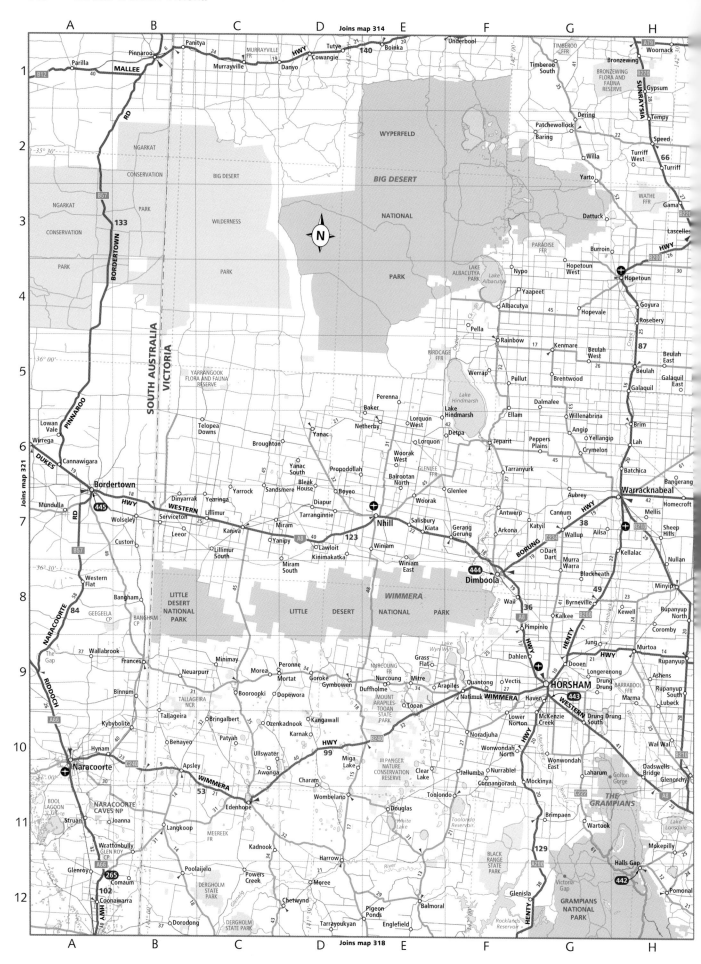

Joins map 314

Joins map 321

Joins map 318

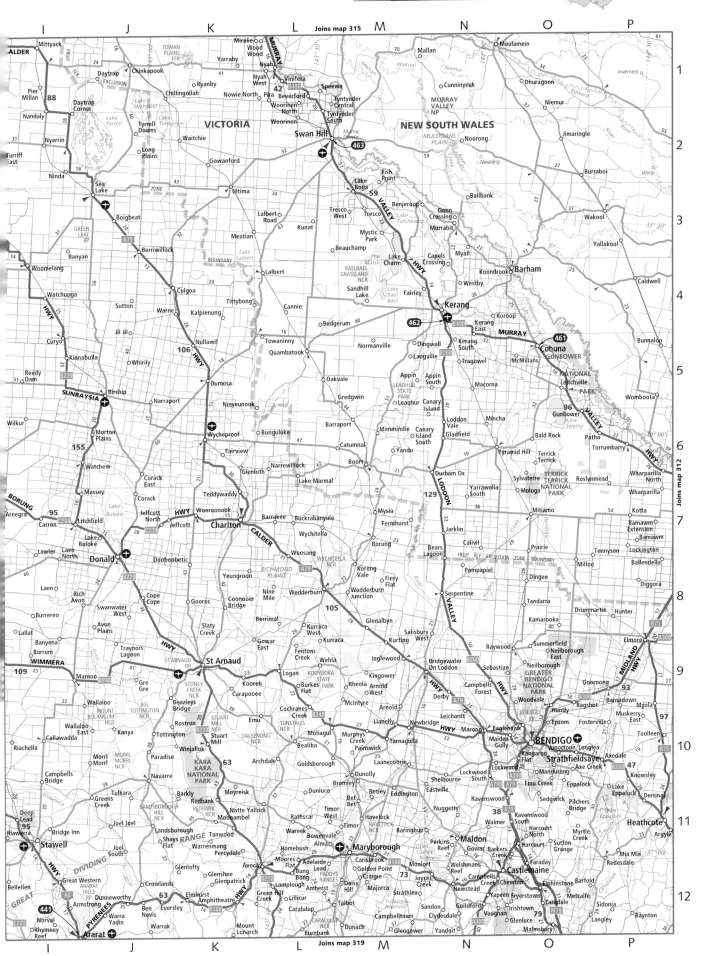

VICTORIA

Joins map 312

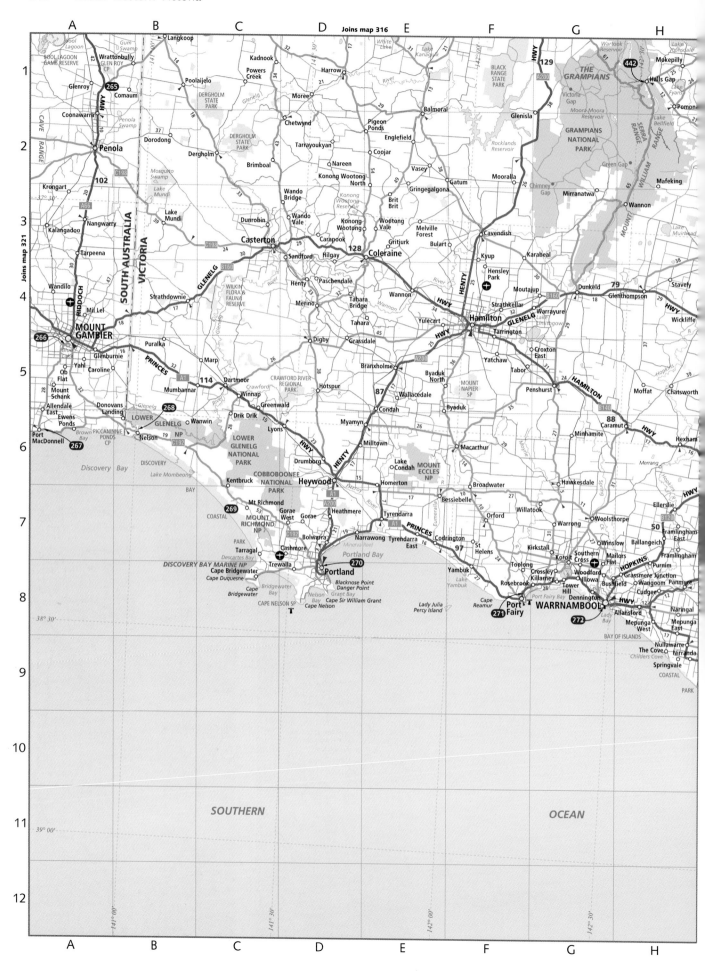

A B C D E F G H

1

Bool Lagoon Game Reserve
BOOL LAGOON GAME RESERVE
Gum Swamp
Langkoop
Wrattonbully
GLEN ROY CP
265
HWY
129
A200
THE GRAMPIANS
Wartook Reservoir
442
Halls Gap
Mokepilly
Kadnook
Powers Creek
Harrow
White Lake
Lake Kanagulk
River

Glenroy
Comaum
Poolaijelo
Moree
Pigeon Ponds
Balmoral
Glenisla
Victoria Gap
Moora-Moora Reservoir
Pomonal

2

CAVE RANGE
Coonawarra
Penola
Penola Swamp
Dorodong
DERGHOLM STATE PARK
Chetwynd
Tarrayoukyan
Konong Wootong North
Nareen
Coojar
Vasey
Gatum
Gringegalgona
Mooralla
Rocklands Reservoir
Chimney Gap
Green Gap
GRAMPIANS NATIONAL PARK
Mirranatwa
SERRA RANGE
WILLIAM RANGE
Mafeking

Krongart
102
A66
Dergholm
Brimboal
Konong Wootong
Konong Wootong Reservoir
Brit Brit
Lake Mundi
Wando Bridge
Wando Vale
Wootong Vale
Melville Forest
Bulart
Cavendish
Kyup
Karabeal
Stavely
Wannon

3

Joins map 321
Nangwarry
Kalangadoo
Tarpeena
Lake Mundi
Dunrobin
Casterton
128
Coleraine
Konong Wootong
Gritjurk
Hensley Park
Moutajup
Dunkeld
79
Glenthompson
Wickliffe

SOUTH AUSTRALIA
VICTORIA
Wandilo
Strathdownie
GLENELG
B160
Sandford
Hilgay
Carapook
Henty
Paschendale
Wannon
Strathkellar
HWY
GLENELG
Warrayure
Croxton East
18
HAMILTON
B160

4

RIDDOCH
Mil Lel
MOUNT GAMBIER
266
Puralka
Marp
PRINCES
Merino
Tabara Bridge
Tahara
Digby
Grassdale
Yulecart
Hamilton
Tarrington
Lake Linlithgow
Yatchaw
Tabor
Penshurst
Moffat
Chatsworth

5

Glenburnie
Yahl
Caroline
A1
114
Dartmoor
Mumbannar
CRAWFORD RIVER REGIONAL PARK
Hotspur
Branxholme
87
Wallacedale
Byaduk North
MOUNT NAPIER SP
Byaduk
Caramut
88
HWY
Hexham

Ob Flat
Mount Schank
Allendale East
Ewens Ponds
Winnap
Greenwald
Drik Drik
Lyons
Condah
Myamyn
Minhamite
Merang

6

Port MacDonnell
267
DONOVANS LANDING
LOWER GLENELG
268
Wanwin
Nelson
C192
LOWER GLENELG NATIONAL PARK
Drumborg
Milltown
Homerton
Lake Condah
MOUNT ECCLES NP
Macarthur
Broadwater
Hawkesdale
HWY

Brown Bay
PICCANINNIE PONDS CP
Discovery Bay
Lake Mombeong
DISCOVERY
BAY
Kentbruck
COBBOBOONEE NATIONAL PARK
Heywood
HENTY
HWY
Bessiebelle
Orford
Willatook
Warrong
Woolsthorpe
Ellerslie
B120

7

COASTAL
269
Mt Richmond
MOUNT RICHMOND NP
Gorae West
Gorae
Heathmere
Tyrendarra
A200
PRINCES
Narrawong
Tyrendarra East
Codrington
St Helens
Kirkstall
Koroit
Southern Cross
Winslow
Mailors Flat
Framlingham East
Ballangeich
Framlingham
50
Hopkins

PARK
Tarragal
Descartes Bay
Bolwarra
Cashmore
97
Yambuk
Toolong
Crossley
Killarney
Woodford
Illowa
Bushfield
Grassmere Junction
Panmure
Warrgoom
Cudgee
Purnim

8

DISCOVERY BAY MARINE NP
Cape Bridgewater
Cape Duquesne
270
Trewalla
Portland
Blacknose Point
Danger Point
Grant Bay
Cape Sir William Grant
Lady Julia Percy Island
Cape Reamur
Port Fairy
271
WARRNAMBOOL
272
Allansford
Naringal
Mepunga East

Cape Bridgewater
Bridgewater Bay
CAPE NELSON SP
Nelson Bay
Cape Nelson
Portland Bay
Minerva Reef
Lady Bay
Port Fairy Bay
Dennington
HWY
Mepunga West
BAY OF ISLANDS
Nullawarre
The Cove
Nirranda
Springvale

9

COASTAL PARK
Childers Cove

38° 30'

10

11

SOUTHERN   OCEAN

39° 00'

12

141° 00'   141° 30'   142° 00'   142° 30'

A B C D E F G H

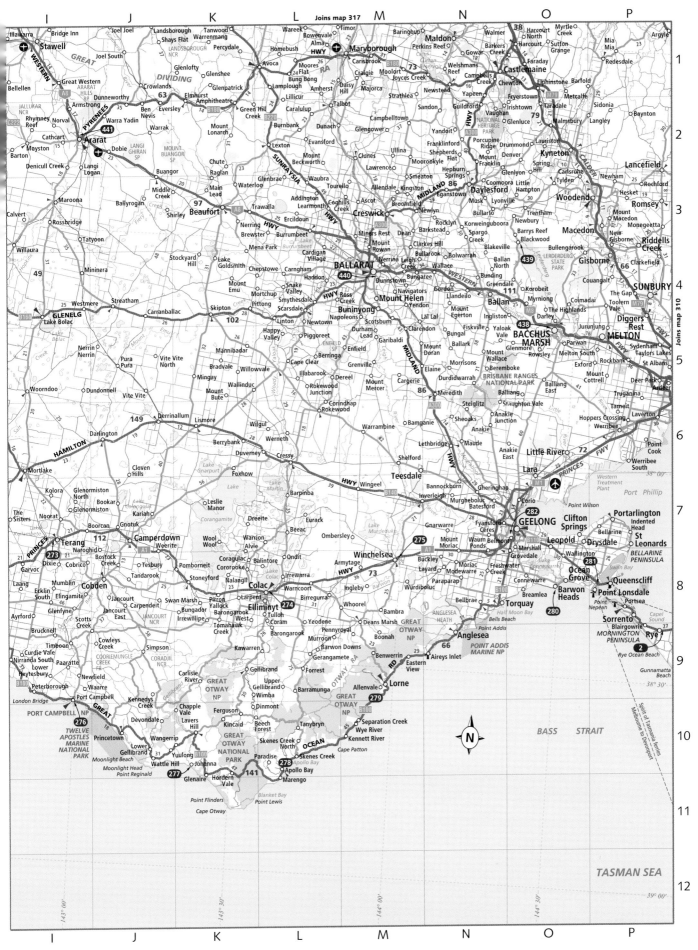

0   10   20   30   40   50 km

Joins map 317

Joins map 310

0 10 20 30 40 50 km

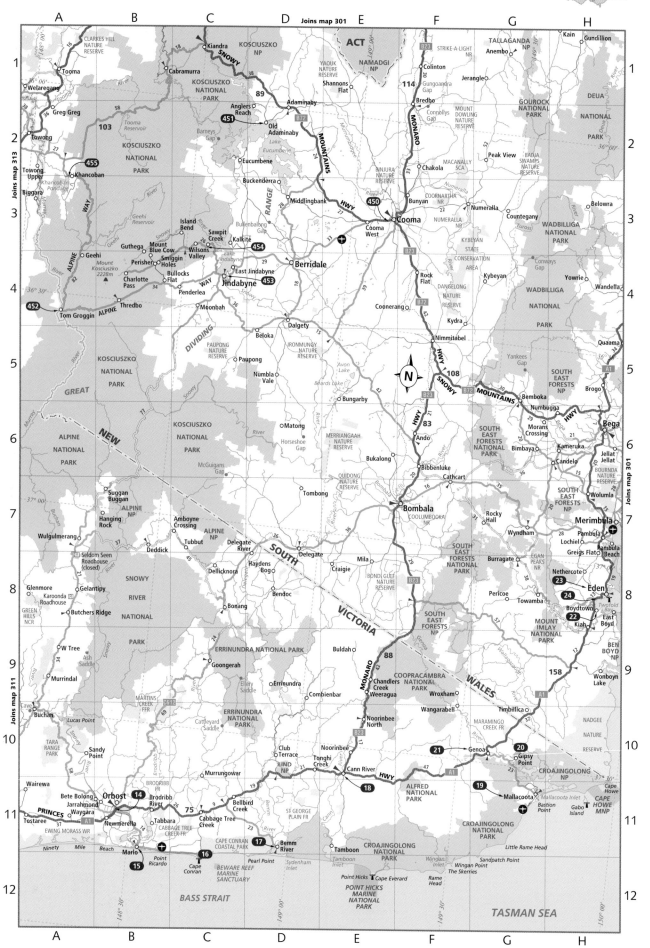

Joins map 301
Joins map 313
Joins map 301
Joins map 311

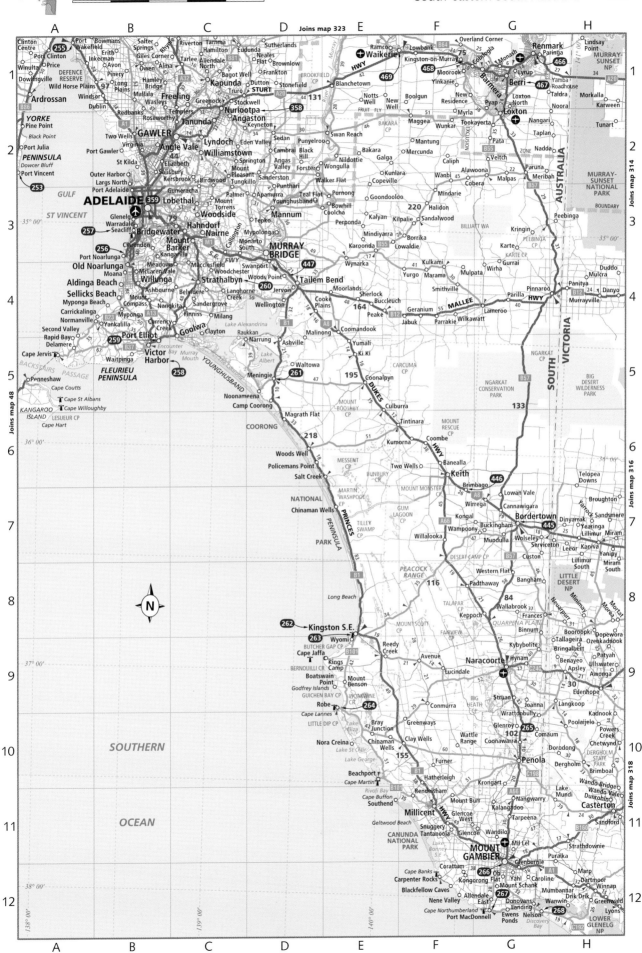

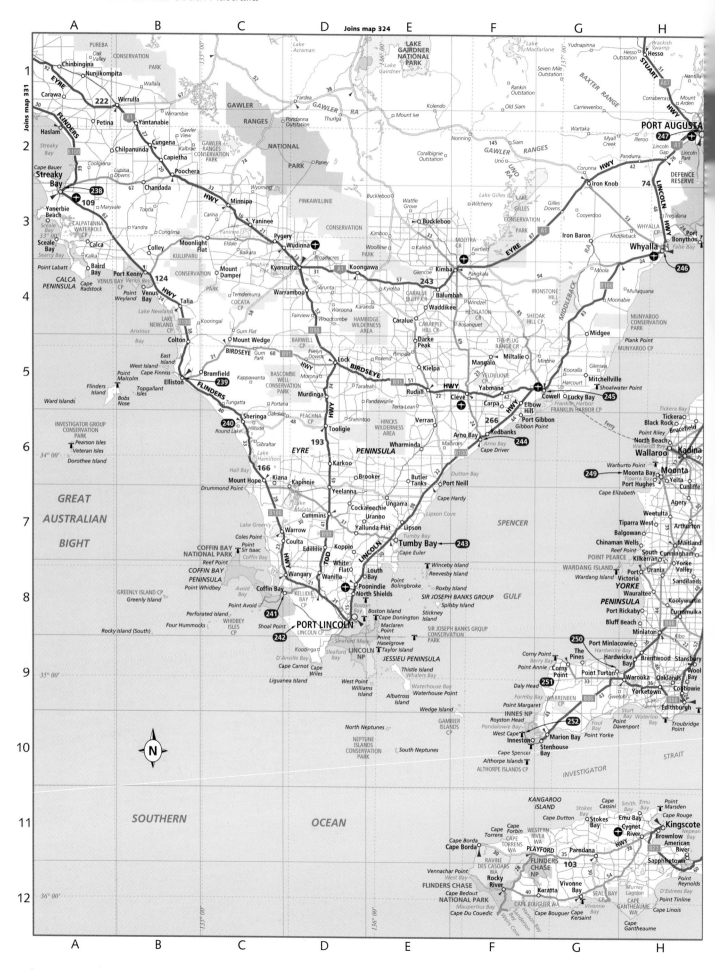

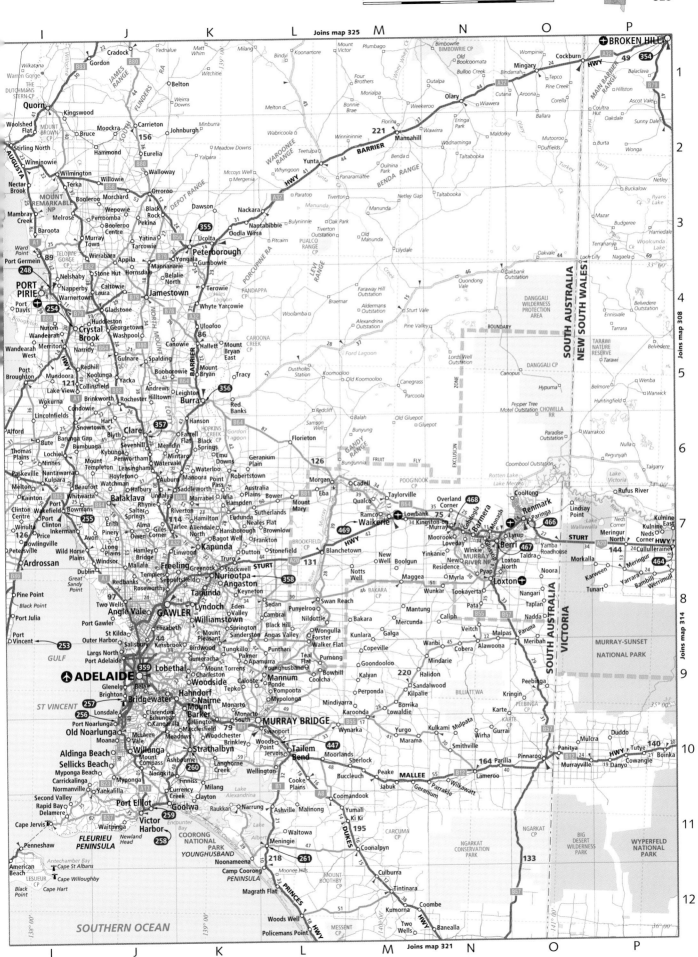

Joins map 325
Joins map 308
Joins map 314
Joins map 321

SOUTHERN OCEAN

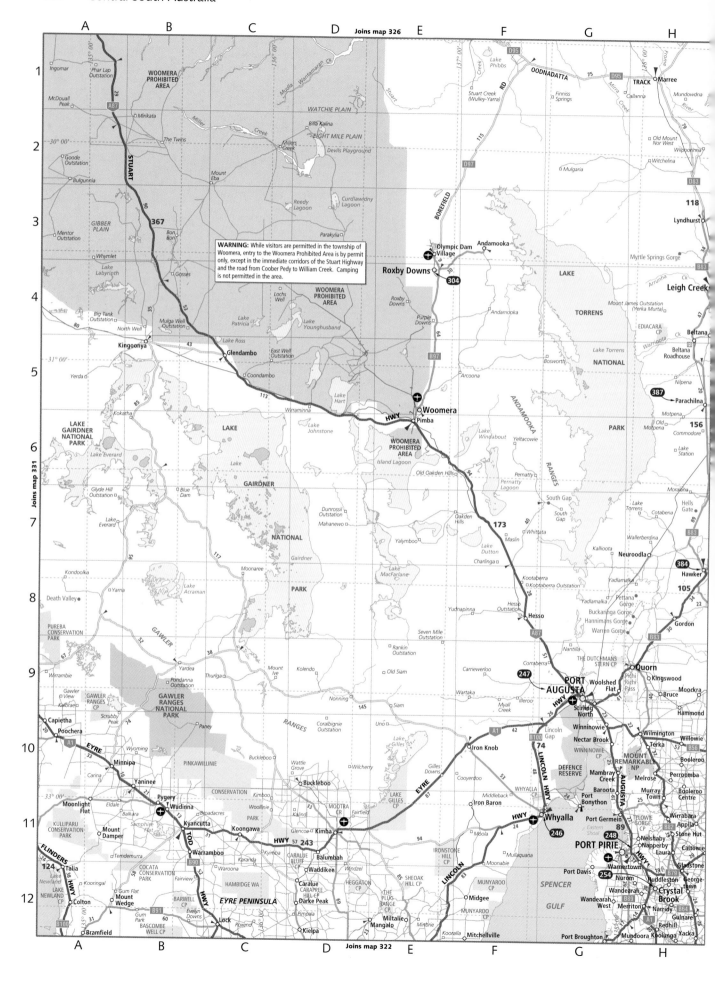

Joins map 326

Joins map 331

Joins map 322

WARNING: While visitors are permitted in the township of Woomera, entry to the Woomera Prohibited Area is by permit only, except in the immediate corridors of the Stuart Highway and the road from Coober Pedy to William Creek. Camping is not permitted in the area.

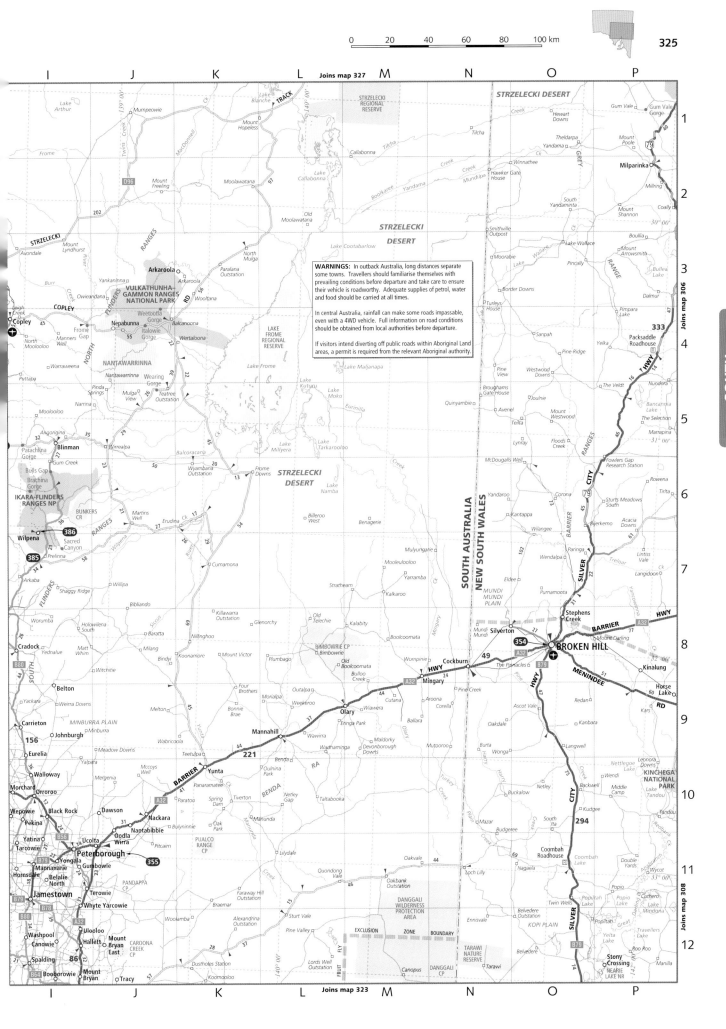

0   20   40   60   80   100 km

SOUTH AUSTRALIA

Joins map 306

Joins map 308

STRZELECKI DESERT

STRZELECKI REGIONAL RESERVE

STRZELECKI DESERT

Lake Arthur

Murnpeowie

Mount Hopeless

Hewart Downs

Gum Vale

Gum Vale Gorge

Tilcha

Theldarpa

Mount Poole

Milparinka

Millring

Coally

Mount Freeling

Moolawatana

Lake Callabonna

Callabonna

Boolkaree

Yandama

Mundlipa

Hawker Gate House

Winnathee

Mount Arrowsmith

Bullea Lake

Dalmur

STRZELECKI

Mount Lyndhurst

Avondale

North Mulga

Old Moolawatana

Lake Cootabarlow

STRZELECKI DESERT

Smithville Outpost

Lake Wallace

Boullia

RANGE

Arkaroola

VULKATHUNHA-GAMMON RANGES NATIONAL PARK

Paralana Outstation

Arkaroola

Wooltana

Moorabie

Border Downs

Mount Arrowsmith

Pimpara Lake

COPLEY

Copley

Owieandana

Frome Gap

Nepabunna

Weetootla Gorge

Italowie Gorge

Balcanoona

Wertaloona

LAKE FROME REGIONAL RESERVE

Turleys House

Sanpah

Avenel

Pincally

Yelka

333

Packsaddle Roadhouse

HWY

North Moolooloo

Manners Well

NANTAWARRINNA

Naritawarrina

Wearing Gorge

Teatree Outstation

Lake Maljanapa

Pine View

Westwood Downs

Joulnie

Pine Ridge

The Veldt

Nundora

Warraweena

Pinda Springs

Mulga View

Narrina

Lake Kutyu

Lake Moko

Eurinilla

Quinyambie

Mount Westwood

Teilta

Bancannia Lake

The Selection

Moolooloo

Brughams Gate House

Marrapina

Angorigina

Blinman

Wirrealpa

Balcoracana

Lake Tarkarooloo

McDougalls Well

Corona

Floods Creek

Fowlers Gap Research Station

Rowena

Tirtla

Patachilna Gorge

Bulls Gap

Brachina Gorge

Gum Creek

Wyamba Outstation

Frome Downs

Lake Namba

Yandaroo

Lynray

Kantappa

Wilangee

BARRIER

Bjerkerno

Sturts Meadows South

Acacia Downs

IKARA-FLINDERS RANGES NP

BUNKERS CR

386

Martins Well

Erudina Ck

Lake Millyera

Curnamona

Benagerie

Mooleulooloo

Yarramba

Paringa

Wendalpa

Lintiss Vale

Langidoon

Wilpena

Sacred Canyon

Prelinna

385

Arkaba

Shaggy Ridge

Willipa

Bibliando

Strathearn

Kalkaroo

Eldee

Purnamoota

Mundi Mundi PLAIN

Treloar

Worumba

Holowilena South

Baratta

Nilfinghoo

Killawarra Outstation

Glenorchy

Old Telechie

Kalabity

Boolcoomata

Mundi Mundi

Silverton

Stephens Creek

Cradock

Yednalue

Milang

Bindyi

Koonamore

Mount Victor

Plumbago

BIMBOWRIE CP

Bimbowrie

Old Boolcoomata

Bulloo Creek

Wompinie

354

BROKEN HILL

Mount Darling

HWY

Belton

Matt Whim

Witchitie

Four Brothers

Morialpa

Weekeroo

Cockburn

HWY

Mingary

The Pinnacles

49

Kinalung

Yackara

Weirra Downs

Melton

Bonnie Brae

Olary

Wiawera

Cutana

Aroona

Corella

Ascot Vale

Redan

Horse Lake

Kars

MENINDEE

RD

Carrieton

Johnburgh

Minburra

MINBURRA PLAIN

Mannahill

Eringa Park

Wawirra

Maldorky

Mutooroo

Oakdale

Kanbata

Langwell

156

Eurelia

Yalpara

Mccoys Well

Mergenia

Teetulpa

221

Yunta

Benda

Wadhaminga

Devonborough Downs

Ballara

Burta

Wonga

Buckalow

Netley

Wendi

Leonora Downs

Nettleson Downs

KINCHEGA NATIONAL PARK

Walloway

Morchard

Orroroo

Meadow Downs

Panaramatee

Paratoo

Spring Dam

Tiverton

Netley Gap

Taltabooka

Turkey Plain

Mazar

Budgeree

South Itta

Middle Camp

Lake Tandou

Tandou

Wepowie

Pekina

Black Rock

Dawson

Nackara

Nantabibbie

Oak Park

Manunda

BENDA RA

Lilydale

Oakvale

Loch Lilly

Nagaela

294

Coombah Roadhouse

Coombah Lake

Double Yards

Wycot

Yatina

Tarcowie

Ucolta

Oodla Wirra

Pitcairn

PUALCO RANGE CP

Quondong Vale

Oakbank Outstation

Belvedere Outstation

KOPI PLAIN

Popio Lake

Cuthero

Peterborough

355

PANDAPPA CP

Faraway Hill Outstation

DANGGALI WILDERNESS PROTECTION AREA

Twin Wells

Popiltah Lake

Popiltah

Mindona Lake

Hornsdale

Belalie North

Gumbowie

Terowie

Whyte Yarcowie

Braemar

Sturt Vale

Ennisvale

Belvedere

SILVER CITY

Yelta Lake

Travellers Lake

Jamestown

Washpool

Canowie

Uloolo

Hallett

Mount Bryan East

CAROONA CREEK CP

Woolamba

Alexandrina Outstation

Pine Valley

EXCLUSION   ZONE   BOUNDARY

TARAWI NATURE RESERVE

DANGGALI CP

Tarawi

Roo Roo

Manilla

Spalding

86

Booborowie

Mount Bryan

Tracy

Dustholes Station

Koolloo

Lords Well Outstation

FRUIT FLY

Canopus

Stony Crossing

NEARIE LAKE NR

WARNINGS: In outback Australia, long distances separate some towns. Travellers should familiarise themselves with prevailing conditions before departure and take care to ensure their vehicle is roadworthy. Adequate supplies of petrol, water and food should be carried at all times.

In central Australia, rainfall can make some roads impassable, even with a 4WD vehicle. Full information on road conditions should be obtained from local authorities before departure.

If visitors intend diverting off public roads within Aboriginal Land areas, a permit is required from the relevant Aboriginal authority.

SOUTH AUSTRALIA / NEW SOUTH WALES

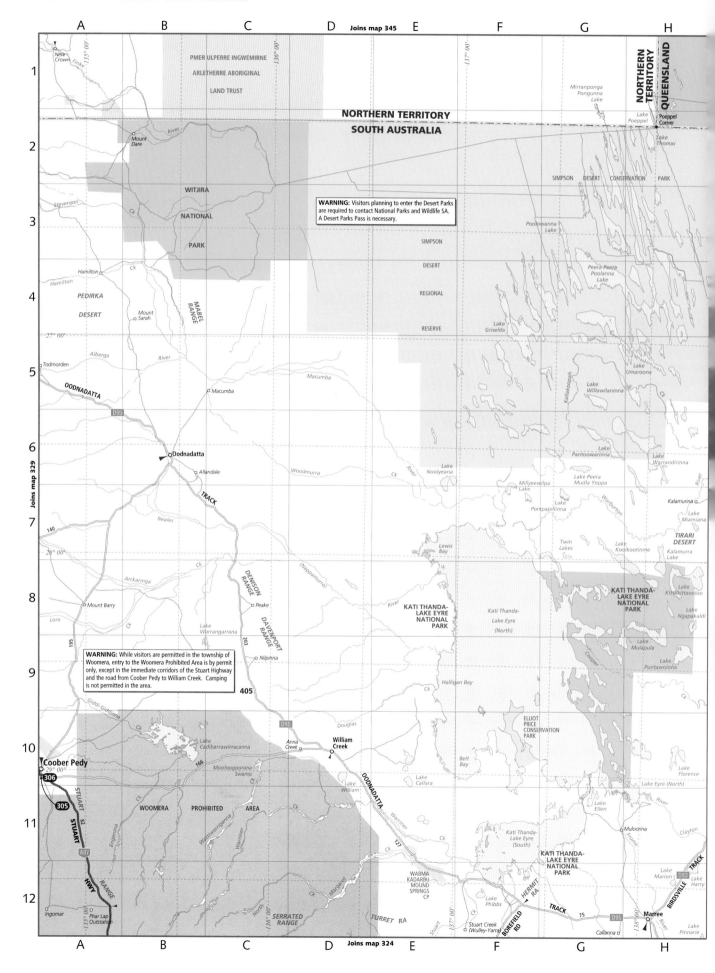

Joins map 345

PMER ULPERRE INGWEMIRNE

ARLETHERRE ABORIGINAL

LAND TRUST

NORTHERN TERRITORY

SOUTH AUSTRALIA

NORTHERN TERRITORY

QUEENSLAND

New Crown

Mount Dare

Finke

River

Mirranponga Ponggunna Lake

Lake Poeppel

Poeppel Corner

Lake Thomas

WITJIRA

NATIONAL

PARK

Stevenson

Ck

WARNING: Visitors planning to enter the Desert Parks are required to contact National Parks and Wildlife SA. A Desert Parks Pass is necessary.

SIMPSON   DESERT   CONSERVATION   PARK

SIMPSON

DESERT

REGIONAL

RESERVE

Poolowanna Lake

Peera Peera Poolanna Lake

Hamilton   Ck

Hamilton

PEDIRKA

DESERT

Mount Sarah

MABEL   RANGE

Lake Griselda

Kallakoopah

Lake Willawilaninna

Lake Umaroona

27° 00'

Alberga   River

Todmorden

Macumba

OODNADATTA

Macumba

Woodmurra

Ck

River

Lake Noolyeana

Lake Pantoowarinna

Lake Warrandirrinna

Lake Kalamurina

D95

Oodnadatta

Allandale

Millyeewilpa Lake

Lake Peera Mudla Yeppa

TRACK

Neales

Lake Pompapillinna

Warburton

River

Kalamurina

Lake Miamiana

140

28° 00'

Arckaringa

Ck

Lewis Bay

Twin Lakes

Lake Koolkootinnie

TIRARI

DESERT

Lake Kamurra Lake

Mount Barry

Lora

DENISON   RANGE

Peake

(Nappamurra)

River

KATI THANDA-LAKE EYRE NATIONAL PARK

Kati Thanda-Lake Eyre (North)

KATI THANDA-LAKE EYRE NATIONAL PARK

Lake Kittakittaooloo

195

203

DAVENPORT   RANGE

Lake Warrangarrana

Nilpinna

Cooper

Lake Mulapula

Lake Puntawonolna

Lake Ngapakaldi

WARNING: While visitors are permitted in the township of Woomera, entry to the Woomera Prohibited Area is by permit only, except in the immediate corridors of the Stuart Highway and the road from Coober Pedy to William Creek. Camping is not permitted in the area.

405

Halligan Bay

Ck

ELLIOT PRICE CONSERVATION PARK

Giddi-Giddinna

Ck

D95

Douglas

Coober Pedy

29° 00'

306

166

Lake Cadibarrawirracanna

Anna Creek

William Creek

Mooloogoorana Swamp

Belt Bay

Lake Callara

Lake Florence

Lake Eyre (North)

305

STUART

82

Engenina

WOOMERA

PROHIBITED

AREA

Wittiwarrigarrana

Warren

Lake William

OODNADATTA

Warriner

Lake Ellen

Muloorina

Kati Thanda-Lake Eyre (South)

Clayton

Frome

A87

STUART

HWY

RANGE

127

Ck

Ck

KATI THANDA-LAKE EYRE NATIONAL PARK

Lake Marion

B83

BIRDSVILLE   TRACK

Lake Harry

Ingomar

Phar Lap Outstation

North

Margaret

SERRATED RANGE

TURRET RA

WABMA KADARBU MOUND SPRINGS CP

Lake Phibbs

Stuart Creek (Wulley-Yarra)

HERMIT RA

BOREFIELD RD

TRACK

75

D95

Callanna

Marree

Lake Pinnarie

Joins map 324

Joins map 329

135° 00'   136° 00'   137° 00'

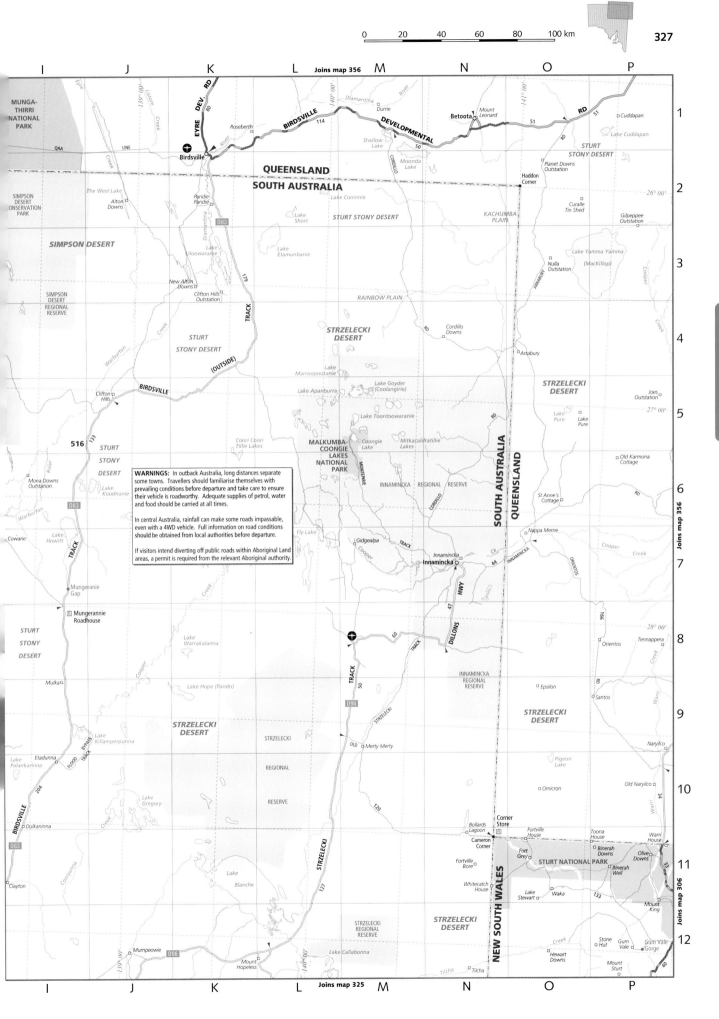

0 20 40 60 80 100 km

SOUTH AUSTRALIA

MUNGA-THIRRI NATIONAL PARK

EYRE DEV. RD

BIRDSVILLE

DEVELOPMENTAL

Betoota
Mount Leonard

RD

Cuddapan

Lake Cuddapan

STURT STONY DESERT

Roseberth

Diamantina
Durrie

River

Birdsville

QAA LINE

Eyre

Listore

Creek

QUEENSLAND

SOUTH AUSTRALIA

Shallow Lake

CORDILLO

Moonda Lake

Haddon Corner

Planet Downs Outstation

26° 00'

SIMPSON DESERT CONSERVATION PARK

The West Lake

Alton Downs

Pandie Pandie

D83

Lake Coninnie

Lake Short

STURT STONY DESERT

KACHUMBA PLAIN

Curalle Tin Shed

Gilpeppee Outstation

SIMPSON DESERT

Lake Ulooawaranie

Diamantina

Lake Etamunbanie

ARRABURY

Nulla Outstation

Lake Yamma Yamma
(MacKillop)

Cooper

New Alton Downs

SIMPSON DESERT REGIONAL RESERVE

Clifton Hills Outstation

Creek

671

TRACK

RAINBOW PLAIN

STRZELECKI DESERT

RD

Cordillo Downs

Arrabury

STRZELECKI DESERT

Joes Outstation

27° 00'

STURT STONY DESERT

Warburton

(OUTSIDE)

Lake Marroopootanie

Lake Apanburra

Lake Goyder (Coolangirie)

Lake Toontoowaranie

RD

Lake Pure
Lake Pure

Clifton Hills

BIRDSVILLE

516

133

STURT STONY DESERT

Coori Coori Tillie Lakes

MALKUMBA-COONGIE LAKES NATIONAL PARK

Coongie Lake

Mitkacaldratillie Lakes

Old Karmona Cottage

Mona Downs Outstation

Lake Koodnanie

D83

Warburton

WARNINGS: In outback Australia, long distances separate some towns. Travellers should familiarise themselves with prevailing conditions before departure and take care to ensure their vehicle is roadworthy. Adequate supplies of petrol, water and food should be carried at all times.

In central Australia, rainfall can make some roads impassable, even with a 4WD vehicle. Full information on road conditions should be obtained from local authorities before departure.

If visitors intend diverting off public roads within Aboriginal Land areas, a permit is required from the relevant Aboriginal authority.

MONTENNIE

INNAMINCKA REGIONAL RESERVE

CORDILLO

RD

St Anne's Cottage

SOUTH AUSTRALIA

QUEENSLAND

Cowarie

Lake Howitt

TRACK

Fly Lake

Gidgealpa

Cooper

TRACK

Innamincka

INNAMINCKA

Nappa Merrie

Ck

INNAMINCKA

44

Cooper Creek

ORIENTOS

Mungeranie Gap

Innamincka

Mungerannie Roadhouse

HWY

DILLONS

161

28° 00'

STURT STONY DESERT

Lake Warrakalanna

60

TRACK

47

Orientos
Tennappera

Creek

Warri

Mulka

Lake Hope (Pando)

TRACK

50

INNAMINCKA REGIONAL RESERVE

Epsilon

Santos

Cooper

D96

STRZELECKI

STRZELECKI DESERT

STRZELECKI DESERT

Etadunna

Lake Killamperpunna

FLOOD BYPASS TRACK

Creek

STRZELECKI

REGIONAL

OLD

Merty Merty

Naryilco

Lake Palankarinna

204

Lake Gregory

RESERVE

120

Pigeon Lake

Omicron

Old Naryilco

34

BIRDSVILLE

D83

Dulkaninna

Cooryenna

STRZELECKI

Lake Blanche

Bollards Lagoon

Corner Store

Fortville House

Toona House

Warri House

Cameron Corner

Fort Grey

Binerah Downs

Olive Downs

33

Clayton

127

Fortville Bore

STURT NATIONAL PARK

Binerah Well

NEW SOUTH WALES

Whitecatch House

Lake Stewart

Waka

133

Mount King

STRZELECKI REGIONAL RESERVE

STRZELECKI DESERT

Creek

Stone Hut

Gum Vale

Gum Vale Gorge

Murnpeowie

D96

Mount Hopeless

Lake Callabonna

Tilcha
Tilcha

Hewart Downs

Mount Sturt

40

SOUTH AUSTRALIA

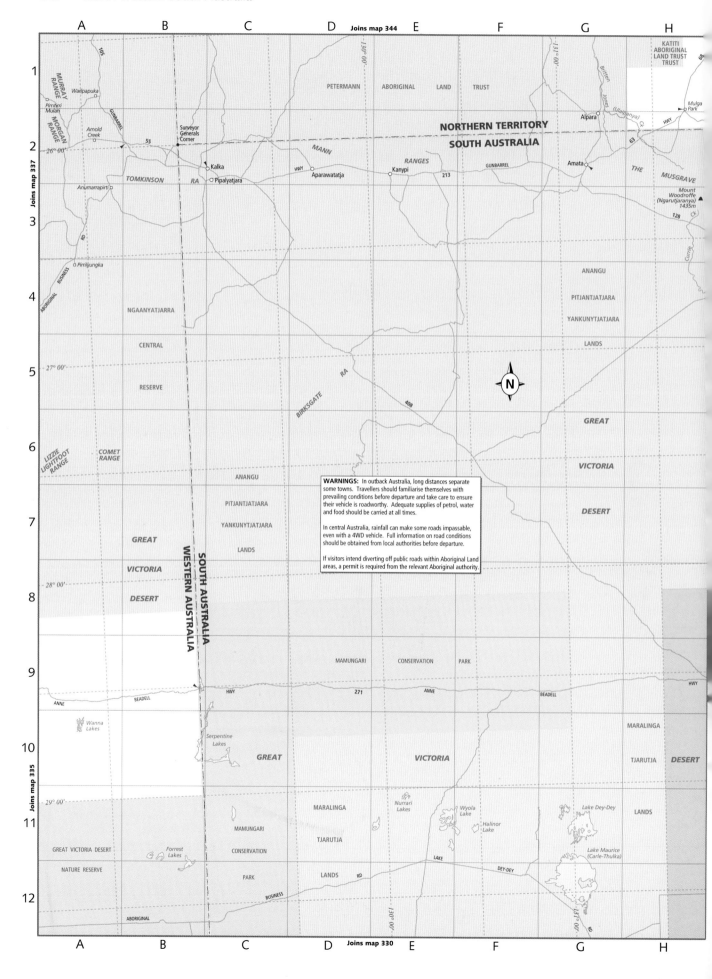

WARNINGS: In outback Australia, long distances separate some towns. Travellers should familiarise themselves with prevailing conditions before departure and take care to ensure their vehicle is roadworthy. Adequate supplies of petrol, water and food should be carried at all times.

In central Australia, rainfall can make some roads impassable, even with a 4WD vehicle. Full information on road conditions should be obtained from local authorities before departure.

If visitors intend diverting off public roads within Aboriginal Land areas, a permit is required from the relevant Aboriginal authority.

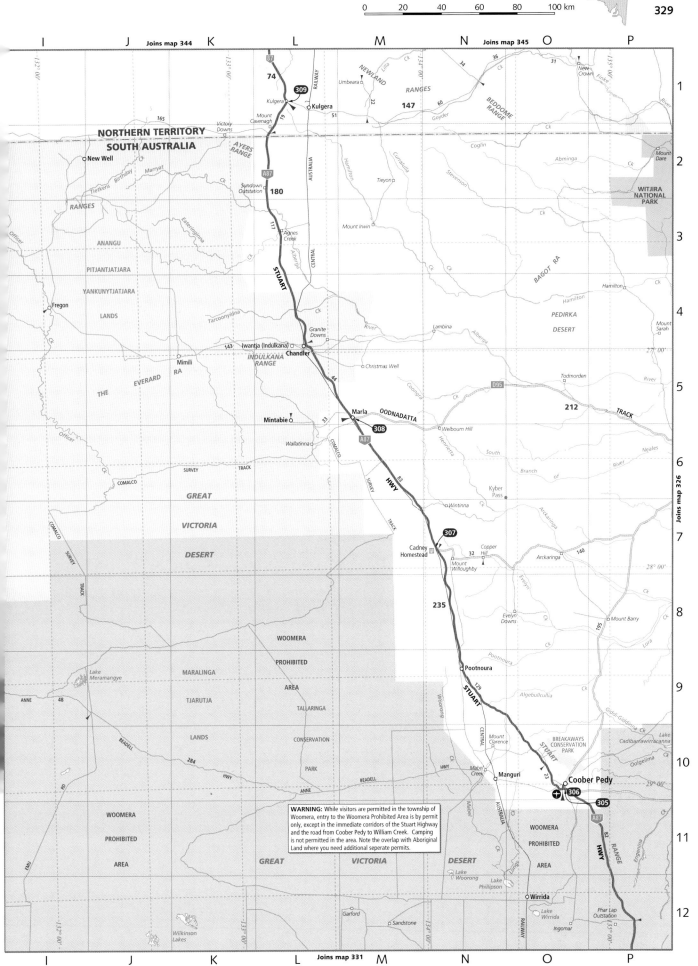

0   20   40   60   80   100 km

SOUTH AUSTRALIA

74

309

Kulgera

Kulgera

Mount
Cavenagh

19

51

Victory
Downs

165

NORTHERN TERRITORY
SOUTH AUSTRALIA

NEWLAND

Umbeara

Lila

Ck

RANGES

147

Goyder

60

22

34

36

31

New
Crown

Finke

River

AYERS
RANGE

A87

AUSTRALIA

CENTRAL

New Well

RANGES

Tietkens

Birthday

Marryat

180

Sundown
Outstation

117

Hamilton

Tieyon

Curraulla

Mount Irwin

Coglin

Stevenson

Abminga

Ck

Mount
Dare

WITJIRA
NATIONAL
PARK

ANANGU

PITJANTJATJARA

Eateringinna

STUART

Agnes
Creek

Alberga

Ck

Ck

River

Hamilton

Ck

BAGOT RA

YANKUNYTJATJARA

LANDS

Fregon

Tarcoonyidna

Granite
Downs

Lambina

Alberga

PEDIRKA

DESERT

Hamilton

Mount
Sarah

143 Iwantja (Indulkana)

Chandler

44

INDULKANA
RANGE

Christmas Well

Coongra

Todmorden

River

27° 00'

Mimili

Marla

OODNADATTA

Welbourn Hill

D95

THE   EVERARD   RA

Mintabie

33

308

A87

Henrietta

South

212

TRACK

Wallatinna

COMALCO

HWY

83

Branch

Neales

River

of

SURVEY   TRACK

GREAT

COMALCO

SURVEY

HWY

Kyber
Pass

Wintinna

Arckaringa

Joins map 326

VICTORIA

SURVEY   TRACK

307

Cadney
Homestead

32 Copper
Hill

Mount
Willoughby

Arckaringa

140

28° 00'

DESERT

235

Evelyn

Evelyn
Downs

195 Mount Barry

Ck

TRACK

WOOMERA

PROHIBITED

STUART

129

Pootnoura

Pootnoura

Ck

Algebullcullia

Lora

Giddi-Giddonna Ck

Lake
Cadibarrawirracanna

ANNE 48

MARALINGA

AREA

Lake
Meramangye

Woorong

BREAKAWAYS
CONSERVATION
PARK

Oolgelima

TJARUTJA

TALLARINGA

Mount
Clarence

STUART

29° 00'

BEADELL

LANDS

CONSERVATION

284

Mabel
Creek

HWY

Manguri

CENTRAL

Coober Pedy

306

305

BEADELL

PARK

ANNE

Mabel

23

AUSTRALIA

A87

EMU

80

WOOMERA

PROHIBITED

AREA

WARNING: While visitors are permitted in the township of
Woomera, entry to the Woomera Prohibited Area is by permit
only, except in the immediate corridors of the Stuart Highway
and the road from Coober Pedy to William Creek. Camping
is not permitted in the area. Note the overlap with Aboriginal
Land where you need additional seperate permits.

GREAT

VICTORIA

DESERT

WOOMERA

PROHIBITED

AREA

RANGE

HWY

82

Lake
Woorong

Lake
Phillipson

Ck

Donga

Engenina

Wirrida

Lake
Wirrida

Phar Lap
Outstation

Wilkinson
Lakes

Garford

Sandstone

RAILWAY

Ingomar

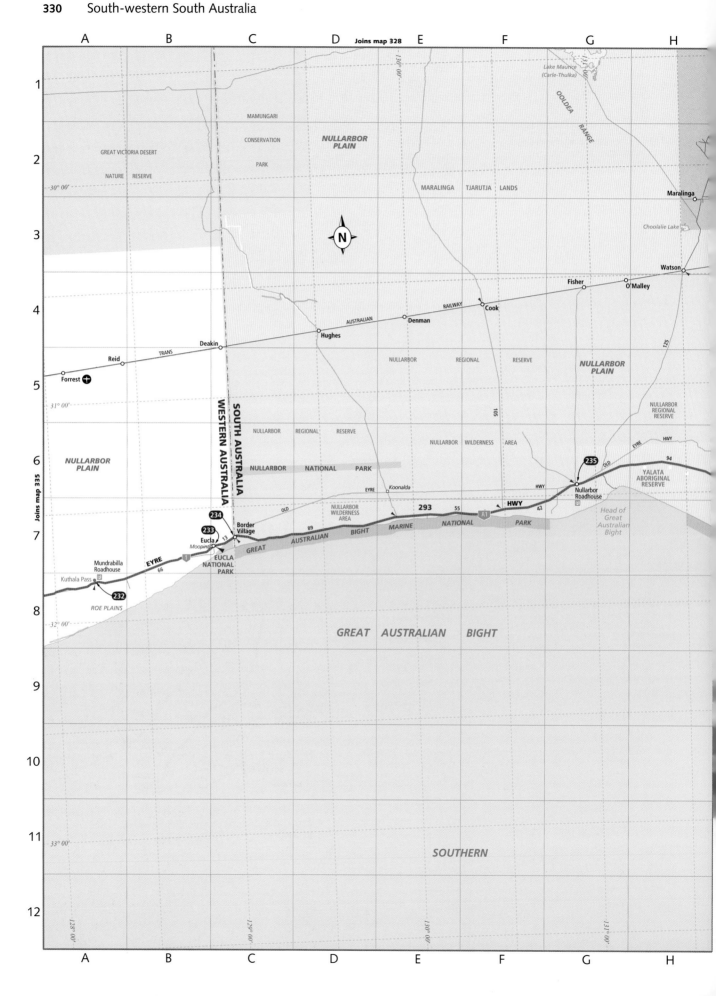

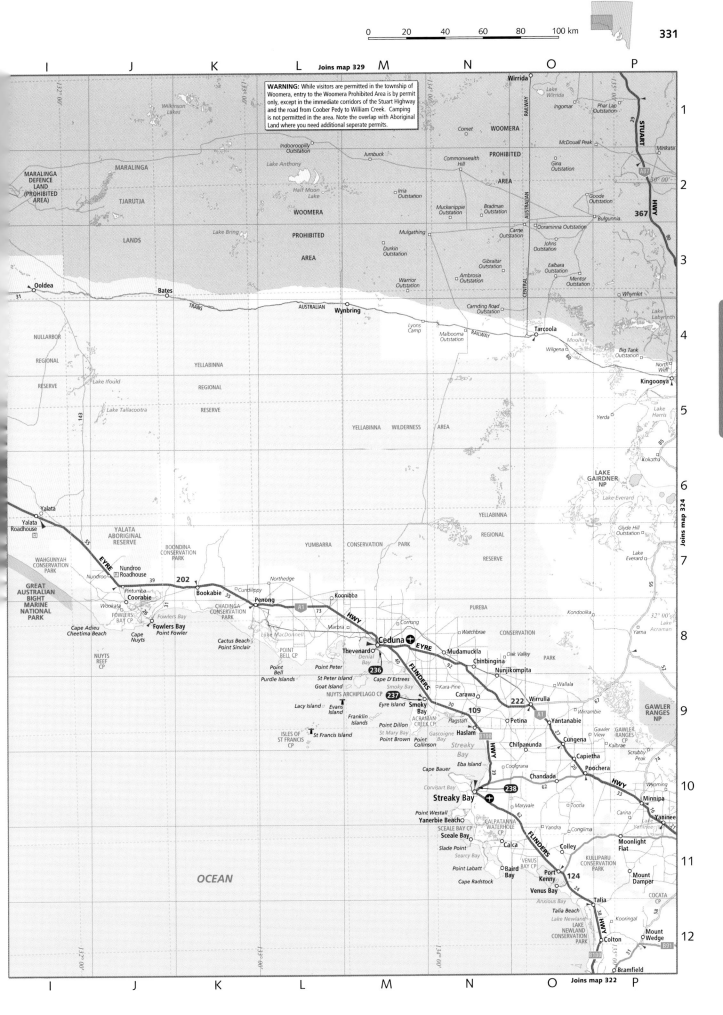

0 20 40 60 80 100 km

WARNING: While visitors are permitted in the township of Woomera, entry to the Woomera Prohibited Area is by permit only, except in the immediate corridors of the Stuart Highway and the road from Coober Pedy to William Creek. Camping is not permitted in the area. Note the overlap with Aboriginal Land where you need additional seperate permits.

I J K L M N O P

Wirrida

Lake Wirrida

Ingomar

Phar Lap Outstation

Mirikata

Wilkinson Lakes

WOOMERA

McDouall Peak

Comet

Commonwealth Hill

PROHIBITED

Gina Outstation

STUART HWY

367

MARALINGA

Indooroopilly Outstation

Lake Anthony

Jumbuck

AREA

Goode Outstation

MARALINGA DEFENCE LAND (PROHIBITED AREA)

TJARUTJA

Half Moon Lake

Irria Outstation

Muckanippie Outstation

Bradman Outstation

Bulgunnia

Ooraminna Outstation

WOOMERA

Durkin Outstation

Mulgathing

Carne Outstation

Johns Outstation

LANDS

Lake Bring

PROHIBITED

Gibraltar Outstation

Ealbara Outstation

AREA

Warrior Outstation

Ambrosia Outstation

Mentor Outstation

Whynlet

Lake Labyrinth

Ooldea

Bates

TRANS

AUSTRALIAN

Wynbring

Lyons Camp

Malbooma Outstation

CENTRAL

Tarcoola

Lake Moolkra

Big Tank Outstation

Lake Harris

31

NULLARBOR

RAILWAY

Wilgena

North Well

REGIONAL

Lake Ifould

YELLABINNA

Kingoonya

RESERVE

Lake Tallacootra

REGIONAL

Yerda

143

RESERVE

YELLABINNA   WILDERNESS   AREA

Kokatha

LAKE GAIRDNER NP

Lake Everard

Glyde Hill Outstation

YELLABINNA

Lake Everard

Yalata

REGIONAL

Yalata Roadhouse

YALATA ABORIGINAL RESERVE

BOONDINA CONSERVATION PARK

YUMBARRA   CONSERVATION   PARK

RESERVE

WAHGUNYAH CONSERVATION PARK

EYRE

Nundroo

Nundroo Roadhouse

39

202

Northedge

GREAT AUSTRALIAN BIGHT MARINE NATIONAL PARK

Pintumba

Coorabie

Wookata

31

Bookabie

35

CHADINGA CONSERVATION PARK

Cundilippy

Penong

A1

73

Koonibba

HWY

PUREBA

Watchbrae

CONSERVATION

Kondoolka

Lake Acraman

Yarna

Fowlers Bay CP

Fowlers Bay

Cape Nuyts

Point Fowler

Lake MacDonnell

Marbra

Corrong

Ceduna

EYRE

Mudamuckla

Oak Valley

PARK

Wallala

Cape Adieu Cheetima Beach

Cactus Beach Point Sinclair

POINT BELL CP

Thevenard

Denial Bay

40

FLINDERS

Chinbingina

92

NUYTS REEF CP

Point Bell

Point Peter

236

Cape D'Estrees

Kara-Pine

Nunjikompita

Point Bell CP

St Peter Island

Smoky Bay

Carawa

Wirrulla

Purdie Islands

Goat Island

237

Eyre Island

Smoky Bay

30

109

222

Wirrambie

GAWLER RANGES NP

Lacy Island

Evans Island

NUYTS ARCHIPELAGO CP

ACRAMAN CREEK CP

Flagstaff

A1

Yantanabie

Franklin Islands

Point Dillon

St Mary Bay

Haslam

B100

Petina

GAWLER RANGES CP

Gawler View

ISLES OF ST FRANCIS CP

St Francis Island

Point Brown

Point Collinson

Streaky Bay

Cungena

Kalbare

Scrubby Peak

Gascoigne Bay

Chilpanunda

Capietha

Cape Bauer

Eba Island

Coolgrana

Poochera

HWY

Wyoming

Corvisart Bay

238

Chandada

62

Minnipa

Streaky Bay

Maryvale

Tootla

Carina

Yaninee

Point Westall

Yanerbie Beach

CALPATANNA WATERHOLE CP

Yandra

Conglima

Yantaree

Moonlight Flat

SCEALE BAY CP

Sceale Bay

Calca

Colley

KULLIPARU CONSERVATION PARK

Slade Point

Searcy Bay

FLINDERS

Mount Damper

Point Labatt

Baird Bay

VENUS BAY CP

Port Kenny

124

COCATA CP

OCEAN

Cape Radstock

Venus Bay

24

Talia

Anxious Bay

Talia Beach

Lake Newland

Kooringal

Mount Wedge

LAKE NEWLAND CONSERVATION PARK

HWY

B91

B100

Colton

Bramfield

SOUTH AUSTRALIA

1 2 3 4 5 6 7 8 9 10 11 12

0 20 40 60 80 km

A B C D E F G H

LESUEUR NP
Halfway Mill Roadhouse
ALEXANDER MORRISON NP
WATHEROO NP
Hamersley Lakes
Lake De Courcy
Lake Moore
Lake Hillman
Lake Harvey
Lake O'Grady
Dalwallinu
Watheroo
Kalannie
Beacon
Wialki
Bonnie Rock
WALYAHMONING NATURE RESERVE
Lake Deborah West
Badgingarra
BADGINGARRA NP
Coomberdale
Pithara
HWY
Miling
Bindi Bindi
Balidu
Cadoux
Koorda
Bencubbin
Mukinbudin
CHIDDARCOOPING NR
Warralakin
BALADJIE LAKE NR
Bullfinch
Cervantes
BRAND
Moora
Dandaragan
Mogumber
New Norcia
Piawaning
Yerecoin
Wongan Hills
Manmanning
Ejanding
Minnivale
Trayning
Kununoppin
Nungarin
Lake Brown
LAKE CAMPION NR
Westonia
Bodallin
109
HWY
JURIEN BAY MP
LANCELIN TRAINING AREA
Cataby Roadhouse
349
MOGUMBER
Gillingarra
Calingiri
Dowerin
Wyalkatchem
Konnongorring
Goomalling
Walgoolan
Burracoppin
Carrabin
Merredin
Nangeenan
Hines Hill
478
Muntadgin
Windmill Roadhouse
Regans Ford
Dide Bay
NORTHERN
110
Wyening
Bolgart
Baandee
Doodlakine
Korbel
Belka
479
Bungulla
Nukarni
Ulva
Kellerberrin
Lancelin
Ledge Point
Breton Bay
MOORE RIVER NP
Bindoon
Chittering
Dewars Pool
Toodyay
Meckering
Waeel
Tammin
Cunderdin
162
EASTERN
Jura
Bruce Rock
Narembeen
Gabbadah
Seabird
Guilderton
Woodridge
Gingin
GREAT
AVON VALLEY NP
Lower Chittering
Ringa
Northam
Quellington
Youndegin
Kwolyin
Shackleton
Ardath
SEAGROATT NR
Two Rocks
Yanchep
YANCHEP NP
Muchea
Bullsbrook
Clackline
Bakers Hill
York
Greenhills
Belmunging
Mawson
Yoting
Pantapin
Babakin
South Kumminin
Eglinton
Quinns Rocks
Joondalup
Wanneroo
Woorooloo
Upper Swan
Gidgegannup
Dangin
Quairading
Bilbarin
NORTH KARLGARIN NR
Hillarys
Scarborough
Midland
Mundaring
WANDOO NP
Jacobs Well
Nornakin
Kunjin
Corrigin
Hyden
PERTH
Claremont
Canning Vale
202
101
Beverley
GREAT
Aldersyde
Kweda
Bulyee
Notting
Karlgarin
Rottnest Island
Fremantle
Jandakot
Armadale
BROOKTON
143
Brookton
Nalya
Bullaring
Gnarming
Pingaring
HARRIS NR
80
Kwinana
Byford
Westdale
HWY
Pingelly
Yealering
Kulin
ROCKINGHAM
203
Waikiki
117
Serpentine
Keysbrook
Jarrahdale
Popanyinning
Malyalling
Wickepin
Jitarning
Singleton
Madora
North Dandalup
199
Wandering
121
Yornaning
Cuballing
Ockley
Harrismith
Toolibin
Dudinin
MANDURAH
204
Furnissdale
Florida
North Pinjarra
Bannister
WANDERING
Minniging
Boundain
Tincurrin
Pinjarra
49
Dwellingup
Coolup
Nanga
Curara
Crossman
Boddington
Marradong
Narrogin
Dummerning
Highbury
205
YALGORUP
206
Waroona
Hamel
Wagerup
Williams
Josbury
Geealying
Tarwonga
Piesseville
Gundaring
Nippering
Wishbone
Kukerin
Moulyinning
Lake Grace
107
INDIAN
Lake Clifton
Preston Beach
NATIONAL
Yarloop
Quindanning
Culbin
SOUTHERN
Dardadine
Hillman
Arthur River
29
Wagin
Ballaying
Dumbleyung
Nyabing
Kuringup
Pingrup
OCEAN
Warawarrup
PARK
60
Harvey
Myalup
Binningup
Wokalup
Benger
Brunswick Junction
Allanson
Boolading
Darkan
146
Warup
Woodanilling
Katanning
Coyrecup
Australind
BUNBURY
207
Dalyellup
Burekup
Waterloo
Collie
Buckingham
Bowelling
Cordering
Duranillin
Boscabel
Geographe Bay
WELLINGTON
Dardanup
Boyanup
Stratham
Lowden
Mumballup
McAlinden
GREATER PRESTON NP
Holly
Broomehill
Peppermint Grove
Ludlow
Capel
Donnybrook
89
Newlands
Wilga
Kulikup
Muradup
Kojonup
211
Gnowangerup
Ongerup
Cape Naturaliste
Dunsborough
Yallingup
BUSSELTON
Vasse
Yoongarillup
Kirup
Mullalyup
Balingup
Bpyup Brook
Dinninup
Jingalup
Tambellup
Borden
210
211
Chapman Hill
Jarrahwood
Greenbushes
208
Mayanup
213
Cowaramup
Gracetown
145
Osmington
Mowen
Nannup
Bridgetown
GREATER KINGSTON NP
228
STIRLING NATIONAL
RANGE PARK
Wellstead
Margaret River
212
Prevelly
Witchcliffe
Rosa Glen
Forest Grove
135
Palgarup
Manjimup
Cranbrook
Tenterden
Kendenup
South Stirling
214
NATIONAL
Karridale
HILLIGER NP
Deanmill
Jardee
209
246
Frankland
Mount Barker
Kamballup
HASSELL NP
215
Hamelin Bay
PARK
216
Quinninup
MUIRS
Pemberton
Rocky Gully
Porongurup
Woodlands
Manypeaks
Cheynes
222
Augusta
Cape Leeuwin
Flinders Bay
NGARI CAPES MARINE PARK
D'ENTRECASTEAUX
Northcliffe
270
MT FRANKLAND NORTH NP
MT ROE NATIONAL PARK
Narrikup
Redmond
King River
Kalgan
Two Peoples Bay
NATIONAL
SHANNON NP
WESTERN
Denmark
Marbelup
ALBANY
221
PARK
Point D'Entrecasteaux
Windy Harbour
Broke Inlet
Cliffy Head
Walpole
Nornalup
218
DENMARK HWY
219
Little Grove
Big Grove
Torbay
WALPOLE-NORNALUP NP
217
Peaceful Bay
220
West Cape Howe
SOUTH COAST
SOUTHERN   OCEAN

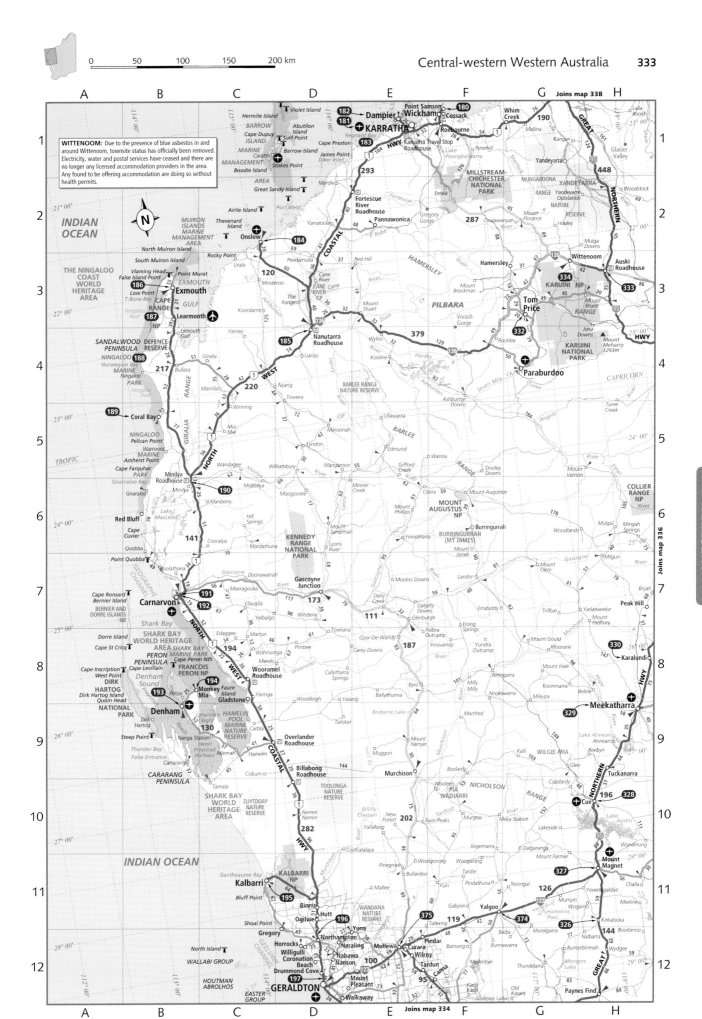

Joins map 336

WESTERN AUSTRALIA

WITTENOOM: Due to the presence of blue asbestos in and around Wittenoom, townsite status has officially been removed. Electricity, water and postal services have ceased and there are no longer any licensed accommodation providers in the area. Any found to be offering accommodation are doing so without health permits.

INDIAN OCEAN

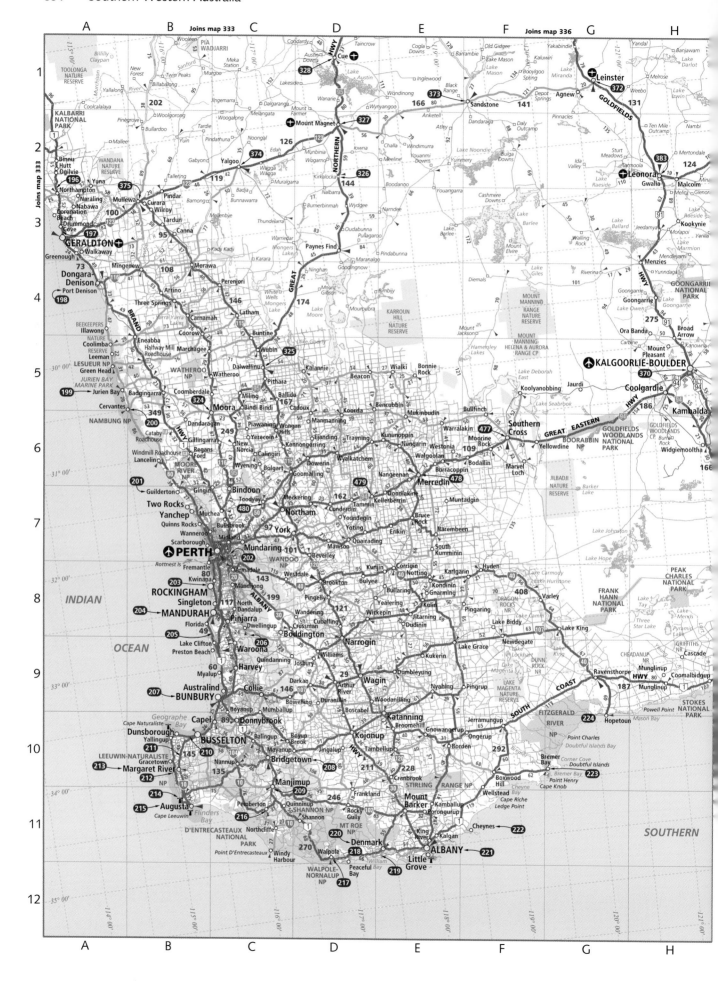

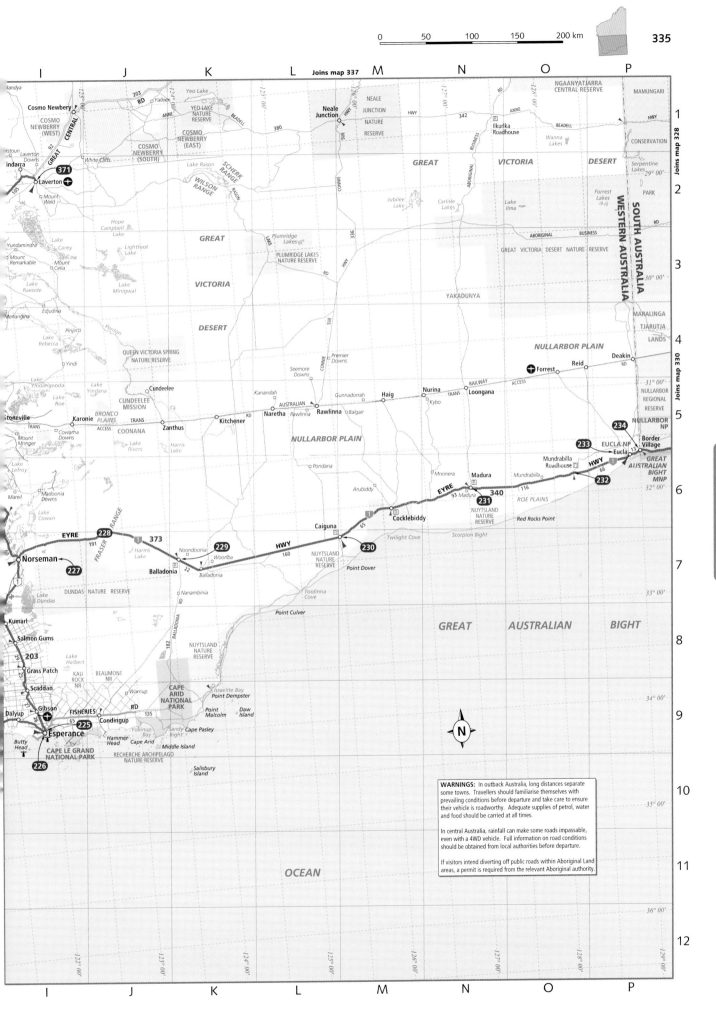

0   50   100   150   200 km

WESTERN AUSTRALIA

Joins map 328

Joins map 330

WARNINGS: In outback Australia, long distances separate some towns. Travellers should familiarise themselves with prevailing conditions before departure and take care to ensure their vehicle is roadworthy. Adequate supplies of petrol, water and food should be carried at all times.

In central Australia, rainfall can make some roads impassable, even with a 4WD vehicle. Full information on road conditions should be obtained from local authorities before departure.

If visitors intend diverting off public roads within Aboriginal Land areas, a permit is required from the relevant Aboriginal authority.

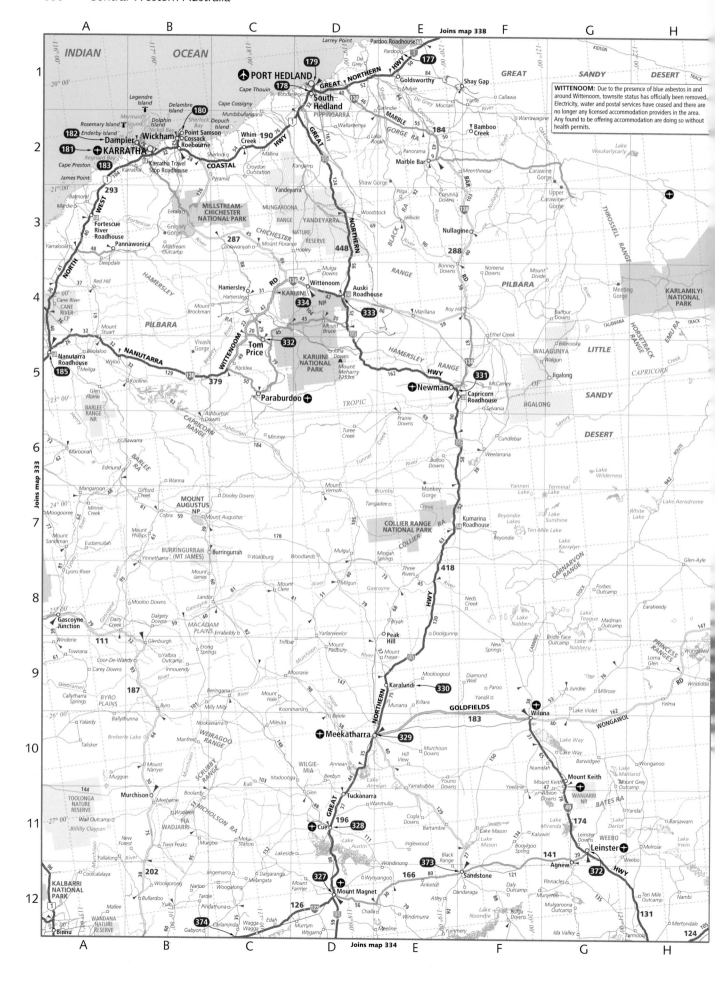

Joins map 338

Joins map 333

Joins map 334

WITTENOOM: Due to the presence of blue asbestos in and around Wittenoom, townsite status has officially been removed. Electricity, water and postal services have ceased and there are no longer any licensed accommodation providers in the area. Any found to be offering accommodation are doing so without health permits.

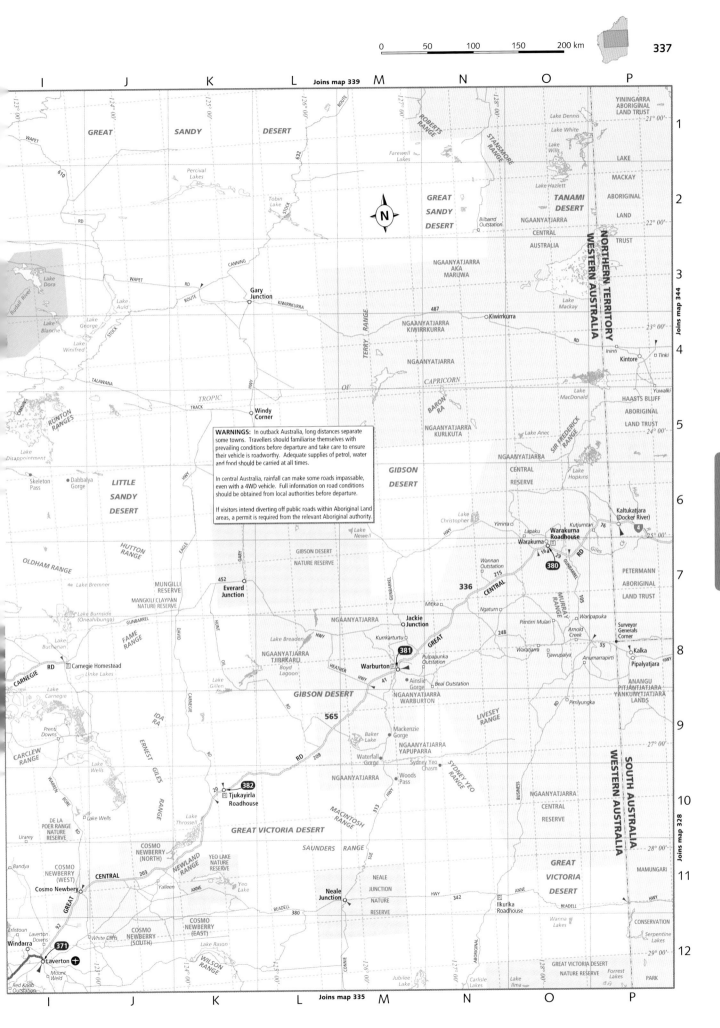

WESTERN AUSTRALIA

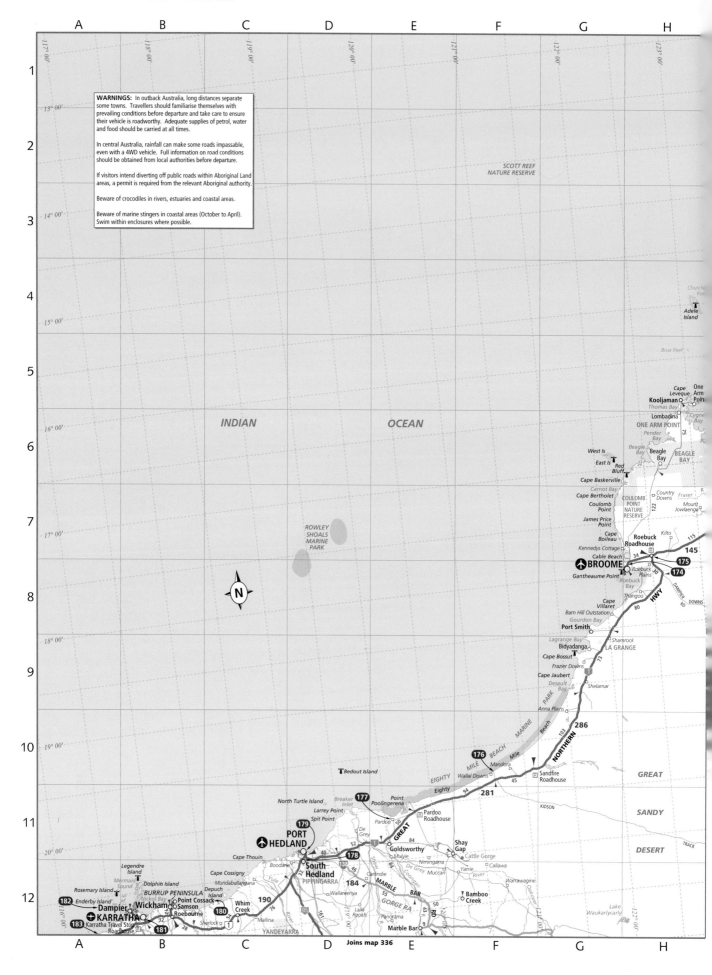

Joins map 336

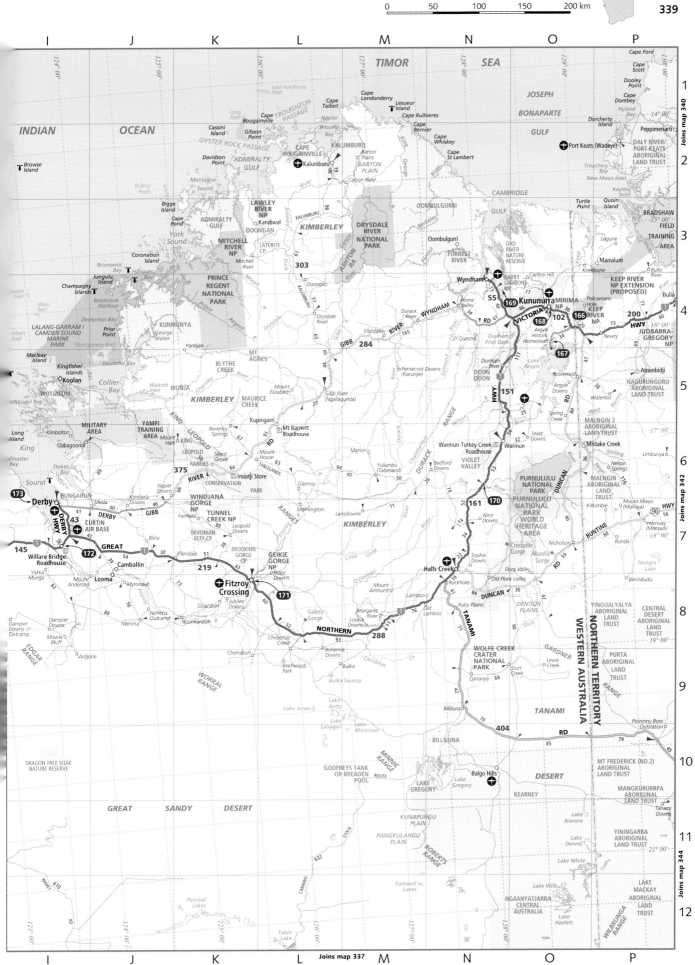

0   50   100   150   200 km

TIMOR   SEA

INDIAN   OCEAN

Cape Ford
Cape Scott
Dooley Point
Cape Dombey
Hyland Bay

Long Reef
East Holothuria Reef
Cape Talbot
Cape Londonderry
Lesueur Island
Cape Rulhieres
Cape Bernier
Cape Whiskey
Cape St Lambert

JOSEPH
BONAPARTE
GULF

Peppimenarti
DALY RIVER/
PORT KEATS
ABORIGINAL
LAND TRUST

Browse Island
Cape Bougainville
Napier Broome Bay
Barton Plains
BARTON PLAIN
Carson River

Port Keats (Wadeye)
Treachery Bay
New Moon Inlet

Cassini Island
Gibson Point
Davidson Point
ADMIRALTY GULF
OYSTER ROCK PASSAGE

CAPE BOUGAINVILLE
Kalumburu
KALUMBURU

King George
Berkeley River
OOMBULGURRI

CAMBRIDGE

Turtle Point
Quoin Island

BRADSHAW
FIELD
TRAINING
AREA

Bigge Island
Montague Sound
Robroy Reefs

LAWLEY RIVER NP
Kandiwal
DOONGAN
MITCHELL RIVER NP
Mitchell River
LATERITE CP

KIMBERLEY
DRYSDALE RIVER NATIONAL PARK
Doongan

303

Oombulgurri
FORREST RIVER

ORD RIVER NATURE RESERVE
Carlton Hill
Legune
Kneebone

Keeling Inlet

Marralum

KEEP RIVER
NP EXTENSION
(PROPOSED)

Bulla

Cape Pond
York Sound
Coronation Island
Brunswick Island
Jungulu Island
Hanover Bay
Champagny Islands
Brecknock Harbour
Deception Bay
Prior Point
Montgomery Reef

ADMIRALTY GULF
PRINCE REGENT NATIONAL PARK
KUNMUNYA
George Water
Pantijan

Drysdale River
KALUMBURU

GIBB 284
Ellenbrae
RIVER
El Questro

Wyndham
WYNDHAM
Home Valley
55
Kununurra
169
VICTORIA
168
102
166
167
200 HWY
JUDBARRA-GREGORY NP

40

Macleay Island
Kingfisher Islands
Koolan
Collier Bay
Doubtful Bay
Walcott Inlet

LALANG-GARRAM / CAMDEN SOUND MARINE PARK
WOTJALUM
trickland Bay
Cone Bay
MUNJA
Charnley River
BLYTHE CREEK
MT AGNES

Mount Elizabeth
Gibb River (Ngallagunda)
21

Durack River
DOON DOON
Dunham River
Argyle Historic Homestead
Dunham River
Lake Argyle

MIRIMA NP
KEEP RIVER NP
Newry

151
Argyle Downs
Rosewood
Waterloo
West
Amanbidji

NAGURUNGURU ABORIGINAL LAND TRUST

Long Island
Disaster Bay
Stokes Bay
King Sound

Kimbolton
Cobagooma
MILITARY AREA
YAMPI TRAINING AREA
Mount Hart
Beverley Springs
Silent Grove
Kupingarri
Mt Barnett Roadhouse

KING LEOPOLD RANGES
375
Napier Downs
Leopold Downs

Marion
Yulumbu (Tableland)
50

DURACK RANGE
Wilson
Bow
Spring Creek
29
Texas Downs

Argyle Downs
Stirling
Nelson

MALNGIN 2 ABORIGINAL LAND TRUST
Mistake Creek
Limbunya

173
Derby
43
DERBY
CURTIN AIR BASE
GIBB
RIVER
CONSERVATION PARK
WINDJANA GORGE NP
Imintji Store
Fairfield
TUNNEL CREEK NP
DEVONIAN REEF CP
Leopold Downs

Mornington
Lansdowne
KIMBERLEY

Warmun-Turkey Creek Roadhouse
Bedford Downs
Warmun
161
170
PURNULULU NATIONAL PARK

MALNGIN ABORIGINAL LAND TRUST
Kirkimbie
Mount Maiyo (Mulliya)
Inverway (Mamadi)
Bunda
Nongra Lake
HWY
96

145
Willare Bridge Roadhouse
172
DERBY HWY
GREAT
Camballin
Looma
219
Fitzroy Crossing
171
Ellendale
BROOKING GORGE CP
GEIKIE GORGE NP
Fossil Downs

VIOLET VALLEY
Ord
Alice Downs
Sophie Downs
Halls Creek
Rockhole
Old Flora Valley
Flora Valley
Crocodile Gorge
Nicholson
Marella Gorge
59

PURNULULU NATIONAL PARK WORLD HERITAGE AREA
DUNCAN
BUNTINE

80
Birrindudu

Yakka Munga
Dampier Downs
Mount Anderson
Myroodah
Noonkanbah
Quanbun
Jubilee Downs
Louisa Downs
O'Donnell River
Mount Amhurst
Lamboo
Old Lamboo
Margaret River
Ruby Plains
DUNCAN
Sturt Creek
Old Flora Valley

NORTHERN
288
TANAMI
Billiluna
DENISON PLAINS

YINGUALYALYA ABORIGINAL LAND TRUST
CENTRAL DESERT ABORIGINAL LAND TRUST
PURTA ABORIGINAL LAND TRUST

Dampier Downs Outcamp
Mowla Bluff
Ardjorie
EDGAR RANGE

Christmas Creek
Cherrabun
Bohemia Downs
Bulka
Beefwood Park
Bulka Swamp

WOLFE CREEK CRATER NATIONAL PARK
Carranya
Sturt Creek
Lewis Creek

WESTERN AUSTRALIA
NORTHERN TERRITORY

GARDNER RANGE

WORRAL RANGE

Lake Jones
Lake Betty
Lake Lanagan
Lake McLernon

404
RD

Billiluna
Balgo Hills
DESERT
KEARNEY

MANGKURURRPA ABORIGINAL LAND TRUST

MT FREDERICK (NO.2) ABORIGINAL LAND TRUST
Picininny Bore Outstation

DRAGON TREE SOAK NATURE RESERVE
GODFREYS TANK OR BREADEN POOL
MINNIE RANGE
LAKE GREGORY
Lake Gregory
KUNAPUNGU PLAIN
ROBERTS RANGE

YININGARRA ABORIGINAL LAND TRUST
Lake Jeavons
Lake Dennis
Tanami Downs

GREAT   SANDY   DESERT
PANGKULANGU PLAIN
Lake White

LAKE MACKAY ABORIGINAL LAND TRUST

Percival Lakes
Farewell Lakes
Lake Wills
Tobin Lake
Lake Hazlett

NGAANYATJARRA CENTRAL AUSTRALIA
WILBRUNGA RANGE

WESTERN AUSTRALIA

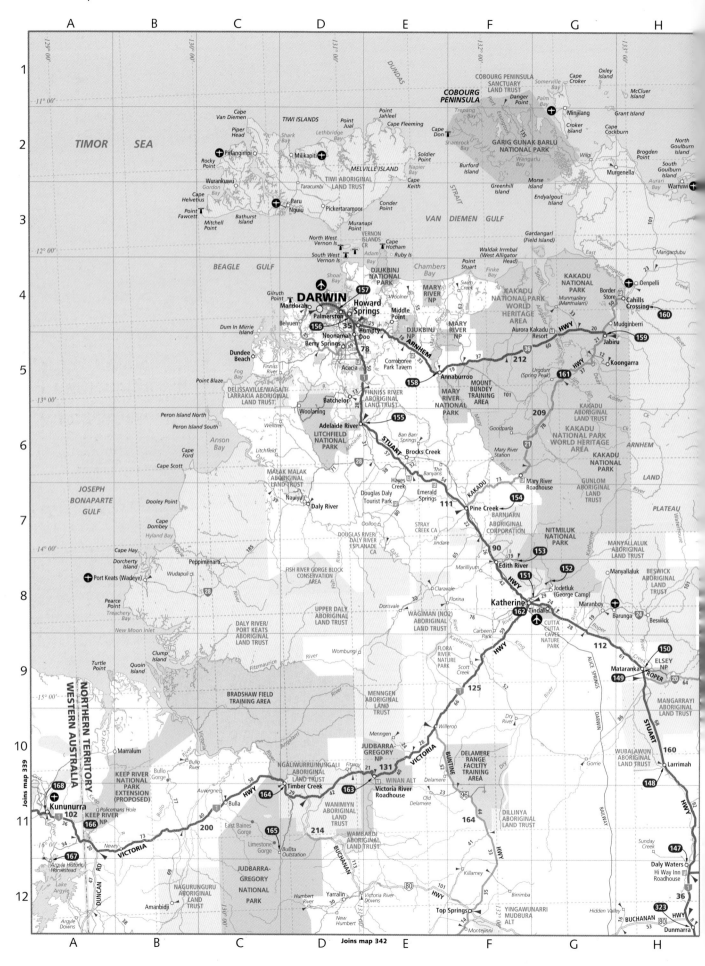

Joins map 339

Joins map 342

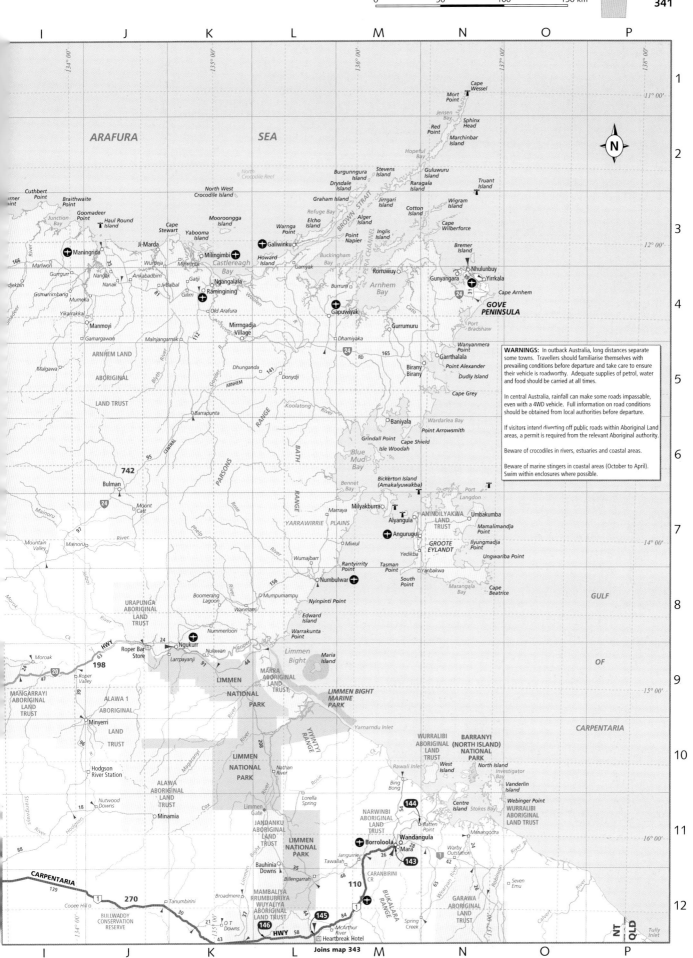

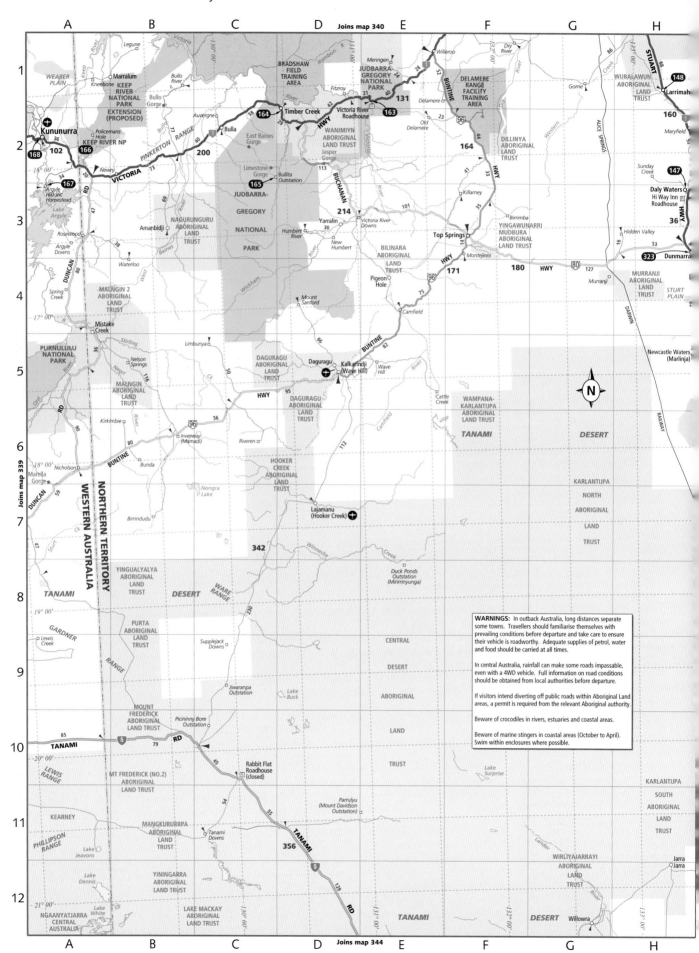

Joins map 340

Joins map 339

Joins map 344

WARNINGS: In outback Australia, long distances separate some towns. Travellers should familiarise themselves with prevailing conditions before departure and take care to ensure their vehicle is roadworthy. Adequate supplies of petrol, water and food should be carried at all times.

In central Australia, rainfall can make some roads impassable, even with a 4WD vehicle. Full information on road conditions should be obtained from local authorities before departure.

If visitors intend diverting off public roads within Aboriginal Land areas, a permit is required from the relevant Aboriginal authority.

Beware of crocodiles in rivers, estuaries and coastal areas.

Beware of marine stingers in coastal areas (October to April). Swim within enclosures where possible.

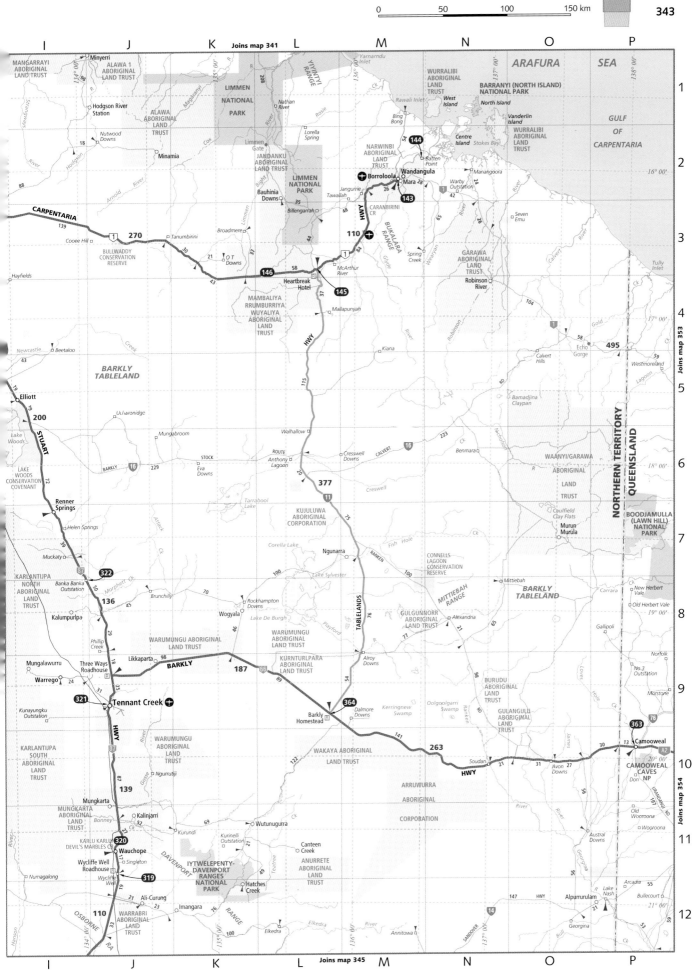

Joins map 341
Joins map 353
Joins map 354
Joins map 345

NORTHERN TERRITORY

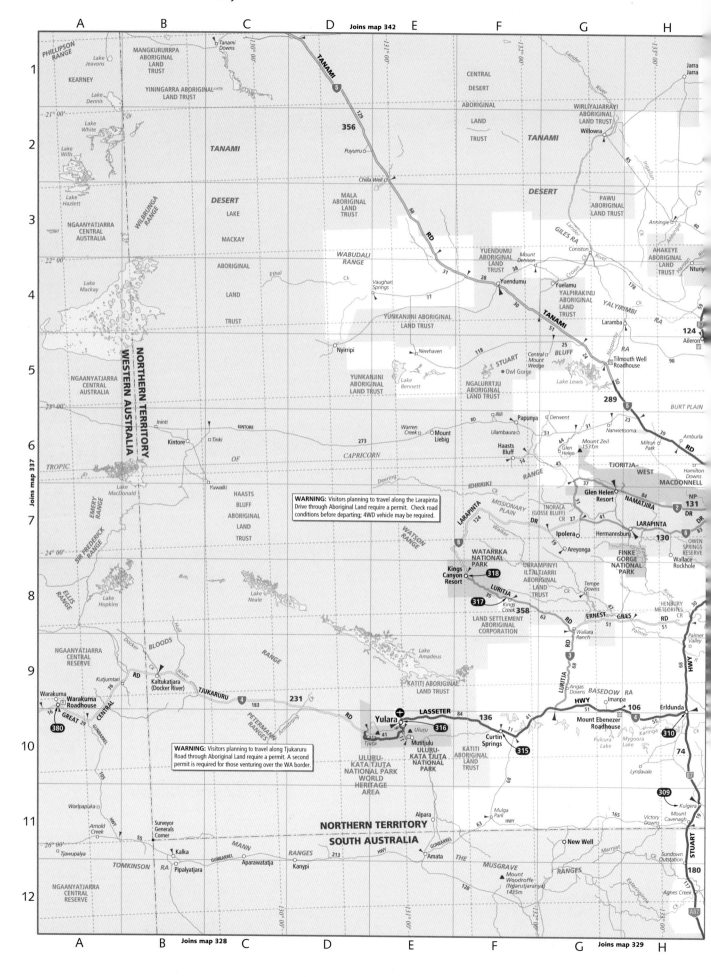

Joins map 342

Joins map 337

Joins map 328

Joins map 329

WARNING: Visitors planning to travel along the Larapinta Drive through Aboriginal Land require a permit. Check road conditions before departing; 4WD vehicle may be required.

WARNING: Visitors planning to travel along Tjukaruru Road through Aboriginal Land require a permit. A second permit is required for those venturing over the WA border.

NORTHERN TERRITORY
SOUTH AUSTRALIA

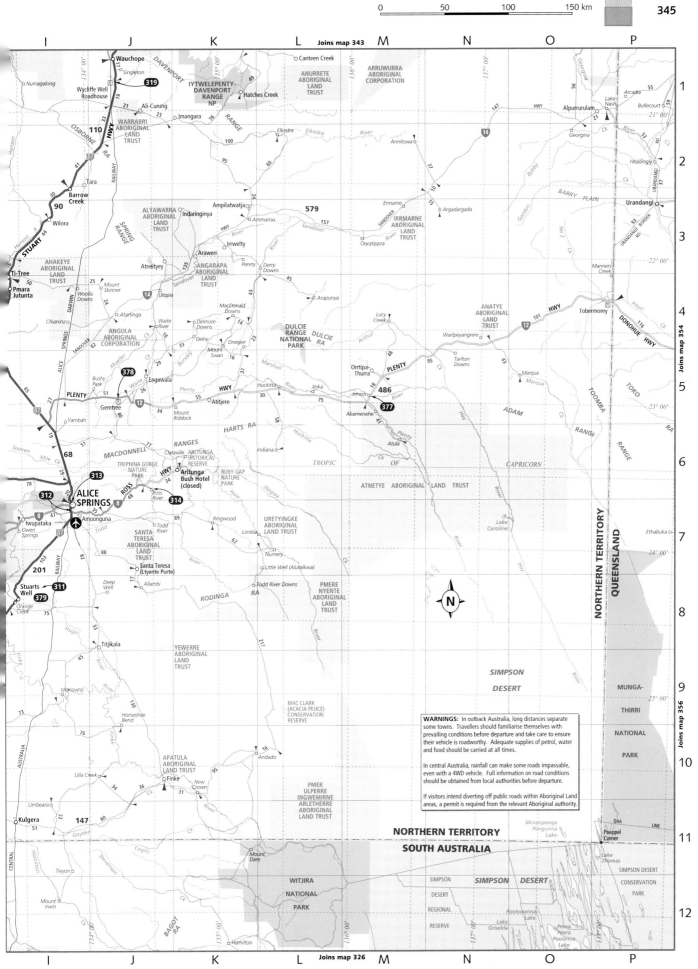

I   J   K   L   Joins map 343   M   N   O   P

Numagalong

Wauchope
Singleton
319

Wycliffe Well
Roadhouse
Ali-Curung   21
23   Imangara   16
Canteen Creek
ANURRETE
ABORIGINAL
LAND
TRUST
ARRUWURRA
ABORIGINAL
CORPORATION
Arcadia   55
Lake
Nash
Bullecourt   59

110   DAVENPORT
IYTWELEPENTY-
DAVENPORT
RANGE
NP
Hatches Creek   49
49
147   HWY
Alpurrurulam   21
Georgina   56
-21° 00'
53   RD

OSBORNE RA   HWY   WARRABRI
ABORIGINAL
LAND
TRUST
100
95   Elkedra   Elkedra
50   River
Georgina
Headingly   37

41   Tara
RAILWAY   SPRING   ALYAWARRA
ABORIGINAL
LAND
TRUST
Ampilatwatja
Indaringinya   24
Ammaroo   157   **579**
Sandover   River   River
Annitowa   31
Ermarne   15   Argadargada
BARRY   PLAIN   Gordon   No 2   Ck   Urandangi
93   URANDANGI

30   Barrow
Creek
90
Wilora   44   Arawerr
Atneltyey   135   Irrwelty
ANGARAPA
ABORIGINAL
LAND
TRUST
Perety   Derry
Downs
45
Ooratippra   SANDOVER   **14**
-22° 00'

Ti-Tree   50
Pmara
Jutunta
AHAKEYE
ABORIGINAL
LAND
TRUST
25   Mount
Skinner
Woolla
Downs   24   Atartinga
14   Utopia
MacDonald
Downs   14
43   Arapunya
Lucy   48
Creek
ANATYE
ABORIGINAL
LAND
TRUST
Tobermorey   116
Manners
Creek   DONOHUE
HWY
-22° 00'

Chianina   SANDOVER   ANGULA
ABORIGINAL
CORPORATION   Waite
River   18   Delmore
Downs
Delny   33   Mount
Swan   16   Dneiper   23
DULCIE
RANGE
NATIONAL
PARK   DULCIE RA   Arthur   HWY   101
Warlpeyangrere   43   Marqua
Marqua
TOOMBA   TOKO

65   ALICE SPRINGS   Bushy
Park   **378**   Mueller   Ck   29   Bundey
Engawala   34   Plenty   River   37   Huckitta   River   Jinka   Orritpa-
Thurra   PLENTY
18   **486**   95   Tarlton
Downs   ADAM   RANGE   RANGE   -23° 00'

PLENTY   51   Gemtree   **12**   34   55   Atitjere   30   Mount
Riddock   58   Huckitta   75   Jervois   41   **377**
Akarnehe   Plenty   CAPRICORN

19   **68**   HARTS RA   RANGES   Claraville   ARLTUNGA
HISTORICAL
RESERVE   Indiana   Hale   Atula
Ck   OF

Sixteen   Mile   Ck   29   77   MACDONNELL   TREPHINA GORGE
NATURE
PARK   HWY   34   Arltunga
Bush Hotel
(closed)   RUBY GAP
NATURE
PARK   Illogwa   TROPIC
ATNETYE ABORIGINAL LAND TRUST

78   **313**
312   20   ROSS   48   Ross
River   **314**   Ringwood   URETYINGKE
ABORIGINAL
LAND
TRUST   Lake
Caroline   Ethabuka   -24° 00'
ALICE
SPRINGS   **8**   35   Todd
River   89   Limbla   62   Numery
Amoonguna

6   47   Iwupataka
Owen
Springs   82   88   SANTA
TERESA
ABORIGINAL
LAND
TRUST   Santa Teresa
(Lyente Purte)   River   Little Well (Alunalkwa)   Hay   River   MUNGA-

7   RAILWAY   82   17   Allambi   Todd River Downs   PMERE
NYENTE
ABORIGINAL
LAND
TRUST   SIMPSON   THIRRI
201   Deep
Well   RODINGA   RA
Stuarts
Well   **311**
379   33   217   DESERT   NATIONAL
Orange
Creek   75   Hugh   Titjikala   YEWERRE
ABORIGINAL
LAND
TRUST   River   PARK   -25° 00'

13   45   Idracowra   130   Horseshoe
Bend   Finke   MAC CLARK
(ACACIA PEUCE)
CONSERVATION
RESERVE

Lilla Creek   36   16   Andado   APATULA
ABORIGINAL
LAND
TRUST   95   Finke   New
Crown

Umbeara   22   **147**   60   Finke   River   PMER
ULPERRE
INGWEMIRNE
ARLETHERRE
ABORIGINAL
LAND
TRUST   Mirranponga
Pangunna
Lake   QAA   LINE   Poeppel
Corner   -25° 00'
Kulgera   51   Goyden

NORTHERN TERRITORY
SOUTH AUSTRALIA   Lake
Thomas
SIMPSON DESERT

CENTRAL   Hamilton   Tieyon   Coglin   Mount
Dare   SIMPSON
DESERT   **SIMPSON DESERT**   CONSERVATION
PARK

Mount
Irwin   Stevenson   WITJIRA
NATIONAL
PARK   DESERT
REGIONAL
RESERVE   Poolowanna
Lake   Lake
Griselda   Peera
Peera
Poolanna
Lake

BAGOT
RA   Hamilton

I   J   K   L   Joins map 326   M   N   O   P

NORTHERN
TERRITORY

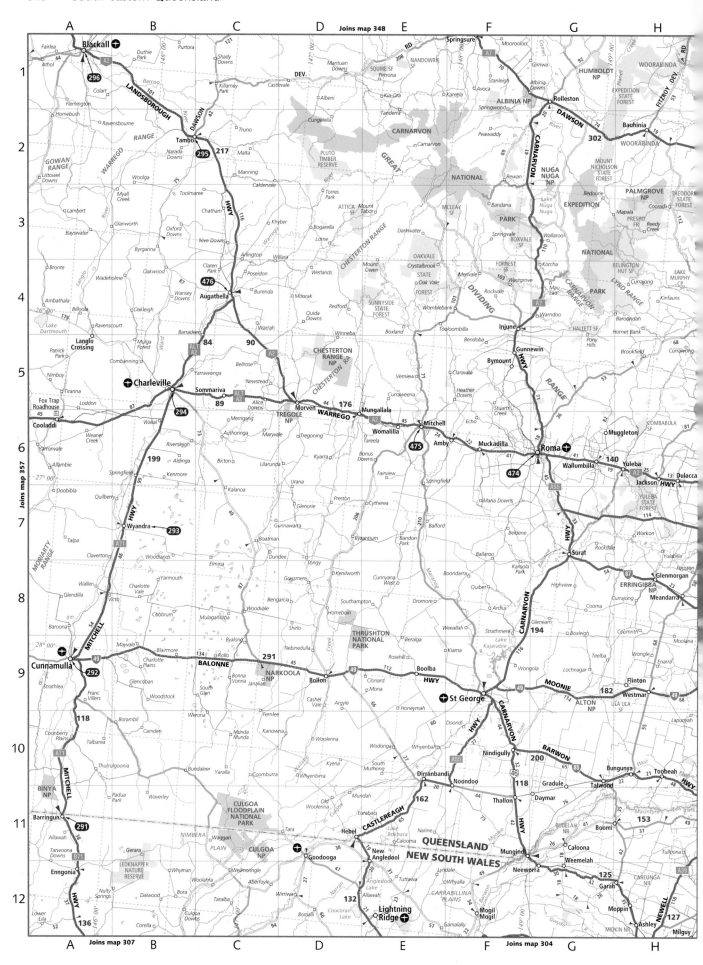

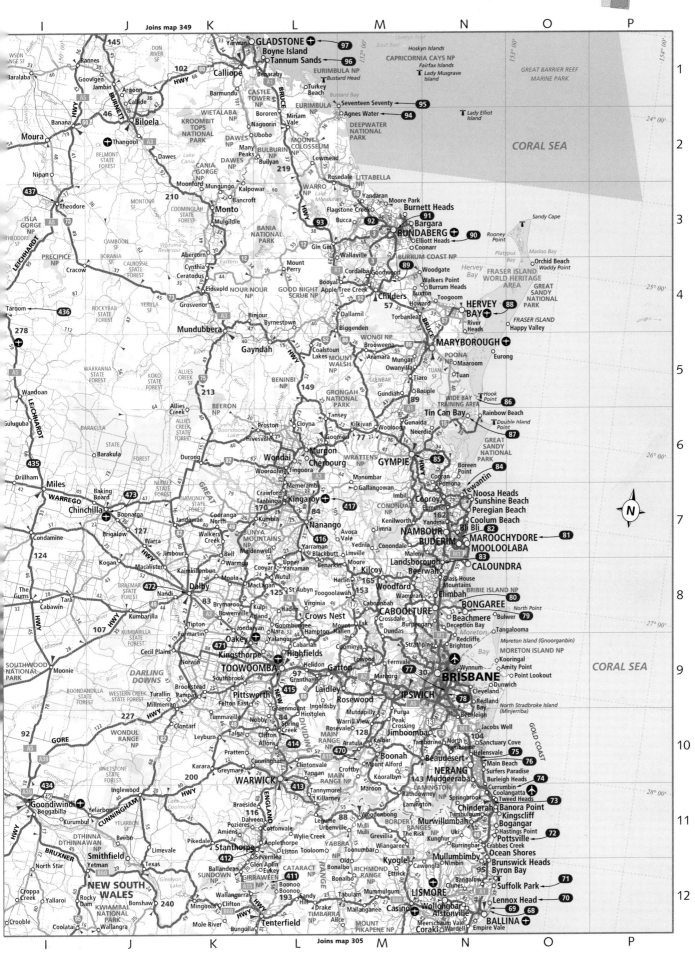

0   25   50   75   100 km

CORAL SEA

GREAT BARRIER REEF
MARINE PARK

CAPRICORNIA CAYS NP
Fairfax Islands

GLADSTONE
Boyne Island
Tannum Sands
Calliope
Benaraby
EURIMBULA NP
Bustard Head
Turkey Beach
Seventeen Seventy
Agnes Water
DEEPWATER NATIONAL PARK

Lady Musgrave Island
Lady Elliot Island

Sandy Cape

Rooney Point

Orchid Beach
Waddy Point

FRASER ISLAND
WORLD HERITAGE AREA

GREAT SANDY NATIONAL PARK

FRASER ISLAND
Happy Valley

Hervey Bay

BUNDABERG
Bargara
Burnett Heads
Moore Park

HERVEY BAY
River Heads

MARYBOROUGH

Tin Can Bay
Rainbow Beach
Double Island Point

Hook Point

WIDE BAY TRAINING AREA

GREAT SANDY NATIONAL PARK

GYMPIE

Noosa Heads
Sunshine Beach
Peregian Beach
Coolum Beach
MAROOCHYDORE
MOOLOOLABA
CALOUNDRA

NAMBOUR
BUDERIM
Landsborough
Beerwah

BRIBIE ISLAND NP
BONGAREE
Beachmere
Deception Bay
Tangalooma

CABOOLTURE

MORETON ISLAND NP

Moreton Bay

BRISBANE
Wynnum
Cleveland
Redland Bay

North Stradbroke Island
(Minjerribah)

Point Lookout

CORAL SEA

IPSWICH

GOLD COAST

Sanctuary Cove
Helensvale
Main Beach
Surfers Paradise
Burleigh Heads
Currumbin
Coolangatta
Tweed Heads

NERANG
Mudgeeraba

Banora Point
Kingscliff
Bogangar
Hastings Point
Pottsville
Crabbes Creek
Ocean Shores
Brunswick Heads
Byron Bay
Suffolk Park
Lennox Head

LISMORE
Alstonville
Wollongbar
BALLINA
Empire Vale

NEW SOUTH WALES

TOOWOOMBA
WARWICK

Stanthorpe

Goondiwindi

Moura
Biloela
Theodore
Monto
Mundubbera
Gayndah

Miles
Chinchilla
Dalby
Nanango
Kingaroy
Wondai
Murgon
Cherbourg

Oakey
Highfields

Pittsworth

QUEENSLAND

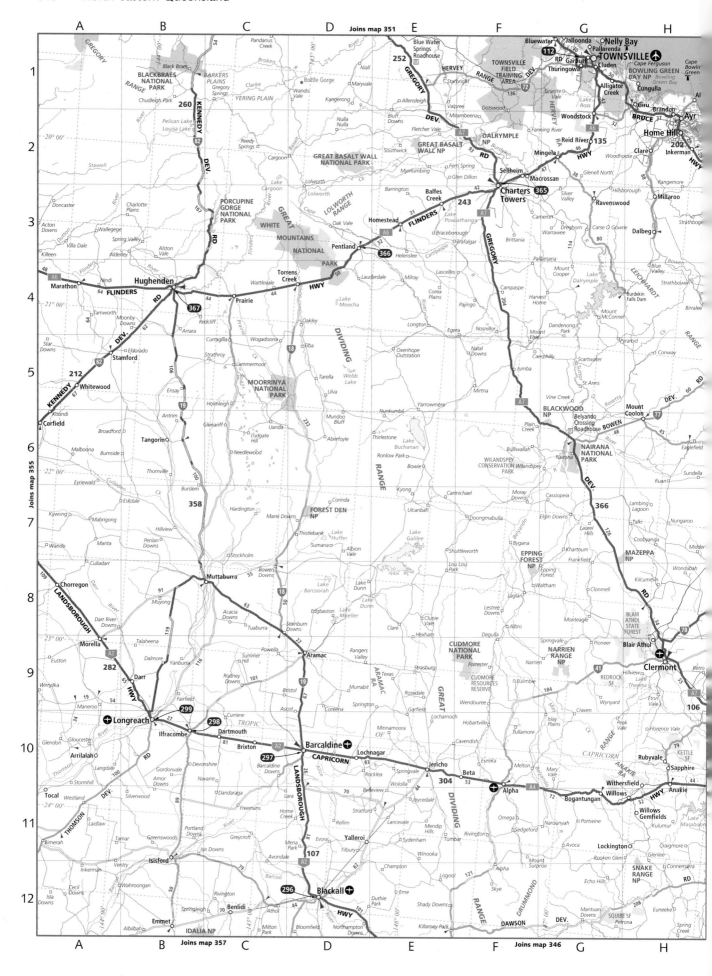

Joins map 351
Joins map 355
Joins map 357
Joins map 346

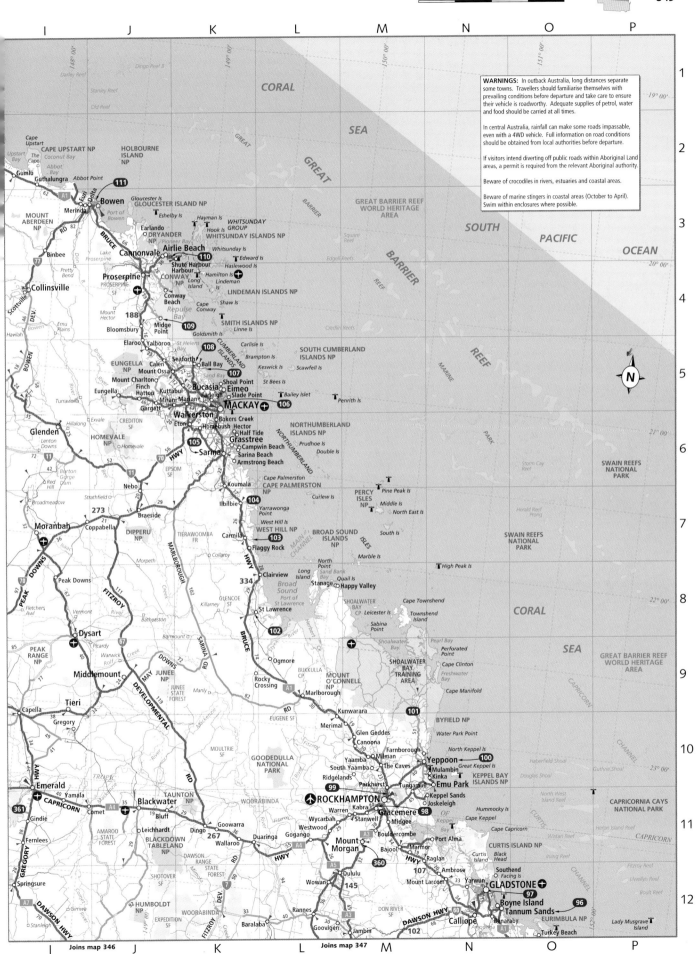

0   25   50   75   100 km

WARNINGS: In outback Australia, long distances separate some towns. Travellers should familiarise themselves with prevailing conditions before departure and take care to ensure their vehicle is roadworthy. Adequate supplies of petrol, water and food should be carried at all times.

In central Australia, rainfall can make some roads impassable, even with a 4WD vehicle. Full information on road conditions should be obtained from local authorities before departure.

If visitors intend diverting off public roads within Aboriginal Land areas, a permit is required from the relevant Aboriginal authority.

Beware of crocodiles in rivers, estuaries and coastal areas.

Beware of marine stingers in coastal areas (October to April). Swim within enclosures where possible.

CORAL

SEA

GREAT

BARRIER

REEF

SOUTH PACIFIC OCEAN

GREAT BARRIER REEF WORLD HERITAGE AREA

CORAL SEA

GREAT BARRIER REEF WORLD HERITAGE AREA

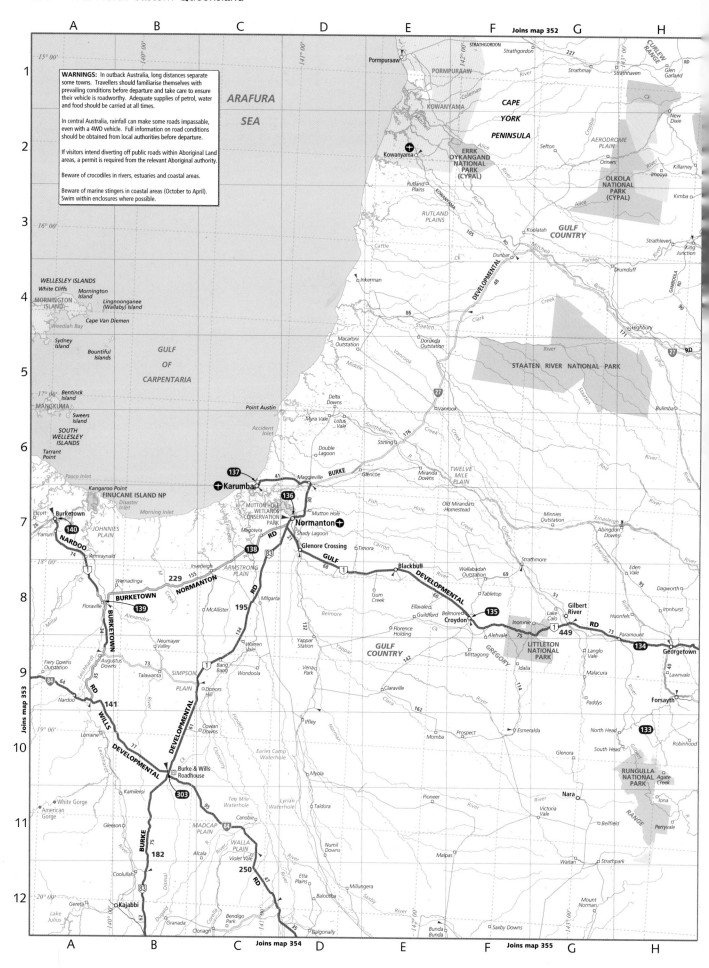

Joins map 352

Joins map 353

Joins map 354

Joins map 355

WARNINGS: In outback Australia, long distances separate some towns. Travellers should familiarise themselves with prevailing conditions before departure and take care to ensure their vehicle is roadworthy. Adequate supplies of petrol, water and food should be carried at all times.

In central Australia, rainfall can make some roads impassable, even with a 4WD vehicle. Full information on road conditions should be obtained from local authorities before departure.

If visitors intend diverting off public roads within Aboriginal Land areas, a permit is required from the relevant Aboriginal authority.

Beware of crocodiles in rivers, estuaries and coastal areas.

Beware of marine stingers in coastal areas (October to April). Swim within enclosures where possible.

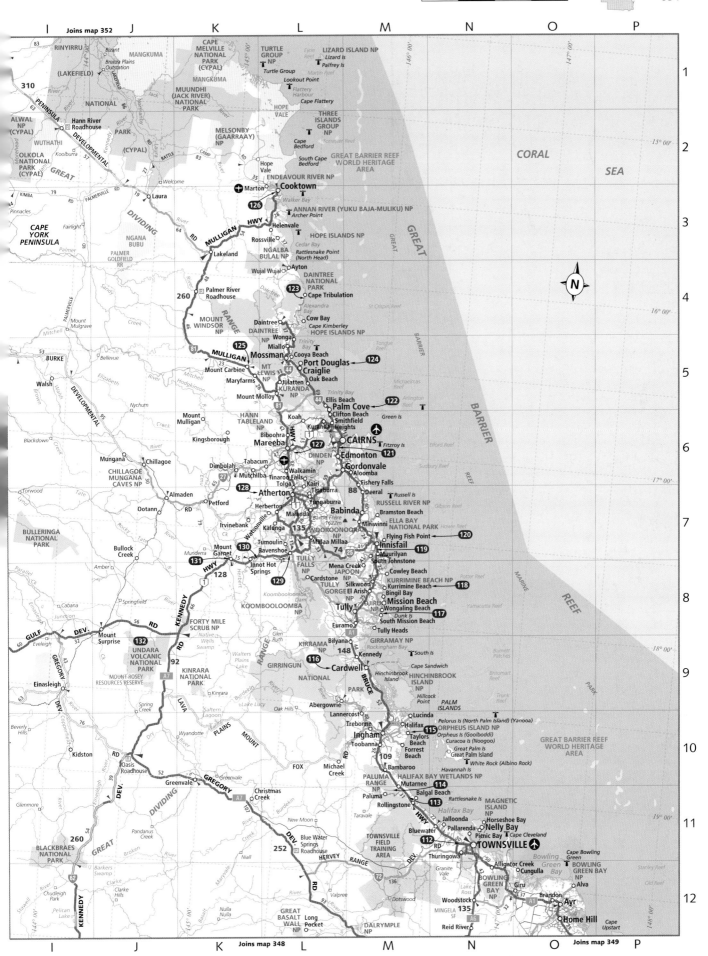

0 25 50 75 100 km

I J K L M N O P

1
2
3
4
5
6
7
8
9
10
11
12

CORAL

SEA

RINYIRRU
(LAKEFIELD)
NATIONAL

Bizant
Breeza Plains
Outstation

MANGKUMA

CAPE
MELVILLE
NATIONAL
PARK
(CYPAL)

TURTLE
GROUP
NP

Eyrie
Reef

LIZARD ISLAND NP
Lizard Is
Palfrey Is

310

MUUNDHI
(JACK RIVER)
NATIONAL
PARK

Turtle Group
Lookout Point

MANGKUMA

Flattery
Harbour
Cape Flattery

Hann River
Roadhouse

PARK
(CYPAL)

MELSONBY
(GAARRAAY)
NP

HOPE
VALE

THREE
ISLANDS
GROUP
NP

Cape
Bedford

GREAT BARRIER REEF
WORLD HERITAGE
AREA

ALWAL
NP
(CYPAL)

WUTHATHI

Koolburra

South Cape
Bedford

OLKOLA
NATIONAL
PARK
(CYPAL)

KIMBA

Hope Vale

ENDEAVOUR RIVER NP

Pinnacles

Fairlight

Laura

Marton

Cooktown

Walker Bay

126

ANNAN RIVER (YUKU BAJA-MULIKU) NP
Archer Point

CAPE
YORK
PENINSULA

NGANA
BUBU

Helenvale

Rossville

HOPE ISLANDS NP

Cedar Bay

GREAT

PALMER
GOLDFIELD
RR

Lakeland

NGALBA
BULAL NP

Rattlesnake Point
(North Head)

Ayton

260

Palmer River
Roadhouse

DAINTREE
NATIONAL
PARK

123

Cape Tribulation

MOUNT
WINDSOR
NP

Alexandra
Bay

St Crispin Reef

Daintree

Cow Bay
Cape Kimberley

HOPE ISLANDS NP

BURKE

Bellevue

DAINTREE
NP

Wonga
Miallo

81

125

MULLIGAN

Mossman
MT
LEWIS
NP

Cooya Beach
Port Douglas

124

Walsh

Mount Carbine

Craiglie

Maryfarms

Julatten

Oak Beach

Mungana

Mount Molloy

KURANDA
NP

Ellis Beach

122

Chillagoe

Mount
Mulligan

HANN
TABLELAND
NP

Koah

Clifton Beach
Smithfield
Kuranda Heights

Palm Cove

Green Is

CHILLAGOE
MUNGANA
CAVES NP

Kingsborough

Biboohra

Mareeba

127

CAIRNS

121

Fitzroy Is

Elford Reef

Almaden

Petford

Dimbulah
Tabacum
Mutchilba
Walkamin

DINDEN
NP

Edmonton
Gordonvale
Aloomba

128

Atherton

Tinaroo Falls
Tolga
Kairi
Timburra

Fishery Falls

88

Deeral

RUSSELL RIVER NP

Russell Is

Gibson Reef

BULLERINGA
NATIONAL
PARK

Irvinebank

Herberton

Yungaburra

Bartle Frere
1622m

Bramston Beach

ELLA BAY
NATIONAL PARK

Bullock
Creek

Watsonville
Kalunga

135

Malanda

WOOROONOORAN
NP

Miriwinni

Howie Reef

Mount
Garnet

130

Tumoulin
Ravenshoe

Millaa Millaa

74

Flying Fish Point

120

131

128

Innot Hot
Springs

129

TULLY
FALLS
NP

Mena Creek

Mourilyan
South Johnstone

Innisfail

119

Cardstone

JAPOON
NP

TULLY
GORGE
NP

Silkwood
El Arish

Cowley Beach

Kurrimine Beach

118

KURRIMINE BEACH NP

Potter Reef

KOOMBOOLOOMBA
NP

Tully

Bingil Bay
Mission Beach

117

FORTY MILE
SCRUB NP

Euramo

Wongaling Beach
South Mission Beach
Tully Heads

Dunk Is

Mount
Surprise

132

Bilyana

KIRRAMA
NP

GIRRAMAY NP

Rockingham Bay

South Is

Cape Sandwich

UNDARA
VOLCANIC
NATIONAL
PARK

92

116

148

Kennedy

Einasleigh

KINRARA
NATIONAL
PARK

GIRRINGUN

Cardwell

Hinchinbrook
Island

HINCHINBROOK
ISLAND
NP

NATIONAL

Hillock
Point

PALM
ISLANDS

GREAT BARRIER REEF
WORLD HERITAGE
AREA

Abergowrie

PARK

Kidston

Oasis
Roadhouse

Lannercost

Trebonne

Lucinda

Pelorus Is (North Palm Island) (Yanooa)

Greenvale

Ingham

Halifax
Taylors
Beach

ORPHEUS ISLAND NP
Orpheus Is (Goolboddi)
Curacoa Is (Noogoo)

109

Toobanna

Forrest Beach

Great Palm Is
Great Palm Island

White Rock (Albino Rock)

Christmas
Creek

Bambaroo

Havannah Is

Michael
Creek

PALUMA
RANGE
NP

Mutarnee

HALIFAX BAY WETLANDS NP

Balgal Beach

114

Blackbraes
National
Park

Blue Water
Springs
Roadhouse

252

Paluma

113

Rollingstone

Rattlesnake Is

MAGNETIC
ISLAND
NP

Halifax Bay

Horseshoe Bay

260

Jalloonda
Pallarenda

Nelly Bay

Picnic Bay

Cape Cleveland

112

Bluewater

TOWNSVILLE
FIELD
TRAINING
AREA

Thuringowa

TOWNSVILLE

Bowling

Cape Bowling
Green

BOWLING
GREEN BAY
NP

Woodstock

MINGELA
SF

135

Granite
Vale

BOWLING
GREEN
BAY NP

Alligator Creek
Cungulla

Giru

Brandon
Ayr

Alva

Reid River

Home Hill

Cape
Upstart

QUEENSLAND

0   25   50   75   100 km

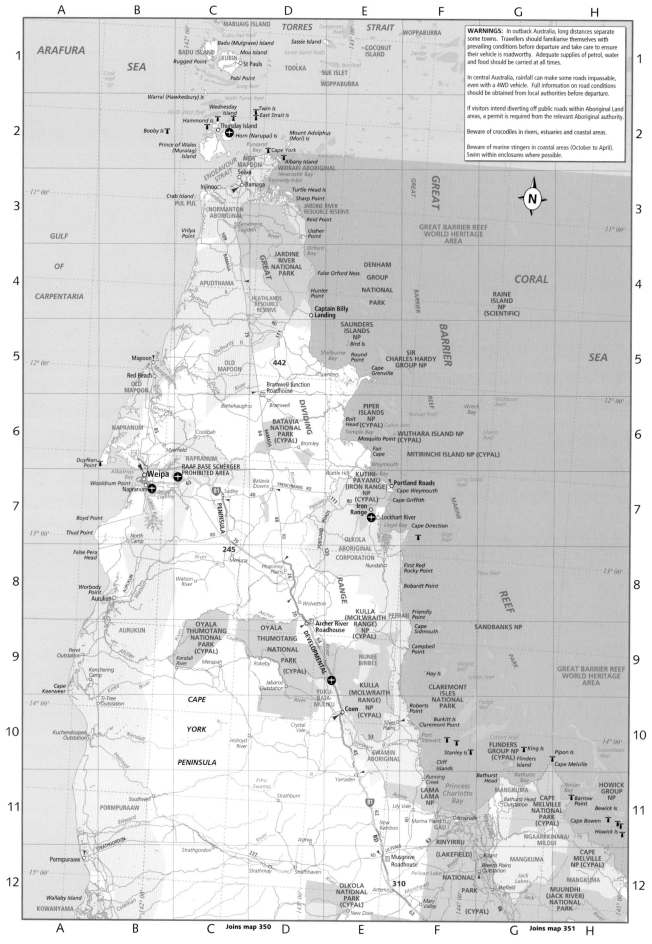

ARAFURA

SEA

MABUAIG ISLAND
TORRES   STRAIT   WOPPABURRA
Kulku Pad Reef
Badu (Mulgrave) Island
BADU ISLAND   Moa Island   COCONUT
Rugged Point   KUBIN   St Pauls   ISLAND
Pabi Point   TOOLKA   SUE ISLET
Long Reef   WOPPABURRA

Warral (Hawkesbury) Is
Wednesday Island   Twin Is
Hammond Is   East Strait Is
Booby Is   Thursday Island   Mount Adolphus
Horn (Narupai) Is   (Mori) Is
Prince of Wales   Punsand
(Muralag)   Bay   Cape York
Island   NEW   Albany Island
MAPOON   WIRRARI ABORIGINAL
Seisia   Newcastle Bay
Injinoo   Bamaga   Kennedy Inlet

11° 00'
Crab Island   Turtle Head Is
PUL PUL   Sharp Point
NORMANTON   JARDINE RIVER
ABORIGINAL   RESOURCE RESERVE
Reid Point
Sanamere
Lagoon   Ussher
Vrilya   River   Point
Point

GULF

OF

CARPENTARIA

GREAT   GREAT BARRIER REEF
WORLD HERITAGE
AREA

N

JARDINE   Orford
RIVER   Bay
NATIONAL   DENHAM
APUDTHAMA   PARK   False Orford Ness   GROUP
CORAL
Hunter   NATIONAL   RAINE
HEATHLANDS   Point   PARK   ISLAND
RESOURCE   NP
RESERVE   Captain Billy   (SCIENTIFIC)
Landing
SAUNDERS
ISLANDS
Mapoon   NP   SEA
Red Beach   OLD   Bird Is
MAPOON   Shelburne   Round   SIR
Bramwell Junction   Bay   Point   CHARLES HARDY
442   Roadhouse   Cape   GROUP NP
Spencers   Grenville
Bertiehaugh   Bramwell   REEF   Wreck
PIPER   Bay
NAPRANUM   BATAVIA   ISLANDS
Coolibah   NATIONAL   Bolt   NP (CYPAL)   Nomad Reef
Myerfield   PARK   Head   Gallon Reef
(CYPAL)   Bromley   Temple Bay   WUTHARA ISLAND NP
Mosquito Point   (CYPAL)
Duyfken   NAPRANUM   Fair   MITIRINCHI ISLAND NP (CYPAL)
Point   RAAF BASE SCHERGER   Cape   Weymouth
Albatross   PROHIBITED AREA   Wattle Hill   Bay
Bay   Weipa   Batavia   KUTINI-   Portland Roads
Wooldrum Point   Downs   FRENCHMANS RD   PAYAMU   Cape Weymouth
Napranum   Sudley   (IRON RANGE)   Cape Griffith
NP   Iron
Boyd Point   (CYPAL)   Range   Lockhart River
North   Lloyd Bay   Cape Direction
Thud Point   Camp   Bligh Reef
False Pera   River   245   MARINE
Head   Meriuna   OLKOLA   First Red
Picaninny   ABORIGINAL   Rocky Point
Worbody   Watson   Plains   CORPORATION
Point   River   Nundah   REEF
Aurukun   Wolverton   RANGE   Bobardt Point
Archer   KULLA   Friendly
AURUKUN   (MCILWRAITH   Point
OYALA   OYALA   RANGE)   Cape   SANDBANKS NP
THUMOTANG   THUMOTANG   NP   Sidmouth
Peret   NATIONAL   NATIONAL   (CYPAL)   Campbell
Outstation   PARK   PARK   Point
Kendall   (CYPAL)   (CYPAL)   Archer   NUNEE   GREAT BARRIER REEF
Kenchering   River   Merapah   Rokeby   BINBEE   Hay Is   WORLD HERITAGE
Camp   River   KULLA   CLAREMONT   AREA
Cape   Jabaroo   (MCILWRAITH   ISLES
Keerweer   Ti-Tree   Outstation   RANGE)   Roberts   NATIONAL
Outstation   YUKU-   NATIONAL   Point   PARK
CAPE   BAJA-   PARK   Burkitt Is
MULKU   Coen   (CYPAL)   Claremont Point
Kuchendoopen   YORK   Crystal   Silver   Port   FLINDERS
Outstation   Vale   Plains   Stewart   GROUP NP   King Is
Holroyd   53   Stanley Is   (CYPAL)   Pipon Is
PENINSULA   River   EWAMIN   Cliff   Flinders   Cape Melville
ABORIGINAL   Islands   Island
Running   HOWICK
Emu   Yarraden   Creek   Bathurst   GROUP
Swamp   LAMA   Head   NP
Strathburn   LAMA   Princess   Barrow
PORMPURAAW   NP   Charlotte   MANGKUMA   Point
Edward   Lily Vale   Bay   Bathurst Head   CAPE   Bewick Is
New Bamboo   Marina Plains   Outstation   MELVILLE   Cape Bowen
Strathgordon   GAU   Aloszville   NATIONAL   Howick Is
Pormpuraaw   RINYIRRU   PARK
STRATHGORDON   Strathmay   Strathhaven   Musgrave   (LAKEFIELD)   (CYPAL)   MANGKUMA
15° 00'   Roadhouse   Bizant   NGAARRKINABA/
Wallaby Island   Strathgordon   Breeze Plains   MILDUI   CAPE
KOWANYAMA   River   310   Outstation   MANGKUMA   MELVILLE
OLKOLA   Pelican Lake   Lakefield   NP (CYPAL)
NATIONAL   Artesia   Jack   MUUNDHI
PARK   Mary   Lakes   MANGKUMA   (JACK RIVER)
(CYPAL)   Valley   NATIONAL
New Dixie   Morehead   Jack   PARK

Joins map 350   Joins map 351

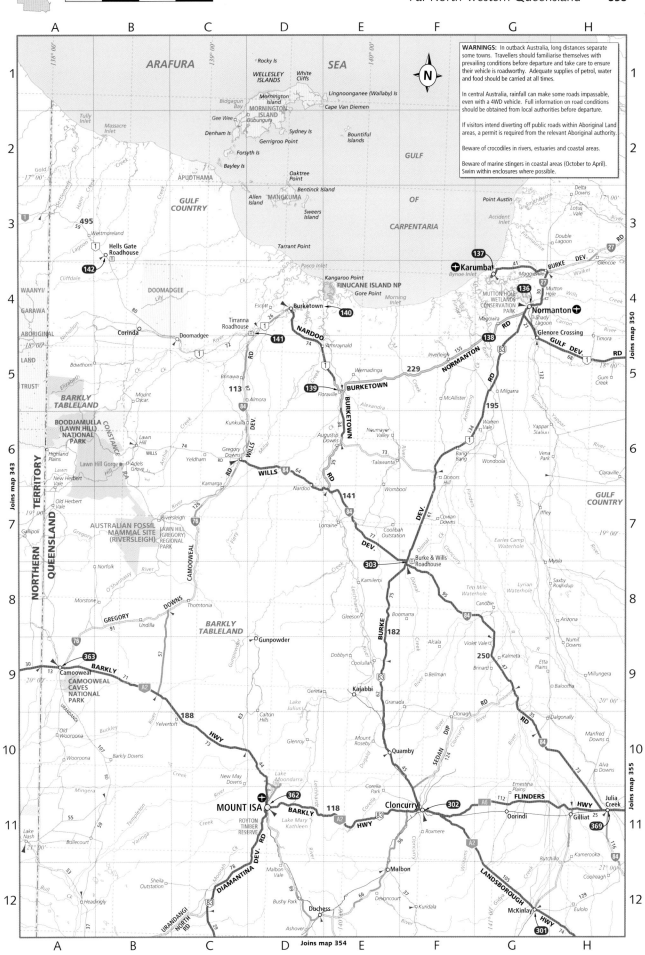

QUEENSLAND

WARNINGS: In outback Australia, long distances separate some towns. Travellers should familiarise themselves with prevailing conditions before departure and take care to ensure their vehicle is roadworthy. Adequate supplies of petrol, water and food should be carried at all times.

In central Australia, rainfall can make some roads impassable, even with a 4WD vehicle. Full information on road conditions should be obtained from local authorities before departure.

If visitors intend diverting off public roads within Aboriginal Land areas, a permit is required from the relevant Aboriginal authority.

Beware of crocodiles in rivers, estuaries and coastal areas.

Beware of marine stingers in coastal areas (October to April). Swim within enclosures where possible.

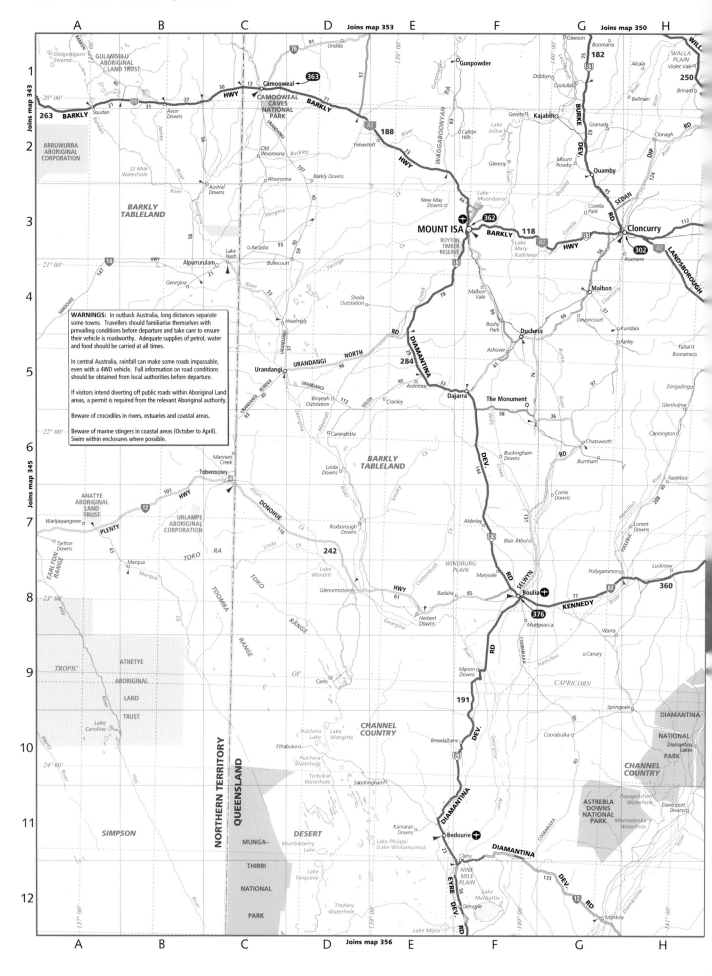

WARNINGS: In outback Australia, long distances separate some towns. Travellers should familiarise themselves with prevailing conditions before departure and take care to ensure their vehicle is roadworthy. Adequate supplies of petrol, water and food should be carried at all times.

In central Australia, rainfall can make some roads impassable, even with a 4WD vehicle. Full information on road conditions should be obtained from local authorities before departure.

If visitors intend diverting off public roads within Aboriginal Land areas, a permit is required from the relevant Aboriginal authority.

Beware of crocodiles in rivers, estuaries and coastal areas.

Beware of marine stingers in coastal areas (October to April). Swim within enclosures where possible.

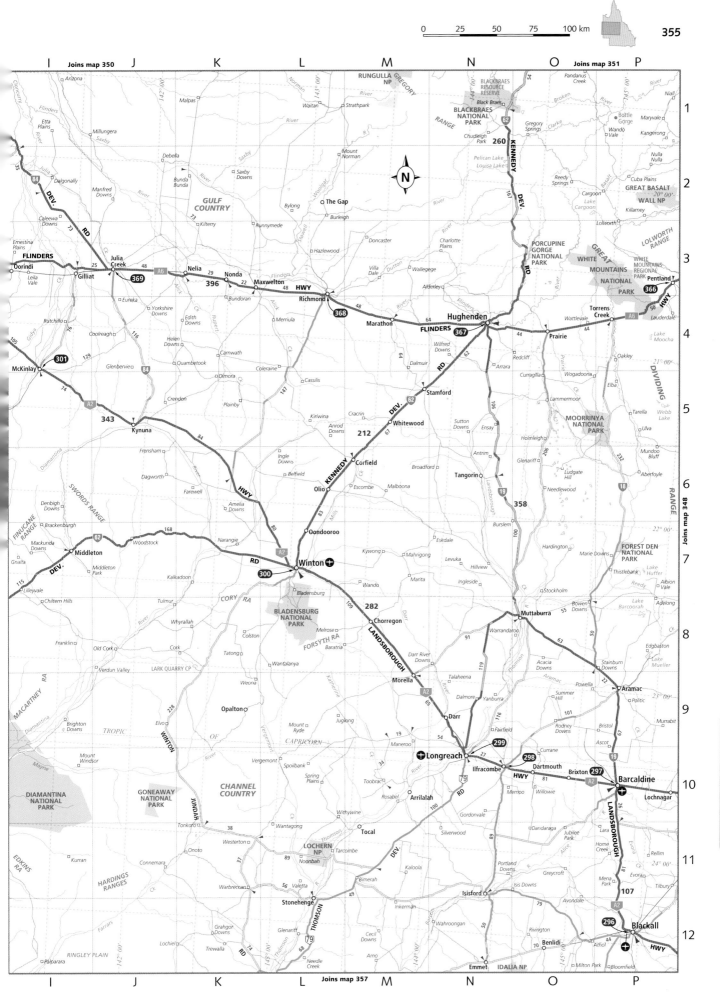

QUEENSLAND

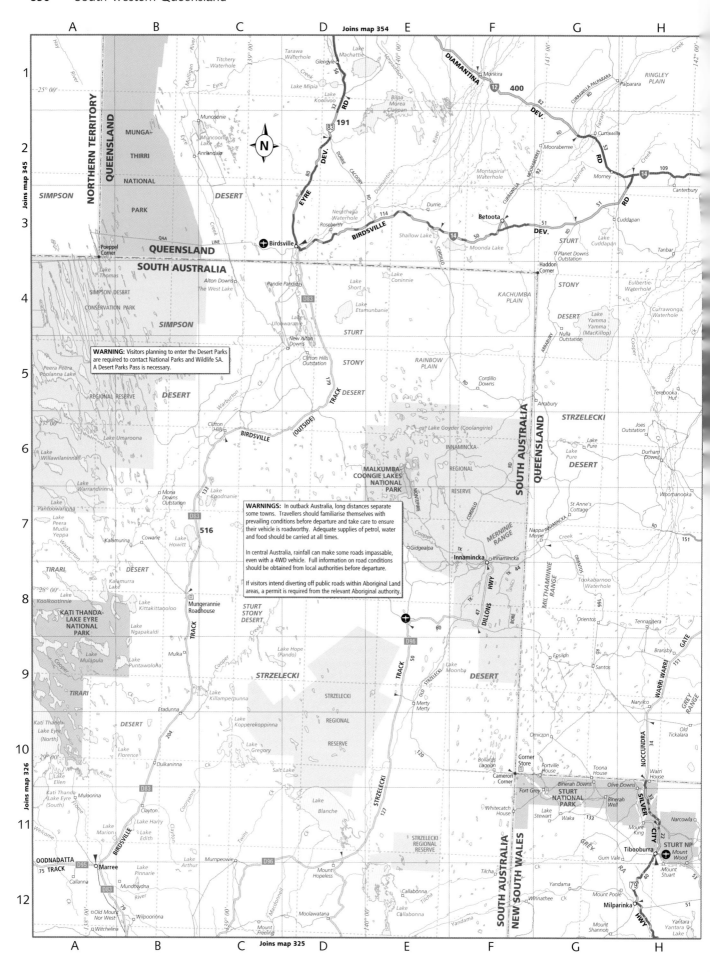

WARNING: Visitors planning to enter the Desert Parks are required to contact National Parks and Wildlife SA. A Desert Parks Pass is necessary.

WARNINGS: In outback Australia, long distances separate some towns. Travellers should familiarise themselves with prevailing conditions before departure and take care to ensure their vehicle is roadworthy. Adequate supplies of petrol, water and food should be carried at all times.

In central Australia, rainfall can make some roads impassable, even with a 4WD vehicle. Full information on road conditions should be obtained from local authorities before departure.

If visitors intend diverting off public roads within Aboriginal Land areas, a permit is required from the relevant Aboriginal authority.

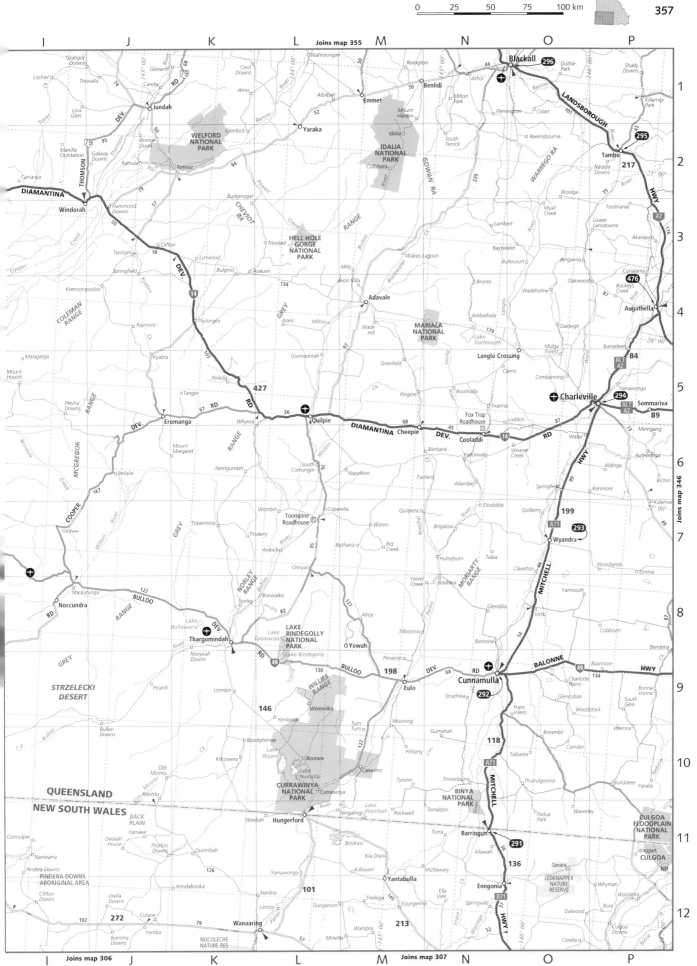

0 25 50 75 100 km

Joins map 355

Joins map 346

Joins map 306

Joins map 307

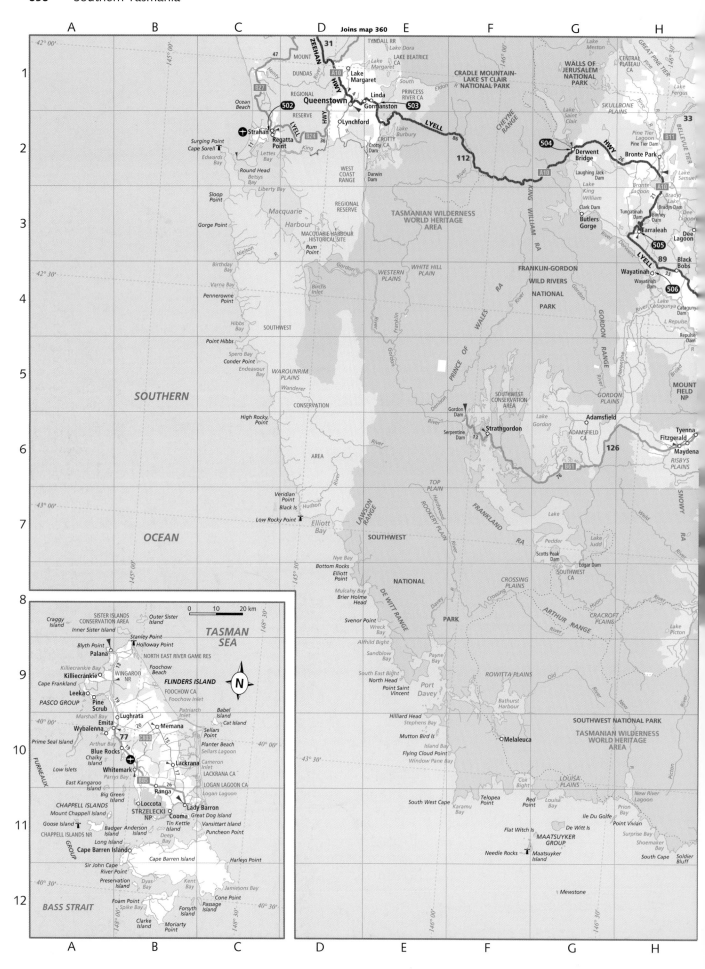

Joins map 360

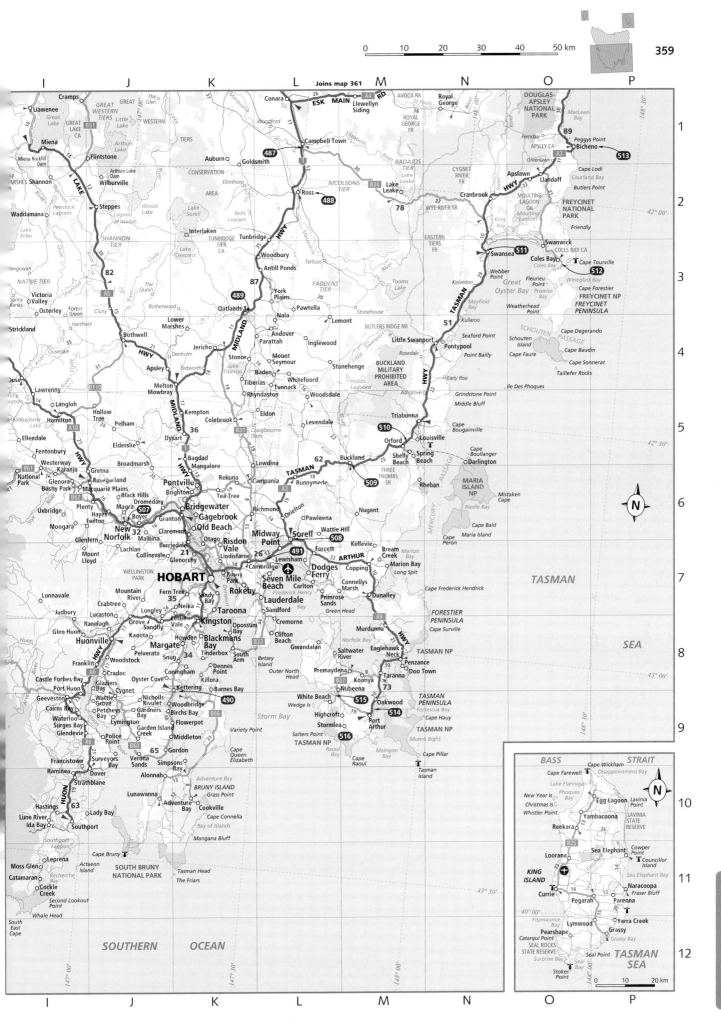

0 10 20 30 40 50 km

Joins map 361

I   J   K   L   M   N   O   P

SOUTHERN   OCEAN

TASMAN

SEA

BASS   STRAIT

KING ISLAND

TASMAN SEA

0 10 20 km

TASMANIA

Joins map 358

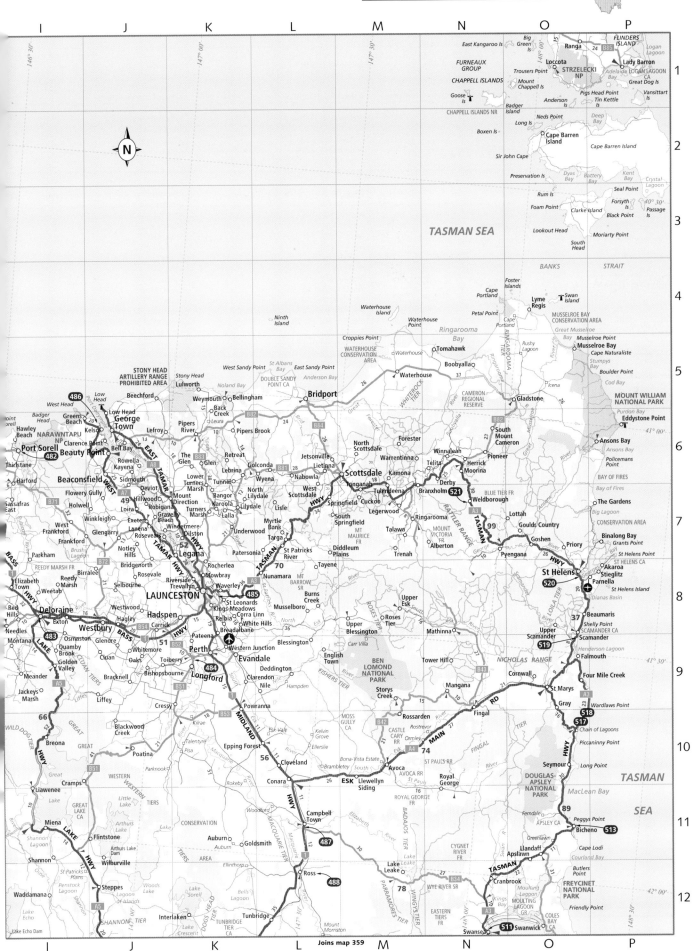

0 10 20 30 40 50 km

TASMAN SEA

I J K L M N O P

FURNEAUX GROUP

CHAPPELL ISLANDS

East Kangaroo Is

Big Green Is

Ranga

FLINDERS ISLAND

Loccota

Lady Barron

STRZELECKI NP

Trousers Point

Mount Chappell Is

Adelaide

LOGAN LAGOON CA

Logan Lagoon

Great Dog Is

CHAPPELL ISLANDS NR

Goose Is

Pigs Head Point

Tin Kettle Is

Vansittart Is

Badger Island

Anderson Is

Long Is

Neds Point

Deep Bay

Boxen Is

Cape Barren Island

Cape Barren Island

Sir John Cape

Preservation Is

Dyas Bay

Battery Bay

Kent Bay

Crystal Lagoon

Rum Is

Seal Point

Foam Point

Clarke Island

Forsyth Is

40° 30'

Black Point

Passage Is

Lookout Head

Moriarty Point

South Head

BANKS   STRAIT

Foster Islands

Cape Portland

Swan Island

Lyme Regis

MUSSELROE BAY CONSERVATION AREA

Waterhouse Island

Cape Portland

Great Musselroe Bay

Musselroe Point

Musselroe Bay

Cape Naturaliste

Waterhouse Point

Ringarooma Bay

Stumpys Bay

Boulder Point

Croppies Point

Waterhouse

Icena

Cod Bay

MOUNT WILLIAM NATIONAL PARK

West Sandy Point

St Albans Bay

East Sandy Point

Anderson Bay

Waterhouse

Tomahawk

Boobyalla

CAMERON REGIONAL RESERVE

Gladstone

Purdon Bay

Eddystone Point

41° 00'

Ninth Island

Double Sandy Point CA

Noland Bay

Bridport

South Mount Cameron

Ansons Bay

Ansons Bay

STONY HEAD ARTILLERY RANGE PROHIBITED AREA

Stony Head

Lulworth

Weymouth

Bellingham

Back Creek

Leura

North Scottsdale

Forester

Winnaleah

Herrick

Pioneer

Policemans Point

BAY OF FIRES

Beechford

Low Head

George Town

Lefroy

Pipers River

Pipers Brook

Jetsonville

Scottsdale

Kamona

Telita

Moorina

The Gardens

West Head

Low Head

Kelso

Glen

Golconda

West Scottsdale

Tonganah

Tulendeena

Branxholm

Derby

Weldborough

BLUE TIER FR

Lottah

Big Musselroe Bay

CONSERVATION AREA

Badger Head

Greens Beach

Clarence Point

Bell Bay

Rowella

Kayena

The Glen

Lebrina

Tunnel

Bangor

Nabowla

Lietinna

Warrentinna

Springfield

Cuckoo

Legerwood

Ringarooma

Goulds Country

Binalong Bay

Grants Point

Hawley Beach

NARAWNTAPU NP

Sidmouth

Lower Turners Marsh

North Lilydale

Lilydale

South Springfield

Talawa

Goshen

Priory

Port Sorell

Beauty Point

Deviot

Hillwood

Mount Direction

Karoola

Lalla

Myrtle Bank

Targa

MT MAURICE FR

Trenah

Pyengana

St Helens CA

Akaroa

Stieglitz

Thirlstane

Beaconsfield

Loira

Robigana

Gravelly Beach

Windermere

Underwood

Patersonia

St Patricks River

Diddleum Plains

Alberton

St Helens

Parnella

Harford

Flowery Gully

Holwell

Exeter

Lanena

Rosevears

Dilston

Rocherlea

Nunamara

Tayene

St Helens Island

Sassafras

Frankford

Glengarry

Winkleigh

Notley Hills

Bridgenorth

Mowbray

MT BARROW SR

Burns Creek

Upper Esk

Roses Tier

Beaumaris

West Frankford

Riverside

Trevallyn

Waverley

Mathinna

Shelly Point

SCAMANDER CA

Parkham

Birralee

Rosevale

Selbourne

LAUNCESTON

St Leonards

Kings Meadows

Corra Linn

White Hills

Musselboro

Upper Blessington

Roses Tier

Upper Scamander

Scamander

Elizabeth Town

Westwood

Hagley

Hadspen

Carrick

Relbia

Breadalbane

Blessington

Tower Hill

NICHOLAS RANGE

Falmouth

Red Hills

Deloraine

Exton

Westbury

Whitemore

Perth

Western Junction

Pateena

English Town

Deddington

Mangana

Cornwall

Four Mile Creek

Needles

Osmaston

Glenore

Oaks

Toiberry

Evandale

Clarendon

Nile

St Marys

Gray

Montana

Quamby Brook

Cluan

Bishopsbourne

Longford

Hampden

BEN LOMOND NATIONAL PARK

Storys Creek

Fingal

Wardlaws Point

Meander

Golden Valley

Bracknell

Cressy

Powranna

FISHERS TIER

Rossarden

Rostrevor

Chain of Lagoons

Jackeys Marsh

Liffey

Blackwood Creek

Epping Forest

MOSS GULLY CA

Kelvin Grove

CASTLE CARY RR

Ormley

Avoca

Seymour

Piccaninny Point

Breona

Poatina

Cleveland

Ellerslie

Bona-Vista Estate

Brambletey

South

AVOCA RR

St Pauls RR

Royal George

DOUGLAS-APSLEY NATIONAL PARK

Long Point

TASMAN

Liawenee

Cramps

Pisa

Parknook

Conara

ESK

Llewellyn Siding

ROYAL GEORGE FR

Ferndale

MacLean Bay

SEA

WILD DOG TIER

GREAT LAKE

WESTERN

Rokeby

BADAJOS TIER

Peggys Point

Bicheno

Miena

Flintstone

Woodford

Campbell Town

Elizabeth River

Apsley CA

Llandaff

Apslawn

Cape Lodi

Shannon Lagoon

Arthurs Lake

Arthurs Lake Dam

Auburn

Goldsmith

Auburn

Ross

Greenlawn

Courland Bay

Shannon

Wilburville

CYGNET RIVER FR

Cranbrook

Butlers Point

FREYCINET NATIONAL PARK

St Patricks Plains

Steppes

Lake Leake

TASMAN

MOULTING LAGOON GR

42° 00'

Waddamana

Penstock Lagoon

Interlaken

Tunbridge

Mount Morriston

EASTERN TIERS FR

PARAMOORES TIER

YINGYS TIER

WYE RIVER SR

Kings Bay

COLES BAY CA

Friendly Point

Lake Echo

Lake Echo Dam

SHANNON TIER

DOGS HEAD

TUNBRIDGE TIER CA

Bells Lagoon

Swansea

Swanwick

I J K L M N O P

Joins map 359

TASMANIA

INDEX OF PLACE NAMES

This index includes all towns, localities, roadhouses, national parks and islands shown on the maps and mentioned in the text. Place names are followed by a map page number and grid reference, and/or the text page number on which that place is mentioned. A page number set in bold type indicates the main text entry for that place.

The alphabetical order followed in the index is that of 'word-by-word' – a space is considered to come before 'A' in the alphabet, and punctuation marks are ignored. Names beginning with Mc are indexed as Mac and those beginning with St as Saint.

The following abbreviations and contractions are used in the index:

ACT – Australian Capital Territory
JBT – Jervis Bay Territory
NSW – New South Wales
NP – National Park
NT – Northern Territory
Qld – Queensland
SA – South Australia
Tas. – Tasmania
Vic. – Victoria
WA – Western Australia

EXPLORE AUSTRALIA BY CARAVAN & MOTORHOME

Bald Rock Vic. 309 I12, 312 A5, 317 O6
Bald Rock NP NSW 305 L3, 347 L12
Baldry NSW 302 E3
Balfes Creek Qld 348 E3, **190**
Balfour Tas. 360 B6
Balgal Beach Qld 351 M11
Balgo Hills WA 339 N10
Balgowan SA 322 H7
Balingup WA 332 C9, 334 C10
Balintore Vic. 319 L8
Ball Bay Qld 349 K5
Balladonia WA 335 K7, **108**
Balladonia Roadhouse WA 335 K7, **108**
Balladoran NSW 304 C11
Ballalaba NSW 301 E5, 302 G11
Ballan Vic. 319 N4, **242**
Ballan North Vic. 319 N4
Ballandean Qld 305 K3, 347 K12
Ballangeich Vic. 318 H7
Ballarat Vic. 319 M4, **242, 243**
Ballarat Vic. to Horsham Vic. **244–5**
Ballark Vic. 319 N5
Ballaying WA 332 F8
Ballbank NSW 308 H10, 317 N3
Balldale NSW 309 N11, 313 J4
Ballendella Vic. 312 B6, 317 P8
Balliang Vic. 310 A4, 319 O5
Balliang East Vic. 310 A4, 319 O5
Ballidu WA 332 D1, 334 C5
Ballimore NSW 302 F1, 304 D12
Ballina NSW 305 O3, 347 N12, **33**
Ballina NSW to Tweed Heads NSW **35–6**
Ballyrogan Vic. 319 J3
Balmattum Vic. 312 F9
Balmoral Vic. 316 E12, 318 E2
Balnarring Vic. 310 C7
Balook Vic. 311 I8
Ralranald NSW 308 H7, 315 M9, **172**
Balrootan North Vic. 308 C12, 316 E7
Balumbah SA 322 E4, 324 D11
Bamaga Qld 352 C3
Bamawm Vic. 309 I12, 312 B6, 317 P7
Bamawm Extension Vic. 312 B6, 317 P7
Bambaroo Qld 351 M10
Bambill Vic. 308 C6, 314 E7, 323 P8
Bamboo Creek WA 336 F2, 338 F12
Bambra Vic. 319 M8
Bamganie Vic. 319 M6
Ban Ban NP Qld 347 L5
Banana Qld 347 I2
Bancroft Qld 347 K3
Bandiana Vic. 302 A12, 313 K6, **251**
Bandon Grove NSW 303 M2
Banealla SA 321 F6, 323 N12
Bangadilly NP NSW 301 F2, 303 I8
Bangalow NSW 305 O3, 347 N12, **35**
Bangerang Vic. 316 H6
Bangham SA 316 B8, 321 G8
Bangor Tas. 361 K7
Bania NP Qld 347 L3
Baniyala NT 341 M6
Banka Banka Station NT **162**
Bannaby NSW 301 F2, 302 H8
Bannerton Vic. 308 F7, 315 J9
Bannister NSW 301 E2, 302 G8
Bannister WA 332 D6
Bannockburn Vic. 319 N7
Banora Point NSW 305 O2, 347 N11
Banrock Station SA **258**
Banyan Vic. 317 I3
Banyena Vic. 317 I9
Baradine NSW 304 D8
Barakee NP NSW 305 J11
Barakula Qld 347 J6
Baralaba Qld 347 I1, 349 L12
Baranduda Vic. 313 K6
Barayamal NP NSW 305 I5
Barcaldine Qld 348 D10, 355 P10, **146, 186, 187**
Barcaldine Qld to Winton Qld **148–9**
Barellan NSW 302 A7, 309 N7
Barfold Vic. 312 A11, 317 P12, 319 P1
Bargara Qld 347 M3, **43**
Bargo NSW 301 G2, 303 J8
Barham NSW 309 I10, 312 A2, 317 O4
Baring Vic. 308 D9, 314 G12, 316 G2
Baringhup Vic. 317 N11, 319 N1

Barjarg Vic. 312 G10
Barkers Creek Vic. 312 A10, 317 O11, 319 O1
Barkly Vic. 317 K11
Barkly Homestead NT 343 L9, **188**
Barkstead Vic. 319 N3
Barmah Vic. 309 J12, 312 D5
Barmah NP Vic. 309 K11, 312 D4
Barmedman NSW 302 C6, 309 P6
Barmera SA 308 A6, 321 G1, 323 N7, **257**
Barmundu Qld 347 K1
Barnadown Vic. 312 B8, 317 P9
Barnard Island Group NP Qld 351 M8
Barnawartha Vic. 302 A12, 309 N12, 313 J6
Barnawartha North Vic. 313 K6
Barnes NSW 309 J12, 312 C5
Barnes Bay Tas. 359 K8
Barongarook Vic. 319 L9
Barongarook West Vic. 319 K8
Barooga NSW 309 L11, 312 G4
Barool NP NSW 305 L5
Baroota SA 323 I3, 324 G11
Barpinba Vic. 319 L7
Barraba NSW 304 H7
Barragga Bay NSW **18**
Barrakee Vic. 317 L7
Barramunga Vic. 319 L9
Barranyi (North Island) NP NT 341 N10, 343 N1
Barraport Vic. 308 H11, 317 M6
Barringo Vic. 310 B2, 312 B12
Barrington NSW 303 M1, 305 J12
Barrington Tas. 360 H7
Barrington Tops NP NSW 303 L1, 305 I12, **28**
Barringun NSW 307 M2, 346 A11, 357 N11, **142**
Barringun NSW to Augathella Qld **144–5**
Barron Gorge NP Qld 351 L6
Barrow Creek NT 345 I2
Barrow Island WA 333 C1
Barry NSW 302 G5, 305 I11
Barrys Reef Vic. 310 A2, 319 O3
Barton Vic. 319 I2
Barunga NT 340 G8
Barunga Gap SA 323 I6
Barwidgee Creek Vic. 313 K8
Barwo Vic. 312 D5
Barwon Downs Vic. 319 L9
Barwon Heads Vic. 310 A7, 319 O8, **130**
Baryulgil NSW 305 M4
Basket Swamp NP NSW 305 L3, 347 L12
Bass Vic. 310 E8
Batavia NP (CYPAL) Qld 352 D6
Batchelor NT 340 D5, **74**
Batchica Vic. 308 E12, 316 H6
Batehaven NSW 302 H12
Batemans Bay NSW 301 F6, 302 H12, **18, 248, 249**
Batemans Bay NSW to Adelaide SA **210–11**
Batemans Bay NSW to Canberra ACT **248–9**
Batemans Bay NSW to Nowra NSW **20–1**
Bates SA 331 J3
Batesford Vic. 319 N7
Bathumi Vic. 312 H5
Bathurst NSW 302 H5, **176, 177**
Bathurst Island NT 340 C3
Batlow NSW 301 A5, 302 D11, 313 P3
Bauhinia Qld 346 H2
Bauhinia Downs NT 341 L11, 343 L2
Bauple Qld 347 M5
Baw Baw NP Vic. 310 H5, 311 I5
Bawley Point NSW 301 F5, 303 I11, **20**
Baxter Vic. 310 D6
Bay Rock Qld 351 N11
Bayles Vic. 310 E6
Baynton Vic. 312 B11, 317 P12, 319 P2
Beachmere Qld 347 N8
Beachport SA 321 E10, **120**
Beacon WA 332 F1, 334 D5
Beaconsfield Tas. 361 J6, **276**
Beaconsfield Vic. 310 E6
Beagle Bay WA 338 H6
Bealiba Vic. 317 L10
Beardmore Vic. 311 I5
Beargamil NSW 302 E3
Bearii Vic. 309 K11, 312 E4
Bears Lagoon Vic. 308 H12, 317 N7
Beauchamp Vic. 317 L3
Beaudesert Qld 305 N1, 347 M10, **33**

Beaufort SA 323 I6
Beaufort Vic. 319 K3, **244**
Beaumaris Tas. 361 O8, **292**
Beauty Point NSW 301 E8
Beauty Point Tas. 361 J6, **276**
Beazleys Bridge Vic. 317 J9
Beckom NSW 302 B7, 309 O7
Bedarra Island Qld 351 M8
Bedgerebong NSW 302 D4
Bedourie Qld 354 E11
Beeac Vic. 319 L7
Beebo Qld 305 I2, 347 J11
Beech Forest Vic. 319 K10
Beechford Tas. 361 J5
Beechwood NSW 305 L11
Beechworth Vic. 313 J7
Beelbangera NSW 309 M7
Beelu NP WA 332 C5, 334 C7
Beenleigh Qld 347 N10
Beeron NP Qld 347 K5
Beerwah Qld 347 N8, **40**
Bega NSW 301 E9, 320 H6, **16**
Bega NSW to Batemans Bay NSW **18–19**
Beggan Beggan NSW 301 B2, 302 D8
Beilpajah NSW 308 H2
Belair SA 323 J9
Belair NP SA 321 B3, 323 J9
Belalie North SA 323 J4, 325 I11
Belbora NSW 303 N1, 305 K12
Belconnen ACT 300 D4, 301 C4, 302 F10
Belford NSW 303 L3
Belford NP NSW 303 L3
Belgrave Vic. 310 E5
Belka WA 332 G4
Bell NSW 303 I5
Bell Qld 347 K7
Bell Bay Tas. 361 J6
Bellarine Vic. 310 B6, 319 P7
Bellarwi NSW 302 B6, 309 P6
Bellata NSW 304 F5, **236**
Bellbird NSW 303 L4
Bellbird Creek Vic. 301 B12, 320 C11
Bellbrae Vic. 319 N8
Bellbridge Vic. 313 L6
Bellbrook NSW 305 L9
Bellellen Vic. 317 I12, 319 I1
Bellingen NSW 305 M8
Bellinger River NP NSW 305 M8
Bellingham Tas. 361 K5
Bellmount Forest NSW 301 D3, 302 F9
Bells Beach Vic. **128**
Bellthorpe NP Qld 347 M8
Belltrees NSW 303 K1, 305 I12
Belmont NSW 306 B10
Belmont Vic. 310 A6, 319 O7
Belmunging WA 332 E4
Beloka NSW 301 B8, 320 D5
Belowra NSW 301 E7, 320 H3
Beltana SA 324 H4
Beltana Roadhouse SA 324 H4
Belton SA 323 K1, 325 I9
Belvidere SA 321 C4
Belyando Crossing Roadhouse Qld 348 G6
Belyuen NT 340 D4
Bemboka NSW 301 D9, 320 G5
Bemm River Vic. 301 B12, 320 D11
Ben Boyd NP NSW 301 E10, 320 H9, **17**
Ben Bullen NSW 303 I4
Ben Halls Gap NP NSW 305 I11
Ben Lomond NSW 305 J6
Ben Lomond NP Tas. 361 M9
Ben Nevis Vic. 317 J12, 319 J2
Bena NSW 302 B5, 309 P5
Bena Vic. 310 F8
Benalla Vic. 312 G8, **212**
Benambra Vic. 311 N1, 313 N11
Benambra NP NSW 302 B11, 309 O11, 313 L4
Benaraby Qld 347 L1, 349 N12, **45**
Benarkin Qld 347 L7
Benarkin NP Qld 347 L8
Benayeo Vic. 316 B10, 321 H9
Bencubbin WA 332 F2, 334 D5
Bendalong NSW 301 G5, 303 I11, **21**
Bendemeer NSW 305 I9
Bendick Murrell NSW 301 B1, 302 E7
Bendidee NP Qld 304 H1, 347 I10

Bendigo Vic. 312 A9, 317 O10
Bendoc Vic. 301 B10, 320 D8
Bendolba NSW 303 M2
Beneree NSW 302 G5
Benetook Vic. 308 D6, 314 G7
Benger WA 332 C8
Bengworden Vic. 311 M6
Beni NSW 302 F1, 304 C12
Beninbi NP Qld 347 L5
Benjeroop Vic. 308 H10, 317 M3
Benlidi Qld 348 C12, 355 O12, 357 M1
Bennies Vic. 313 I11
Bentinck Island Qld 350 A5, 353 D2
Bentley NSW 305 N3
Benwerrin Vic. 319 M9
Berat Qld 305 L1
Beremboke Vic. 319 N5
Berendebba NSW 302 D6
Beresfield NSW 303 L4
Bergalia NSW 301 F7
Bermagui NSW 301 E8, **18**
Bermagui South NSW 301 E8
Bernier Island WA 333 B7
Berri SA 308 A6, 321 G1, 323 N7, **257**
Berridale NSW 301 B8, 320 D4
Berriedale Tas. 359 K6
Berrigan NSW 309 L11, 312 G3
Berrima NSW 301 G2, 303 I8, **218**
Berrimal Vic. 317 L8
Berringa Vic. 319 L5
Berringama Vic. 313 N7
Berriwillock Vic. 308 F10, 317 J3
Berry NSW 301 G3, 303 J9, **22**
Berry Springs NT 340 D5, **73**
Berrybank Vic. 319 K6
Berwick Vic. 310 D6
Bessiebelle Vic. 318 E7
Beswick NT 340 H8
Bet Bet Vic. 317 M11
Beta Qld 348 F10
Bete Bolong Vic. 301 A12, 311 P5, 320 B11
Bethanga Vic. 313 L6
Bethungra NSW 301 A3, 302 D8
Betley Vic. 317 M11
Betoota Qld 327 N1, 356 F3
Beulah Tas. 360 H8
Beulah Vic. 308 E11, 316 H5
Beulah East Vic. 308 E11, 316 H5
Beulah West Vic. 308 E11, 316 G5
Bevendale NSW 301 D2, 302 F8
Beverford Vic. 308 G9, 315 L12, 317 L1
Beveridge Vic. 310 C2
Beverley WA 332 E5, 334 D7
Bexhill NSW 305 O3
Biala NSW 301 D2, 302 G8
Biamanga NP NSW 301 E8, 320 H5
Bibbenluke NSW 301 C9, 320 F6
Biboohra Qld 351 L6
Bicheno Tas. 359 O1, 361 O11, **289, 292**
Bicheno Tas. to Launceston Tas. **292–3**
Bickerton Island (Amakalyuwakba) NT 341 M6
Biddon NSW 304 D10
Bidyadanga WA 338 G9
Big Bell WA **166**
Big Caroline Rock Tas. 358 E9
Big Grove WA 332 G12
Big Rocky NSW 303 M4
Bigga NSW 301 D1, 302 G7
Biggara Vic. 301 A7, 313 P7, 320 A3
Bigge Island WA 339 K2
Biggenden Qld 347 L4
Bilbarin WA 332 G5
Bilbul NSW 309 M7
Billabong Vic. 308 E6, 314 G6
Billabong Roadhouse WA 333 D10
Billimari NSW 302 E5
Billinudgel NSW 305 O2
Billys Creek NSW 305 M7
Biloela Qld 347 J2
Bilpin NSW 303 J5
Bilyana Qld 351 M9
Bimbaya NSW 320 G6
Bimberamala NP NSW 301 F5, 302 H11
Bimbi NSW 302 D6
Bimbimbie NSW 301 F6, 302 H12
Binalong NSW 301 C2, 302 E8

Brooms Head NSW 305 N6
Brooweena Qld 347 M5
Broughton Vic. 308 C12, 316 D6, 321 H7
Broughton Island NSW 303 N3
Broula NSW 302 E6
Broulee NSW 301 F6, 302 H12
Brownlow SA 321 D1, 322 H11, 323 L7
Browns Plains Vic. 313 J6
Bruarong Vic. 313 K8
Bruce SA 323 I2, 324 H9
Bruce Rock WA 332 G4, 334 E7
Brucefield SA 322 H6
Brucknell Vic. 319 I9
Brungle NSW 301 A4, 302 D10
Brunswick Vic. 310 C4
Brunswick Heads NSW 305 O3, 347 N12, 36
Brunswick Junction WA 332 C8
Bruny Island Tas. 359 K10, 289
Brushgrove NSW 305 I8
Bruthen Vic. 311 N5
Brymaroo Qld 347 K8
Buangor Vic. 319 J3
Bucasia Qld 349 K5
Bucca Qld 347 M3
Buccleuch SA 321 E4, 323 M10
Buchan Vic. 301 A11, 311 P4, 320 A10
Buchan South Vic. 311 O4
Bucheen Creek Vic. 313 N8
Buckenderra NSW 301 B7, 320 D3
Bucketty NSW 303 K4
Buckingham SA 308 A12, 321 G7
Buckingham WA 332 D8
Buckland Tas. 359 M5, 288
Buckland Vic. 313 K10
Buckleboo SA 322 E3, 324 D10
Buckley Vic. 319 N8
Buckrabanyule Vic. 308 G12, 317 L7
Budawang NP NSW 301 F5, 302 H11
Buddabaddah NSW 307 O11
Budderoo NP NSW 301 G3, 303 J9, 23
Buddigower NSW 302 B6, 309 O6
Buderim Qld 347 N7
Budgeree Vic. 310 H8
Budgeree East Vic. 310 H8
Budgerum Vic. 317 L4
Buffalo Vic. 310 G9
Buffalo Creek Vic. 313 J9
Buffalo River Vic. 313 J9
Bugaldie NSW 304 D9
Bugilbone NSW 304 D5
Bugong NP NSW 301 G3, 303 I9
Builyan Qld 347 L2
Bukalong NSW 301 C9, 320 E6
Bukkulla NSW 305 I5
Bulahdelah NSW 303 N3, 27
Bulart Vic. 318 F3
Bulburin NP Qld 347 L2
Buldah Vic. 301 C10, 320 E9
Bulga NSW 303 K3
Bulgandramine NSW 302 E2
Bulgobac Tas. 360 E8
Bulla NT 339 P4, 340 C11, 342 C2
Bulla Vic. 310 B3
Bullala NP NSW 304 H4, 347 I12
Bullarah NSW 304 E4
Bullaring WA 332 F6, 334 E8
Bullarook Vic. 319 M4
Bullarto Vic. 319 N3
Bullengarook Vic. 310 A2, 319 O4
Bullengarook East Vic. 310 A2
Bulleringa NP Qld 351 I7
Bullfinch WA 332 H2, 334 F6
Bullhead Creek Vic. 313 M8
Bulli NSW 22, 23
Bullioh Vic. 313 M7
Bullock Creek Qld 351 J7
Bullocks Flat NSW 320 B4
Bullsbrook WA 332 C4, 334 C7
Bullumwaal Vic. 311 M4
Bulman NT 341 J6
Buln Buln Vic. 310 G6
Buln Buln East Vic. 310 G6
Bulwer Qld 347 N8
Bulyee WA 332 F5, 334 D8
Bumbaldry NSW 302 E6
Bumberry NSW 302 E4

Bumbunga SA 323 I6
Bunbartha Vic. 309 K12, 312 E6
Bunbury WA 332 C8, 334 C9, 99
Bunbury WA to Manjimup WA – South-west
   Capes Diversion 102–3
Bundaberg Qld 347 M3, 42
Bundaburrah NSW 302 D5
Bundalaguah Vic. 311 K6
Bundalong Vic. 309 M12, 312 H5
Bundalong South Vic. 312 H6
Bundanoon NSW 301 G3, 303 I9
Bundarra NSW 305 I7
Bundeena NSW 303 K7
Bundella NSW 304 F10
Bunding Vic. 319 N4
Bundjalung NP NSW 305 N5, 33
Bundook NSW 303 N1, 305 K12
Bundure NSW 309 M9
Bunga NSW 301 E8
Bungador Vic. 319 K8
Bungal Vic. 319 N5
Bungarby NSW 301 C9, 320 E5
Bungaree Vic. 319 M4
Bungawalbin NP NSW 305 N4, 347 N12
Bungeet Vic. 312 H7
Bungendore NSW 300 H5, 301 D4, 302 G10, 248
Bungil Vic. 302 B12, 313 M6
Bungonia NSW 301 F3, 302 H9
Bungonia NP NSW 301 F3, 302 H9, 218
Bungowannah NSW 302 A12, 313 K5
Bungulla NSW 305 L4, 347 L12
Bungulla WA 332 F4
Bunguluke Vic. 308 G12, 317 L6
Bungunya Qld 304 F1, 346 H10
Bungwahl NSW 303 N3
Buninyong Vic. 319 M4
Bunnaloo NSW 309 J11, 312 B3, 317 P5
Bunnan NSW 303 J1, 304 G12
Buntine WA 334 C5
Bunurong Marine NP Vic. 310 E9
Bunya Mountains NP Qld 347 K7, 229
Bunyah NSW 303 N2
Bunyan NSW 301 C7, 320 F3
Bunyip Vic. 310 F6
Buraja NSW 309 M11, 313 I4
Burbong NSW 300 G5
Burcher NSW 302 C5, 309 P5
Burekup WA 332 C8
Burgooney NSW 302 A4, 309 N4
Burke and Wills Roadhouse Qld 350 B10,
   353 F8, 151
Burkes Flat Vic. 317 L9
Burketown Qld 350 A7, 353 D4, 66
Burleigh Head NP Qld 305 O1, 347 N11
Burleigh Heads Qld 305 O1, 347 N11
Burnbank Vic. 317 L12, 319 L2
Burnett Heads Qld 347 M3
Burnie Tas. 360 F5, 280
Burns Creek Tas. 361 L8
Burnt Yards NSW 302 F5
Buronga NSW 314 G6
Burpengary Qld 347 N8
Burra SA 323 K5, 184, 185
Burraboi NSW 309 I10, 312 A1, 317 O2
Burracoppin WA 332 G3, 334 E6
Burraga NSW 302 G6
Burragate NSW 320 G8
Burral Yurrul NP NSW 305 I3, 347 J12
Burramine South Vic. 312 G5
Burrandana NSW 302 B10, 309 P10, 313 M2
Burrawang NSW 301 G3, 303 I9
Burrell Creek NSW 303 N1, 305 K12
Burren Junction NSW 304 D6
Burrereo Vic. 317 I8
Burrill Lake NSW 301 G5, 303 I11
Burringbar NSW 305 O2, 347 N11
Burringurrah WA 333 F6, 336 C7
Burrinjuck NSW 301 B3, 302 E9
Burroin Vic. 308 E10, 316 H3
Burrowa-Pine Mountain NP Vic. 302 C12,
   309 P12, 313 N6
Burroway NSW 304 B11
Burrowye Vic. 302 C12, 309 P12, 313 N6
Burrum Vic. 317 I9
Burrum Coast NP Qld 347 M4

Burrum Heads Qld 347 N4, 42
Burrumbeet Vic. 319 L3
Burrumbuttock NSW 302 A11, 309 N11, 313 K4
Burton Rocks WA 335 I9
Bushfield Vic. 318 G8
Bushy Park Tas. 359 I6
Bushy Park Vic. 311 K5
Busselton WA 332 B9, 334 B10, 102
Butchers Ridge Vic. 301 A10, 311 P2, 320 A8
Bute SA 323 I6
Butler Tanks SA 322 E6
Butlers Gorge Tas. 358 G3
Butmaroo NSW 301 D4, 302 G10
Butterleaf NP NSW 305 K5
Buxton NSW 301 G2, 303 I8
Buxton Qld 347 M4
Buxton Vic. 310 F2
Byabarra NSW 305 L11
Byaduk Vic. 318 E5
Byaduk North Vic. 318 E5
Byawatha Vic. 313 J7
Byfield NP Qld 349 N10
Byford WA 332 C5
Bylands Vic. 310 C2, 312 C12
Bylong NSW 303 I2
Bymount Qld 346 F5
Byrne Vic. 313 I8
Byrneside Vic. 312 D7
Byrnestown Qld 347 L4
Byrneville Vic. 316 G8
Byrock NSW 307 N7, 142
Byron Bay NSW 305 O3, 347 N12, 35, 36

C

Cabarita Vic. 308 D6, 314 G6
Cabarlah Qld 347 L9
Cabawin Qld 347 I8
Cabbage Tree Creek Vic. 301 B12, 320 C11
Cable Beach WA 338 H8
Caboolture Qld 347 N8, 39
Caboonbah Qld 347 M8
Cabramatta NSW 301 H1, 303 J7
Cabramurra NSW 301 B6, 302 D12, 320 B1, 250
Cadell SA 323 M6
Cadney Homestead SA 329 N7, 154
Cadoux WA 332 E2, 334 D6
Cahills Crossing NT 340 H4
Caiguna WA 335 M7, 109
Caiguna Roadhouse WA 335 L7, 109
Cairns Qld 351 L6, 55, 58, 61
Cairns Qld to Cooktown Qld 58–60
Cairns Qld to Darwin NT 4–5
Cairns Qld to Mount Garnet Qld 61–2
Cairns Bay Tas. 359 I9
Calala NSW 305 I9
Calca SA 322 A3, 331 N11
Calder Tas. 360 E5
Caldwell NSW 309 I10, 312 B2, 317 P4
Calen Qld 349 J5
Calingiri WA 332 C3, 334 C6
Caliph SA 321 F2, 323 N8
Calivil Vic. 317 N7
Callala Bay NSW 301 G4, 303 J10
Callawadda Vic. 317 I10
Calleen NSW 302 B5, 309 O5
Callide Qld 347 J1
Callignee Vic. 311 I8
Callignee North Vic. 311 I8
Callington SA 321 C3, 323 K10
Calliope Qld 347 K1, 349 N12, 45
Caloona NSW 304 E2, 346 G11
Caloote SA 323 K9
Caloundra Qld 347 N8, 39
Caltowie SA 323 J4, 324 H11
Calulu Vic. 311 M5
Calvert Vic. 319 I3
Camballin WA 339 J7
Cambarville Vic. 310 G3
Camberwell NSW 303 K2
Cambewarra NSW 301 G3, 303 I9
Cambrai SA 321 D2, 323 L8
Cambridge Tas. 359 K7
Camdale Tas. 360 F5
Camden NSW 301 H1, 303 J7
Cameron Corner NSW 306 B1, 327 N11, 356 F10
Camira Creek NSW 305 N4

Camooweal Qld 343 P10, 353 A9, 354 C1, 188,
   189
Camooweal Caves NP Qld 343 P10, 353 A9,
   354 C1, 188
Camp Coorong SA 321 D5, 323 L12
Campania Tas. 359 K6
Campbell Town Tas. 359 L1, 361 L11, 278
Campbells Bridge Vic. 317 I10
Campbells Creek Vic. 317 N12, 319 N1
Campbells Forest Vic. 317 N9
Campbelltown NSW 301 H1, 303 J7
Campbelltown Vic. 317 M12, 319 M2
Camperdown Vic. 319 J7, 125
Campwin Beach Qld 349 K6
Camurra NSW 304 G4
Canbelego NSW 307 M9
Canberra ACT 300 E5, 301 D4, 302 F10, 217,
   248, 249
Canberra ACT to Albury NSW 250–2
Candelo NSW 301 D9, 320 H6, 17
Cangai NSW 305 L5
Cania Gorge NP Qld 347 K2
Caniambo Vic. 312 F8
Cann River Vic. 301 C11, 320 E10, 14
Canna WA 333 F12, 334 B3
Cannawigara SA 308 A12, 316 A6, 321 G7
Cannie Vic. 308 G11, 317 L4
Canning Vale WA 332 C5
Cannon Creek Qld 305 K2
Cannonvale Qld 349 J3
Cannum Vic. 316 G7
Canomodine NSW 302 F5
Canonba NSW 307 P9
Canowie SA 323 K4, 325 I12
Canowindra NSW 302 F5
Canteen Creek NT 343 L11, 345 L1
Canunda NP SA 321 F11
Cape Arid NP WA 335 K9
Cape Barren Island Tas. 358 B12, 361 O2
Cape Borda SA 322 F11
Cape Bridgewater Vic. 318 C8
Cape Byron NSW 36
Cape Clear Vic. 319 L5
Cape Conran Coastal Park Vic. 14, 15
Cape Crawford NT 69
Cape Hillsborough NP Qld 349 K5, 52
Cape Howe Marine NP Vic. 301 E11, 320 H11
Cape Jaffa SA 321 E9
Cape Jervis SA 321 A5, 323 I11, 118
Cape Keraudren WA 87
Cape Le Grand NP WA 335 I9, 106, 107
Cape Leeuwin WA 102
Cape Melville NP (CYPAL) Qld 351 K1, 352 H2
Cape Otway Vic. 127
Cape Palmerston NP Qld 349 K6, 50
Cape Paterson Vic. 310 E9, 10
Cape Range NP WA 333 B3, 91, 93
Cape Tribulation Qld 351 L4, 56, 58, 59
Cape Upstart NP Qld 349 I2, 351 P12
Cape Woolamai Vic. 310 D8
Capel WA 332 B9, 334 C10
Capella Qld 349 I9
Capels Crossing Vic. 317 N4
Capertee NSW 303 I4
Capertee NP NSW 303 I4
Capietha SA 322 B2, 324 A10, 331 O10
Capoompeta NP NSW 305 K5
Capricorn Coast NP Qld 349 N10
Capricorn Roadhouse WA 336 E5
Capricornia Cays NP Qld 347 N1, 349 P11
Captain Billy Landing Qld 352 D4
Captains Flat NSW 300 G9, 301 D5, 302 G11
Carabost NSW 302 C11, 309 P11, 313 O4
Caragabal NSW 302 D6
Caralue SA 322 E4, 324 D12
Caralulup Vic. 317 L12, 319 L2
Caramut Vic. 318 H6
Carapooee Vic. 317 K9
Carapook Vic. 318 D3
Carawa SA 322 A1, 331 N9
Carboor Vic. 313 J9
Carboor Upper Vic. 313 J9
Carcoar NSW 302 G5
Cardigan Village Vic. 319 L3
Cardinia Vic. 310 E6

Coombell NSW 305 N4
Coomberdale WA 332 B1, 334 C5
Coominya Qld 347 M9
Coomoora Vic. 319 N3
Coonabarabran NSW 304 E9, **236**
Coonalpyn SA 321 E5, 323 M11
Coonamble NSW 304 C8
Coonarr Qld 347 M3
Coonawarra SA 316 A12, 318 A2, 321 G10
Coonerang NSW 301 C8, 320 F4
Coongulla Vic. 311 J5
Coongulmerang Vic. 311 L5
Coonong NSW 309 M9
Coonooer Bridge Vic. 317 K8
Coopernook NSW 303 O1, 305 L12
Coopers Creek Vic. 311 I6
Cooplacurripa NSW 305 K11
Coopracambra NP Vic. 301 C11, 320 F9
Coorabakh NP NSW 303 O1, 305 L12
Coorabie SA 331 J8
Cooran Qld 347 N6
Cooranbong NSW 303 L4
Cooranga North Qld 347 K7
Coorong NP SA 321 D6, 323 K11
Coorow WA 334 B4
Cooroy Qld 347 N7
Cootamundra NSW 301 A2, 302 D8
Cooya Beach Qld 351 L5
Cooyal NSW 302 H2
Cooyar Qld 347 L8, **228**
Cope Cope Vic. 317 J8
Copeland NSW 303 M1, 305 J12
Copeville SA 321 E2, 323 M9
Copley SA 325 I4
Copmanhurst NSW 305 M5
Coppabella Qld 349 I7
Copping Tas. 359 M7
Coppins Crossing ACT 300 D5
Cora Lynn Vic. 310 E6
Corack Vic. 308 F12, 317 J7
Corack East Vic. 308 F12, 317 J6
Coragulac Vic. 319 K8
Coraki NSW 305 O4, 347 N12
Coral Bank Vic. 313 L9
Coral Bay WA 333 B5, **91**, **92**
Coram Vic. 319 L8
Coramba NSW 305 M7
Corang NSW 301 F4, 302 H10
Corattum SA 321 F12
Cordalba Qld 347 M4
Cordalba NP Qld 347 M4
Cordering WA 332 E8
Coreen NSW 309 M11, 313 I4
Corfield Qld 348 A6, 355 M6
Corinda Qld 353 B4
Corindhap Vic. 319 L6
Corindi NSW 305 N7
Corindi Beach NSW 305 N7
Corinella Vic. 310 E8
Corinna Tas. 360 C8
Corio Vic. 310 A6, 319 O7
Corner Inlet Marine NP Vic. 310 H10
Corner Store Qld 306 B1, 327 N11, 356 F10
Cornwall Tas. 361 O9
Corny Point SA 322 G9
Corobimilla NSW 309 N8
Coromby Vic. 316 H8
Coronation Beach WA 333 D12, 334 A3
Coronet Bay Vic. 310 E8
Corop Vic. 312 C7
Cororooke Vic. 319 K8
Corowa NSW 309 M12, 313 I5, **253**
Corra Linn Tas. 361 K8
Corrigin WA 332 F5, 334 E8
Corrimal NSW **22**
Corringle NSW 302 C5, 309 P5
Corroboree Park Tavern NT 340 E5
Corryong Vic. 313 O7, **252**
Cosgrove Vic. 312 F7
Cosmo Newbery WA 335 I1, 337 I11, **201**
Cossack WA 333 F1, 336 B2, 338 B12, **89**
Costerfield Vic. 312 C9
Cottan-Bimbang NP NSW 305 K10
Cottonvale Qld 305 L2, 347 L11
Couangalt Vic. 310 B3, 319 P4
Cougal NSW 305 N2

Coulta SA 322 D7
Countegany NSW 301 D7, 320 G3
Couradda NP NSW 304 G6
Couta Rocks Tas. 360 A5
Coutts Crossing NSW 305 M6
Cow Bay Qld 351 L4
Cowabbie West NSW 302 A8, 309 O8
Cowan NSW 303 K6
Cowangie Vic. 308 C9, 314 D11, 316 D1, 323 P10
Cowaramup WA 332 B9
Cowell SA 322 G5, **112**
Cowes Vic. 310 D8
Cowley Beach Qld 351 M8
Cowleys Creek Vic. 319 J9
Cowper NSW 305 N5
Cowra NSW 302 F6
Cowwarr Vic. 311 J6
Coyrecup WA 332 G8
Crabbes Creek NSW 305 O2, 347 N11
Crabtree Tas. 359 J7
Cracow Qld 347 I4
Cradle Mountain-Lake St Clair NP Tas. 358 F2, 360 F9, **282**, **283**, **284**
Cradle Valley Tas. 360 F9
Cradoc Tas. 359 J8
Cradock SA 323 J1, 325 I8
Craigie NSW 301 C10, 320 E8
Craigie Vic. 317 M12, 319 M1
Craigieburn Vic. 310 C3
Craiglie Qld 351 L5
Cramenton Vic. 308 E8, 314 H9
Cramps Tas. 359 I1, 361 I10
Cranbourne Vic. 310 D6
Cranbourne South Vic. 310 D6
Cranbrook Tas. 359 N2, 361 N12
Cranbrook WA 332 F10, 334 E10
Crater Lakes NP Qld 351 L7
Craven NSW 303 M2
Cravensville Vic. 313 N8
Crawford Qld 347 L7
Crawney Pass NP NSW 305 I11
Crayfish Creek Tas. 360 D4
Creek Junction Vic. 312 G9
Creighton Vic. 312 E9
Cremorne Tas. 359 L8
Crescent Head NSW 305 M10, **30**
Cressy Tas. 361 K9
Cressy Vic. 319 L6
Creswick Vic. 319 M3, **242**
Crib Point Vic. 310 D7
Croajingolong NP Vic. 301 C12, 320 E11, **14**, **15**
Croftby Qld 305 M1, 347 M10
Croker Island NT 340 G1
Cronulla NSW 303 K7
Crooble NSW 304 H4, 347 I12
Crooked River Vic. 311 K3
Crookwell NSW 301 E2, 302 G8
Croppa Creek NSW 304 H3, 347 I12
Crossdale Qld 347 M8
Crossley Vic. 318 G8
Crossman WA 332 D7, 334 C8
Crossover Vic. 310 G6
Crowdy Bay NP NSW 303 O1, 305 L12, **29**
Crowlands Vic. 317 J12, 319 J1
Crown Rock NT 341 O11, 343 O2
Crows Nest Qld 347 L8, **228**
Crows Nest NP Qld 347 L8, **228**
Crowther NSW 301 B1, 302 E7
Croxton East Vic. 318 F5
Croydon Qld 350 F8, **64**
Crymelon Vic. 308 E12, 316 G6
Cryon NSW 304 D5
Crystal Brook SA 323 I4, 324 H12
Cuballing WA 332 E6, 334 D8
Cubbaroo NSW 304 E6
Cuckoo Tas. 361 M7
Cudal NSW 302 F4
Cuddell NSW 309 N8
Cudgee Vic. 318 H8
Cudgewa Vic. 313 O7
Cudgewa North Vic. 313 O6
Cudmore NP Qld 348 F9
Cue WA 333 H10, 334 D1, 336 D11, **166**
Culbin WA 332 E7
Culburra NSW 301 H4, 303 J10
Culburra SA 321 E5, 323 M12

Culcairn NSW 302 B11, 309 O11, 313 L4
Culgoa Vic. 308 F10, 317 K4
Culgoa Floodplain NP Qld 304 A2, 307 O2, 346 C11, 357 P11
Culgoa NP NSW 304 A2, 307 O2, 346 C11, 357 P11
Cullen Bullen NSW 303 I5
Cullendulla NSW 302 H12
Culloden Vic. 311 K5
Cullulleraine Vic. 308 C6, 314 E6, 323 P7
Cumberland Rock WA 332 B11, 334 B11
Cumborah NSW 304 B4
Cummins SA 322 D7
Cumnock NSW 302 F3
Cundeelee WA 335 J5
Cunderdin WA 332 E4, 334 D7
Cungena SA 322 B2, 331 O9
Cungulla Qld 348 H1, 351 O12
Cunliffe SA 322 H6
Cunnamulla Qld 346 A9, 357 N9, **143**, **144**
Cunnawarra NP NSW 305 L8
Cunningar NSW 301 B2, 302 E8
Cunningham Qld 305 K1, 347 K10
Cunningham SA 322 H7
Cunninyeuk NSW 308 H9, 315 N12, 317 N1
Cuprona Tas. 360 F6
Curara WA 332 D7, 333 E12, 334 B3
Curban NSW 304 D8
Curdie Vale Vic. 319 I9, **128**
Curlewis NSW 304 G9
Curlwaa NSW 308 D5, 314 G5
Currabubula NSW 304 H10
Curracabundi NP NSW 305 I11
Curramulka SA 322 H8
Currarong NSW 301 H4, 303 J10
Currawang NSW 301 E4, 302 G10
Currawarna NSW 302 B9, 309 O9
Currawinya NP Qld 307 I1, 357 L10
Currency Creek SA 321 C4, 323 J10
Currie Tas. 359 O11
Currowan Creek NSW 301 F6, 302 H12
Currumbin Qld 305 O1, 347 N11, **38**
Curtain Fig NP Qld 351 L7
Curtin Springs NT 344 F10, **157**
Curtis Island Qld 347 L1, 349 N11
Curtis Island NP Qld 349 N11
Curyo Vic. 308 F11, 317 I5
Custon SA 308 B12, 316 B7, 321 G7
Cuttabri NSW 304 E6
Cuttagee NSW **18**
Cygnet Tas. 359 J9
Cygnet River SA 322 H11
Cynthia Qld 347 K4

D

Dadswells Bridge Vic. 316 H10
D'Aguilar NP Qld 347 M8
Daguragu NT 342 D5
Dahlen Vic. 316 G9
Daintree Qld 351 L4, **56**, **58**
Daintree NP Qld 351 L4, **59**
Daisy Dell Tas. 360 G8
Daisy Hill Vic. 317 M12, 319 M1
Dajarra Qld 354 F5
Dalbeg Qld 348 H3
Dalby Qld 347 K8, **229**, **262**, **263**
Dalby Qld to Roma Qld **264–5**
Dalgarup NP WA 332 C9, 334 C10
Dalgety NSW 301 B8, 320 D4
Dallarnil Qld 347 M4
Dalmalee Vic. 308 D11, 316 G5
Dalmeny NSW 301 F7, **18**
Dalmorton NSW 305 L6
Dalrymple NP Qld 348 F2, 351 M12
Dalton NSW 301 D3, 302 F9
Dalveen Qld 305 L2, 347 L11
Dalwallinu WA 332 D1, 334 C5, **164**
Daly River NT 340 D7
Daly Waters NT 340 H12, 342 H3, **69**, **162**
Daly Waters NT to Katherine NT **71–2**
Dalyellup WA 332 C8
Dalyston Vic. 310 E9
Dalyup WA 335 I9
Dampier WA 333 E1, 336 B2, 338 B12, **89**
Dampiers Monument WA 339 I5
Dan Dan NP Qld 347 K1, 349 N12

Danbulla NP Qld 351 L6
Dandaloo NSW 302 D1, 304 A12, 307 P12
Dandaragan WA 332 B2, 334 B6
Dandenong Vic. 310 D5
Dandenong Ranges NP Vic. 310 E5
Dandongadale Vic. 313 J10
Dangarfield NSW 303 K1, 304 H12
Dangarsleigh NSW 305 J8
Dangin WA 332 E5
Danyo Vic. 308 C9, 314 D11, 316 D1, 321 H4, 323 P10
Darby Falls NSW 302 F6
Darbyshire Vic. 313 M6
Dardadine WA 332 E8
Dardanup WA 332 C8
Dareton NSW 308 D5, 314 G5
Dargo Vic. 311 L3
Dargo High Plains Vic. 311 L1
Dark Corner NSW 302 H5
Darkan WA 332 E8, 334 D9
Darke Peak SA 322 E5, 324 D12
Darkwood NSW 305 M8
Darley Vic. 310 A3, 319 O4
Darling Downs Qld **229**
Darlington Tas. 359 N5, **289**
Darlington Vic. 319 J6
Darlington Point NSW 309 M7, **140**, **170**
Darnick NSW 308 H2
Darnum Vic. 310 G7
Daroobalgie NSW 302 D4
Darr Qld 348 B9, 355 N9
Darraweit Guim Vic. 310 C2, 312 C12
Darriman Vic. 311 J9
Dart Dart Vic. 308 D12, 316 G7
Dartmoor Vic. 318 C5, 321 H12, **123**
Dartmouth Qld 348 C10, 355 O10
Dartmouth Vic. 313 M9
Darwin NT 340 D4, **73**, **74**
Darwin NT to Port Hedland WA **4–5**
Dattuck Vic. 308 E10, 316 G3
Davies Creek NP Qld 351 L6
Davis Creek NSW 303 L2
Dawes Qld 347 J2
Dawes NP Qld 347 K2
Dawson SA 323 K3, 325 J10
Dawson Vic. 311 J6
Dawsons Hill NSW 303 L2
Daydream (West Molle) Island Qld 349 K3
Daylesford Vic. 319 N3, **242**
Daymar Qld 304 E1, 346 G11
Daysdale NSW 309 M11, 313 I3
Daytrap Vic. 308 F9, 315 J12, 317 J1
Daytrap Corner Vic. 308 F9, 315 J12, 317 I2
De Witt Island Tas. 358 G11
Deakin WA 330 C4, 335 P4
Dean Vic. 319 M3
Deanmill WA 332 D10
Deans Marsh Vic. 319 M8
Deception Bay Qld 347 N8
Deddick Vic. 301 A10, 320 B7
Deddington Tas. 361 L9
Dederang Vic. 313 L8
Dee Lagoon Tas. 358 H3
Deep Lead Vic. 317 I11
Deepwater NSW 305 K5
Deepwater NP Qld 347 L2, **45**
Deer Park Vic. 310 B4, 319 P5
Deer Reserve NP Qld 347 M8
Deeral Qld 351 M7
Delamere SA 321 A5, 323 I11
Delatite Vic. 310 H1, 312 H11
Delburn Vic. 310 H8
Delegate NSW 301 C10, 320 D7
Delegate River Vic. 301 B10, 320 D8
Delicate Nobby NSW **30**
Dellicknora Vic. 301 B10, 320 C8
Deloraine Tas. 361 I8, **276**
Delta Qld 349 J3
Delungra NSW 305 I5
Denham WA 333 B9, **94**, **95**
Denham Group NP Qld 352 E4
Denicull Creek Vic. 319 I2
Deniliquin NSW 309 J10, 312 D2
Denison Vic. 311 J6
Denman NSW 303 J2
Denman SA 330 E4

Glengarry Tas. 361 J7
Glengarry Vic. 311 I7
Glengower Vic. 317 M12, 319 M2
Glenisla Vic. 316 G12, 318 G1
Glenlee Vic. 308 D12, 316 E7
Glenlofty Vic. 317 K12, 319 K1
Glenloth Vic. 308 G12, 317 K6
Glenluce Vic. 317 N12, 319 N2
Glenlyon Vic. 319 N2
Glenmaggie Vic. 311 J5
Glenmore Vic. 310 A3, 311 O2, 319 O5, 320 A8
Glenmorgan Qld 346 H8
Glenora Tas. 359 I6
Glenorchy Tas. 359 K7
Glenorchy Vic. 316 H10
Glenore Tas. 361 J9
Glenore Crossing Qld 350 D7, 353 G5
Glenormiston Vic. 319 I7
Glenormiston North Vic. 319 I7
Glenpatrick Vic. 317 K12, 319 K1
Glenreagh NSW 305 M7
Glenrowan Vic. 312 H8, **212**
Glenrowan West Vic. 312 H8
Glenroy NSW 301 A6, 302 C11, 303 I5, 313 O4
Glenroy SA 316 A12, 318 A1, 321 G10
Glenshee Vic. 317 K12, 319 K1
Glenthompson Vic. 318 H4
Glenvale Vic. 310 D2
Gliddon Reef SA 331 M9
Glossop SA 308 A6, 314 A6, 323 N7, **258**
Gloucester NSW 303 M1, 305 K12, **28**
Gloucester Island Qld 349 J3
Gloucester Island NP Qld 349 J3
Gloucester NP WA 332 D11, 334 C11
Gnarming WA 332 G6, 334 E8
Gnarwarre Vic. 319 N7
Gnotuk Vic. 319 J7
Gnowangerup WA 332 G9, 334 E10
Gobondery NSW 302 C2
Gobur Vic. 312 F11
Gocup NSW 301 A4, 302 D10
Godfreys Creek NSW 301 C1, 302 F7
Gogango Qld 349 L11
Gol Gol NSW 308 E6, 314 G6
Golconda Tas. 361 L6
Gold Coast Qld **37**, **38**
Golden Beach Vic. 311 L7
Golden Point Vic. 312 A10, 317 M12
Golden Valley Tas. 361 I9
Goldfields Woodlands NP WA 334 G6, **268**
Goldsborough Vic. 317 L10
Goldsmith Tas. 359 K1, 361 K11
Goldsmith Island Qld 349 K4
Goldsworthy WA 336 E1, 338 E11
Gollan NSW 302 G1, 304 D12
Golspie NSW 301 E2, 302 H8
Goneaway NP Qld 355 J10
Gongolgon NSW 307 O6
Gonn Crossing Vic. 317 N3
Goobang NP NSW 302 E2
Goobarragandra NSW 301 B5, 302 E11
Good Night Scrub NP Qld 347 L4
Goodedulla NP Qld 349 L10
Goodnight NSW 308 G8, 315 L10
Goodooga NSW 304 A2, 346 D11
Goodwood Qld 347 M4
Goolawah NP NSW 305 M10
Goold Island NP Qld 351 M9
Goolgowi NSW 309 L6
Goolma NSW 302 G2
Goolmangar NSW 305 N3
Gooloogong NSW 302 E5
Goolwa NSW 321 C4, 323 J11, **120**
Goomalibee Vic. 312 G8
Goomalling WA 332 D3, 334 C6
Goomboorian NP Qld 347 N6
Goombungee Qld 347 L8
Goomburra Qld 305 L1
Goomeri Qld 347 L6, **228**
Goon Nure Vic. 311 M6
Goondah NSW 301 C3, 302 E9
Goondiwindi Qld 304 H1, 347 I11, **238**, **260**, **261**
Goondooloo SA 321 E3, 323 M9
Goonengerry NP NSW 305 O3, 347 N12
Goongarrie WA 334 H4
Goongarrie NP WA 334 H4

Goongerah Vic. 301 B11, 320 C9
Goonoo NP NSW 302 F1, 304 C11
Goonumbla NSW 302 E3
Gooram Vic. 312 F10
Goorambat Vic. 312 G7
Goornong Vic. 312 B8, 317 P9
Gooroc Vic. 317 K8
Gooseberry Hill NP WA 332 C5, 334 C7
Goovigen Qld 347 J1, 349 L12
Goowarra Qld 349 K11
Gorae Vic. 318 D7
Gorae West Vic. 318 D7
Gordon SA 323 J1, 324 H8
Gordon Tas. 359 J9
Gordon Vic. 319 N4
Gordonvale Qld 351 L6, **55**
Gormandale Vic. 311 J8
Gormanston Tas. 358 E1, 360 E11
Goroke Vic. 316 D9
Gosford NSW 303 L5, **25**
Goshen Tas. 361 O7
Goughs Bay Vic. 310 H1, 312 H12
Goulburn NSW 301 E3, 302 H9, **216**, **218**
Goulburn NSW to Sydney NSW 218–19
Goulburn River NP NSW 303 I2, 304 F12
Goulburn Weir Vic. 312 D9
Gould Island Qld 349 J4
Goulds Country Tas. 361 O7
Gourock NP NSW 300 G12, 301 D6, 302 G12, 320 G1
Gowanford Vic. 308 G10, 317 K2
Gowangardie Vic. 312 F8
Gowar Vic. 317 N11, 319 N1
Gowar East Vic. 317 K9
Gowrie Park Tas. 360 G8
Goyura Vic. 308 E11, 316 H4
Grabben Gullen NSW 301 D2, 302 G8
Grabine NSW 302 F6
Gracemere Qld 349 M11
Gracetown WA 332 B9, 334 B10
Gradgery NSW 304 B9
Gradule Qld 304 E1, 346 G10
Grafton NSW 305 M6, **32**
Graman NSW 305 I4
Grampians NP Vic. 316 G12, 318 G2, **244**
Granite Flat Vic. 313 M9
Granite Island SA 321 B5, 323 J11
Grantham Qld 347 L9
Granton Tas. 359 K6
Grantville Vic. 310 E8
Granville Harbour Tas. 360 B9
Granya Vic. 302 B12, 309 O12, 313 M6
Grass Flat Vic. 316 E9
Grass Patch WA 335 I8
Grassdale Vic. 318 D5
Grassmere Junction Vic. 318 H8
Grasstree Qld 349 K6
Grassy Tas. 359 P12
Gravelly Beach Tas. 361 J7
Gravesend NSW 304 H5
Grawin NSW 304 B4
Grawlin NSW 302 D5
Grawlin Plains NSW 302 D5
Gray Tas. 361 O9
Graytown Vic. 312 C9
Gre Gre Vic. 317 J9
Great Australian Bight Marine NP SA 330 D7, 331 I7, 335 P6
Great Barrier Reef Marine Park Qld 347 O2, 348 H1, 349 N4, 351 N7, 352 F5, **51**
Great Basalt Wall NP Qld 348 D2, 351 L12, 355 P2
Great Keppel Island Qld 349 N10
Great Northern Vic. 313 J6
Great Ocean Road Vic. **127–9**
Great Otway NP Vic. 319 K9, **127**
Great Palm Island Qld 351 N10
Great Sandy NP Qld 347 N6
Great Western Vic. 317 I12, 319 I1, **244**
Greater Beedelup NP WA 332 C10, 334 C11
Greater Bendigo NP Vic. 312 A8, 317 O9
Greater Dordagup NP WA 332 D11, 334 C11
Greater Kingston NP WA 332 D10, 334 D10
Greater Preston NP WA 332 D8, 334 C10
Gredgwin Vic. 308 G11, 317 L5
Green Head WA 334 A5

Green Hill NSW 305 M10
Green Hill Creek Vic. 317 K12, 319 K2
Green Island (Cairns region) Qld 351 M6
Green Island (Mackay region) Qld 349 K5
Green Island (Milwarpa) (Brisbane region) Qld 347 N9
Green Island NP Qld 351 M6
Green Point NSW 303 O2
Greenbushes WA 332 C9
Greendale Vic. 310 A3, 319 O4
Greenethorpe NSW 302 E6
Greenhills WA 332 E4
Greenmantle NSW 302 F6
Greenmount Qld 347 L9
Greenmount Vic. 311 I9
Greenmount NP WA 332 C5, 334 C7
Greenock SA 321 C1, 323 K8
Greenough WA 334 A3
Greens Beach Tas. 361 I6
Greens Creek Vic. 317 J11
Greensborough Vic. 310 D4
Greenvale Qld 351 K10
Greenwald Vic. 318 C5, 321 H12
Greenways SA 321 F10
Greenwell Point NSW 301 G4, 303 J10
Greg Greg NSW 301 A6, 302 D12, 313 P6, 320 A2
Gregory Qld 349 I10, **67**
Gregory WA 333 D12, **94**
Gregory NP NT 339 P4
Greigs Flat NSW 301 E10, 320 H7
Grenfell NSW 302 D6
Grenville Vic. 319 M5
Gresford NSW 303 L2
Greta Vic. 313 I8
Greta South Vic. 312 H9
Greta West Vic. 312 H8
Gretna Tas. 359 J6
Grevillia NSW 305 N2, 347 M11
Grey Peaks NP Qld 351 M6
Greymare Qld 305 K1, 347 K10
Griffith NSW 309 M7, **140**, **141**, **170**
Gringegalgona Vic. 318 E2
Gritjurk Vic. 318 E3
Grogan NSW 301 A1, 302 D7
Grong Grong NSW 302 A8, 309 O8
Grongah NP Qld 347 L5
Groote Eylandt NT 341 N7
Grosvenor Qld 347 K4
Grove Tas. 359 J7
Grovedale Vic. 319 O8
Gubbata NSW 302 A5, 309 N5
Guilderton WA 332 B4, 334 B7
Guildford Tas. 360 E7
Guildford Vic. 317 N12, 319 N2
Gulaga NP NSW 301 E8
Gular NSW 304 C9
Gulargambone NSW 304 C9
Gulf Creek NSW 304 H7
Gulgong NSW 302 H2
Gull Rock WA 332 G11, 334 E11
Gull Rock NP WA 332 G11, 334 E11
Gulnare SA 323 J5, 324 H12
Guluguba Qld 347 I6
Gum Lake NSW 306 F12, 308 G1
Gumbaynggirr NP NSW 305 L8
Gumble NSW 302 F4
Gumbowie SA 323 K3, 325 I11
Gumeracha SA 321 C2, 323 K9
Gumlu Qld 349 I2
Gumly Gumly NSW 302 C9, 309 P9, 313 N1
Gunalda Qld 347 M6
Gunbar NSW 309 L6
Gunbower Vic. 309 I11, 312 A4, 317 O6
Gunbower NP Vic. 309 I11, 312 A4, 317 O5, **255**
Gundabooka NP NSW 307 L6
Gundagai NSW 301 A3, 302 D9, 313 P1, **170**, **215**
Gundagai NSW to Goulburn NSW 216–17
Gundagai NSW to Hay NSW 170–1
Gundagai NSW to Mildura Vic. **136**
Gundaring WA 332 F7
Gundaroo NSW 300 F2, 301 D4, 302 G10
Gundary NSW 301 E3, 302 H9
Gundiah Qld 347 M5
Gundillion NSW 301 E6, 302 G12, 320 H1
Gundowring Vic. 313 L8
Gundowring North Vic. 313 L7

Gundowring Upper Vic. 313 L8
Gundy NSW 303 K1, 304 H12
Gunebang NSW 302 A3, 309 O3
Gungahlin ACT 300 E3, 302 F10
Gungal NSW 303 J2
Gunnary NSW 301 C2, 302 F7
Gunnedah NSW 304 G9
Gunnewin NSW 346 F5
Gunning NSW 301 D3, 302 G9, **216**
Gunningbland NSW 302 D4
Gunns Plains Tas. 360 G6
Gunpowder Qld 353 D9, 354 F1
Gunyangara NT 341 N4
Gunyerwarildi NP NSW 304 H4, 347 I12
Gurley NSW 304 F5, **236**
Gurrai SA 308 A8, 314 A10, 321 G4, 323 N10
Gurrumuru NT 341 M4
Gurrundah NSW 301 D3, 302 G9
Guthalungra Qld 349 I2
Guthega NSW 301 A8, 320 B4
Guy Fawkes River NP NSW 305 L7, **224**
Guyong NSW 302 G5
Guyra NSW 305 J7, **224**
Guys Forest Vic. 302 C12, 313 N6
Gwabegar NSW 304 D7
Gwalia WA 334 H2, **194**
Gwandalan Tas. 359 L8
Gwydir River NP NSW 304 H6, 305 I6
Gymbowen Vic. 316 D9
Gympie Qld 347 M6, **39**, **228**
Gympie Qld to Gin Gin Qld 42–4
Gympie NP Qld 347 M6
Gypsum Vic. 308 E9, 314 H12, 316 H1

H

Haasts Bluff NT 344 F6
Haddon Vic. 319 L4
Haddon Corner Qld 327 O2, 356 G4
Haden Qld 347 L8
Hadspen Tas. 361 K8
Hagley Tas. 361 J8
Hahndorf SA 321 C3, 323 K9
Haig WA 335 M5
Halbury SA 323 J6
Half Tide Qld 349 K6
Halfway Creek NSW 305 N6
Halfway Mill Roadhouse WA 332 A1, 334 B5
Halidon SA 321 F3, 323 M9
Halifax Qld 351 M9
Halifax Bay Wetlands NP Qld 351 M10
Hall ACT 300 D3
Hallett SA 323 K5, 325 I12
Hallidays Point NSW 303 O2
Halls Creek WA 339 N7, **83**, **84**
Halls Gap Vic. 316 H12, 318 H1, **244**, **245**
Hallston Vic. 310 G8
Halton NSW 303 L2
Hamel WA 332 C7
Hamelin Bay WA 332 B10
Hamersley WA 333 G3, 336 C4
Hamilton SA 321 C1, 323 K7
Hamilton Tas. 359 I5, **286**
Hamilton Vic. 318 F4
Hamilton Island Qld 349 K4
Hamley Bridge SA 321 B1, 323 J7
Hammond SA 323 J2, 324 H9
Hampden SA 323 K7
Hampshire Tas. 360 F6
Hampton NSW 303 I6
Hampton Qld 347 L9
Hampton NP Qld 347 L9
Hanging Rock Vic. 311 P1, 313 P12, 320 B7
Hann River Roadhouse Qld 351 I2
Hann Tableland NP Qld 351 K6
Hannahs Bridge NSW 304 E11
Hannan NSW 302 A5, 309 N5
Hansborough SA 323 K7
Hanson SA 323 K6
Hansonville Vic. 313 I8
Hanwood NSW 309 M7
Happy Valley Qld 347 O4, 349 L8
Happy Valley Vic. 308 F7, 313 K9, 315 I9, 319 L5
Harcourt Vic. 312 A10, 317 O11, 319 O1
Harcourt North Vic. 312 A10, 317 O11, 319 O1
Harden NSW 301 B2, 302 E8
Hardwicke Bay SA 322 H9

Mount Egerton Vic. 319 N4
Mount Eliza Vic. 310 C6
Mount Emu Vic. 319 K4
Mount Etna Caves NP Qld 349 M10
Mount Fairy NSW 301 E4, 302 G10
Mount Field NP Tas. 358 H5, 359 I5, **287**
Mount Frankland NP WA 332 E11, 334 D11
Mount Frankland North NP WA 332 E11, 334 D11
Mount Frankland South NP WA 332 E11, 334 D11
Mount Franklin Vic. 319 N2
Mount Gambier SA 318 A5, 321 G12, **120**
Mount Gambier SA to Port Fairy Vic. 123–4
Mount Garnet Qld 351 K7, **62**
Mount Garnet Qld to Karumba Qld 63–5
Mount George NSW 303 N1, 305 K12
Mount Hallen Qld 347 M9
Mount Helen Vic. 319 M4
Mount Hope NSW 309 M2
Mount Hope SA 322 C6
Mount Horeb NSW 301 A4, 302 D10, 313 P1
Mount Hotham Vic. **212**
Mount Hypipamee NP Qld 351 L7, **62**
Mount Imlay NP NSW 301 D10, 320 G8
Mount Isa Qld 353 D11, 354 F3, **66**, **188**
Mount Jerusalem NP NSW 305 O2, 347 N11
Mount Jim Crow NP Qld 349 M10
Mount Kaputar NP NSW 304 G6, **236**
Mount Keith WA 336 G10
Mount Lambie NSW 303 I5
Mount Larcom Qld 349 N12
Mount Lewis NP Qld 351 L5
Mount Liebig NT 344 E6
Mount Lindesay NP NSW 332 F11, 334 D11
Mount Lloyd Tas. 359 I7
Mount Lonarch Vic. 317 K12, 319 K2
Mount Macedon Vic. 310 B2, 312 B12, 319 P3
Mount Mackay NP Qld 351 M8
Mount Magnet WA 333 H11, 334 D2, 336 D12, **164**, **196**, **197**
Mount Magnet WA to Newman WA 166–7
Mount Martha Vic. 310 C7
Mount Martin NP Qld 349 K5
Mount Mary SA 323 L7
Mount Mercer Vic. 319 M5
Mount Molloy Qld 351 L5
Mount Morgan Qld 349 M11, **240**, **241**
Mount Moriac Vic. 319 N8
Mount Mulligan Qld 351 K6
Mount Nothofagus NP NSW 305 M2, 347 M11
Mount O'Connell NP Qld 349 L9
Mount Ossa Qld 349 J5
Mount Ossa NP Qld 349 J5
Mount Perry Qld 347 L4
Mount Pikapene NP NSW 305 M4, 347 M12
Mount Pinbarren NP Qld 347 N6
Mount Pleasant SA 321 C2, 323 K9
Mount Pleasant WA 333 D12, 334 H5
Mount Remarkable NP SA 323 I3, 324 H10
Mount Richmond Vic. 318 C7
Mount Richmond NP Vic. 318 C7
Mount Roe NP WA 332 F11, 334 D11
Mount Rowan Vic. 319 M3
Mount Royal NP NSW 303 L2
Mount Schank SA 318 A5, 321 G12
Mount Seaview NSW 305 K11
Mount Seymour Tas. 359 L4
Mount Spurgeon NP Qld 351 K5
Mount Surprise Qld 351 J8, **63**
Mount Tamborine Qld **37**
Mount Taylor Vic. 311 M5
Mount Templeton SA 323 J6
Mount Thorley NSW 303 K3
Mount Torrens SA 321 C3, 323 K9
Mount Victoria NSW 303 I6
Mount Walker WA **270**
Mount Wallace Vic. 319 N5
Mount Walsh NP Qld 347 L5
Mount Warning NSW **35**
Mount Webb NP Qld 351 L2
Mount Wedge SA 322 C5, 324 A12, 331 P12
Mount White NSW 303 K5
Mount William NP Tas. 361 P5
Mount Wilson NSW 303 I5
Mount Windsor NP Qld 351 K4

Mountain River Tas. 359 J7
Moura Qld 347 I2
Mourilyan Qld 351 M7, **55**
Moutajup Vic. 318 G4
Mowbray Tas. 361 K8
Mowbray NP Tas. 351 L5
Mowen WA 332 B10
Moyhu Vic. 313 I8
Moyreisk Vic. 317 K10
Moyston Vic. 319 I2
Muchea WA 332 C4, 334 C7
Muckadilla Qld 346 F6
Mudamuckla SA 331 N8
Mudgee NSW 302 H2
Mudgeeraba Qld 305 O1, 347 N10
Mudgegonga Vic. 313 K8
Mudginberri NT 340 G4
Mudlo NP Qld 347 M6
Muggleton Qld 346 G6
Mukinbudin WA 332 G2, 334 E6
Muknab Rock Qld 352 C1
Mulcra Vic. 308 B9, 314 C11, 321 H4, 323 O10
Mulgildie Qld 347 K3
Mulgoa NSW 303 J6
Mullaley NSW 304 F9
Mullalyup WA 332 C9
Mullaway NSW 305 N7
Mullenderee NSW 302 H12
Mullengandra NSW 302 B12, 309 O12, 313 L5
Mullengudgery NSW 304 A10, 307 P10
Mullewa WA 333 E12, 334 B3, **196**, **197**
Mulli Mulli NSW 305 M2, 347 M11
Mullindolingong Vic. 313 L9
Mullion Creek NSW 302 G4
Mullumbimby NSW 305 O3, 347 N12, **35**
Mulpata SA 308 A8, 321 F4, 323 N10
Mulwala NSW 309 M12, 312 H5, **253**
Mumballup WA 332 D8, 334 C9
Mumbannar Vic. 318 C5, 321 H12
Mumbil NSW 302 G3
Mumblin Vic. 319 I8
Mummel Gulf NP NSW 305 J10
Mummulgum NSW 305 M3, 347 M12
Mundaring WA 332 C5, 334 C7, **270**
Mundijong WA 334 C8
Mundoona Vic. 312 E6
Mundoora SA 323 I5, 324 H12
Mundrabilla Roadhouse WA 330 A8, 335 O6
Mundubbera Qld 347 K4
Mundulla SA 308 A12, 316 A7, 321 G7
Munga-Thirri NP Qld 326 H1, 327 I1, 345 P9, 354 C12, 356 B1
Mungalawurru NT 343 I9
Mungallala Qld 346 D6, **266**
Mungana Qld 351 J6
Mungar Qld 347 N6
Mungerannie Roadhouse SA 327 I8, 356 B8
Mungeribar NSW 302 E1, 304 B12
Mungery NSW 302 D2
Mungindi NSW 304 E2, 346 F11
Mungkarta NT 343 J11
Munglinup WA 334 H9
Mungo NP NSW 308 F3, 315 K1, **172**
Mungungo Qld 347 K3
Munro Vic. 311 L6
Muntadgin WA 332 H4, 334 E7
Muradup WA 332 E9
Murchison Vic. 312 D8
Murchison WA 333 E9, 336 B11
Murchison East Vic. 312 E8
Murdinga SA 322 D5
Murdunna Tas. 359 M8
Murga NSW 302 E4
Murgenella NT 340 G2
Murgheboluc Vic. 319 N7
Murgon Qld 347 L6
Murmungee Vic. 313 J8
Murphys Creek Vic. 317 M10
Murra Warra Vic. 316 G8
Murrabit Vic. 308 H10, 317 N3, **255**
Murramarang NP NSW 301 F6, 302 H12, 303 I12, **20**
Murrami NSW 309 N7
Murrawal NSW 304 E10
Murray Bridge SA 321 D3, 323 K10, **120**, **258**

Murray River NSW/SA 251, 253, 254, 255, 257, 258
Murray River NP SA 308 A6, 314 B5, 321 G1, 323 N8
Murray-Sunset NP Vic. 308 C7, 314 D9, 321 H2, 323 P9, **256**
Murray Town SA 323 I3, 324 H11
Murray Valley NP NSW 309 K11, 312 D3
Murrays Run NSW 303 K4
Murrayville Vic. 308 B9, 314 C11, 316 C1, 321 H4, 323 O10
Murrindal Vic. 301 A11, 311 P3, 320 A9
Murrindindi Vic. 310 E2, 312 E12
Murringo NSW 301 B1, 302 E7
Murroon Vic. 319 L9
Murrumbateman NSW 300 D1, 301 C3, 302 F9
Murrumburrah NSW 301 B2, 302 E8
Murrungowar Vic. 301 B11, 320 C10
Murrurundi NSW 304 H11, **222**
Murrurundi Pass NP NSW 304 H11
Murtoa Vic. 316 H9
Murun Murula NT 343 O7
Murwillumbah NSW 305 O2, 347 N11, **35**
Musgrave Roadhouse Qld 352 E12
Musk Vic. 319 N3
Muskerry East Vic. 312 B8, 317 P10
Musselboro Tas. 361 L8
Musselroe Bay Tas. 361 O5
Muswellbrook NSW 303 K2, **220**, **222**
Muswellbrook NSW to Tamworth NSW 222–3
Mutarnee Qld 351 M10
Mutawintji NP NSW 306 E7
Mutchilba Qld 351 K6
Mutdapilly Qld 347 M10
Mutitjulu NT 344 E10
Muttaburra Qld 348 C8, 355 O8
Muttama NSW 301 A3, 302 D9
Mutton Bird Island Vic. 319 J10
Muttonbird Island NSW 305 N8
Muundhi (Jack River) NP (CYPAL) Qld 351 K1, 352 H12
Myall Vic. 308 H10, 317 N3
Myall Lakes NP NSW 303 N3, **27**
Myall Mundi NSW 304 B11
Myall Plains NSW 309 M10, 312 H2
Myalla Tas. 360 E5
Myalup WA 332 C8, 334 C9
Myamyn Vic. 318 E6
Mylestom NSW 305 M8
Myola Vic. 312 B8, 317 P9
Mypolonga SA 321 D3, 323 L9
Myponga SA 321 B4, 323 J10, **118**
Myponga Beach SA 321 B4, 323 J10
Myrla SA 321 F2, 323 N8
Myrniong Vic. 310 A3, 319 O4
Myrrhee Vic. 310 H4, 313 I9
Myrtle Bank Tas. 361 L7
Myrtle Creek Vic. 312 A10, 317 O11, 319 O1
Myrtleford Vic. 313 J8
Myrtleville NSW 301 E2, 302 H8
Mysia Vic. 308 H12, 317 M7
Mystic Park Vic. 308 H10, 317 M3
Mywee Vic. 312 F4

N

Nabageena Tas. 360 C4
Nabawa WA 333 D12, 334 A3
Nabiac NSW 303 N2
Nabowla Tas. 361 L6
Nackara SA 323 L3, 325 J10
Nadda SA 308 B7, 314 B8, 321 H2, 323 O8
Nagambie Vic. 312 D9, **230**
Nagoorin Qld 347 K2
Nairana NP Qld 348 G6
Nairne SA 321 C3, 323 K9
Nala Tas. 359 L4
Nalangil Vic. 319 K8
Nalinga Vic. 312 G7
Nalya WA 332 E5
Namadgi NP ACT 300 C8, 301 C5, 302 F12, 320 E1
Nambour Qld 347 N7, **39**
Nambrok Vic. 311 J6
Nambucca Heads NSW 305 M9, **30**
Nambung NP WA 332 A2, 334 B5, **97**
Nana Glen NSW 305 M7
Nanango Qld 347 L7

Nanarup WA 332 H11
Nandaly Vic. 308 F9, 315 I12, 317 I1
Nandi Qld 347 K8
Nanga WA 332 C7
Nangana Vic. 310 E5
Nangar NP NSW 302 E5
Nangari SA 308 B6, 314 B7, 321 H2, 323 O8
Nangeenan WA 332 G3, 334 E6
Nangiloc Vic. 308 E7, 314 H7
Nangur NP Qld 347 L6
Nangus NSW 301 A3, 302 D9, 313 P1
Nangwarry SA 318 A3, 321 G11
Nanneella Vic. 312 C6
Nannup WA 332 C10, 334 C10
Nanson WA 333 D12
Nantabibbie SA 323 K3, 325 J10
Nantawarra SA 323 I6
Nanutarra Roadhouse WA 333 D4, 336 A5
Napoleons Vic. 319 M4
Napperby SA 323 I4, 324 H11
Napranum Qld 352 B7
Nar Nar Goon Vic. 310 E6
Nara Qld 347 L8, 350 G11
Naracoopa Tas. 359 P11
Naracoorte SA 316 A10, 321 G9, **246**
Naracoorte Caves NP SA 316 A11, 321 G9, **121**
Naradhan NSW 309 N5
Naraling WA 333 D12, 334 A3
Narawntapu NP Tas. 361 I6
Narbethong Vic. 310 F3
Naree Budjong Djara NP Qld 347 N9
Nareen Vic. 318 D2
Narellan NSW 301 H1, 303 J7
Narembeen WA 332 G4, 334 E7, **270**
Naretha WA 335 L5
Nariel Vic. 313 O8
Naringal Vic. 318 H8
Narkoola NP Qld 346 C9
Naroghid Vic. 319 J7
Narooma NSW 301 F8, **18**
Narrabri NSW 304 F7, **236**
Narrabri West NSW 304 F7
Narracan Vic. 310 H7
Narrandera NSW 302 A8, 309 N8, **170**, **234**
Narraport Vic. 308 F11, 317 J5
Narrawa Tas. 360 G7
Narrawong Vic. 318 D7
Narre Warren Vic. 310 D6
Narrewillock Vic. 317 L6
Narridy SA 323 J5, 324 H12
Narrien Range NP Qld 348 G9
Narrikup WA 332 G11
Narrogin WA 332 E7, 334 D9
Narromine NSW 302 E1, 304 B12, **180**
Narrung SA 321 C5, 323 K11
Narrung Vic. 308 G8, 315 K9
Nashdale NSW 302 F4
Nathalia Vic. 309 K12, 312 E5
Natimuk Vic. 316 F9
National Park Tas. 359 I6
Natone Tas. 360 F6
Nattai NSW 301 G1, 303 I7
Nattai NP NSW 301 G2, 303 I8
Natte Yallock Vic. 317 L11
Natural Bridge Qld 305 O1
Natya Vic. 308 G8, 315 K10
Nauiyu NT 340 D7
Navarre Vic. 317 J10
Navigators Vic. 319 M4
Nayook Vic. 310 G5
Neale Junction WA 335 M1, 337 M11
Neales Flat SA 321 D1, 323 K7
Nebo Qld 349 J7
Nectar Brook SA 323 I2, 324 G10
Neds Corner Vic. 308 C6, 314 E6, 323 P7
Needle Rocks Tas. 358 F11
Needles Tas. 361 I8
Neerabup NP WA 332 B4, 334 B7
Neerdie Qld 347 N6
Neerim Vic. 310 G5
Neerim East Vic. 310 G6
Neerim Junction Vic. 310 G6
Neerim South Vic. 310 G6
Neeworra NSW 304 E3, 346 G12
Neika Tas. 359 K7

EXPLORE AUSTRALIA BY CARAVAN & MOTORHOME

INDEX OF CARAVAN PARKS

PHOTOGRAPHY CREDITS

Page ii TEQ; vii (a) DNSW (b) TA; viii TEQ; ix TNT; x TA; xi TV; 1 TEQ; 2 DNSW; 3 James Horan/DNSW; 4 Matt Raimondo/TEQ; 5 Graham Freeman/TNT; 8 Phillip Island Nature Park/TV; 10 Gavin Hansford/TV; 12 Josie Withers/TV; 14 (a) Andrew Barnes/TV, (b) Andrew Barnes/TV; 16 Claudine Thornton/DNSW; 20 Discover Jervis Bay/DNSW; 24 Destination Southern Highlands/DNSW; 27 Brett Gregory/DNSW; 30 Kempsey Shire Council; 33 Dallas Kilponen/DNSW; 37 TEQ; 45 Darren Jew/TEQ; 46 Vince Valitutti/TEQ; 49 TEQ; 51 Jason Hill/TEQ; 53 TEQ; 55 TEQ; 56 TEQ; 57 TEQ; 58 TEQ; 59 Murray Waite & Associates/TEQ; 60 TEQ; 61 TEQ; 68 Reichlyn Aguilar/TEQ; 72 Shaana McNaught/TNT; 75 Shaana McNaught/TNT; 77 Shaana McNaught/TNT; 78 Shaana McNaught/TNT; 79 Nick Rains/TNT; 80 Jan Butchofsky-Houser/Alamy Stock Photo; 81 Oliver Strewe/TA; 82 Rich Keam/ TA; 83 Australian Pacific Touring Pty Ltd/TA; 84 Nick Rains/TA; 85 Virgin Australia/TA; 87 Mark Higgins/Alamy Stock Photo; 89 TA; 90 Mackerel Islands/TA; 91 Australia's Coral Coast/TA; 92 (a) TA, (b) Australia's Coral Coast/TA, (c) Australia's Coral Coast/TA; 94 TA; 95 (a) Australia's Coral Coast/TA, (b) Australia's Coral Coast/TA; 97 Australia's Coral Coast/TA; 98 Australia's Coral Coast/TA; 100 TA; 105 TA; 112 (a) TA, (b) TA; 114 TSA; 115 Greg Snell/TA; 123 Robert Blackburn/ TV; 124 Robert Blackburn/TV; 125 Robert Blackburn/TV; 126 Robert Blackburn/TV; 128 Robert Blackburn/TV; 130 Robert Blackburn/TV; 132 robertharding / Alamy Stock Photo; 137 TEQ; 139 TA; 140 DNSW; 144 TEQ; 145 (a) TEQ, (b) TEQ, (c) TEQ; 146 TEQ; 147 TEQ; 149 TEQ; 153 TA; 155 Steve Strike/TNT; 155 Sarena Hyland/TNT; 157 Shaana McNaught/TNT; 160 Shaana McNaught/TNT; 161 Peter Eve/TNT; 163 Ingo Oeland/Alamy Stock Photo; 163 (a) ScotStock/ Alamy Stock Photo, (b) Andrew Michael/Alamy Stock Photo; 164 blickwinkel/Alamy Stock Photo; 165 Duncan Sharrocks/Alamy Stock Photo; 166 Manfred Gottschalk/Alamy Stock Photo; 167 Adwo/Alamy Stock Photo; 168 TA; 169 (a) Karijini Eco Retreat /TA, (b) TA; 175 DNSW; 176 Emirates One&Only Wolgan Valley/DNSW; 177 DNSW; 178 (a) Taronga Western Plains Zoo/DNSW, (b) DNSW; 181 Gecko Photographics/DNSW; 186 Blink Photography/TEQ; 187 TEQ; 188 Garry Norris/TEQ; 189 TEQ; 190 TEQ; 191 (a) TEQ, (b) TEQ; 192 TEQ; 193 TEQ; 196 Australia's Coral Coast/TA; 197 (a) Australia's Coral Coast/TA, (b) Australia's Coral Coast/ TA; 201 ZUMA Press, Inc./Alamy Stock Photo; 203 TA; 204 Maxime Coquard/TA; 205 Maxime Coquard/TA; 206 Viktor Posnov/Alamy Stock Photo; 208 MJK Creative/DNSW; 209 Julian Kingma/TV; 210 TEQ; 212 Victorian Wine Industry Association/TV; 213 Robert Blackburn/TV; 214 Robert Blackburn/TV; 215 Dee Kramer Photography/ DNSW; 216 Dee Kramer PhotographyDNSW; 217 Paul Livingston/Capital Country Tourism; 218 Paul Livingston/Capital Country Tourism; 219 Lawrence Furzey/DNSW; 220 Murray Vanderveer/DNSW; 221 Hunter Valley Gardens/DNSW; 222 Tao Jones/DNSW; 223 Grenville Turner/DNSW; 224 DNSW; 225 (a) DNSW, (b) DNSW; 226 TEQ; 227 TEQ/Jewels Lynch; 228 TEQ; 229 TEQ; 230 Victorian Wine Industry Association/TV; 231 (a) TV, (b) David Hannah- Victorian Wine Industry Association TV; 232 DNSW; 233 Robert Blackburn/ TV; 234 Dee Kramer Photography/DNSW; 237 DNSW; 238 TEQ; 239 (a) Ben Nott/TEQ, (b) TEQ; 240 TEQ; 241 OZSHOTZ/Alamy Stock Photo; 243 (a) TV, (b) Robert Blackburn/TV; 244 Roberto Seba/TV; 245 Victorian Wine Industry Association/TV; 246 Heather Farish/Alamy Stock Photo; 247 Southern Grampians Shire/TV; 248 James Horan/DNSW; 249 TA; 250 Robert Blackburn/TV; 250 Don Fuchs/DNSW; 251 Ben Coope/ DNSW; 253 Emily Godfrey/TV; 256 (a) Robert Blackburn/TV, (b) Robert Blackburn/TV; 255 Emily Godfrey/TV; 257 TA; 258 TA; 259 TA; 260 TEQ; 261 TEQ; 262 TEQ; 263 TEQ; 264 TEQ; 265 (a) TEQ; (b) TEQ; 266 Andrew Sole/Alamy Stock Photo; 267 TEQ; 268 Virgin Australia/TA; 269 Iain Dainty/ Alamy Stock Photo; 270 TA; 272-273 David Kleyn/Alamy Stock Photo; 274 Cradle Mountain Huts/TA; 275 (a) TA, (b) Port Arthur Historic Site Management Authority/TA; 276 Rob Burnett- Launceston Tamar Valley TA; 277 Tourism Tasmania & Rob Burnett/TA; 278 TA; 280 TA; 281 TA; 282 Sean Scott Photography/TA; 283 David Noton Photography/Alamy Stock Photo; 284 TA; 285 TA; 286 Tourism Tasmania & Rob Burnett/TA; 287 TA; 290 Sean Scott Photography/TA; 291 Port Arthur Historic Site Management Authority/TA; 294 Twelve Apostles Lodge Walk/TV; 298 Shaana McNaught/TNT

Abbreviations

DNSW Destination New South Wales	TEQ Tourism and Events Queensland
TA Tourism Australia	TV Tourism Victoria
TNT Tourism NT	TSA Tourism South Australia

Published in 2018 by Hardie Grant Travel, a division of Hardie Grant Publishing

Hardie Grant Travel (Melbourne)
Building 1, 658 Church Street
Richmond, Victoria 3121

Hardie Grant Travel (Sydney)
Level 7, 45 Jones Street
Ultimo, NSW 2007

www.hardiegrant.com/au/travel

Explore Australia is an imprint of Hardie Grant Travel

Assistance with research: The publisher would like to thank the following organisations for assistance with data and information: Australian Bureau of Statistics, Bureau of Meteorology, National Road Transport Commission, Tristate Fruit Fly Committee; *New South Wales* Roads and Traffic Authority, NSW Department of Environment Climate, Change and Water, Destination New South Wales; *Australian Capital Territory* ACT Planning and Land Authority, Australian Capital Tourism Corporation; *Victoria* VicRoads, Department of Sustainability and Environment, Victoria, Tourism Victoria; *South Australia* Transport SA, Primary Industries and Resources South Australia, Department of Environment and Natural Resources, South Australian Tourism Commission; *Western Australia* Main Roads Western Australia, Department of Indigenous Affairs Western Australia, Aboriginal Lands Trust, Department of Environment and Conservation, Western Australia Tourism Commission; *Northern Territory* Department of Transport and Infrastructure, Northern and Central land councils, Department of Natural Resources, Environment, The Arts and Sport, Parks Australia, Northern Territory Tourist Commission; *Queensland* Department of Main Roads, Department of Environment & Resource Management, Queensland Parks & Wildlife Service, Tourism Queensland; *Tasmania* Department of Infrastructure, Energy & Resources, Parks and Wildlife Service, Tourism Tasmania.

A catalogue record for this book is available from the National Library of Australia

Explore Australia by Caravan & Motorhome (6th Edition)
ISBN 9781741175523

10 9 8 7 6 5 4 3 2 1

Publisher
Melissa Kayser

Project manager
Megan Cuthbert

Project Editor
Natalie Wilson

Editorial assistant
Rosanna Dutson

Proofreader
Scott Forbes

Cartographer
Emily Maffei, Robyn Hinchliffe and Claire Johnston

Design
Nanette Backhouse, Seiso Design

Typesetting
Megan Ellis

Index
Max McMaster

Prepress
Megan Ellis and Splitting Image Colour Studio

Printed and bound in China by LEO Paper Group

FUEL

Fuel is readily available across Australia, particularly in the more populated areas. The cost of fuel has increased dramatically in recent times and there is a large price difference between some states and between city and country areas. Most towns have a petrol station or two but in remote regions you will have to consider the distances between isolated roadhouses, and decide on whether you need to carry additional

Fuel consumption										
Litres per 100 km	Km per litre	Miles per gallon	100	150	200	250	300	350	400	45
8.0	12.5	35.6	8.0	12.0	16.0	20.0	24.0	28.0	32.0	36
8.5	11.8	33.5	8.5	12.8	17.0	21.3	25.5	29.8	34.0	38
9.0	11.1	31.6	9.0	13.5	18.0	22.5	27.0	31.5	36.0	40
9.5	10.5	29.9	9.5	14.3	19.0	23.8	28.5	33.3	38.0	42
10.0	10.0	28.4	10.0	15.0	20.0	25.0	30.0	35.0	40.0	45.
10.5	9.5	27.1	10.5	15.8	21.0	26.3	31.5	36.8	42.0	47.
11.0	9.1	25.9	11.0	16.5	22.0	27.5	33.0	38.5	44.0	49.
11.5	8.7	24.7	11.5	17.3	23.0	28.8	34.5	40.3	46.0	51.
12.0	8.3	23.7	12.0	18.0	24.0	30.0	36.0	42.0	48.0	54.
12.5	8.0	22.8	12.5	18.8	25.0	31.3	37.5	43.8	50.0	56.
13.0	7.7	21.9	13.0	19.5	26.0	32.5	39.0	45.5	52.0	58.
13.5	7.4	21.1	13.5	20.3	27.0	33.8	40.5	47.3	54.0	60.8
14.0	7.1	20.3	14.0	21.0	28.0	35.0	42.0	49.0	56.0	63.0
14.5	6.9	19.6	14.5	21.8	29.0	36.3	43.5	50.8	58.0	65.
15.0	6.7	19.0	15.0	22.5	30.0	37.5	45.0	52.5	60.0	67.
15.5	6.5	18.4	15.5	23.3	31.0	38.8	46.5	54.3	62.0	69.8
16.0	6.3	17.8	16.0	24.0	32.0	40.0	48.0	56.0	64.0	72.0
16.5	6.1	17.2	16.5	24.8	33.0	41.3	49.5	57.8	66.0	74.
17.0	5.9	16.7	17.0	25.5	34.0	42.5	51.0	59.5	68.0	76.
17.5	5.7	16.3	17.5	26.3	35.0	43.8	52.5	61.3	70.0	78.8
18.0	5.6	15.8	18.0	27.0	36.0	45.0	54.0	63.0	72.0	81.0
18.5	5.4	15.4	18.5	27.8	37.0	46.3	55.5	64.8	74.0	83.3
19.0	5.3	15.0	19.0	28.5	38.0	47.5	57.0	66.5	76.0	85.5
19.5	5.1	14.6	19.5	29.3	39.0	48.8	58.5	68.3	78.0	87.8
20.0	5.0	14.2	20.0	30.0	40.0	50.0	60.0	70.0	80.0	90.0
20.5	4.9	13.9	20.5	30.8	41.0	51.3	61.5	71.8	82.0	92.3
21.0	4.8	13.5	21.0	31.5	42.0	52.5	63.0	73.5	84.0	94.5
21.5	4.7	13.2	21.5	32.3	43.0	53.8	64.5	75.3	86.0	96.8
22.0	4.5	12.9	22.0	33.0	44.0	55.0	66.0	77.0	88.0	99.0
22.5	4.4	12.6	22.5	33.8	45.0	56.3	67.5	78.8	90.0	101.3
23.0	4.3	12.4	23.0	34.5	46.0	57.5	69.0	80.5	92.0	103.5
23.5	4.3	12.1	23.5	35.3	47.0	58.8	70.5	82.3	94.0	105.8
24.0	4.2	11.9	24.0	36.0	48.0	60.0	72.0	84.0	96.0	108.0
24.5	4.1	11.6	24.5	36.8	49.0	61.3	73.5	85.8	98.0	110.3
25.0	4.0	11.4	25.0	37.5	50.0	62.5	75.0	87.5	100.0	112.5